Ashley Road
Epsom
Surrey                           Tel:      01372 202461
KT18 5BE              E-mail: libraryepsm@uca.ac.uk

The AF Encyclopedia of Textiles was planned and directed by
William C. Segal and the Editors of American Fabrics Magazine

© 1960, 1972 by

Doric Publishing Company

Library of Congress
Catalog Card Number: 70-167915

Printed in the United States of America
ISBN-0-13-276568-3

B & P

# ENCYCLOPEDIA

of

# TEXTILES

(Second Edition)

By the Editors of American Fabrics Magazine

*An illustrated and authoritative source book on textiles, presenting a complete and practical coverage of the entire field — its history and origins, its art and design, its natural and man-made fibers, its manufacturing and finishing processes, color and dyes, textile printing, specialty end uses.*

..........Plus A Comprehensive Dictionary of Textile Terms.........

Prentice-Hall, Inc.          Englewood Cliffs, N. J.

# STAFF

## for the

## AF Encyclopedia of Textiles

THE AF ENCYCLOPEDIA of Textiles was prepared by the Editorial Board of American Fabrics Magazine, assisted by technical experts and writers in specialized fields of textile knowledge. The program of research, writing, editing, visualization and production of the second edition was directed by the following team:

| | |
|---|---|
| MANAGING DIRECTOR: | William C. Segal |
| EXECUTIVE EDITOR: | Cecil Lubell |
| MANAGING EDITOR: | Harvey S. Turner |
| MARKETING EDITOR: | Joseph C. Stein |
| ASST. EDITOR: | Estelle K. Silvay |
| TECHNICAL EDITOR: | Dr. George E. Linton |
| CONSULTING EDITORS: | G. Robert Stetson |
| | A. C. Tanquary |
| RESEARCH EDITOR: | Margaret Walch |
| ART EDITOR: | William Lully |

Entire contents copyright

THE PRODUCTION OF TEXTILES is one of civilization's earliest accomplishments, reflecting man's successful struggle to control and adapt himself to his environment. But never before in the 8000-year history of textiles have we seen such revolutionary developments as have taken place since the rise of the man-made fibers and the modern finishing processes. To describe and interpret these changes and to understand them from the perspective of world textile history, is one of the major objectives of the AF Encyclopedia of Textiles. Such understanding is vital to every practitioner in the world's second largest industry — *The Editors*

# ENCYCLOPEDIA of TEXTILES

# CONTENTS

## THE TEXTILE FIBERS

  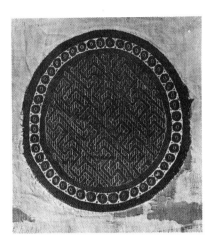

# HISTORY & ORIGINS

## CHRONOLOGICAL HISTORY . . . . . . . . . . . . . . . .

From pre-history to the 20th Century • Origins • The four great natural
fibers • Textiles in prehistoric times • Oldest continuous industry known
to man • Archeological discoveries • Textiles in ancient literature •
Arab traders in the 2nd Century • Beginnings of industry in the 8th Century
• Textile production in the 10th Century • British leadership in the 12th
Century • The Middle Ages • Textiles in the Renaissance • The New
World enters the picture • First inventions • Effect of the Industrial Revolution • Early developments in America • The great period of textile inven-
tion in the 18th Century • American competition and growth • The 19th
Century brings more inventions • Rise of the chemist and engineer • The
20th Century brings new fibers, new finishes • The contributions of science

## INVENTORS & THEIR INVENTIONS . . . . . . . . . .

The great inventors who laid the foundations of the modern textile industry •
From Arkwright to Wyatt

## ORIGINS OF FABRIC NAMES . . . . . . . . . . . . . . .

Tracing to their country of origin the fabric names which are most widely used
today • Derivations from Africa • Arabia • Asia Minor • Austria •
Belgium • China • Denmark • Egypt • England • France •
Germany • Greece • India • Italy • Japan • Malaya
• Mesopotamia • Palestine • Panama • Persia • Russia •
Scotland • South America • Spain • Switzerland • Tibet • Turkey

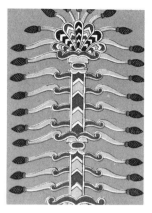

TEXTILE DESIGN

## MASTERPIECES OF TEXTILE DESIGN

Design evolution in textiles • Earliest known fabrics • Coptic, Persian and Byzantine influences • British design • New World contributions • A 48-page portfolio of black and white reproductions showing historic textiles from the great periods of design

## TEXTILES IN THE AMERICAS

## PERUVIAN TEXTILES

Peruvian weaving techniques and innovations • Design symbols • Fabrics reflect Peruvian culture • Influence of cultural exchanges • Materials

## TEXTILES IN THE NEW WORLD

Historical development • Early character of fabrics produced • Power politics and industrial growth • Early production techniques • Weaving and fulling methods • American inventions • Social effects of the textile industry • Effect of fashion changes • The U. S. textile industry today

# THE MANUFACTURING PROCESSES

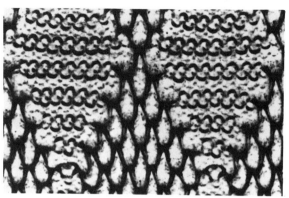

INTRODUCTION TO THE SECOND EDITION . . . . . . . . . . . . . . . .

Textiles and their end products constitute the world's second largest industry — ranking only below food products. At least 10% of the world's productive energies are devoted to this activity and a huge segment of our global population earns its living and obtains its creative satisfaction from the same source.

The Encyclopedia of Textiles is directed to the men and women in this field. It has been designed as an authoritative reference guide for every person concerned with the production and marketing of fibers and fabrics, for the professions of design and advertising which service the textile industry, for the teacher and for the student.

More specifically, the aim of the editors has been to provide in one comprehensive volume a much-needed source of inspiration and up-to-date fact for the practical work of creating, designing, producing, selling and advertising textiles and textile products.

The editorial approach has been geared to interpreting, condensing and illustrating the complicated technical information which is basic to the field, so that it will become readily available for day-to-day use. The method of presentation is based on the successful practices developed by American Fabrics Magazine during twenty-five years of publication.

The concept of a single-volume encyclopedia on so vast a subject as textiles is in itself a bold one. Each branch of this wide ranging field is worthy of encyclopedic treatment. We therefore began this work with an understandable degree of trepidation.

It is gratifying to report that the first edition of the AF Encyclopedia was well received and filled an existing need. That need is now greater than ever and has made necessary this revised and thoroughly updated second edition.

In the decade since 1960, when the first edition was published, technological advances in textiles have been more far-reaching than at any other time in history—with the possible exception of the mid-eighteenth century. These advances are now covered in the present volume.

New developments in fibers, in fabric-forming processes, in electronic controls, and particularly in fabric finishing, have all been included in this new edition.

The text has been carefully revised throughout in order to conform to existing practices in the industry. Obsolete processes have been eliminated and over 150 pages of new material have been added, covering more than thirty major new developments in the field.

The dictionary has also been revised and updated.

THE EDITORS
New York—1971

# PHOTOGRAPHIC CREDITS

Acknowledgments are made to the following institutions, corporations and individuals for their generous and continuing cooperation in the preparation and loan of illustrative material used in the various sections listed here. The numbers following each name refer to pages on which pictures appear.

## MAN-MADE FIBERS:

E. I. Du Pont de Nemours & Co., Inc., 2, 3; Monsanto Co., 4; ITT Rayonier, 6; United States Testing Laboratories, 7; FMC American Viscose, 8; Union Carbide Corp., 10; Beaunit Corp., 11; Celanese Corp., 14; U.S. Testing, 15; Celanese, 17–19; Du Pont, 20; U.S. Testing, 21; Du Pont, 23, 24; Monsanto, 25–27; Du Pont, 28; U.S. Testing, 29; Du Pont, 30, 32; Goodyear Tire & Rubber Co., 33; Du Pont, 34; U.S. Testing, 35; Monsanto, 37; Hercules Inc., 38; U.S. Testing, 39; Montecatini, 40; Phillips Fibers Corp., 41; FMC American Viscose, 42, 43; Du Pont, 44, 45; Owens-Corning Fiberglas Corp., 48; U.S. Testing, 49; Owens-Corning Fiberglas, 52, 53; Johns Manville Corp., 54–56; Du Pont, 58; Standard Oil Co. of New Jersey, 60; U.S. Testing, 61; Celanese, 62; Du Pont, 64, 65; Hystron Fibers Inc., 69.

## COTTON:

National Cotton Council of America, 70; FMC American Viscose, 70; Textile Research Institute, 71; The Smithsonian Institution, 75; Fruit of the Loom Corp., 76; Indian Head Inc., 76; Iselin-Jefferson Co. Inc., 76; Dan River Inc., 77; National Cotton Council, 78–81; Dixie Mercerizing Corp., 82, 83, 84; Reeves Brothers Inc., 85.

## WOOL:

Wool Bureau Inc., 90, 91, 94, 95, 98, 99; Security Mills Inc., 100; Wool Bureau, 101; British Information Services, 102; Wool Bureau, 102, 104; Smithsonian Inst., 106; The British Museum, 108; Wool Bureau, 109–111.

## SPECIALTY FIBERS:

S. Strook & Co., 115; Wool Bureau, 116; American Cyanamid Co., 117; Wool Bureau, 119; American Museum of Natural History, 121; Wool Bureau, 122, 123.

## SILK:

The International Silk Assoc., 126; Metropolitan Museum of Art, 127; International Silk Assoc., 128; Kanegafuchi Spinning Co., 129; International Silk Assoc., 130–133; Japan Travel Information Office, 135; International Silk Assoc., 136, 137.

## BAST FIBERS:

Belgian Linen Assoc., 140; Irish Linen Guild, 141–143, 145; Almedahl Factories, Sweden, 145; Irish Linen Guild, 146; Sea Island Mills, 148; U.S. Dept. of Agriculture, 150, 151.

## HISTORY OF TEXTILES:

British Museum, 154; Metropolitan Museum, 155; Smithsonian, 155; Metropolitan Museum, 156; U.S. Dept. of Agriculture, 162; Smithsonian, 167, 169, 171; Ciba-Geigy Corp., 182; Irish Linen Guild, 185.

## ORIGIN OF FABRIC NAMES:

Metropolitan Museum, 197–199; Kanegafuchi Spinning Co., 200; Metropolitan Museum, 201; Scalamandré Museum of Textiles, 202; Cooper Union Museum, 203; Metropolitan Museum, 204, 206, 207.

## MASTERPIECES OF TEXTILE DESIGN:

Metropolitan Museum, 213, 216; Kanegafuchi Spinning Co., 218; Metropolitan Museum, 219–222; Anne Freemantle, 223; Metropolitan Museum, 224, 226, 230–235; Cooper Union Museum, 236; Museum of Primitive Art, 237; Metropolitan Museum, 238–246; Hispanic Society of America, 247; Springs Mills Inc., 248; Metropolitan Museum, 249–251; Hambro House of Design, 252; Cooper Union Museum, 254; Boston Museum of Fine Arts, 255; Metropolitan Museum, 256, 259, 261.

## PERUVIAN TEXTILES:

British Museum, 263; Kanegafuchi Spinning Co., 265; Cooper Union Museum, 266; Kanegafuchi Spinning Co., 267.

## TEXTILES IN THE NEW WORLD:

Museum of Modern Art, 269; Indian Head Inc., 273; Celanese, 277.

## SPINNING:

National Cotton Council, 280; J. P. Stevens & Co., Inc., 281; Wool Bureau, 282; U.S. Dept. of Agriculture, 283; Rieter, Switzerland, 284; Smithsonian, 285; Rieter, Switzerland, 287, 288; Johns-Manville Corp., 289; J. P. Stevens, 290; Wool Bureau, 291; Elitex Textile Machine Co., 293; J. P. Stevens, 294; Fiber Controls Corp., 296; Monsanto, 298, 299; Dow Badische Co., 300; Monsanto, 301; Leesona Corp., 302; A.R.C.T., 302; Monsanto, 304; Rohm & Haas Co., 308; Monsanto, 308; Rohm & Haas, 309; Waumbec Mills, 312; Rohm & Haas, 313; Du Pont, 314–316.

# The MAN-MADE FIBERS

*A comprehensive review of the scientific fibers made by man, both cellulosic and non-cellulosic, whose production poundage overtook that of natural fibers in the United States during 1970 and whose development represents the most significant contribution of the 20th Century to textiles.*

1

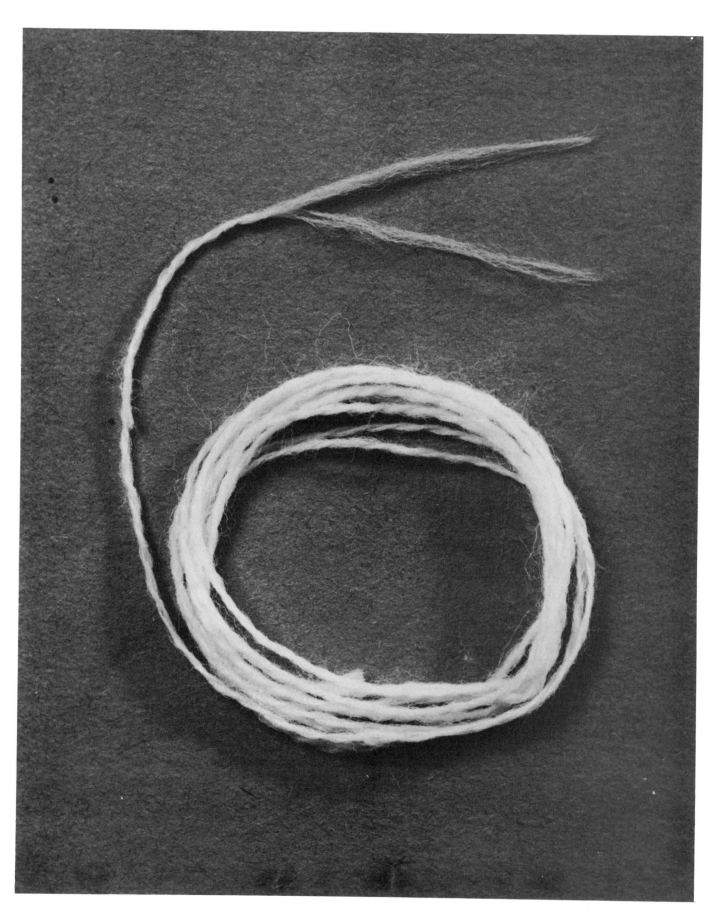

Push-button control in man-made fiber production.

# The

# MAN-MADE

# FIBERS

(*Photo opposite*) Spun yarns from staple—whether cotton, wool, any natural or man-made fiber—are bulky and fuzzy compared with smooth continuous-filament yarn.

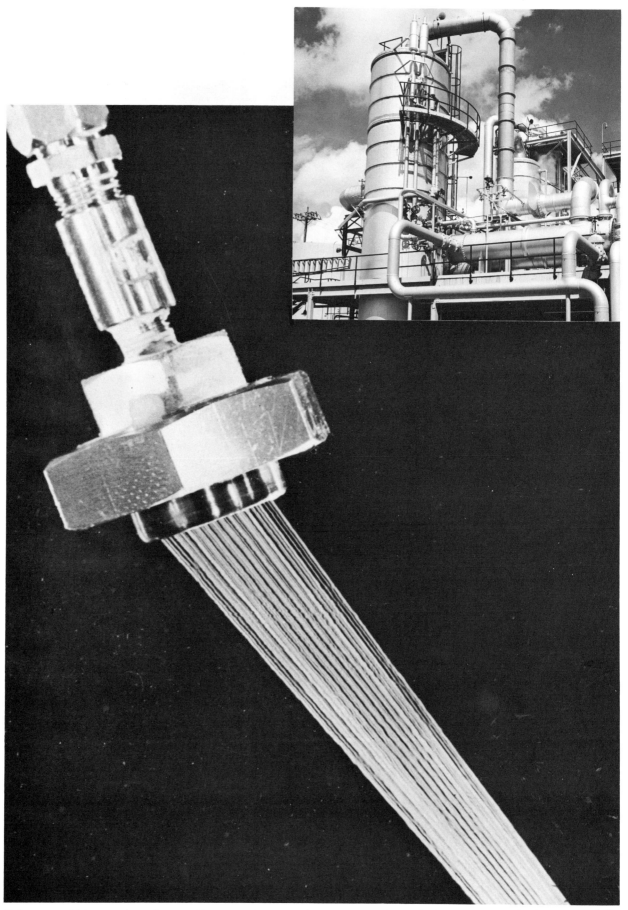

Spinneret, which contains minute orifices, expels chemicals into a coagulation bath; this causes the formation of filaments or fibers as illustrated here. The liquid from bath is pumped through system (*top right*) and the solvent recovered.

# The Genesis of
# Man-Made Fibers

*Observation of the silkworm as it made its cocoon gave the
clue to the processes needed for creating man-made fibers.*

In its simplest form the manufacture of a man-made fiber simulates the process by which a silkworm produces its filament.

The silkworm extrudes through its glands a liquid substance which solidifies into a continuous filament as it emerges and is subjected to cool air.

Chemists watching this mysterious and fascinating process conceived the idea that a man-made liquid substance, forced through fine holes, could also be solidified into a continuous filament or fiber.

From this simple idea grew the vast and flourishing industry of the man-made fibers.

There are three basic techniques by which a man-made fiber can be produced but all three are variations on a single technique using the spinneret:

1. DRY SPINNING METHOD. A polymer solution in a solvent can be forced through tiny holes into warm air. The solvent evaporates in the warm air and the liquid stream solidifies into a continuous filament.

2. WET SPINNING METHOD. A polymer solution can be forced through tiny holes into another solution where it is coagulated into a continuous filament.

3. MELT SPINNING METHOD. A solid polymer can be melted and forced through tiny holes into cool air which solidifies it into a continuous filament.

The key word here is POLYMER. This is the base or substance from which the viscous liquid is made.

## What Is a Polymer?

A polymer is the union of simple molecules or monomers, into a giant molecule (macro-molecule) or polymer. The process is called polymerization.

All fibers found in nature are composed of molecules. They are held together in a chain-like formation within a macro-molecule by strong electronic forces known as valency bonds. For instance: cellulose, which is the base of cotton, is formed by the polymerization of small, simple molecules into a larger, complicated macro-molecule.

In the case of cellulose such chemical action takes place in nature. Why not in the laboratory? This was the obvious question for scientists to ask themselves once they had learned to break a natural fiber down to its molecular structure. Why could they not duplicate or synthesize such chain-like macro-molecules from known simple molecules such as are found in wood, coal-tar and petroleum, and which they knew would react together?

As the result of much research and experimentation based on this research, man-made fibers were created in the laboratory.

Most important to the whole concept was the ability to cause these macro-molecular chains to line up parallel to each other in order to create a fiber.

The spinneret (which looks something like a shower head) with its tiny holes, supplied the solution. It is made of iridium and platinum.

After extrusion, the polymer molecules are aligned by stretching (an operation called drawing). This operation is important to the ultimate strength and elasticity of the filament.

This, basically, is a simplified explanation of the complicated chemistry by which man-made fibers are produced. In essence man is arranging molecules in the same way as nature arranges them, and is then converting them into flexible fibers by the same technique nature devised for the silkworm.

Based on trees and cotton linters, rayon stands close to many natural fibers in chemical composition.

# Rayon

*Regenerated cellulose from natural sources, rayon was the first major fiber engineered by man.*

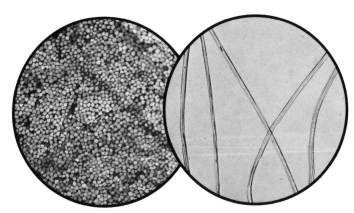

Longitudinal and sectional views of rayon fibers, many times enlarged.

RAYON is a regenerated man-made textile fiber made from chemically treated cellulose. The cellulose source used is either wood pulp or cotton linters. Today, pine wood is the dominant raw material.

The word rayon is also man-made. It was coined by Kenneth Lord, Sr. in 1924 during an industry-sponsored contest to find a generic name for what was then known as "artificial silk."

## How Rayon Is Made

Simply stated, rayon is formed in this manner:

Cellulose, with the aid of chemicals, is reduced to a honey-like solution. This viscous liquid is forced through the holes of a spinneret—a tiny instrument that looks like a very fine shower nozzle. As the slender, hair-like filaments stream out, they are so-lidified—and twisted together to form a rayon yarn of any desired size or denier (a measure of weight indicating the number of grams in each 9,000 meters of yarn).

Through use of different types of cellulose, different chemicals and different manufacturing techniques, three major types of rayon are produced. They are: viscose rayon, Cuprammonium rayon, nitro-cellulose rayon (now practically extinct).

## Characteristics of Rayon

Rayon remembers its cellulose origin, and all rayons pick up many qualities and characteristics of this vegetable matter common to the rayon family background. This vegetable origin explains rayon's strong resemblance in chemical—and some physical —properties to cotton, a natural fiber which comes from plant life.

Like cotton, rayon fibers are strong. They are extremely absorbent—a quality which makes rayon highly receptive to a wide variety of dyes and special finishes. This ability to soak up moisture explains why rayon dries more slowly than some man-made fibers. The tendency to shrink, which is characteristic of an absorbent fiber, can be controlled in the production of the fiber and in the finishing of the final fabric.

Rayon reacts to heat in a cotton-like way. It does not melt; it does burn at a high temperature. It is mothproof. It is not affected by ordinary household bleaches and chemicals.

## Stages in Viscose Rayon Production

1. Cellulose xanthate crumb is dissolved in caustic soda to form solution from which rayon is spun.

2. The spinning solution is dark and of high viscosity, which characteristic gives process its name.

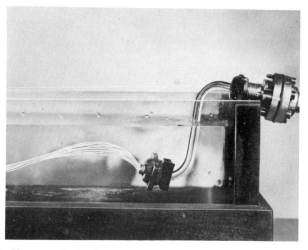

3. Viscose solution being forced through holes in spinneret into bath where it coagulates as filaments.

4. The continuous filaments formed by spinnerets will be either spun into yarns or made into staple.

5. Continuous filaments are given crimp prior to cutting into correct lengths for various yarn types.

6. The finished viscose rayon staple is stored in bulk ready for spinning into staple type yarns.

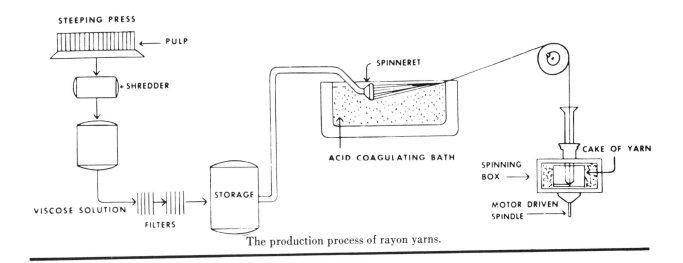

The production process of rayon yarns.

## The Viscose Process

The viscose process of rayon manufacture takes the form of processing natural cellulose, derived from wood pulp or cotton linters as raw material, by a series of chemical treatments. In this transformation, sheets of purified natural cellulose are converted into a solution and subsequently reconverted into a solid in the form of a fine filament without molecular or chemical degradation.

1. White sheets of bleached cellulose sulphate pulp, resembling large pieces of blotting paper, are steeped in a solution of caustic soda after blending to ensure uniformity. The resultant product is known as alkali cellulose.

2. After steeping, the sheets are crumbled by the revolving blades of a *pfleidering* machine, and stored in bins to undergo aging.

3. With addition of carbon disulphate the crumbs turn a bright orange, at which point the product is known as *xanthate crumb*.

4. This is ready for dissolving in a dilute solution of caustic soda.

5. The resulting product is a thick, honey-colored liquid known as the viscose solution, from its physical character and sluggish flow.

6. This liquid has the property of hardening when passed through a dilute solution of sulphuric acid, which enables fine filaments, extruded through holes in a spinneret into a sulphuric acid bath, to be withdrawn, dried and skeined.

7. The filament now can be prepared in one of several ways—either by spinning as continuous filament yarn, or by cutting into staple of desired length or of mixed lengths, or by direct spinning, according to the type of fabric and end use in view. The staple may be spun on the woolen, worsted or cotton system.

## The Cuprammonium Process

The following are the most important steps in the manufacture of cuprammonium cellulose yarns by the Bemberg stretch-spinning process. These process steps give Bemberg rayon its distinctive qualities of evenness, fineness, suppleness, characteristic luster and strength.

1. RAW MATERIAL is cotton linters or wood pulp.

2. RAW MATERIAL is bleached a pure white in washing machine. The only bleaching required of Bemberg rayon yarn is accomplished at this point.

3. SOLUTION MIXER is used where the bleached cotton or wood pulp is dissolved into a cellulose solution by the addition of copper-ammonium (ammoniacal copper oxide) liquid.

4. IMPURITIES are filtered out in solution filter, leaving a pure, clean spinning solution of a dark blue color.

5. AGING takes place in spinning solution storage tanks where the solution is brought to maturity.

6. SPINNING BATH SUPPLY uses a liquid that brings about coagulation of the filaments after they leave the spinneret.

7. STRETCH-SPINNING APPARATUS. The cuprammonium spinning solution after being forced through holes in a spinneret is stretched and spun here into the finest filaments produced by man commercially. The size of Bemberg rayon filaments is not limited by the size of the spinneret holes, but achieves

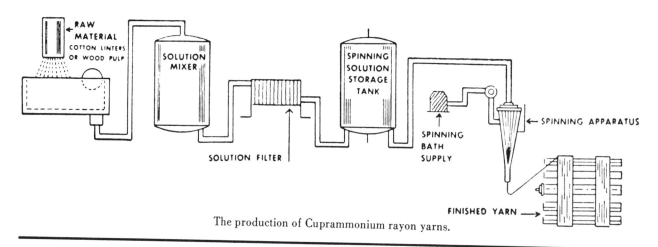

The production of Cuprammonium rayon yarns.

fineness through the use of the unique stretch-spinning device.

8. FINISHED YARN is wound on reels in skein form. Later put in skeins and cones for use by manufacturers.

## High-Performance Rayon

High-performance rayon (often called high-wet-modulus rayon) became one of the most sophisticated blending fibers of the 1960's. Its performance is much like that of fine cotton, with the added property of deep luster.

HP rayon has good stability in washing, good strength and accepts vat dyes. It can be Sanforized and mercerized. When blended with carded cotton, it is believed to match the performance of combed cotton on the more economical carded system.

The development of HP rayon was a by-product of

High-performance rayon yarn.

the search for a stronger tire yarn after World War II. Scientists learned to improve the fiber's molecular structure, improving rayon's strength and dyeability. They also developed a latent crimping process in the fiber.

HP rayon is spun on two systems: The Zinc-Based System, by which 95% of U.S. rayon production is achieved, and the Non-Zinc System, which is used in France and other countries to produce HP rayons classified under the generic name, "polynosic."

## Non-Woven Fabrics Built on Rayon

Since the mid-1960's rayon has become an important fiber in the growing field of non-wovens. There are two basic non-woven categories in which rayon plays a significant role:

1. Non-Woven Durables, where rayon has been a big factor for many years. This field includes interlinings, carpet backings, drapery headers, coated fabrics such as wall coverings, tapes, ribbons, shades, casket linings, book-bindings and filters.

2. Non-Woven Disposables, which is the fastest-growing market for non-woven fabrics, as well as the newest. Here, rayon is an important factor in the hospital/institutional end uses, including disposable gowns, masks, caps, foot coverings, throw-away sheets, pillowcases, mattress covers, divider drapes and scrub suits; the industrial/commercial market, which includes uniforms, coveralls, aprons, headrest sheets, jackets, wipe towels, pillows for gas stations, restaurants and industrial plants; and in consumer markets, including everything from cleaning cloths to sheets, pillowcases, aprons, baby diapers, panties and sleeping bag liners.

## History of Rayon

Rayon is generally looked upon as a European in-

## Stages in Cuprammonium Rayon Production

1. An operator loading fluffed wood pulp into chute leading to one of the dissolving tanks for solution.

2. The spinning solution is stored in big containers and aged before being moved to the spinning machines.

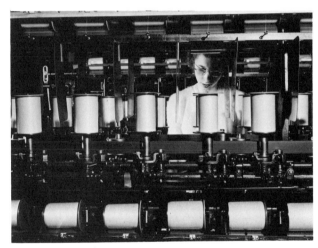

3. After spinning the Bemberg filaments are passed through twisting machine to give yarn desired twist.

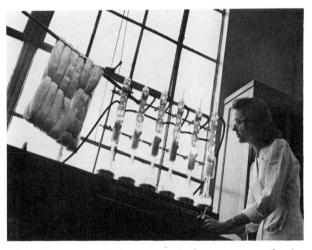

4. Laboratory controls are exercised over yarn production at every stage from wood pulp to shipping.

5. Skeins of Bemberg yarn are passed through washing bath by lowering in racks while being revolved.

6. Cones pass through final inspection check point before being packed for shipment to mills for use.

vention of the 19th Century and a 20th Century development in America. Actually its roots burrow deep in antiquity, for chemically treated cellulose was pounded (felted) into tapa cloth by the natives of the Marquesa Islands in the dawn of their history. It is interesting to learn that the cellulose used in making tapa cloth was derived from the bark of the mulberry tree, the same substance which George Audemars used in his experiments at Lausanne in 1855. It was Audemars' work which furthered the commercial development of "artificial silk," since his laboratory efforts produced the first synthetic filament which could be cut.

Rayon is a product of no one person's ingenuity; no one group's activity; no one century's development. As far back as 1664 the eminent British scientist Dr. Robert Hooke predicted the coming of "artificial silk" in his famous book "Micrographia." In the early 18th Century René A. F. de Reaumur, French naturalist and physicist, posed a problem to scientific investigators in his "L'Histoire des Insectes."

He questioned, "Why cannot one spin out a fiber like silk, since it is possible to make varnishes that possess the qualities of silk?"

## Swiss Patent Is Issued

Reaumur suggested no method for drawing the varnishes into threads. It remained for Audemars to achieve laboratory success. In 1855 the latter was granted a Swiss patent for transforming nitro-cellulose into fine threads which he called "artificial silk."

In contrast to Audemars' success, his contemporary Louis Schwabe of Manchester experimented with substances which could be drawn out through fine holes into filaments or threads. His efforts found little support and collapsed with his suicide.

Up to this point rayon was only a success in laboratories. It awaited a practical demonstration of its commercial possibilities.

## Chardonnet Perfected Process

In 1886 Count Hilaire de Chardonnet worked and experimented beyond the findings of Swann, Wynne-Powell, Swinburne, Crookes, and others, upon a commercial process for manufacturing artificial silk. The finished product was first exhibited at the Paris Exhibition in 1889. From that time onward rayon has been produced in plants all over the world.

France established Les Etablissements de Chardonnet à Besançon. Germany started La Société des Fabriques de Soie Artificielle à Frankfort. Switzerland opened L'Usine de Spreitenbach, canton d'Argonie. Belgium built Les Fabriques de Tubize et d'Obourg.

Because rayon was evolved from several sources of thought, both related and independent, it was only natural that several different processes should be brought into being.

France started the nitro-cellulose process, Germany developed the cuprammonium process, England introduced the viscose process and the United States spun the first cellulose acetate.

## First Rayon Hosiery

In 1910 the first successful industrial plant for the manufacture of rayon by the viscose process was started at Marcus Hook, Pa. It was the first plant of the American Viscose Company, which produced 375,000 pounds of rayon yarn in its initial year.

The year 1912 brought to market the first rayon hosiery in quantity. This is important because it brought "silk" stockings within the reach of the mass markets for everyday wear, pointing out vast commercial possibilities for rayon. Four years later the first knitted rayon fabric for outerwear made its appearance on the market. It was at this time that the rayon business started to give stiff competition to its natural fiber rivals.

During World War I . . . with the submarine menace interrupting shipping; with cargo space needed for troop and munition transport; in short, with all of the war-time urgency of self-sufficiency brought home in a dramatic manner . . . America determined to produce her own silk-like fabrics at home and to depend less upon imports.

Immediately following the war, the rayon department of E. I. du Pont de Nemours established a plant in Buffalo. In conjunction with the Tubize Chatillon Corporation of Belgium, a plant for the making of nitro-cellulose rayon was established in Hopewell, Va. (However, this process of making rayon has since been abandoned by DuPont.) Following rapidly, the National Artificial Silk Co. was set up in Cleveland. This company is now the Industrial Rayon Company with plants in Cleveland, Painesville and Covington.

Simultaneously, the first acetate yarn to be made in this country was produced in East Boston by the Lustron Company, which soon became part of the Celanese Corporation.

## Development in Rayon

The year 1925 launched the greatest period of the rayon industry's growth. Many new plants were established and, as a result, the market became glutted with rayons, both good and inferior. Consumer reaction brought about the rayon depression (both in demand and price) and led to general improvements in standards of quality. It was the shortest depression in history, for the rayon industry was quick to correct its own errors.

The following year brought Bemberg of Germany to this country. The first Bemberg plant producing cuprammonium rayon in the United States was erected at Johnson City, Tenn. Glanzstoff, a German company, following the lead of its countryman, commenced plans to erect its first American viscose unit at Elizabethton, Tenn. In 1928, Enka of Holland opened a unit at Asheville, N. C.

## Technical Advances in Rayon

Rayon made significant strides in technical improvement between the two world wars. In the early 1930's de-lustering techniques were developed to remove viscose rayon's characteristic high shine, thus improving its optical properties and covering powers, and reducing its tendency to show dirt.

In the late 1930's, rayon's tensile strength was increased to 3.5 grams/denier to develop a higher-tenacity rayon yarn for tire cord as a substitute for war-short cotton. This was achieved by a fiber-stretching process and by adding more zinc to the spinning bath.

In the 1940's, new cross sections—crenulated, round, flat, etc.—were developed, which improved rayon's covering power and resistance to soiling. Between 1945 and 1950, the industry produced solution-dyed rayons for color fastness and uniformity, and in 1950 the industry developed a "Super" tire yarn with tensile strength of 4 grams/denier. Through the 1950's and 1960's rayon became the predominant tire yarn for original-equipment tires, developing tensile strengths of up to 10 grams/denier.

But rayon as an apparel fiber went into a decline during the 1950's because of competitive pressure from other man-made fibers, particularly nylon and polyester, with considerably higher wet moduluses. Finally, when the high-wet-modulus (high-performance) rayons were developed by FMC American Viscose in the late 1950's and early 1960's, rayon began to recapture many apparel and home furnishings markets. It gradually became one of the prime blending fibers with polyester, especially in permanent-press wear, just at the time when polyester was beginning to challenge rayon decisively in original-equipment tire cord yarns.

---

### Some Major U.S. Producers of Rayon Fiber and Yarn:

American Cyanamid Co., Fibers Div.
American Enka Corp.
Beaunit Corp.
Courtaulds North America Inc.
FMC Corp., American Viscose Div.
Fair Haven Mills

---

## Uses of Rayon

WOMEN'S AND CHILDREN'S APPAREL.

| | |
|---|---|
| Dresses | Rainwear |
| Suits | Lingerie |
| Blouses | Accessories |
| Sportswear | Millinery |
| Coats | Coat and suit linings |

MEN'S AND BOYS' WEAR.

| | |
|---|---|
| Sport shirts | Jackets |
| Summer and year-round suits | Raincoats |
| | Work clothes |
| Slacks | Ties |
| Rugged outerwear | |

HOME FURNISHING FABRICS.

| | |
|---|---|
| Decorative draperies and slip covers | Tablecloths |
| | Bedspreads |
| Curtains | Blankets |
| Upholstery | Carpets |

INDUSTRIAL FABRICS AND PRODUCTS.

| | |
|---|---|
| Automobile tires | V-belts |
| Hose | Conveyor belts |

## Care of Rayon

Rayon fabrics are either washable or dry cleanable. Washable rayon fabrics shed dirt quickly and easily when hand or machine washed. Sheer, dainty rayons should be treated as other fine fabrics— warm water, mild soap, gentle handling, careful rinsing. Sturdy rayons can be treated like other sturdy fabrics.

The acetate process is basically the transformation of cellulose from tree trunks or cotton linters into a textile filament which can be spun as yarn.

# Acetate Fibers

*A major group of fibers with a cellulose base; how it differs from other fibers; its characteristics; its manufacture, uses, and care.*

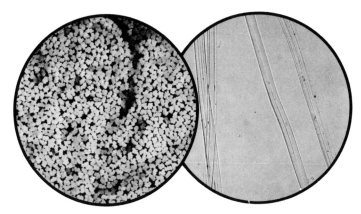

Once grouped with rayon in one category, acetate has long since developed characteristics and identity of its own.

ACETATE is a textile fiber man-made from a chemical compound of cellulose. It takes its name from one chemical used, which is acetic acid. It must be distinguished from rayon, with which it was originally lumped into one category. Its physical and chemical properties and its reaction to dyes are different from those of rayon.

## How Acetate Is Made

Acetate fibers are formed when a solid substance is first changed to a liquid, and then converted to a solid form once again. Generally speaking, all man-made fibers are made in this manner. Their differences (and there are many) spring from the use of different raw materials, different chemicals, different production techniques.

The major ingredient of acetate is cellulose—wood pulp or cotton linters (the short fibers that stick to the cotton seed when the long fibers are removed). When this cellulose is treated chemically an entirely new substance, called cellulose acetate, is formed. Cellulose acetate has qualities and characteristics all its own—it does not resemble cotton or cellulose.

This cellulose acetate is dissolved to form a liquid. The solution is then streamed out through the holes of a spinneret. As each slender stream is exposed to air, it hardens and forms a long, hair-like acetate filament.

## Engineered for End Use

Because acetate is a man-made product, acetate fibers can be "engineered" to meet different end uses. Features that affect the appearance and performance of a fabric can be controlled. These variations are achieved in many interesting ways. For example :

The shape and appearance of the acetate filament itself can be created to exact specifications. It can be varied in size and weight. It can be thick, thin, or thick-and-thin, the latter being like linen in appearance, and bright or dull luster. The filament can be round and smooth, with gentle luster. It can be flat and ribbon-like, with a mirror-like glint and sparkle. It can be made curly and kinky—a quality needed for textured fabrics.

Acetate filaments may be twisted together to form long continuous strands of smooth filament yarns. These yarns are at their best in smooth-surfaced fabrics.

## Dyed in the Solution

Colors are sometimes added to the solution before the acetate filaments are formed. This solution-dyeing process provides deep and glowing colors, which become a basic part of the fiber and are uniform throughout the length of the fabric. They do not dim through washing or dry cleaning—cannot wash away or streak—and do not fade from exposure to salt water, gases or perspiration.

15

## Characteristics of Acetate

Acetate has certain basic properties which have a great effect on the appearance and performance of the fabrics in which they are used.

1. Acetate does not absorb moisture readily. This contributes to speedy drying—is responsible for resistance to shrinking.

2. Acetate fibers and yarns are pliable and supple. This gives fabrics a soft, pleasant touch and good drape.

3. Acetate fibers and yarns are resilient. This means they resist wrinkling—then spring back into shape.

4. Acetate is thermoplastic. This means that the fiber or yarn becomes more pliable when subjected to high heat—then hardens when cool. This trait makes it possible to heat-set durable pleats into acetate fabrics—to imprint patterns and decorations on the surface. This thermoplastic quality also means that only light pressing with a low-heat iron is necessary to restore the original appearance of acetate fabrics.

5. Acetate, a chemical product, has built-in resistance to moths, perspiration, mildew, and mold. A note of caution—Acetone and alcohol dissolve acetate fibers, so nail polish remover and perfumes should be used with care around acetate fabrics.

6. Acetate takes only its own dyes—does not accept dyes used for rayon or natural fibers. This selectivity about dyes makes it possible for fabric designers to achieve special color or two-tone effects when acetate is combined with other fibers in a fabric.

## Uses of Acetate

| | |
|---|---|
| Evening gowns | Bathing suits |
| Dresses | Curtains |
| Sportswear blouses | Draperies |
| Uniforms | Automobile upholstery |
| Knitted jerseys | Men's wear |
| Lingerie | Children's wear |
| Carpets | Interlinings |
| Rugs | Fillings for pillows |

### Some Major U.S. Producers of Acetate Fibers:

Celanese Corp.
E. I. du Pont de Nemours
& Co. Inc.
Tennessee Eastman Co.
FMC Corp., American Viscose Div.

## History of Acetate

In 1865, the acetate radical, acetyl, was combined with cellulose to produce cellulose acetate, but it was not spun successfully until World War I.

Cellulose acetate actually found its first application in plastics. In Basle, Switzerland, the chemists Henri and Camille Dreyfus patented a process for manufacturing flameproof films, lacquers and plastics in 1901 and 1911. During World War I, they built plants in France and England to make waterproof varnishes for the fabric-covered airplanes of that period. In 1920, British Celanese Limited made the first feasible acetate fiber.

The first U.S. acetate production took place at the Cumberland, Md. plant of British Celanese (now Celanese Corp.) in 1924. Triacetate was first made by Bayer & Co. in 1901 and was duplicated by the Lustron Company in 1914 and by the Germans in 1936 under the tradename "Triceta." But the use of an expensive and toxic element, chloroform, barred its economical production.

It wasn't until 1954, when Celanese discovered an easier method of production, that triacetate was commercialized under the tradename *Arnel*. By dissolving triacetate in methylene chloride, to which alcohol has been added, the fiber can be easily brought into solution and spun.

Acetate had a slump during the mid-1950's, as did rayon, but recuperated by the early 1960's when the industry introduced textured acetate doubleknit fabrics and solution-dyed acetate. It also became very popular in tricot, which became widely used in the growing field of bonded fabrics. As tow, it became very successful as cigarette filter material.

Arnel triacetate has been basically popular as an apparel fiber and has broadened its market range by combining with nylon to give it manufacturing and wearing strength.

## Triacetate Fiber

ARNEL is cellulose triacetate, which has many important different physical properties from acetate. In general, while preserving the desirable hand and beauty of acetate, Arnel offers vastly improved characteristics in ease of care, especially in laundering. These superior properties are achieved through heat treatment of the finished fabric. Some of these basic properties that contribute towards ease of care are:

1. Higher heat resistance—fabrics made of Arnel may be ironed safely at temperatures up to 450° F. without damage or with the cotton setting on an iron.

## Final Steps in Producing Acetate Fibers

1. Purified wood pulp or cotton linters **are** mixed with acetic acid, acetic anhydride and catalyst.

2. Cellulose acetate solution is poured from acetylating mixer into storage tanks for ripening.

3. Cellulose acetate from storage tanks is chilled in water, forming flakes, now dissolved in acetone.

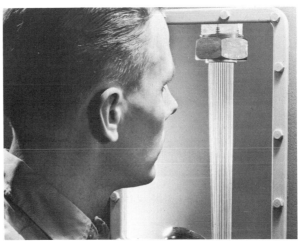

4. Solution in acetone, either plain or with color added, is forced through spinneret, forming filaments.

5. Continuous filament yarn comes from spinneret and this, after twisting, is rewound on cones.

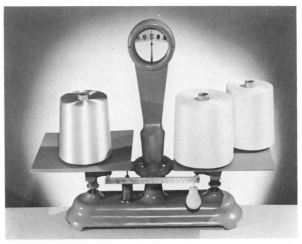

6. The finished yarn may be in regular form or it may be lofted by special **process**, giving double bulk.

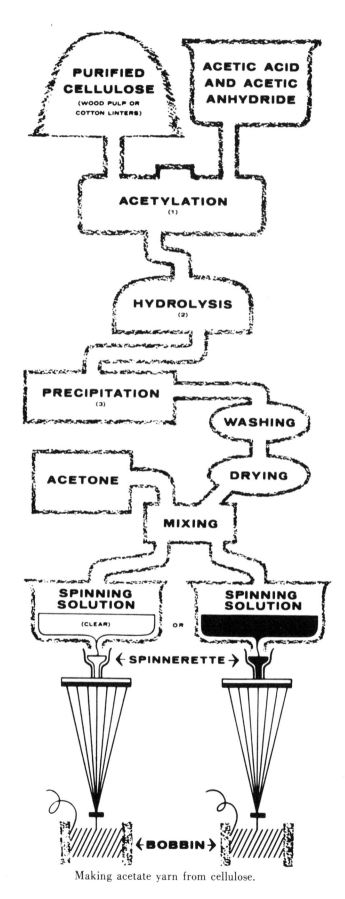

Making acetate yarn from cellulose.

2. Superior wrinkle resistance. Fabrics of Arnel are extremely resistant to wrinkling and mussing, due to the fact that the fiber is hydrophobic.

3. Crease and pleat retention. As a thermoplastic fiber Arnel endows fabrics with excellent crease retention, even where the fabric contains up to 30% of nonthermoplastic fiber, under proper pleating conditions.

4. Color-fastness to washing. Arnel is dyed with acetate dyes, but colorfastness to washing is greatly increased by the heat treatment in finishing.

5. Rate of drying. Since Arnel is hydrophobic, it dries very fast.

6. Pilling. Fabrics containing Arnel staple fiber, whether in blends or all-Arnel, have no tendency to pill.

7. Fungus and mold resistance. Arnel has very high resistance to mold and mildew.

8. Dimensional stability.

## Steps in Producing Cellulosic Fibers

### First Steps in Producing Acetate Fibers

The production of cellulosic fibers starts in the forests. Some of the steps preceding the processing are shown in the photographs below and on the opposite page.

1. Scientific logging techniques protect forest wealth. Healthy trees around area cut supply seeds for new crop.

## Cellulose—The Raw Material

2. Foresters mark trees which are felled by logging crews using chain saws and modern handling equipment.

3. Logs are carried to the mill by trucking over forest roads or by waterways; then stored near mill to "age."

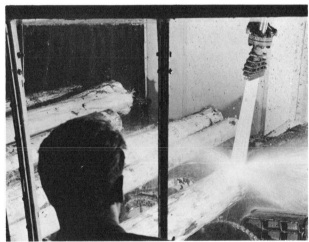

4. Logs are cut to twenty-foot lengths, barked under hydraulic pressure, as shown here, and taken to chipper.

5. The chipper which consists of a conveyor and revolving blades, reduces logs to chips less than 1″ square.

6. The chips are digested with chemicals into pulp stock, then to machines for washing, bleaching and drying.

7. The purified cellulose is dried and wound in rolls for shipping to cellulosic fiber producing plant.

(*Above*) General view of a modern nylon plant shows the tremendous complication of synthesizing on industrial scale and demonstrates importance of instrumentation techniques.

(*Below*) Inside the central control room of the plant where six men, with aid of fine instrumentation techniques, are continuously monitoring every process of manufacture.

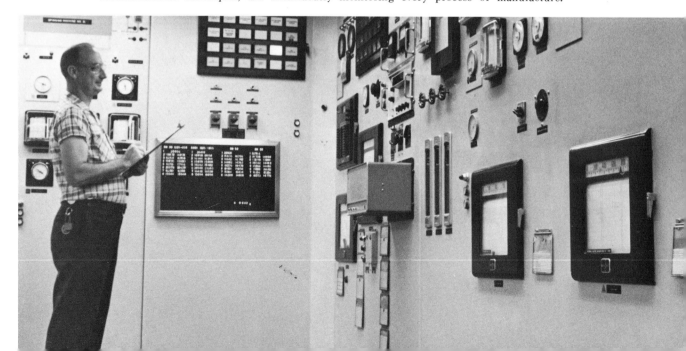

# Polyamide Fibers (Nylon)

*Since DuPont introduced Nylon in America, numerous specific types have been engineered through changes in the formula to fill different needs for different end uses.*

The first fiber to be manufactured by a process of chemical synthesis, nylon paved the way for development of a continuing series of man-made textile fibers based on common raw materials and industrial chemicals.

The polyamide fibers are synthetic fibers made from basic chemicals which are found in coal, oil, water, corncobs, oats and rice hulls, bran, gas, and petroleum. In the United States polyamide fibers are known by the generic name of nylon.

## How Nylon Is Made

Nylon is a family of many related chemical compounds. A nylon molecule contains atoms of hydrogen, nitrogen, oxygen, and carbon in controlled proportions and structural arrangement. The process of manufacturing nylon is a highly complex one. Here are the basic steps:

1. By high pressure synthesis, two chemicals called hexamethylene diamine and adipic acid are made in a series of chemical steps. They are then com-

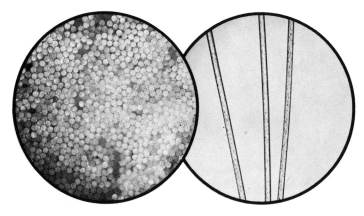
Crystalline lattice of nylon.

bined, and the resultant product is called nylon salt.

2. For ease in handling, the salt is dissolved in water and shipped to various plants for manufacture into yarn, bristle and other forms.

3. To make yarn, the first step is to evaporate a portion of the water from the salt.

4. The salt is then placed in an autoclave, a piece of equipment like a giant pressure cooker. Here heat combines the molecules of the two chemicals into giant ones, called linear superpolymers. It is this process which gives nylon a molecular structure similar to materials like wood and silk. It is also the source of nylon's strength and elasticity.

5. The nylon is then removed from the autoclave, cooled, hardened and ground up into little chips for efficient handling.

6. Spinning is done by melting the chips over heating grids, and pumping the melt out through tiny holes in a spinneret or metal disc about the size of a silver dollar.

7. The solution emerges from the spinneret in thin strands which can be stretched like warm taffy. These strands, after cooling, can be further stretched to three or four times their original length. When so drawn out the strands take on even greater strength and elasticity.

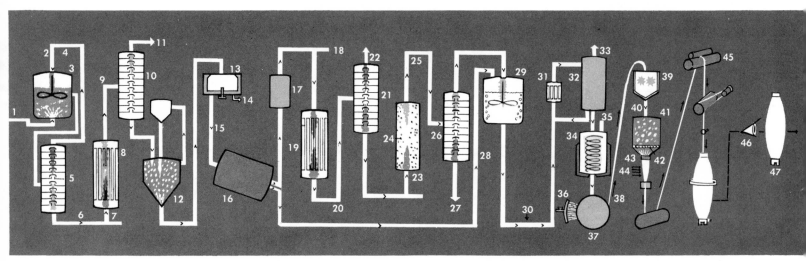

Flow chart showing the synthesis by stages of nylon salts from raw materials: air, cyclohexane and ammonia; and the spinning of the nylon salts into continuous filament form, ready for manufacture into various types of yarns.

## Key to the Chart above:

1. Air
2. Cyclohexane from Petroleum
3. Reactor
4. Recycle Cyclohexane
5. Still
6. Cyclohexanol Cyclohexanone KA
7. HNO$_3$
8. Converter
9. Adipic Acid Solution
10. Still
11. Impurities
12. Crystallizer
13. Centrifuge
14. Impurities
15. Adipic Acid Crystals
16. Drier

17. Vaporizer
18. NH$_3$
19. Converter
20. Crude Adiponitrile
21. Still
22. Impurities
23. H$_2$
24. Converter
25. Crude Diamine
26. Still
27. Impurities
28. Nylon Salt Solution
29. Reactor
30. Stabilizer
31. Calandria
32. Evaporator

33. Excess water
34. Autoclave
35. Delustrant
36. Water Sprays
37. Casting Wheel
38. Polymer Ribbon
39. Grinder
40. Polymer Flake
41. Spinning Machine
42. Heating Cells
43. Spinnerette
44. Air
45. Drawtwisting
46. Inspection
47. Nylon Bobbin

These strands, or filaments, are used in three ways:

A. A single solid strand may be used alone to make a fine yarn of great strength and smoothness. This is called monofilament yarn, and is used in sheer hosiery, blouses, veils and gowns. Monofilament yarn can be textured to provide yarn with more bulk, opacity, reflectance and a more natural hand than untextured yarn.

B. A number of tiny, endless strands can be twisted together to form a yarn. The size and number of strands used, as well as the amount of twist, can be varied to form yarns of various sizes. This is called multifilament yarn, and is the most widely used type. The surface texture, softness, and drape which this yarn gives to fabrics makes it appropriate for many ready-to-wear and home furnishings uses. Multifilament yarn can also be textured to provide yarn with more "natural" properties.

C. Nylon filaments are also cut into short, wavy strands varying in length from one and one-half to five inches. These cut strands, called nylon staple, are spun into soft, springy yarns used especially in rugs and carpets, sweaters and socks.

Dr. W. H. Carothers, inventor of nylon.

## Background for Nylon

In 1926, the DuPont Laboratories initiated a chemical research program which, during the next ten years, was destined to produce a whole new field of man-made fibers—the synthetics. Synthetic fibers bear no relation to plant life, but are wholly compounded from chemicals.

In its early stages, the first synthetic fiber was known in the laboratory as Fiber 66. Still in the experimental stage, it was used for the bristles in tooth brushes, in yarn from which stockings were knitted, in sewing thread. It proved itself to have many desirable properties.

In 1938, the DuPont Company gave to Fiber 66 the name it bears today—NYLON—and began widespread production for commercial uses. Two years later, nylon hosiery was on sale in stores throughout the country. Surgeons were using nylon sutures. Sportsmen were fishing with nylon lines. Nylon began finding its way into every part of living. Other companies were licensed to produce nylon under DuPont patents, and nylon became a household word.

In 1942, nylon was called into service with the armed forces. The War Production Board allocated the total production of nylon for military purposes—parachutes, flak vests, combat uniforms, tires, and a host of other vital military purposes. Not until the close of the war were civilians able again to buy quantities of products containing nylon.

Following its return from the war, nylon began the first of several major metamorphoses by which it has become one of the most versatile of the synthetics. From its beginnings as a hosiery yarn, nylon was soon adapted for use in tricot, woven fabrics, industrial applications and carpeting, while continuing to dominate the hosiery field. Other companies were licensed to produce nylon under Du Pont patents, and nylon became a household word.

The introduction of bulked continuous filament nylon for tufted carpets in 1958 signalled the second major change in nylon—not merely adaptations of the initial yarn concept, but major revisions in the nature of the yarn to fit it for special applications.

Du Pont's long experience with the fiber led to the introduction during the 1960's of a host of second- or third-generation nylon products: Antron, a yarn with unique optical properties; Nomex, a high-temperature-resistant nylon; Cantrece, a bicomponent yarn with built-in coil or crimp; and Qiana, a luxury fiber with excellent performance characteristics.

Other manufacturers developed specialty versions of the first of the synthetics. Monsanto's ribbon form of nylon goes into AstroTurf synthetic playing fields. American Enka developed producer-textured Crepeset, and Allied produces Source, a nylon matrix with polyester constituents incorporated in the fiber, for luxury carpet markets.

Today, there are two types of nylon which dominate world production, nylon 66 and nylon 6. They are used almost interchangeably since they have only minor technical differences. Nylon 66 was the industry standard for the Allies during World War II, while nylon 6 was the standard for the Axis. These relationships remained practically unchanged until the mid-1960's, since few companies in the two areas wanted to change a well-rationalized production system for minor advantages.

But during the late 1960's, nylon 66 began to penetrate some nylon 6 markets on the Continent, and some nylon 6 went into the USA and UK. In addition, nylon 4, which had long resisted efforts to spin it stably, has now been developed for commercial markets with an arrangement between the appropriate American and Japanese fiber companies. Nylon 4 purportedly offers a higher moisture absorption rate than nylon 6 or 66, thus making it more like cotton for apparel end uses.

### The Qualities of Nylon

The final appearance and performance of a fabric are dependent to some degree on each of the five elements or processes which go into its making—the fiber, the yarn, the construction, the dyeing and finishing. Engineered into the nylon fiber are many properties which play an important part.

1. Perhaps the outstanding property of nylon is its unusual strength. Nylon is stronger, yet weighs less, than any other commonly used fiber.

2. Nylon is elastic and resilient. Fabrics of nylon return readily to their original shape whether stretched or crushed. Part of this property is in the fiber itself and part of it comes from a process called "heat-setting" which comes at the finishing stage in the fabric production. Nylon is particularly responsive to heat-setting because it permanently takes the shape or form desired, yet remains resilient and pliable after cooling.

3. Nylon fibers are smooth, non-absorbent and dry quickly. Dirt does not cling, and can be quickly removed. This non-absorbent quality makes nylon resist some dyes, but dye producers have met this challenge by producing a full range of new dyes with special properties which appeal to nylon and produce bright, colorful hues with long-lasting resistance to many color-destroying factors.

4. The chemical composition of nylon holds no attraction for moths and other insects. Water, perspiration, or standard dry-cleaning agents have no weakening effect on the fiber.

### Uses of Nylon

Nylon is used in fabrics in three principal ways. Each time it contributes its key properties to the fabric.

1. ALL NYLON. Fabrics made entirely from nylon.

2. BLENDS AND COMBINATIONS. Nylon staple is often mixed with one or more other fibers (either natural or man-made) before the yarn is made. Fabrics made from such yarns are called blends.

In some fabrics, yarn made from nylon and yarn made entirely from another fiber are knitted or woven together. These are called combination fabrics, to which nylon adds strength, resistance to wear, and shape retention. Because some dyes have no effect on nylon, yet are quite effective with other fibers, some interesting and unusual color effects are to be found in blend and combination fabrics.

3. REINFORCEMENTS. Nylon is often added in small amounts to a final product to provide reinforcement. Nylon yarn knitted into toes and heels greatly increases the wear life of socks made from another fiber.

### Products of Nylon

IN WEARING APPAREL, nylon is used for women's hosiery, knitted or woven lingerie, socks and sweaters for men, women, and children. Tightly constructed nylon weaves are used in snow suits, ski clothes, windbreakers, and raincoats. Loose and open weaves are used in sheer blouses, dresses, and men's shirts.

IN HOME FURNISHINGS, nylon is used for lamp shades, curtains, draperies, bedspreads, rugs, and carpets.

Spinnaker made from Du Pont nylon.

IN SPORTING GOODS, nylon is used for tents, sleeping bags, duffel bags, racquet strings, football pants, fishing lines and leaders, sails.

IN INDUSTRIAL FABRICS, it is used for tire cord, machine belting, filter netting, fish nets, laminates, ropes, and other widely used textiles.

---

### Some Major U.S. Producers of Polyamide Fibers:

| | |
|---|---|
| Allied Chemical Corp. | Fiber Industries, Inc. |
| American Enka Corp. | Firestone Synthetic |
| Beaunit Corp. | Fibers & Textiles Co. |
| Courtaulds North | Monsanto Co., Textiles |
| America Inc. | Div. |
| Dow Badische Co. | Phillips Fibers Corp. |
| E. I. duPont de | Rohm and Haas Co. |
| Nemours & Co., Inc. | UniRoyal Fibers & |
| Enjay Fibers & | Textile, Div. of |
| Laminates Co. | UniRoyal, Inc. |

Nylon is beamed from creel ready for weaving into apparel, decorative, sports or industrial fabrics.

## Stages in the Making of Polyamide Fibers

1. Cyclohexane, primary material for nylon manufacture is stored in tanks, fed to plant by pipes.

2. Overall view of some of the Girdler Absorber towers used in making the intermediates needed.

3. Bank of autoclaves in which the concentrated nylon salt solution undergoes polymerization.

4. An operator regulates a valve at the burner face of a Dowtherm Vaporizer at the plant.

5. At the spinning stage an operator supplies a hopper with nylon flake ready for spinning.

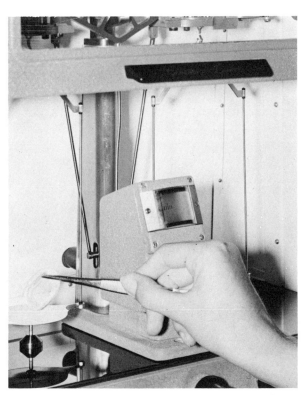

6. Spun filaments are checked in Physical Testing Laboratory, reporting to controls room.

7. Spun nylon yarn is beamed from creels on warp beams ready for shipment to customer's plant.

8. A beam of nylon yarn hoisted to storage rack prior to shipment to the customer's mills.

Moving down across the picture from the upper right corner, polyester fiber in rope-like tow form passes into a drawing machine (*not shown*) where all fibers are stretched to give them proper strength. This is one of many steps through which staple and tow must pass before they are ready to be shipped to textile mills. At each chasm-like can, another strand of tow is added until a total of 20-odd endless strands flows continuously.

# Polyester Fibers

*Wrinkle-resistance and strength make polyester fibers especially desirable for permanent-press blends and for the ease-of-care demands of the consumer.*

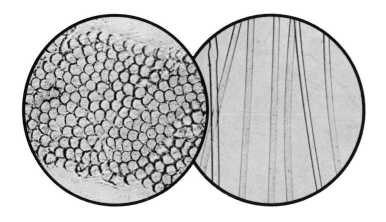

Polyester fibers are formed when several different esters are combined. The *ester* is formed from the reaction of an acid and an alcohol, involving the loss of water.

PRODUCTION of the polyester fiber is similar in many ways to the intricate process used in the manufacture of a polyamide fiber like nylon. The chemical components, however, are quite different—and account for differences in the behavior and appearance of these two synthetic fibers.

The original method for producing polyester is the batch method, which rests on the reaction of dimethyl terephthalate with ethylene glycol (commonly known as anti-freeze). The second and more recent method is continuous polymerization, which rests upon the reaction of terephthalic acid with ethylene glycol. Whatever system is used, polyethylene terephthalate is produced.

The basic chemicals from which the polyester fiber is made come from coal, air, water, and petroleum. These chemicals are "cooked" in a vacuum at very high temperatures until they combine to form a hard, porcelain-like substance. This material is melted down to a honey-like liquid which is then forced through the tiny holes in a metal disk, which is called a spinneret.

As the streams of molten liquid emerge from the spinneret, they are cooled and solidified into long, slender hair-like strands or filaments. These filaments are then stretched out to many times their original length. This stretching process imparts great strength to each filament.

## Four Forms of Polyester

Polyester fiber is produced and marketed in four basic forms:

*Filament.* An individual strand that is indefinite or continuous in length. Yarns are made by twisting together several continuous filaments. Smooth-surfaced, untextured filament yarns are used in sheer, crisp fabrics such as women's underwear and lingerie, sheer curtains and draperies. Monofilament is used in tire cord. And textured filament yarns are widely used in many apparel markets, especially knit fabrics for both women and men.

*Staple.* Fiber in short, controlled lengths cut from continuous filament. Yarns spun from it are known as staple yarns. Staple yarns are a major factor in the large and varied blend markets of polyester, especially in permanent-press wear. Staple spun yarns are also widely used in carpets.

*Tow.* A continuous, loose rope of filaments drawn together without a twist.

*Fiberfill.* A lofty or voluminous assembly of fibers used for quilting, pillows, upholstery and comfort pads. It is now available in continuous filament or crimped staple form.

## Also Used as Film

Polyester is also produced by DuPont and Celanese in the form of film, under the trade names of Mylar and Celanar. Its chief textile use is in metallic yarn laminations. Its other uses include computer and recording tapes, electrical and electronic insulation and packaging.

## Background for Polyesters

The development of man-made fibers to fill specific textile needs is an exciting story of scientific achievement. In 1926, the DuPont Laboratories initiated a research program which laid the groundwork for a whole family of synthetic fibers. The

Dr. Alfred Caress , polyester inventor.

DuPont chemists were particularly interested in determining how and why certain molecules unite to form "giant" molecules. The research revealed that giant molecules form in a variety of ways.

Rather than pursue a thorough study of all the different structural forms, DuPont concentrated its early efforts on one particular type. From this phase of the research, the nylon fiber (first of the synthetics) was developed.

British scientists became interested in the DuPont study, and selected another type of giant molecule structure for further research. This type, bearing the scientific name of "polyester," also showed traits which predicted useful textile properties. From this research came the first of the polyester fibers, known in England as TERYLENE, developed by The Calico Printers Association.

In 1946, DuPont secured the exclusive right to produce this polyester fiber in the United States. Then began a period of intensive study and experimentation directed toward practical commercial uses.

In November, 1950, ICI authorized its first major

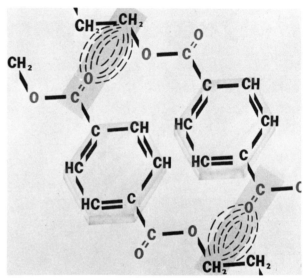

Crystalline lattice of Dacron.

polyester plant with a capacity of 11 million pounds a year, to be built at Wilton, Yorkshire, at the cost of £11 million. In December, 1950, DuPont announced plans to build its first plant at Kinston, N.C., with a capacity of 36 million pounds a year and a cost of $40 million.

To reach these points, ICI had spent $14 million, DuPont $6 million on polyester research. The $8 million difference was largely attributed to the fact that ICI had to learn melt-spinning technology from the beginning, while DuPont already had it from its nylon know-how.

All during development, DuPont called the fiber, Fiber V. In 1951, when it was unveiled at its now-famous press conference, the new fiber, now named Dacron, was displayed in the memorable "swimming pool" suit which had been worn 67 days continuously without pressing. It was dunked in the pool twice, washed in a washing machine and was still presentable after its ordeal, without pressing.

The first markets for polyester were men's suits, women's blouses and men's shirts. It quickly became a good blending fiber in men's suits, especially cord suits of Dacron/nylon and Dacron/wool.

In the mid-1950's ICI began to license world rights for polyester production, first in Canada, then to Rhodiaceta in France, Montecatini/Rhodiaceta in Italy, Hoechst and Glanzstoff in Germany, A.K.U. in Holland, Toyo Rayon and Teijin in Japan. Later ICI-licensed production units were set up in India, Australia, South Africa, Portugal, Poland, Czechoslovakia and the U.S.S.R. In 1958, when DuPont's U.S. patent was close to expiration, ICI also entered the U.S. market through Fiber Industries, Inc., a joint venture with Celanese.

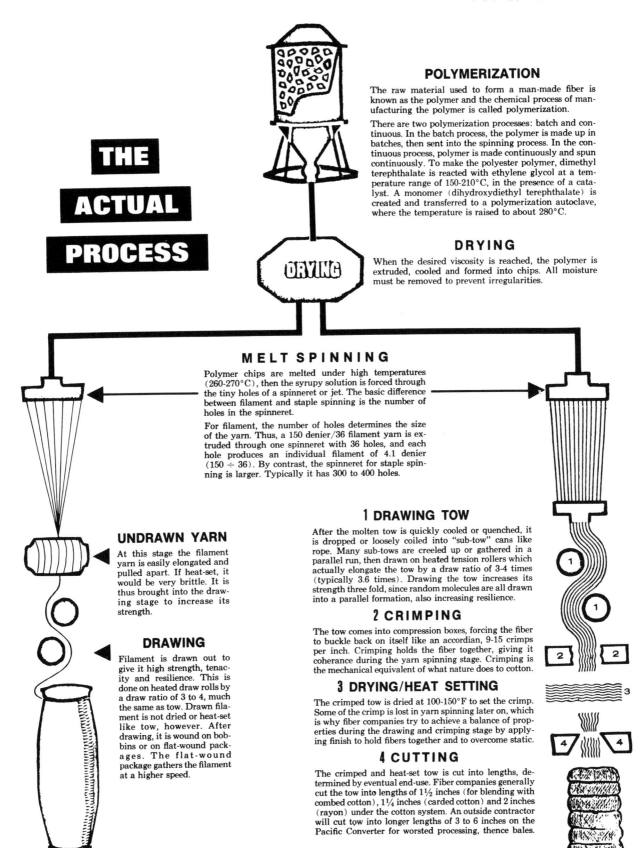

# THE ACTUAL PROCESS

## POLYMERIZATION

The raw material used to form a man-made fiber is known as the polymer and the chemical process of manufacturing the polymer is called polymerization.

There are two polymerization processes: batch and continuous. In the batch process, the polymer is made up in batches, then sent into the spinning process. In the continuous process, polymer is made continuously and spun continuously. To make the polyester polymer, dimethyl terephthalate is reacted with ethylene glycol at a temperature range of 150-210°C, in the presence of a catalyst. A monomer (dihydroxydiethyl terephthalate) is created and transferred to a polymerization autoclave, where the temperature is raised to about 280°C.

## DRYING

When the desired viscosity is reached, the polymer is extruded, cooled and formed into chips. All moisture must be removed to prevent irregularities.

## MELT SPINNING

Polymer chips are melted under high temperatures (260-270°C), then the syrupy solution is forced through the tiny holes of a spinneret or jet. The basic difference between filament and staple spinning is the number of holes in the spinneret.

For filament, the number of holes determines the size of the yarn. Thus, a 150 denier/36 filament yarn is extruded through one spinneret with 36 holes, and each hole produces an individual filament of 4.1 denier (150 ÷ 36). By contrast, the spinneret for staple spinning is larger. Typically it has 300 to 400 holes.

## UNDRAWN YARN

At this stage the filament yarn is easily elongated and pulled apart. If heat-set, it would be very brittle. It is thus brought into the drawing stage to increase its strength.

## DRAWING

Filament is drawn out to give it high strength, tenacity and resilience. This is done on heated draw rolls by a draw ratio of 3 to 4, much the same as tow. Drawn filament is not dried or heat-set like tow, however. After drawing, it is wound on bobbins or on flat-wound packages. The flat-wound package gathers the filament at a higher speed.

## 1 DRAWING TOW

After the molten tow is quickly cooled or quenched, it is dropped or loosely coiled into "sub-tow" cans like rope. Many sub-tows are creeled up or gathered in a parallel run, then drawn on heated tension rollers which actually elongate the tow by a draw ratio of 3-4 times (typically 3.6 times). Drawing the tow increases its strength three fold, since random molecules are all drawn into a parallel formation, also increasing resilience.

## 2 CRIMPING

The tow comes into compression boxes, forcing the fiber to buckle back on itself like an accordian, 9-15 crimps per inch. Crimping holds the fiber together, giving it coherance during the yarn spinning stage. Crimping is the mechanical equivalent of what nature does to cotton.

## 3 DRYING/HEAT SETTING

The crimped tow is dried at 100-150°F to set the crimp. Some of the crimp is lost in yarn spinning later on, which is why fiber companies try to achieve a balance of properties during the drawing and crimping stage by applying finish to hold fibers together and to overcome static.

## 4 CUTTING

The crimped and heat-set tow is cut into lengths, determined by eventual end-use. Fiber companies generally cut the tow into lengths of 1½ inches (for blending with combed cotton), 1¼ inches (carded cotton) and 2 inches (rayon) under the cotton system. An outside contractor will cut tow into longer lengths of 3 to 6 inches on the Pacific Converter for worsted processing, thence bales.

**FILAMENT YARN**

**STAPLE FIBER**

Polyester was the fastest growing U.S. fiber in the 1960's. Its popularity as a blend fiber with cotton and rayon, along with its permanent-press capacity, made polyester staple the predominant growth fiber in the industry. Filament polyester began to rise dramatically in the U.S. in the late 1960's, with the great popularity of textured polyester doubleknits.

Polyester is an excellent ease-of-care fiber made even more versatile by a wide range of variants, which give the fiber loft, bulk, reflectance, softer hand, soil-releasing qualities, anti-static properties, and many other advantages.

## Qualities of Polyester Fiber

The polyester fiber is an extremely resilient and springy fiber. It has the ability to spring back to its original position, wet or dry—regardless of the twisting or crushing it may undergo.

It is a smooth, crisp fiber that keeps its shape even in damp, muggy weather. Fabrics of all polyester fibers do not wilt or droop. And polyester/cotton or rayon fabrics, treated with permanent-press resins, are quite wrinkle-resistant—and crease-retentive.

It is virtually insensitive to moisture. Water does not penetrate its slick surface—doesn't affect the shape, size or resiliency of the fiber itself.

It is a thermoplastic fiber. This means that once the fiber is set to a shape by the application of heat it stays that way. This trait makes it possible to control shrinking and sagging in the final fabric—to heat-set pleats and creases that stay put through many washings and wearings.

It is a lightweight, strong fiber that resists abrasion. It is not damaged by sunlight or weather. It is not appetizing to moths nor is it harmed by mildew. Its flammability is low in fabrics when properly selected dyes and finishes are used.

## Blended with Other Fibers

Just as good cooks blend different ingredients to produce new taste treats, so do textile experts combine different fibers to produce new blended fabrics. Their goal is to create the best possible fabric for whatever end use is intended. When two or more fibers are properly combined in a single fabric it is possible to capitalize on each fiber's strong points —to offset any natural limitations or weaknesses.

Polyester adds its qualities of wrinkle-resistance, crease and shape retention, insensitivity to moisture, to a wide range of blended fabrics. Generally speak-

ing, it has been found that 50% or more of polyester is needed in the blend to bring out its best qualities. Here are some examples of typical blended fabrics in which polyester plays a strong role:

1. When polyester is properly combined with wool the resulting blended fabric has a wool-like feel and appearance—and has the added advantages of polyester's durability and easy maintenance. Many of these polyester/wool blends retain permanent pleats and creases.

2. A combination of polyester and cotton is being used extensively for men's shirts. This shirting washes easily and needs little or no ironing. Fine cotton and polyester yarns are used in dainty fabrics for women's blouses.

3. When blended with rayon or acetate in suiting fabrics, polyester brings added durability, shape retention, and lasting crispness to suits. Polyester and acetate are also combined successfully in sheer, dainty, durable lingerie fabrics.

Du Pont's Dacron plant at Old Hickory, Tenn.

### Some Major U.S. Producers of Polyester Fibers:

Allied Chemical Corp.
American Cyanamid Co. Fibers Div.
American Enka Corp.
Beaunit Corp.
Dow Badische Co.
E. I. du Pont de Nemours & Co., Inc.
Tennessee Eastman Co. Div.
FMC Corp., American Viscose Div.
Fiber Industries, Inc.
Firestone Synthetic Fibers & Textiles Co.
The Goodyear Tire & Rubber Co.
Hystron Fibers Inc.
Monsanto Co., Textiles Div.
Phillips Fibers Corp.

Polyester filament making, from pouring
of the pellets to tire cord application.

Modern bulk-handling equipment used in manufacturing Orlon acrylic fiber includes automatic weigh-tanks as shown here.

# Acrylic Fibers

*Including Modified acrylic fibers, known in the United States as Modacrylic fibers.*

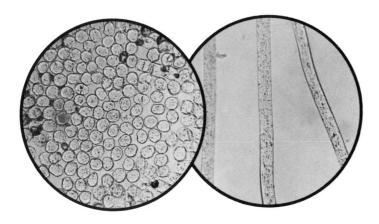

Acrylics add valuable characteristics to hundreds of textile articles, whether used alone or in blends with other fibers, natural or man-made.

ACRYLIC fibers are made from a chemical compound called acrylonitrile. This compound (from which the acrylic fiber takes its name) is made from chemicals derived from elements found in coal, air, water, petroleum and limestone. After a series of complicated chemical reactions, a solution is formed which is forced (extruded) through a spinneret, a round metal plate with tiny holes in it. Some acrylics—DuPont's Orlon, for example—are dry spun, while Monsanto's Acrilan, American Cyanamid's Creslan and Dow Badische's Zefran are wet spun. The long slender threads or filaments that stream out are dried and stretched. This "drawing" controls the stretchiness and improves the strength of the newly-formed acrylic fiber.

Acrylic fibers are used in staple fiber form. Staple fibers are made when acrylic filaments are crimped (given a permanent wave) and then chopped into any desired length, one of the many advantages of man-made fibers. These staple fibers are spun into yarns used in woven and knitted fabrics.

Bi-component acrylic yarns, which are made from two different acrylic variants, provide the industry with yarns which have very wool-like characteristics. Because of differing shrink rates, these bi-component acrylic yarns have a special crimp, which results in more loft, cover and bulk.

Modacrylic fibers are made from copolymers of acry-lonitrile and other materials such as vinyl chloride, vinylidene chloride or vinylidene dicyanide. These are derived from elements in natural gas, coal, air, salt and water. Modacrylic fibers are dry spun. The chief difference between acrylic and modacrylic fibers is that modacrylic fibers are fire-resistant.

## The Qualities of Acrylic Fibers

Acrylic fibers may be fine or heavy. The finer fibers are soft and luxurious in feeling. The heavier fibers have the bulk and hand of heavy wool.

Acrylic fibers are light in weight and springy. Because of this resilience and special textile operations, they have a fluffy quality (a loftiness) that holds up through long wear and use.

Acrylic fibers are strong despite their look of fluffiness. They have excellent resistance to sunlight, soot, smoke, fumes, and chemicals. They have no food value for moths and they resist mildew. They are non-allergenic.

Acrylic fibers are thermoplastic. This trait makes it possible to heat-set durable pleats and creases in fabrics containing acrylic fibers—contributes to shape retention.

Acrylic fibers have low moisture absorbency like most chemical fibers. This means they dry very

35

quickly. Although the fiber does not soak up water, its physical properties help a fabric made of acrylic fibers draw moisture away from the body. This contributes to body comfort, prevents any feeling of clammy dampness.

Acrylic fibers can be dyed in a wide range of colors that have excellent fastness to the elements fabrics encounter in use. Originally, the acrylics were difficult to dye, but new dyes and certain fiber changes have corrected this disadvantage. Dyes may be applied at the fiber stage, the yarn stage, the fabric stage. Some fibers are dyed at the solution stage. And some acrylics have been designed to permit piece-dyed, cross-dyed variations, producing two colors and a third tone in a single dye bath.

## Background for Acrylics

Following the development of cellulose-based fibers, research continued. The first completely synthetic fiber—nylon—was developed in 1938.

No fiber is considered an all-purpose fiber able to meet all the varied requirements of apparel, home furnishings, and other textile uses. Therefore, scientists continued the development of new, different, and varied fibers. Chemists began to look for a fiber with warm and luxurious feel—with lightness and fluffiness—with resistance to harmful elements.

The first of the acrylics of major importance — Orlon — was introduced by DuPont to the general public in the early 1950's. Now there are several additional acrylic fibers on the market — Acrilan, produced by Monsanto; Creslan, produced by American Cyanamid Company; and a nitrile alloy fiber called Zefran, produced by the Dow Badische Company, for example. Acrylics, long overshadowed by nylon and polyester, are nearly as versatile as both. They do not have nylon's durability and polyester's excellent ease-of-care properties, but they are sufficiently performance-oriented to capture many markets, both in apparel and home furnishings. In addition, they are important in many industrial and indoor/outdoor carpeting markets because of their chemical inertness, which makes them very resistant to sunlight and chemical degradation.

As an apparel and home furnishings fiber, acrylics are as versatile as polyester and even more versatile than nylon. Acrylics go into everything from luxurious sweaters to bonded knits, from hand knitting yarns to indoor/outdoor carpets.

Fibers classed as modacrylics are those such as Dynel, produced by the Union Carbide Chemicals Company; and Verel, a product of the Tennessee Eastman Company. Modacrylics have grown impressively in pile fabrics, particularly "fun" or "fake" furs. Their flame-resistant qualities make them valuable in a number of textile end uses.

## How Acrylics Are Used

Acrylic fibers have a wide variety of uses in apparel, home and industrial fabrics. They are found in:

| | |
|---|---|
| Blankets | Molded fabrics |
| Coverlets | Infants' wear |
| Draperies | Men's suitings |
| Upholstery | Snow suits |
| Pile fabrics | Scarves |
| Sweaters | Swim suits |
| Men's hose | Shirtings |
| Resist yarns | Work clothing |
| Filter cloths | Insulation fabrics |
| Dust fume bags | Floor coverings |
| Water softener filters | Knit dresses |
| Stiffened fabrics for | Paint rollers |
| collars, hats, visors | Doll wigs |
| Carpets | Hand knitting yarns |

## Use in Blends

Fabrics of several fibers blended together are becoming more and more important in the clothing and home furnishings field. Since there is no all-purpose fiber, two or more fibers are often blended into one yarn or combined in a fabric in order to obtain the benefits offered by each fiber, to decrease the disadvantages of any of the component fibers. The acrylic fibers are important in blends, both with man-made and natural fibers.

---

### Some Major U.S. Producers of Acrylic and Modacrylic Fibers:

| *Acrylic:* | *Modacrylic:* |
|---|---|
| American Cyanamid Co., Fibers Div. | Tennessee Eastman Co. Div. |
| Dow Badische Co. | Union Carbide Corp. |
| E. I. duPont de Nemours & Co., Inc. | Monsanto Co., Textiles Div. |
| Monsanto Co., Textiles Div. | |

---

## Some Stages in Acrylic Fiber Production:

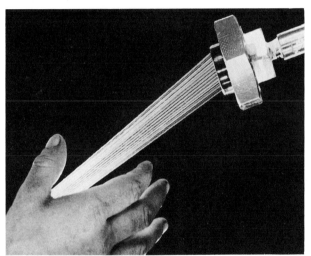

1. Unloading acrylonitrile, the basic raw material.

2. Plant where polymer is dissolved forming "dope."

3. Fibers are extended from spinneret in filament form.

4. Fiber strands are stretched, and washed in bath.

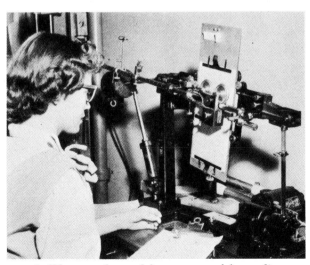

5. Fiber samples are laboratory tested for quality.

6. Baled fiber is loaded for shipment to the mill.

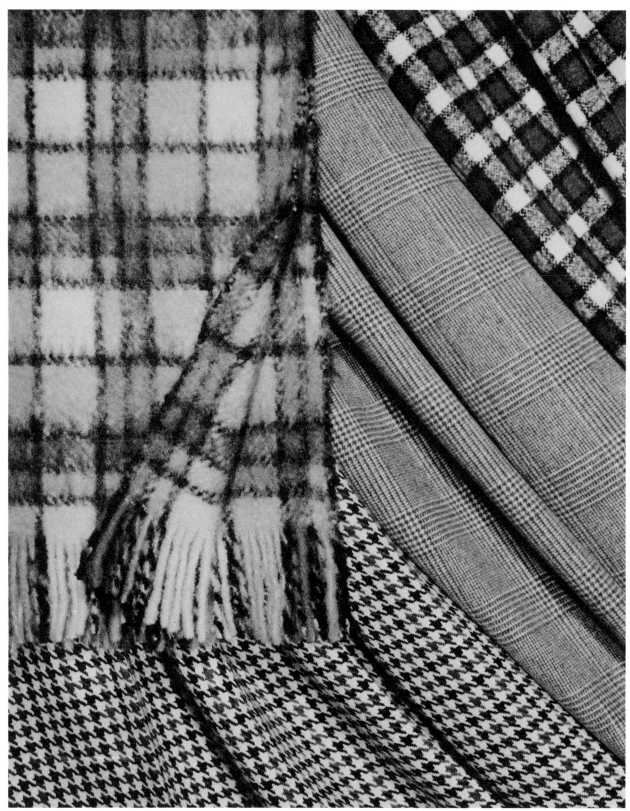

Polypropylene fibers can be used alone or blended with wool and cotton. Shown in the upper left corner is a blanket of pure polypropylene. At the lower left and upper right corners are suitings also made of the pure synthetic. The glen plaid fabric in the center is a polypropylene-wool blend.

# Olefins (Polyethylene, Polypropylene)

*Polyolefins have great chemical inertness and a growing role in textiles, particularly carpets.*

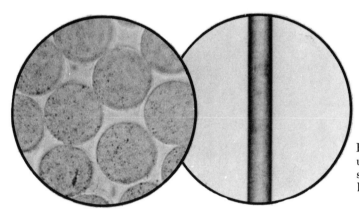

By the mid-1960's, olefins had become a widely used textile fiber in carpeting, cordage, upholstery, fishing gear, blankets and in cellulosic blends.

Olefin fibers (polyethylene and polypropylene) are man-made fibers derived from petroleum products, particularly propylene and ethylene gases. Their chief characteristics are moisture resistance and chemical inertness. Polypropylene is by far the more popular for textile applications, especially carpeting.

Polyethylene fibers are polymerized by two methods, a high pressure/high temperature process and a low pressure/low temperature process. Both low-density and high-density polyethylene are extruded into monofilaments of round, flat or other cross-sections. High-density polyethylene is drawn to a higher degree than low-density polyethylene (10:1 as opposed to 4-10:1).

The actual conditions of polymerizing polypropylene are not divulged by the manufacturers, but it is speculated that polymerization, using Ziegler-type catalysts, takes place under 25-30 atmospheres of pressure at about 100°C. Polymer of high viscosity is spun to maximize fiber properties. Filaments are air-cooled as they emerge from the spinneret, then collected on bobbins.

## Background for Olefins

Isobutylene, the first olefin, was polymerized as long ago as 1873, but the first commercialization of the major olefin, polypropylene, as a textile fiber had to wait until the early 1960's. During the 1920's, many efforts were made to polymerize ethylene, the simplest olefin. But, because of many technical difficulties, it resisted polymerization until the early 1930's. Even then, it had to wait until World War II before it had an important commercial role to play—and then as a plastic, not as a textile fiber.

In 1954, the Ziegler Process for ethylene polymerization provided polyethylenes of higher melting points, which were capable of being spun into filaments and monofilaments for small-volume textile applications.

Because of its low softening or melting point, polyethylene has been confined to non-apparel fields. Even high-density polyethylene softens at 126-132°C. Its resistance to rot, to water and to chemical erosion make it suitable for cordage and netting, while its strength and cleaness make it a good fiber for car upholstery fabrics, protective clothing, tarpaulin and related end-uses.

Polypropylene vastly expands the use of olefins as the raw material base for man-made fibers. With the successful polymerization of ethylene, the search for an even more successful textile fiber was started. Professor Guilio Natta filed the first patent applica-

(*Above*) Source of propylene gas, the basic material for manufacture of polypropylene fiber, is oil refinery. (*Below*) Production of polypropylene thread in **Montecatini** spinning plant, Terni, **Italy**.

tions on polypropylene, in conjunction with Professor Karl Ziegler, in 1954. Polypropylene production was begun by Montecatini Societa Generale in 1957 in Italy, and, in the U.S., by Hercules in 1961.

Polypropylene fiber has properties most suitable for textile applications. It softens at over 300°F. and melts at about 345°F., so that it can be melt-extruded with ease. It is light in weight, having a specific gravity of 0.91. Moisture absorbency is low and it has high wet strength and high electrical insulation properties. Chemically inert, it is resistant to acids and alkalis, to mildew and moths. It is soft to the touch when spun, and blends extremely well with natural wool.

Although the tensile strength of polypropylene when extruded is low, drawing processes aimed at alignment of the polymer construction have been perfected which give the fiber a good tensile strength. It has natural abrasion resistance. Being liquid-spun it can easily be pigmented before extrusion; dyeing is difficult and appropriate techniques are being developed to overcome its non-absorbent nature.

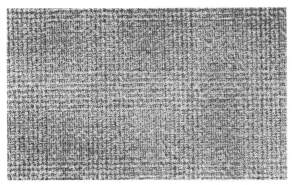

Glen plaid in polypropylene and wool.

By the mid-1960's polypropylene had become a widely used textile fiber of diversified application. It entered the same markets as its technical cousin, polyethylene—cordage, upholstery and fishing gear —then burgeoned into carpeting, which is its most impressive textile application to date. It has also had some success in sewing thread, blankets, some knitwear, hosiery, and in cellulosic blends.

Despite the original hope that polypropylene fibers would one day rank with nylon and polyester, it has been hampered by dyeing difficulties and relatively low melting point. It had a rapid and broad growth rate during the 1960's, however, and may well reach something approximating its original forecasts if technology can overcome its remaining inhibitions to growth. One mark of its success is the fact that there are more plants producing it in the world than any other man-made fiber.

Checkerboard carpet made from polypropylene.

## Uses of Olefins (Primarily Polypropylene):

Carpeting
Non-Woven Felts
Laundry Bags
Dye Nets
Hosiery
Sweaters
Upholstery
Rope
Ties
Undergarments
Pile Fabrics
Filters
Sewing Thread

### Some Major U.S. Producers of Olefin Fiber:

Burlington Industrial Fabrics Co.
Celanese Corp.
CF & I Steel Corp.
Chevron Chemical Co.
Columbian Rope Co.
Deering Milliken, Inc.
Enjay Fibers & Laminates Co.
Fibron, Inc.
Hercules Inc.

International Harvester Co.
Ozite Corp.
Phillips Fibers Corp.
Thiokol Chemical Corp.
UniRoyal Fiber & Textile, Div. of UniRoyal, Inc.
Vogt Plastics

# Polyvinyl

*Polyvinyl chloride is the basis of fibers
classed as vinyons in the United States.*

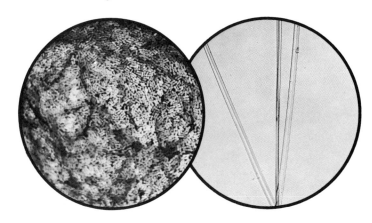

Photomicrographs of a polyvinyl
fiber, showing smooth surface
and elongated cross-section
which determine its performance.

Polyvinyl fibers are man-made from basic chemicals found in salt water and petroleum. The chemical compound is called vinylidene chloride. In the chemical process ethylene is obtained from petroleum by cracking, and chlorine is extracted from salt water by electrolysis. Chlorine and ethylene combine to form a simple molecule or monomer called trichloroethane, which is then polymerized into the basic vinylidene chloride resin. This is melted, extruded and stretched into filaments.

## Background for Polyvinyl

Vinylidene chloride was discovered experimentally by the French chemist Regnault in 1840, but was not developed until 1939, when the Dow Chemical Company began research in the field.

The first fibers produced were named SARAN and were in the form of heavy denier monofilament. They were used in tapes, outdoor furniture seats, screening, auto covers, upholstery, agricultural shade cloth, bristles, grille cloth. To expand the field, the Saran Yarns Company was formed and began to produce finer denier monofilaments and fiber. Curled staple fiber opened up new fields because it closely approximated the natural crimp of multifilaments. They also added a new curled staple wool fiber and added new characteristics such as being moth and mildew-proof, non-absorbent, stain-resistant, and flame resistant.

Because of their non-flammability and resistance to chemical degradation, polyvinyl chloride fibers play a significant role in industrial markets, particularly in filters, battery fabrics, tarpaulins, fishing nets, orthopedic materials and canvas awnings for aircraft.

As an upholstery fabric, p.v.c. is dominant in car seat covers and very popular in tropical countries because of its resistance to deterioration. P.v.c. fiber has never been a significant apparel fiber because of its susceptibility to shrinkage and distortion at relatively low temperatures, which makes fabrics of p.v.c. difficult to wash and iron.

*Opposite:*

Some key steps in the making of vinylidene chloride yarns:

1. A small batch of resin is mixed with color, then blended in a ball mill and mixed with other batches of resin and color.

2. The ingredients of resin and color are unloaded from a cone blender into drums for handling prior to extrusion process.

3. An operator checks the extrusion process by which the melted resin mixture is formed into filaments and cooled in tank.

4. After extrusion and cooling the strands of polyvinyl fiber are oriented or stretched to the desired diameter, and wound.

5. In product control laboratory a technician examines samples in Fade-Ometer to determine aging resistance under ultra-violet light.

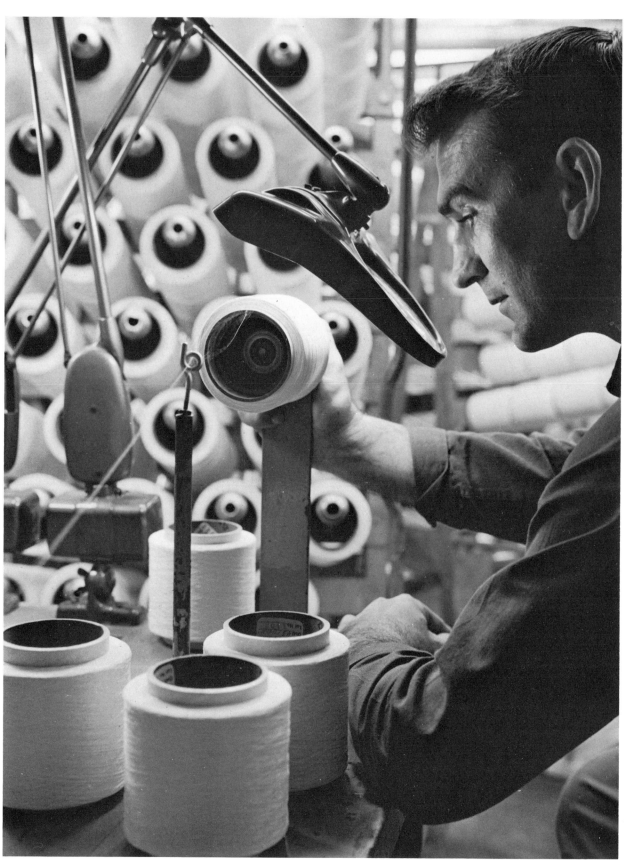

Introduced by Du Pont in 1960, spandex fiber requires one of the most complex chemical technologies in man-made fibers. Spandex is a generic term used to describe elastomerc fibers which stretch and snap back into shape like natural rubber.

# Spandex

Spandex yarn being creeled, for hosiery, swimwear, foundation garments.

## Definition

Spandex is a generic term used to describe a family of elastomeric man-made fibers. Spandex has elastic properties which allow the fiber to stretch and snap back into shape like natural rubber.

The term "spandex" was adopted by the Federal Trade Commission to identify synthetic elastomers which are chemically different from natural or synthetic rubbers. Technically, spandex describes a man-made fiber in which the fiber-forming substance is a long chain synthetic polymer comprised of at least 85% of a segmented urethane, which is the same chemical substance widely used as a foam in bonded and laminated fabrics, and in furniture. Urethane (the term is interchangeable with polyurethane) has been regarded in the rubber and textile industries as a development of major importance.

Spandex is extruded as a monofilament or in a multiplicity of fine filaments which immediately form a monofilament.

## History of Spandex

The origins of spandex go back to World War II when chemists began to search for a man-made fiber which would replace scarce rubber. An additional impetus was the urge to offset the price gyrations of rubber and thus create greater economic stability in the market. The research that began at that time had as its goal the development of a durable elastic strand, particularly one that would stand up to dry cleaning and oxidation.

Though the research objective was not to find a *finer* elastic thread (rubber threads of extreme fineness had already been achieved but had gained little acceptance in the market), nevertheless fineness of thread became a highly promotable factor in the first spandex garments, and as a result spandex became associated with lightness of weight. Later there was a return to the use of coarser spandex yarns, particularly in fabrics for foundation garments.

Final achievement of spandex fiber was due to basic research over a number of years by the Du Pont and U.S. Rubber (now UniRoyal) Companies. In each case the research was conducted independently. Du Pont named its new elastic fiber "Lycra." UniRoyal's spandex is registered under the name "Vyrene."

In addition to these two pioneer developments, at least six other U.S. companies have expanded their operations to include the production of spandex fiber in response to strong trade and consumer demand. Others are in the experimental stage or in pilot operation.

## Research and Development

Soon after nylon was invented by Du Pont in 1939—marking the beginning of a new era in textiles—research teams began to explore the concept of stretchable yarns made of nylon fibers, which would take the rigidity out of woven textiles and give fast recovery to knits.

The groundwork for Du Pont's "Lycra" was laid by a research team seeking ways to produce a fiber with the elastic qualities of rubber, but at the same time a textile fiber in the truest sense. In 1958 the experimental fiber was introduced for trade evaluation and, during the next year and a half, was tested extensively by foundation garment manufacturers. Plans for commercialization were announced in October 1959. First quantities introduced for trade use were produced at Du Pont's pilot plant in 1960, but by February 1961 construction was started at a commercial-scale plant, and production increased six to ten times by mid-1962.

Concurrently, the UniRoyal spandex fiber, under the registered trademark "Vyrene," was produced after more than ten years of research, development and testing of the unique method used in the fiber's manufacture.

## Two Types of Spandex

At this point a distinction must be made between the two pioneer spandex brands—Lycra and Vyrene. Both are classified as spandex, but they differ in their physical construction. Vyrene is a monofilament spandex fiber which was designed as a covered yarn by its producer. It was covered with various other fibers, depending on the end use for which it was made, and these could be nylon, acetate, cotton, acrylic or other textile yarns.

In contrast, Lycra is a multifilament bundle joined together to form a monofilament yarn. It can be used "bare" or covered. To the eye, multifilament Lycra appears to be a single continuous thread, but actually is composed of many threads so tiny that, singly, they are invisible to the eye.

## Properties of Spandex

The basic properties of spandex may be listed as follows:

1. HIGH STRETCH. It compares well with natural rubber in its high degree of stretch—over 500% without breaking.

2. LOW SET. This refers to its remarkable ability to spring back to its original shape or set. After repeated stretching it shows only an extremely small change in length.

3. HIGH DURABILITY. Its tensile strength is substantially higher than that of rubber. Its resistance to chafing under stress and strain is superior to rubber or synthetic elastomers. And it resists deterioration due to oxidation.

4. EASY TO CLEAN. It stands up well under both dry cleaning and laundering. It can be machine washed and dried.

5. UNIFORMITY. Even in extrusions as fine as human hair it has excellent uniformity of structure.

6. VERSATILITY. It can be used either "bare" or as a core fiber covered by any other textile fiber, natural or man-made.

Because of these varied properties, spandex makes possible durable elastic fabrics which weigh much less than previous elastic fabrics, resulting in a wide range of sheer, lightweight cloths with surprising control power and many end uses.

## Spandex for Core-Spinning

Spandex—which takes dyes and can be successfully used in its bare state to produce fabrics—is the essential ingredient in core-spinning. Core-spinning is a method by which the elastic filament is fed into the twisting zone of the spinning frame under predetermined tensions. It thus produces a yarn whose core is the elastic filament and whose outer sheath is composed of any staple fiber used in spinning. When tension is removed from the spandex core, it returns to its normal length, pulling the sheath fibers into a more compact formation.

There are two significant advantages of core-spinning with spandex:

1. The use of as little as 5% to 10% spandex can produce a yarn with high stretch and excellent recovery. The degree of elongation can also be controlled from a very low percentage to one as high as 200%, depending on the yarn construction.

2. The core-spun yarn takes on the aesthetic characteristics (hand and appearance) of whatever fibers are used in the outer sheath. Since the elastic core is buried in the casing of sheath fibers, it does not appear on the fabric's surface.

## Spandex a Tool in Knit Designs

Though elasticity is a natural characteristic in knit products, spandex used in knitted fabrics serves to achieve quick recovery from stretching and therefore more perfect garment fit. At the same time, spandex also serves as a design tool to achieve stitch effects not previously attainable in machine knit production.

One example is the use of feed devices to supply spandex yarn to the knitting needles of the mechanism at precisely controlled sequences, in a range of yarn-delivery variations beyond the capacity of non-elastic yarns. Thus the stitch quality may be varied, or fabric modifications may be imposed through regular or random phasing which depends on the setting of the feed mechanism. Unusual fashion fabrics can be produced by this principle on the most simple knitting equipment, without patterning or selecting mechanisms.

When applied to fancy-patterning circular knitting equipment—capable of needle selection by jacquard, pattern wheel or electronic controls—spandex yarns at chosen yarn feeds can achieve precise forms of fashion and design expression.

---

### Lastex Yarn

Perhaps the best-known name in elastic yarns is Lastex, produced by the United States Rubber Company. Lastex followed the successful extrusion of a fine latex strand by U.S. Rubber in 1925. This rubber strand could be made both continuous and very fine in size, which meant that an elastic yarn could be produced that could be so fine as to be run through a knitting needle or a shuttle. This was a marked advance over the earlier technique of wrapping textile yarns around heavier and coarser-cut rubber strands which, up to that time, had a comparatively short life-span compared to the new latex type. Further development work led to patenting Lastex in 1931. This came after much work with fiber textile yarns and on special covering equipment.

How Lastex is made. Manufacturing procedures on the main types of Lastex yarn fall into two parts: blending, extrusion, and curing of the fine latex strand for the core; and wrapping or covering this core with textile strands. In most constructions, the latter covering consists of spinning textile yarn about the rubber core, which is drawn through the hollow spindles of two cones as they revolve in opposite directions. The resulting elastic yarn can be taken up either on skeins or on cones, the use to be determined by fabric manufacturers.

---

## Wide Range of Apparel Uses

Spandex was recognized from the beginning as a natural and ideal medium for swimwear, where the fiber's virtues are shown to good advantage and where it has achieved important fashion functions of great variety. In swimwear spandex provides superior fit with a minimum of complicated tailoring. Equally successful is the role of spandex in foundation garments where there are almost no limits to the types of textiles in which the fiber can be utilized. These include elastic laces, jacquards, lenos, knits—all of which can be made to exact specifications of stretch and tension, either woven or knitted right into the fabric.

Other apparel uses include hosiery, especially sock tops, support and surgical stockings. Spandex allows lightweight freedom of movement in pants, sportswear—especially active skiwear—slacks.

---

### Anim/8 Fiber

In 1969 Rohm and Haas introduced the anidex fiber, Anim/8, an elastomeric, the first generic fiber to be introduced in the United States since 1961. Anim/8 was reported to have recovery qualities superior to any previous elastomeric fiber. It can also be bleached with chlorine and blends with all natural and man-made fibers. Its other characteristics include: equal adaptability to weaving and knitting; applicability to corespun, covered, plied or bare constructions; affinity for dispersed dyes, permanent press and soil-release finishes; dyeing, printing and finishing by traditional processes; and retention of elasticity after washing or dry cleaning. The Federal Trade Commission ruled that Anim/8 was a generic fiber in 1970. It has since been introduced in a number of fabric constructions and end-uses, from apparel to upholstery. The F.T.C. defines anidex as a manufactured fiber in which the fiber-forming substance is any long chain synthetic polymer composed of at least 50% by weight of one or more esters of a monohydric alcohol and acrylic acid. Rohm and Haas reputedly spent $20 million and 10 years of research time to develop Anim/8.

Glass marbles are the base material from which filaments are drawn to be woven into glass fiber textiles.

# Glass Fibers

*One of the most remarkable achievements in modern textiles is the conversion of solid glass marbles into soft, durable and luxurious, decorative fabrics.*

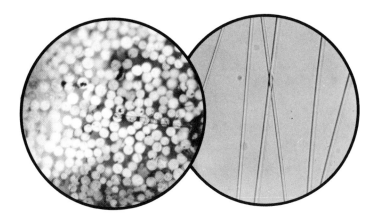

Cross sectional and longitudinal views of glass fibers used in textiles.

A group of textile fibers and yarns is made of glass. The reason they are pliable and can be woven—when most glass is brittle—is that the individual fibers are extremely fine—so fine that it takes from 100 to 12,500 filaments fibers to make a fine yarn. The finest filament is one-quarter denier or 3.8 microns in diameter.

## Characteristics

The chief characteristics of glass fiber fabrics are:

1. NON-INFLAMMABLE. They do not burn and can be subjected to temperatures as high as 1200°F. before they show signs of deterioration.

2. NON-ABSORBENT. Being glass, they do not absorb moisture. They also do not absorb dirt. This makes it possible to wash glass fabrics easily and to dry them damp in as little as seven minutes. They require no ironing.

3. IMPERVIOUS. They are mothproof, mildew-proof, and will not deteriorate in sunlight or with age. They resist most chemicals. Being impervious to water, glass fabrics will not shrink when washed.

4. STRONG. Fibers made of glass are among the strongest produced by man-made means. Owing to their tensile strength they are stable in fabric; in addition, when used as reinforcement in plastics they serve the function of the steel rods in rein-

forced concrete, producing a very light yet strong material.

## Uses of Glass Fibers

Glass fiber textiles are used in a wide variety of products. The chief ones are:

| | |
|---|---|
| Decorative fabrics | Electrical and thermal |
| Fireproof clothes | insulation |
| Soundproofing | Air filters |
| | Reinforcement for plastics |
| | Tires |
| | Upholstery |

## Background for Glass Fibers

While the Venetians contrived to attenuate glass into fairly flexible strands for decorative purposes, the first glass fabrics did not make their debut until the Columbian Exposition of 1893 in Chicago, when an actress by the name of Georgia Cayvan appeared in a glass dress and drew gaping crowds who thought the dress would be transparent. Even today a lot of people can't seem to understand that glass textiles are first and foremost *not* transparent.

The man responsible for this strange departure in couture was Edward D. Libbey, of the Libbey Glass Company, who had succeeded in drawing coarse fibers from the heated ends of glass rods. A warp made up of these fibers was worked together with a filling of silk threads to make Miss Cayvan's dress.

In the dawn of the 20th Century a number of patents were issued in Germany and England for drawing fibers from glass. Though too coarse for weaving, they were used to some extent in thermal insulation by the Germans, prior to World War I.

## First Explorations

It was not until the early thirties that the possibility of manufacturing glass fibers was first seriously explored in the United States, with considerable research undertaken by Owens-Illinois Glass Company and Corning Glass Works—at first independently and later on a joint basis. There were numerous discouragements and setbacks before any substantial progress was noted. At length, in November, 1938, Owens-Corning Fiberglas Corporation was organized as an independent company to make and market Fiberglas products. The men chiefly responsible for this development were Games Slayter and John H. Thomas and Harold Boeschenstein.

The first Fiberglas products which enjoyed any considerable commercial acceptance were filters. Then in rapid succession came thermal insulation materials, plastic reinforcements, electrical insulation, curtains, draperies.

Today, technology permits yarn-dyeing of glass fibers. Prior to this development, glass fiber fabrics could be colored only after the fabrics are woven. Glass fabrics with the same color depth and pattern variation achieved in other yarn-dyed fabrics are obtainable in glass fiber fabrics.

## How Glass Fibers Are Made

1. PRELIMINARY YARN PROCESSING. Two processes —continuous filament and staple fiber—are employed to produce glass fiber yarns. Both begin with accurate batch formulation, glass melting, and refining. Throughout the entire operation the processes are subject to an unusually high degree of scientific control and inspection. The raw materials comprising the glass batch are inspected, analyzed, and mixed in accordance with formulas adapted to the end uses of the fibers. From precisely controlled furnaces, the molten glass flows to marble-forming machines which turn out small glass marbles of one inch in diameter.

One reason for forming these marbles is to permit visual inspection of the glass for the purpose of eliminating impurities such as bubbles or bits of refractory material that would lower the uniform fiber quality or interfere with subsequent operations. The marbles are then remelted in small electric furnaces as a part of the fiber-forming operation. Recent improvements enable textile fibers also to be drawn from the original melt, eliminating this marble operation.

2. CONTINUOUS FILAMENT PROCESS. The continuous filament process provides filaments of indefinite length measurable in miles. The fibers are formed by mechanical attenuation. Molten glass flows downward through temperature-resistant metal alloy feeders having more than 200 small orifices. As the fine streams of molten glass emerge from these

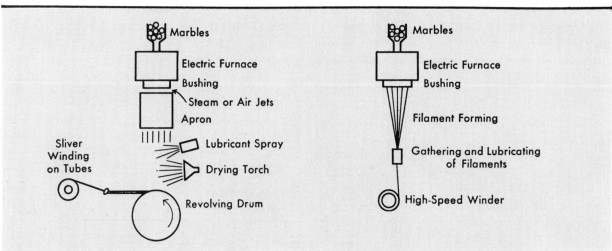

### Staple Fiber Process

### Continuous Filament Process

Marbles
Electric Furnace
Bushing
Steam or Air Jets
Apron
Sliver Winding on Tubes
Lubricant Spray
Drying Torch
Revolving Drum

Marbles
Electric Furnace
Bushing
Filament Forming
Gathering and Lubricating of Filaments
High-Speed Winder

Diagram of the staple fiber and continuous filament processes of producing fibers from glass.

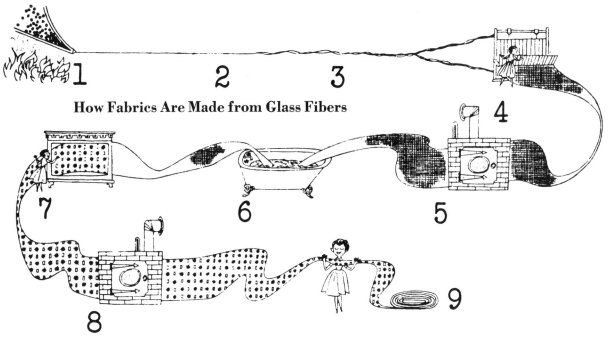

**How Fabrics Are Made from Glass Fibers**

1. Glass marbles are melted over intense heat.
2. Yarn is processed by plying filaments.
3. Yarns textured by jets of air.
4. Weaving of yarns on standard looms.

5. Coronizing fabrics heat sets them at 1200°.
6. Fabric passes through bath of finishing resins.
7. Fabric is roller or screen printed with dye.
8. Baking at 320° sets the finish for fastness.

feeders having up to 1,200 small orifices. As the fine streams of molten glass emerge from these holes, they are gathered together, run over an applicator where a sizing is picked up, and then carried to a high-speed winder. Because the winder revolves at a much faster rate than the stream flows from the melting chamber, the tension attenuates the glass while it is still molten and thus draws out filaments that are a mere fraction of the diameter of the orifices. The winder draws out the continuous filaments at rates above two miles a minute.

After being drawn onto a forming tube, the continuous filaments are subsequently processed into glass fiber yarns and cords through conventional twisting and plying operations on standard textile machinery.

3. WOOL PROCESS. In addition to the various glass-fiber yarns and the fabrics woven from them, there is another important substance in this family—glass-fiber wool. As a matter of fact, glass-fiber wool came first. The preliminary processing follows the familiar pattern of melting and refining. Once again the molten glass flows through tiny orifices in thin streams. It is caught by the impact of high-pressure steam jets that attenuate it into long, resilient fibers.

These are gathered at the base of the forming chamber, on a traveling conveyor, as a white fleecy mass of fine fibers, intricately interlaced with each other.

The product may be used for thermal insulation in substantially the form thus produced; or it may be fabricated into such items as filters, mats, or blankets with a variety of facings; or it may be treated with a thermo-setting resin binder, compressed to the desired density and thickness, and passed through an oven where the binder takes its final set. The resultant product may range from a flexible batt to a semi-rigid or rigid board.

4. STAPLE FIBER PROCESS. The staple fiber process forms a fiber having long-staple characteristics. It uses jets of compressed air to attenuate or draw out the molten glass into fine fibers. The molten glass flows through orifices in special temperature-resistant metal alloy feeders at the base of each furnace. The impact of the compressed air literally yanks the thin stream of molten glass into fine fibers varying in length from 8 to 15 inches. The fibers are driven down onto a revolving drum on which they form a thin veil resembling a cobweb.

In their almost instantaneous descent to the drum, the fibers pass through a spray of lubricant and a drying flame. This web of fibers is then gathered from the drum into a strand that is lightly drafted in the ensuing winding operation so that the majority of the fibers lie parallel with the length of the strand. This soft strand can be further reduced in diameter, if desired, and then twisted and plied into yarns of various sizes, using textile machinery and processes similar to those employed for long-staple materials.

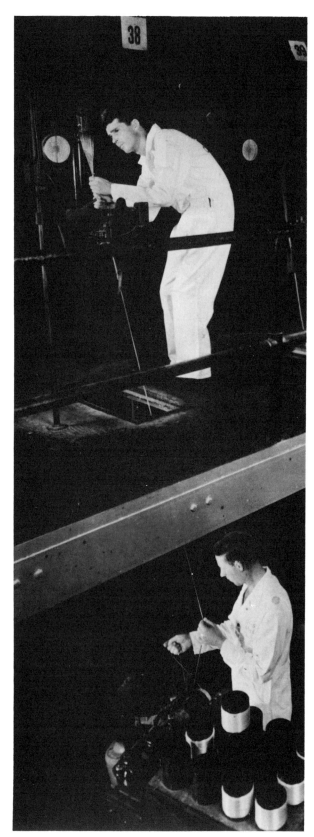

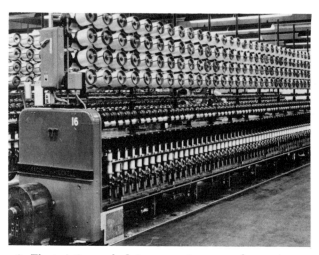

2. The twisting and plying operation turns the continuous filaments into yarns for weaving.

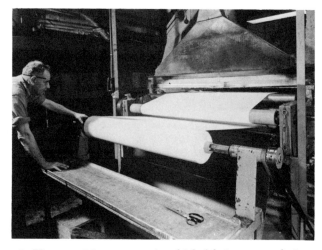

3. The coronizing process in which fabric woven of glass fibers is heated, cleaned, and the weave set.

1. Continuous filaments of glass fiber are extruded from spinnerets and wound on bobbins on lower floor.

4. Inspection of a fine glass fiber marquisette curtain fabric before shipping from the mill.

## Coronizing Solved Many Problems

The first household fabrics made of glass left a great deal to be desired. They had an inferior hand and poor draping character. These difficulties were caused by the fact that the fiber is made up of innumerable tiny glass rods, which have an intrinsic tendency to remain in a straight line. This would occur the minute the materials were handled; hence the wrinkles and other fabric faults. There was also trouble with tiny skin-irritating spicules in the glass yarns.

All these fabric faults have been entirely corrected by Coronizing. This process puts a permanent crimp into the tiny glass rods by subjecting them to intense heat, approximately 1200°F. After Coronizing, the fibers can never straighten out again. In other words, this gives a permanent set to the weave and makes the fabric permanently wrinkle-proof, in addition to softening it. The cloth is then passed through a finishing bath in which resin and pigment are applied, improving its resistance to abrasion, and leaving the surface soft and smooth.

## The Aerocor Process

Fiberglas textured yarn is standard continuous yarn which, after plying, is textured by means of concentrated air pressure. This is done as it winds past a nozzle on a machine which looks like a twisting frame. One current technique of texturing is the process known as Taslan, patented by the DuPont Company. Most of the textured Fiberglas yarns today have been put through the Taslan process. Owens-Corning is a licensee, as are the major weavers of Fiberglas fabrics. Another form of Fiberglas continuous yarns are the bulked or lofted yarns, which are put through an Owens-Corning bulking process. These are known as Fiberglas 401 yarns.

The 401 yarn is entirely different in appearance and hand from continuous Fiberglas yarns. The bulking process increases the diameter of the strand by from 30 to 40%. Fabrics woven from these yarns have a different feel and texture. This yarn gives a natural fiber look and a drier, softer hand to fiberglas fabrics.

Fiberglas 401 yarns, due to their bulk, have a degree of wicking action. Accordingly, the fabric may require a longer drip-drying time than regular continuous fabrics. The fiber itself does not absorb water.

Other developments in glass-fiber technology have led to softer, more pliable fibers. Fiberglas Beta yarn, for example, is less than four microns in diameter or about one-half the diameter of any previously used in Fiberglas textiles. It is 1/6 the fineness of silk, 1/3 the diameter of Vicuna and 1/6 the denier of the finest acrylics, nylon or viscose rayon. This imparts a softer hand to organic fibers to which it is blended.

Beta is a product of fusion under high temperatures. It will not yield at temperatures under 945°F, lending it properties of perfect elasticity, dimensional stability, high strength, fire proofness and temperature resistance.

## Rapid Growth in Tires

The most dramatic recent development in glass fibers for industrial use is tire cord. During the late 1960's bias/belted polyester and glass tires became a dominant factor in original equipment markets. A typical polyester/glass tire features a bias-ply polyester cord for the body or envelope of the tire and fiberglass belts under the tread for high strength. The fiberglass belt is a key factor in excellent tread life and overall tread performance.

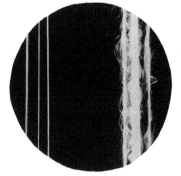

Photomicrograph of continuous filament (*left*), and textured Aerocor Fiberglas yarn (*right*).

## Care of Glass Fiber Fabrics

Glass fiber materials, like any other materials, are not indestructible. If used as draw or traverse draperies they should be hung just off the floor and slightly away from protruding window sills or other objects which might cause abrasion and snag the fabric.

### Some Major U.S. Producers of Glass Fibers for Textiles:

Fiber Glass Industries Inc.
Glass Fiber Products, Inc.
Johns-Manville Fiber Glass Inc.
Modiglass Fibers Div.,
Reichold Chemicals, Inc.
Owens-Corning Fiberglas Corp.
PPG Industries, Inc.
Uniglass Industries

World's largest asbestos mine, John's-Manville's Jeffrey Mine, located in Asbestos, Quebec.

Asbestos in the natural mineral state, after it has been separated from the matrix rock in which it is mined.

After the asbestos fibers have been cleaned and graded according to length, they are carded and made into roving, ready for spinning.

# Asbestos Fibers

*While asbestos is a natural fiber, it is close to man-made products, being formed under heat and pressure inorganically.*

Photomicrograph of chrysotile asbestos fibers seen under an electron microscope magnified 41,200 diameters.

Asbestos is a fibrous mineral mined from rock deposits. There are approximately thirty different mineral types in the asbestos group. Six of these have commercial importance and of these six, only one—chrysotile—is used in textile processing.

Asbestos was known to the ancient Greeks as early as the 1st Century A.D. The name asbestos is derived from the Greek term which means inconsumable. However, the mineral did not assume commercial importance until the invention of the steam engine, with its need for packing and insulation.

Chemically, chrysotile asbestos is a hydrated silicate of magnesium which contains small amounts of ferrous, ferric and aluminum oxides.

## Physical Properties

The commercial value of asbesos textiles is built on two main factors:

1. Asbestos will not burn. Its quality will not deteriorate at temperatures up to 750°F. and its structure remains stable up to 1490°F.

2. It can be spun and woven into textiles. The best grades of chrysotile with the longest fibers are used in textile processing. The fibers are silky and extremely fine in diameter, among the finest fibers now in commercial use.

## Sources of Asbestos

The world's leading sources of chrysotile asbestos are Canada and Russia. In 1969, the total Canadian production was approximately 1,577,000 short tons. The Province of Quebec, in an area of no more than 750 square miles, accounted for about 85% of this production. Russia has large chrysotile deposits and it is estimated that its 1969 production was about 2,200,000 tons. Other countries which produce this material include South Rhodesia, the United States, Swaziland (South Africa), Turkey, Venezuela and Colombia.

## How Asbestos Fibers Are Produced

According to chemical and mineralogical studies, asbestos is solely of mineral origin and theory holds that it was formed when deposits of rock composed of iron, magnesia and silica were acted upon by hot waters containing carbon dioxide and dissolved salts while under high pressure. Through the ages the product of this chemical process slowly formed into layers of closely packed fibers. When separated, this yields the workable form in which asbestos is now used.

Asbestos is mined either by the open pit or underground method. It takes about 20 tons of asbestos-bearing rock to produce one ton of fiber which can be successfully processed. Following are the main steps in processing:

1. COBBING. The longer fibers—from ⅜ to ¾ of an inch—are separated from the adhering rock by pounding or cobbing. This is done by hand with a cobbing hammer.

2. MILLING. Shorter fibers—up to ⅜ inch long—are separated from the rock by mechanical milling. This involves crushing and screening.

Among the uses of woven asbestos fiber is fire-resistant cloth (above) which can be made into special clothing, and asbestos tape (below), also known as listing, which is used for heat insulation.

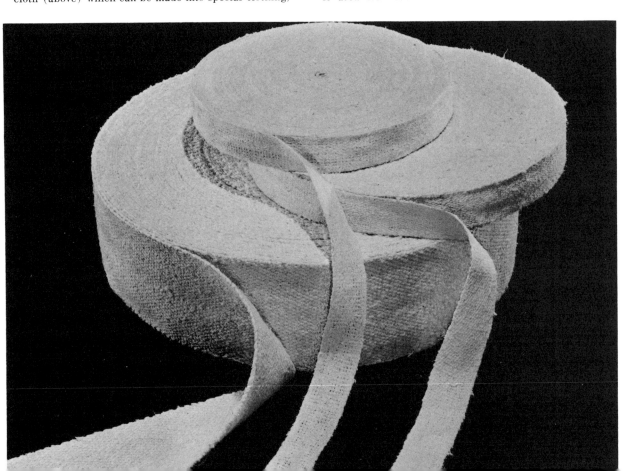

3. GRADING. The fibers are accurately graded according to length. The screen or shaker box method is the one most commonly used.

4. FIBERIZATION. The fibers are further cleaned and separated.

5. BLENDING AND MIXING. Different grades of fiber are blended together. Asbestos fibers are relatively short and smooth with most spinning-quality lengths being three-quarters of an inch or less. Because of this shortness, cotton or synthetic carrier fibers of somewhat longer staple are added to the asbestos fibers to aid in carding and spinning operations. The amount of such carrier fiber is restricted because the finished fabric must be highly heat-resistant.

6. CARDING. Fibers are combed, cleaned, and paralleled into a web, as in wool or cotton processing.

7. ROVING. The carding web is separated into ribbons or rope-like strands called roving, as in the woolen process.

8. LAPPING. Slivers are formed into laps or rolls. In this form asbestos is used for electrical insulation.

9. SPINNING. The roving strands are spun and twisted into yarns of various sizes depending on end use. The process is the same as is used in the manufacture of either cotton or wool. Reinforced asbestos yarns are also produced. These have inserts of cotton, rayon, or glass filament as well as brass wire.

10. WEAVING. Yarns are woven into fabric just as in the case of wool or cotton yarns.

11. BRAIDING. Much asbestos yarn is also plaited into braids by mechanical braiders.

## U.S. Rubber Adds Finer Yarn

Early methods of making yarn from asbestos consisted largely of obtaining a rope-like strand of the approximate desired yarn weight, and merely adding twist to give the yarn strength and to reduce its diameter. Only the longest fibers available were used due to difficulty in carding and spinning, and yarns so made were coarse and heavy. Fabrics woven from these early asbestos yarns had limited applications, due to the thick and bulky constructions.

In 1934 textile engineers at U.S. Rubber's research laboratories conceived a new and practical method of spinning short asbestos fibers into commercially valuable yarns. They had four objectives:

(1) a drafted and twisted yarn which could use shorter length fibers, (2) a yarn with a fine gauge or diameter, (3) a stronger yarn, (4) a more uniform yarn. These objectives were achieved and patents were granted in 1937 and 1939. Commercial production on Asbeston by United States Rubber Company started in 1941 at the Stark Mills in Hogansville, Ga.

## Man-Made Fibers Added

The fineness and high strength of asbestos yarn is illustrated by a fire-fighting suit developed for military use during World War II; this garment weighed 13 pounds when fabricated with asbestos fabric, compared with 25 pounds for the type of asbestos materials previously used.

With the advent of the new man-made fibers, technicians successfully blended in various synthetic fibers to give asbestos yarns and fabrics new and unique properties for special purposes. A typical fabric using synthetic fibers is a dry-cleaning press cover fabric, which is made with one series of yarns composed of asbestos-cotton blend interwoven with a series of nylon filament yarns. This combination gives the fabric smoothness and increased strength, yet retains its heat resistance and imparts long service life to the cover.

Other synthetic fibers that have been incorporated in asbestos fabrics are Dynel, Orlon, Dacron and Arnel. Glass fiber is also used in asbestos to make a braided cigarette lighter wicking.

## Uses of Asbestos Fibers

Typical applications of asbestos yarns and fabrics are:

Safety clothing
Thermal insulation jacketing fabrics
Barbecue mitts
Commercial laundry and dry cleaning press covers
Conveyor belts
Dust filters
Heating and ventilating ducts
Electrical insulating tapes
Yarns for electric wire insulation and for paper maker's felts
Fireproof draperies
Fire-smothering blankets
Brake linings

Mylar polyester film, a basic material in manufacture of metallic yarns, is made in rolls like this one; the rolls are slit into narrower widths and, after lamination, finally slit into yarn widths and reeled as yarn.

# Metallic Yarns

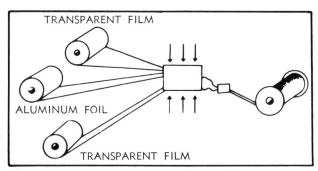 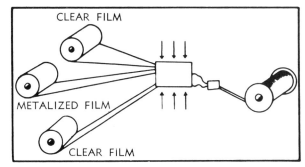

The diagrams above illustrate two methods of making metallic yarns. That on the left shows aluminum foil being sandwiched between two sheets of transparent film, giving a silver colored yarn. If other colors are desired the adhesive used is colored accordingly. The diagram at right shows a process in which a layer of film, which has been exposed to aluminum vapor under high vacuum and thus metallized, is being sandwiched between two clear sheets.

Metallic yarns have been used since earliest times to achieve luxury in the decoration of clothing and hangings. Early civilizations knew them as tinsel yarns and made them of silver and gold. The Bible is full of references to gold and silver threads, and the civilization of Alexander the Great (356-323 B.C.) developed the art of weaving with tinsel to a high degree. In spite of their weight and harshness they were widely used in royal and ecclesiastical garments and in religious decorations of all kinds.

Today gold and silver yarns are seldom used, but their effect has been duplicated by the use of aluminum in combination with man-made substances. Modern metallic yarns are soft, light in weight, and do not tarnish.

## How Metallic Yarns Are Made

The first widely used type of metallic yarn was manufactured by Dobeckmun (now a division of Dow Chemical Co.) Cleveland under the trade name of *Lurex*. It consisted of a three-layer sandwich: the top and bottom layers were clear polyethylene film; a center layer of aluminum foil was laminated in between. After this the three-ply sheet was mechanically sliced to the desired widths.

Today, two types of metallic yarn are available through these processes:

1. *The Foil Type* has an inside layer of metal (generally aluminum foil) which is sandwiched between two layers of clear plastic film. Where a silver color is desired, the adhesive is clear in color; where gold or other colors are desired, pigments are added to the adhesive or printed on film before laminating.

2. *The Metalized Type* is also a "sandwich" of clear plastic film. However, the inside layer consists of a clear plastic film which has been vacuum-plated with the vaporized metal (generally also aluminum). The desired coloring, achieved as described above, therefore shines through the outside layers.

**Some Major U.S. Producers of Metallic Yarns:**

Dow Badische Co.
Malina Co., Inc.

## Properties and Uses

Modern metallic yarns do not tarnish, they can be either dry cleaned or washed, and can be ironed at low temperatures.

Metallic yarns are used largely in combination with other yarns for a wide variety of products. They are found in:

| | |
|---|---|
| Draperies | Coats |
| Upholstery | Hats |
| Fabrics | Shoes |
| Tablecloths | Accessories |
| Mats | Knitting and crocheting |
| Evening dresses | yarns |
| Blouses | Beltings |
| Sweaters | Ribbons |
| Sportswear | Trimmings |
| Negligees | Tapes and braids |
| Suits | Shoelaces |
| Bathing suits | |

Corn, like peanuts or soybeans, is employed as a source of natural proteins for the fibers industry.

# Protein Base Fibers

*Textile chemists synthesize man-made fibers from the natural proteins found in milk, fish or vegetables such as peanuts and corn. Protein base fibers are called Azlon fibers.*

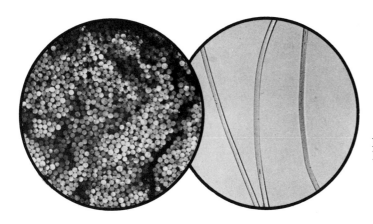

Photomicrographs of a typical protein base fiber based on corn proteins.

## How Protein Base Fibers Are Made

Corn (or maize), soybean, and peanut fibers are produced as follows:

1. Vegetable matter is crushed and oil is extracted.
2. In the remaining meal is a protein substance.
3. This protein, in powdered form, is dissolved in a caustic solution and allowed to age.
4. The resulting viscous solution is then extruded through the spinneret and passed through an acid bath which coagulates the filaments.
5. The fiber tow is then cured and stretched to give it strength.
6. It is washed, dried, and used either in filament or staple form, often with a pre-set crimp to give it the hand of wool.

CASEIN fibers follow a similar procedure. A protein powder is extracted from skim milk. It is dissolved in water and extruded under heat and pressure. The resulting filaments are hardened and aged in an acid bath. They are then washed, dried, and used either in filament or staple form, also crimped.

SEAWEED fibers are made by extracting the chemical, sodium alginate, from brown seaweed by the use of an alkali. The resulting solution is purified, filtered, and wet-spun into a coagulating bath to form the fibers.

---

**Some Major Producers of Protein Base Fibers:**

None in U.S.
European producers exist in Belgium, East Germany, Italy, Poland and the United Kingdom.

---

## Used in Blends

Protein base fibers, especially in the form of cut staple with curl or crimp, have been used chiefly in blends with other fibers. They impart a wool-like hand to other fibers and add loft, softness and resiliency. Protein fiber has been successfully blended with almost all the natural and man-made fibers. It resists moths and mildew, does not shrink, and imparts a "quality" cashmere-like hand to fabrics in which it is used.

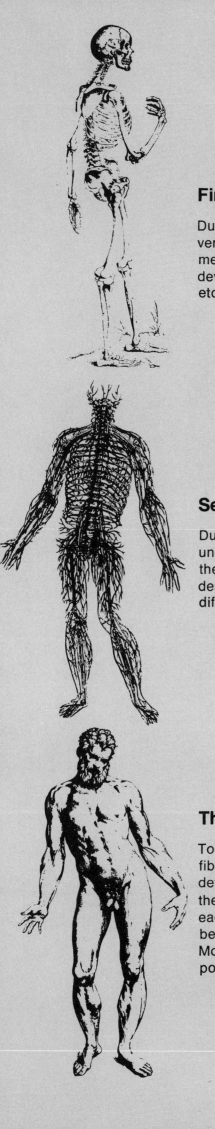

### First Generation: <u>INVENTION</u>

During the first generation of man-made fibers, chemists invented the basic technology for fibers made by man — to supplement and simulate those grown by nature. In this phase of development each of the fibers — rayon, nylon, polyester, acrylic etc. — was first made only in one form.

### Second Generation: <u>DIVERSIFICATION</u>

During this phase of development, each of the generic fibers underwent modification to improve both performance and aesthetics. It was a time of problem-solving and the exploration of design for end use. Now, most generic fibers are made in many different versions, each engineered to suit a particular product.

### Third Generation: <u>SOPHISTICATION</u>

Today, we are entering a new phase of development in which the fibers are being custom-tailored for specialized markets. Predetermined aesthetics and performance are now being built into the fibers at the production level and it begins to seem as though each generic fiber can be changed in so many ways that we may be on the road to one "universal" fiber modified for all purposes. Most representative of the third generation fibers are the Bi-Components, the Bi-Constituents and the Blended Filaments.

# Evolution of Man-Made Fibers

*The needs of expanding populations and advances in textile technology have combined to create new fibers which did not exist a generation ago.*

The history of man-made fibers has followed an evolutionary course which represents the impact of modern chemistry on the textile process. What follows is a capsule review of this history through its various stages of development. It begins with the cellulosics—rayon and acetate.

## First Came the Cellulosics

Rayon (viscose) is the oldest commercial man-made fiber and on a world-wide basis (in 1969) it was the second largest category of textile raw materials after cotton. It is produced in countless variations to suit differing end uses, ranging from dresses to tire cord. Being a cellulosic, many of its properties are similar to those of cotton, but it has high moisture absorption and subsequent swelling which leads to dimensional instability and loss of strength. As a result it has been used primarily in blends with the natural and synthetic fibers where it lends evenness to the yarns and fabrics as well as offering a price advantage.

As in all areas of the textile industry, the scientists have been busy with improvements in viscose rayon. These chiefly apply to the development of High Wet Modulus or high performance fibers. The degree of polymerization of the modified fibers is twice or even three times that of the ordinary viscose, leading to much higher strength both wet and dry. Moisture regain suffers to some extent, but is higher than in the synthetic fibers.

Acetates are the other branch of the cellulosic family and have been with us since the 1920's. Their basic structure is the cellulose chain (40–60 percent), to which acetyl groups have been added, resulting in their having the cellulosic properties, but to a lesser degree. Easy dyeing is a characteristic of acetates, but sensitivity to abrasion, especially in the wet state, plus lack of dimensional stability, have been problems. The introduction of the triacetate fiber in the 1950's has considerably solved the shrinkage factor and has opened up end uses which acetate could not have gained before.

## Next Came the Synthetic Fibers

The versatility of the synthetic fibers has provided the base for their penetration into almost every phase of our modern life.

The successful synthetics have found their place in textiles because they possess one or more outstanding aesthetic advantages. In addition, they all have the easy-care virtues that have become essential in today's demanding society—controlled shrinkage, pleat and crease retention, wrinkle resistance and the need for little or no ironing. It is in this combination of so many desirable properties that the synthetics have the advantage over natural fibers. And that is why they continue to advance.

It was thought at one time that nylon was the universal fiber, the best for all applications. But experience proved that nylon has limitations, such as relatively poor recovery from deformation. Hence it is prone to wrinkling in wear and is not well adapted to many outerwear applications.

Shortly after nylon came the acrylic and polyester fibers, the former lauded for its wool-like bulk and hand, the latter for its remarkable wrinkle recovery and continued freshness of appearance. These were important additions to the family of fibers and it is mainly because of these three that the tremendous growth of the synthetics has been achieved.

## The Rise of Blends

Originally conceived as continuous filament yarns, the early synthetics attempted to replace silk, nature's own continuous filament yarn. But these fibers were so versatile that their makers soon learned to chop them up, crimp them, bulk them and otherwise prepare them to contribute their strength, abrasion resistance, crease resistance and easy-care properties to blends with cotton for many applications.

Adding further impetus to the blends of polyester and cotton was the development of permanent press

Magnified close-up of a polyester filament fiber revealed by zoom lens. The fiber, which looks like peeled corn, has been magnified 3,600 times. The picture shows the extremely precise, longitudinal fibrillation of a typical polyester filament structure. These photos reveal to the fiber scientist whether the spinneret is functioning properly.

Closer magnifications of the same polyester filament fiber: above, it is magnified to a power of almost 4,000X; below, the same polyester filament is magnified to a power of 12,000X. Investigation of normal man-made fibers has led to the invention and engineering of a third generation of man-made fibers, primarily fibers with modified cross-sections.

finishes. Initially applied to garments of cotton, it was found that the finishes degraded the cotton, requiring polyester to give the fabric sufficient strength. It was this blend that made permanent press an outstanding success.

Blends of the synthetics with wool for suitings have also found favor and, again, the ability to make long and short staple, fine and coarse staple, bright and dull staple—each with various bulking and dyeability properties—has enabled them to be used in areas previously reserved for wool and silk.

Industrial products, as well, have felt the impact of the synthetics, despite the price advantage of cotton. Synthetics have very nearly taken over the tire cord market and there are the nylon-supported inflatable structures, carpet backings, outdoor-indoor carpeting and filter fabrics of many types being made from the synthetics. A later addition to this group is narrow polypropylene film woven into fabric to replace burlap bags. Because of its resistance to mildew and sunlight degradation, easier handling, cleaning and storage, as well as its low cost, polypropylene has made giant strides to replace jute.

## Physical Modification of Synthetics

While the basic synthetics were good in themselves and contributed greatly to ease-of-living patterns, it was found that greater versatility in appearance, hand and comfort were required to sell the output of the synthetic plants. This led to a long list of inventions and patents designed to alter the synthetics in their physical appearance and adapt them to many and more varied end uses.

These changes in fiber form resulted in the second generation of fibers and there are countless examples at this level. For example, Du Pont advertises 70 types of nylon and 31 types of "Dacron" for texturing alone, with many more for other applications. To these must be added the variations of the other yarn producers and the multiplying factor of the modifications introduced by the throwsters with their many methods of bulking or texturing the raw yarns. The range of this second generation of fibers is thus very great.

## Sophistication of Fiber Science

At the second stage in synthetic fiber development one could obtain a vast range of effects—fabrics like silk, wool, worsted, linen, dull and bright surfaces, soft, hard, smooth or textured surfaces. Many in the textile industry felt there was little more to be accomplished. But the scientists soon created the

A close-up of a looped bundle of textile filaments shot by the magnification lens at a power of 100X.

third generation of fibers, with a potential to match that of the previous stages (see section on Third Generation Man-Made Fibers).

## How Fibers Are Changed

Man's ingenuity has developed at least thirteen ways to change or modify a man-made fiber:

1. Bi-component technology.

2. Bi-constituent technology.

3. Blended filament yarns.

4. Graft polymerization of other fiber types.

5. Chemical modification of the polymer's molecular structure.

6. Chemical additives to the solution.

7. Cross-sectional modification.

8. Changing the denier or size of yarn.

9. Changing the fiber's length from continuous filament to short staple.

10. Texturing yarn by bulking, crimping, looping, or other texturing procedure.

11. Changing the yarn's luster.

12. Roughening the fiber's surface.

13. Increasing the fiber's stiffness.

All these techniques have played a role in making man-made fibers more natural—softer, more lustrous, more comfortable, easier to care for, more pleasing to the eye and hand.

# Third Generation Man-Made Fibers

*The third generation of man-made fibers represents the third phase of development in which fibers are engineered at the production level for specialized end uses.*

Since the invention of the first man-made fiber, rayon, textile scientists have constantly been inventing new fibers and improving those already in existence. In the United States, rayon was first commercially launched in 1910, followed by acetate (1924), nylon (1939), acrylic (1950), polyester (1953), triacetate (1954), and polypropylene (1961). The use of these fibers has expanded dramatically so that in 1968 they surpassed natural fibers in U.S. consumption—5 billion pounds to 4.57 billion pounds.

This success has been based largely on the scientist's ability to adapt man-made fibers to an ever-increasing variety of end uses. During the last fifty years, textile research has actually brought man-made fibers through three generations: (1) invention, (2) diversification, and (3) sophistication.

**Invention.** During this phase, chemists invented the basic polymer technology for man-made fibers.

**Diversification.** During this phase, scientists modified generic fibers to improve their performance and aesthetics, so that they would be more competitive with natural fibers.

**Sophistication.** During this phase, scientists began to custom-tailor fibers for specialized end uses.

All three phases or technical movements are still under way. Scientists are still concerned with invention, diversification and sophistication of man-made fibers, but latest emphasis is decidedly focused on the second and third generation fibers, particularly the third.

The objective, in most cases, is to create a filament yarn with texture; that is, a yarn which simulates the unevenness of organic natural fibers (see section on Textured Yarns).

Third generation fibers generally fit into three basic categories: (1) bi-components, (2) bi-constituents, and (3) blended filaments.

BI-COMPONENT FIBERS. These are fibers composed of two generically similar but chemically or physically different polymers, physically joined in a single filament.

The bi-component was originally conceived as a means of self-bulking or self-crimping, since two polymers with differing shrinkage rates were joined at the spinneret. In processing, or in later fabric finishing, one component shrinks more than the other, thus pulling the whole yarn into a crimped conformation.

Bi-components can only result from compatible polymers made by the same process, with good adhesive qualities at the interface. This probably rules out polypropylene, which has poor adhesive qualities, and probably rules out polymers with low melting points that may decompose at the higher temperatures required in self-crimping or bulking—the main object of bi-components.

A well-known example of a bi-component is "Cantrece," a combination of nylon fibers produced by Du Pont.

BI-CONSTITUENT FIBERS. These are filaments composed of two generically different compounds physically joined or dispersed one within the other in solution, before extrusion through the spinneret.

Bi-constituents can be produced in three distinct ways:

1. By mixing polymers to produce an entirely different fiber.

2. By introducing additives to change functional or aesthetic properties such as dyeability or soil-releasing capability.

3. By adding components which can be removed to modify optical properties or to change specific gravity.

In the last method, for example, one can add a water-soluble component to the solution which will percolate out later (leach), leaving hollow spaces on the surface for light reflectance and luster.

# Bi-Component

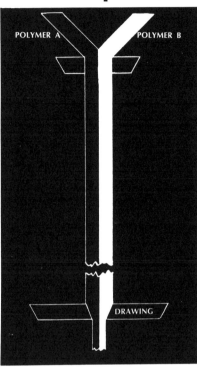

The bi-component fiber is a fiber composed of two generically similar but chemically or physically different polymers, physically joined in a single filament. The bi-component fiber was originally conceived as a means to self-bulking or self-crimping, since two polymers with differential shrinkage rates were joined in the process of fiber creation.

The bi-constituent fiber is a filament composed of two generically different compounds physically joined together or dispersed one within the other. The first bi-constituent fiber was Source, from Allied Chemical, a composition of 70% polyamide (matrix) and 30% polyester (the fibrils within the matrix). Obviously the most difficult of all third-generation fibers to make.

# Bi-Constituent

# Blended Filament

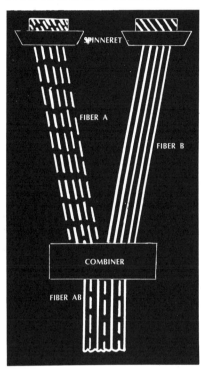

The blended filament is a yarn made by intimate blending, that is, twisting, interlacing or otherwise making a coherent bundle of dissimilar filaments. Arnel plus nylon from Celanese is the only blended filament yarn yet made, but its potential seems to be rather significant, since it doesn't seem to require the chemical wizardry of the other third-generation processes.

Three third-generation man-made fibers: bi-component, bi-constituent and blended filament yarn.

An example of a bi-constituent fiber is "Source," a composition of 70 percent polyamide (matrix) and 30 percent polyester (the fibrils within the matrix). It is a lustrous carpet fiber produced by Allied Chemical.

**BLENDED FILAMENT YARNS.** These are yarns made by intimate blending of dissimilar filaments to form a coherent bundle.

Blended filament yarns, which are produced from solid fibers, not from modified polymers in the solution state, lend themselves to a wider variety of final products than is possible with bi-component or bi-constituent technology. A much greater range of fibers can be combined into blended filament yarns than can be compatibly mixed or joined in the solution state or at the spinneret. And it is much easier and quicker to make up experimental yarns and fabric with this method.

An example of a blended filament yarn is "Arnel Plus" an apparel yarn of Arnel and nylon produced by Celanese.

# DESIGN A FIBER TO ORDER

BI-COMPONENT

SHEATH-CORE

BI-COMPONENT

SKIN-CORE

**One of the critical differences between natural and man-made fibers is the ability of man-made fibers to be tailored for end-use. Today, with sophisticated third-generation technology, fibers can literally be designed at the spinneret.**

The following formulations illustrate the complexity of fiber modification and the ingenuity of the textile technologists.

1. **For improving luster (sheen, not shine):**
   - Modification of cross-section.
   - Roughening of fiber surface.

2. **For improving tactile touch and scroop:**
   - Modification of cross-section.
   - Roughening of fiber surface.
   - Increase of fiber surface.
   - Bulked or permanently crimped fiber.

3. **For improving or modifying dyeability:**
   - Mainly chemical additives.
   - Graft polymerization of other fiber types.

4. **For loft and bulk:**
   - Chemical treatments or additives.
   - Physical treatments.
   - Bi-component fibers.
   - Blended fibers.
   - Mixed polymer fibers.

5. **For reducing static electricity and increasing moisture absorbency:**
   - Chemical treatments or additives.
   - Graft polymerization of other fiber types.

6. **For improving whiteness retention:**
   - Chemical treatment or additives.

7. **For reducing or eliminating pilling:**
   - Chemical or physical treatments.

8. **For improving washing performance (wrinkle resistance):**
   - Chemical modifications.

9. **For making a fiber that can be fulled for greater aesthetics:**
   - Chemical or physical modifications or treatments.

10. **For temperature control via conductive polymers:**
    - Chemical modifications, additives or treatments.

11. **For making filaments with spun-like aesthetics.**
    - Physical modifications or treatments.

12. **For making moldable fibers:**
    - Chemical modifications.

13. **For improved flame retardancy:**
    - Chemical modifications or additives.

## New Fibers Project Luxury

The most exciting developments can be expected through the introduction of entirely new fibers that offer more luxury in hand, drape, appearance, more comfort, as well as more performance features, especially wrinkle resistance, pleat and press retention and no ironing at all.

"Qiana" fiber by Du Pont is one answer to this demand. It has the drape, hand, scroop and luster of silk, outstanding wrinkle resistance and pleat retention.

Other companies have been working in the same direction and here are some of the things projected:

A hollow polyester filament with a triangular cross section gives the yarn in textured form a light and bulky touch, luxurious for high fashion women's apparel.

A protein-polyvinyl compound grafted copolymer is claimed to be the closest synthetic yarn to natural silk. The new yarn can be commercially produced at approximately half the cost of silk.

One new fiber has both ester and ether linkages, and claims to achieve a luxurious silky hand, immediate wrinkle recovery, good pleat and crease retention and excellent dyeability.

Another new fiber is a wool substitute made through the combination of protein with polyvinyl alcohol. This fiber is much stronger than casein fibers, has wool-like properties, high moisture absorption and is easily dyed.

Still another yarn grafts polyvinyl chloride and polyvinyl alcohol to produce a wool-like staple with excellent properties for apparel, carpeting and home furnishings.

The process for the manufacture of nylon 4, long considered too difficult to produce, has been perfected. The new nylon has been produced in experimental quantities and indications are that its price can be approximately the same as that of nylon 6. The chief virtue of nylon 4 is that, unlike other polyamides, it absorbs water like cotton, with a moisture regain of nine percent. That means it is low in static build-up and can be ironed like cotton. Its hand is very close to that of cotton, yet in spun for it has the feel of wool.

Nylon 4 should have important applications in all end uses with permanent press. It provides the necessary strength to resist degradation from permanent press resins and, at the same time, offers comfort in wear. Other end uses may be toweling, carpets and tire cord.

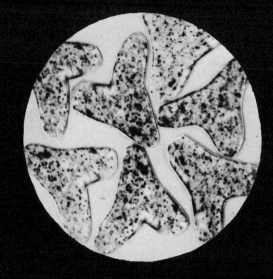

Above, a trilobal, below, a pentalobal and normal round fiber.

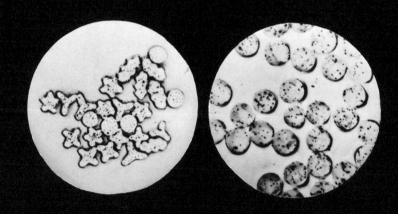

**Various Engineered Fibers**

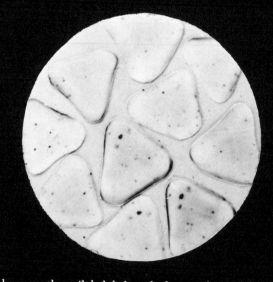

Above, another trilobal, below, dogbone and pentalobal fibers.

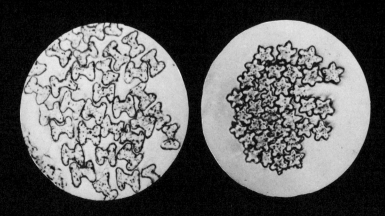

A cotton field at harvest time and, *inset*, two fully mature cotton bolls which have opened, showing cotton within.

# COTTON

*Cotton in its pure form and in blends is the principal clothing fiber of the five continents of the world. Its production is one of the major factors in world prosperity and economic stability.*

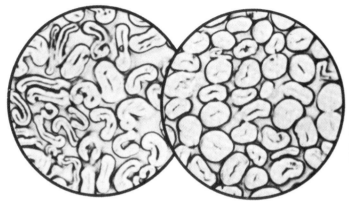

Photomicrographs of two different types of cotton magnified about 500 times. At left, Rowden, at right, Empire cotton.

COTTON is a vegetable seed fiber. Botanically, the fibers are the protective covering of the seeds in the cotton plant *Gossypium*. This is a shrub which grows from 4 to 6 feet high.

## Under the Microscope

Cotton fiber is a single cell. Seen under the microscope while growing it resembles a cylindrical tube with a central canal or lumen, a secondary wall, a primary wall and a thin outer film or cuticle. After it is picked the fiber becomes flat and ribbon-like and is twisted throughout its length. The number of twists vary from 150 to 300 per inch depending on the type and quality of the fiber. The finest cotton (Sea Island) averages about 300 twists to the inch. The poorest grade (Indian) has about 150. These twists give cotton its excellent spinning qualities. They provide the friction needed to make the fibers cling together.

When mercerized (treated under tension with a 25 to 30% solution of caustic soda) the fiber swells and straightens out permanently; becomes smooth, rod-like, and uniform in appearance, and develops a high luster.

## Chemical Properties

When dry, cotton fiber is almost entirely made up of cellulose—88 to 96%. After scouring, bleaching,

and drying it is about 99% cellulose. Its formula reads $(C_6H_{10}O_5)_n$. In addition to cellulose it contains small amounts of protein, pectin, wax, ash, organic acids, and pigment.

## Physical Characteristics

STRENGTH: The tensile strength of the cotton fiber is greater when wet than when dry. It can withstand pressures of from 30,000 to 60,000 pounds per square inch, depending on quality.

ABSORBENCY: It has remarkable capacities for absorbing moisture. When rid of impurities, the so-called absorbent cotton will retain 24 to 27 times its own weight in water. Because of this, it can absorb and release perspiration quickly, has great affinity for dyestuffs, and bleaches excellently to a clear white.

HEAT ACTION: It can be sterilized at boiling temperatures without disintegration. It withstands dry heat up to 248°F and can therefore be ironed at relatively high temperatures without damage.

WASHABILITY: Because it is stronger wet than dry it stands up well under the rigors of repeated launderings. It also has good resistance to alkalies.

DURABILITY: It stands up well in abrasion tests, and a fiber can be bent as many as 50,000 times without rupture.

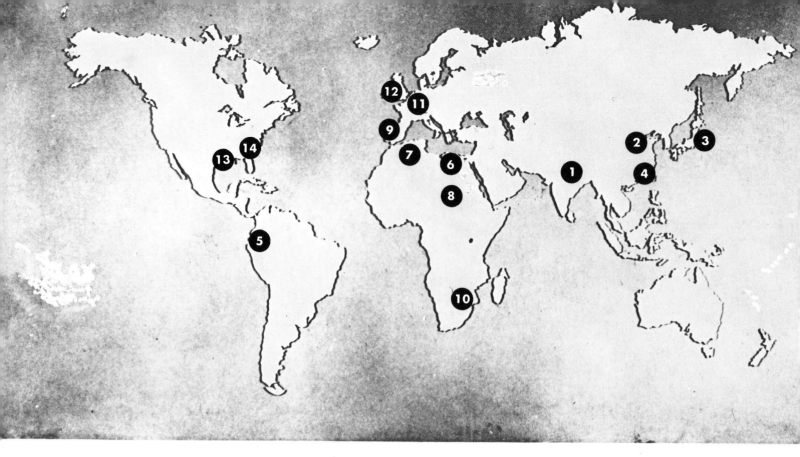

## Capsule History of Cotton

1. Cotton appears in India about 5,000 B.C. and moves east and west.
2. Chinese use cotton and develop the spinning wheel.
3. Japanese learn about cotton from the Chinese invaders.
4. Possibly Chinese bring cotton to America before white men.
5. Pre-Inca use of cotton beginning as early as 2,500 B.C. in Peru.
6. Arab traders travel to Egypt and bring cotton with them.
7. Arabs carry cotton further west along the coast of North Africa.

8. Egyptians give cotton to Ethiopians and its use spreads south.
9. Moors conquer Spain and bring the use of cotton to the Iberian Peninsula.
10. Vasco de Gama, Portuguese explorer, finds cotton in Africa.
11, 12. British and Flemish weavers use cotton during the industrial revolution.
13. Early Americans grow cotton which possibly is indigenous plant.
14. Development of industrial methods of cotton spinning and weaving in America, Europe and the Far East.

# History of Cotton

Cotton has been the companion of civilization for over fifty centuries. It has also been its king . . . it has clothed nations . . . it has made slaves of men . . . it has monopolized labor . . . and has given rise to new industries. It has produced more economic paradoxes than any other natural product, for cotton has created cotton cloth and cotton linters serve as the base for acetate and rayon.

The first historical mention of cotton is found in the writings of the Greek historian Herodotus, who lived some 484 years before the Christian era. The father of history, returning from a trip to India, wrote, "There are trees in which fleece grew surpassing that of sheep and from which the natives made cloth."

His fellow Greeks scoffed at the report, yet for

many centuries the legend took hold that cotton bolls were vegetable "lambs." Our forefathers believed that the mythical "lambs" reached down and grazed until the stalks grew too high. Then they starved and their bodies turned into "fleece."

## Cotton Has a Romantic History

In 1350 the English explorer, Sir John Mandeville, returned from a visit to India with a story that "there grew there a wonderful tree which bore tiny lambs on the endes of its branches. These branches were so pliable that they bent down to allow the lambs to feed when they are hungrie."

It was natural for cotton to become confused with wool in the minds of many. Even today, the German word for cotton is "baumwolle" which, literally translated, means tree-wool.

All ancient writings credit the Old World origin of cotton to India. Archeological discoveries in the valley of the Indus in Sind date cotton at about 3000 B.C. or even earlier. Nearchus, admiral to Alexander the Great, settled a colony of Macedonians on the Indus River. His reports speak of the chintz or flowered cotton fabrics which rival the sunlight and resist washing.

A few centuries later from Periplus on the Erythrean Sea comes the first trade account in which manifests of cotton goods are mentioned describing trading in the Red Sea, Arabia, the eastern coast of Africa, and the western coast of India.

## Egyptian Cotton Prospered

Then two great causes brought cotton stuffs in profusion to the world which was Europe. Alexander's armies amid other marauding bands had introduced the culture of cotton into Northern Africa. The fertile soil of the Nile valley was admirably suited to raising the "wool-plant." Soon Egyptian cotton surpassed the cotton of India in excellence. First Hebrew and Phoenician traders spread the cotton trade. In the 7th and 8th Centuries the Arab conquests and the Crusades brought the art of spinning and weaving of cotton from Egypt into Spain. The art was introduced by the Moors and then taken eastwards by the Spaniards into northern Africa and along the coasts of the dark continent, reaching as far south as the island of Madeira.

That Columbus was familiar with cotton is evidenced by his report that he had discovered a new route to Asia, when he discovered cotton plants on islands in the Caribbean.

An old wood cut of the "Wool Plant."

## Portuguese Helped Spread Cotton

In 1497 Vasco da Gama set sail to find the western route to India. Leaving Lisbon he rounded the "Story Cape" (Cape of Good Hope) and arrived at Calcutta. On his return to Europe, his cargo consisted in part of "pintadores," which we now call calico.

Thus, between Portugal and Spain, the cotton traffic was divided by virtue of their tremendous sea power and by grace of the Pope who divided all newly discovered lands between them. However, a tight little isle off the coast of Europe was soon to bring Spanish sea domination to an end. Admiral Sir Charles Howard destroyed the vast Spanish Armada; and for hundreds of years Britannia ruled the waves . . . and the cotton trade.

Egyptians began cotton pre-shrinking. This tomb panel shows yarn inspection, water pre-shrinking, hand twisting, loom and woven fabric preparation.

West Indian plantation of middle of 18th Century; a workman stands inside a hanging bag stamping on and pressing cotton while another sprays water on the bag to make it contract around cotton, prevent cotton fluffing; in the background is a gin of the roller type quite different from that later invented by Whitney.

With colonies on the other side of the Atlantic climatically perfect, it was almost automatic that the English should become cotton planters. But the English did not introduce the cotton plant into America. Cotton seemed to be an indigenous plant in the New World, existing long before the first white man ever trod upon its shores.

## Columbus Found Cotton

In Columbus' journal dated Oct. 12th, 1492, the Admiral of Isabella writes of the natives of Watling's Island: "They came swimming toward us and brought us parrots, and balls of cotton thread and many other things which they exchanged with us for other things which we gave them such as strings of beads and little bells."

Cortez, Pizarro, De Soto, and other Conquistadores discovered finely woven cotton fabrics manufactured in Peru, Mexico, and what is now Southwestern United States. The high status of this cotton culture reveals the fact that it existed hundreds of years before the European invasion. Latest estimates based on carbon 14 tests show that domesticated cotton was grown and woven in Peru as early as 2500 B.C.

To the present day, the prevalence of the cotton plant and cotton culture on two continents separated by thousands of miles of ocean is a problem which has puzzled scientists.

## Virginia Planted First for Profit

The first planting of cotton for commercial purposes in the New World was accomplished in Virginia in

1607, with seed brought from the West Indies. Cotton in those days was planted by hand . . . not a difficult task; but the picking by hand was another matter. The cotton lint must be torn from its case and kept free from leaves and twigs. It must be picked when it is perfectly dry, which means the hottest part of hot days; and it must be gathered before the wind could scatter the fluffy seeds. Naturally, this task was not to the liking of early colonists, who had many irons in the fire. Slaves had previously been imported to work the indigo and rice fields in Louisiana, and the British colonists took a labor cue from their Spanish predecessors.

## Ancient Indian Method Used

The earliest method of preparing cotton fibers for weaving was derived from the ancient Indian method.

The cotton fleece was hand picked and *churga ginned*, a process of cleaning the hairy, seeded South Atlantic cotton. The method was too gentle and too slow, and did not compete favorably with hand cleaning. (That's why cotton did not assume its kingship until Whitney's invention.) The cotton fibers were then spun into a thread. The Chinese had invented a foot treadle which replaced the ancient hand crank, and to this invention Leonardo da Vinci added the flyer (known to the colonies as the Saxony Wheel). This was the first successful application of continuous motion to the production of cotton yarn. It became the basic principle of the great English machines invented by Arkwright and others, which became the germ of the Industrial Revolution.

Next the raw stock was *bowed*. A workman struck a

string of a bow with a mallet and the vibration opened knots, shook out dust and raised it to a down fleece. The homemade thread was then woven on hand looms in the household.

*Bowed Cotton from Georgia* was a regular commodity in English markets in the 18th Century.

## King Cotton Born with the Gin

The coronation of Cotton as King of American crops was due in the main to a chance visit by Eli Whitney, fresh from Yale, to friends in Savannah. Young Whitney liked the indolent life of the South and decided to stay a while. He soon learned another side of it . . . a side that was sweat and tears instead of magnolias and moonlight. His farmer friends complained bitterly of the expense and difficulty of separating cotton from the seed by hand or by *churga ginning.* Young Eli, who had a tremendous mechanical bent, worked for a few months and produced the *saw-gin.* This little hand-operated gadget made the United States a world factor.

In 1791, a year prior to Whitney's invention, America shipped 400 bales of cotton to Europe. In 1800, these same states shipped 30,000 bales! In 1810, nearly 180,000 bales!

## Cotton Increased Slave Need

But with the good came evil. In the few decades before Whitney's invention, the principle of slavery had been growing more and more distasteful to the American people. State after state made laws prohibiting the extension of slavery and the importation of slaves. Only six years before the appearance of the cotton gin the entire South voted unanimously against slave importation. But with the sudden and unprecedented increase in cotton growing, the South saw no way of carrying out the possibilities so alluringly opened up by the cotton gin, except by slave labor. In the decade between 1790 and 1800 the slave population of the Southern states was increased 33%. At the end of the next ten years (1810) there were more than a million slaves in the Southern states.

Before the sudden growth of cotton production. wool and linen had formed the chief clothing of the American people (linsey-woolsey). The making of cloth had been confined to the homes, but with this new fiber produced in prodigious quantity at their very doors, enterprising men began to build factories here and abroad for the manufacture of cotton cloth.

With a prescience that must have anticipated Whit-

The cotton gin invented by Eli Whitney in 1793. The model made by the inventor in about 1800.

Cotton carding machine built by Samuel Slater in 1790 in Pawtucket, Rhode Island.

ney's cotton gin, Quaker merchant Moses Brown engaged Samuel Slater to operate a cotton mill which was built in Pawtucket, R.I., in 1793. The rapid waterways of New England, coupled with its climatic condition, made it a rival to England for the production of cotton cloth. Mr. Slater's mill employed a widow and five children in addition to himself. Their pay, according to his journal, was $1.60 per week for the widow and 60 cents per week for the children. The latter worked 12 hours a day in the winter and 14 hours a day in the summer. Slater developed a modified spinning frame which was the first spinning machinery built in the

SEEK NO FURTHER

"SELL AND REPENT"

Two well-known symbols of the 19th Century cotton picture. (*At left*) The original Fruit of the Loom label, said to be the first pictorial label ever used on cotton goods. (*At right*) The famous "Sell and Repent" figure which became a symbol of Worth Street philosophy.

United States. For this achievement history has dubbed him the "Father of American Mechanical Water-power Spinning."

## Abundant Water Power Meant Mills

Other mills soon sprang up where water power was abundant. The North gave rise to many, but the South built mills in 1817-1822 in North Carolina.

In 1822, also, the Merrimack Manufacturing Company started its first mill at Lowell, Mass. Soon New Bedford rivaled England in the production of cotton and was called the "Bolton of America."

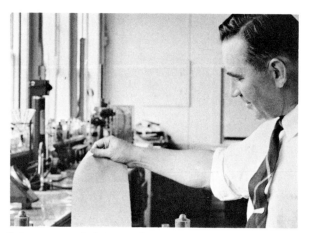

Laboratory technician performing one of the phases in the sample dyeing of fast color cotton.

But the South did not confine its products to domestic markets. Savannah, New Orleans, and other Southern seaports became metropoli. By 1860 "King Cotton" was a common expression all over the country, but along with the growth of King Cotton there had developed a situation in the South which was not anticipated in the beginning. By 1860 the South had a slave population of over 4 million.

Immediately before the Civil War, the South was of vital importance to the British textile industry. During 1859-60 the United States exported to England 2,522,000 bales of cotton, and was followed next by the East Indies, exporting only 563,000 bales.

## War and Industrial Expansion

Four years of bitterly contested war, a complete breakdown of commerce and industry, the change from slave to free labor, together with the frustration and futility of the reconstruction period, placed the South in a position where it could be saved only by the energy and self-devotion of its own people. But the South met the challenge. Stirred by the success of William Gregg, Southern business men were convinced that industry could flourish in Dixie. Their ambitions were stimulated by the International Cotton Exposition of 1881 in Atlanta, which was staged primarily to encourage better methods of planting and ginning. The new machines shown there inspired many who saw them. Mills sprang up throughout the South, where more than 80% of the industry is located today. By 1895 the South had safely passed beyond embryonic industrialism, and the dreams of men of vision had become reality in the New South.

The years between the first and second World Wars marked another great period of Southern textile industrialization. In the last year of World War I there were 14,529,063 active spindles in place in the South, and 18,065,857 in the North. At the beginning of World War II, the South had increased its capacity to 17,939,000, while New England's spindles had declined to 5,334,000.

## The Blend Revolution

Since the end of World War II, cotton has been under severe pressure from the man-made fibers, particularly polyester. Though world cotton production was still the greatest of all fibers in 1968, it constitutes a steadily declining percentage of the world fiber output. Total world-wide cotton production in 1968 amounted to 22.5 billions pounds, compared to 3.2 billion pounds of nylon and 2.5 billion pounds of polyester. Cotton production declined from 25.1 billion pounds during 1962–65, while nylon and polyester production steadily increased during that same time.

Cotton's declining importance in world markets can be attributed to two factors: the incursion of polyester and the shrinking availability of cotton-growing acreage around the world. Polyester in blend form has penetrated many end-uses such as shirts, sheets, underwear, dresses, pants and other apparel which were once 100% cotton; today these markets are blend markets of polyester/cotton, with many of them in the permanent-press category. Cotton remains predominant in the underdeveloped world, however, and will probably retain its prominence for years to come.

## Cotton Cultivation

Cotton is best cultivated in a warm, humid climate and sandy soil. Under the most favorable conditions it has 6 to 7 months of warm or hot weather and 3 to 5 inches of rainfall during growth. From planting to flowering of the plant takes from 80 to 110 days; from flowering to opening of the cotton boll, another 55 to 80 days. For the United States planting begins in early February in the southern part of Texas and extends to the end of May or early June in the northern areas of the cotton belt. The United States is the world's leading cotton grower. Other important growers include India, China, Russia, Egypt, South America, the coast of Africa, the West Indies, Mexico, Brazil and Central America.

It has been estimated that about one out of every eight bales of cotton is destroyed by insect pests,

The oldest cotton baler , at Tarboro, North Carolina.

the chief of which is the *boll weevil*. To control this damage cotton farmers must spray their fields with insecticides many times during the growing season. In large operations this is done by sprays and dusters mounted either on tractors or airplanes.

Harvesting cotton is done either by hand or by mechanical means. Mechanical harvesting has the disadvantage of picking up much waste matter with the lint. However, it is many times faster. A hand picker can gather about 15 pounds in an hour. The mechanical picker (spindle type) can harvest up to 650 pounds in an hour. Another type of mechanical picker, called a stripper, can harvest nearly a bale (about 500 pounds) in an hour. This machine is used mostly in Texas.

## Ginning—Cleaning the Cotton

After cotton has been picked it must be cleaned in preparation for spinning. When first picked it is known as seed cotton. Only about a third of this is fiber; the rest is seed and has other uses.

The principle of ginning is basically the same now as it was in 1793 when Eli Whitney revolutionized the industry with his mechanical cotton gin. The seed cotton is fed into the gin stand. This consists of a series of circular saws which project through

Cotton is sent from the grower to the spinner in bales of 478 pounds weight, wrapped in jute. *(Above)* the bales leaving the press box; *(below)* opening the bale at the mill ready for processing.

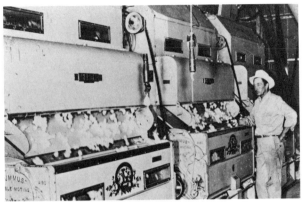

An operator supervises the processing of raw cotton from the field through automatic gin.

Cotton bales are stacked outside gin awaiting shipment to customer's mills.

Raw cotton is carefully tested and graded for cleanliness, length of fiber and strength.

steel ribs. They separate the lint or fiber from the seeds. It is then carried to the baling press.

The baling press compresses the fiber to a density of about 28 pounds per cubic foot. Each bale, wrapped in jute, weighs about 478 pounds, and measures 54 x 27 x 27 inches.

Since the first ginning does not remove all the fiber from the seeds, they are put through a second ginning process which removes the short fibers known as linters. These are extensively used in the manufacture of rayon, plastics, paper, guncotton, stuffing, etc.

## How Cotton Is Graded

The two chief methods of classifying cotton are: (1) By fiber length or *staple* and (2) by *grade* or degree of quality.

STAPLE CLASSES. There are five basic groupings:

(1) *Very short*. Not more than ¾-inch in length. Coarse in texture. Used chiefly as batting and wadding.

(2) *Short staple*. Between $1\frac{3}{16}$ and $\frac{15}{16}$ of an inch. Used in cheaper fabrics.

(3) *Medium staple*. Between $\frac{15}{16}$ and $1\frac{1}{8}$ inches. the bulk of United States production falls into this category. American Upland cotton, the world standard cotton, belongs to this group.

(4) *Ordinary long staple*. Between $1\frac{1}{8}$ and $1\frac{3}{8}$ inches.

(5) *Extra long staple*. From $1\frac{3}{8}$ to $2\frac{1}{2}$ inches long.

Lustrous Egyptian and Sea Island cottons belong in this group.

QUALITY GRADES. There are nine basic divisions, descending in value:

1. Middling. Fair.
2. Strict Good Middling.
3. Good Middling.
4. Strict Middling.
5. Middling—all grades are compared with this type.
6. Strict Low Middling.
7. Low Middling.
8. Strict Good Ordinary.
9. Good Ordinary.

Sections of Cotton Boll

A, Cross section.   B, Vertical section along line shown in A.

## Preparing the Cotton for Spinning

1. The seeds are removed from the cotton.

2. Much of remaining seed is removed by picker.

3. Cotton is then formed into a roll or lap.

Cotton in rolls is ready for carding.

4. In the card the roll is brushed into thin sheet.

5. Combing removes short fibers and forms sliver.

6. Drawing frame takes several slivers and draws them out into one.

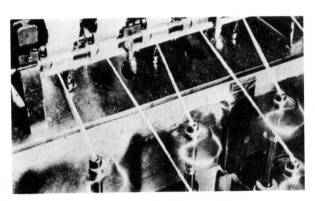

Sliver at top is twisted into roving.

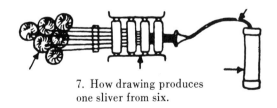

7. How drawing produces one sliver from six.

*On the following pages will be found a more detailed account of how the raw cotton is spun into yarn and finally woven into cloth.*

### From Raw Cotton into Yarn

The transformation of raw cotton fiber into finished yarn involves the following processes:

1. PICKING. When the cotton bales arrive at the mill they are opened and fed into a *blender*, which arranges the fibers for uniformity. They are then processed through the *picker*. This machine removes or picks out the heavier impurities such as seed and dirt. It then forms the lint into *laps*, which resemble rolls of absorbent cotton. Each lap runs about 45 inches wide and 18 inches in diameter.

2. CARDING. From the picker the lap goes to the *carding machine*. This straightens the mass of fibers and lays them in parallel rows by drawing them over a revolving cylinder with teeth. They emerge as a wide thin *web*, which still resembles absorbent cotton. The web is then gathered together into a rope or strand known as a *sliver*.

3. COMBING. Some fabrics are made from carded yarns, but if a higher quality is desired the fiber goes from the carder to the combing machine. Here the fiber is again straightened by fine-tooth combing until all short lengths (*noils*) are removed. It is then formed into *comber slivers*.

4. DRAWING. From the carding or combing machines the slivers then pass through the *drawing* operation. Several slivers are combined and are drawn out or pulled into thinner strands. The fibers remain parallel.

5. ROVING. Now the twisting process begins. The sliver may move through several slubbing frames, depending on the fineness of yarn required. The first stage is known as the *slubber*. Here the sliver is drawn out into a thinner strand, and is given a few twists. The cotton is now known as a *roving*.

6. SPINNING. The spinning frame takes the roving and continues the process of drawing out and twisting until the finished yarn emerges and is wound on bobbins. *Warp* or lengthwise yarns usually require more twisting than *filling* yarns because they are subjected to more tension in the weaving process.

CLASSIFYING YARNS. Yarns are classified by thickness. The basic unit of measurement is the *hank*. One hank is 840 yards long and weighs one pound. This is classed as *1s*. A finer yarn, which takes twice the yardage to make one pound, would be classed as *2s* in count—and so on. A *30s* count, which is common, means there are 25,200 yards of yarn in each one-pound hank.

Spinning the yarn. A spinning frame showing the roving (*above*) being spun into cotton yarn on spools (*below*).

1. Expert examines cotton staple for defects.

2. Scientific testing of staple for fineness.

3. Yarn uniformity assured by blending machines.

4. Pickers remove trash and make the lap.

5. Uniformity of picker lap is checked.

6. Carding parallels fibers, produces sliver.

7. Drawing or drafting on modern equipment.

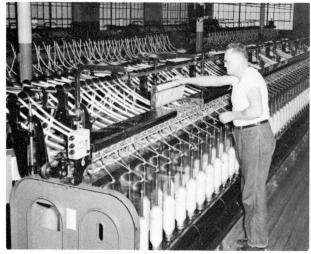

8. Drafting is completed by further stages.

9. Spinning in a modern cotton yarn mill.

10. Winding is done on automatic equipment.

11. Electronic testing to assure yarn quality.

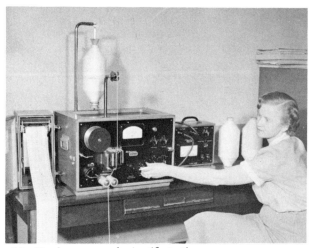

12. Further stages of scientific testing.

13. Visual inspection of test knit with yarn.

14. Visual inspection of finished yarn.

15. Automatic control on processing chemicals.

16. Modern dye production department.

17. Control laboratory with equipment.

18. Yarn is given final check before shipping.

1. Preparing warp on beam.

2. Warp on the loom ready for weaving.

3. Shuttle passing through the shed.

4. Weaving a cotton jacquard design.

## Weaving the Fabric

Weaving cotton yarn is basically the same as weaving any other fiber. It consists of interlacing the lengthwise *warp* yarns with the crossing or *filling* yarns. In the case of cotton the warp yarns, which are subjected to considerable tension, may first be coated with starch or sizing to prevent breaking or injury. Cotton looms operate at high speed. For example, a typical speed might be 180 *picks* a minute. A *pick* is a filling thread. This means that 180 filling threads are interlaced with the warp thread each minute. If the cloth has a filling count of 60 picks to the inch, a yard has 2160 picks and takes 12 minutes to weave. (See WEAVING section.)

KNITTING. Cotton yarns can be knitted as well as woven. Modern automatic knitting machines are high speed and are either of the *circular* or *flat* type. They can produce as many as 1,000,000 stitches a minute and can turn out a yard of fabric from two to five times faster than a modern weaving loom. (See KNITTING section.)

An operator watches the weaving of cotton fabric on a high speed loom.

# WOOLENS AND WORSTEDS

*What wool is, where it comes from, the differences in wool,
and how it is processed from a raw fiber to finished fabrics.
A brief lexicon of important names and terms in wool.*

## Definition

Wool is the fiber of a living animal. It forms the protective covering of the sheep, insulating it against both heat and cold and keeping its body temperature even.

Chemically wool is described as a protein called *keratin*. Keratin contains 18 of the known amino acids which are basic to living matter and is built up through a complex molecular structure known as a polypeptide chain. In general composition it is somewhat similar to human hair.

## Chemical Properties

The chemical formula for wool reads:

$(C_{42} H_{157} O_{15} N_5 S)$ n

Its average composition is:

Carbon—50%

Hydrogen—7%

Oxygen—22% to 25%

Nitrogen—16% to 17%

Sulphur—3% to 4%

## Under the Microscope

Wool is a living fiber. Under the microscope it shows three distinct parts:

1. EPIDERMIS. The outside surface consists of a series of serrated scales which overlap each other much like the scales of a fish. Wool is the only fiber with such serrations; these make it possible for the fibers to cling together and so produce *felt*. The serrations may run anywhere from 600 to 3000 per inch. The higher the number, the choicer the quality of the fiber.

2. CORTEX. A series of fibrous, spindle-shaped cells which form the center of the fiber. They supply elasticity and strength.

3. MEDULLA. The pith or core of the living fiber. This is the channel through which it receives nourishment.

## Physical Characteristics

DIMENSIONS: From 1 to 14 inches or more in length. From 1/600th to 1/3000th of an inch in diameter.

STRENGTH: Can be bent 20,000 times without breaking. Extremely flexible.

ELASTICITY: Can be stretched to an additional 25 to 35% of its own length without breaking.

RESILIENCY: Natural elastic recovery causes it to return to original position after being stretched or creased. Is therefore wrinkle-resistant.

CRIMP: Natural crimp or waviness of the fiber gives it bulk, enables it to trap air and so provide insulation.

ABSORBENCY: Will absorb up to 30% of its weight in moisture without feeling damp. This explains its affinity for dyes. It also explains why wool feels warm. Perspiration is absorbed and so does not cool the body by evaporation.

HEAT ACTION: Begins to disintegrate at 212°F.

**GREASY WOOL (Fine)**

**SCOURED WOOL**

**CARDED WOOL**

**COMBED WOOL**

**WORSTED ROVING**

## Some key stages in processing wool.

Rambouillet sheep, the largest and strongest-bodied wool sheep.

Carding room overseer holds in left hand picked wool ready for carding, in right, rovings after carding. (*Left*) Five steps in preparation of wool from the raw state to roving, from which the yarn will be spun.

# Wool

*What the Electron Microscope Shows*

MORE AND MORE LIGHT is being thrown by science on the structure of molecules which go to make up natural proteins, such as those from which wool fibers are composed. We can picture a wool fiber as built up of a great number of chain molecules crimped like springs. When the fiber is put under tension these chains are pulled out straight and extend to about twice their natural length.

These protein molecule chains are known to the chemist as polypeptide chains and their thickness is not over one 25-millionth of one inch. Every individual wool fiber is composed of a tremendous number of them arranged side by side; they are not completely separate, being tied together by cross links resembling the rungs of a ladder, which are, in reality, chemical bonds. The sides of the ladder are the crimped chains; when the fiber is under tension the crimped sides of the ladder straighten out.

When the extended fiber is released the cross links help to pull the fiber back into its original crimped form, thus contributing to the elasticity shown by woolen materials. If, however, the fiber is held in extension for a long time, new cross links tend to form, which have the effect of setting the fabric in its extended state, thus delaying recovery.

When a fiber is moist it has an improved recovery, since the water forms a molecular lubricant and enables the chains to resume their crimped shape rapidly. Dry fabrics have rather less rapid recovery. This is why fabrics of wool are steamed when pressing and why, once dry, they retain their press more strongly.

This process of shortening or lengthening by means of molecular chain folding can be carried to exaggerated degrees under certain conditions; a fiber of wool can be shortened to two-thirds of its normal length, if it is stretched and held extended in steam for two minutes and released while still in the steam. The stretching and steam act together to break down the molecular cross links and allow the chains to take much more crimp than they can when linked. They thus become shorter than their original length.

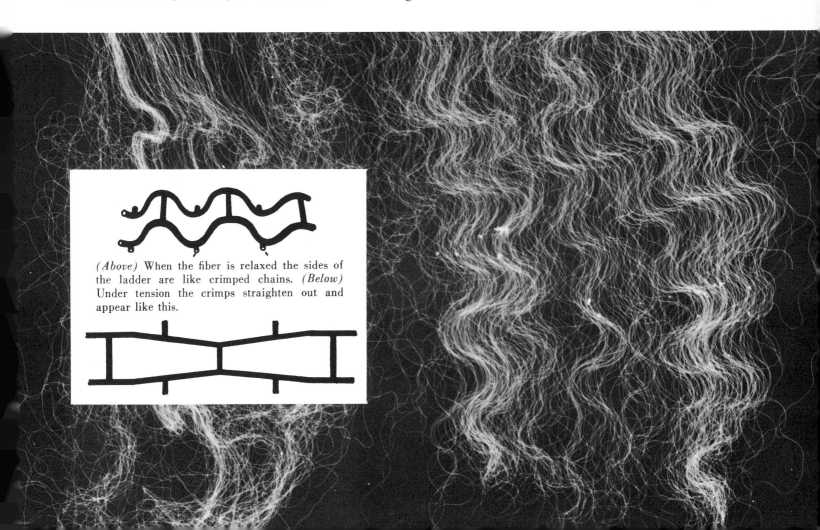

*(Above)* When the fiber is relaxed the sides of the ladder are like crimped chains. *(Below)* Under tension the crimps straighten out and appear like this.

# Wool from Sheep's Back to Finished Fabric

*The key stages in manufacturing wool . . . the differences between Woolens and Worsteds; how to determine the specific characteristics.*

Shearing sheep with power clippers

### First Step Is Shearing

The first step in the process of converting wool fiber into fabric is the shearing of the sheep.

Clipping the fleece from the hide of the animal is done annually in the spring, except in Texas and California, where, due to climatic conditions, the sheep are shorn biannually. Texas and California wools may bring a lower price in the market because the fleeces are more or less infested with small spiral burrs that are detrimental until removed from the fleece. Much of this wool, however, is of good quality.

Hand or power clippers are used in shearing. There are professional shearers who travel from place to place to perform the work. They are paid so much per fleece. In the shearing season these workers shear from sun-up to sun-down on a piece-work basis. Good shearers are usually extremely well-paid.

They clip as many as 200 sheep a day and can clip the whole fleece in one continuous piece in the shape of a sheepskin.

The fleeces, as they are taken from the sheep, are thrown to a helper who stands at the top of a high stand which has the top of the burlap bag fastened to it. This tender boy drops the fleeces, as he catches them, into the bag so that they can be moved quickly from place to place. A bag may weigh 300 lbs.

### Sorting the Fleece

Each wool fleece yields several different grades of wool fiber. A skilled sorter can separate them by qualities known as sorts. The shoulder wool has usually the best fiber. Next come side, neck, back, etc., in a descending order of quality. The numbered sketch below shows the order of preference generally used by the wool sorter.

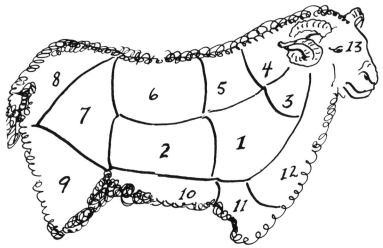

SHEEP FLEECE: the best area of wool fiber on any sheep is generally the back and sides near the head. The weight of a fleece ranges from 6 to 18 or 20 pounds, dependent on the breed and local conditions. The fleece, when received at the mill, must be sorted. From four to twenty distinct grades may be obtained from the one fleece, dependent on the rigidity of selection. The numbers show the approximate order of preference.

On this page are photographs of typical woolen cloths. Note the pronounced nap which gives each fabric a soft appearance and a lofty hand. At the bottom-right is a knitted woolen cloth.

## Characteristics of Woolen Fabrics

1. Woolen fabrics generally have a soft feel and fuzzy surface.

2. They have little shine, or sheen.

3. Woolens do not hold a crease well.

4. Their tensile strength is relatively low.

5. As a rule, woolens use less expensive yarns than worsteds.

6. Woolens take great depth of color in dyeing.

7. Woolens are generally heavier and bulkier than worsteds.

8. Woolens are more suited to casual fashions.

# Woolens and the Woolen Process

Woolen yarn. Note random arrangement of fibers yielding bulky yarn with soft and fuzzy surface.

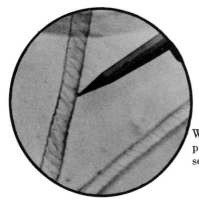

Wool fibers seen through a micro-projector; the pencil points to scales on surface of the fiber.

### Wool—Fiber to Finished Fabric

From the time raw wool enters the mill until it is ready to be cut up into apparel it may go through more than seventy special handlings in order to produce the quality of finished fabric expected by the consumer. Some of the basic steps in this production line are outlined below, with a division into the woolen and the worsted processes.

### The Woolen Process

1. Wool is sorted into different grades by hand; it takes years of experience to become a good sorter.

2. Wool is scoured to remove all dirt and yolk, to prepare the fleece for dyeing.

3. Wool may be dyed after it has been scoured and dried, in colors which are blended to attain the required shades. This is known as *stock-dyed*. Dyeing may also take place at later stages.

4. Wool tops are inspected to ascertain that the wool is of the required quality prior to woolen or worsted yarn spinning.

5. Wool is carded by a machine which opens the fibers, makes a homogeneous mix, and rolls the fibers into a roving.

6. Fiber is spun by drawing out and twisting the fibers in a continuous strand called yarn, which is wound on a bobbin. If wool is dyed at this stage it is called *yarn-dyed*.

7. Yarn is conditioned for efficient weaving; all kinks are removed by steam pressure.

8. Yarn is dressed by beaming the warp yarn to pattern specifications for color and size.

9. Yarn is drawn-in by the operator; each of the threads in the warp is drawn through small eyes in wires called heddles which are set in harnesses. The drawing-in is done according to the designer's plan, and the drawing-in controls the fabric pattern.

10. Yarn is woven by interlacing the yarns running lengthwise in the loom (the warp) with a series of yarns running crosswise (the filling) at true right angles . . . thus making up the basic fabric structure. If wool is dyed at the fabric stage it is called *piece-dyed*.

11. Cloth is perched, which means that it is perched on high frames and then closely scrutinized as a final examination.

12. Cloth is burled, which means that all knots, loose threads, and slubs are removed before the finishing process begins.

13. Cloth is fulled (or milled) by a process combining heat, moisture, friction, and pressure to shrink the cloth considerably in both width and length. The fabric loses its open-weave appearance in this essential operation after weaving.

14. Cloth is washed and rinsed to remove all impurities and dirt picked up through the previous operations.

15. Cloth is dried and straightened to remove all wrinkles, on a high speed set of over-and-under heated rollers.

16. Cloth is sheared on a machine with revolving razor-sharp blades to attain a uniformly even pile or nap.

17. Cloth is pressed after being moistened on a dewing machine, by passing through heated rollers.

1. An eighteen-month-old Australian ram with fine fleece which will provide long-staple wool after shearing.

2. Scouring the wool. The wool drops from feed at right into soap and soda solution, is moved along by spikes.

3. Oil emulsion being sprayed on scoured wool as it goes into mixing picker in order to lubricate the fibers.

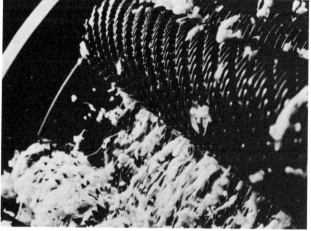

4. Wool being blended in the mixing picker, the revolving wheels of which open up and blend fiber masses.

5. Loading scoured and blended wool into Bramwell hopper which controls weight of batches fed to first card.

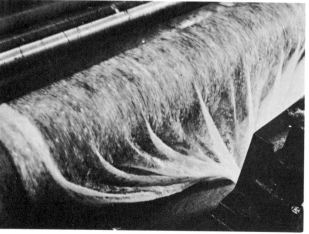

6. Web of carded wool as it comes from first card after passing through peralta rollers to pulverize seeds.

*For continuing steps see "Weaving" and "Finishing" sections.*

WORSTED CLOTH: (the word "worsted" was first associated with the parish of Worstead, in Norfolk, England). Worsted cloth is made from worsted yarns, tightly woven and with a smooth "hard" surface, and little or no nap. *Unfinished worsteds* are slightly softer to the touch, having a light covering of wool fibers or nap which is retained, instead of being completely sheared off as in the case of clear finished worsteds. Photograph shows typical men's wear worsted suitings. Note the closeness of weave and smooth finish.

## Characteristics of Worsted Fabrics

1. Worsted cloths generally have a smoother texture than woolens.

2. They take a shine more easily, because of the twist.

3. Worsteds do not sag, and they hold a crease well.

4. Worsteds have greater tensile strength than woolens.

5. On the whole worsteds use a better grade of yarn.

6. Worsted cloth is lighter and less bulky than woolen.

7. It is easier to tailor and drape worsteds.

8. You may expect longer wear from worsted cloth.

# Worsteds... How They Differ from Woolens

*The difference begins with the yarn. Worsted yarns require a greater number of processes, during which the fibers are arranged parallel to each other. The smoother, harder-surface worsted yarns produce smoother fabrics with a minimum of fuzziness and nap.*

*Worsted Yarn*

1. Carded and combed
2. Substantial, harder than wool
3. Smooth, even, uniform fibers
4. Stronger
5. Fibers are parallel
6. Even and greater twist
7. Uniform in diameter

*Woolen Yarn*

1. Carded only
2. Soft, slubby
3. Fuzzy, uneven fibers
4. Weaker
5. Fibers in conglomerate mass
6. Uneven twist
7. Bulky, uneven yarn

## The Worsted Process

Up to a certain point, the process for producing worsted fabrics is almost identical with that which results in the production of woolens. The raw wool is sorted, then scoured; it may be dyed, and the tops are inspected exactly as in the woolen process. At this point, however :

1. The wool is combed. This process removes foreign matter and noils; it parallels the wool fibers into a uniform staple length to ensure both the purity and the evenness of the yarn which is to be spun in preparation for weaving the cloth.

This step is possibly the most important departure on the road to weaving a worsted cloth, for it is most essential that the fiber be of uniform length in order to attain the twist which is the nub of a worsted cloth. After combing, comes another unique operation:

2. Packing tops in the dye vat is an operation in which the wool is wound on perforated tubes through which dyes are forced at tremendous pressure in order to set the colors evenly on yarn. This is done only on the worsted system, and so also is the next step in the production of worsted fabrics.

3. Washing tops after dyeing, to remove any surface or ingrained impurities or extraneous matter.

After this step the yarn is spun, conditioned, dressed, drawn-in, woven, burled, and fulled, as in the case of woolens; then come the final steps of washing, drying, shearing, pressing, and perching the finished worsted fabric.

Several important points differentiate the woolen and worsted system, as you may have already gathered. For one thing, worsteds are chosen for particular uses where it is desirable to obtain a hard surface finish, greater durability, and sharper colorings. Under the worsted system, the treatment of wool from the raw state to the finished state makes it possible to twist the fibers in such a manner as to create a smoother, harder surface. This is the essential difference between woolens and worsteds; there are other characteristics, but, in essence, it is the ability to twist uniform length fibers prior to the weaving process which paves the way for the worsted cloth.

There is no ground for the common notion that all worsteds are better than all woolens. Actually, a good woolen is a fine and desirable cloth, much more desirable than a poorly woven worsted made of yarns lower in quality than three-eighths. The final determinant is the purpose to which the cloth is to be put; if you know the advantages of each type of cloth, as well as their differences, you can then decide whether you should take the woolen or the worsted.

1. Carded wool is passed through back washing machine, dried, and made ready for processing into tops.

2. In gill box the wool slivers pass through the fallers, which parallel fibers and reduce strand.

3. Noble comb is key in worsted yarn spinning; removes short fibers and straightens long ones.

4. Wool tops are further processed on can gill box, and small percentage of oil is added to the wool.

5. The wool sliver is passed through the drawing box to reduce the slivers in thickness and even them.

6. Roving is final operation before spinning; here the slivers have been greatly reduced in thickness.

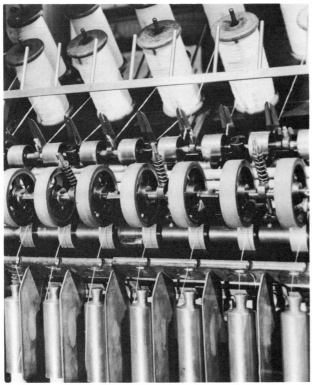

7. The rovings are spun into yarn on a ring spinning machine, being drawn out and twist being inserted.

8. Operator adjusting self-doffing mechanism on spinning frame, saving time in replacing bobbins.

Adjusting circular knit machine.

Taking samples of non-woven fabric.

## Knitting, Felting, and Pile Weaves

In addition to the weaving process, wool fiber can be converted into fabric by other processes. After the yarn has been made it can be knitted into a fabric either by hand or by machine. The basic principle is the same in both, and involves the use of a single strand of yarn which is knitted over itself into a series of interloops as distinct from weaving, which uses at least two yarns interlacing at right angles to each other. (See KNITTING SECTION)

The felting process takes place before the fibers have been spun. They are scoured, carded, and then set down in layers (or webs), one on top of the other. By the application of steam, moisture, and a pounding action, and the natural clinging properties of the fiber itself, it forms a strong non-woven cloth which is then finished and sheared.

A pile fabric is the basic principle which underlies most carpet making. While the method used is still weaving, it calls for the use of an additional filling or warp yarn which emerges as a loop or pile on the surface of the basic weave. This pile can be cut or left uncut. Plush fabrics are also made in this manner by cutting the pile evenly after weaving.

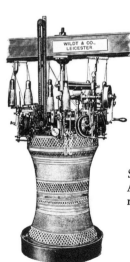

Sketch of a 19th Century American wool-knitting machine.

Bowing wool, from a 19th Century drawing.

Fulling the woolen cloth.

Natural teasels are used for raising.

## Shrinking the Wool Fabric

Before being cut up into garments all wool fabrics should be pre-shrunk. When properly shrunk, a piece of fabric which emerged from the loom with a width of 72 inches and a length of 60 yards will be reduced to a length of approximately 50 yards. Most woolens and worsteds, generally speaking, go to the apparel houses in lengths which range from 60 to 80 yards. The most popular method used is known as the London Shrinking process. It originated in London when that city became a garment-making center, and name is still used in the trade.

## Teaseling or Raising Wool Fabrics

Woolen fabrics are often raised during finishing. This is done in various styles, divided into wet and dry raising. Wet raising is employed for such goods as doeskins, beavers, and others where the weave is not shown. When wet-raised goods are shorn, only the loose, straggling threads are removed, as the pile raised lies flat on the surface. Dry raising is often done on machines where the cloth is brought into contact with rotating banks of teasels, as shown above, which produces a soft pile surface. Teasels are often replaced by wire for raising today.

Fulling, from a 19th Century illustration.

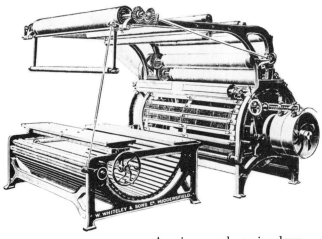

American wool-weaving loom of the late 19th Century.

# Wool Historicals

Open market at Witney, famous English wool blanket town.

In the Book of Samuel, they spoke of Goliath thus: *And the staff of his spear was like a weaver's beam.*

Having spoiled the Midianites, a part of the booty which the men of war had caught was 675,000 sheep.

In Proverbs and in Exodus, we are told that *the virtuous woman seeketh Wool and Flax and worketh willingly with her hands. She layeth her hands to the spindle, and her hands hold the distaff.*

From Exodus we learn: *And all the women that were wise-hearted did spin with their hands, and brought that which they had spun, both of blue and of purple, and of scarlet.*

It is recorded in Deuteronomy that *it shall be the Priest's due, the first of the fleece of thy sheep shalt thou give him.*

The Spanish Order of the Golden Fleece was a tribute to the merino sheep. Ferdinand and Isabella pawned the tax income from the merino revenues to finance the voyage of Columbus to America.

Elizabeth I, Queen of England, decreed that nobles should take the oath of fealty to the crown while kneeling upon a woolsack, to remind them that the power of England was built upon wool.

In ancient Aramaic it was called KMR. The Greeks called it Lenos, the Romans named it Lana, the Gauls spoke of Laine, the Germans and Saxons said Wolle. We call it wool.

New South Wales, Australia, is spoken of as the world's merino breeding bowl. The largest merino stud properties cover over 500,000 acres and about 125,000 sheep are grazed annually in the area. To this blooded flock are related 80% of Australia's 700 registered merino studs. About 12,000 merino rams are sold annually to the growers. It has not been uncommon for a prize stud to bring its owner from $5,000 to $20,000.

The Spaniards brought sheep to Santo Domingo and Cuba and, sailing west to conquer Mexico, introduced them to the mainland. From this beginning sheep were soon grazing as far south as Oxaca and as far north as New Mexico.

In New England the Dutch and English settlers established wool growing at the start of the 17th Century and thus began the textile industry which is still active in New England.

When the opening up of the West began and was followed by the California Gold Rush, sheep were in great demand to provide food and clothing. Wootton made his celebrated drive with 9,000 sheep from Taos, New

Shepherds use stilts in parts of the Near East and France.

Mexico to Sacramento, California, the trip taking a whole year, and the sheep fetching a price of over $50,000 on arrival, in 1852.

The King of Spain made a gift of six Merino sheep to the government of the Netherlands, and these were sent to the Dutch East India Company in South Africa. From these six sheep are descended the South African, and also the Australian flocks.

Perhaps as early as 4000 B.C., the Babylonians wore woven wool garments. Inscribed seals from that period, found by archaeologists in Asia Minor, indicate that wool trading had already begun.

By 2500 B.C. wool growing was a major industry in Mesopotamia; clay tablets record the accounts of Sumerian wool and sheep merchants of the day, who seem to have sold wool to the surrounding areas.

The nomads from the Asian steppes, who were sheep raisers and breeders, introduced carpets and tent hangings of wool and probably tailored clothing for the use of their horsemen.

The Spanish sheep were introduced by the Romans who conquered Spain; they found the climate to be especially suitable, and the sheep they bred became, after a lapse of many centuries, the famous Merino breed, which produces some of the finest wool in the world today.

The Romans are also said to have taught the craft of wool manufacture to the Britons after the conquest of Britain in 55 B.C., thus laying the foundation of British power which was built on wool.

*(At right)* Sculpture on the Cathedral of Chartres, dating from 12th Century, depicts shepherds with their flock.

# The History of Wool

*Wool has a long and exciting history. It parallels the advance of civilization and the course of empire. The beginnings of man's early culture, his first faltering steps as a social creature, are associated with the domestication of sheep.*

### Food, Clothing, and Shelter

We know that the Swiss Lake Dwellers who lived in the Later Stone Age kept sheep and used their wool. Like other early peoples they had discovered sheep could supply the basic necessities of life. They were food, they supplied clothing and even shelter in the form of tents. They were easy to domesticate and herd and they lived on what the land had to offer.

### Six Thousand Years Ago

The Scriptures are replete with references to sheep and shepherds. Abel was a keeper of sheep. The Israelites were, above all, shepherds; their flocks were their pride and wealth. In the Biblical lands of Babylonia and Mesopotamia, as early as the year 4000 B.C., people wore garments of wool and the fleece of the sheep had become a commodity in trade. In Britain, during the Bronze Age (3000 B.C.), woolen garments were worn, and the nomadic tribes from the Asian steppes in the second millennium B.C. insulated their tents with wool carpets, and made shirts and trousers out of wool.

### Romans Gave the World Merinos

The Greeks, the Romans, and the Persians had access to the sheep of all the known world. They selected and cross-bred those which had the finest fleeces. As the Roman empire made its way from the Mediterranean to the Danube, the Romans and the colonies they created scattered sheep throughout Europe. They made spinning and weaving the labor of all the women of the Roman world.

The Romans brought sheep to Spain because the climate was considered ideal for sheep raising. In the province of Tarraconensis they crossed the Tarrentine sheep with the Laodicean sheep of Asia Minor to produce the ancestor of today's most important wool bearer: the merino. The Moors, while they dominated Spain, improved the breed and for centuries thereafter the wealth of the Spanish empire was built on the fleece of the merino. It was guarded as a national treasure. Laws were passed to protect its use, and death was the penalty for illegal traffic. When Spanish royalty married into other royal families, part of the dowry was always merino sheep.

It was only by this method and by the illegal method of smuggling that merinos got out of Spain and began to infiltrate other countries of the world.

### Sheep in the New World

Columbus carried sheep to America on the Santa Maria, and the Spanish Conquistadores who followed him in 1540 introduced wool to Mexico. Under Spanish domination the Pueblos and the Navajos wove magnificent wool blankets which have seldom been equaled.

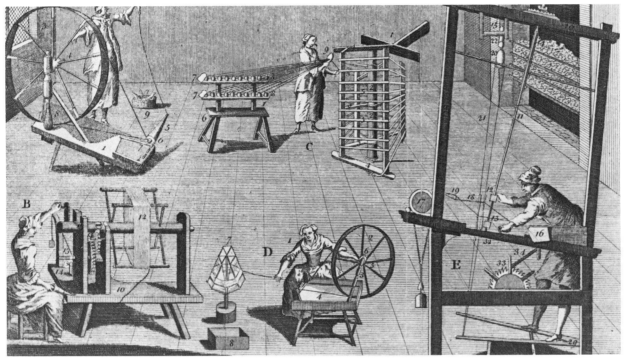

*Woolen manufacturing in England* during the 18th Century, as depicted in this engraving. Steps shown are (a) spinning, (b) reeling, (c) warping, (d) re-reeling, and (e) weaving.

## An Empire Built on Wool

Through the years of the Middle Ages, Spain and Britain were the two world rivals as producers of wool. Eventually England won the battle and thus laid the foundation of her riches and her wealth as a world power. The Empire was literally built on the wool she grew, processed, and traded with the rest of the world. The world demand for British woolens was so great that in the 19th Century England had to turn to her overseas colonies for raw wool. South Africa, Australia, and eventually New Zealand began the foundation of their great sheep-raising industries and are today among the world's six largest producers of raw wool.

## Home Industry to Factory System

In the New World, following the example of Columbus and the Spanish Conquistadores, the early settlers also began to grow wool. In 1607 the London Company sent to its Virginia colony a flock of sheep "to raise for peltrys and to fertylize ye soil." Thirteen years after Plymouth Rock, sheep were introduced into Massachusetts, and by 1640 the colonists had a flock of 3000. The Dutch also sent sheep to their settlers in the New World.

In the early colonies wool growing and weaving was a home industry. The first break in American household self-sufficiency came with the establishment of fulling mills (shrinking, shearing and finishing of woven woolen cloth) in 1643. The product of the first of the mills established by John Pearson at Rowley, Mass., was of such superior finish that a great demand for it was established. A second mill sprang up in Watertown in 1662, and the third in Dedham in 1681. The rest of the Colonies soon followed suit and by 1700 mills were numerous. It was not until 1794, however, that the first water-power operated factory was established at Byfield, Mass.

## Wool and Revolution

The art of the weaver of wool was destined to influence the shaping of the thinking and destiny of America. From these humble beginnings arose the "Manufactories." These establishments served a worthy purpose. They supplied work to the worthy poor, making them self-supporting, and helped sever American economic bondage to Europe. While these manufacturers did not have power equipment and even the "modern" machinery of their times, they turned out enough woolen stuffs to make America a power to be reckoned with in wool fabric production. This did not set well with British weavers,

Before the Industrial Revolution women spun the wool with yarn in hand. Then came James Hargreaves' invention of the Spinning Jenny which did the same work much faster and cheaper by machine.

whose nagging at the Crown was one of the underlying causes of the American Revolution. In 1767, James Hargreaves of Standhill invented the spinning jenny, by which one person unassisted could operate sixteen threads at once. Immediately Colonial production was stepped up.

Then came the shot that was heard 'round the world. The Revolutionary War was on. America learned that wool constituted the real sinews of war.

Valley Forge proved the vital necessity for wool clothing, wool blankets, wool hose. The records show that more men left the army because of an insufficiency of woolen stuffs than for any other reason.

## A Full Suit of Broadcloth

The lesson learned in war swiftly applied in peace. In 1780, a woolen factory was established in Hartford, Conn., which General George Washington visited and commented on in his diary, stating that "Their broadcloths are not of the first quality as yet. . . . I ordered a suit to be sent to me at New York." He is said to have read his inaugural speech to Congress in the ensuing January in a full suit of broadcloth made at the Hartford factory and presented to him by the owners.

While the English had lost the Colonies, they did not relinquish their hold on the woolen industry in America. Several British operators incorporated the first woolen organizations at this time. These were the largest organizations then in the country. However, Britain would not allow English makers to export wool machinery to America. Schofield had to construct his own machinery without patterns or drawings, and he was compelled to return to England to refresh his memory before he could complete a wool-carding machine.

In 1808 he manufactured a piece of black broadcloth of thirteen yards and presented it to President Madison. The President had a very stylish suit tailored from this fabric, and wore it at his inauguration. The vogue for American broadcloth spread and in 1811 "On motion of Mr. Clinton, the Senate of New York passed a resolution in which the House concurred, recommending all members of the Legislature to appear in the next session in cloth of American manufacture." Thus, Mr. Clinton became the first wool lobbyist in the United States.

## Necessity the Mother

Many inventions for improving the production of woolen fabrics took place during this era. The first

The photograph below, from the Smithsonian Institution, portrays a model of the Spinning Jenny, made from the original patent specifications in 1767.

wool-spinning machine was in operation at Peace Dale, R.I., in 1804. The first power loom for weaving wool cloth was introduced in Massachusetts in 1823. The first loom for weaving fancy cloth was invented by Crompton in 1840.

Because Britain had forbidden export of parts for wool machinery and of machines *in toto*, Americans were forced to create their own. On a par with Crompton were Erastus Bigelow and Lucius K. Knowles.

During the War of 1812 the woolen industry came to a standstill again. Even though at war with the British, woolen blankets for the American army were brought from England by way of France. Once more Britain unwittingly aided its foe.

Two Americans, Lucius and F. B. Knowles, invented powerloom for weaving woolens in Worcester, Mass., 1852.

The import of merino sheep was not an accident. Previously Spain had restricted the export of these fine wool-bearing animals. When Napoleon conquered Spain, she had to sell her flocks to pay the expenses of war. The American consul at Lisbon contracted for the shipment of 3,850 of these merinos to New York and New England.

## The Vogue for Trousers

Early in the 19th Century merino sheep were imported to the United States by Elkanah Watson. They multiplied rapidly and formed the basis of a new type of fabric which was manufactured by General David Humphreys at Seymour, Conn. Humphreys not only established a mill, but incorporated a model village which is still in existence and operation.

One of the most curious outgrowths of the War of 1812 was the popularity of trousers. These shank-covering garments became the American rage as a symbol of revolt against British imperialism, which was associated with knee breeches.

In 1843, the first worsteds were manufactured for women's dress goods but it was not until 1867 that American worsteds were used for men's suiting. England had a monopoly and prohibited the export of worsted machinery but America needed worsteds . . . a fabric much hardier than the woolen materials then in use. A machine was invented here by which worsted yarns could be combed as well as woolens.

## Industry Spreads Westward

In 1854 the Pacific Mills installed the first worsted machines. The Civil War need for uniforms made a great market for its production. New mills sprang up all over the country. Many cotton mills, deprived of raw materials, changed over to the manufacture of woolens and worsteds. More and more inventions came into being, lightening the work so that women could be employed in worsted manufacture. As cotton production fell off, wool manufacture increased. The largest woolen mill in the world was established in Lawrence, Mass.

The production of woolen fabrics had received an increasing impetus with such events as the opening of the Erie Canal in 1825, the opening of the Ohio Canal in 1833, and the 1849 California Gold Rush. The building of railroads, the establishment of clip-

per freight fleets, and the inland waterways communication system gave rise to a vast industry that spread rapidly westward. By 1840, there were 11 million sheep in the middle and Atlantic states alone. However, by 1893, the nation's sheep reached a peak of 63 millions.

## World Wool Statistics

Today the United States has about 19 million sheep and consumed about 275 million pounds of raw wool in 1969. World production of scoured wool was 3,548 million pounds in 1969, a figure which has shown a steady if undramatic increase for the preceding 10 years. The largest wool-producing countries in the world, in order of their 1969 production, are Australia, Russia, New Zealand, Argentina and South Africa. U.S. production of raw wool in 1969 was 197 million pounds, a figure which declined steadily during the 1960's. This decline occurred because of increased use of acrylics in apparel markets once dominated by wool and because of the increase of man-made fibers in carpets which, until 1964, was led by wool and is now led by nylon.

## Second Generation of Wool

Until very recently, wool consumption has been restricted because wool does not have the reputation of being an ease-of-care fiber. With new developments from the laboratory, however, this has changed considerably. A recent technological breakthrough has produced a fully machine-washable/dryable wool fabric which does not shrink. This has been accomplished by finishing the fabric with a resin which covers the scaly surface of the fiber. Thus, when the treated wool fabric is agitated in hot water during the wash cycle, it does not felt as ordinary wool would under similar circumstances. A second development in wool has been permanent-press fabrics. These are produced by treating the washable-wool fabrics with a special resin, which permits the making of garments whose wrinkle-free qualities measure up to the permanent-press qualities of similar garments constructed of man-made fibers. A third development has been a differential dyeing technique called "Multi-Krome." This technique achieves two or even three contrasting colors in a single dye-bath, permitting intricate heather and patterned effects. With developments like these, wool will probably begin to compete on more even terms with man-made fibers such as polyester.

# Sheep Breeds

*Important in wool production are the various breeds of sheep which yield a wide variety of types and qualities of wool. On the following pages are illustrated a number of the more prominent breeds found in wool growing today.*

Pictured above is a domestic ram which appears on an ancient frieze in the British Museum. Probably the sheep which produce the hard carpet wools of Asia Minor are descended from such flocks, recorded in biblical times; and the Merino sheep of Spain are said to have been bred from those introduced there by the Romans when they conquered the country.

## Blood Grades

About 200 different breeds and cross-breeds of sheep in the world produce the many different grades of wool fiber. One method of grading these wools is by *blood*. Using full-blooded merino sheep as the standard, various fractions of 100% merino are used to designate other grades of sheep. There are seven basic grades, descending in quality and fineness. Each blood grade corresponds to a numerical system of grading based on the fineness or count of the yarn; that is, how many threads can be woven to the inch. The seven grades and their corresponding numbers are full-blood or fine, which includes XX and X or ¾ or Delaine, 80's, 70's, 64's; half-blood, 62's, 60's, 58's; three-eighths blood, 56's; quarter-blood, 50's, 48's; low quarter-blood, 46's; common, 44's; and braid, 40's, 36's.

Cheviot Ram

Columbia Ewe

Corriedale Ram

Cotswold Ram

Dorset Ram

Hampshire Ram

Karakul Ram

Kurdy Ram

Leicester Ram

Lincoln Ram

Merino Ram

Oxford Ram

Rambouillet Ram

Romney Marsh Ewes

Southdown Ram

Targhee Ram

Tunis Ram

West Highland Ewes

1. WOOL SORTING: The sorter divides fleece into the qualities which it contains, from finest at neck to coarsest round the tail. As many as six qualities, apart from color, are sometimes taken from one fleece.

2. SPINNING: The workers, known as "piecers," mend or "piece" the threads that break, and "strip" or empty the machine when the bobbins are full and put in a new set of bobbins or "pirns."

3. WOOL DYEING: The wool has to be continually and carefully turned to allow the dye to go on evenly.

4. DRAWING: Preparation of a warp for the weaving. Each thread is separately drawn through a cotton or brass eyelet — known as a "heddle."

5. HAND LOOM WEAVING: Primitive type hand loom used in Scotland, on which Harris Tweed and such like cloths are produced. Competent craftsmen are capable of surprisingly intricate work.

6. KNOTTING AND PICKING: The piece, after leaving the loom, is gone over and the knots and such like blemishes are removed.

**KEY**

**STEPS**

**IN**

**HANDLING**

**OF WOOL**

7. MODERN CARDING MACHINERY: These rotary machines are covered with fine wire brushes, and as the wool passes between the rollers it is disentangled for spinning.

8. MODERN POWER LOOM: This elaborate mass of moving parts has superseded the simple hand loom for most purposes. Speed and accuracy are its features.

9. MENDING OR DARNING: The cloth, when delivered from the weavers, and every thread missed or misplaced by the weaver is replaced in its correct position.

10. SCOURING AND MILLING: After cloth is woven and examined, the piece is scoured and milled. This removes the oils used in spinning, cleans the cloth and shrinks it anything from 10 to 25 per cent, in length and width.

 LPACA

 HINCHILLA

 UTRIA

 NGORA GOAT

 OX

 POSSUM

 NGORA RABBIT

 UANACO

 ABBIT OR CONEY

 EAVER

 ARE OR JACKRABBIT

 ACCOON

 AMEL

 LAMA

 ICUNA

 ASHMERE GOAT

 USKRAT

WEASEL FAMILY

114

# Specialty Fibers

**The animal fibers which are used either for blending with wool to give special qualities and textures, or unblended for weaving fabrics which possess outstanding, hand lightness and warmth.**

The Bactrian Camel of Asia, the fleece of which is used for making fabric with unusual qualities of insulation, affording the wearer protection from extremes of both cold and heat.

Two of the outstanding specialty fibers are camel's hair, used for fine soft blankets and luxury woven coatings, and the hair of Kashmir goats, used in fine knitted goods to give them superlative "hand." (*Above*) Bactrian camel; (*Below*) Himalayan goat.

# Specialty Fibers

*The specialty fibers are the rare animal fibers which possess special qualities of fineness, "hand," or luster. They are a most valuable asset, either alone or in blends, to the weaver of quality textiles.*

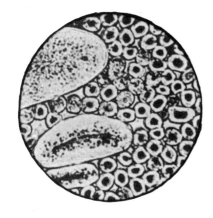

A cross-section of Muskrat fur, showing the coarse guard hairs and fine undergrowth, magnified approximately 1000 times.

Although the qualities which individual specialty fibers give to fabrics are quite different, the animal fibers themselves are in most cases similar. They grow in two principal coats. The outer is called the hair and is shiny and stiff. It overlaps and forms a protective shield around the animal's body against water, rain and snow. The undergrowth is called the fur. It is closer to the skin and is a soft shorter fiber which is much finer than the hair and acts as insulation against heat or cold.

Each fiber type has its place in the blending process depending on the ultimate effect desired. In some cases because of the scarcity of the fiber, the fabric developed becomes quite expensive. The world's total vicuna fleece production one year for example was 10,000 pounds. Compare this to the total wool production of more than 5 billion pounds.

Fabrics which contain specialty fibers are expensive not only because of the difficulty in obtaining the fiber, but also because of the elaborate processing involved. Some animals must be captured and killed. Many are allowed to live so that they may be periodically sheared. Others may be tamed, and bred for obtaining the pelt. Then the fur must be separated from the skin by cutting, and blown or dehaired. Some fibers from the various animals are blended for certain types of cloth. The fiber product might even have to be bleached and sometimes it is static-proofed.

Regardless of how the specialty fiber is obtained, unlimited combinations with wool are possible in the textile mills, since animals have fibers of varying colors, different degrees of fineness, luster, and lengths of staple.

As in sheep wool, usually the lighter the color and the finer and longer the staple of the specialty fibers, the more expensive it will be. Chief exception to this rule is vicuna, which is cinnamon brown. Because of the beauty of the color, this fiber is most frequently woven in its original shade. The rather dark color of vicuna does not prevent it from being woven into fabrics from which coats are tailored valued at $500 or more.

In some instances the luster of the specialty fiber plays the most important part in the finished fabric. This is when a glint or novelty effect is desired on the fabric surface.

Certain animals such as the guanaco and rabbit have the fine undergrowth of their fleece used in its entirety. However, there are some animals . . . the mink, muskrat and beaver . . . whose fibers are not used for the sole and ultimate purpose of blending with wool for textile use. The mink blend for example would be prohibitive in cost if the complete raw skin were to be cut and its fibers used in textile blends. This kind of peltry is used mainly by furriers and only the trimmings or portions of the skins which are not processed by them are diverted to the textile trade.

Specialty fibers have more than ever come into their own in recent years. Specialty fibers such as camel hair, cashmere, guanaco, and vicuna give decided appeal to a fabric, and they reach their peak of desirability in the development of fabrics for women who desire expensive and attractive apparel.

## How some important specialty fiber animals are related to one another:

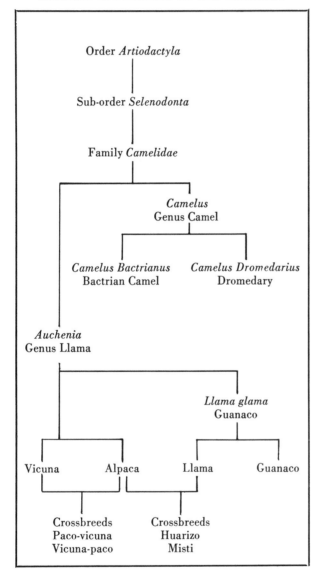

Order *Artiodactyla*

Sub-order *Selenodonta*

Family *Camelidae*

*Camelus*
Genus Camel

*Camelus Bactrianus*
Bactrian Camel

*Camelus Dromedarius*
Dromedary

*Auchenia*
Genus Llama

*Llama glama*
Guanaco

Vicuna     Alpaca     Llama     Guanaco

Crossbreeds
Paco-vicuna
Vicuna-paco

Crossbreeds
Huarizo
Misti

Besides adding softness or luster to fabrics, specialty fibers in many cases also have the glamour of being very rare. Important too is their ability to add warmth to the fabric without the addition of proportionate weight.

## From Skin to Fiber . . . Highlights in Specialty Fur Fiber Processing

KILLING AND SKINNING . . . The animal is either raised in captivity or captured when wild. It is then killed and skinned.

DRYING . . . The pelts are dried by exposure to air. Then they are baled and sold to large-scale purchasers in the textile and hatter markets. The price obtained depends on the season in which the animals are killed. If trapped in the summer, the animals' fur is meager. If in winter, it is luxuriant. Price is also subject to such variables as the region where the animal was caught, its age and size and the color of its fur.

DRUMMING . . . The skins are drummed by the purchaser with wet sawdust until they become pliable and easy to handle.

CLIPPING OR SHEARING . . . The skins are clipped or sheared so that the guard hairs are cut away as close as possible to the soft short undergrowth.

PLUCKING . . . If the guard hairs are to be removed in their entirety, the skins are put through another process called plucking, in which special machines extract the hair from the root and leave only the undergrowth on the skin.

REMOVING THE FIBERS FROM THE SKIN . . . The fibers must be removed from the skin. This is done by a special cutting machine which does not shear the fur fiber from the skin, but paradoxical as it may sound, it shreds the skin from the fibers. Once the fibers are cut off, the shredded skins are sold as a by-product for glue making.

SEPARATING THE FINE FUR UNDERGROWTH FROM THE REMAINING GUARD HAIRS . . . After cutting, the remaining guard hairs and the fine undergrowth must be separated. This is done in blowing machines which enlist the aid of gravity. When blown in enclosed compartments, the guard hair, being heavier, drops to the bottom of the blowing machine and the fur is transported to the second compartment where the process is repeated. This is done several times in a continuous operation so that the ultimate product is a very fine fur containing a minimum of coarse hair. Sometimes this dehairing treatment is very difficult as in the case of cashmere. The coarse hair which accumulates at the bottom of the blowing machine is known to the trade as droppings. It is packed separately and often is used to give certain shiny and lustrous effects when blended with wool.

# The Leading Specialty Fibers

*The following is a description of the more important specialty fibers now being used alone or in blended yarns for luxury woven and knitted materials.*

## Alpaca Widely Used

ALPACA—a smaller member of the South American camel family, it is able to live at altitudes above twelve thousand feet. Its colors are like the llama's —white, black, fawn, or grey. The fleece is very rich and silky with considerable luster. The Suri, a breed of alpaca, has even finer and longer fleece which ultimately helps make a more luxurious fabric. In comparison to the llama, all breeds of the alpaca have fleece containing less coarse fibers, but possessing a higher tensile strength. The average fineness of the alpaca fleece is 26.7 microns and the hair length varies from 8 to 20 inches. It hangs over the body and flanks and often conceals the feet. Roughly six pounds of fleece are produced by the alpaca every two years. It is domesticated. Although alpaca farms exist, most animals are owned and bred by Indians. Arequipa, Peru, is the main collecting and sorting point for alpaca wool.

The Suri breed of Alpaca, prized for its long fleece, source of the finest wool.

## Angora Goat Produces Mohair

ANGORA GOAT—the clipped fiber of the living animal is called mohair. It is used extensively in industries such as carpet, upholstery, curtain and automobile cloth. In the clothing industry, it is used in tropical worsteds. The animal is domesticated and originated in Turkey. It thrives elsewhere only in the Union of South Africa and the southwestern

United States. Scoured mohair which appears smooth and white has a wide range of fineness varying from eleven to ninety microns. It is highly resilient and possesses considerable tensile strength and luster. Its luster, not its softness, determines its value. Mohair is also sold in tops and noils.

## Angora Rabbit for Soft Blending

ANGORA RABBIT—a beautiful animal, this rodent has long, fluffy, white, silky hair. Indigenous to Turkey and Asia Minor, this animal acclimatizes itself to any region. Unlike the hare and the wild rabbit, the angora rabbit is domesticated. It is clipped or combed every 3 or 4 months and the product which approximates 12-14 ounces a year is marketed. The fur fiber is one of the finest. It has an average micron count of 13. Despite United States competition and the clamor of American ranchers for protective tariffs, the cleanest and finest angora rabbit furs still come from France, Italy and Japan. It is used on a large scale by knitting mills. There is a considerable market for the yarn on a retail level. Sweaters, mittens, baby clothes, etc., are fashioned from 100% angora fur dyed in various pastel col-

Angora goat, called for capital of Turkey.

ors, or sold in its pure natural white. It is also sold mixed in a certain percentage with very fine wool.

## Many Uses for Beaver

BEAVER—the largest amphibious member of the rodent family, it is found in Europe and America. Beaver fur, like muskrat, is considered the best for felt-hat manufacture. Coming from an animal which weighs about forty pounds, the fur has an average micron count of 15.8. It is soft and silky and lends itself to textile use. The hair is used by this industry only when certain shiny effects are desired in blends. Considerable demand exists for beaver pelts in the fur industry. They are plucked and sheared and because of the light belly portion, they appear to be striped. Canadian beaver has a blue-brown fur fiber while other animals vary in shading from light brown to pale tawny. Unlike the early 19th Century, when the fur was used in the manufacture of beaver hats and the shiny, coarse guard hair left on the skin for ultimate use as stoles for priests and royal officials, today finds the pelt used in fur coats and in trimming fur and fabric garments.

CAMEL—this is the two humped, or Bactrian species of the Chinese and Mongolian deserts which is distinguished from the dromedary, or one-hump type. It is the source of camel's hair fiber, a mixed wool type having a fine undercoat of about 17 microns and coarse beard fibers. The fibers are obtained by shearing and also by collecting the hair shed during the molting period. This hair is reddish brown or tan. Because of the beauty of the color, fabrics containing camel's hair are left in the natural state or dyed to a darker shade of brown. The fine fur fibers are woven as such, or blended with fine wool for overcoating, topcoating, sportswear and sports hosiery. The coarse hair is used in the manufacture of very strong transmission belts which will withstand dampness and oil. Camel hair is also combed and sold in tops and noils.

CASHMERE GOAT—also known as the KASHMIR GOAT, a domesticated native of Tibet, China, Persia, Turkestan, and Outer Mongolia; this animal sheds during the spring. The hair is plucked either by hand or picked off the shrubs against which the animals rub. The natural color of the fibers is white, black, brown, or grey. The diameter of the cashmere down averages about 15 microns. The beard hairs are extremely irregular, varying from 30 to 140 microns in diameter. As in the case of the camel's hair, the textile industry is interested only in the soft fibers. The separation of fine fibers from the long

coarse hair is a very tedious and difficult operation. It is done in different ways, some of which require several successive steps. As in the case of camel hair, cashmere is often combed and sold in tops and noils.

CHINCHILLA—a squirrel-sized rodent found in the South American Andes, the chinchilla is renowned

Chinchilla.

for its platinum-grey coat of ultra fine fibers. Decimated by hunters in the late 19th Century, the animal is extremely valuable today. It is primarily coveted by furriers, but the price of the finished coats precludes much selling. As a specialty fiber for fabrics the pieces of chinchilla and its cousin chinchillona are used in blends emphasizing pearl grey color combined with an almost unbelievable softness.

Fox.

FOX—an animal well known in every part of the world. It varies in color from black, red, silver, cross, silver grey, and white. Foxes are not only wild, but are also bred in various countries on an extensive scale. A few years ago fox growers surprised the market with an entirely new hybrid animal of an unearthly platinum color which is called platina fox. Fox fur has an average micron diameter of 15.2 and is highly prized by furriers who use it for scarves, muffs, jackets, coats, and trimmings. The fur is also used extensively to provide softness in wool blends for the textile industry. Its price for this use depends on the blend.

Guanaco.

GUANACO—like the alpaca, is related to the llama, but is a larger and more graceful animal. A native of Southern Argentina, it is found not only wild, but also in a domesticated state. Guanaquito, the progeny of the guanaco, produces the fleece of the most glorious natural honey beige color known to man. This inimitable color combines with a very soft handle, which is literally thrilling to the touch of the connoisseur.

Hare or Jackrabbit.

HARE OR JACKRABBIT—one of the well-known animals in the United States, this rodent exists everywhere in the world except on the island of Madagascar. Its hair texture is wooly and of interest not only to the textile trade, but also to hatters and

Camel caravan — Near East.

It cannot be claimed that a camel is beautiful or intelligent. Tradition of the East tells that when Allah had finished making all the other animals he found himself left with several odds and ends, and with these he made the camel. When the camel first saw its reflection in the water it was so ashamed that it fled to the desert, where it has lived ever since.

But in penance, it has been a loyal and faithful servant of humanity. It will carry half a ton of load twenty-five miles a day without water for three days, and its coat provides man with shelter against the sun's heat and the cold at night.

The camel coat is still a favorite far from desert climates, for its light weight and soft texture. It is said that a 22 oz. camel fabric is as warm as a 32 oz. woolen fabric. First popularized by the polo-playing fraternity of Westbury, Long Island, it has long remained a staple for sports and campus wear.

Polo players in the 1920's.

121

Members of the same family, the llamas and alpacas interbreed freely, and out of the crossing of their blood come two hybrids. These are the *huarizo* (*left*) born of a llama sire and alpaca dam, and the *misti* (*right*), sired by an alpaca with a llama dam. The fleeces of these two breeds are not so fine, generally speaking, as those of the alpaca.

furriers. The hare's clipped outer hairs when blended with wool before the fabric is spun give the finished goods an appearance of hairiness. When the fur fibers are used, the end fabric is soft handle. The wooly texture of the hare's coat lends itself particularly well to felting. More than 50% of all fur fibers used in woolen clothing are selected from the hare, the angora rabbit and the plain rabbit.

HUARIZO—see Llama.

LLAMA—the largest of the South American *camelidae*, weighs about 250 pounds. It is used as a beast of burden because of its sure-footedness in the mountain areas. Its long fibers have an average diameter of 27 microns and vary in color from white to brown to black. They are uniform in diameter and length. Llama fleece is obtained by shearing in early December, a warm month in the southern hemisphere. Owned almost exclusively by Indians, the fleece is either woven by them or sold to factors who make it available to the textile industry for use in woolens and hair fiber materials which have an impressive luster, warmth and light weight. Hybrid members of the llama family are huarizo (llama father and alpaca mother) and the misti (alpaca father and llama mother). Both have fleece which can be processed into fine fabrics. In some of the remote regions of South America the huarizo is used as a beast of burden like the llama, but the misti is never so used. All the members of the South American family of *Camelidae* are in a wide sense designated as llamas.

MINK—see Weasel family.

MISTI—see Llama.

MUSKRAT—an aquatic rodent of North America which has never been domesticated, this animal is valued for its thick blue grey brownish fur which resembles the beaver's. The fur fibers are extremely fine and have an average micron count of 11.7. Used primarily by the fur industry, muskrat furs provide the very fine fibers for various textile blends emphasizing a deep softness in the ultimate fabric. For the textile industry the muskrat pieces are collected and dissolved in such a way that the leather is destroyed, and the fur released and almost unaffected by the chemical process necessary to destroy the skin.

NUTRIA—a native of South America, this aquatic rodent has a beautiful silky fine belly undergrowth which is unlike other similar animals because the nutria dwells in streams that are colder than the atmosphere. Remaining in shallow portions, its back is exposed to the air and does not require the fur protection demanded by the stomach. The bellies after the guard hairs are removed are used by furriers. The textile industry also uses nutria fur fibers in blends emphasizing softness.

OPOSSUM—the only marsupial outside of Australia, this beast thrives in Australia, the southern United States and is found as far south as Argentina. It is about cat size, has a white face and fur that is loose, greyish, and white-tipped. The pelting is used chiefly as trimming for cloth coats. In textile fabrics, the hair is separated from the undergrowth and only the latter used. Australia and New Zealand are by far the biggest producers of opossum.

RABBIT OR CONEY—a small rodent, this animal is of the same genus as the hare. It is enormously prolific and its fur, together with that of the hare, forms the backbone of the felt hat industry. Under the name of "Lapin," the sheared pelts dyed in innumerable shades are widely used for coats and trimmings. There are wild and tame rabbits. The wild rabbits are with very few exceptions of a brownish-grey color. Australia is by far the largest producer of wild-rabbit skins. Tame rabbits are being raised all over the world, and they run in colors from white to black. A large part of tame rabbit skins are being used to produce one of the most popular specialty fibers. The guard hairs have an average thickness of 90 microns while the average fineness of the fur varies from 11 to 15 microns. The quality of the fur and hair depends on the season, geographical location, and the age of the animal. Rabbit fibers, both the soft fibers and the hairs, are used in the manufacture of varieties of textile blends. Where the accent is on softness of touch, only the undergrowth is used. Where the fabric is to have a shiny effect, the guard hairs, or both the fur and the guard hairs, are used. Pricing depends on the fineness and the color, with the lighter hues being more expensive.

The Raccoon.

RACCOON—a native American. It is greyish brown in color with a characteristic black and white face and ringed tail. Its pelt is used as trimmings for cloth and fur coats. For sportswear, the pelts are "let out" in long stripes to give the coat an elongated appearance. For textile purposes, only the wooly fur fiber which has an average micron count of 15.3 is used.

SURI—see Alpaca.

The Vicuna.

VICUNA—like the guanaco, it is a member of the llama family. It is the smallest and the wildest. Living at heights above 16,000 feet it generally is killed to obtain the fleece. Its fleece is reddish brown, shading to white on the belly. The amount of coarse hair is negligible with the exception of the breast part which consists of long white beard hairs in the shape of an apron. One of the finest fibers in the world, the vicuna fiber has an average diameter of 13.5 microns. Since 1921, the Peruvian government has protected the vicuna by rigorous conservation measures. The textile industry uses the fibers to manufacture the softest coat cloth in the world.

WEASEL FAMILY—about 175 species are in existence. They have a long cylindrical body and walk on their toes, not on the soles of their feet. Some species are well known, the mink and the ermine for example are ferocious and bloodthirsty animals. Larger than these two and of stouter build is the wolverine which is found in Europe, Asia, and America. Other members with valuable fur are the marten and the sable. Still another group includes the badger. The fur industry uses nearly all the species of the weasel family in making coats, trimmings, capes, etc. The textile industry uses large amounts of their fine fibers, but only those with names that will add to the dignity and glamour of the fabrics. The accent is on luxury.

Silk cocoons yield the raw silk. In modern sericulture the proper
selection and grading of the silk cocoons play an important part.

(*At right*) Cross-section of raw silk threads reeled from six cocoons; each of these cocoon ends being in fact double, the resultant threads contain twelve filaments. Note how the natural gum binds them together at this stage. (Magnification x 150.)

# Silk...Nature's Luxury Fiber

*Nature's luxury fiber is still regarded as the quintessence of quality which many new textile fibers strive to attain.*

## Definition

Silk fiber is a continuous protein filament produced by the silkworm in order to form its cocoon. The principal species used in commercial production is the mulberry silkworm which is the larva of the silk moth, *Bombyx mori*. It belongs to the order *Lepidoptera*.

## Under the Microscope

Magnified many times, the raw silk fiber shows a smooth, translucent, rod-like filament with occasional swellings along its length.

Each silkworm has two glands and from each of these it extrudes a filament called a brin. The two filaments together are called fibroin. This is the insoluble part of the fiber. As the filaments emerge from the glands, the two brins are cemented together by a soluble silk gum called sericin. These three elements taken together are known as the bave. This is the raw silk fiber.

## Chemical Properties

Since the raw silk fiber is made up of two parts—fibroin and sericin—they can be analyzed separately. Fibroin represents from 75 to 90% of the fiber; sericin from 10 to 25%. There are small traces of wax, fat, and salts. Fibroin and sericin are similar compounds and classified as proteins.

The chemical formula for fibroin reads:

$C_{15} H_{23} N_5 O_6$

The chemical formula for sericin reads:

$C_{15} H_{25} N_5 O_8$

## Physical Characteristics

DENSITY: Lower than wool, cotton, linen or rayon, it is therefore lighter in weight than these fibers.

INSULATION: A poor conductor of both heat and electricity, it is therefore warm next to the body and highly valued for electric-wire insulation.

ABSORBENCY: It can soak up 30% of its weight in moisture and still feel dry. It absorbs perspiration without becoming clammy, another reason for its warmth. The same capacity gives it great affinity for dyestuffs at low temperatures.

STRENGTH: It is extremely strong. A filament of silk is stronger than an equal filament of steel. Its breaking strength is reckoned as high as 65,000 pounds per square inch.

ELASTICITY: It will stretch as much as 20% of its length without breaking, but will not spring back if stretched more than 2%.

SCROOP: This is the quality which gives silk fabrics their characteristic rustle. It is not an integral quality of the fiber but is imparted in the finishing process when washed in a bath of dilute acetic acid.

HEAT ACTION: Silk is not injured by temperatures as high as 284°F.

LUSTER: Because it is a smooth, translucent filament, silk when processed becomes a smooth, lustrous, and luxurious fabric.

RESILIENCE: It has remarkable recovery. That is why a silk fabric, if tightly compressed, will quickly spring back to its former position when released.

This quality gives it excellent wrinkle-recovery.

125

Reeling silk in 18th Century.
Japanese Ukiyoe wood block print.

| SILK IN NINE LANGUAGES | |
| --- | --- |
| SPANISH- *Seda* | LATIN—*Sericum* |
| CHINESE—*Si* | FRENCH—*Soie* |
| ITALIAN—*Seta* | GERMAN—*Seide* |
| KOREAN—*Soi* | ENGLISH—*Silk* |
| JAPANESE—*Kinu* | |

# Silk History

Most historians agree that silk and sericulture had their origin in the dim antiquities of China more than four thousand years ago. According to Chinese records, the silk industry became an important factor in Chinese economic life when the Empress Si-ling, wife of the famous Emperor Huang-ti (2640 B.C.) made it fashionable to cultivate the mulberry tree, rear the silk moth (*Bombyx mori*), and reel the silk. Ancient Chinese literature credits Si-ling with devoting herself, personally, to the care of silkworms and to the invention of the silk loom. There is a vast compilation of ancient literature dealing with the importance of Chinese sericulture and the attention bestowed upon it by royal and noble families which followed Si-ling's example. The silken fabrics were used by the aristocracy of ancient China as a medium of exchange.

The Chinese not only used silk fabric for clothing, but soon effected new means of employment for thousands of citizens by employing silks for wall hangings, paintings, religious ornamentation, interior decoration, and for the maintenance of ecclesiastic and imperial records. Caravans from all over the world exchanged their loads for this priceless fabric, and thus China prospered. Naturally, the Chinese guarded the secrets of their precious craft with fierce jealousy. It meant death by torture to spread this knowledge beyond the borders imposed by imperial decree.

## Japanese Beginnings in Sericulture

Many centuries passed before the knowledge of the silkworm and its product were smuggled into Japan through Korea. While silk fabrics were already known to the Japanese as well as to parts of the Western world, the art of sericulture, according to the Nihongi (one of the most ancient of Japanese histories), was not practiced in the Land of the Rising Sun until 300 A.D.

At that time, the Japanese negotiated with Korean agents to engage experts from China to teach the art of weaving and manufacturing silk fabrics. There is a temple in the Province of Settsu which was erected in honor of the four Chinese concubines who were smuggled into Japan to instruct the Japanese court and the nobility in the art of making plain and figured woven silks.

Japan, at this time a nation of two extreme castes, the feudal lords (Daimios) and the peasantry, eked out its economic existence by means of agriculture. It was not only the climate of Japan, but the indefatigable industry of the peasant that gave impetus to the silk industry. The ruling powers realized the importance of this new industry and nurtured the economic infant until it grew to national importance. For 1600 years, silk was the vital factor that transformed these tiny isolated islands into a world power.

About 400 A.D., a Chinese legend says, the eggs of a silk moth and a seed of the mulberry tree were taken to India by a Chinese princess who concealed them in the lining of her head-dress. It is now known that sericulture was first established in India in the tract of land which lies between the Ganges and the Brahmaputra Rivers, a valley admirable for the raising of mulberry trees, and easily reached by the overland route from China. However, certain Sanskrit writings claim that silk manufacture was practiced in India as early as 4000 B.C. Whether this story denotes the manufacture of end products from silk or the weaving of silk is not clear. Probably it is the former. The Rajahs and Brahman caste of India were extremely partial to silk. But it may be noted that conditions were not sufficiently stable to permit of the development of a major silk industry in India until after the Mogul conquest in the course of the 16th Century.

## The Silk Path to Europe

The path of silk followed the westward overland route; slowly it led to Khotan, Persia, and Central Asia. It was in the latter place that the Greeks first became acquainted with the fabulous fabric. The philosopher Aristotle, in his History of Animals, was the first Western writer to describe the silkworm. He called it . . . "a great worm which has horns and so differs from others. At its first metamorphosis, it produces a caterpillar, then a bombylius and, lastly, a chrysalis . . . all these changes taking place within six months. From this animal, women separate and reel off the cocoons and afterwards spin them. It is said that this was first spun in the Island of Cos by Pamphile, daughter of Plates."

When the seat of the Roman Empire was moved to Constantinople, the Emperor Justinian monopolized the trade for himself and also sought to divert the trade from the Persian route (over which raw silk was then imported from the East and into Europe) through Abyssinia. He was not successful; but two Nestorian monks who had lived a long time in China acted as his spies and smuggled in silkworm eggs and mulberry seeds in a hollow bamboo cane. In this memorable year, A.D. 550, the varieties of silkworms which stocked and supplied the Western world for more than 1400 years were generated. The silken textures of Byzantium became world-famous. The spread of the demand for silk was in part propagated by early prelates of the Christian church, whose vestments and altar cloths were made of priceless silks. The feudal lords envied the luxury displayed by the early churchmen; soon they adopted silk for themselves, their ladies, and their courts. In the many wars during the next few hundred years, silken booty was diverted into every part of the Western world. Men-at-arms brought home bits of silk as treasures for their mothers and wives. Silk was a treasure coveted all over Europe.

## Development of Manufacture in the West

The conquering Saracens next gained mastery over Egypt, North Africa and Spain, and their conquests spread the knowledge of silk weaving throughout the West. The Islamic culture continued traditional themes, but eliminated representation of the human form, substituting for it as a decorative theme, the use of Kufic lettering in panels and borders. By the 10th Century there were Arab mills in Sicily.

The excellence of their products is verified in the written testimony of Ordericus Vitalis, who writes, "A Bishop of France brought with him from Southern Italy (Sicily) several large pieces of silk, out of the finest of which four copes were made for the cathedral chanters."

In this period of history, most of the great wealth of Europe lay in the hands of the nobles and the church. Since the cultivation and manufacture of silk was a profitable business, these lords encouraged the making of silk in such towns as Florence,

Hsuan Tsung's Kittens, attributed to Emperor Hsuan Tsung (reign 1426-1435) in the Ming dynasty (1368-1644). In the A. W. Bahr collection of Chinese paintings at the Metropolitan Museum of Art.

Milan, Genoa, and Venice, which have given their names to silken products ever since.

Just twelve years before Columbus discovered America, Louis XI started the first silk mill at Tours. Columbus set out, not to discover the new world, but to find (among other things) a new route to the East by which trading in silks could be made easier. By the 17th Century a wise Frenchman, Colbert, had done much to stimulate the silk industry in France by offering premiums for the planting of mulberry trees.

In the meantime, England did not lag far behind the Continent countries in silk manufacture. Although silk-making was introduced in the British Isles during the reign of Henry VI, the war between Holland and Spain gave the first real impetus to British silk-making when a large body of expert Flemish weavers emigrated from the Low Countries. The revocation of the Edict of Nantes 100 years later sent a large group of the most skilled silk workers from France to England. The bulk of these French workers settled at Spitalfields and set up a guild of silk workers in 1629. James I used all possible inducements to encourage the growth of the industry.

Silk manufacture in England was at the mercy of the Continent countries where most of the thrown silks were obtained. In 1718, one Lombe of Derby entered Italy disguised as a laborer. He smuggled out drawings of the machinery used for silk throwing and was then subsidized by the English government to build a plant on the banks of the Derwent. The Irish, too, came in for their share of sericulture when in 1825 the British, Irish, and Colonial silk companies, with a capital of a million pounds, tried to introduce silk growing into Ireland, but this was a failure. Vying for leadership, the Spaniards under Cortez tried to introduce sericulture into Mexico; in 1522 the writer Acosta mentions the fact that the first mulberry trees were planted and eggs were brought from Spain. It was not long before this industry died out in Mexico.

## Attempts at Sericulture in America

In 1609, King James, straining every effort to make England a world silk leader, tried to introduce the silkworm into the British segment of the New World. Due to a shipwreck, his first venture was a failure. In 1619, an all-out effort was again made in Virginia to encourage sericulture. The industry was bolstered by means of bounties and rewards, and laws were passed to stimulate its development.

When the Revolutionary War broke out, Benjamin Franklin was at work trying to establish a silk filature at Philadelphia. After the Colonies won their independence, Connecticut tried by means of the bounty system to encourage home silk raising. In fact, practically every state in the Union tried such a measure until as late as 1872.

A state of frenzy in silk production took place in 1838. The South Sea Islands' mulberry tree was claimed by Samuel Whitmarsh to be ideal for feeding silkworms. Plants, crops, trees, and houses were razed to make room for mulberry plantations. Mulberry plants were sold two and three times over, at an advance in prices for every sale, the buyers never seeing the actual shrub itself. Seedlings of a year's growth were sold at the almost unheard of price of one dollar each, and as much as $3,300,000 changed hands for these plants in one week in Philadelphia. But the speculation collapsed in 1839 when the South Sea Island mulberry tree—the *moris multicaulis*—was found to be unfit for silkworm rearing. The financial ruin that attended this collapse effected a tremendous pressure on many American economies.

Silk manufacturing in Japan in the 19th Century.

## Nylon Invades Silk Field

The field of women's hosiery, silk's largest single market, was taken over by nylon after World War II. Many other silk markets such as apparel and scarves have also been taken over by nylon, polyester and acetate during the postwar era, particularly in textured form. Silk production world-wide, however, remains stable at about the 80 million pound level, though the silk market in the United States has declined significantly. Total U.S. silk consumption in 1969 was 9-million pounds.

Silk moth laying eggs.

Section of modern silk-weaving mill, Nagahama, Japan.

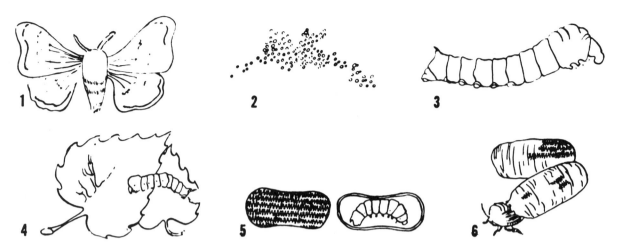

Stages in the life cycle of the silkworm: (1) the silk moth lays the eggs (2) which emerge as tiny, newly-hatched silkworms and (3) grow into adult silkworms through continuous feeding on mulberry leaves (4). It begins to spin its silk cocoon about itself (5) and develops into the chrysalis and then into a moth (6) ready to begin the cycle anew.

# Silk  *how it is made. From moth to cocoon; from cocoon to silk reeling.*

Silk is the filament a silkworm spins for its cocoon. The silkworm is actually the caterpillar of the silk moth (*Bombyx mori*), and its cocoon is the shell it constructs to protect itself during its growth from caterpillar to chrysalis to moth. A single cocoon is made of a continuous filament of silk which the silkworm extrudes from its body and throws about itself, layer upon layer, making a thick, smooth, symmetrical wall. Along with the silk filament, the silkworm emits a gummy substance called sericin. This is the cement that glues the silk filament into a firm, hard cocoon.

## Sericulture

Sericulture, the culture of silk, is the care of the little creature that produces the silk filament, from egg through to cocoon (and, with breeders, to the moth as well). It is a most delicate process, requiring scrupulous care and tireless patience throughout the entire cycle. In Japan, from which we receive the bulk of our raw silk, and in Italy, from which a fine grade of silk is imported in comparatively small quantities, the culture of silk of a uniformly high grade has been developed with enormous scientific research and governmental regulation.

Silk cocoons require airy and fresh surroundings.

The silkworms are kept under conditions of scrupulous cleanliness on bamboo trays. A Japanese girl is here seen feeding fresh mulberry leaves to the silkworms on tray at left.

The breeder moths are selected with the utmost care. The eggs undergo many tests to insure perfect, disease-free worms. They are put in cold storage until the early spring, when the mulberry trees begin to leaf. Then they are incubated, and hatch, in a week or so, into tiny silkworms, which are kept under rigidly clean conditions on trays which must constantly be refilled with mulberry leaves. The silkworms have finicky and insatiable appetites. They demand the freshest of mulberry leaves every two or three hours, and they eat voraciously night and day for five weeks. Enough silkworms to produce a pound of silk eat two hundred pounds of mulberry leaves. During this time they grow to seventy times their original size.

It is estimated that one acre of mulberry trees can provide enough leaves to raise about 160,000 silkworms a year, which produce about 528 pounds of cocoons or fiber for about 1300 square yards of silk crepe.

When the high value of pure silk fabric is considered, this represents a rich return for the grower.

### Spinning the Cocoon

When the silkworm has eaten its fill, it is placed on a pile of straw or heather which has been provided for it, and begins spinning its cocoon. First it attaches itself to a twig, then, moving its head from side to side, it spins the filaments of silk in an endless series of figure eights which build up wall within wall, held firm by the gummy sericin that dries and hardens soon after it has been exposed to the air.

In the natural course, the worm inside the cocoon would develop into a chrysalis, and the chrysalis into a moth. The moth would then burst the cocoon and break the one long silk filament into many short ones. It is necessary, therefore, to destroy the worm inside the cocoon if the silk is to be reeled. This is done by stifling it with heat.

A male and a female moth photographed during the process of mating, followed by egg fertilization.

The silkworm in its cocoon after ten or twelve days is transformed into a chrysalis.

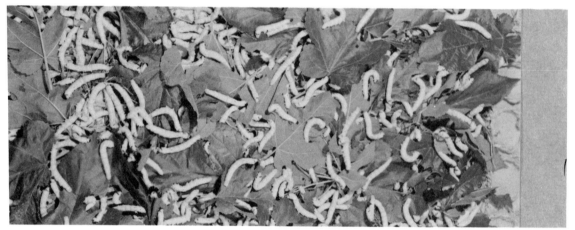

The young silkworms are voracious and are fed on tender young leaves from the mulberry tree.

The female lays her eggs in an orderly array, side by side, in tremendous quantities.

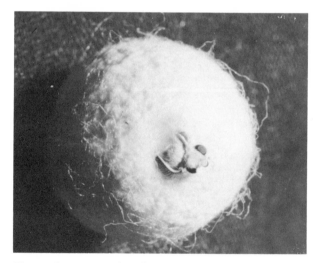

The moth emerges (as shown here) by emitting a liquid which dissolves the silk on contact.

The unwinding of the silk filament onto reels is done by the process called reeling. Since one silk filament is too fine to reel, eight are reeled together.

The selected cocoons are immersed in boiling water for ten or twelve minutes. The process releases the ends of the filament and make for easier reeling. Basically. this is the process used 4,600 years ago.

## Reeling—Unwinding the Cocoon

Each cocoon yields from 300 to 1600 yards of filament. The process of unwinding the filament is called reeling, and is performed in a reeling factory known as a filature. In order to produce a uniform strand of raw silk for commercial use, the filaments of from 5 to 10 cocoons must be united into a single thread. This is done by soaking the cocoons in hot water, brushing them to find the ends of the filaments, and then leading these filaments through porcelain guides so they can be twisted together into a fiber of uniform strength and regularity. It is done either by hand or by an automatic machine which unwinds and reels five cocoons at one time. This is the raw silk which, when wound into skeins, is then ready for commercial use.

Thirty skeins of raw silk make up what is called a book. It weighs about 4.3 pounds. Thirty books make a bale, which weighs 132.3 pounds. This is the basic unit in commercial transactions. It requires about 100 kan, or 900 pounds, of cocoons to produce one bale of raw silk.

## Throwing—Twisting the Threads

Before the raw silk can be woven it must go through a series of operations which condition it for the loom. The raw silk fiber as it comes from the filature is too fine to withstand the rigors of weaving. It must therefore be made into a thicker and more substantial yarn.

This involves a series of operations which are known as throwing. The term itself comes from the Anglo-Saxon word *thraw* which means to twist or spin. Throwing calls for the following processes:

SORTING: The raw-silk skeins are separated for quality.

SOAKING: Some skeins are soaked to soften the sericin. Others are wound without soaking.

DRYING: If soaked, the skeins are dried by a centrifugal extractor and circulating warm air.

WINDING: The skeins are now rewound from reels onto bobbins. Knots and irregularities are removed at the same time.

DOUBLING: Also known as low twisting. At this stage the threads from two or more bobbins are twisted together (doubled) to form a single strand. This first twist is a downward process on the machine and calls for no more than ten twists. If the yarn is used for weaving at this stage it is called tram, and usually goes into the filling of the fabric.

UPTWISTING: Also known as high twisting. The doubled thread is now wound upwards onto new bobbins and acquires as many as 75 twists per inch (for crepe) in the process. Such reinforced yarn is usually used for the warp of a fabric and is known as organzine. Filling yarn is called tram.

CONDITIONING: High-twist thread is then placed in an oven which sets the twist so it will not unravel.

## Silk Is Also Spun Like Cotton

Not all silk is thrown. Some silk is spun on the cotton system. Such silk is not a continuous fila-

A close-up of silk cocoons. Notice that the two groups of cocoons differ in shape. The Japanese have lavished a great deal of scientific patience and skill to improve the strains of silkworms.

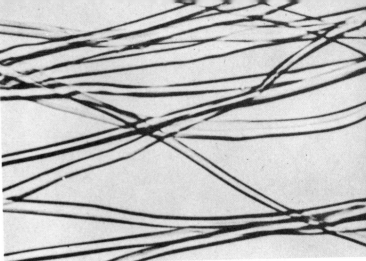

A single thread of raw silk after removal of the gum by boiling. The twelve filaments which are shown separated are magnified 150 times in this microphotograph.

ment like reeled silk. It is a short length fiber like cotton and is therefore spun into yarn by the same methods.

Spun silk comes from cocoons which have been pierced by the emerging silk moth. It also comes from the beginnings and the ends of the cocoon filament, which are of inferior quality, as well as from silk waste which results from the various stages of processing.

Before spun silk can be processed, the gum or sericin must be removed. This is done by boiling off the waste silk in soapy water. It is then washed in clear water, dried and processed like cotton lint.

## Degumming—Yarn-Dyed or Piece-Dyed

If silk is to be dyed in the yarn stage it must first be degummed. This is a process which removes the sericin by boiling it off. It is therefore referred to as boil-off. An olive-oil soap bath is the usual method of degumming. It leaves the yarn white and soft, and reduces its weight by as much as 25%. The more sericin boiled off, the better the quality of the filament.

*Weighting.* Because of this drop in weight, various methods have been used to make up the loss. Since silk is sold by weight this is a serious consideration to the mill and weighting is widely used. Hence the term weighted silk. If used in moderation (up to about 25%) no harm is done. However, there have been many abuses of this process and the result is inferior silk, which splits and cracks because of the excess of tin and iron salts with which it is weighted. In the United States the Federal Trade Commission has ruled that silk fabrics dyed black may be weighted up to 15% and still sold as "pure dyed silk." Only 10% is allowed for other colors.

*Piece-Dyed.* If silk is to be dyed in the piece, after weaving, it can be woven without boiling off the sericin. The finished fabric is then degummed before being dyed and is seldom weighted.

## Tussah Silk Grows Wild

Aside from the cultivated *Bombyx mori* silk, only one other type of silk has proven commercially practical for textile manufacture. This is the wild, uncultivated silk known as tussah. The tussah silkworm grows wild and feeds on the leaves of the oak tree, castor oil plant, cherry tree, and uncultivated mulberry tree. The filament it spins is not round like that of the *Bombyx mori*. It is flat and ribbonlike, is generally considered hardier than the cultivated type, and is about three times as thick in structure. It is used extensively in making heavier drapery fabrics and especially for rough-textured shantung weaves. Often it is blended with cultivated silk to add body and strength to a fabric. Tussah is ideal as filling yarn in many types of fabrics because of its natural tensile strength.

Tussah silk fiber is brown in color and the filaments are quite hairy, and there is less cohesion in it, compared with the true silk fiber.

Cocoons of tussah silkworm.

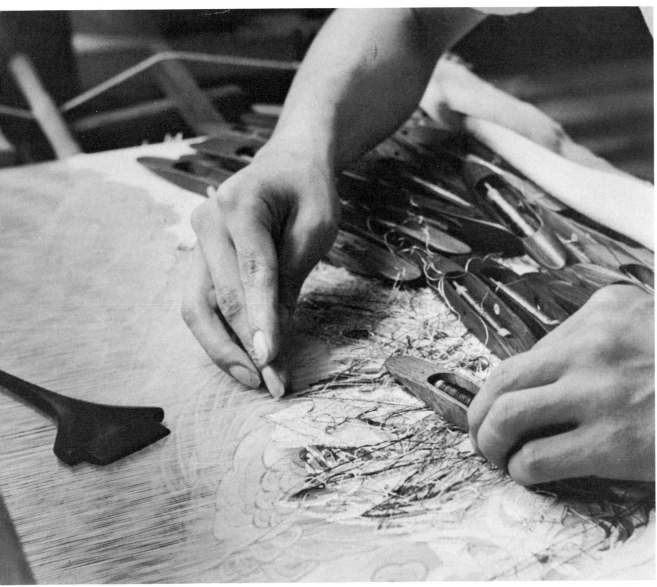

The ancient craft of Nishijin silk hand-weaving, with weaver using serrated finger nail, is still practiced in Kyoto, Japan.

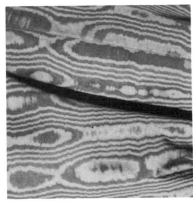

Moire

Crepe

Jacquard

Traditional Silk Fabrics

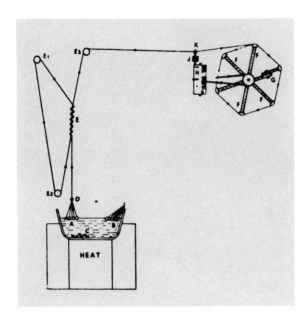

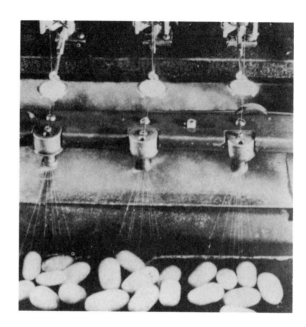

## Silk Reeling

Silk reeling is one of the most fascinating processes in the field of textiles. Great strides have been made in automatic silk reeling. The diagram (*above left*) is a schematic outline of the reeling process. A close-up of automatic silk reeling is shown in the photograph (*above right*). Explanation of diagram: **BASIN**—A. Cocoons being reeled. B. Cocoons after removal of knubbs, with ends anchored to a hook, ready to replace spent cocoons. C. Spent cocoons, sunk to bottom of basin with thin envelope of silk remaining around the chrysalis. **TAKE-UP MOTION**—D. Porcelain button guide, drilled with vertical hole gauged to denier required. E. 'Croisure'—crossing of the thread with itself to dissipate water and to assist cohesion of baves. F. Rotating six-armed winding reel. G. Collapsible arm for eventual removal of hank. **TRAVERSE**—H. Drum rotated by belt from winding reel. J. End of sliding rod, pinned eccentrically to drum top, causing to and fro movement across the direction of the thread. K. Guide eye, set on sliding rod, to spread the ends and so give width to the hank.

The cocoons are being removed from their "Mabushi" or straw beds. These are delicately made and collapsible for easy removal of the cocoons.

The cocoons are dried in large cabinets before going to the filature for reeling. The drying helps to preserve the quality of the silk filament.

## Life of the Silkworm from Mulberry Leaf to Raw Silk.

Silkworms, which feed on mulberry leaves and nothing else, lay eggs the size of the head of a pin. Carefully hand fed, the silkworm increases to 30 times its original length and 10,000 times its original weight in about 30 days. At that time, it begins to spin a liquid silk filament 1,100 yards long, which solidifies into a cocoon upon contact with the air. These delicate silk filaments are stronger than like filaments of steel. Silk cocoons come in different shapes: Chinese cocoons are round and oval; Japanese are peanut-shaped; and European cocoons are long and oval.

## Silk in Modern Japan

*A great deal of Japan's silk production is used in the domestic market of that country. Silk is highly valued for its qualities—especially by wearers of the kimono. Fine examples of silk weaving are eagerly bought by men and women alike. The beauty of the silk kimono continues to be appreciated in Japan, and most of the best-dressed Japanese women include these silk kimonos in their wardrobe.*

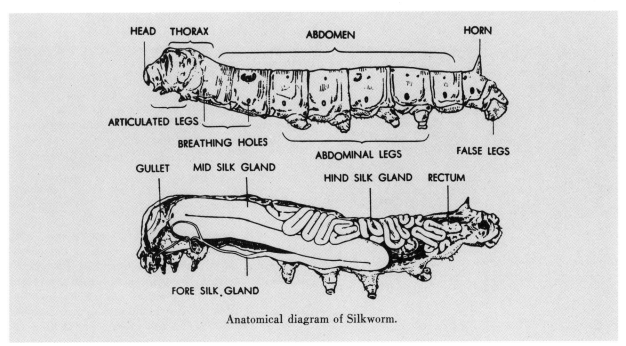

Anatomical diagram of Silkworm.

Jute is still used extensively in industry, though man-made fibers are replacing it in many areas of end-use. Here it is used as covering for cotton bales during transit from grower to mill.

# The BAST FIBERS

- Jute
- Flax
- Hemp
- Sunn
- Ramie
- Kenaf
- Urena

Little known as a group, seven of the Bast Fibers alone represent a leading segment of all plant fibers, second only to cotton. The Bast (or Stem) fibers come from the fibrous bundles in the inner bark—fhloem or bast—of the stems of dicotyledenous plants, plants which form two seed leaves.

Since earliest times, the bast fibers have been used for making textiles. When man first learned that the fibrous mass which lies between the outer covering and inner core of certain plants could be converted to a useful fiber is not recorded; but at widespread points of the globe such knowledge came to light, and today, out of a great number of different bast fibers, seven have attained commercial prominence in the industry. In order of importance from the production standpoint are:

1. Jute
2. Flax
3. Hemp
4. Sunn
5. Ramie
6. Kenaf
7. Urena

Their end uses range from fashion to industrial fields. While basically similar, each of the above varities has certain characteristics which lend themselves to specific engineering possibilities. However, individuals with imagination have been able to adapt bast fiber fabrics from industry to fashion quite successfully. The use of jute hopsacking (a bagging cloth) for men's sportswear is an example.

Jute Plant (*Corchorus capsularis.*) 1. Flower 2. Fruit

## JUTE

*First among the Bast Fibers in poundage is Jute, which finds its way mainly into industrial and decorative fabrics.*

### Definition

Jute is a bast fiber obtained from the stalks of two plants known botanically as *Corchorus capsularis* and *Corchorus olitorius*. The word *jute* comes from the Indian name for the plant, which has the same sound. The jute plant grows from 5 to 16 feet high and averages a growth of 10 to 12 feet. The stalk is from $\frac{1}{2}$ to $\frac{3}{4}$ inches in diameter. The fibers range from 4 to 7 feet in length and are prepared by rippling, retting, scutching, and hackling, very much like the flax fiber. The yield of fiber from the jute plant is 2 to 5 times greater than from the flax stalk.

### Chemical Properties

Chemically, jute is composed chiefly of cellulose like the other bast fibers, but it has a larger percentage of gum than either flax or ramie. Typical samples show 64% cellulose, 24% gum, and small amounts of water, fat, wax and ash.

Jute fiber is moderately strong and lustrous and yellowish-brown in color. It tends to disintegrate in water and has poor elasticity. However, this rigidity becomes a virtue in bagging materials because the fabric does not shift readily. It can be bleached and dyed but considerable care is necessary or the fiber may be injured.

### Largest Bast Fiber

In terms of quantity, jute is still the most impor-

tant of the bast fibers. It is thought to have originated in the Mediterranean in prehistoric times and to have been transplanted later to India and Pakistan, which are today the leading world producers of jute. China and Brazil are the next most important producers, while small quantities are being raised in Nepal, Burma, Vietnam, Taiwan, Thailand, Cambodia and Peru. The Far East produces the greatest quantity of jute by far, with Latin America second and Africa third. Europe and the Near East produce hardly any jute in comparison with these countries.

Total world production is about 6-billion pounds a year. Production reached a peak of about 8.4-billion pounds in 1966 but has declined ever since because of the inroads of man-made fibers.

The most important use of jute in the world today is in bagging cloth. It is also used for carpet backing and for home furnishings and decorative fabrics. Others uses for jute are rope and twine, electrical uses, paper and tape reinforcement and roofing materials.

Apart from carpet backing yarn, however, none of the above uses for jute have much of a future because of competition from man-made fibers. Jute bags for agricultural products such as sugar and tobacco—once a necessity throughout the world—are rapidly being replaced by polypropylene sacks, which are lighter in weight and cheaper to produce than sacks made of jute. This man-made fiber is just as sturdy as jute and can be woven into a fiber which "breathes"—a necessity for bagging foodstuffs. Use of jute for bagging is decreasing in all countries except Japan, where it has increased because of its use in rice bags.

139

Today flax crop is harvested by pulling machines.

# FLAX
*The most ancient and best known of the bast fibers, is the material from which linen fabrics are made.*

## Definition

Flax is a bast fiber taken from the stalk of the plant *Linum usitatissimum.* When processed into yarn or fabric it is called linen. The word flax comes from the Anglo-Saxon *fleax.* The word linen comes from the Anglo-Saxon *lin,* but also appears in many other languages in similar forms.

## Under the Microscope

The flax fiber is a long, smooth, cylindrical tube interrupted along its length by swellings or joints which have somewhat the appearance of bamboo. The tube is composed of a fine central channel surrounded by fibrous cells.

The flax stalk from which the fibers come is composed of a woody central portion, the cell wall which supplies the fibers, and an outer bark. These parts are firmly held together by a gum or pectin which is dissolved in processing the fibers.

## Chemical Composition

Flax is composed largely of cellulose. In its raw state it contains over 70% cellulose with water, fat, wax, ash, and intercellular matter making up the remainder. After boiling, bleaching, and drying it is almost pure cellulose.

## Physical Characteristics

LENGTH. Flax is a long fiber. It runs from 6 to 40 inches with an average of 15 to 25 inches.

TEXTURE. It is a smooth fiber and is therefore lint-free, since there are no short fiber ends to work loose. It has good luster because of its natural wax content.

COLOR. It is creamy white to light tan in color. Hence the use of the words *natural* or *linen* as a color designation.

STRENGTH. It is considered the strongest of the vegetable fibers, having two to three times the strength of cotton.

ABSORBENCY. It is highly absorbent and allows moisture to evaporate quickly. As a result it has good affinity for dyes and crease-resistant finishes.

HEAT ACTION. It is an excellent conductor of heat and is therefore cool as an apparel fabric.

RESILIENCY. It has poor elasticity and does not spring back readily after creasing because the fiber is smooth and has no crimp. This same quality gives it strength and rigidity in a finished fabric. Crease-resistant finishes supply resiliency.

WASHABILITY. It is completely washable and can be boiled without harm.

## Cultivating the Plant

The flax plant *Linum usitatissimum* is cultivated in two ways:

1. *For seed*. The flax seed is the base for linseed oil. When grown for this purpose, the plants are placed farther apart, so that they grow shorter in length with more seed branches.

2. *For fiber*. When grown for fiber, the plants are set very close together so they branch only at the top and produce a long fibrous stalk.

The flax plant grows from 2 to 4 feet tall. It grows best in sandy loam soil, in temperate climates with ample rainfall. However, the number of countries which grow flax indicates that it adapts itself to many different climates. The yield per acre varies greatly in different parts of the world, from a low of 180 pounds per acre amongst major growers to a high of approximately 1,000 to 1,150 pounds per acre in Spain, France, the Netherlands and Belgium. The growing period is about three months.

## Harvesting Flax

Until recently flax was largely harvested by hand, but today much flax harvesting is done by pulling machines. The flax plant must be pulled up

After retting, flax is spread in fields, so it will dry an even color.

Flax being stacked in retting dam; it steeps in warm water for seven days.

rather than cut because the fiber extends to the roots. After harvesting it is usually dried in the field, seeds are removed by combing or *rippling*, and it is then ready for *retting*.

## From Fiber to Fabric

The processes involved in converting the flax fiber into finished fabric follow:

1. RETTING. This involves soaking the flax stalks in warm water to rot away the woody core and to dissolve the gums so the fibers can be loosened and pulled away. In some areas of the world, like Ireland and Belgium, this is still done in natural outdoor pools, ponds, lakes, and rivers. The stalks are weighted with stones and submerged. In other areas, like the United States, retting is done in man-made tanks where water is heated to between 80 and 90 degrees. The water must be clean, soft, and free from impurities like iron which would discolor the flax. The water of the River Lys in Belgium is especially adaptable and this accounts for the fame of this area in the production of the well-known Courtrai flax. Flax is also retted in the field by the action of dew and bacteria but this is a very primitive method. The retting process may take from 4 days to 3 weeks, depending on the methods used.

Getting in the flax near Londonderry, Ireland.

2. SCUTCHING. After the flax is retted and dried, it is sent to the mill where scutching rollers break up and separate the woody portions of the stalk from the usable fiber.

3. HACKLING. The next step is called hackling. This involves cleaning and straightening the fibers

141

Open stacking of flax, which was formerly practiced in Michigan, is still the custom in many foreign countries.

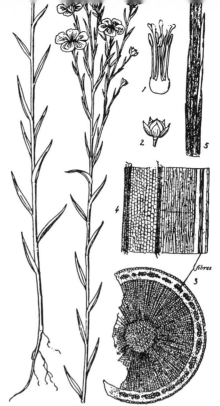

Flax plant. 1. Stamens and pistil. 2. Fruit. 3, 4. Sections of stem. 5. Fibers of flax.

by the use of combs and is basically the same as the carding and combing process in cotton manufacture.

4. CARDING, DRAWING, ROVING, SPINNING, WEAVING. The fiber now goes through the same processes used in preparing cotton yarn for the weaving operation. It consists of further cleaning, drawing out and doubling the fibers into strong yarn for warps and filling.

5. FINISHING. Linen requires very little finishing. Boiling and bleaching are again basically the same as in the cotton process. Some linen fabrics are also beetled. This involves pounding the cloth with large wooden blocks to give it the permanent sheen characteristic of many linen tablecloths.

## Russia Is World's Largest Producer

Today world production of flax is estimated at close to 1.3 billion pounds. Russia is by far the largest producer, accounting for nearly 900-million pounds in 1968, or nearly two-thirds of the world's production.

Other leading countries in the order of their productive capacities follow:

| | |
|---|---|
| Poland | Spain |
| France | Turkey |
| Czechoslovakia | Bulgaria |
| Belgium | Argentina |
| Netherlands | Taiwan |
| Africa | Yugoslavia |
| Romania | Chile |
| Hungary | Korea |
| East Germany | Japan |

142

## History—Oldest of the Textile Fibers

Flax is generally considered to be the most ancient of textile fibers. The archeological remains of Stone Age man in the Swiss Lake Dwellings show bundles of flax fibers, spun linen yarn, and even fragments of linen fabric. The ancient peoples who lived in Mesopotamia, Assyria, and Egypt 5000 and more years ago, had learned to cultivate flax and weave linen fabrics. Egyptian wall paintings illustrated the process of preparing the fiber, and Egyptian mummy wrappings were largely made of linen. Until the end of the 14th Century, Egyptian flax was exported to all parts of the commercial world.

The Old Testament has many references to linen, and early Greek and Roman writings show how important it was to the economy of the ancient world. The Finns are said to have carried it to Northern Europe, and the Phoenecian traders to other parts of the world. Until near the end of the 18th Century, it was the world's most important textile fiber and its leading producers were Russia, Austria, Germany, Holland, Belgium, France, England, Northern Ireland, and Scotland. But it was always largely a domestic industry. With the advent of the industrial revolution and the great textile inventions, it was replaced by cotton, which was easier and cheaper to raise and process.

Linen—widely used in handkerchiefs.

(*Above*) A bundle of flax from which Irish linen is made. (*Left below*) Flax straw bundling in Ireland.

143

Gathering flax in a field.

## LINEN

*The most ancient of fabrics, linen is beginning to enjoy the advantages of modern finishing techniques. Modern linens differ from their predecessors in that they are lighter in weight and muss less easily due to improved finishing processes which give permanent wrinkle-resistant qualities to the traditional weaves.*

Manufacturers of linen dress fabrics and suitings had always realized that a disadvantage (as compared to fabrics made of animal fiber such as wool and silk) had been the lack of crease-resistance. They knew that if they could discover a method of treating linen fibers so that they would resist and recover from creasing, it would be of tremendous benefit to the linen industry.

Research laboratories, after more than a decade of experimenting with the various processes, ultimately solved the problem; today there are available on the market linen fabrics which resist and recover from creasing in a manner similar to wool and fine silk.

The wrinkle-resistant process consists of impregnating the fabric with a synthetic resin in such a manner that the resin itself penetrates the fiber. The linen is first given a boiling-off treatment (similar to the process which precedes vat dyeing) to remove all traces of dirt and oil. The fabric is then run through a caustic bath. This shrinks the material considerably but opens up the fibers to permit absorption of the resin. After being put through the resin solution, the linen is stretched back to its original width on mechanical frames and run through a curing chamber to fix the resin in the flax fiber and make its resistance to creasing permanent. The fixing process is followed by whatever type of finish is desired.

(*Below*) Preparation and spinning of flax in ancient times. (From a wall painting in the tomb of Daga at Thebes, Egypt—about 2000 B.C.)

## How to Care for Linens

Linens require little care, but since many linen cloths are regarded as heirlooms their life expectancy may be increased by the following simple rules:

1. Many breaks or tears are not caused by self-breaking or abrasion of the linen yarn; they generally come from careless scrapes with knives, forks, razor blades or other sharp or pointed instruments. These cause tiny yarn breaks which, under the strains of laundering, develop into large tears.

2. Linens should be folded with the least possible number of creases, and preferably with soft creases, since constant creasing with sharp folds will tend to break the threads.

3. Excessive starching causes a coating to form which, when the fabric is folded, may cause threads to crack.

4. When boiling linen, the use of washing soda, or alkaline or other caustic solutions, may cause threads to separate and lose strength. A mild soap, with no free alkali, is best to use in washing linen.

5. It is advisable, from time to time, to change the fold line so that the same threads are not constantly being bent and unbent.

6. It is best to remove stains, whenever possible, before laundering.

7. To remove grease spots use benzine, gasoline, kerosene, carbon tetrachloride, chloroform or similar compounds . . . always applying them to the underside of the article, with a blotter or absorbent cloth pressed to right side.

8. Stains of fruit juice, tea or coffee can be removed by pouring boiling water through the cloth; hold the kettle at some distance above the cloth, so that the water strikes with some force.

9. Acetic acid or vinegar will generally remove rust stains; salt and lemon juice may also be used.

10. Many rust stains come from bluing containing aniline dyes. They should be avoided.

11. Alternate applications of ammonia and hydrogen peroxide will remove grass stains.

12. Fresh mildew stains may be removed by washing in a strong soap solution, then exposing to the sun.

13. Linen should be ironed while damp, using a moderately hot iron to avoid scorching. To preserve the luster, iron on both sides.

14. Colored linens should be washed in suds made of a pure soap, in tepid water, and then rinsed in two clear waters; first-washed printed linens should be rinsed until the water is clear, to remove excess color.

Transparent linen drape— Swedish.

A fine damask cloth, traditional in linen, being rolled.

Linen tablecloth and napkin— Swedish.

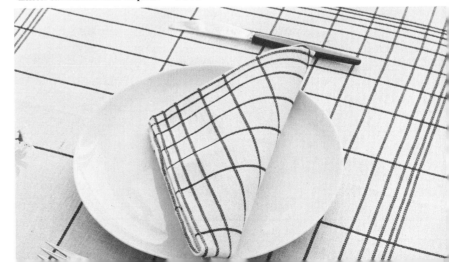

1. Fibers are combed by hand, then drawn over steel combs.

2. Flax in the hackling machine.

3. *Above:* After spinning, wet yarn hanks are dried.

4. Linen damask designers at work.

5. Grass bleaching of Irish linen.

## Making Linens in Ireland

The largest part of the world's flax production is used in countries where it is raised. The exceptions are Northern Ireland and Belgium, both of which are leading exporters of linen fabrics. Ireland grows some of its needs but imports more from Belgium, Holland, Germany and France. No figures are available for Russia, which consumes most of its flax production domestically.

6. *Below:* Linen yarn being wound on wooden bobbins.

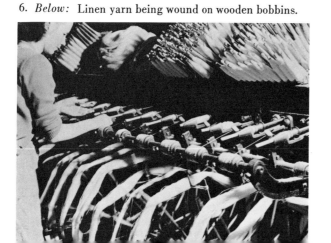

7. *Below:* Irish linen weavers examine samples.

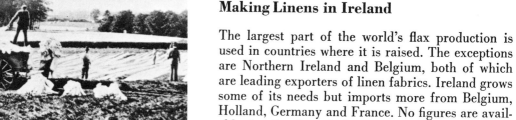

Hemp Plant—1. Male plant. 2. Female spike 3. Male flower 4. Female flower 5. Fruit

## HEMP

*Main source for making cordage, Hemp has other uses, such as linen-type woven fabrics and a base for sponges.*

True hemp is a bast fiber obtained from the stalk of the plant known botanically as *Cannabis sativa*. There are at least fifty other fibers known as hemp but they are all different botanical species and the word hemp is always qualified by a descriptive phrase such as African bowstring hemp or Manila hemp, grown in the Philippines (see ABACA in this section).

The true hemp plant grows from 7 to 10 feet high. The stalk is about half an inch in diameter. It is retted and processed much like flax.

### Chemical Properties

Like the other bast fibers, hemp breaks down into cellulose, water, ash, fat, wax, and gum. In this case cellulose is about 77% of the composition.

### Characteristics

The hemp fiber runs 40 to 80 inches in length, is generally yellowish-brown in color and fairly lustrous. It has good breaking strength and looks very much like flax in general appearance.

### History and Production

Hemp, like flax, is a prehistoric fiber and is thought to have been used first in Asia. It was also known in ancient China and Persia, and was the first tex-tile fiber developed by the Japanese.

It was widely used throughout the history of most European countries and was cultivated in Russia from earliest times. Russia is still the most important producer of hemp fiber.

Today, world production of hemp amounts to approximately 660 million pounds. As such, it ranks third among the bast fibers, after jute and flax. One-third of this total is grown in Russia; 25% in India; and nearly 10% apiece in Hungary, Romania and Poland. The remaining 15% is divided among the following countries, listed in the order of their productivity:

| | |
|---|---|
| Pakistan | Chile |
| Yugoslavia | Taiwan |
| Turkey | East Germany |
| Bulgaria | Spain |
| Korea | Japan |
| Czechoslovakia | Syria |
| Italy | France |

Hemp production has fallen steadily since 1966 because of the influx of man-made fibers into many of its markets, particularly cordage. Production in Italy, for example, shrunk from 115 million pounds in 1956 to 10.5 million in 1968.

### Uses of Hemp

Today the principal use for hemp is in the manufacture of cordage. However, fine Italian hemp is made into woven fabrics not unlike linen. It is also used as a base for cellulose sponges.

147

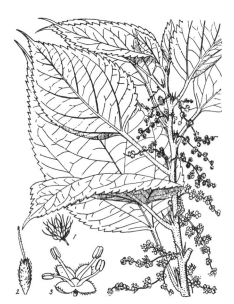 

(*Left*) The female flower (cluster) of the Ramie plant, from the stalk of which the fiber is drawn. (*Right*) Various stages of the fiber, from raw material to woven cloth.

# RAMIE   *The chief obstacle, in the development of this bast fiber, is the difficulty of degumming.*

## Definition

Ramie, also known as China-grass, is a bast fiber obtained from the stalk of a stingless nettle plant whose botanical name is *Boehmeria nivea*. The word ramie is derived from the ancient Malayan.

The ramie plant grows from 5 to 8 feet high and the diameter of the stalk is from ½ to ¾ of an inch. The length of the ramie fibers range from ½ to 20 inches with an average of between 5 and 6 inches.

## Chemical Properties

Chemically, the ramie fiber is about 83% cellulose, with small amounts of ash, moisture, fat, wax and gum. After degumming and drying it is 96 to 98% cellulose.

## Characteristics

The ramie fiber is naturally white in color, has a high luster and unusual resistance to bacteria and mildew. It is extremely absorbent, dries quickly and has good affinity for dyes. Perhaps its chief virtue is its strength. It has excellent abrasion resistance and has been tested to be three to five times stronger than cotton and twice as strong as flax.

## Difficulties of Production

Ramie ranks as a classic fiber in that it has been grown and used—under the names of China-grass, rhea and ramie—in a score of countries from immemorial times. The reasons why it has always played a relatively minor role are mostly of a technical nature. Like linen, it is difficult to decorticate; it offers resistance to degumming and above all it is difficult to obtain from this springing green nettle plant an even growth and consistent quality of fiber.

## Traditional Techniques

Until recently, the only methods known for separating and cleaning the useful fibers from the stalk of the ramie plant required exhaustive hand labor and the cost was prohibitive. Before the war the Japanese had achieved some progress with the use of hand-operated machinery for processing the stems, and the English had built or adapted special machinery for spinning the fibers. The whole question of commercial production was still, however, tied up with hand methods of cropping and laborious techniques for decortication. Only recently have discoveries of new methods for separating the fiber made ramie commercially available. This has resulted from approaching the combined problems of cultivation, fiber-extraction and processing, methodically and scientifically, with the aim of securing regular delivery and fiber uniformity on a productive scale.

## Some Modern Methods

The character of the methods adopted in Florida for producing ramie in the ten-foot loam beds of the Everglades is of interest. First is the production of ramie in conjunction with other crops using similar machinery; the equipment can thereby be put to year-round use, with resulting cut in overhead cost. Next is control of moisture by selecting a locality where the water table can be controlled, ensuring so far as possible uniform growth under varying seasonal conditions. Third is the use of every scientific aid for securing uniformity, such as defoliation by spraying from the air, and degumming in accordance with latest scientific procedures. Newly adapted machines which ensure uniformity have been substituted for the old hand-decorticating machinery.

## Three Crops Annually

The cropping period is divided into three sixty-day periods running through May-June, July-August and September-October. By the use of this plan, in combination with measures described above, a regular growth in each crop is achieved and uniformity results. Reports have been received from mills in France, Germany, Italy, and Japan, to which shipments have been made, that the fiber produced by these methods is the top-ranking quality obtainable anywhere in the world.

## Leading Producers

Today the world produces an estimated 28-million pounds of ramie annually. However, this figure does not include China, for which no figures are available. It is known that during the 1930's China alone produced an average of 150,000,000 pounds a year. Other leading producers today are Japan, the Philippines, and the United States. Small amounts, chiefly for domestic production, are also produced in several Asiatic countries, in Africa, in parts of Europe, Russia, Latin America, and the West Indies.

## Uses of Ramie

Now that production has been somewhat mechanized, ramie is being used for apparel fabrics, either alone or in blends with other fibers like cotton and rayon. It is also used in fish nets, industrial threads, canvas, fire hose, filter cloths, upholstery fabrics, and packings for propeller screws.

Fabric of unspun, fully degummed ramie combined with cotton warp—fine cotton; weft—unspun, commercially degummed ramie. Fabric construction—tabby. Sample of fiber used in weft shown at left.

The fiber of Kenaf (*Hibiscus cannabinus*) drying in the sun at a Cuban plantation.

## The Bast Fibers (continued)

### SUNN

Sunn is a bast fiber obtained from the stalk of the plant whose botanical name is *Crotalaria juncea*. Fibers are 4 to 5 feet long and are retted and prepared like other bast fibers. Sunn contains over 80% cellulose and has good resistance to water and mildew. Most of the world production of some 140-million pounds comes from India. Small amounts are grown in Uganda. It is used principally for cordage, rug yarns, and paper. In India it is also used for fish nets and sometimes as a substitute for jute in bagging cloths.

### KENAF

Kenaf is a bast fiber obtained from the stalk of the plant *Hibiscus cannabinus*. The stalks grow 8 to 12 feet high and about half an inch in diameter. The plant is processed much like jute and yields a fiber much like jute in appearance, and of about the same strength. It also has about the same cellulose content as jute. Leading producing areas

Abaca (or Manila hemp) fiber drying on bamboo racks in the open air in Ecuador.

are India and Pakistan. It is also grown in Africa, South East Asia, Indonesia, Russia, Cuba, Mexico, the Philippines, and the United States. Annual world production is estimated at about 100,000,000 pounds. Its principal uses are cordage, canvas, and sacking is sometimes used as a substitute for jute.

### URENA

A bast fiber from the plant *Urena lobata*. It grows 3 to 7 feet high in its wild state and from 10 to 12 feet high under cultivation. Strands of fiber are 3 or more feet long, creamy white in color and with good luster. It has about the same strength as jute, is processed the same way, and has the same end uses. World production is generally estimated at about 12-million pounds. The Congo area is the chief source of supply. Smaller amounts are raised in French Equatorial Africa, Brazil, Madagascar, India, the Philippines and Indonesia.

### OTHER PLANT FIBERS

While the bast group is the best known and most important of the textile plant fibers after cotton, it is not the only source of fibers in the vegetable world. Many other plants, growing wild or under cultivation, yield fibers capable of being spun and woven. However, most of them have been found commercially impractical for conversion into cloth. They have found other important uses such as cordage, stuffing materials and brushes.

The most important category of such non-textile fibers is the leaf species, of which abaca, sisal, and henequen are the best known. These three are the world's most important cordage fibers. Between them they yield an annual production of about 1,855-million pounds.

## Abaca for Cordage

ABACA is a vegetable leaf fiber derived from the *Musa textilis* plant. The fiber itself is taken from the outer layer of the leaf sheath. It is separated and mechanically decorticated into lengths varying from 3 to 9 feet. Because of its high strength and luster and its unusual resistance to disintegration in salt water, it is the world's most desirable cordage fiber. Approximately 158-million pounds of this fiber were produced in 1968. The overwhelming bulk of this production comes from the Philippines; smaller quantities are raised in Malaysia, Costa Rica, Indonesia and Africa, with production declining because of the inroads of man-made fibers.

## The Agave Fibers

SISAL AND HENEQUEN are generally grouped together and are classified as agave fibers. They are also vegetable leaf fibers, as is abaca, and find similar uses in ropes and twine. Sisal is derived from the plant *Agave sisalana* by machine decortication, into strands from 40 to 50 inches in length. It is white and lustrous and ranks next to abaca in strength and in resistance to salt-water disintegration.

HENEQUEN is derived from the leaves of the plant *Agave fourcroydes*, which is native to Mexico. It is produced by mechanically decorticating the leaves into strands of from 4 to 5 feet. In strength it is about on a par with that of sisal.

Sisal and henequen together accounted for a world production of 1,696 million pounds in 1968. Chief producing countries in the order of their importance are Tanganyika, Brazil, Mexico, Kenya, Mozam-

The ropes are made from Roselle fiber plants (in background of photo) in El Salvador.

bique, Madagascar, Haiti, Venezuela and Cuba. Tanganyika is the largest producer of sisal; Mexico is first in henequen production.

Other fibers which deserve mention are:

COIR, a seed fiber obtained from the husk of the coconut. It is used for brush-making, door mats, and sometimes for fish nets and cordage.

KAPOK, a seed fiber or floss obtained from the cotton tree. It is used chiefly for stuffing pillows.

IXTLE, a leaf fiber obtained from the *Tula ixtle* plant, which is native to Mexico. It is used for brush-making.

REDWOOD BARK FIBER, obtained from the bark of the California redwood tree. It is used for insulation and sometimes for blending with other fibers such as wool and cotton.

(*Left*) Henequen fiber ready to be processed into ropes and bags, in El Salvador. (*Right*) Sisal area in Haiti.

Roman sculpture circa 5th Century B.C.

# THE HISTORY OF TEXTILES FROM PREHISTORIC TIMES TO THE 20th CENTURY

# THE HISTORY OF TEXTILES

*Every fabric woven today bears the imprint of the accumulated knowledge of centuries of fine craft, and these origins often go further back into the past than we suspect. Here are highlights in the history of textiles, the manufacture of which is probably the oldest continuous industry known to man.*

FOR AT LEAST seven thousand years—until man-made fibers were developed at the end of the 19th Century—the history of textiles was the developing story of the four great natural fibers. As far as we can tell from archeological discoveries, flax, wool, cotton, and silk appeared on the stage of civilization in that order and each, in its turn, reflected the successful struggle of man to control and adapt himself to his environment.

First came *flax*. Some five thousand years before the birth of Christ, linen-like fabrics made of flax were used by the early cultures along the Nile River in the region now known as Egypt. Still earlier, many primitive peoples separated the strands of the bast fibers (of which flax is one) from their stalks, plaited or wove them into simple textiles and used them as covering for their bodies.

The Swiss Lake Dwellers, who flourished in the Later Stone Age, were spinners and weavers of flax.

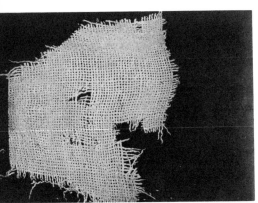

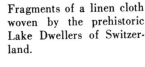
Fragments of a linen cloth woven by the prehistoric Lake Dwellers of Switzerland.

Diggings at the site of one of their earliest villages in the bed of the lake at Robenhausen, Switzerland, have revealed actual bundles of flax fiber, spun threads, fragments of cloth, and pieces of the primitive mechanisms by which they were produced. For centuries they were preserved in the mud and waters of this lake.

Next came *wool*. It is more than likely that Neolithic Man in the Later Stone Age used wool as well as flax, because the Swiss Lake Dwellers were known to have domesticated the sheep. However, the earliest date of which we have any accurate knowledge is about 4000 B.C. The place is the Great Hill Region on the banks of the Euphrates River in ancient Mesopotamia. Sheep were raised there and wool was used for the spinning and weaving of primitive textiles. The early Babylonians and Assyrians were also believed to have worn robes of woolen cloth and in the Biblical land of Ur near the Iranian Gulf archeologists unearthed an ancient mosaic which depicts domesticated sheep. It dates from the year 3500 B.C.

The third—and most important—fiber in the time sequence of civilization was *cotton*. Its earliest origins have been fixed at about 3000 B.C. by archeological discoveries in the valley of the Indus at

Example of twill weave, Persian, Sassanian Period, 6th Century.

Sind, India, though some researchers claim it was used much earlier in Egypt. Arab traders carried cotton from India to the Near East, to Central Asia, and then to China. The very word cotton comes from the Arabic word *quoton*.

And it is here that we come upon one of the fascinating mysteries of the world's early civilizations. At the same time that cotton was being grown, spun, and woven in Asia, the ancient Inca culture of Peru . . . half-way across the globe in the *still undiscovered* Americas . . . was producing some of the richest and most exciting colored cotton fabrics the world has ever seen. No studies have yet determined how cotton developed almost simultaneously in two such unconnected parts of the prehistoric world. Perhaps here is further evidence to support the Theory of the Moving Continents and speculation about the lost continent which is said to have flourished in the middle of the Pacific Ocean before recorded time.

This is fascinating speculation but it is no speculation at all that by 2500 B.C. the Egyptians were weaving fabrics so fine that they have rarely been equaled. An Egyptian mummy from this period was wrapped in a cloth which counted 540 warp threads to the inch. The best comparable British fabrics today run about 350 warp threads to the inch.

The fourth of the great natural fibers—*Silk*—probably originated in China. Legend attributes its discovery and development to the Chinese Empress Hsi-Ling-Chi about 2640 B.C. She is said to have accidentally dropped a silk cocoon into hot water. Noticing the fine silk filament separated from the

cocoon, she realized its possibilities and so fostered sericulture, which is the cultivation of the silkworm and the white mulberry tree whose leaves it eats.

Whether or not this legend is true becomes unimportant. Some such discovery certainly occurred either in China or other regions of the Far East before the period of recorded history. It was the Chinese who brought sericulture to a point of near perfection and by 1400 B.C. woven silk fabrics of many types were established as valuable commodities in China. The early document known as the Tribute of Yu records silk fabrics used as a method of paying tribute.

These, then, were the four most important fibers used by all early peoples for the spinning and weaving of textiles. The simple handicraft methods they developed seven or more thousand years ago have not changed from then until now. All we have added through the centuries are mechanization and speed. The fragments of spindles and looms found in the Robenhausen diggings are based on the same simple principles used in the production of today's giant textile machines. As the story of textiles is unfolded through the years, the phrase "warp and weft of civilization" takes on new and more literal meaning.

Roller cotton gin from India.

### ARCHEOLOGY REVEALS TEXTILE ORIGINS

**PREHISTORIC TIMES:** The ruins of the Swiss Lake Dwellers, discovered in the winter of 1853-54, offer sufficient proof that the art of textiles was known in the earliest era of the Stone Age, the period of the mammoth and the cave bear. Yarns of linen and wool were found in plaited and woven constructions. Strings, cordage, rope, and linen yarns were also found.

**SCRIPTURE:** These contained many references to sheep, shepherds, cotton, linen, wool, weaving, etc. In Genesis it is reported that "Abel was the keeper of the sheep, Cain, a tiller of the soil." There is a passage in Deuteronomy concerning the dispute between the children of Israel, who wore wool, and the Egyptians, who wore linen.

**4200 B.C.:** Sheep were kept in the Tel Asman or Great Hill region on the banks of the Euphrates River in Mesopotamia. The earliest known representation of sheep is in a mosaic of Ur, not far from the Iranian Gulf. This dates to about 3500 B.C. Around 3000 B.C. people in Britain wore crude forms of woolen garments.

**2640 B.C.:** According to legend, the Chinese Empress Hsi-Ling-Chi fostered the silk industry by encouraging the cultivation of the mulberry tree, the raising of silkworms, and silk reeling.

**2500 B.C.:** It is said that the Egyptians placed a shuttle in the hands of the goddess Isis to signify her having devised the art of weaving.

### ANCIENT LITERATURE DESCRIBES ADVANCES

**1500 B.C.:** India was raising cotton and spinning yarn to be woven into fabric. The ancient Laws of Manu specified that the sacrificial thread of the Brahmin had to be made of cotton (*karpasi*), that the theft of cotton thread was punishable by fines, and that rice-water (*possibly the first starch*) was used in the weaving.

**1000 B.C.:** The Phoenicians were carrying on active trade in raw wool and all types of woven goods with the Spaniards in the port of Cadiz.

**715 B.C.:** Wool dyeing was established as a craft in Rome.

Terra cotta. Black Greek pottery, about 450 B.C.

**450 B.C.:** Herodotus, 484-425 B.C., stated that the Babylonians wore a linen shirt or covering which reached to the ground, and was worn over a white tunic. He reported also that the Indian auxiliaries of the Persian King Xerxes were clothed in cotton, and that fabrics made of this exotic fiber owed their perfection to the craftsmanship practiced by the Indians for more than 1,000 years.

**327 B.C.:** Alexander the Great, at the time of the invasion of India, expressed wonderment at the beautiful cotton prints made there. Mention was also made of the flax and linen industries. Dating from these discoveries, cotton became the main apparel fabric along the shores of the Mediterranean Sea for the next 300 years.

**200 B.C.:** The Romans were practicing scientific sheep raising and breeding. They developed the famous Tarrentine breed of sheep, forerunner of the present-day merino breed, by crossing Colchian rams imported from Greece with Italian-bred ewes.

**100-44 B.C.:** Caesar, with the aid of his animal-husbandry expert, Lucius Junius Columella, fostered the breeding and raising of sheep, the production of wool, and the manufacture of woolen cloth for his legions.

Columella was a Roman living in Cadiz, Spain, where he crossbred Tarrentine sheep with native white sheep of the wandering tribes and conducted other experiments in breeding. He is considered to be the actual developer of the merino sheep. His principles of animal husbandry in his *De Re Rustica*, are still adhered to in many parts of the world.

### EARLY WRITINGS ON SILK, WOOL, COTTON

**75 B.C.:** Pompey, 106-48 B.C., Roman general and a member of the First Triumvirate, returned from China laden with beautiful silk fabrics. During this era silk became the leading cloth of the Roman Empire.

**63 B.C.:** Cotton awnings made their first appearance in Rome.

**54 B.C.:** Silk was introduced into Rome following the Parthian Wars. Marcus Antonius sent a delegation to Seres (ancient name for China) to arrange for the importation of silks to Rome. The mission, however, did not prove fruitful and Persia remained the main source of supply of Chinese silks.

**EARLY ANNO DOMINI YEARS:** Ovid explained the processes involved in making woolen fabric. Shortly after, Pliny stated that woolen garments could be made without the spinning and weaving processes. He also made reference to the finest wool sheep in the world of his time, the original Tarentine sheep. The growing of cotton and the raising

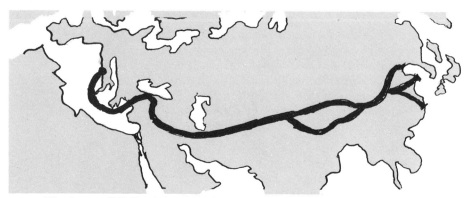

The famous Silk Road (opened about 126 B.C.) was a 6,000-mile-long route by which precious silk was transported from China to Greece and Rome.

of sheep in Egypt did not escape the observations of Pliny, who extolled the work being done there in cotton culture and animal husbandry.

Seneca wrote about the lustrous, shiny thread (silk) gathered by the Seres (Chinese) from the boughs of trees.

Pausanias, noted traveler and geographer of this era, believed that silk came from an animal twice the size of a large beetle which resembled a spider. He also thought that the Chinese fed the silkworms on green reeds until they burst, whereupon the filaments were found within the body.

## ARAB TRADERS SPREAD KNOWLEDGE

**SECOND CENTURY:** Elis, Greece, was the homeland of the first cotton raised on European soil.

Arab traders were the first to import cotton in quantity to Italy and Spain. Arrian, an Egyptian-Greek, in his *Circumnavigation of the Erythraean Sea*, was one of the first to mention cotton. A century before this time, Arab traders brought Indian calico, muslin, and other cotton fabrics to ports on the Red Sea and thence to Europe. It is said of Omar, one of the caliphs of Mahomet, that "he preached in a tattered cotton gown, rent in twelve places."

**THIRD CENTURY:** Japan began to learn much more about sericulture from Koreans who had gained their knowledge from the Chinese. Though silkworms were introduced in Japan as early as 195 A.D., it was not until this time that the Japanese began to take genuine interest in sericulture.

**273:** Emperor Aurelian refused the plea of his wife for a single garment of purple silk on the ground that it was too sheer, and sheer extravagance. A pound of silk at that time was worth its weight in gold.

**FOURTH CENTURY:** Ammianus Marcellinus, Roman historian, speculated that the soil in China was as soft as wool, and that after sprinkling with water and then combing, it would be possible to form cloths such as silks. This was still another effort to explain silk, which was a mystery in Europe.

The cultivation of silk started in India when, according to legend, a Chinese princess, given in marriage to an Indian prince, brought him silkworm eggs and mulberry tree seeds hidden in the lining of her headdress.

## INDUSTRY BEGINS TO GROW

**552:** Two Nestorian monks succeeded in bringing from China a few fertile silkworm eggs hidden in the hollow of their canes, which they presented to the Emperor Justinian. This was the beginning of a silk industry in the West. In a short time, under the direction of the monks, eggs were hatched, worms raised, black mulberry trees planted, and Constantinople was on its way to becoming a silk center.

**EARLY EIGHTH CENTURY:** The Saracens overran Spain and introduced to Europe beautifully woven textiles which became highly prized.

**EIGHTH CENTURY:** Chinese manuscripts mention the decoration of textile fabrics by coating with wax, a method now known as batik dyeing.

**712:** The first known mention of sheep in England relates that the price of a sheep was one shilling "until a fortnight after Easter."

**768:** Charlemagne became king of France. He favored the textile industry and established the two world-renowned textile centers of Lyons and Rouen; the former city is still the silk designing and weaving center of the world. A few years later, Charlemagne instituted the cloth fairs throughout western Europe. These centers are still the clearing houses for world buyers and sellers.

**796:** Charlemagne of France and Offa, King of Mercia, in north-midland England, made a treaty in which the length of woolen cloths and cloaks was discussed.

Charlemagne granted charter to English pilgrims in France to carry on trade in English Monastery Wool. This is often referred to as the first English trade agreement.

## SILK CULTURE SPREADS

**NINTH CENTURY:** The knowledge of sericulture spread from Greece to what is now Italy, Spain, and Portugal. In time, other European nations learned of the wonders of silk, especially France, which today is one of the leading silk designing and silk weaving centers.

**804:** Hamburg and Lübeck were founded by Charlemagne. These cities became clearing-house ports and supplied the rest of the world with many products, including textiles. Itinerant textile workers of all types gathered there, as well as textile merchants, cloth brokers, etc.

**877:** The Mohammedan Wars interfered with the importation of silks from the Far East, and caused the Greeks to take more than passing interest in sericulture. Around this time the Chinese rebel, Baichu, destroyed Canfu, the great Chinese city noted for its silk exports. The destruction of this city cut off all silks intended for the then known Western World.

## TEXTILE PRODUCTION UP

**EARLY TENTH CENTURY:** Cotton raising and cotton weaving were developed in Spain. The Arabians fostered cotton culture in Sicily.

**900:** Alfred the Great, who reigned from 871 to 901, did much to stimulate the wool industry in England. His mother fostered spinning among the women at home, to increase the supply of yarn available for weaving.

**925:** Wool dyers' guilds initiated in Germany.

**961:** Indoor cloth halls were established in Flanders in the cities of Bruges, Ghent, and Ypres; the idea came from methods of bartering observed by travelers to the Orient.

**979:** The Teutonic Guilds were founded in London under charter granted by King Ethelred II in return for twenty pounds of pepper each year. These mercantile groups carried on successful business in England until they were banished by Queen Elizabeth in 1578 as a retaliatory measure against Germany.

**ELEVENTH CENTURY:** During the 10th and the 11th Centuries, Flanders clothed Europe in woolens, and Flanders, Brabant, some of the German towns, and France were producing fine linens. The rise of the guild system was instrumental in the growth of the textile industry.

**1000:** Venice dominated the textile raw material and finished products markets and retained this position for many years, since it was the center of Asiatic and European trade.

York, England, had an extensive trade in raw wool and woolen cloth.

Around this time cotton began to be raised commercially in China, fostered by the Tartar tribes. For three hundred years before this it was used in China as an ornamental shrub.

**1066:** With the arrival of the Norman conquerors, Bristol and Exeter in England became great centers for sheep raising.

ENGLAND BECOMES CENTER

**TWELFTH CENTURY:** The conquest of Constantinople by the Venetians in this century gave the latter access to the rarest types of silk fabrics. Raw silk was shipped to Venice whose looms now began to supply all in Europe who could afford to buy the luxury material.

**1111:** Henry I of England established the Scottish woolen industry at the mouth of the Tweed, which separates England and Scotland.

**1120:** Henry I, England, scattered and relocated the skilled Flemish workers then in England among the towns, villages, and hamlets so as to increase the textile knowledges and skills of his own people. He sponsored the first merchant guild about this time, the woolen cloth weavers. Other guilds soon came into being. At this time the guilds were composed of those who did not sell their labor but only the product of that labor. This method laid the economic foundation of medieval textile activity.

**1128:** The famous Cistercian monks, also known as the Trappists, arrived in England from France. They settled first in Waverley and Surrey and in time built abbeys in Yorkshire and the Welsh marches. In a few years the monks were to become the largest sheep producers in the world. By 1143 they had built 50

abbeys and the one at Fountains had 15,000 sheep while Rievaulx boasted of 12,000 sheep.

**1146:** With the exception of Constantinople, the silk industry had made very little progress in the Western World in the past 400 years. Greece and northern Africa, thanks to the Saracens, had made some progress but the industry, although given encouragement, could not be classed as flourishing. The only places up to this time where silk was produced were Sicily and southern Spain under Saracen influence.

The first Norman king of Sicily, Roger, fought the Greek Empire and in the course of the struggle was able to capture many silk producers and silk weavers as towns capitulated. These artisans were sent to Palermo, Sicily, where the industry was a flourishing one.

**1147:** The first white mulberry trees for sericulture were planted in France by Guipape de St. Aubon. The trees had come from Syria, where he had observed their value at the time of the Second Crusade.

BRITAIN CONCENTRATES ON WOOL

**1150:** Some Hebrew cloth manufacturers from Flanders went to England. In spite of persecution, they participated in the woolen trade and gave it impetus.

**1153:** Under King Stephen, English woolen production reached a point where a royal charter was solicited and granted to the Priory of St. Bartholomew to hold an annual cloth fair, the first to be held in England.

**1154-1189:** During these years of the reign of Henry II, England, a charter was granted to the guild of woolen-cloth weavers who were allowed the exclusive privilege of importing raw wool to London. This grant was opposed by English sheep growers who desired to ban the importation of the superior Spanish wool.

**1164:** Weavers' and fullers' guilds were now established in seven English cities.

**1173:** The Spanish rabbi of the Kingdom of Navarre went to Jerusalem and reported that the only dealers in wool were Hebrews. Two hundred of them were in this business.

**1188:** First mention of guilds for dyers of textiles in England.

**1193:** There were guilds for weavers in Florence. Cloth merchants' guilds were also founded around this time—*arte della Callimali.* These guilds prevented, for the time being, the formation of guilds for dyers, since they were considered as weavers' assistants.

**1195:** Wool raised by the Cistercians paid a part of the ransom for Richard Coeur de Lion.

**1197:** King John, of English Magna Carta fame, persuaded Parliament to regulate the dyeing of woolen cloth which was offered to the buying public.

EUROPE CONCENTRATES ON SILK

**THIRTEENTH CENTURY:** Cardinal Barberini reported 16,000 looms in Seville, Spain, and that Catalonia, because of its excellent output of high-quality woolen cloth, had good trade relations

The sheep, probably the animal kingdom's greatest gift to man, was valued in Asiatic countries not only for its wool and mutton but for the fat stored up in its tail, which was and is considered a great delicacy. Two methods of protecting the tail of the Fat or Broad-Tailed Sheep are illustrated.

with Byzantium, Egypt, and Greece. Barcelona was also coming into its own as a noted textile center.

St. Adhemar, in England, spoke of weaving and dyeing woolen cloth, with purple and red colored fabric used for religious rituals.

This century saw the rise of the famous Monastery Wool, which was grown under the auspices of the many abbeys in England, Scotland, and Wales.

The Florentine, Rucellai, re-discovered the ancient art and the method of making purple dyes from certain lichens that had been sent him from Asia Minor.

**1203-1209:** The Venetians scored many victories over the Greek Empire and their booty included silk districts in Greece.

They introduced the industry to other Italian city-states. By 1300, several thousand persons were in the silk business in cities like Bologna, Genoa, and Milan. Bologna became known for the only successful silk-throwing mill in Italy, a position it held until around 1500 when other cities established throwing plants of their own.

**1210:** Alexander II, King of Scotland, chartered cloth-merchant guilds in Aberdeen, Perth, and Sterling.

**1212:** By this time, the flourishing city of Florence had about two hundred wool dyers, fullers, and cloth cutters or tailors, and published a directory of weavers and spinners.

**1221:** Henry III, England, ordered the mayor of London to burn every piece of woolen cloth which contained Spanish wool. This action was designed to protect and foster home production and consumption.

**1240:** Imported fabric of good quality reappeared in England. English wool merchants began to export some of their wool to Flanders. By 1248, wool merchants were quite well established in London, with a well-welded organization that was powerful in the textile trades.

**1250:** Flanders was sending much linen fabric to England, where it was now in great demand.

Satins were now being woven in the southern European nations—Spain, Portugal, and Italy. Almeria, in Andalusia,

Spain, was particularly noted for its richly woven silks.

Silk fabrics were now being made to some degree in England, but they could not compete with the silks from the south of Europe. The higher classes in England were now wearing costly silks that came chiefly from Italy. One thousand knights appeared in silk raiment at the wedding of the daughter of Henry III, the sponsor of the silk industry in England.

**1252:** The Humble Fathers of St. Michael moved from Alexandria, Egypt, to Florence, Italy, and took with them their knowledge and skill in spinning yarn, and weaving and dyeing cloth. They had looms capable of the most intricate weaving.

## LAWS TO CONTROL TEXTILES

**1253:** Marco Polo, in his account of the Persians, observed that "there are excellent artificers in the city who make wonderful things in gold, silk, and embroidery. The women make excellent needlework in silk with all sorts of creatures very admirably wrought therein."

Some fine linen goods were being made in England; Sussex and Wiltshire were the weaving centers at the time.

**1261:** Henry III, England, noting conditions on the Continent, prohibited "export of any or all English wools."

Coventry was at this time noted for its raw wool, woolen fabrics, and cap cloth. The King allowed the people of this city to tax all wool processed locally into cloth in order to raise funds for public improvements. He sanctioned the plan for five years and then it was cancelled.

**1270:** The first banking law on record emanated from Venice. It was to protect depositors in transactions, textiles and otherwise, with other nations; merchant-operated banks came into being.

**1271:** "All workers, male and female, as well of Flanders, as of other lands, may safely come to our realm, there to make cloth." This was a decree from Henry III, England. A year later he was to speak of the great raw-wool business in the Kingdom and of the amount of commerce done with the city-state of Florence.

**1273:** Alfonso the Learned, Spain, decreed that "all shepherds of Castile are to be incorporated into the Honourable Assembly of the Mesta of the Shepherds." The group received a charter and for over 500 years exerted the greatest care for the merino sheep of Spain. No other nation was able to obtain any of these prized sheep until 1765.

**1275:** So vast were the numbers of sheep raised for their wool in England that even the serfs in the village of Swyncombe averaged 50 sheep on a per capita basis.

## BANKING ENTERS THE PICTURE

**1285:** Florentine banking houses were making generous advances in money to English abbeys in return for their entire raw-wool output. The merchants and banking houses of Florence and the English abbeys enjoyed many years of good business intercourse, chiefly in wool transactions.

**1290:** Woad, the only blue dyestuff known at this time, began to be extensively raised in Germany. The three major dyes were now madder, weld, and woad.

**1298:** Around this time the more affluent people were wearing woolen shirtings, linen fabrics were becoming more prevalent, and silk gowns, some of which were embroidered with gold and silver, were favored by the ladies.

## FLEMISH WOOLENS—ENGLISH SHEEP

**FOURTEENTH CENTURY:** Venice had over 17,000 woolen cloth workers. Philip the Fair of France, 1285-1314, was so jealous and alarmed at the popularity of Flemish woolens that he forbade their purchase by his people. It did not, however, prevent his agents from buying them for his own wardrobe since they were definitely much superior to comparable French cloths.

Sheep raising was now the most profitable agricultural pursuit in England. The abundance of wool was an important factor in the growth of a native woolen industry. Merchant guilds such as the *Gilda Mercatoria* were organized to handle the situation.

Pedro IV, Castile, Spain, imported Barbary rams to be used in cross-breeding with his own sheep to improve the wool staple fiber.

Silk manufacture was now in a flourishing condition in the Italian city-states of Bologna, Florence, Genoa, Lucca, and Modena.

**1305:** Louvain and the surrounding country in Flanders boasted of about 150,000 journeymen weavers.

**1307:** Edward II, successor of Edward I, England, decided to rid himself of all creditors, whose number had waxed great under "Longshanks," a nickname applied to Edward I. By 1311, on the pretext that foreign creditors in England were considering leaving England en masse, Edward confiscated all the English property of the supposed aggressors. The largest group among these recalcitrants was the Florentine contingent. Many were merchant-bankers who had large interests in the famed Monastery Wool. By 1320, most Florentine merchants had left England, leaving their interests there.

English wool sent to Florence was now shipped via the port of Genoa. Frequent city-state wars in Italy, however, greatly interfered with this method of shipping wool by sea from England to Italy.

**1310:** Florence produced over 100,000 pieces of woolen cloth on an annual basis. The wool came chiefly from England, Sardinia, and Spain.

**1315:** First mention of the word, *worsted*, dates from the reign of Edward II.

**1326:** Foreign-made cloth was forbidden within the confines of England, Ireland, and Wales by Edward II.

### THE ROYAL WOOL MERCHANT

**1327-1377:** Edward III has always been known in history as the "Father of English Commerce" and the "Royal Wool Merchant" for he did much to make the importance of his land felt in world commerce. He offered protection to all foreigners living in England and to those who might come to improve the textile industry.

**1336-1360:** The earliest recognition of silk occurred in an act decreed by Edward III, England, whereby English merchants were restricted to a single line of goods. Many of the merchants, a great number of whom had come from Italy, had been offering the various types of silk fabrics that were being made in Italy. Edward followed up his laws as rigorously as possible, but *owling*, or smuggling, became rampant.

**1337:** Flemish textile workers began to pour into England as a result of the earlier edict of King Edward III. Wool was now a Crown commodity and the king announced that he would buy all English wool. Much of the wool had to be seized since many growers were not in sympathy with the rulings on wool. Disappointed merchants received promissory notes for their investments and then Parliament had to pass drastic laws prohibiting the export of English raw wool. Smuggling had become such a problem that it is said to have been the reason for the rise of the British navy.

**1339:** Bristol, England, began to set up looms for the manufacture of woolen goods.

### FLORENTINE CRAFTSMEN

**1340:** The Humiliates and the Benedictines joined orders and made the city-state of Florence just about the most powerful city-state in Europe. The religious orders had over 200 communities in Florence and were growing in numbers and in importance. There were 30,000 craftsmen in Florence who were producing some 100,000 pieces of cloth per year. These figures do not include cotton and linen goods.

The famous de Medici family were the patrons of textiles, merchandising, and also of the textile-banking business. These Florentines laid the foundation for world commerce, trade and banking, local and foreign. Members of this re-

Catherine de Medici.

nowned family were members of the various textile guilds and many of them were well versed in the respective fields. It may be said that the Medici founded banking as a necessary adjunct to the great textile industry and its far-reaching branches.

### ENGLISH-FLEMISH COMPETITION

**1346-1350:** Another great influx of Flemish workers went to England. This laid the genuine groundwork for the present British woolen and worsted industries.

**1349:** This was the year of the Black Death in England. In the chaos, stress, and strife, sheep raising became most unpopular because "Sheep have eaten up our meadows and our downs, Our corn, our wood, whole villages and towns."

**1350:** Sir John Mandeville, English explorer, on his return from India wrote that, "there grew there a wonderful tree which bore tiny lambs on the end of its branches. These branches were so pliable that they bent down to allow the lambs to feed when they are hungrie." He was speaking of cotton.

Around this time, satin was first mentioned in England when Bishop Grandison made a gift of choice satins to Exeter Cathedral.

**1351:** A Flemish decree prohibited the sale of woolen cloth beyond a distance of three miles from the town in which it was made. Alarmed at the English attitude of this time, the Flemings passed laws which were intended to improve the quality of their fabrics offered to the buying public and to keep the standards in accordance with the seals of the respective Flemish cities. Every city had its Cloth Examining Board, which was made up of three persons chosen by local authorities. The Flemings were of the opinion that quality counted more than quantity, and that quality would sell their products. These decrees caused many weavers to go to England for work.

**1380:** Louvain, Flanders, lost much of its textile manufactures because of the insurrection of journeymen weavers, a severe blow to this great city.

**1385:** The six-hundred-year-old city of Bruges in Flanders was now the "center of commerce of all Christendom."

**1386:** The organization of the Linen Guild in London, England.

**1394:** The King of France sent fine linens made in Rheims as a ransom to the Sultan for some noblemen who had fallen into the hands of the latter.

**1398:** Much ado about the ban on woolen cloth in England, the beginning of a long struggle between the woolen manufacturers and the Crown.

**FIFTEENTH CENTURY:** Ypres, in western Flanders, because of its thriving textile industry, was larger, more populous, and of greater importance than London.

Early in this century, Cennino Cennini of Padua described a *Method of Painting Cloths by Means of Moulds.* Today this method is known as block printing. This is the oldest form of printing textiles known to man.

**1400:** About this time, the Wool Wheel or High Wheel, with an intermittent motion, came into being.

**1429:** The first European book on dyeing appeared under the title of *Mariegola dell' arte de Tentori.*

**1436:** Coventry, England, became noted for its manufacture of woolens and woolen caps.

**1455:** Silk was being manufactured in England, and the British, in hopes of making England a leading silk center, passed a law forbidding the importation of foreign goods, which was in force for five years.

BRITAIN EXPORTS WOOL

**1461-1483:** Edward IV, England, modified the rather harsh law of Edward III concerning the non-exportation of raw wool from England. Citizens were permitted to sell their wool outside of the country provided it was sent to Calais, France, for distribution. The law was not lifted until the time of Queen Elizabeth, who allowed full exportation of English wool.

**1466:** Edward IV, England, in order to curry favor with Henry of Castile and John of Aragon allowed the shipment of some English sheep to Spain. The catch in the gift was that the sheep were not of high quality and much below Spanish merino sheep in classification.

Earliest illustration of Spinning Wheel. From the "Housbuck" of the Waldburg family, 1480.

**1470:** York and Beverley, during this time of the War of the Roses, suffered great losses in sheep, and woolen-cloth industries were disrupted.

**1472:** Edward IV incorporated the Dyer's Company of London.

**1480:** Louis XI, King of France, became a patron of the silk industry in Tours.

**1488:** Knitted caps became very popular with the poorer classes in England, so much so that a law was passed placing ceiling prices on them. The word knit was rapidly becoming a very common term at this time.

Another English decree stated that woolen fabrics could not be sent out from England unless they were fully dressed, or finished.

**1490:** This era may be said to mark the decline of Spain as a textile power, not so much in sheep but in the fabric markets. Just prior to this year, Ferdinand V banished about 100,000 woolen workers from Spain because they were of Saracenic origin. Philip III in this year, "in an endeavor to drive all heathens from the country," banished 700,000 aliens, many of whom were textile workers.

NEW WORLD COTTON DISCOVERED

**1492:** Columbus discovered that the Indians of the New World had cotton cloth which they used for mantles, bags, and breeches. He took samples of Sea Island cotton back to Spain where it evoked great curiosity. Knowledge of the cotton fiber, gained during the Crusades by way of Egypt, Persia, and the Far East, was now spreading throughout Europe.

**1496:** The Magnus Intercursus Act of England was drawn up to assure a free market for the sale of woolen cloths to the Netherlands.

**1497:** Vasco da Gama sailed around the Cape of Good Hope and discovered a new route to India. This voyage has had much to do with the changes in the social, political, and economic phases of world commerce and culture, down to the present day.

**1507:** France, Germany, and Holland began the cultivation of dye plants.

LEONARDO INVENTS FLYER

**1516:** Leonardo da Vinci invented the spinning flyer, considered to be the first continuous movement in textile history. Henry VIII placed many Flemish workers in Coventry. They introduced new spinning and weaving methods which made the city famous as a textile center for centuries. The famous woolen fabric called Coventry Blue originated there.

Da Vinci's Spinning Flyer.

Leonardo da Vinci.

**1519:** Pizarro and Cortez found the "little white flower" cotton in Mexico, Central and South America. Cortez sent to the Spanish king many cotton cloths and garments with red, yellow, green, blue, and black figures on them, proof that these American natives knew about the block-printing method of coloring textiles. Red cochineal from Mexico and Peru was now being sent to Spain for use as a dye.

### FRANCE FOSTERS SILK INDUSTRY

**1520:** Francis I, the father of the silk industry in France, brought silkworms from Milan, Italy, to the Rhone Valley, where they have been reared ever since. Francis laid the foundation for Lyons and Paris; the former as the world center for design and motif in fabrics of high quality, the latter as the world center of fashion and style in apparel.

**1522:** Cortez, the noted Spanish explorer, appointed some officials to introduce sericulture in what is now Mexico. Acosta, the Spanish chronicler of records, says that the venture died with the century.

**1529:** The distaff was introduced into England by Anthony Bonvoise, an Italian.

### SAXONY WHEEL INVENTED

**1533:** A citizen of Brunswick, Germany, Johann Jurgen, a wood carver by trade, invented the so-called *bobbing-wheel*, also known as the Saxony Wheel. This was a regular spinning wheel with a cranked axis on the large wheel, and an added treadle by which the spinner could rotate the spindle with one foot. The wheel improved the quality of yarn for handloom weaving and did it faster than previous models. Jurgen received his ideas from sketches of Leonardo da Vinci. Jurgen also designed the flyer used in processing cotton into yarn.

Pizarro, conqueror of Peru, said that Peruvian woven fabrics were superior to those made in Spain and that their woolen cloths were comparable with linens made in Egypt.

**1536:** First mention of cotton growing in America made by the explorer, De Vaca, who explored what is now Louisiana and Texas.

Present-day Navajo Indians still spin wool (above) and weave rugs and blankets as they did in the days of the Conquistadores.

**1539:** Henry VIII, England, suppressed 190 abbeys and monasteries in Great Britain, which resulted in the demise of Monastery Wool, a product which had been in great demand from the 6th Century to this time. These communities housed upwards of 50,000 persons at the time of the suppression; their annual income was close to $12 million.

### MEXICANS WEAVE WOOL

**1540:** Spaniards brought sheep to Mexico and native Indians began to weave wool into blankets. The Pueblo Indians became expert weavers, but in time rebelled against the Conquistadores. The Navajo Indians received the sheep of the conquered and dispersed Pueblos. Only the best of present-day textures compare with the Pueblo and Navajo weaving.

Queen Elizabeth I.

**1541:** Coronado had about 5,000 sheep with him on his trip from Mexico City across the Rio Grande into what is now the United States. His voyage took him to about the present site of Dodge City, Kansas. He was searching for the "Seven Cities of Cibala." Some of the sheep died en route, some were eaten, and some were captured by various Indian tribes encountered on the way.

**1549:** Edward VI, England, encouraged foreign Protestants to come there to work in the textile industry. Varying numbers did bring their talents, chiefly Germans, Walloons, French, and some few workers from Italy, Poland, and Switzerland.

**1555:** The Weavers' Act in England limited those who lived outside the old urban limits of towns and cities to two looms for making woolen fabric. The law was not too rigidly enforced, however.

**1561:** Pillow-lace method invented by Barbara Uttmann.

**1562:** The Guild for silk throwers founded in Spitalfields, England.

### QUEEN BESS FOSTERS TEXTILE GROWTH

**1567-1575:** Queen Elizabeth was instrumental in bringing about the immigration of Dutch and Flemish refugees, many of whom were textile workers who were fleeing the Spanish invasion of Flanders and the Netherlands. The work and influence of these workers did much to enhance the British textile industry, particularly in woolens and worsteds.

**1573:** John Tice, England, claimed to have perfected tufted taffetas and wrought velvets.

**1578:** Antwerp, then a Dutch possession, was sacked by the Spaniards; and the powerful Merchant Adventurers, trading companies, fled to the city of Hamburg, but the Germans forbade their staying there. Queen Elizabeth, in support of the English merchant groups, then banished all German merchants from England, including many long-established textile traders with offices there. The Teutonic Traders, some with 600 years of residence, left England.

**1582:** During this chaotic period on the Continent and in Great Britain, the English boasted of the fact that they were exporting annually 200,000 pounds worth of fabric, about one million dollars worth per annum.

**1585:** Philip II, Spain, invaded Flanders. The Dukes of Alba and Parma made shambles of Antwerp, Bruges, Ypres, and other Flemish cities. Thousands of skilled workers had to flee to other nations and many of these went to England, France, and Ireland. Elizabeth welcomed all the workers who came to British shores and these groups did much to make England more of a textile power.

## MONOPOLY ON MERINO SHEEP

**1588:** Spain had a world-wide reputation for its merino sheep, which they kept as a monopoly until the time of the defeat of the Spanish Armada by the English. Despite the defeat and the treaties made concerning sheep, it was not until 1765 that other nations suc-ceeded in receiving merino sheep from Spain. England was supposed to have received some merino sheep shortly after the Spanish defeat but it took almost 200 years to fulfill the arrangement.

## LEE INVENTS KNITTING FRAME

**1589:** William Lee invented the knitting frame. This stocking frame knitted only woolen stockings until 1598, when Lee perfected his machine so that he could knit silk stockings. Queen Elizabeth was presented with the first pair made on the machine, and was much pleased since they were not as cumbersome as the woolen stockings and possessed a kindlier feel.

**1590:** After the defeat of the Spanish Armada, the British, conscious more than ever of their sea power, began the manufacture of their own sailcloth, the beginning of an important segment of the textile industry.

A knitting school for children was begun in York; three teachers were employed.

**1598:** Juan de Onate, Spanish explorer, set out to explore the American Southwest and covered about the same route as Coronado in 1541. He had 3,000 sheep with him, the Churro type, a low-grade breed. De Onate gave some of the sheep to each Indian tribe encountered on the way. The Franciscan and the Jesuit missionaries on the voyage with him included several animal-husbandry experts. They aided the Indians in caring for the sheep left with them, taught them pastoral life, and gave general instructions for breeding.

**1600:** American cotton was offered to English cloth makers, who were buying supplies from the Near East, and the response was small.

*1607–1831: In these years the advent of the industrial revolution quickens the pace of textile development; an amazing number of new machines are invented, steam power replaces hand and horse, England becomes a major manufacturer, America starts its own textile industry.*

**1607:** The London Company sent a flock of sheep to Virginia.

**1614:** "Dyeing of cloth in the wood" was introduced in England; the use of logwood, madder, quercitron, etc., soon became popular.

**1620-1630:** The era of the Great Depression in England. Exports were off one-third, there was a marked drop in the price of wool, unemployment was rampant, and many men once affluent became poor. After 1625 some recovery was made but it was not until 1630 that England came out of the depression.

## VIRGINIA TRIES SERICULTURE

**1623:** Virginia plantation owners were to be fined ten pounds if they did not produce at least ten mulberry trees for each one hundred acres. This was part of the English plan to establish sericulture in the colonies.

**1625:** The Dutch East India Company sent a flock of sheep to what is now New York City.

**1629:** At Spitalfields, London, England, an incorporation of silk workers was formed. James I was the sponsor of the incorporation.

**1630:** The Dutch chemist, Drebbel, produced a new scarlet dyestuff for wool by using tin and cochineal. The Gobelin Dye Works in France and the Bow Dye Works, England, used the dye.

**1631-1633:** The East India Company began the importation of calico from Calicut, a city in India. The fabric at this time was judged to be a soft linen fabric. In 1633, Samuel Pepys, the great English diarist, referred to the problem as follows: "Sir Martin Noell told us of the dispute between him as a farmer of the additional duty and the East India Company, whether calico be linen or no: which he says it is, having been ever esteemed so; they say it is made of cotton woole that grows upon trees, not like flax or hemp. But it was carried against the company though they stand out against the verdict." The result is not known.

**1633:** The Massachusetts Colony received its first flock of sheep from England, which were scattered and given to settlers. By 1640, about 3,000 sheep were in this colony.

## FIRST U.S. FULLING MILL BUILT

**1634:** John Pearson built the first fulling mill for treating woolen cloth in Rowley, Mass.

**1635:** Dutch Texel sheep from Holland were purchased by Massachusetts Colonists. These were to be used in crossbreeding since the Massachusetts sheep were of low classification.

**1638:** The first cloth manufacture in the American Colonies was established in Rowley, Mass., by the same individual who had erected a fulling mill there in 1634, John Pearson. About twenty families had come from England and knew something of cloth manufacture, hence the project.

A spinning wheel was now valued at three shillings in Massachusetts.

The first ship to bring cotton to Boston arrived. The *Trial* had picked up the cargo in the West Indies.

**1641:** Ireland had a lucrative business in flax spinning for the mills of Manchester, England; much of the woven cloth came back to Ireland for sale.

## FIRST U.S. COTTON MILL

**1643:** The first cotton manufactory in this country was established in Rowley, Mass.

**1646:** The French began manufacture of exceptionally fine woolens in Sedan, France. Cardinal Mazarin, the successor of the first great French nationalist, Cardinal Richelieu, sponsored the efforts.

**1649:** English cloth merchants were now free to trade with the world except for African ports, the Levant, and Russia.

**1650:** Cotton plantations were established in the Colony of Virginia.

Norwich, England, incorporated its worsted manufactures.

There was a bleaching plant in Southwark, England, at this time. Shakespeare mentioned "whiting time" or "bleaching period" and described the workers in the process as "whitsers."

**1652:** The Dutch, under Van Riebeck, visited Cape of Good Hope to use the cape as a base for the Dutch fleets. They found that the Hottentots were very good sheep raisers, but were interested in raising sheep for mutton rather than for wool.

## CROMWELL A TEXTILE WORKER

**1654-1658:** Cromwell forbade during his tenure the exportation of sheep, raw wool, or yarn to the American colonies. Cromwell knew what this would mean since he was a textile man himself, a fuller of woolen cloth. The colonists retaliated to this Non-Exportation Act by conserving their own wool and ar-

ranging for credits with Holland to purchase sheep. Agreements were also made with Spain.

Holland was receiving much woolen broadcloth from England; the material was dyed and finished by the Dutch, who were very adept in this art.

**1656:** Some skilled English weavers slipped through the various English embargoes and settled near what is now Lowell, Mass. Land grants were given to these workers who taught their skills to the colonists.

Linsey-woolsey, one of the most popular cloths of the time, was made in a 27-inch width and it was about twice as expensive as woolen homespun. This fabric was in demand, at all times, until the Civil War, 1861-1865. Kersey, flannel, and worsted serge were the other popular fabrics until about 1863.

**1657:** The Virginia Assembly offered 10,000 pounds of tobacco to any planter who exported 200 pounds worth of raw silk or cocoons per annum. These, and other bounties, were withdrawn in 1666, renewed in 1669, but no claims were ever presented.

Oliver Cromwell granted a charter for machine-made hosiery.

**1660:** England passed a series of acts that forbade the export of wool. These laws put teeth in prior laws that were not followed too closely in the past. These restrictions remained in effect until 1825.

**1661:** The government of Poland suppressed the first power loom which had been made by a citizen of Danzig because the invention, it was thought, would cause chaos among the citizenry. The inventor was subsequently drowned "to protect the poor."

A fulling mill was established in Watertown, Mass.

## TEXTILE DEPRESSION IN ENGLAND

**1662:** The textile industry in England was in a depressed state around this time. A commission was set up to find out the trouble. The board was composed of twelve men who made a survey, discussed the problems at hand, and then filed a report which was varied in opinion and diversified in remedial measures

that should be taken. It was the consensus, however, that unemployment was caused by the English people wearing too many foreign-manufactured goods, especially silk materials, and too little of the domestic cloth.

**1663:** 40,000 men, women, and children now employed in the silk-throwing industry in and around London.

**1664:** In his book *Micrographia*, Dr. Robert Hooke, an English naturalist and scientist, mentioned the possibilities of making an artificial yarn by mechanical means.

There were now about 100,000 sheep in the Massachusetts Bay Colony.

First mention of cotton raising in another Southern Colony, South Carolina.

## ORIGIN OF SPINSTER

**1665:** Massachusetts decreed that every household spin yarn and weave cloth in proportion to the number of females in the family. Incidentally, the term, spinster, grew out of this decree. The law required that each family make at least three pounds of wool, cotton, or linen.

The islands near Narragansett Bay: Block Island, Nantucket, and Martha's Vineyard, became centers of sheep raising. These were good places to raise sheep since the Indians were no menace on these islands and it was difficult for the Crown agents to find out where the sheep owned by the colonists were kept. The colonists were now self-sufficient from raw wool to finished garments, and the Crown could not understand how that was possible.

**1667:** The Flannel Act, decreed after the English Reformation, stated that "dead men must be buried in woollen cloth." A wag of the time said that "it forced the dead to consume what the living were not able to purchase."

**1668:** The Scots began sending linen yarn to England.

England passed a resolution which enjoined "all persons whatsoever to wear no garment, stockings or other sort of apparel but what is made of sheep's wool only, from the Feast of All Saints to the Feast of the Annunciation of Our Lady, inclusive."

## RESTRICTIONS ON COLONIES

**1669:** England passed a law aimed at the American Colonies—"no wool, woollen yarn, cloth, serge, bays, kersies, says, friezes, druggets, cloth-serges, shalloons, or other drapery, stuff or woollen manufactures whatsoever should be exported from the colonies or even transported from one colony to another."

**1671:** Edmund Blood received patent rights for the carding and spinning of waste silk, probably the first effort to do so in Europe.

**1675:** The Massachusetts Bay Colony was now trading wool for linen with France, and wool for wine with Portugal and Spain.

**1677:** Linen-spinning schools were organized in England. They followed the pattern of those in Germany which had already proved to be very efficient.

**1680:** About this time Indian uprisings in the South, Southwest, and West drove out the Spaniards from many strongholds. The Indians remembered the teachings in animal husbandry from the missionaries who accompanied De Onate almost one hundred years before this time. They tended to their flocks and kept the industry alive and thriving, knew how to cross-breed, and sold much of their wool to white traders each season. The foundations of the sheep industry remained in these areas and cross-breeding began to take on scientific aspects around the time of the Civil War and shortly thereafter.

**1681:** Dedham, Mass., joined Rowley and Watertown in fame with the establishment of a woolen mill.

## GERMANTOWN KNITTING CENTER

**1683:** The Mennonites from the Rhenish Palatinate settled in what is now Germantown, a part of the city of Philadelphia. Many of these were experienced textile workers. They introduced the art of knitting there, and contributed to the rise of Germantown as a knitting center —a position that it held for a great many years in this country. This group of Mennonites formed a plant to make linen about five years after their arrival in Germantown.

**1687:** A patent was taken out in England on a device which replaced the boy-helper who used to draw the cords which controlled the warp on the draw loom.

**1688:** James II, England, prohibited exportation of un-dyed woolen cloth; he wanted to bolster home industries since Scotland was a close competitor of England and James wanted to stifle the Scots.

## GERMAN TEXTILE PRINTING

**1689:** The first calico printworks were established in Germany at Augsburg, the beginning of this industry there. The Jeremy Neuhofers, father and son, directed the work, which soon reached mammoth proportions since their product became popular on the Continent.

Sir William Dampier, who circled the globe in 1689-91, published a book, *A New Voyage Around the World*, London, 1698, in which he described fabric made by the natives of Mindinao from the "bonono tree like a plaintain." What he described is now known as abaca fiber.

**1693:** First fulling mill for woolen fabrics established in Connecticut.

Francis Pousset, in England, received patent rights for the weaving of silk crepe; he was a Huguenot who came to England around 1685.

**1695:** First worsted mill in America was established in Boston. The founder was John Cornish, a comber, and dyer.

## IRELAND TAKES OVER LINEN

**1696:** Ireland was exporting wool and cloth to about every nation except England, where the acceptance of Irish fabrics was forbidden. The flax and linen industry, which England tried very hard to promote, was a dismal failure. England, as a gesture, thought it would be well for Ireland to take over the industry, but there was reciprocity in their madness. Ireland did take over the industry, and made a grand success with both flax and linen, but England forbade the Irish to export wool or woolen cloth. Irish goods found in England were to be confiscated. The Lord Deputy, a Home Office appointee, had the Irish Legislature place heavy export duties on Irish raw wool and woolen cloth which Irish weavers could make cheaper than could be made in England. This action caused an exodus of Irish workers that seriously crippled business.

**1698:** Parliament passed the Woolen Act, which forbade shipment of wool from the American Colonies to England, despite the fact that England was in need of raw wool.

## BELGIAN LINEN FAMOUS

**EIGHTEENTH CENTURY:** Many European nations became interested in flax and linen. Courtrai, on the famous Lys River in Belgium, became the flax-retting city of Europe. It still holds this position despite the ravages of wars fought in that area. Flax retted along the Lys River is the best in the world.

The foundations of the industrial revolution were laid in these family workshops. In pre-Colonial days, almost every home around Philadelphia contained a knitting frame, making what came to be known all over the Colonies as Germantown stockings.

Wool was still the most important textile fiber in England, as it is today. East Anglia was the most important worsted center while the West of England was noted for its woolens. Coarse woolen fabrics were being produced in North England. Cloth halls for woolens began to appear in England—Halifax, 1700, Wakefield, 1710, Leeds, 1711, 1755, 1756.

**1700:** In France, Oliver de Serres and M. Laffemas, somewhat against the will of the great Sully, obtained royal edicts which favored the raising of mulberry trees on plantations and the cultivation of silk. Their plan was to increase employment opportunities for the peasants. Later on, Colbert gave much time and attention to the promotion of the silk industry and offered bounties for efforts made.

Cotton goods were forbidden in England; wool and worsted fabrics were the choice because of deep-rooted tradition and the interest England had in the industry.

**1701:** England passed laws forbidding the importation of silks from China, France, India, and Persia.

**1703:** The English Treaty of Methuen with Portugal permitted the entry of English woolen goods on the condition that Portuguese wines come to England at two-thirds the duty levied on comparable French wines.

**1708:** King William, III, signed a law in England to prohibit the importation of Indian silk prints for inland use, on penalty of a 200-pound fine to be paid by the wearer or the seller. The law, however, was not successful, since these fabrics were smuggled into the country by way of other European nations. The law boomeranged, since it spurred on the popularity and sale of Indian calico and silk prints in England.

Caleb Heathcote, an industrialist, wrote that "three-quarters of the linen and wool used in the American Colonies is made domestically."

## Anti-Cotton Laws

**1712:** England passed another law against cotton which forbade the wearing of cotton fabrics in the British Isles.

**1716:** There now were 30 laws in England which prohibited the importation of calico. Despite these, however, the prints became more popular than ever.

**1718:** The silk industry of England owes much to John Lombe of Derby. He went to Italy, disguised himself as a common laborer, obtained employment in one of the leading silk-throwing plants there, and, by bribing two workmen, was allowed to remain in the plant after working hours. He studied the machinery, made drawings, improved his findings, and soon had acquired much knowledge about the manufacture of silk. The trio were discovered and he succeeded in escaping on a ship bound for England after many harrowing events. On his return to England, he built the first real throwing plant there, on the Derwent in Derby.

**1724:** The Dutch were now in possession of Cape Colony and tried to build up the merino sheep raising industry. This venture was not successful. When the Colony was ceded to Great Britain, the British raised the sheep with great success around Port Elizabeth, Durban, and in the Transvaal. It took them about 200 years to improve the breeds to the point where these sheep compare favorably with the best breeds in the world. About 38 million head are now raised there, most of them are merino. This is around 6% of world production.

Richard Rogers, New London, Conn., had eight looms that he used for weaving duck.

The demise of the aulnager or cloth inspector of goods for proper high quality occurred in England. It was now the custom for the English to allow poorer-quality woolens to be bought and sold. England had begun the blending of fibers in fabrics to vary the quality of the goods.

## Bleaching Method Introduced

**1727:** In 1727, the Board of Trustees of Edinburgh established a charter to encourage, foster, and protect Scotch manufactures and fisheries. At this time, the only progress made by Scotland had been in processing flax into linen yarn and fabric. In 1759, however, a branch of the silk business was set up in Paisley by transfer from Spitalfields, England.

A method of bleaching by means of kelp (seaweed) was introduced in Dundee, Scotland, by an Irishman named R. Holden. The process was used to bleach linen.

**1733:** John Kay, England, invented the fly shuttle.

**1734:** René de Réaumur, the French scientist, tried to develop an imitation of the silkworm and spider filaments by drawing out a continuous strand of some waterproofed varnish. He met with little success but left the thought and foundation for future experimentation.

**1735:** Governor Oglethorpe, Georgia, took eight pounds of silk with him on a visit to Queen Caroline of England. Around this time, South Carolina and Georgia were vigorously promoting sericulture.

First mention of cotton growing in Georgia.

**1736:** The cotton plant, while known in England, was considered mainly as an ornamental plant. England, of course, was importing cotton at this time but only about 200,000 pounds a year from cotton-raising areas.

## Two Major Inventions

**1737:** John Wyatt and Lewis Paul, England, invented drawing rollers to draft fibers so that spinning of yarn would be possible by machine.

Calico printing was now being done in Scotland. The Claytons of Bamber Bridge, Preston, established the first English plant for this type of work a few years later.

**1739:** Ten thousand pounds of silk cocoons received in Savannah, Ga. Efforts were made to establish the industry there. There is a possibility that silk reeling might have been successful in time, but the arrival of Eli Whitney's cotton gin, about fifty-five years later, spelled the demise of silk culture in the South.

**1742:** First cotton mill built in Birmingham, England. Because of limited power the mill was not a success.

**1745:** Indigo, used as a blue dye, now being raised in South Carolina. It was a very profitable crop until after the American Revolution, when it was found that indigo could be imported more cheaply from the East Indies.

## More Wyatt-Paul Inventions

**1748:** John Wyatt and Lewis Paul, England, invented the revolving cylinder, later to become an essential part of a carding machine.

Daniel Bourn, England, obtained patent No. 268, for a carding machine. He owned a cotton mill in Leominster in Herefordshire and it appears that he was in partnership with Henry Morris of Lancashire, who purchased his spindles from Lewis Paul, a name to conjure with in the early textile industry. Bourn's carder, it is said, was inspired by the necessity of feeding Paul's spinning machine, invented in 1738.

**1749:** A silk filature was established in Savannah, Ga. Silk could now be sent to England free of duty and Georgia and the Carolinas began to take an interest in silk as a source of revenue. In due time, good-sized shipments were sent to the mother country and some of the prices exceeded those accorded Italian silk, which was already of proven quality.

**1754:** Bourn's cotton mill in Leominster, England, burned down and with it went the interest for improvements in mechanical carding. A decade was to pass before interest was renewed.

**1755:** South Carolina was experimenting with silk around this time. In fact, Mrs. William Pinckney, wife of the statesman, took enough silk with her on a trip to England to make three silk dresses. One of these she presented to the Princess Dowager of Wales.

**1756:** Cotton velvets and quiltings first made in England.

Silesian sheep were introduced into Magdeburg, Prussia, the beginning of sheep raising there. Silesian wool is now a Class One merino.

## Stocking Frame Patented

**1758:** Jedediah Strutt, England, patented his ribbed stocking frame and he soon had a hosiery mill in operation in Derby.

Johann Heinrich von Schule, "the pioneer of modern industry in technical organization," established the first large plant of any type, when he opened his large printworks in Augsburg, Germany.

By 1760 there were more than 1,500 employees in the plant.

Collapse of the wage assessment system in England was an indication of the growth of *laissez-faire* philosophy which was to dominate the economic thinking of the 18th Century.

**1759:** In this year Christophe Philippe Oberkampf established his factory for printing textiles at Jouy, France, and began a great era of production which holds an important place in textile history. Of Bavarian origin, Oberkampf had gained experience in his father's factory at Wisenbach. On May 1st, 1760, he issued the first Toile de Jouy, designed, printed and dyed in his factory. Toile de Jouy had an immediate success. Due to Oberkampf's artistic perception and to his business capability, he was able to attract artists of high caliber and inventiveness to work for him. By 1783 his factory had been granted Royal status and the Court was using his products both for furnishings and apparel. In 1781 J. B. Huet began to use metal plates similar to those used in printing illustrations for books, and toward the end of the century printing from wooden rollers was introduced, probably by Oberkampf himself, though it may have been taken from Bell in Scotland. Among the famous artists employed at the factory, in addition to Huet, were Horace Vernet, Le Bas, Pillement and others. This factory, owing to the rapid nature of printing design, was able to introduce a topicality into textiles which had not existed before. An example is the "Baloon Ascension" in which a dog motif was removed from a popular design and replaced by the balloon, to commemorate the first balloon ascent in Paris in 1783, creating a textile still famous among Toiles de Jouy.

**1759:** Georgia evidently did make some progress in sericulture by this time. The filature that had been established in Savannah received about 10,000 pounds of cocoons for manipulation. Tobacco and cotton, however, soon sounded the death knell for silk. By 1772 the silk bubble in Georgia had burst.

**1760:** Robert Kay, son of John Kay, England, invented the drop-box loom.

**1762:** Dr. Aspinwall of Connecticut sent silkworms and mulberry trees to Mansfield and New Haven in an effort to establish a silk industry in the north.

**1763:** The Connecticut Assembly offered 10 shillings bounty for each 100

Model of a hand loom with a fly-shuttle.

mulberry trees planted and kept in good condition for three years; another of 3 pence was offered for each ounce of raw silk produced. In order to spread the culture, one-half ounce of seed was sent to each parish in the Colony. The plan did stir interest in sericulture and it soon took on rather good proportions.

**1763-1790:** Dr. Stiles, president of Yale University, was very interested in silk and kept a diary on the subject during these years. A woman and three children could make 10 pounds of raw silk worth $50 in five weeks. He did much to promote interest in sericulture.

## Merinos Come to England

**1765:** Spain finally lived up to the terms of the treaty with England made after the defeat of the Spanish Armada in 1588, and began shipping merino sheep to England. It took about 200 years for the English to obtain the prized and cherished merinos from Spain.

**1765:** Sheep from the colony of New York were now being exported to the West Indies for molasses, sugar, rum, etc.

The Stamp Act was passed and stipulated many things most disagreeable to the Colonists. The populace was forbidden to wear imported fabrics; by this time, however, the Colonists were doing very well in providing their own garments from wool raised here.

### THE SPINNING JENNY

**1767:** James Hargreaves, England, invented the spinning jenny, named in honor of his wife. Drawing of the roving on the machine was done by means of the carriage on the frame.

**1768:** George Washington had at least one yard of woolen cloth woven daily on his hand looms which, incidentally, may still be seen at Mount Vernon.

The commencement exercises of Harvard College were highlighted by the fact that all graduates wore Colonial-made fabrics.

### THE SPINNING FRAME

**1769:** Sir Richard Arkwright, England, invented the spinning frame which did its drawing by means of rollers on the frame. He had the famous Jedediah Strutt and Samuel Weed as partners in the enterprise. Horses were used to supply the power to turn the machines.

**1770:** George Washington imported merino rams to increase his flock in Mount Vernon.

A filature was established in Philadelphia with money raised by popular subscription.

Thomas Bell, England, conceived the idea of printing calico by using flat engraved copper plates similar to those employed to print mezzotints and copies of pictures.

**1770:** Benjamin Franklin induced John Hewson, the first calico printer, to come to Philadelphia from England and ply his trade there. The Revolution interrupted his work and he served in the Continental armies, being made prisoner at the Battle of Monmouth. He escaped, with a price of 50 guineas on

(*Left*) Arkwright's water frame for spinning was a remarkable invention and a milestone in the textile industry's history.

(*Below*) Hargreave's Spinning Jenny, named for his wife, was another great textile invention.

his head, and continued his business after the war. In 1789 he received a loan of 200 pounds from the state treasury to carry on his business.

Samuel Wetherill, Jr., a very prominent Quaker leader in Philadelphia, formed a partnership with other business leaders and established "The United Company of Philadelphia for Promoting American Manufactures." Woolens, cottons and linens were made in a house located at the southwest corner of Ninth and Market Streets. The undertaking flourished until British occupation of Philadelphia during the American Revolution necessitated its going out of business. After the end of the war, Mr. Wetherill began business operations once more in South Alley between Market and Arch Streets and between Fifth and Sixth Streets.

**1771:** Robert Frost devised a machine for making coarse, square net, used for wigs.

Richard Arkwright founded the first great cotton mill in Cromford, Derbyshire, England. His spinning frames did their drafting by rollers while the twisting was done by flyers. This was the first mill in England to employ children.

Henry Marchant, of Providence, R.I., while in Nottingham, England, observed the following: "The wheels for spinning cotton were very curious, one woman drawing 24 threads at once. . . . In two rooms there were at work at least 130 girls all briskly singing at their work."

Maria Theresa negotiated for the importation of Spanish merino sheep into Austria-Hungary, where they were established on a government experimental farm.

**1772:** The first American-woven broadcloth was exhibited in Philadelphia. By this time the Colonists were cooperating to the fullest degree with each other in opposition to the Stamp Act, which seemed to weld all the people into one homogeneous group. Contests and competitions were held locally in carding, spinning, weaving, and cloth finishing, etc.

John Lee, England, invented the feeder device for carding frames.

**1774:** England passed a bill to prohibit exportation of cotton textile machinery.

Edmund Cartwright, England, invented the power loom and the comber frame.

William Calverly became the first person to manufacture carpets in Philadelphia.

Dr. James Ferguson, Belfast, received a premium of 300 pounds from the Irish Linen Board for his application of lime in the linen bleaching process.

C. W. Scheele, the great Swedish chemist, discovered that chlorine destroyed vegetable colors. This discovery came about through his observation, quite by accident, of the manner in which the cork in a bottle of hydrochloric acid was affected.

Prussian blue and sulphuric acid were perfected for commercial use.

## ARKWRIGHT'S INVENTIONS

**1775:** Arkwright invented the coiler can attachment for the carding machine, and the flyer for slubbing and roving frames in cotton manufacture. He also took out patents for a complete set of cotton machines—carding, drawing, roving, and spinning.

There were about 150 knitting frames in America at this time with Germantown, Pa., the center of the industry.

## CROMPTON'S MULE

**1779:** Samuel Crompton, England, invented the mule spinning frame. The machine was a combination of ideas derived from the spinning jenny of Hargreaves, and the spinning frame of Arkwright. Drawing of the fibers was done by the carriage idea of Hargreaves, and the roller plan of Arkwright; thus, the name mule, a hybrid. Mule-spinning still exists today.

**1780:** George Washington visited a woolen mill in Hartford, Conn. He commented on the superb quality of the broadcloth made there.

A few sheep were brought to Australia by settlers from England.

The London merchant, Crawford, patented a silk doubling frame. This machine was noteworthy because it was the first attempt to devise a machine which would stop automatically when a thread became broken.

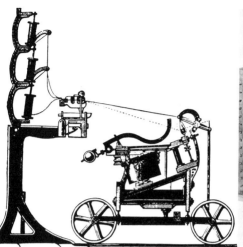

(*Left*) Crompton's Mule (1779). (*Right*) Cartwright's power loom (1785), reconstructed from the original patent specifications.

## STEAM ENGINE DEVELOPED

**1782:** English officials, apparently at the behest of woolen merchants, began to protest the use of cotton machinery which had recently been installed in England. Cotton was looked upon with disfavor and some people saw that the rise of the cotton industry would seriously affect the woolen and worsted industry.

The Watt steam engine was brought out during the year.

**1783:** Bounties were granted by England for the export of certain cotton goods. England was now going all-out for cotton, and importing about two million pounds a year. Only a year before the English were wary about the future of cotton and its possible inroads upon the woolen and worsted industries.

The popular textile fabrics of this era included "Bed tickings, Bird's-eye, Corduroy, Dimotys, Denim, Feathered Stripes, Fustian, Jean, Jeanett, Ribclure, Ribdurant, Royal Rib, Satin-stripes, Satinett, Satin-cord, Stockinett, Thicksett, and Zebray."

**1785:** Edmund Cartwright, England, received a second set of patents for the power loom. He also invented the warp stop-motion for a loom. Cartwright's loom was equipped with a vertical warp. Steam was first used as the source of power for textile machinery.

## EXPERIMENTS IN BLEACHING

Claude Berthollet, France, recommended chlorine-water for industrial bleaching of textiles. Other oxidizing agents began to be used at this time: sodium perborate, sodium peroxide, and hydrogen peroxide.

One of the first improvements in chlorine based on the findings of Bertholet was made by Javel in Paris. Chlorine was dangerous to use, its odor was pungent, and there were other disadvantages. Javel used what is now known as *Eau de Javel*, (Javelle Water). This is ideal for bleaching cottons and linens. He used a solution of potash, one part to eight of water, until effervescence began.

**1785:** Patrick Walsh, Kingston, Jamaica, persuaded his friend, Frank Levett, along with his family and his Negroes, to settle on Sapelo Island, off the coast of Georgia. Walsh sent Levett a large quantity of cotton seeds from Jamaica and Pernambuco. This was the birth of the famous Sea Island cotton industry in this country. The resultant cotton was superior in all respects to all other staples, and soon many of the other coastal islands raised the fiber.

## ROLLER PRINTING STARTS

**1785:** Bell, England, who had invented printing from plates, developed the roller-printing of textiles.

There were now 20 water-frame factories in England using Arkwright's patents. Ten years later the number had risen to 150 in England and Wales alone.

**1786:** Ipswich, Mass., was a lace-making center in this country.

Louis XVI, King of France, bought 380

*(Left)* Don Pedro was believed to be the first pure-blood Merino ram to come to America. His fleece weighed eight and a half pounds, compared to the three or four-pound fleece of the early American native breeds. *(Right)* Slater Mill, oldest cotton mill in America.

merino ewes from Spain. He desired to establish a high-grade sheep industry. The sheep were placed in Rambouillet Forest, near Paris, and served as the basis for French merino wool.

**1787:** John Kendrew and Thomas Porthouse, in Darlington, England, obtained patents on a machine for spinning yarn from hemp, tow, flax, or wool.

Around this time steam power came into being and England and Scotland soon adopted it for driving textile machinery.

James Watt, the inventor, who was also a chemist, and his father-in-law, Mr. MacGregor, successfully used chlorine on a bleach field, the first time it was used for bleaching in England.

Cotton was now being manipulated in 143 mills in England, Scotland, and Wales.

A Scotsman by the name of McClure was the first weaver in the United States to weave fabric by hand with a fly shuttle. This took place in a mill in Bridgewater, Mass., where jean and corduroy were woven in this manner.

Tench Coxe, subsequently Assistant Secretary of the Treasury under Alexander Hamilton, Samuel Wetherill, Jr., and others formed in Philadelphia "The Pennsylvania Society for the Encouragement of Manufacturers and the Useful Arts." This was an outgrowth of the old United Company formed there in 1775 and then interrupted by the Revolution. The United Company was in business as late as 1782, but this new organization, founded at the University of Pennsylvania, was the venture that now attracted considerable numbers of the industrialists of Philadelphia.

## U.S. MILLS IN PRODUCTION

**1788:** Bissel, American, invented the roller gin for cotton ginning.

Cotton manufacturing in Rhode Island began under the aegis of Daniel Anthony, Andrew Dexter, and Lewis Peck, all of Providence.

Picric acid was now made available for commercial purposes.

John Fullem began operation of his stocking loom in Providence, R.I. A year later a calendering machine was set up in Providence.

The first woolen mill that used water power was founded in Hartford, Conn. Fulling mills, of course, had used water power prior to this time. Two of the stockholders were Oliver Wolcott, a signer of the Declaration of Independence, and Peter Colt, uncle of the man who originated the famous revolver.

A three-story brick mill was erected in Beverly, Mass. This was, no doubt, the first textile plant to be built in this nation. The Philadelphia mill of Samuel Wetherill, Jr., while somewhat older, was set up in an old wooden building taken over for the purpose. The Beverly mill, however, closed its doors in 1807 for lack of orders. The mill trademark, brought out in 1788, was the first to appear on textiles in this country.

**1789:** Samuel Slater sailed secretly from England for America. He came to Providence, R.I., where he formed a partnership with Moses Brown and William Almy. He began work on building his machine solely from memory since England forbade exportation of any machinery or plans for machines. The mill he built in Pawtucket, R.I., was named after him.

Captain Waterhouse, a native Australian, returned there from a voyage to the Cape of Good Hope with 29 merino sheep. The sheep were of Bengal or Dutch origin.

First cotton mills begun in the South; mill erected near Statesburg, S.C., while a second one began operations on James Island, near Charleston, S.C. Mules actually furnished the power for the latter mill.

The first woolen mill in Connecticut was built by John Schofield in Montville. First corduroy fabric made in this country in Worcester, Mass.

The first advertising of textiles in this country was done by Beverly Cotton Manufactory in December; the agency was Baker & Allen.

## BLOCK PRINTING UNDERWAY

**1790:** An English mill that had been equipped with 400 looms made by Cartwright was burned to the ground. The workers were against "modern textile machinery." Cartwright's development of the loom had effectively supplemented the work done by Richard Arkwright.

Around this time, the Dutch tried to revive the long-dead sheep industry in Africa. The Dutch of Cape of Good Hope imported 4 ewes and 2 rams from

Holland; they had been given to Holland by the King of Spain. This small flock served as the nucleus for future sheep raising by the Dutch in their holdings in Africa.

Josef Leitenberger, Germany, invented a block-printing machine that was a vast improvement on all others used up to this time.

The Northwest Fur Company was founded by Canadian merchants with headquarters established in Montreal. By 1803 trading posts had been established all the way to the Pacific Coast.

**1791-1810:** America shipped 400 bales of cotton to Europe. In 1800, after the cotton gin of Eli Whitney became an actuality, close to 30,000 bales went to England and the Continent; by 1810 the number was close to 180,000.

**1792:** Kirk and Leslie, Americans, received patents for the first American loom.

### WHITNEY TO JACQUARD

**1792-1794:** Eli Whitney, American, invented the saw gin for the ginning of cotton.

**1792-1801:** Joseph-Marie Jacquard, France, invented his famous Jacquard Loom, which made it possible to control each and every warp end so that it could be raised or lowered at will to form intricate design. He was a friend of Napoleon, who decreed that a pension be given him in his later years of life.

**1793:** The first American-built wool carding machine was made in Newbury-port, Mass. It was set up in a mill in Byfield village.

Three pedigreed merino sheep were sent to Andrew Craigie of Cambridge, Mass., by William Foster, a Bostonian, who obtained the sheep in Spain. Mr. Craigie, not knowing the value of the sheep, had them slaughtered and used as food. Ten years later this same Mr. Craigie paid one thousand dollars for one merino ram.

The Slater Mill, Pawtucket, R.I., was now spinning yarn by the Arkwright System. Slater, in his youth, had been apprenticed to Jedediah Strutt, a partner of Arkwright. He spent eight years with Strutt, the latter part of the time as superintendent of the mill in Belper, England. Slater's original finisher card and his 48-spindle spinning frame are now in the Smithsonian Institute, Washington, D.C. Arkwright's work and influence bore fruit with Slater's accomplishments in America.

The Schofield brothers emigrated from England to the United States. They were master mechanics in the field of making woolens and worsteds on power looms and were the first to attempt the manufacture of woolen cloths in this country by power-driven looms.

### U.S. COMPETES WITH BRITAIN

**1794:** Byfield, Mass., is known in textile history as the home of the first mill to be run by water power.

Cotton production, because of Eli Whitney's invention, rose to about six million pounds.

Spanish merino sheep introduced into the Argentine and the present nation of Uruguay.

The second cotton mill in Rhode Island was founded by Colonel Job Green and John Allen, in Warwick. In 1799 the mill was bought for $2,500 by Almy & Brown Co.

Three Frenchmen, Schaub, Tissot, and Dubosque, set up a calico printing mill in Providence, R.I. They performed their calendering by creating friction with flint stone.

The first successfully operated woolen mill in this country, with power-driven machinery, was built in Newburyport, Mass. John and Arthur Schofield were the managers.

James Davenport, an American mechanic, received the first American patent on any kind of textile machinery from the government. On February 14th, his carding and spinning patents were granted and he established the Globe Mills, north end of Second Street, Philadelphia, Pa. His mill wove linen and hemp fabrics by water power. The labor was furnished by boys who were able to spin in a ten-hour day 290 feet of hemp or flax, and one boy could weave fifteen to twenty yards of sailcloth a day.

About this time, in England, woolen fabrics were classified as follows: woolens were made from short carded wool; worsteds from long combed wool; with a third group of materials being made from combed worsted warp and carded wool filling. Incidentally, the word stuff at this time implied a fabric made of both worsted warp and filling.

The following worsted fabrics were be-

Samuel Slater.

Whitney's Cotton Gin.

Eli Whitney.

ing featured in England at this time. Many of them are still made although present-day spelling differs somewhat—baize, bombazine, callimanco, camlet, crape, drugget, duroy, estamene, russell, lasting, poplin, sanford, shalloon.

**1795:** Several knitters from Nottingham and Leicester, England, came to Germantown, Pa., to augment the number of workers in this growing knitting industry. At this time, Germantown was the knitting center of the country.

The first mill to manufacture woolen goods in Maryland was founded in Elkton, the Cecil Manufacturing Company under the direction of Col. Henry Hollingsworth.

## Beginnings of Australian Wool

**1797:** Captain Macarthur began crossbreeding sheep in Australia and purchased various types of rams and ewes. He watched his efforts and saw that Australia could become a world wool-raising area.

**1799:** About 200 merino sheep from Spain were added to those bought by Louis XVI in 1786. These sheep were the nucleus for the present Rambouillet merino breed of sheep, Class One wools in wool grading.

Robert Miller, Glasgow, invented a power loom; adapted by John Monteith in 1801. There were 200 of these looms soon at work in a plant in that city.

**1800:** Ireland's exports in linen fabric reached 25 million yards.

Progress was now being made in our own Southwest with sheep raising. Churro, the low-grade sheep left there by Coronado and De Onate, had continued to multiply. These descendants of the original sheep were now being cross-bred and the quality of the wool was being improved.

Importation of women's ready-made clothing from Europe begins the story of apparel made outside the home.

## Sheep Raising in U.S.

**1802:** Chancellor Robert R. Livingston sent six rams and a flock of Rambouillet sheep from France to his estate on the Hudson River. Cross-breeding produced good results. His *Essay on Sheep* is the first paper written about sheep husbandry in this country.

Colonel David Humphrey, American, sent 100 choice merino rams from Lisbon, Portugal, to Derby, Conn. Nine died on the way over but the nucleus served as the basis for the present merino sheep industry in this country. Ohio is now the center of this industry.

Sir Robert Peel, England, brought out the resist method of printing textile materials. He bought the idea from a man named Grouse, a commercial traveler, for five pounds, less than $25. The principle was to print the goods with wax or some other substance that would resist the dye. After dyeing, when the wax was removed the figures would be seen on an undyed background. It is really a type of batik dyeing which developed to great proportions.

## New Textile Patents

**1803:** Captain Macarthur visited London with some samples of his Australian wool and with some help set up plans for the colonization of Australia. He promoted the Pastoral Company of English Investors to aid him.

Radcliffe and Ross, England, took out patents for the takeup of cloth by the motion of the lathe, and also for new methods of warping and dressing. These patents were taken out in the name of Johnson, an employee, who received a bonus of 50 pounds for the favor.

William Horrocks, Stockport, England, patented looms at this time. In 1805 and in 1813, he improved his efforts and brought out what was known as the Crank or Scotch loom.

**1804:** First cotton mill in New Hampshire established in Ipswich.

The first wool spinning machine in operation at Peace Dale, R.I.

**1805:** First power looms successfully operated in England.

The Pearce Manufacturing Company founded a blanket mill in Harmony, Pa. Incidentally, this plant is still operating and has the distinction of being the oldest blanket mill in the nation. It is now located in Latrobe, Pa.

**1808:** The King of Spain sold 2,000 of his best merino sheep to England because it was feared at the time that the armies of Napoleon would overrun the country. Other favored nations were also able to obtain some of the prized merino flocks.

The embargo on foreign goods stimulated the woolen manufacturing industry in the United States. Up to this time, homespuns and tweeds were popular. With the rise of the merino sheep industry in the northern part of the country, broadcloths of several types became very popular. The price of merino grease wool rose from 75 cents to over $2.00 a pound.

**1809:** John Heathcoat invented the bobbinet lace-making frame.

Northbridge Cotton Mfg. Co., established in Northbridge, Mass. Paul Whitin was one of the original founders.

Daniel Day built a woolen mill in Uxbridge, Mass.

Parker & Hugh, the forerunner of the present Parker, Wilder Co., Inc., began operations in Boston. The latter concern was set up in 1850.

**1810:** Napoleon became a patron of the flax and linen industries. Philippe de Gérard was the winner of a prize offered by the Emperor for improvements made in machinery to be used in linen manufacture. Although De Gérard soon passed into oblivion, his ideas and efforts laid the foundation for the types of machinery used in linen manufacture to this day.

## Vermont Big Sheep Area

William Jarvis, United States Consul in Lisbon, sent 4,000 merino sheep to his home in Vermont. Within a year this state was the leading merino area in the nation.

Rodney and Horatio Hanks built a small mill in Mansfield, Conn., to make sewing silk and twist. The Hanks brothers used water power and built their own machinery in their 12-foot-square mill.

London, Tolland, and Windham Counties in Connecticut were producing a combined total of about $30,000 worth of silk annually, and about $15,000 worth of waste silk.

The invasion of Spain by two hostile armies during the Napoleonic Wars caused over 20,000 pure-bred merino sheep to be sold to Americans to prevent their confiscation. Prior to this time, the Spanish Government forbade the exportation of sheep, except when the King of Spain presented flocks to the principal crowned heads of Europe. Of course, sheep were regularly smuggled out of Spain.

The first regular machinery for cotton manufacturing was established in Holmesburg, Pa., by Alfred Jenks. Jenks, who was a disciple of Samuel Slater, also invented a power loom for weaving checks in 1830.

**1811:** De Witt Clinton, Governor of New York, decreed that the Senate of the state appear at the next session in cloth made of American manufacture.

**1812:** Merino wool, because of the embargo, now sold for three dollars a pound in the grease state. Our own embargo acts on foreign products did much to strengthen the textile industry.

There were now 38 cotton mills in Rhode Island with a total of over 30,000 spindles. Three years later, at the close of the War of 1812, there were 99 mills, with over 75,000 spindles.

The War of 1812 threw the country on its own resources, and the household industry was taxed to capacity to supply cloth and blankets for the armed forces. Broadcloth was sold for $8 to $12 a yard. The United States became sheep-

raising conscious and from this time forward the sheep industry thrived and became a very important item in our economy.

Cotton manufacturing was making rapid strides in England. There were over 4½ million spindles working on mule frames which were using 40 million pounds of cotton annually. 500,000 persons were employed in cotton manufactures at this time.

**1812-1815:** The introduction of trousers was an outgrowth of the War of 1812. The garb was worn as a revolt against British imperialism, which was personified by men dressed in knee breeches.

**1813:** John Leavers perfected a machine able to make practically all types of lace.

Michael Schenck, a native of Lancaster County, Pa., founded the first successful Southern cotton mill in Lincolnton, N.C.

William Gilmore landed in Boston, Mass. He had a great knowledge of the Scotch dressing frame and the Scotch power loom. He tried in vain to interest the Slaters in the weaving end of the textile industry. Finally, he did form a partnership with John Slater. The War of 1812, however, caused them to cancel their plans to build power looms.

### SHEEP NOW BIG INDUSTRY

**1814:** The textile industry in this country had become such an important factor that merino wool rose in price to about four dollars per pound. The price of a merino ram increased from about $500 to $1500.

Creighton, England, devised a cotton opener with lap attachment.

The sheep population of the United States increased from 7 million head to over 14 million head. The War of 1812 was the chief reason for the rise, along with our favorable economic status at this time.

**1814-1835:** The last remnants of the English cloth guilds disappeared. The guilds were not able to cope with the volume of men, material, machinery, and money involved in the factory system.

**1815:** With the War of 1812 ended, British manufacturers began to come into our markets, thereby causing a drop in prices. Sheep raising began its decline. Vermont, Massachusetts, and Pennsylvania had the bulk of the sheep in this country. The DuPont family of Delaware, around this time, had a flock of about 4,500 sheep. 746 were of the pure merino type.

First mill for the weaving of silk ribbon, trimmings, and fringes established in Philadelphia under the aegis of William H. Horstmann.

At this time there were 170 textile mills in America. There were about 135,000 spindles in operation.

**1816:** Founding of Draper Company, Hopedale, Mass. Ira Draper invented the loom temple and an improved fly-shuttle hand loom; the first self-acting loom temple of Draper's was the second American textile invention.

England now had about 2,400 power looms in operation.

The first power-loomed goods in this country sold by the Waltham Manufacturing Company, Waltham, Mass.

There were 170 textile mills in this country; Rhode Island and Massachusetts were the two leading textile states.

M. I. Brunel invented the circular knitting machine.

The application of power to textile machinery began to break up the **household**

Hogarth's famous engraving of the apprentices at their looms, shows loom and equipment in a typical home-weaving factory. The master at right, stick in hand, is ready to mete out punishment at the slightest sign of idleness in the apprentice weavers.

industry in textiles. By 1816 only 5% of our textile manufactures were made in factories but from this time on factories began to spring up in New England. This year may be said to mark the beginning of the woolen industry in America.

**1817:** Joel Battle, Rocky Mount, N.C., founded a cotton mill along the rocky bed of the Tar River. This plant is the oldest cotton mill in the South still in operation. Burned during the War Between the States, it was re-built and continues to function. The Battle family is still prominent in the operation of the plant.

Gilmore and Daniel Lyman, in North Providence, R.I., formed a partnership to build looms. By the end of the year they had turned out 12 looms, all of which were in operation.

The first power weaving done in Fall River, Mass., under direction of Dexter Wheeler.

**1818:** Medway, Mass., became the home of the first machine-made lace plant in America.

Ira Draper, American, invented the self-moving temple. This invention enabled a weaver to run two looms instead of the customary one.

### First Knitting Mill

The first knitting mill in New England was built in Ipswich, Mass. In 1818, Benjamin Fewkes and George Warner, stocking knitters, had smuggled a knitting frame out of England by burying it under a cargo of salt to avoid a payment of 500 pounds export duty. This machine became the core of the knitting industry in Ipswich.

**1819:** George Rapp, founder of the Cooperative Colony in Harmony, Ind., fostered what is known at present as the Ohio-Delaine breed of sheep, which is still the best in this country.

**1820:** United States cotton production approximated 125 million pounds.

There were 14,150 power looms in England at this time.

Lt. John White, U.S. Navy, brought samples of abaca to the Navy Yard, Salem, Mass. The samples were well received and demand for the fiber in-

creased steadily, particularly during the later era of the clipper and whaling ships which made Salem famous in maritime circles.

**1821:** Ireland's exports of linen reached 43 million yards of fabric; spinning of yarn and weaving of fabric were done by hand and not by machine.

About 325 bales of Australian wool brought high prices in the London market.

**1822:** First cotton mill in Lowell, Mass.

D. & J. Anderson Company founded in England; reputed to be the oldest textile concern still in business there.

Samuel Slater began the manufacture of textiles at Amoskeag Falls, N.H. This was the beginning of the Amoskeag Mills, Manchester, N.H.

### The Compound Gear

One of the greatest improvements in any type of machinery was the famous Compound Gear device of Asa Arnold of Rhode Island. He succeeded in combining a train of three bevel gears so as to regulate the variable velocity needed for winding filaments of cotton onto the bobbin of a roving frame. Although the invention was in use at this time, the actual patent was not taken out until January 21st, 1823.

India began the raising of abaca on a commercial basis; the fiber is still raised there to considerable degree.

**1823:** First power loom in operation in this country, Southbridge, Mass.

**1824:** Stephen Wilson devised a new method of weaving velvet; it was the weaving of velvet double, face-to-face, and then cutting the two fabrics apart.

George Danforth took out patents for his Taunton Speeder—designed for cotton manufacture.

The first company in America to build mule spinning frames founded in Pawtucket, R.I.; the James Brown Machine Shop.

Ipswich, Mass., with large numbers of knitters from Nottingham, England, became the knitting center of America at this time. South Boston, Mass., and Belmont, N.H., were also knitting areas. Augustine Heard of Ipswich put the knitting industry on a firm footing.

### First U.S. Clothing Factory

**1825:** First men's clothing factory in the United States was established to make sailor suits.

There was formed in England a public company that was incorporated under the name of The British, Irish, and Colonial Silk Company with a capital of one million dollars. Ireland was chosen for sericulture but the enterprise was a complete failure.

Roberts of England obtained patents on the self-acting mule frame.

New Bedford, Mass., was a great cotton center and referred to as the Bolton of America.

Wet-spinning method of spinning linen yarn began in Ireland. This sounded the death-knell for the hand-processing of flax into linen yarn.

Mathias Baldwin, subsequently of locomotive fame, inaugurated the first American production of engraved metal rollers for calico printing. Used by established calico printers in and near Philadelphia. Around this time a cotton printing mill established in Stockport, N.Y. was capable of printing 300 yards a day.

Even at this late date it was an offense, punishable by death, to export sheep from England.

A model of the Compound Gear, brought out in 1822 by Asa Arnold of Rhode Island, was taken to Manchester, England, and an Englishman, Henry Houldsworth, Jr., managed to appropriate the action for his own use. He took out a patent for himself and called it the English Equation Box, sometimes known as the "Bag of Tricks." Consequently, Arnold did not receive any of the pecuniary advantages that he should have for his outstanding work.

The Erie Canal, connecting the Great Lakes and the Atlantic seaboard, caused the development of the Ohio and Mississippi Valley areas as important wool-growing sections. Prior to this time all wool not consumed by the grower had to be sent to New Orleans by river routes.

### Silk Boom in U.S.

**1826:** The boom in silk in the United States got under way by means of the tree, *Morus multicaulis*. This mulberry

Exchange Place, after New York's Great Fire, 1835.

tree was used in China, and Gideon B. Smith of Baltimore, Md., imported it into this country by way of the Philippines and France. Smith's trees, when compared with the black or the Italian white mulberry, far outstripped these by producing larger leaves and maturing quicker.

Paul Moody, one of the incorporators of the Merrimack Mill, was the first man to use belts for transmission purposes for power from the engine to the shafting on the several floors of the mill.

English patents for the speeder frame of Danforth's, brought out a year before this, were obtained by an inventor named Dyer, of Manchester. The original Taunton speeder replaced the fly frame in England to considerable degree.

## Year of Inventions

**1828:** William H. Horstmann brought the first jacquard looms, shipped to this country from France, to Philadelphia.

The famous Henry Clay Tariff made the raising of sheep and the manufacture of cloth profitable enterprises here.

The English now recognized that Australian wool was superior in all qualities and characteristics when compared with British wool; and it went into the best of English fabrics.

Thorp of England obtained patents for his ring spinning frame.

First steam-driven flax spinning mill built in Belfast, Ireland.

John Sharp invented the ring spinning frame in this country.

The Danforth, or cap, spinner was invented by George Danforth of Paterson, N.J. An Englishman, John Hutchinson of Liverpool, appropriated the idea in 1830 and the invention became popular in England and on the Continent, chiefly for spinning filling yarn.

Addison and Stevens received patent rights for a traveler or wire loop which slid around on a single ring, and from this the present form of ring spinning has been derived and adopted by manufacturers throughout the world.

Gilbert Brewster invented a roving frame in Poughkeepsie, N.Y. This machine provided temporary twist to the roving during the passage from rolls to spools by passing the roving between two leather bands, or belts, moving in opposite directions. This was called the Eclipse Speeder and it had considerable use for quite some time because of the small cost of the frame and the large production received from it. The Compound or Equation Box replaced it in popularity around 1835.

**1829:** Johannes Schwarzenbach founded the concern now known as Schwarzenbach Huber Company. Mill established in Thalwill, near Zurich, Switzerland. By the end of the 19th Century, Schwarzenbach enterprises were in England, France, Germany, Italy, and this country. First American plant established in Hoboken, N.J.

## Australia Leads in Wool

**1830:** Australia became decidedly merino-wool conscious and the saying was "Put everything in four feet." At the present time, this country produces about one-quarter to one-third of the world's supply of wool and 85% of it is merino stock. About one-sixth of the sheep in the world are raised there.

Roberts invented the quadrant for the mule spinning frame.

Josué Heilmann, Alsatian, invented the single-nip type of combing machine. He conceived the idea from watching his daughters comb out their hair.

Patents taken out for the first circular knitting frame.

The United States had enough sheep to supply the needs of all the woolen mills of the country. Western Massachusetts, Vermont, and up-state New York expanded sheep facilities to considerable degree. By 1850, however, because of many factors, Ohio took the lead in the merino sheep industry. As man "went West" so did his animals.

The first inventor to build a sewing machine in Europe was Barthélemy Thimmonier of France. His machines, unfortunately, were destroyed by workers who feared for their jobs. Thimmonier's machine was of the chain-stitch type and he was interested in making uniforms for the French armies on a mass production basis. Opposition, however, caused him to give up his plans.

**1831:** "Indian Head" trade name used on sheetings made by Nashua Manufacturing Co., Nashua, N.H. Name registered in November, 1871.

In the past six years many clothing factories for men's clothing came into being; they originated in the so-called slop shops, which catered to clothing for sailors.

The ring spinning frame developed by Sharpe in 1828 had been greatly improved by this time and was taking on added importance.

175

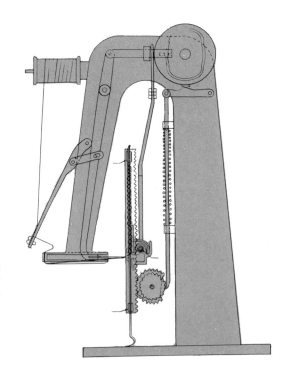

A drawing of Walter Hunt's sewing machine (1832-1834). This tracing was made from an illustration in the Sewing Machine News, Vol. 2, No. 8, 1881.

*1832–1919: The syntheses of artificial silk, of dyes, and such finishing discoveries as mercerization, bring the chemists and engineers into textiles, and the groundwork is laid for the current era of synthetics. Among the continuing flow of mechanical innovations is the sewing machine, which makes possible the mechanization of the apparel industry.*

**1832:** Bachelder invented stop motion for the drawing frame.

### HUNT'S SEWING MACHINE

In his little shop in what is now downtown New York City, a Quaker, Walter Hunt, made a sewing machine that would "sew, stitch and seam cloth." It incorporated two new ideas: an eye-pointed needle and lockstitching.

The first fashioned hosiery mill was established in Germantown, Pa., by Thomas Jones.

**1833:** The Ohio and Erie Canal was opened from Portsmouth on the Ohio River to Cleveland on Lake Erie. This furnished an all-water route from the Mississippi River system to Atlantic coastal markets, a great transportation improvement of the time.

**1834:** Reid and Johnson in England developed the shuttle-changing loom.

Ramsbottom and Hope developed a feeler stop motion for filling yarn on a loom.

Cheney Brothers established their first nursery in South Manchester, Conn., still the home of the world-renowned Cheney Silks. An item of the times from the family papers shows that the mulberry trees on which the silkworms fed were priced at $4 a hundred; in 1835, the price was $10 and a year later it was $30.

James Smith, Scotsman, incorporated revolving flats on cards for the first time. Prior efforts by other inventors had proved futile.

The year of the Great Trek in South African history. Seven thousand people trekked northward from South Africa, taking their sheep with them, to form the Transvaal and the Orange Free State, both of which were outside the sphere of British control and were recognized by the British Government as independent republics. In a short time Saxony, Rambouillet, and Vermont merino sheep were imported and the sheep-raising industry stood on a firm footing. Cross-breeding was actively pursued to improve the stock.

### PERROTINE PRINTING

The French master mechanic, Perrot, invented a new type of printing machine which simulated the hand printing frame for coloring textiles. Called the Perrotine, it could print several colors on cloth at one time.

The production of cotton cloth grew by leaps and bounds in England and now exceeded the production of wool fabrics. Wool, at this time, was not readily adaptable to mechanical handling.

Runge, German chemist, noticed that one of the products obtained by distilling coal-tar, namely, aniline, gave a bright blue coloration under the influence of bleaching powder. This paved the way for development of aniline dyes, the first departure from natural dyestuffs.

### BRUSSELS REPLACES AXMINSTER

**1835:** Brussels carpeting, because of cheaper labor costs, began to replace Axminster carpeting. Axminster had waned to such a degree that what remained of the industry was moved to Wilton, England.

The first knitting mill, the Wakefield Mill, in America was founded in Germantown, Pa., by Thomas R. Fisher.

London Wool Auctions established.

There were over 14,000 power looms in England making woolen fabric; there were close to 39,000 looms employed in the manufacture of worsted cloths. Yorkshire had over 2800 worsted looms, while Lancashire was the leader in woolen looms, with about 1150.

**1836:** New York City merchants began to advertise the sale of women's machine-made cloaks and mantillas.

## WILDCAT SILK SPECULATION

**1837:** The panic of this year threw America into chaos, and people were anxiously embracing any scheme for making money. Samuel Whitmarsh of Philadelphia had little trouble convincing people that the mulberry tree from the South Sea Islands would bring riches and establish sericulture in this country. In a short time, other crops were ignored for this "eighth wonder of the world." In Pennsylvania alone, over $300,000 changed hands in one week in the purchase of trees. By 1839, the South Sea Mulberry was found to be no golden tree, and the wildcat speculation stopped.

**1839:** The decline of the clipper ship brought lean times to Salem, Mass. Some ship owners turned to a new enterprise and organized the Naumkeag Steam Cotton Co., Inc.

## CROMPTON'S FANCY LOOM

**1840:** First loom for weaving fancies invented by William Crompton. The loom could make from 45 to 85 picks a minute. Crompton, along with Lucius Knowles, established the famous Crompton-Knowles Loom Works, Worcester, Mass. Their power loom plant spelled the decline of hand looms in this country. Erastus Bigelow was also an outstanding loom inventor of this period. These three men put American weaving on a par with that done in British mills.

19,300,000 sheep in the United States gave a yield of 45 million pounds of wool. New England and the Middle Atlantic states each raised one-third of the sheep in this country. Twenty percent was raised in the South, chiefly in Virginia, Kentucky, and Tennessee. The remainder, raised principally in Ohio, was known as Northwestern sheep. From this time forward sheep-raising began to move west.

## FATHER OF U.S. SILK INDUSTRY

**1842:** The first loom for weaving silk was set up in Paterson, N.J., by John Ryle, the father of the silk industry in America. Paterson was the silk center of the world until the early '30s.

Louis Schwabe, silk fabric manufacturer to Queen Victoria, read a paper in which he outlined his plans for a machine that would spin what he called artificial silk. The paper was presented before the British Association for the Advancement of Science and elicited great interest at the time.

**1843:** First worsted looms were installed in a plant in Ballardale, Mass. The first worsted cloth was styled for the women's wear trade. Men's wear worsteds did not make their appearance until the time of the War Between the States, about twenty years later.

The average wage in the Cheney Brothers' silk mill, for men and women employees, was fifty-one cents per day.

**1844:** Those still hanging on to the numerous silk ventures in this country in the hope that losses would be retrieved received a final blow—a blight destroyed all remaining traces of the mulberry trees. The raising of silk was even abandoned at this time by the Cheney Brothers Co. in Connecticut. Cheney was now dyeing silk in their plant. Sewing silk was selling for about $7 a pound.

The climate of New Zealand, unlike that of Australia, compares favorably with that of England. As a result many sheep were sent to New Zealand from England: Lincoln, Leicester, Border Leicester, Romney Marsh. Southdown sheep were imported by New Zealand around 1860 to give a good foundation to the flocks. The famous Corriedale crossbreed of sheep was developed by crossing Lincoln luster sheep with purebred merinos.

A popular book on the history of cloth printing, *Geschichte des Zeugdrucks*, appeared in Germany. It was written by Von Kurrer, and disseminated printing knowledge all over the world.

## MERCERIZED COTTON

John Mercer, a Lancashire calico printer, discovered that treating cotton with strong caustic soda would make it stronger, more lustrous, more absorbent, and more susceptible to dyes. He developed this knowledge into the process named for him, mercerization.

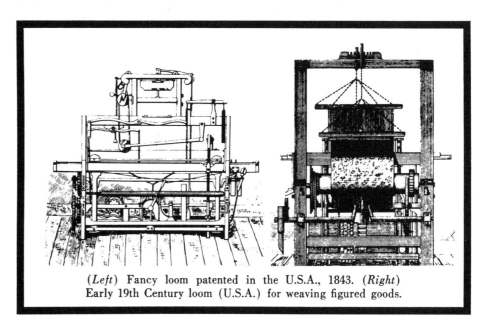

*(Left)* Fancy loom patented in the U.S.A., 1843. *(Right)* Early 19th Century loom (U.S.A.) for weaving figured goods.

  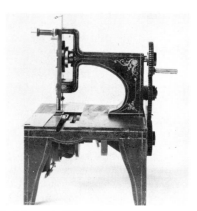

(*Left*) Original Elias Howe sewing machine, made by the inventor in 1845. (*Center*) Elias Howe.
(*Right*) Original patent model of Isaac Singer, patented Aug. 12, 1851.

### HOWE'S SEWING MACHINE

**1845:** Elias Howe, a twenty-six-year-old watchmaker apprentice in Boston, made his first sewing machine, which incorporated the curved eye-pointed needle and the underthread shuttle. A machine was perfected that could run 250 stitches a minute, five times greater than the speed of a swift hand-sewer.

German scientists mixed cotton cellulose with sulphuric acid and nitric acid to make guncotton, a substitute for gunpowder. This cellulose nitrate in time was to be the basis for what is now known as the nitro-cellulose method of making rayon.

Worsted fabrics began to appear on the American market. These domestic fabrics found favor with the public.

The average number of sets of woolen cards per factory in the United States was 1.75.

The Miami Canal was opened from Cincinnati to Toledo to relieve the congestion on the Ohio Canal; a factor that aided the growth of the sheep industry.

**1845-1855:** Period of extensive emigration of many Irish linen workers to the Continent and the United States.

### SINGER MACHINE PERFECTED

**1846:** Elias Howe raised money to perfect his second sewing machine. Patent Number 4750 was granted him on September 10.

In the latter part of the year Howe, becoming more or less disgusted with the lack of interest shown in his sewing machine, made a third machine and sent his brother to England to demonstrate his invention. English rights to the machine were soon bought with the proviso that Elias Howe go to England to make the machine adaptable for sewing leather. Disputes arose in England between Howe and his cohorts and he soon returned to America. Finally, his machine made headway in this country and it was not long before he was reaping vast royalties for his genius.

Isaac Singer also perfected his sewing machine and this year marked the debut of the sewing machine in factories.

Wamsutta Mills began operations in a plant at New Bedford, Mass.

W. W. Dutcher, American, patented the first parallel underpick shuttle motion, in use for many years in weaving fabric.

**1848:** William Skinner came to America from London and in 1848 founded the first Skinner silk mill on Mill River near Williamsburg, Mass. The mill prospered and the site became Skinnerville, a model industrial community of its time. In 1874 the Williamsburg Reservoir dam burst and the mill was swept away. William Skinner was left penniless, but his reputation was such that the Holyoke Water and Power Company offered him a mill site and enough money at fair interest rate to rebuild at Holyoke, Mass. where the mills of William Skinner & Sons stand today.

American Silk Journal founded.

**1849:** The ready-to-wear industry was born in New York City as a result of the introduction of the sewing machine.

The gold and silver rush to California and Nevada caused the exportation of large numbers of sheep to these territories from the Middle West. The animals were used, however, chiefly for food.

Australia, New Zealand, and the Cape Colony were now important factors in the world's wool supply.

### 50,000 WOOL WORKERS

**1850:** The British woolen and worsted industry was now fully mechanized. This made it capable of competing with the growing popularity of cotton cloths.

There were 1,600 woolen plants, not counting fulling plants, in thirty-two states of the United States. Close to 50,000 workers were employed, and the finished product was in excess of 40 million dollars. Capital investment was $28 million.

Power knitting machines introduced in New York City. The Baily Company was the first to use these frames for knitted underwear.

The beginning of the rapid growth of Ireland as a linen producer dates from the installation of machinery for processing flax fibers into linen yarns and fabrics at this time. Power looms began to make their appearance in linen weaving mills. To this day, however, much linen is still made on hand looms.

Bates Manufacturing Company incorporated, and running by 1852.

Around this time, women's magazines in this country began to feature clothes patterns. These were rather crude but, at least, a beginning had been made to promote patterns.

Total production of cotton goods in the United States amounted to about 60 million dollars. Imports were about the same amount.

## SHEEP-RAISING MOVES WEST

At this time the Middle West became an important factor in the wool production of America. This new source of supply caused a lowering in wool prices and some havoc in the East. Eastern wool growers could not compete with Western growers, since shelter and fodder had to be provided for the sheep during five months of the year, and grazing lands averaged about $30 value per acre. The West used free public lands, and required little shelter and fodder. The growth of cities and towns in the East created excellent markets for vegetable and dairy products, and this made for a decline in the desire to raise sheep. Increased acreage was devoted to food crops to supply city consumption and less ground was available for grazing purposes.

**1851:** Donisthorpe and Lister, England, invented their nip-comber. Lister improved upon the machine and today it bears his name.

Nathan Wheeler's sewing machine, introduced into the collar business around Troy, N.Y., made mass production possible.

**1852:** First New York State Law aimed at elimination of child labor; the Truancy Law passed as well.

Machine-twist yarn now being manufactured in Cheney silk mill.

**1853:** Holden and Lister, England, devised the square-motion combing machine, which Lister later improved. The machine is today known by his name alone.

Pacific Mills, Inc., incorporated at this time, was the largest mill of its kind in the world. Abbott Lawrence was the first president. Original capital was two million dollars.

**1854:** Pacific Mills, Lawrence, Mass., installed the first complete worsted machinery layout.

Wellman, American, brought out his stationary flat card fitted with a mechanism for raising selected flats.

**1855:** Anthony Street, New York City, was renamed Worth Street, in honor of General Worth of Mexican War fame. Worth Street is the market place and clearing house for cotton textiles in this country.

Railroads had now crossed the Mississippi River into Iowa and these opened up new lands for sheep breeders.

## MAUVE—FIRST ANILINE DYE

**1856:** The year of the opening of the era of synthetic dyestuffs. Sir William H. Perkin, the famous English scientist, applied the previous findings of Runge to develop the first aniline dye, mauve. Soon many aniline dyes began to appear on the market—magenta, aniline blue, Hoffman's violet, etc. By 1858 aniline dyes were much in demand and they have more than held their own to the present.

Only about one half of the woolen workers in the great center of Yorkshire, England, at this time were working in textile factories; the rest performed their work outside of a plant.

## SCHWEITZER'S REAGENT

**1857:** Snell and Bartlett, Americans, invented the let-off motion for looms. This Draper Corporation patent, improved and now known as the Bartlett Let-off Motion, is a standard motion used in weaving rayon.

Schweitzer, a great German chemist, discovered that cellulose could be dissolved in an alkaline solution of copper. This solution is still known as Schweitzer's Reagent, as is the cuprammonium solution used in the manufacture of cuprammonium rayon.

A patent was recorded in England for a "glass-like fiber."

Revolving, self-stripping flats on cards brought to final perfection by Evan Leigh, England. Leigh's card of 1857 could almost be said to be the modern card of today.

Extravagant clothes worn by women cited as a cause for the industrial crisis prevalent at this time.

First knitting mill in New York State established in Amsterdam.

Sir William Henry Perkin, the discoverer of the first synthetic dye and the first manufacturer of coal-tar dyes on a commercial scale.

**1858:** Townsend and Moulding, England, perfected the latch-needle knitting machine.

Cooper and Tiffany perfected a spring needle for the knitting of ribbed-effect underwear. Prior to this time only the latch needle had been used. The knitting industry thus became well established in New York City.

The first automatic knitting machines were set up for use in Canada. Hand-knitting frames were used to great degree there up to this time.

## WORSTED BECOMES IMPORTANT

**1860:** Around this time mutton became very popular for food, and sheep owners turned to raising the English mutton breeds instead of merinos. Broadcloth was no longer a popular staple fabric, which caused a decline in the demand for merino wool. Worsteds began to take on importance and the types made at this time were using longer stapled and coarser stock than those used in making broadcloths. Serges and cassimeres of the day were harsh in feel because of the type of fiber stock employed. The English breeds of sheep produced the ideal staple fiber for these worsteds and, at the same time, produced a very good quality mutton. Thus, these British breeds became popular here, chiefly Southdown, Cotswold, Lincoln, Leicester, and Romney Marsh.

Wool growing was now definitely declining in the Eastern states. Household manufacture had all but disappeared. Improved machinery now run by power, better transportation facilities, improved techniques, and wider and larger markets had great effect on the shifting of the sheep industry toward the West.

Rambouillet or French merino became popular around this time in America because this breed, in addition to good staple fiber, was capable of giving an ideal mutton that met with great favor.

Texas began the raising of sheep in a determined manner. Large flocks could be found there, some of them numbering in the thousands. California and Oregon became established wool-raising states.

The United States was now consuming about 100 million pounds of wool a year. About half was raised here, the rest was imported.

By this time it can be stated that the design and set-up of modern carding machines were perfected; to the present day there has been little change, certainly not in fundamentals.

The Eighth Census showed that the women's clothing industry had 96 plants which did an annual business of about $260 million. New York and Boston were the centers and over 90% of the workers were women.

Argentina and Uruguay were now exporting wool all over the world, much of it to the United States and England.

Nine million pounds of wool were being used in the manufacture of floor coverings. Ingrain carpeting was the popular type.

Machine-knitted products in the United States rose from one million dollars in 1850 to seven million in 1860. The rise is attributed to the invention of the circular knitting machine in 1851.

**1861:** Henry Rice, William Stix, and Henry Eiseman founded the house of Rice-Stix, Inc., in Memphis, Tenn. This concern. now located in St. Louis, Mo., is the oldest dress house in the United States.

### Effect of Civil War

**1861-1865:** The Civil War caused the sagging wool and sheep industries in New England to revive. Every effort was now being made to augment flocks of sheep, to increase the fabric supply, particularly for the armed forces. It was estimated that each Federal soldier needed fifty pounds of grease wool a year. Uniform fabrics were in great demand and these years were the ones that marked the beginning of the men's wear garment industry in New York City. The industry brought mass production, uniform sizes, job specialization, and assembly lines to the clothing field.

**1862:** The land-grant laws aided in the opening of tracts of land in the Southwest and gave impetus to sheep breeding.

### Butterick Patterns Start

**1863:** The Massachusetts tailor, Ebenezer Butterick, made a paper pattern of a gingham dress that his wife had made. The pattern was graded so that copies could be made in different sizes. Soon thereafter, he began making patterns for men's shirts.

George Draper, American, perfected the frog-with-loose-steel device which was first made as an attachment for Mason Looms and later applied to looms made in this country. By decreasing the movement required of the binder it improved boxing of the shuttle.

Q. U. Lamb, American, produced the first flat-bed knitting frame for wide knitting.

Pendleton Woolen Mills began operations in Pendleton, Ore.

**1864:** William Cotton received a patent for shaping knitted hosiery at the time of manufacture; the heel and the toe could now be made on specially constructed machines.

### Cotton Industry 15 Billion

**1865:** With the close of the Civil War, the Cotton Futures Market was established with centers in New Orleans and New York City. By 1950, thanks in large measure to this system of buying, selling, and handling cotton, the industry had grown to an annual business of 15 billion dollars, employing in all its branches 14 million persons, and rating as the top industry in 18 states.

The acetate radical, acetyl, was combined with cellulose to form cellulose acetate, now the basis for the manufacture of cellulose acetate rayon yarn.

With the war's end, wool returned to the doldrums in the east. Cotton came back strongly and the demand for sheep and woolen fabrics declined somewhat. The discharge of the troops lessened clothing demands for woolen fabrics.

In the West, however, wool growing was making rapid progress. The "loyal states east of the Rockies" began founding sheep empires in several areas. There were now 36 million sheep in the United States. Wool prices began to drop but the demand for mutton sheep increased.

The Civil War had caused sheep flocks to increase 140% by 1867; by 1871, however, these same flocks were reduced 45%.

Another cause for the decline in sheep flocks at this time was the increase of all other important agricultural products, while wool and mutton decreased in price.

William Deering and S. M. Milliken founded the mills, well-known in textile circles today, of Deering, Milliken & Co.

**1866:** The long cutting knife was introduced, and its use spread rapidly among the nation's leading clothing manufacturers.

**1867:** A spindle patent was granted to George Draper. By 1887, he held patent rights on twelve named variations of spindles.

Harper's Bazaar founded.

### Metcalf's Shuttle

**1868:** Metcalf, American, produced the first practical self-threading shuttle. This development for the Draper Corporation has much to do with the demise of the "kiss of death" practice of threading a shuttle by sucking the filling through the hole in the shuttle.

John W. Hyatt, Albany, N.Y., when there was a shortage of ivory for billiard balls, hit upon the method of mixing cellulose nitrate, made from cotton linters and nitric acid, with camphor. The product was called Celluloid, the first commercially accepted plastic. Used later for collars, cuffs, shirt fronts, window curtains for early automobile models, and when colored pink, it was widely used to replace hard rubber in making denture plates.

Coon & Co., merged with George B. Cluett Bros. & Co., bringing the Cluetts

A patented cotton picker, 1855.

the trade-name Arrow as well as an enterprising Coon & Co., salesman, Frederick F. Peabody. In 1894, the Cluett, Peabody & Co. name replaced Coon & Cluett Bros. & Co., Troy, N.Y., the name adopted at this merger.

**1869:** Carroll, American, devised the double-flange ring, an original Draper Corporation design now made by all ring manufacturers.

### ACETATE EXPERIMENTS

Mandin and Schutzenberger experimented with what was to become acetate, a cellulose-derivative fiber.

Graebe and Liebermann, German chemists, succeeded in preparing Alizarin, the coloring matter of the madder root, from the coal-tar product anthracene. The first instance of the artificial production of a vegetable dyestuff.

Sheep population in the United States was now 29 million.

### McCALL PATTERNS LAUNCHED

**1870:** James McCall, a tailor and author of The Royal Chart, a system for drafting patterns, commenced the manufacture of dress patterns in New York City. For several years Butterick and McCall had the pattern field to themselves; others did enter the field for a time but did not survive.

There had been a loss in this one year in the sheep population of America of 6 million; population was now 23 million.

**1872:** Forty-three leading silk executives met in the Astor House in New York City to form The National Silk Association for the purpose of establishing the silk industry on a firm basis, to win the respect of the customer, and to combat some of the abuses to which the industry was being subjected. John Ryle was the first president, Ward Cheney, vice-president, and Franklin Allen, executive secretary.

The original idea of this group was an interchange of ideas, increase of information, and harmonious action to promote and foster the trade.

This organization later became the National Federation of Textiles, which now functions with The American Cotton Manufacturers Institute, Inc.

**1873:** Name of The National Silk Association changed to Silk Association of America. A campaign was launched against the adulteration of silk, the first collection of industrial statistics and data was made, and American silk products were displayed at the American Institute exhibit.

**1874:** Further limitation of child labor was obtained by the passage of the Compulsory Education Laws.

**1875:** Moquette, the French *tufts-of-wool* carpeting, made its appearance in the trade. This rib-back fabric, with a deep-tufted pile capable of splendid color treatment, is of American origin. Moquette is now in the Axminster-type of carpeting.

Because of the great interest in knitted fabrics, the knitting industry began to take on major proportions in this country.

There were some 180 silk manufacturing concerns in this country. By this time the number of power looms far exceeded hand looms in this industry.

**1878:** Rabbeth, American, produced a spindle which made ring spinning of yarn practical by doubling the spinning speeds.

Artificial indigo synthesized by Baeyer, another notable advance in the progress from natural dyestuffs to synthetic ones.

### SIXTY TYPES OF COTTON

**1880:** United States Testing Company founded in Hoboken, N.J.

Example of early labeling.

There were almost sixty grades of cotton standardized and raised in this country.

First silk-conditioning house in this country was established. Development was slow at first but it was not long before silk-conditioning was on a firm basis here.

The sword knife and slotted table, standards of measurement forming since the days of tne Civil War, accepted by producers.

The use of B Naphthol for the dyeing of red on cotton perfected by Thomas and Holliday.

Cheney Brothers imported two looms from Germany for the weaving of plush and velvet.

Great influx of Austrian, German, and Hungarian tailors in New York City, which caused lower wages and distressing conditions in the garment industry.

The general range of wool prices was low because of panics, business depressions, and the great increase of flocks in the United States, River Plate region of Argentina, Paraguay and Uruguay, and Australia. Supply and demand were somewhat out of focus and an era of instability and uncertainty prevailed. It

A classic denim mark.

181

is around this time that American wool came nearer to supplying the requirements of the home markets than at any other time since the early part of the 19th Century.

Sir Joseph Swan produced the first artificial fiber in his efforts to devise a filament for an incandescent lamp. He forced collodion through very fine holes or orifices into a coagulating solution to produce tough threads which were carbonized by heat. His basic methods are still in use today in the rayon industry and he may be said to be the real inventor of what was in time to be known as nitro-cellulose rayon.

**1883:** Textile School established in Philadelphia, Pa.; now known as Philadelphia Textile Institute.

New York State Bureau of Statistics of Labor established. The apparel industry was one of the first industries to be studied.

Indigo application print with glucose and alkali made possible by Schlieper. The blue-red style perfected by Schlieper and Baum.

The contract system was making itself felt in the apparel industry in New York City.

## 50 Million Sheep

**1884:** Exclusive of lambs the sheep population in the United States reached its high water mark, 50,627,000. Our population at this time was less than 55 million and there were almost as many sheep as human beings.

The influx of a large farming population into Texas drove many sheep owners out of Texas to the Far West, as the free grazing lands began to disappear in this state.

The estimated cost of keeping sheep in the East was figured to be $2.65 per head; in the Western ranges it was 50 cents. This sharp difference, caused by the abundance of free grazing land in the West, accentuated anew the westward shift of the sheep-growing industry.

## Boom in Dress Patterns

**1885:** In December, the Wilkes-Barre Lace Company made the first pair of lace curtains to be produced in this country.

Para Red (B naphthol and nitraniline) brought out by von Gallois and Ullrich.

Around this time, *Arthur's Home Magazine,* a magazine for women, used Butterick patterns by arrangement. Four pages were inserted in the advertising section of each issue. In 1888, the magazine switched to McCall and Company patterns. The patterns were stapled-in but soon were bound into each issue because of the increased demand. The dress pattern section was offered as a premium to augment the number of subscribers. A year's subscription brought the subscriber 1200 pages of reading matter and three dollars' worth of patterns, all for the sum of one dollar.

## Father of Rayon

**1885-1889:** Count Hilaire de Chardonnet, Besancon, France, used the extract of mulberry leaves to make an artificial silk, the forerunner of rayon of today. His cloth, made from the filaments developed by him, was on display at the Paris Exposition in 1889. Chardonnet, a student of Louis Pasteur, is known as father of the rayon industry. In 1891 Chardonnet built his first commercial plant in Besançon. The method he used at the time is still called by his name.

Count Hilaire de Chardonnet.

**1886:** Office of Factory Inspection set up in New York State. Children under 13 denied employment.

A group of civic-minded people in New York City organized an Anti-sweating League. In two years' time they were instrumental in having wages for apparel workers raised to $12.00 a week.

**1888:** Invention of the Rhoades shuttle-changing loom.

About 45% of the workers in the cloak and suit industry were women.

## Automatic Loom Developed

**1889:** James H. Northrop, an expert English mechanic in the employ of Draper Corporation, Hopedale, Mass., completed a loom, and on October 24th placed it in operation at the Seaconnet Mill in Fall River, Mass. Improvements were made on the loom, and with a warp stop-motion with a filling changer that worked to perfection the looms were fully accepted by customers in 1895. This is said to be the first commercial loom to supply filling automatically, and the first one to supply the thread automatically, either commercially or experimentally. It was also the first loom to incorporate a practical warp stop-motion for general weaving purposes; to automatically supply itself with filling before the exhaustion of the running supply; to do away with the right- and the left-hand system; and to adopt generally the high roll take-up.

Silk Association of America took up the cudgels against misbranding of non-silk fabrics. Names such as *sansilk* and *cilk*, which confused the buying public, were the targets of the Association.

## U.S Interest in Flax

**1890:** United States Department of Agriculture began to take vital interest in the flax-linen industry. Original research and work was done in the states of Michigan, Minnesota, and Oregon. Incidentally, Oregon is the "flax state" of the Union today.

Electrification of sewing machines and the introduction of electric cutting machines were a boon to the apparel industry.

Mutton sheep, chiefly Shropshire and

Southdown, largely replaced merinos in Illinois, Indiana, Michigan, and Ohio. Sheep population in this country now at 48 million.

The sheep industry in America, it may be said, began in the hill areas of the New England and Middle Atlantic states after the close of the War of 1812. By the 1820s it was established. By the 1830s the industry began to move westward. Around 1870 the sheep industry which had been firmly established in the Middle West began to move to the Far West, to the territory states. By 1890 this vast movement was completed and the Far West and the Southwest are today the sheep raising centers for the nation.

**1890-1894:** C. F. Cross and E. J. Bevan, English chemists, used ammoniacal copper oxide to dissolve cellulose, a great aid to the coming rayon industry. About this time, the cellulose acetate method of making artificial silk was given to the world. Cellulose acetate, however, did not come into its own until after the close of World War I.

**1890-1897:** In 1890, L. H. Despaissis, French chemist, patented the making of artificial silk by the cuprammonium method. However, it was not until 1897 that Dr. M. Fremery, and the engineer J. Urban, who had used cuprammonium in making carbon filaments, succeeded in making artificial silk. Their patent was obtained in Germany in the name of Doctor H. Pauly; now used as the J. P. Bemberg Method.

**1891:** U.S. Department of Agriculture discontinued its Department of Sericulture. The Department of Entomology took over affairs which pertain to silk.

Moses H. and Caesar Cone founded the company which, in time, was to be called Cone Export Co., and is now known as Cone Mills, Inc.

**1892:** The English company, Lehner Artificial Silk Co., Ltd., was organized in Glattburg, Switzerland. Lehner published a journal on art of artificial silk. Eight years later the company became a part of Vereinigten Kunstseide-Fabriken A-G of Frankfort-am-Main, Germany. The Chardonnet plant in Spreitenbach, Germany, also joined the combine at this time.

GLASS FIBER DRAWN

**1893:** The Panic caused the price of wool to drop one-third.

Edward D. Libby succeeded in drawing from heated ends of glass rods filaments of very fine size and texture; the forerunner of present day Fiberglas.

At this time New York City had about 100 cloak and suit houses with about 50 of these manufacturing "directly." Cloaks were made almost entirely by sweat-shop labor. The Tenth Ward of the city was notorious for its sweat-shop tenements. Weekly wages ranged from as low as $1.50 per week to as much as $10 per week for the better workers. Many girl workers were paid only 25 cents a garment and they could only produce two per day working at top speed.

From this time forward, Rambouillet sheep have been considered the best breeding type in the United States, and are the most popular sheep in this country to the present day.

The Arkwright Club, famous in textile circles, founded in New York City at 40 Worth Street.

**1894:** Cross and Bevan made further strides in the perfection of acetate rayon filament.

The admission of foreign wool duty free under the Wilson Bill of 1894, was followed by a 50% decline in the value of domestic wool raised in this country.

NORTHROP'S AUTOMATIC LOOM

**1895:** Northrop, American, developed the first automatic bobbin-changing loom in the world. This loom, incidentally, was made for the Gaffney Manufacturing Company, Gaffney, S.C. Restored to its original condition by the Draper Corporation, Hopedale, Mass., in 1941, the loom is now in the Smithsonian Institution, Washington, D.C.

Cross and Bevan, England, developed the viscose method of making rayon.

**1897:** Textile School established in Lowell, Mass. Later known as Lowell Textile School and Lowell Textile Institute, it is known at present as Lowell Technological Institute. Present name adopted in 1953.

Galey & Lord established in Worth St., New York City.

**1898:** C. H. Stearn, England, improved the method of rayon yarn manufacture on the viscose system.

Strong, Hewat & Co. was established in North Adams, Mass.

**1899:** Textile school established at North Carolina State College, Raleigh,

The late 19th Century was an era of inventiveness at all levels. At left is a reproduction of a conewinder system for mechanical looms and machinery. At right, a drawing of Gunning's patented hoop-skirt frame.

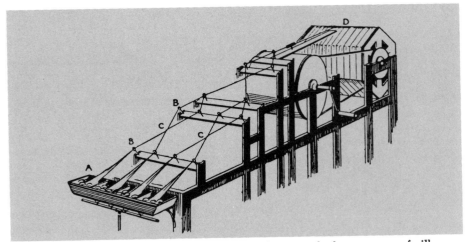

Early silk-reeling machine, part of framework removed, shows course of silk threads. (A) Cocoons in trough of hot water heated by gas jets. (B) Guides for silk threads. (C) Threads twisted. (D) Drum on which silk is wound.

N.C. Now known as the School of Textiles, Raleigh, N.C.

Several viscose plants were in operation in England by this time.

George Mabbett & Sons, Co., established in Plymouth, Mass. The Mabbett family coat-of-arms was adopted as the company trademark.

BOOM IN SILK

**1900:** Silk Association of America issued Statistical Yearbook for which there was a definite need in the trade. Soak-testing of silk was proposed by the Association, which also campaigned against defective twist in Japanese silk.

Dr. E. Bronnert established the first cuprammonium rayon plant in Oberbruck, Germany. He had improved the work done by Despaissis, Fremery, and Urban. His method is now the Bemberg Stretch System Rayon.

Birth of the present International Ladies Garment Workers Union following the decline of the Knights of Labor Cloakmakers.

From 1880 to 1900, the value of the products of the silk industry increased from 12 million to 87 million dollars.

New York City had about 475 shirtwaist factories which gave employment to about 18,000 workers, the result of the Gibson Girl rage brought about by Charles Dana Gibson.

**1901:** Italians and Japanese adopt standard American silk skein designed

to meet the needs of high-powered machinery.

René Bohn obtained patents for his invention of Indanthron, the first synthetic anthraquinone vat color.

RAYON SPINNING BOX

**1902:** C. F. Topham and C. H. Stearn invented the rayon spinning box. This culminated prior efforts in the field and assured success to what is now known as rayon manufacture.

Thesmar, Baumann, Decamps, and Frossard brought out Hydrosulphite and Sulfoxylate-formaldehyde.

Joseph W. Simons patented a machine to hemstitch sheetings after the threads had been drawn out by hand.

**1903:** "Artificial silk," now known as rayon, was being made in England.

A remarkable young man, only 24 years old at the time, brought out a book on "Artificial Silk and Its Manufacture." Joseph Folzer was the author of this first book on the phases of artificial filament making. He was a consulting engineer for mills in France, Germany, and Poland, and his book was published in France.

CASEIN FIBER INVENTED

**1904:** Silk Association of America awarded a special prize for gathering world-wide statistics at the St. Louis Exposition.

Lanital, the first protein fiber made from casein, was invented by Ferretti, Italy, and is still made in Belgium.

Trubenizing process made its debut, credited to Liebowitz.

Kopan process developed by Edelstein.

Samuel Courtauld & Co., Ltd., became interested in artificial silk and bought the British rights to the viscose process; their plant was in operation by 1906.

**1905:** The first patent rights for the viscose method of making rayon were obtained by the General Artificial Silk Company of Lansdowne, Pa. This company produced about 500 pounds a day for about four years. The company failed in 1909.

The Pressing Machine of Adon J. Hoffman began to revolutionize factory pressing.

Introduction of Jeanmaire's method of vat color-printing with metal salts and after-treatment with caustic.

**1907:** The first fair trade practice rules adopted in this country. The Silk Association of America set up the first United States silk-conditioning house. This culminated twenty-seven years of work on the part of the association.

Emil Fisher, German chemist, synthesized the molecule, protein-like in content, with 1,326 atoms.

The depression in this country in 1907-08 caused many of the apparel houses in New York City to fail; only part-time work could be found, there was a great excess of labor, unions disintegrated, strikes were prevalent.

New Bedford, Mass., became the leader in production of fine cotton goods.

RAYON HOSIERY FOR U.S.

**1908:** Imported rayon yarn knitted into hosiery by American knitting mills.

Sunder brought out a method of dyeing with glucose discharge on indigo.

Cellophane was devised by a Swiss chemist, Jaques Edwin Brandenberger, whose work was based on the prior findings of some British scientists. Incidentally, he coined the word, cellophane, by taking the first syllable of cellulose and linking it with the last syllable of the Greek word diaphane, which means clear or transparent.

**1909:** World production of silk totaled 85 million pounds. China led with 36 million, followed by Japan with 30 million, and Italy with 9 million. Silk manufactures in the United States were valued at $200 million, with a capital investment of $150 million, and over 100,-000 employees.

## VISCOSE AT $1.85 A POUND

**1910:** This date marks the beginning of the machine-lace industry in this country. Rhode Island is the leading lace center in America.

Leucrotope for the discharge of indigo and other vat colors announced by "Reinking."

The American Viscose Corporation under the aegis of Sir Samuel Salvage, the representative of Courtaulds, Ltd., which controlled this company, was making a 150-denier, 12-filament, artificial silk yarn. This viscose yarn sold for $1.85 a pound.

The South was now spinning 45% of the cotton spun here.

**1911:** Philadelphia, Chicago, Cleveland, and Boston were the only prominent apparel centers outside of New York City.

## NEW BEDFORD A TEXTILE CENTER

New Bedford, Mass., had almost 3 million spindles, over 50,000 looms, and employed over 31,000 workers. The 67 cotton mills were capitalized for over 36 million dollars. The city had a population of over 100,000.

**1912:** American knitting mills were now making hosiery from domestic rayon.

Silk Association of America approved fair trade practice rules for broad woven goods. Because of the trend to move the silk industry to mid-city, the Association's home was 354 Fourth Avenue, New York City.

## WOOL PRICES UP 50%

**1914:** World War I caused an increase of about 50% in wool values. The supply of fine wools, however, declined greatly. Lower-staple grades were in demand for uniform fabrics.

It was at this time that the Australian methods of shearing were adopted in this country, particularly in the Western states.

## RAYON SUBSTITUTES FOR WOOL

**1915:** The Germans were spinning rayon, cutting it into short staple lengths and using it as a substitute for wool. Many mills were converted to this project which, at the time, was startling and evoked much interest in the entire textile world.

**1917:** Rayon was used in knitted outerwear and underwear for women. American Viscose built a plant to manufacture the yarn for this purpose, in Roanoke, Va. At this time, viscose yarn was selling for $4.00 a pound.

**1918:** Courtaulds, Ltd., began the manufacture of Fibro, a new rayon staple fiber with some properties comparable to wool.

J. P. Bemberg A-G began marketing cuprammonium filament yarn.

## RAYON NOW $5.50 A POUND

**1919:** Rayon production in this country was 8 million pounds a year, and the price was about $5.50 a pound.

There were nearly 8,000 apparel firms in New York City following World War I.

Many chemical plants had large stocks of cellulose acetate, which was used as dope for covering airplane wings, on hand as the war ended. The Dreyfus brothers, Camille and Henri, solved the problem by perfecting acetate filaments. The first acetate rayon was produced in this country.

Casein plastic introduced commercially in America; made from protein of skim milk reacted with formaldehyde.

Even while the textile industry was going through the travails of its own modern evolution, an ancient craft such as handloom weaving continued. It is, to this day, a significant part of the textile field. (*Irish Handloom Weaver*)

*1920–58: In the years from 1920 to 1958 textiles becomes the second largest industry in America and inventiveness keeps pace with growth. This is the era of new fibers. Rayon and acetate are accompanied by nylon, Acrilan, Dacron, Orlon and Dynel and many others. We see the beginning of fabric control with the development of processes to resist wrinkles and shrinkage.*

## Fashion Sells More Textiles

**1920:** Beginning of the decade which had tremendous repercussions on American life. Some of the changes were: the knee-length skirt which helped the hosiery manufacturers; the Charleston, which was a boon to the shoe industry; bobbed hair; flat bosom caused by tight brassieres; the demise of the corset; polo coats, raccoon coats for the male in college; sweaters, the "sloppy stance," the boyish form, and the long cigarette holder. This was the era of Coolidge prosperity and the coming of sportswear, spectator sports clothes, fashion news on the radio and movie shorts on the latest fashions. Styles became fashions overnight in this era of synthetic gin. The automobile did much to change the tempo of life and the fur coat now became a necessity instead of a luxury. Dresses became the best paying proposition in the garment industry. By 1928, Fashion and Style had passed the growing pains stage; they were here to stay and to become a powerful factor in clothing.

About this time the first acetate yarn to be made in this country was produced in East Boston, Mass. This product was made by the Lustron Company. This organization later became the Celanese Corporation of America, a major acetate company today.

Charles B. Johnson perfected the first practical rayon warp sizer for the textile industry. It had been found that the then standard cotton sizers could not give rayon warps the handling they required.

Rayon at the beginning of the year was around $6.00 a pound but sold for about $2.50 by the end of the year.

## Home Sewing Grows Big

**1921:** First International Silk Exposition—still remembered and discussed—was a marvelous success.

In November, the first meeting of the American Association of Textile Chemists and Colorists was held in the Engineer's Club, Boston. Dr. Louis Olney, Lowell Textile Institute, became chairman of the organizing committee and was elected the first president.

Soluble vat colors, the Indigosols, were developed by Dr. Marcel Bader.

McCall introduced the printed pattern, which was a great advance in the development of home sewing. After 1938, when the patents expired and the method became public domain, other companies issued printed patterns.

Draper Corporation built its first loom to weave rayon fabric.

DuPont began commercial production of rayon in its plant in Buffalo, N.Y.

## Colorfast Standards Sought

**1922:** In January, AATCC formed its first sub-committee of the research committees. This committee was authorized to proceed with a study of fastness to washing of dyed and printed cotton fabrics; to formulate methods of procedure, and to establish proper standards to indicate the degree of fastness. The committee has worked on washfastness ever since and the end is not yet in sight.

U.S. Supreme Court upheld the powers of the Federal Trade Commission to act in cases of misbranding textile materials.

## 266 Million Pounds of Wool

**1923:** Japanese earthquake created serious crisis in raw silk trading; trading suspended pending collection of pertinent data by Dr. D. E. Douty, president of U.S. Testing Company, Hoboken, N.J. The Silk Association sent $400,000 collected in one week to stricken Japanese.

DuPont acquired the cellophane rights under the Brandenberger patents of 1908 and in April, 1924, brought out the first cellophane produced in this country. Col. W. C. Spruance directed the work in the DuPont Cellophane plant, Buffalo, N.Y.

Sheep population was a little over 38 million; wool produced was 266 million pounds.

## Word Rayon Coined

**1924:** Kenneth Lord, Sr., of the fabric firm of Galey & Lord, coined the term which today is worth millions—rayon. The name was adopted by all rayon-producing nations as a generic term for chemical yarns. Silk Association polices world industry to prevent private use of the word rayon.

Silk Association established examination bureau for impartial examination of goods in trade disputes. This bureau did yeoman work for the industry.

The original plain, transparent cellophane film was selling at $2.65 a pound.

**1925:** Since 1914 the value of silk manufactured goods in this country increased 218%.

## New Synthetics Appear

**1925-1929:** New concerns came into being in the field of rayon—American Enka Corporation, affiliated with Dutch interests; North American Rayon Corporation; American Bemberg Corporation.

In 1927 and 1928 the Viscose Company and DuPont decided to supplement their production of viscose rayon with additional production of acetate.

The Eastman Kodak Company of Rochester, N.Y., in conjunction with Tennessee Eastman Company and the A. M. Tenney Associates of New York City, began to make acetate. The product was known as Estron.

**1926:** First industry-compiled data available for the rayon industry.

First raw-silk classification and standard methods of testing provided by the Silk Association of America.

## HIGH TENACITY YARNS IMPROVED

**1927:** First acetate rayon and rayon crepes made in Europe.

The plastic resins, Alkyd and Aniline Formaldehyde, made their appearance.

Vinyl resins produced on a commercial basis by Carbide and Carbon Chemicals Corporation, Buffalo, N.Y.

Moistureproof cellophane was introduced by two DuPont chemists, Dr. Hale Church and Dr. Karl Krindle. DuPont was now making 90% of the world output.

American Viscose Corporation announced the invention of the double-godet by Frank H. Griffin. With this invention began the improvement of high-tenacity viscose yarns.

## BEGINNINGS OF NYLON

**1928:** DuPont began fundamental research in the "how and why of molecules." Efforts were being made to determine how these building blocks of nature unite to form giant molecules such as those found in cotton, silk, and rubber. This research gradually developed what is now nylon.

Rayon staple fiber made its debut in the textile industry.

Design Registration Bureau established.

Employment wages in the rayon industry show increase of 38% since 1925.

Delustered rayon of American Viscose Corporation, *Dulesco*, appeared on the market. Delustered rayon was used in hosiery.

By this time Japan was on its way to world leadership in rayon production.

## U.S. WORLD RAYON PRODUCER

**1929:** Second International Technical Raw Silk Conference was held in New York. It consisted of 21 sessions and 85 papers were read in English and Japanese.

American Viscose Company produced 54 million pounds of rayon in 1928 to become America's leading producer.

Soviet Russia began building two rayon plants, with Germany supplying equipment.

Rayon linings were meeting with favor in men's suits since they were now made perspiration-proof, resistant to moths, and had desirable smoothness.

America became world leader in production and consumption of rayon, producing almost 100% more than the next rayon producer.

With the stock market crash in October of this year, it can be stated that the age of the flapper passed into oblivion. The textile and apparel failures were many during the hectic months which were to follow.

Process for imparting crease-resistance to linens, cottons, rayons, and acetates patented by Tootal Broadhurst Lee Co. Ltd.

## HIGH-SPEED LOOM INVENTED

**1930:** Color Coordination Committee established here.

DuPont chemists created a new synthetic substance from which crude filaments could be drawn.

Great strides made in the Arizona cotton belt for improvement of the staple. Sakellarides, the well-known Egyptian cotton, was crossed with the prominent Pima staples of this country. The resultant cotton, known as SXP, gave greater yield per acre than Pima.

Rapidogen colors, synthesized from stabilized diazomines, were announced.

The Circuit Court of Appeals ruled that the term "satin" is the name of a weave construction; thus, rayon satins could now be legally advertised as such.

Mixtures of cotton and rayon proved successful in the rainwear field.

The first Draper high-speed loom invented; loom speed increased by 20%.

## GLASS FIBERS DEVELOPED

**1931:** Silk Association of America saved industry one million dollars by securing a three-dollars-per-100-pounds reduction on transcontinental freight rates. Also helped manufacturers to set up the first standard system for the numbering of spun-rayon yarns.

Design Protection Association formed in New York.

Cluett, Peabody & Co. set up licensing agreement whereby manufacturers of cotton textiles could benefit from the Sanforized Compressive Shrinkage process.

Owens-Illinois Glass Company and Corning Glass Works commenced research and experimentation in glass filaments. The glass marble used in making Fiberglas, five-eighths of an inch in diameter, can be drawn out to a length of 102 miles in filament form. The Fiberglas filament was perfected to the point where it would bend like rubber, could be tied into a knot and woven into a fabric.

Lastex appeared on the market. Made in woven and knitted yarns, it finds much use in horizontal, vertical, and two-way stretch fabrics, chiefly in the foundation garment trade.

## DEPRESSION IN SILK

**1932:** Cellulose Acetate Butyrate, a plastic resin, appeared.

At the bottom of the depression, and with U.S. Steel selling for $26 a share, silk dropped to $153 a bale on the Yokohama Exchange. Japan's farming population constituted about 40% of the people, or 2 million households, all engaged in the cultivation of very small farms devoted almost exclusively to sericulture.

## VISCOSE RAYON 50 CENTS A POUND

**1933:** In November the American Association of Textile Technologists organized. J. J. Reutlinger was made chairman and soon after became the first president.

New York City since 1929 had lost 1,100 dress houses; there were 2,300 in 1929, in 1933 there were only 1,200. Contract shops showed a decline of 80% in the same period.

Viscose rayon was selling for around 50 cents a pound.

## NYLON READY TO EMERGE

**1934:** DuPont chemists perfected synthetic polymers of great strength and elasticity—a step toward nylon.

The Silk Association of America was reorganized to cope with changing conditions and became the National Federation of Textiles.

Tire yarn was first produced on a commercial basis in the Richmond plant of DuPont.

**1935:** Cotton production in this country reached approximately 9 billion pounds, about 18 million bales.

DuPont research brought about a superpolymer of the polyamide type in synthesized form. The superpolymer was called "66" because of the molecular structure. The first "6" indicated the number of carbon atoms in the diamine; the second indicated the number of carbon atoms in the dibasic acid of which the new substance was composed.

Acetate staple was now being produced in this country.

## RAYON PRODUCTION IS 300 MILLION POUNDS IN THE MID 1930'S

**1936:** The famous Rust brothers, Memphis, Tennessee, invented the mechanical cotton picker, the best type to date.

Methyl Methacrylate and Vinyl made their appearance.

Demise of the NRA. National Federation of Textiles returned to the field of general industrial cooperation.

Three hundred million pounds of rayon were produced in this country in 1936, a truly sensational rise from the 6 million pounds made in 1930.

## NYLON STOCKINGS APPEAR

**1937:** Ethyl Cellulose and Lignin, plastic resins, came onto the market. Polystyrene and Vinyl Butyral also made their debut.

DuPont brought out experimental toothbrushes with bristling filaments made of polyamide. These bristles were known as Exton, and were more durable than the usual pig bristles.

Experimental stockings were knitted from the new chemically-produced material developed by DuPont, named Nylon. Dr. W. H. Carothers received patents.

NFT obtained the cooperation of the cotton textile industry in acceptance of one minimum wage for all cotton, rayon, and silk mills. These groups discussed the possibilities of forming a National Council for the Textile Industries.

The New York dress trade was now showing a volume of about $400 million a year; the all-time high was $750 million in 1929.

The Draper Corporation brought out the first pick tension shuttle eye which laid the first pick with the same tension as the other picks in the cloth.

Announcement by DuPont of its Cordura HST viscose rayon for tire cord fabric.

Cuprammonium staple now on the market.

A new continuous process for the manufacture of rayon was developed by Industrial Rayon Corporation, Cleveland, Ohio, and housed in a 12-million-dollar plant.

**1938:** In October, nylon was formally announced to the public.

Owens-Corning Fiberglas Corporation began production of Fiberglas.

## BIG ADVANCES IN SYNTHETICS

**1939:** Vinyon, made from vinyl, was introduced into the commercial field of synthetic filaments. The original patents on vinyl resin were assigned to Union Carbide and Carbon Company, New York. The resin serves as the base for making Vinyon, a product of the American Viscose Company, Marcus Hook, Pa.

Large scale plants to make nylon polymer and yarn on a vast commercial basis were begun in Seaford, Del. One plant was in operation in less than five years after the original invention of the now famous "66" polymer.

Women's nylon stockings displayed at the San Francisco World's Fair.

Asbeston (blend of cotton and asbestos) patented by United States Rubber Co.

Japan led the world in production of raw silk, which constituted 37% of its foreign trade. It supplied the world with 60% of its raw silk goods and the United States took better than 85% of Japanese silk exports.

This country produced 325 millions of pounds of rayon yarn; Japan was in second place with an annual output of 240 million pounds; Germany was third with 155 million pounds; Great Britain and Italy, 120 million pounds each; France, 55 million pounds. Germany and Japan had worked hand in glove in the field of synthetics; textile engineers, technicians, and technologists were exchanged, money was furnished, and factories were built along modern lines.

The old "Truth-in-Fabrics" project of Senator Capper, Kansas, fostered by him since 1923, now blossomed forth with the passage of the Wool Labeling Act of 1939, to protect manufacturer and consumer.

Perlon, the German synthetic fiber that is the counterpart of DuPont's nylon, discovered and invented by Dr. Schlack.

## RAYON PRODUCTION NOW 1,237 MILLION POUNDS

**1940:** Alginate, the fiber produced from seaweed, made its appearance in England.

Dow Chemical Company, Midland, Mich., began commercial production of Saran.

DuPont began to build its second large plant in Seaford, Del., in January. This plant more than doubled nylon production.

Nylon placed on public sale throughout the country on May 15th.

Rayon production reached 1,237 million pounds; in 1930 it was 6 million and in 1936, 300 million. In four years rayon had quadrupled in production, a sensational rise.

The Garment Center in New York provided about 36 weeks of work a year with wages totaling only $1,200 for the inside worker and about $900 for the contract worker.

Carbide and Carbon Chemicals Corporation developed a commercially feasible process for the synthesis of glyoxal; this is 84 years after glyoxal was first synthesized by H. Debus.

The first rayon rugs were made by American Viscose Corp. Tufton is the name given to this viscose carpet-type yarn.

### Nylon Production 20 Million Pounds

**1941:** In November, the Martinsville, Va., plant of DuPont was in full operation, doubling the production of nylon. Twenty million pounds were produced in 1942. This was seven times the production originally planned.

Fortisan appeared on the market under auspices of Celanese Corporation of America.

Founding of the New York Dress Institute, a great clearing house for the apparel trade.

On August 27th, the Government took over all silk stocks in this country.

**1942-1945:** During the war years, NFT served as clearing house for Government procurement agencies in placing contracts for silk and nylon parachute cloths and other products. The Federation did valiant work in expediting manufacture and delivery of vitally needed materials.

### Aluminum Yarn Introduced

**1943:** Silicones came on the market.

Elastic type Vinyon entered the textile field; it is a product of American Viscose Company.

Reynolds Metal Company introduced aluminum yarn.

### Fiber from Peanuts

**1944:** In October, AATCC awarded the first Olney Medal for Distinguished Service to Dr. Louis A. Olney. The medal gives public recognition of outstanding achievement and contributions in the field of textile chemistry.

Polyfiber (polystyrene fiber) introduced to the textile market by Dow Chemical Company.

DuPont and Carbide and Carbon Chemicals Corporation announced Polyethylene.

Ardil, the peanut protein fiber, was announced by Imperial Chemical Industries, Ltd., London, England.

High-heat-resistant thermoplastics such as styrene copolymers commercially produced.

Apparel trade in New York City reached annual production of 1¼ billion dollars.

Founding of the Fashion Institute, New York City. This junior college, the first of its type in the nation, is sponsored by the Board of Education, New York City, State Department of Education, Albany, N.Y., and the Education Foundation for the Apparel Industry, New York City.

**1945:** Filament of stainless steel announced.

Leslie & Co. founded; the original company was Baldwin & Leslie, established in 1906.

### Cotton Prices Fall

**1946:** In February, the price of cotton exceeded that of viscose rayon staple; the first time that a man-made fiber actually undersold cotton.

In early October, cotton tumbled 50 dollars a bale after a meteoric rise in price. This threw the market awry and caused the Cotton Exchange to close three times in a single two-week period. From the 15th to the 17th of October, cotton fell 10 dollars in price each of these three days.

Thomas Jordan, an operator in the New Orleans market, admitted that it was the liquidation of his holdings that forced the closing of the New Orleans and New York Cotton Exchanges. Said to be the greatest cotton operator in the world at the time, he was caught with 140,000 bales long and is supposed to have lost $5 million in the deals.

New York City was now producing close to 80% of the outerwear apparel in this

country, valued at almost $2 billion. Two hundred million dresses and 100 million skirts, slacks, blouses, and jackets were made in this year; a 60% gain over 1944.

Carbide and Carbon Chemicals Corporation built a new plant for the production of glyoxal; demand had been created by the development of Sanforset process for the dimensional stability of rayon. Fabrics of viscose rayon are made permanently resistant to shrinkage through treatment with glyoxal.

### 398,000 Looms in U.S.

**1947:** The New Orleans Cotton Exchange released a three-point program for the Chicago, New York, and New Orleans Exchanges to govern the trading rules with a view to prevent price upheavals in the market. The program dealt with credits to trade accounts, margins for speculative accounts, and an agency to supervise the activities of Exchange members.

Masslinn, a non-woven fabric made from a blend of cotton and rayon fibers by a method that completely eliminates spinning and weaving, announced to the trade.

In March, there were 398,000 looms in place in this country. Loom operation amounted to 486 million hours. A total of 950 million pounds of yarn was consumed in the manufacture of cotton broad woven goods and tire fabric; 877 million pounds were cotton, 61 million pounds rayon, and 12 million pounds other yarns.

Sarelon, a new protein fiber, announced to the textile industry. As far as is known, the Southern Region Laboratory of the Department of Agriculture was the first laboratory in this country to produce fibers from peanuts.

Vinyon N, basically different from other vinyl materials, and produced from a white, powdery resin which results from the copolymerization of vinyl chloride and acrylonitrile, was announced by Union Carbide and Carbon Corporation, Buffalo, N.Y.

The House of Commons passed, 179 to 72, the Government-sponsored bill to continue the buying of raw cotton by a state commission which replaced the privately operated Liverpool Cotton Exchange during the late war. The Government commission's authority is now absolute for buying raw cotton for Britain's huge cotton spinning and weaving industry.

## Japan Back in Textile Business

In June, Japan shipped its first grey goods to England since the close of World War II. One-half of the order for 64 million yards was delivered. Australia took 12 million yards of Japanese cotton grey goods.

Curbs on textiles in Germany eased; U.S. cotton producers agreed to allow mills to sell finished goods where they wish.

Private international trade with Japan was resumed on August 15th, 1947.

President Truman lifted cotton ban and allowed importation or withdrawal from warehouse of an additional 23 million pounds of long-staple cotton during the quota year ending September, 1947.

Pacific Mills announced Pacifix, a process for making wool fabrics washable; it was designed to fix the size of the finished garment by holding shrinkage to a minimum. Shirts of Pacifixed fabrics show less than 2% shrinkage.

Professors Robert B. Woodward and C. H. Schramm of Harvard University rivaled feat of nature in making a substance like protein. Their achievement opened up an entirely new field of plastics—with this technique it was possible to make fur, silk, or wool that would be all but identical to the natural product.

Plastavon, a non-woven fabric made from cotton taken raw from the bale, bleached, dyed or tinted, as desired, and bonded with synthetic resins, which in effect spot-weld the cotton fibers into a uniform sheet, was produced by Avondale Mills, Sylacauga, Ala. It was used in "throw-away napkins."

This year's cotton acreage was 18% higher than in 1946 but yield was about 2 million bales under spring-estimated needs. This was offset, however, by carry-over of 3 million bales. July futures were highest in 27 years, 39.49¢.

The 80th Congress passed the bill which directed the Commodity Credit Corporation to continue price support for domestic wool in keeping with the 1946 support price until December 31, 1948.

Japan began to rebuild its woolen industry; mills to handle 665,000 bales of wool annually and to buy U.S. and Australian wool clips.

Wool production in the United States dropped 40% since 1942. Cause was said to be continued liquidation of the American wool-growing industry under pressure of lower-cost imports.

## Non-Crush Cottons Launched

Dan River Mills began production of several cotton fabrics treated with a new and exclusive chemical process to render them as wrinkle-resistant as woolens or worsteds. The basis of the process was Resloom C, a synthetic resin produced by Monsanto Chemical Co.

The silk of Japan was transferred to the Government by the Supreme Allied Headquarters by direction of General Douglas MacArthur. Japanese silk had been frozen since September, 1945.

Japan had about 100,000 bales of raw silk and about 100 million yards of silk fabrics on hand. The Allied Command supervised distribution in the interest of the nation's economy. Raw silk production in Japan rose from 2,000 bales in January, 1946, to about 10,000 bales monthly during the first half of 1947. Fabric production increased to about 4 million yards monthly from a production of about 2 million yards a month in 1946.

Report of the British cotton industry found Britain still the largest cotton-exporting nation in the world. Cotton trade was about 55% of the 1937 production level, but further comeback was impeded by a severe labor shortage, antiquated equipment and restrictive trade practices.

## Acrilan Appears

Chemstrand Corporation formed to handle sales of nylon and the new acrylic fiber, Acrilan.

High-speed section beam warper developed by Fontana-Lagano, Italy, proved practical.

Shuttleless loom developed by Leontyev of the Moscow Textile Institute; somewhat similar to the shuttleless weaving machine produced by Sulzer of Winterthur.

## Textiles Second Largest Industry

**1948:** Domestic production of rayon for 1947 exceeded 975 million pounds, and represented about 48% of world production.

Textiles became the second largest industry in America: 750,000 electric motors located in 6,203 establishments, employing about 1¼ million people, and paying 1⅓ billions in salaries and wages per annum.

Statistics for the apparel industry revealed there were over one million workers whose earnings totaled 1⅔ billion dollars per year. These workers produced about 9 billion dollars' worth of clothing. New York State produced more than one-half the apparel for the nation, employed more than 40% of the workers, and paid about one-half of the total salaries and wages.

Joseph Bancroft and Sons, Wilmington, Del., announced production of Everglaze on spun rayon, and on blends of cotton and rayon.

For 1947, average consumer consumption of cotton was 27 pounds; rayon, 6.3 pounds; wool, 4.9 pounds.

## Saran and Estron Adopted

The descriptive name Saran was announced by the Dow Chemical Co. The term Saran applies to a series of thermoplastic resins chemically known as vinylidene chloride copolymers, originally developed by Dow in the late thirties.

Tennessee Eastman Corporation adopted the word Estron to identify its cellulose ester textile yarns and staple.

Mandatory labeling of rayon suitings was being sought by the manufacturers of wool fabrics and garments. The claim was made that consumers often confuse the advertising of rayon suitings which use the term "worsted types." Under the Wool Labeling Act of 1939, labels on woolens must specify actual wool con-

*1959–70: In this period man-made fibers surpass natural fibers in U.S. consumption for the first time in history, and technology dominates textile developments. These developments include permanent-press, bonding, soil-release, textured fibers and third-generation fibers. This era also sees the developments of blends and ease-of-care fabrics.*

tent and type, while the rayon manufacturers mark their products only in compliance with fair trade practice rules of the Federal Trade Commission.

Wool boards in South Africa, Australia, and New Zealand, the International Wool Secretariat, and the American Wool Council merged to form The Wool Bureau, Inc., aimed at fostering the wool industry.

## BOOM IN AUTO TEXTILES

General Motors divisions contemplated using more than 10 million linear yards of interior upholstery fabric and approximately 1½ million yards of top material and interior linings for convertibles. Ford Motor Co. to use about 40 million dollars' worth of textile materials.

DuPont Orlon, previously called Fiber A, was now in pilot-plant production.

**1949:** January opened with the Industrial Rayon Corporation's announcement of its continuous process for viscose spinning.

## DYNEL ANNOUNCED

Dynel announced a new name for an acrylonotrilevinyl chloride staple, a product of Union Carbide and Carbon Chemical Corporation.

**1950:** Courtaulds began the commercial production of cellulose triacetate fiber which resulted in a triacetate fiber trade-marked "Courpleta" in 1954.

Du Pont announced the first commercial production of "Orlon" acrylic fiber, originally a "wool substitute."

**1951:** Du Pont announced that it would build a plant in Kinston, N.C., to manufacture Dacron polyester.

The chairman of Courtaulds stated in

London that the newer man-made fibers presented no serious threat to acetate and viscose rayon.

Acrilan, a new acrylic fiber, was announced by Chemstrand Corporation.

**1952:** The sale of Perlon in the United States was licensed by Du Pont, in agreement with seven producers of the fiber in West Germany.

The new J. P. Stevens building opened at 41st Street and Broadway, New York City.

Senator Lister Hill, Alabama Democrat, presented a bill whereby informative labeling would be applied to cotton fabrics; fiber content and materials must be disclosed in percentage terms on labels attached to the fabric or article.

## DACRON LAUNCHED

**1953:** Du Pont produced first commercially successful polyester in the United States, Dacron. Polyester proved to be the fastest-growing man-made fiber of the post-war era, bringing about a revolution in blends, permanent-press and wrinkle-free doubleknits.

From 1947 to 1953 there was a 22 per cent textile employment decline in the New England states, with North Carolina showing the largest textile employment gain in the south.

## ARNEL INTRODUCED

**1954:** Celanese Corporation of America announced commercial production of the first American triacetate fiber, Arnel.

Because of the rise of other man-made fibers, American Viscose ceased manufacture of rayon in its Marcus Hook, Pa., plant which had produced rayon since 1910.

**1955:** Nylon, Perlon, Rhovil and other non-cellulosic man-made fibers continued

to be classified as rayon by the customs bureau.

Exports of cotton textiles from Japan in the month of May were second highest since World War II.

**1956:** J. P. Stevens acquired all the textile properties of the Simmons Company, the leading U.S. manufacturer of sleeping equipment.

Eastman Chemical Products announced Verel, a modified acrylic fiber (modacrylic) with high tensile strength, stretching properties and fire-resistance.

American Cyanamid acquired the Formica Company, one of the leading plastic laminate manufacturers. It also announced its new acrylic textile fiber, Creslan, after nearly a decade of research and development.

One person in 7 in the United States received his wages from work performed in the textile and apparel industries.

Burlington Industries announced a new wash-and-wear shirting made with Taslan, the textured Dacron polyester fiber developed by Du Pont.

Tufted carpets accounted for 46 per cent of all carpet sales in the United States in 1956, a 900 per cent increase since 1951.

Wash-and-wear apparel increased its total sales 633 per cent from 1952 to 1956 ($45 million to $285 million).

## POLYPROPYLENE DEVELOPED

**1957:** A new man-made fiber polypropylene, was developed in Italy by the country's largest chemical producer, Montecatini, under the aegis of Professor Giulio Natta.

The directors of Courtaulds and British Celanese announced merger plans, Courtaulds acquiring British Celanese in the largest industrial merger in Great Britain in many years.

Since 1940 it has been estimated that 5-million people have left the cotton farms of Alabama, Georgia, North Carolina and South Carolina to obtain work in industry, 4-million having migrated to the north.

A seamless stocking for women is knitted in about 15 minutes, composed of about 925 thousand stitches.

The "sack" look for women, which created considerable furor in apparel circles, has been sacked.

## ZEFRAN INTRODUCED

**1958:** Dow Chemical Company announced commercial production of Zefran "acrylic alloy."

Allied Chemical & Dye Corporation changed its name to The Allied Chemical Corporation.

Eastman Chemical announced production of Kodel polyester fiber.

U.S. Rubber Company announced new experimental fiber, Vyrene, undergoing market evaluation.

A new law required that fabrics and apparel be labeled with fiber names by weight.

## FASHION INSTITUTE OPENED

**1959:** The Fashion Institute of Technology opened its new $13-million building at 227 West 27th Street, New York. Du Pont announced plans to produce its elastic textile fiber "Lycra."

Vycron is the name of a new polyester fiber announced by Beaunit Mills, coming in filament, staple, tow and direct spun yarn.

Zantrel, a high-wet modulus cellulosic fiber, announced by Hartford Fibres, a division of Bigelow-Sanford.

**1960:** American Viscose announced a new type of cellulosic fiber, Avlin, which has a triangular rather than a conventional round cross-section.

Fiber Industries announced the new name, Fortrel, to replace Teron polyester fiber. Fiber Industries is a joint venture of Celanese Corporation of America and Imperial Chemical Industries, Great Britain.

Joseph Bancroft announced a new Ban-Lon warp knit fabric of permanently crimped Textralized yarn.

**1961:** Beaunit Corporation acquired Du Pont rayon technical data.

The Celanese Camille Dreyfus Laboratories dedicated in Research Triangle Park, N.C.

## DU PONT WITHDRAWS FROM RAYON

**1962:** Du Pont announced its withdrawal from rayon production, which it had been making since 1921.

Du Pont also announced development of its poromeric material, Corfam, and launched "Antron" nylon, a tri-lobal fiber and "Orlon Sayelle," a self-crimped acrylic fiber.

American Enka bought Hartford Fibers, together with the trademark Zantrel.

"Herculon" announced as name for olefin fiber produced by Hercules Powder Company.

## FMC BUYS AMERICAN VISCOSE

**1963:** FMC Corporation bought the operating assets of American Viscose Corporation for $116-million cash.

Courtaulds North America announced "Teklan," a flame-resistant modacrylic, and "Sarille," a producer-crimped rayon staple.

Du Pont announced "Nomex" as the trademark for its high-temperature-resistant nylon; also "Cantrece" as the trademark for its textured hosiery yarn.

**1964:** American Enka announced "Crepeset" as the name of its crimped monofilament nylon, especially designed for use in tricot fabrics.

First parmanent-press garments commercially marketed; popularly received.

## DU PONT LAUNCHES REEMAY

**1965:** Du Pont announced first commercial applications for its "Reemay" spun-bonded polyester fabric.

Courtaulds announced "Celon," a nylon 6 fiber.

**1966:** Deering Milliken announced "Visa" cloth with soil-release properties plus permanent-press performance.

American Enka named its new polyester fiber "Encron." Another new Enka name was "Enkasheer," for a new stretch nylon used in women's hosiery.

## CELANESE INTRODUCES CELABOND

**1967:** "Celabond" trademark introduced by Celanese to identify bonded fabrics which meet fixed performance standards.

Avisun Corporation purchased by Standard Oil (Indiana).

Phillips Fibers announced Marvess olefin fiber, Phillips 66 nylon and Quintess polyester.

Hystron Fibers registered the name "Trevira" for its polyester fiber.

## QIANA LAUNCHED

**1968:** "Qiana" nylon unveiled by Du Pont. It offers the aesthetics of silk combined with the performance of nylon.

"Nomelle" introduced as certification mark for Du Pont's "soft" acrylic fiber.

"Source," new bi-constitutent fiber from Allied Chemical, launched. It is a union of nylon and polyester.

"Frontera" introduced by Tenneco Chemicals. This is a new polymer development which can be formed to resemble anything from suede to tiles.

## MAN-MADE TOPPED NATURAL FIBERS

For the first-time in history, man-made fiber consumption (5-billion pounds) surpassed natural fiber consumption (4.6-billion pounds) in the United States, polyester growth being the key factor in this development.

**1969:** Collins & Aikman developed the first non-static nylon tricot fabric.

American Cyanamid agreed in principle to acquire IRC Fibers Division, a main producer of polyester tire cord.

Rohm and Haas launched a new anidex stretch fiber called Anim/8.

# Inventors and Their Inventions

*Out of the fertility of a handful of great inventive minds has germinated much of the rich diversity of textile technology of today. These men were the forerunners of such moderns as Carothers, Camille Dreyfuss and Whinfield.*

**ARKWRIGHT, SIR RICHARD:** Invented, in 1769, the spinning frame which did its drawing by the use of rollers on the frame. Incidentally, horses were used to supply the power to turn the machines. His partners were the noted Jedediah Strutt and Samuel Weed. In 1771 he built the first great cotton mill in England, which was the first to employ children. He was awarded a second set of patents for his further inventions for carding, drawing, and spinning frames.

**ARNOLD, ASA:** This American invented the compound-gear device, which combined a train of three bevel gears in order to regulate the variable velocity needed for winding cotton fibers in slubbing form onto the bobbin of a roving frame to be made into roving, one step removed from being completed spun yarn. While this gear arrangement was in use in 1822, it was not until 1823 that the patent was granted. The device is now called the differential-motion.

**BALDWIN, MATHIAS:** Brought out the first engraved metallic rollers for calico printing, in Philadelphia (1825).

**BANKS, NATHANIEL:** See ELIAS HOWE.

**BARLOW, ALFRED:** Inventor of the double-jacquard loom (1849).

**BARTLETT, WILLIAM:** See SNELL.

**BATCHELDER, SAMUEL:** Invented the stop motion on drawing frames in 1832.

**BELLOUGH, J.:** Devised, in 1842, the separate cylinder motion for use on a jacquard loom. It was operated from the crank shaft of the loom.

**BENVOISE, ANTHONY:** This Italian inventor introduced the distaff into England (1529) shortly after he perfected it in Italy.

**BEVAN:** See CROSS.

Richard Arkwright

**BISSEL, ———— :** This American inventor brought out a roller gin for ginning of cotton, in 1788.

**BLOOD, EDMUND:** Received patent rights for the carding and spinning of waste silk from his findings in research and discovery; done in England in 1671.

**BOURN, DANIEL:** This Englishman patented a carding machine in Leominster, England, in 1748. Bourn's carder, it is believed, was inspired by the necessity of feeding Lewis Paul's spinning machine, invented in 1737. Bourn and Paul were friends.

**BREWSTER, GILBERT:** In 1828, he invented a roving frame in Poughkeepsie, N.Y. Provided temporary twist to the roving fibers during their passage from rolls to spools by passing the stock between two leather bands, or belts, moving in opposite directions. Was obsolete, however, by 1835 when the Equation Box replaced it.

**BRONNERT, DR. E.:** From his discoveries he invented, in 1900, the methods necessary to make cuprammonium rayon.

**BRUNEL, M. I.:** Invented the circular knitting machine in France in 1816.

**CARROLL, W. T.:** American inventor of the double-flange ring for use in ring spinning, a Draper Corporation patent (1869).

**CARTWRIGHT, EDMUND:** This Englishman invented, in 1774, the power loom and the comber frame for combing fibers. In 1785, he received his second set of patents for his further inventions on the power loom. At this time he brought out the warp-stop motions on a loom.

**CHARDONNET, COUNT HILAIRE DE:** This great French benefactor to mankind used the extract of mulberry leaves to make what was called artificial silk, forerunner of rayon of today. Cloth made from his yarn was shown at the Paris Exposition in 1889.

His process of manufacture is known as the nitro-cellulose method.

**COOPER, GEORGE, AND TIFFANY, ELI:** New York City inventors who made possible, in 1858, an improved spring needle and presser bar arrangement for knitting of ribbed-effect fabric.

**CREIGHTON, ———— :** English inventor who devised a cotton opener machine with lap attachment (1814).

**CROMPTON, SAMUEL:** Invented in 1779 the mule spinning frame by combining the ideas taken from Hargreaves's jenny and Arkwright's spinning frame —drawing by means of a carriage and rollers, respectively. Since his machine combined these actions in the one frame, he called the machine a mule, a name which remains to this day since the mule is a hybrid and so is his spinning frame in its action, the so-called "hybrid action."

**CROSS, C. F., AND BEVAN, E. J.:** English discoverers of the viscose method of making rayon. Arthur Little, in the United States, also produced viscose rayon in the same year (1895). Little at the time did not know that Cross and Bevan were working on a project similar to his own, nor did they know of his work.

**DANFORTH, GEORGE:** This American inventor brought out the Taunton Speeder in Taunton, Mass., in 1824. It was designed for cotton manufacture. In 1826, Dyer, an inventor in England, took out patents for Danforth's speeder with the result that the Taunton Speeder replaced the fly frame in England to con-

Samuel Crompton

siderable degree. In 1828, Danforth invented the cap spinning frame.

**DAVENPORT, JAMES:** This American mechanic received the first patent of any type for textile machinery in the United States (1794). He invented new methods for carding and spinning in Philadelphia, Pa.

**DONISTHORPE, GEORGE E. AND LISTER, SAMUEL CUNLIFFE:** British inventors who brought out an improved nipcomber in 1851. Lister, afterwards Lord Masham, improved the comber and it still carries his name to the present time.

**DRAPER, GEORGE:** American inventor, in 1863, of the frog-with-loose-steel device which was first made as an attachment for the Mason looms and later applied to other looms made in the United States. In 1867, a spindle patent was issued to him by the United States Patent office. By 1887, he had rights on twelve named-variations of spindles.

**DRAPER, IRA:** Founded, in 1816, the Draper Corporation, Hopedale, Mass. He invented the loom temple and an improved type of fly-shuttle hand loom. In 1818 he brought out his self-moving temple for use on a loom. In 1829, Draper made further improvements on loom temples.

**DREBBEL, C. VAN:** This Dutch chemist discovered in 1630 a new scarlet dyestuff for use on wool. Cochineal and tin were used to produce this particular shade, which was used by the Gobelin Dye Works in France in dyeing yarns for tapestries.

**DUTCHER, W. W.:** American who invented the first parallel underpick shuttle motion for a loom (1846).

**DYER:** See DANFORTH.

**FERRETTI, ANTONIO:** In 1904, this Italian scientist made possible commercial Lanital, the first protein textile fiber. Now made only in Belgium.

**HARGREAVES, JAMES:** Invented the spinning jenny in 1764. It was said to be named in honor of his wife. This machine or frame performed its drawing by means of the carriage.

**HEATHCOAT, JOHN:** This English inventor brought out the bobbinet lace-frame in 1809.

**HEILMANN, JOSUÉ:** French inventor of the single nip comber frame in 1830. He conceived the idea from watching his daughters comb out their hair. Still called the Heilmann comber.

**HOFFMAN, ADON, J.:** American inventor, in 1905, of the pressing machine, which revolutionized the garment industries throughout the world.

Dr. Edmund Cartwright

**HOLDEN, ISAAC:** Discovered how to bleach linen by the use of kelp or seaweed. An Irishman, he perfected his work in Dundee, Scotland, in 1727.

**HOLT, PETER F.:** Invented machinery for preparing sewing cotton, in 1818.

**HOOKE, DR. ROBERT:** This English naturalist and scientist in his book, "Micrographia," discussed the possibilities of making an artificial yarn by mechanical means—the forerunner of man-made and synthetic fibers in use today (1664).

**HOPE:** See RAMSBOTTOM.

**HORROCKS, WILLIAM:** In Stockport, England, he received patents for power looms. In 1805 and 1813, he improved his inventions and brought out what was known as the Crank or Scotch loom.

**HOULDSWORTH, HENRY, JR.:** In 1825, this Englishman in some manner appropriated a model of the compound-gear motion of Asa Arnold of America. He took out a patent in England and called the device the English Equation Box, known as "The Bag of Tricks."

**HOWE, ELIAS AND BANKS, NATHANIEL:** These American inventors, brothers-in-law, made a sewing machine which incorporated the curved eye-needle and the underthread shuttle. The machine was perfected to run 250 stitches a minute, five times greater than the speed of a swift hand sewer.

**HUNT, WALTER:** In his little shop in New York City, this Quaker made a machine that would "sew, stitch, and seam cloth." It incorporated two ideas —an eye-pointed needle and lockstitching (1832).

**JACQUARD, JOSEPH M.:** After about ten years of intensive work and research, this great Frenchman invented the loom that carries his name, one which makes it possible to control each and every warp end so that any end can be raised or lowered at will to form an intricate motif or design. He was a friend of Napoleon, who decreed that Jacquard be given a pension for life. His machine was first shown at the Paris Exposition in 1801.

**JOHNSON:** See RADCLIFFE.

**JOHNSON:** See REID.

**JURGEN, JOHANN:** A woodcarver of Brunswick, Germany, he invented (1533) the so-called bobbing-wheel, commonly known as the Saxony Wheel. This was a regulation spinning wheel with a cranked axis on the large wheel, and there was an added treadle by which the spinner could rotate the spindle with one foot. Jurgen conceived his idea for the wheel from sketches of Leonardo da Vinci, made about sixty years before his time.

**KAY, JOHN:** English inventor of the fly shuttle for use on a loom (1733).

**KAY, ROBERT:** The son of John Kay. He invented the dropbox loom in 1760.

**KENDREW, JOHN AND PORTHOUSE, THOMAS:** In 1787, they obtained patents on a machine to spin yarn from hemp, tow, flax, or wool. Perfected their inventions in Darlington, England.

**KIRK, TIMOTHY AND LESLIE, ROBERT:** American inventors who obtained in 1792 the first patents for a power loom in the United States.

**LAMB, Q. U.:** American who invented in 1863 the first flat-bed knitting frame for knitting wide fabric. Invented device, in 1864, for shaping hosiery at the time of manufacture; the heel and the toe could now be made on specially constructed machines.

**LEAVERS, JOHN:** English inventor who perfected, in 1813, a machine that could make practically any type of lace.

**LEE, JOHN:** Invented the feeding device for carding frames, in England, in 1772.

**LEE, WILLIAM:** This English minister invented the knitting frame in 1589. Until 1598 the frame could knit only woolen yarn; in 1598 he perfected a frame that could knit silk stockings.

**LEIGH, EVAN:** English inventor of revolving, self-stripping flats on cotton cards (1857).

**LEITENBERGER, JOSEF:** German inventor of a really workable block printing machine (1790).

**LESLIE:** See KIRK.

John Kay

**LIBBY, EDWARD D.:** American who succeeded, in 1893, in drawing, from heated ends of glass rod, filaments of very fine size and texture; forerunner of glass fibers of today.

**LITTLE, ARTHUR:** See CROSS.

**LISTER:** See DONISTHORPE.

**LOMBE, JOHN:** The first Englishman who learned how to manufacture silk filament into yarn after spending some time on the Continent. The first throwing plant was built by him at Derby on the Derwent River (1718).

**METCALF, J. A.:** American who made the first practical self-threading shuttle, a Draper Corporation patent (1868).

**MOODY, PAUL:** Conceived the idea of using belts for transmission purposes for power from the engine to the shafting on the several floors of a mill (1826).

**MOULDEN:** See TOWNSEND.

**MILLER, ROBERT:** A Glasgow inventor who brought out, in 1799, an improved type of power loom which met with much success.

**NOBLE, JAMES:** English inventor of the circular comber machine still used today (1853).

**NORTHROP, JAMES:** This expert English mechanic in the employ of Draper Corporation, Hopedale, Mass., perfected a loom that was, at the time, considered to be the "last word" in looms. Known as the Northrop Loom, it is said to be the first commercial loom to supply filling automatically, and to include a warp stop-motion for general weaving purposes. In 1895, he developed the first automatic bobbin-changing loom in the world. The original is in the Smithsonian Institution, Washington, D.C.

**PAUL, LEWIS:** See JOHN WYATT.

**PEEL, SIR ROBERT:** This British peer perfected in 1802 a resist method, for use in printing textile fabrics.

**PORTHOUSE, THOMAS:** See JOHN KENDREW.

**POUSSET, FRANCIS:** He received patent rights in 1693 for his efforts in England for the weaving of silk crepe fabric. Pousset was an experienced Huguenot weaver who came to England about 1685.

**RABBETH, F. J.:** American inventor of a spindle which made ring spinning of yarn practical by doubling the spinning speeds (1878).

**RADCLIFFE, WILLIAM; ROSS, ————; AND JOHNSON, THOMAS:** The first two inventors received patents for fabric takeup by the motion of the lathe, as well as new methods for dressing and warping warp yarns. For some reason these patents were taken out in the name of Johnson, an employee who received a bonus of fifty pounds for the part he played in the matter (1803).

**RAMSBOTTOM, JOHN AND WATSON, THOMAS:** Invented, in 1858, a feeler stop motion for filling yarn on a loom in England.

**REID, JOHN P. AND JOHNSON, THOMAS:** These two Englishmen developed a shuttle-changing loom (1834).

**RHOADES, A. E.:** Inventor of the Rhoades shuttle-changing loom (1888).

**ROBERTS, RICHARD:** English inventor who received patents for improvements on the self-acting mule frame (1825). Roberts also invented the quadrant on the mule spinning frame in 1830.

**ROSS:** See RADCLIFFE.

**RUST, JOHN AND MACK:** Brothers and native Texans, they invented the automatic cotton picking machine in 1936. This mechanical picker revolutionized the industry and increased production a great deal. It is estimated that four thousand previous attempts had been made to develop the mechanical cotton picker.

**SHARP, JOHN:** American inventor of the ring spinning frame in this country (1828).

Richard Roberts

**SINGER, ISAAC:** Invented his sewing machine in 1846 and this was the year in which these machines were used in factories.

**SMITH, JAMES:** A Scotsman who made revolving flats on carding frames workable for the first time. Prior efforts by other inventors were not practical (1834).

**SNELL, DANIEL W, AND BARTLETT, S. S.:** Americans who invented, in 1857, the let-off motions for looms, a patent of the Draper Corporation and a standard motion today.

**STEARN, C. H.:** This British inventor improved the method of making viscose rayon yarn in 1898.

**STRUTT, JEDEDIAH:** Patented his ribbed stocking frame in Derby, England, in 1758.

**SWAN, SIR JOSEPH:** English inventor and discoverer (1880) of the first artificial fiber known to mankind. His basic methods are still in use today in the manufacture of man-made filaments.

**THIMMONIER, BARTHELEMY:** This Frenchman was the first to receive recognition for a sewing machine in 1830. However, his machines were destroyed by workers who feared that the sewing machine would cause them to lose their jobs. His machine was of the chain-stitch type and he was interested in making uniforms for the armies of France on a mass production basis. Opposition, however, caused him to give up his plans.

**THORP, J.:** Invented improvements for his ring spinning frame which then became a powerful factor in the manufacture of cotton yarn in England (1828).

**TIFFANY:** See COOPER.

**TOWNSEND, MATTHEW AND MOULDEN, DAVID:** English inventors who made possible the latch needle knitting machine, in 1849.

**WATT, JAMES:** This renowned inventor received his first patents for the steam engine in 1769. In 1782 this Scotsman perfected his steam engine for practical mill purposes. In 1785 steam was first used as the source of power for textile machinery. In 1787 he suc-

cessfully used chlorine in a bleach field to bleach linen and cotton cloth.

**WEED, SAMUEL:** See SIR RICHARD ARKWRIGHT.

**WHEELER, NATHAN:** His sewing machine was introduced around Troy,

Samuel Cunliffe Lister

New York, in 1851, to serve the collar trade. This machine actually made mass production possible as we know it today.

**WHITNEY, ELI:** This great American invented the saw gin for ginning of cotton, 1794.

**WILLIAMSON:** Perfected stop motion device on ring spinning frames (1834).

**WILSON, STEPHEN:** This Englishman, a silk manufacturer, invented, in 1824, a reading machine and a punching apparatus for the cards which are used on a jacquard loom to control the pattern or design. Wilson also devised a new method for weaving velvets; it was the weaving of velvet in a double formation, face-to-face, and then cutting the two fabrics apart by the use of a razor-tipped blade which ran from side to side on the loom cutting the pile yarns in the cloth.

**WYATT, JOHN AND PAUL, LEWIS:** These English inventors brought out drawing rollers in 1737 to draft fibers so that the spinning of yarn could be done by machine. Also, in 1748, they invented the revolving cylinder, later to become a very essential part of the carding machine.

XVIIth Century Indian painted and printed cotton hanging.

# Origins of Fabric Names...

*On the following pages the most significant and widely used fabric names are traced to their sources. For the reader's convenience, they have been grouped in alphabetical order under the name of the country where they originated or with which they are ordinarily associated.*

## Africa

**BERBER** is a lightweight, satin-faced fabric, made of all silk or of cotton back and silk face; it came into prominence at the turn of the present century when the famous English general, Gordon of Khartoum, defeated the Berber tribes in his campaign in North Africa.

**MOGADOR,** a corded, plain weave material of rayon warp and a cotton or linen filling to give it firmness or stiffness. This neckwear material comes in regimental, college, blazer, Algerian and Moroccan stripes, in a wide range of qualities, and some of it is moired.

**MOZAMBIQUE,** named for the island off the east coast of Africa, is a staple decorative cloth of the grenadine type made with large floral effects in relief to form the motif. Originally made of silk and thus one of the more expensive materials, now available in acetate and rayon.

## Arabia

**MOHAIR** comes from the Arabic *mukhayyar*, which means fabric made from the hair of goats.

**QUOTON,** as the Arabs speak of cotton, is a derivative of the Egyptian term for cotton, *goton.*

**SARSANET,** in Arabic, implies a silk veiling or net. The cloth is still popular in the veiling and millinery trades today.

## Asia Minor

**BIAZ** is a linen or cotton fabric used as dress goods and is still a staple fabric in the area. Cotton cloth of this name is finished to simulate more expensive linen fabrics.

**DAMASK,** which originally meant any richly decorated silk fabric, was brought to the Western world in the 13th Century by Marco Polo from the Far East. Damascus was the chief city or clearing center between East and West and its name was given to these exquisite, expensive silks. Damasks, brocades, brocatelles, and comparable fabrics have different characteristics today, but they are all manufactured on the general principles of the original damasks and all are now made on Jacquard looms.

## Austria

**AUSTRIAN CLOTH** is one of the finest woolen or worsted fabrics to be found anywhere today. Made in Austria for many years, the fabric is produced from the highest grades of merino wool obtainable, either Austrian Silesia or Botany Bay-Australian wool. It is used for men's formal wear.

**LODEN CLOTH** is a woolen coating, fleecy in nature, which originated in a small village in Austria. It is today used widely in casual types of coats for men, women and children because it is quite durable.

**SILESIA** is a popular lining fabric known by its smooth finish and good structure when made from combed cotton yarns. There is today, however, a wide range of lining material known by this name. The weave is a small twill—1-up and 2-down, right-hand or left-hand construction. In the woolen trade, Silesia or Silicia implies a high-grade suiting fabric made for over two centuries in Austria. Merino wool, Class One in grade, is known as Silesia wool in Austria.

Fragment of Egypto-Arabic linen and silk; from the Fatimid Period (10th Century).

## Belgium

**DIAPER** fabric of silk, with small square or diamond effects, was originally made in Ypres. The word *diaspron*, from the Greek, means small-figured, and present-day diaper fabric, well-known in many households, received its name from *Cloth d'Ypres*, which has been contracted into the English word diaper.

**MALINES** is one of the oldest and best known of lace, net, and silk fabrics diaphanous in nature, and named for this city of Belgium.

**CANTON FLANNEL,** identified by its nap on one or both sides, is a medium-to-heavy weight cotton goods. It is made with a 3-up and 1-down or a 4-up and 1-down right-hand twill weave.

**CHINA SILK,** when used as a fabric term, is any lightweight cloth made of silk produced in China. Much of the goods is flimsy; and the texture and grade have wide variance.

**CREPE DE CHINE,** a very fine, lightweight silk made with a crepe weave, is usually constructed with raw-silk warp and crepe-twist silk filling, alter-

**NANKEEN** is named for the ancient city of Nankin where the cloth was first woven on hand looms with cotton yarn in warp and filling. It is usually made with local cotton, which has a natural yellowish tint, and is dyed buff or yellow when made from other cottons.

**PONGEE,** from the Chinese word *pen-chi*, which means "home loom," is made from wild or tussah silk in the natural or écru color of the filament. Very uneven in yarn and texture, it is noted for its many nubs and slubs in the yarn.

**SATIN** was first made from silk and

A Chinese pure silk brocade, 16th Century.

## China

**CANTON** silk was first made in Canton, one of the oldest silk areas in the world. Made with a satin weave, the fabric has long served as a popular staple dress-goods throughout the world.

**CANTON CREPE,** which uses silk from the Canton area, is identified by its crepe weave, a derivation of the plain weave, in which certain raisers are left out in the weaving in order to make small floats in the goods for a pebbled effect and feel. The yarn is of high twist, which adds to its wearing quality and its ability to resist friction and chafing.

nating with 2-S twist and 2-Z twist. Usually piece-dyed or printed.

**HABUTAI** means *soft* or *spongy*, an appropriate name for this fabric commonly made on hand looms in China and Japan; it is heavier than its counterpart, China silk, a fabric which it resembles in other respects.

**HONAN** is a silk pongee cloth made from wild silkworms raised in the Honan area of China. The fabric is noted for its uniformity of color, because these worms are the only wild type which gives uniform dyeing results. The name is also applied to fabrics made of manmade fibers.

woven in satin weaves, either in warp effect or in filling effect. The original fabrics were called *sztun* until the Renaissance; then the Italian silk manufacturers changed the term to *saeta* to imply *hair* or *bristle*, a term which can be applied to fabrics of this type since they show a hairline and glossy surface.

**SHANTUNG** comes from the province of this name and is a native reeled silk. Many types of natural imperfections characterize the goods and at times the more uneven and nubbier the fabric the better it was supposed to be. Shantung is still a favorite for women's wear.

(*top*) An eight-flower rondel design in 8th Century Chinese textile from the Shoso-in Collection in Nara.

(*alongside*) Emperor's dragon medallion of embroidered textile, from the Ming Dynasty (1384-1644 A.D.)

Egypto-Coptic fragment, circa 3rd Century.

## Denmark

**BURLAP,** strange as it may seem, comes from the Danish *boenlap,* a rubbing cloth that withstands hard usage.

## Egypt

**ALMA,** a mourning fabric which has been known among the Egyptians for centuries, is made from cotton or linen and dyed black or purple.

**FUSTIAN** was a low quality, coarse cotton cloth first made in the Fustat or Ghetto area outside the city of Cairo. The Egyptians used a double cloth construction to make this goods which, despite the fact that it was regarded as an inferior material, gave long wear. Some better-grade cloths were made from linen. The fustian of today has changed much from the original material and implies, as a generic term, the rather high pick, heavy cotton goods on the order of beaverteen, corduroy, doeskin, moleskin, and velveteen.

**GOTON** means cotton to the Egyptians. (See *Arabia—Quoton*).

**MUMMY CLOTH** is the name given to the linen or cotton fabric used to encase dead persons in Egypt. It may be seen in museums throughout the world. The yarn used was very fine in diameter and high in yarn count. The fabric was plain weave and left unbleached.

## England

**AXMINSTER** is a popular, low-priced carpeting which was first made in Axminster. Not a yard of it, however, has been made there for many years but there are several other world carpet centers that make this floor covering. The number of colors that may be used and the intricacy of design, plus the economic possibilities in the use of the pile yarn, make Axminster the largest-selling type of carpeting today.

**BEDFORD CORD,** one of the best fabrics made today, was first made in Bedford, England. It is also claimed by New Bedford, Mass., where it was made as early as 1845. The fabric is a simulation of the pile cloth corduroy, which originated in France (the *cord-du-roi,* cord of the king)—during the 17th Century. It was first made in worsted yarn, but cotton and woolen fabrics of this name are also popular. Much of the material sold today as piqué is in reality Bedford cord and the warp-effect construction is still used. It is ideal for riding habits, uniforms, slacks, and casual clothes.

**BLANKET** received its name from a combination of *blanc,* the French for white or undyed, and *kett,* the Anglo-Saxon word for covering; hence, a white or undyed covering. There is also the legend that the fabric was introduced in England about 600 years ago by Thomas Blanquette, a Flemish textile worker who settled there. The word, however, has come to mean any warm, heavy, bed covering.

**CLAY WORSTED,** which is also known as Chain Twill, since the fabric is made with a 3-up and 3-down twill and gives a sort of chain surface effect to the goods, is named for its originator, J. T. Clay of Rastrick, Yorkshire, England. This cassimere-type cloth has been made for about 100 years in England and in this country.

**CORONATION CLOTH** made its debut in 1901 when Edward VII was crowned king of England. The fabric is a full mixture suiting in red, blue, and black, and made of wool.

**CRAVENETTE** signifies waterproofed fabrics. The first of this type of goods was introduced by the inventor, Thomas Craven, Bradford, England. It is now a generic term signifying cloth that repels rain.

**DOILIE** is a corruption of the name *Doyley,* a linen merchant of London who brought out this linen napery material in 1707-1714.

**FLANNEL,** a low-textured, soft woolen goods, received its name from the Welsh term *gwlamen* which implies "allied with wool." The English contracted the term into *flannen* and then to *flannel*. Flannel is now made from other fibers as well as wool for specific purposes.

**HARRIS TWEED,** one of the oldest hand-woven fabrics in current use, was originally produced on the islands of Harris and Lewis and dyed by the islanders for their own apparel. It is known to have existed for at least 300 years and was originally produced from local hand-spun and hand-woven wool. It was first introduced to the mainland of Great Britain about 100 years ago, and the first registration of a trademark occurred in 1908.

**HENRIETTA,** although not popular at present, has had its waves of popularity in the women's and misses' dress trade in days gone by. This soft, lustrous dress goods was first made with silk warp and high-grade worsted filling with a 1-up and 2-down twill weave. It was named for Henrietta Maria, Queen and Consort of Charles I (1625-1649).

**JERSEY,** either woven or knitted, first appeared on the English Channel island of that name. First used by fishermen, the back of the goods was often napped to provide extra warmth to the wearer. The jersey of today is much different from the original fabric.

**KERSEY,** a heavy, face-finished, conventional and popular overcoating given a high satin-like finish, was first made in the woolen goods center of that name in England. Kersey, melton, beaver, and broadcloth are the four most popular face-finished overcoating fabrics of today.

**LINSEY-WOOLSEY,** often mentioned in early American writings, was any material made with varying amounts of linen and wool in it.

**LINTON TWEED,** a distinctive range of tweed fabrics used for summer and winter coatings and for women's ensembles, is a product of Linton Tweeds, Ltd., Carlisle, England. Made for a great many years, the fabric weight runs from 8 to 18 ounces per yard with most of the cloth averaging 12 to 14 ounces. It is known for extreme softness, wide variance in design, and an appealing hand.

**LOVAT** was named after Lord Lovat in Scotland. It is reported that he preferred greyed-down hues; these gave his name to such tones, especially greens.

**MELTON,** closely allied with kersey, received its name from the town of this name. The cloth is fulled the most and has the shortest nap when compared with its related fabrics . . . beaver, kersey, and broadcloth.

**MERCERIZATION** was discovered by John Mercer in 1844. It is one of the greatest textile phenomena of all time, and a boon to the finishing of cotton fabrics. Cotton yarn and fabric, because of this accidental discovery, shows a silken-like, permanent luster that lasts for the life of the fabric; the cloth, so treated, becomes stronger. Only about seven-tenths as much dyestuff is needed to dye mercerized goods as compared with dyeing of non-mercerized fabrics. Done in a cold bath of caustic soda, at a strength of about 25 to 45 degrees, Twaddle thermometer, mercerizing can be performed in an ordinary room temperature. Surprisingly enough, John Mercer was a calico dyer and interested chiefly in the affinities of dyestuff for fabric and not in fabric development.

**NORFOLK SUITING,** at one time very popular in this country for suits with pleats and belted effect, came into being in the English county of that name.

**OXFORD** is named for the university city and was first produced by Flemish weavers who had migrated to England at the time of the revocation of the Edict of Nantes, 1685. The fabric simulates a type of basket weave made possible by the bulky, rounded, or flat filling used in the goods and the fine diameter of the warp yarn. The word also implies grey mixtures used in woolen and worsted suitings today.

**TATTERSALL,** a cloth that has cycles of popularity, is a rather gaudy checked or block-effect material whose name comes from the famous horse auction

Elizabethan needlework.

201

An ancient Millefleurs tapestry, from about 1650 A.D.

rooms of London owned by Tattersall. It is believed that the ideas for the cloth were taken from the horse blankets which were usually made with some checks.

**WORSTED** goes back to the day of William the Conqueror. The story goes that, when he came to Britain, he noted that the peasants were manipulating woolen fibers with a type of card or comb to work the fibers into a sliver and slubbing form so that they might be hand-spun into a yarn. William became much interested in the work and, not knowing what to call the task being done, and, since he had worsted the people by conquest, he called the area *Worsted*. In due time, the finished yarn as well was given this name. The village of Worstead where he is supposed to have observed the carding and combing is in Norfolk County. About 1340, fabric of this name was being made in Suffolk County, England. Worsted fabric, as it is known today, did not become a winner in the trade until the 1890's.

**YARD** is a 36-inch measure in America, while the English yard is a standard established by the government, indicated by two marks on a metal rod embedded in the masonry of the House of Parliament in London. The American yard, which is 1/100,000 of an inch longer than the English yard, is not fixed by government standards. The foot of today, which measures 12 inches, is supposed to have been the length of the foot of James I, 1603-1625.

### France

**ARMURE** is named for the weaves that show small, interlaced designs of chain armor which was popular for military equipment during the Crusades. The name is still used for types of metallic fabric for evening wear, handbags, and other accessories.

**BATISTE,** named for Jean Batiste, a French weaver who lived in Cambrai and first produced the cloth, is noted for its fine yarn, high texture, and softness. It is made with cotton or linen yarn.

**BEIGE,** a popular shade, is the French term for natural or neutral color.

**BOMBAZINE,** probably first produced by the Greeks, comes from the Grecian word for silkworm. This lightweight silk mourning cloth, still made in France, became popular there about 400 years ago.

**BOUCLE** is a curled-face fabric which received its name from the French verb *boucler*, which means to curl or to buckle into ringlets.

**BOURETTE** derives its name from the French *bourre*, which means hairy in appearance. The material has a hairy effect on the surface, since the yarn is interspersed with nubs.

**BROCADE** comes from the French verb *brocart*, meaning ornamented. Brocade is a very rich looking, expensive, decorative fabric.

**BROCATELLE** is on the order of brocade. The original fabric featured raised figures made of woolen yarn on a background of silk. It is still a staple decorative and upholstery material.

**BROCHE,** another name for a hairline or pinstripe fabric, implies that the single color of the goods is broken up and decorated by a stripe.

**CAMBRIC** is a very fine, thin white cloth made of cotton or linen of which it has been stated that the "greatest thread was not even the size of the smallest hair." The old Flemish name for cambric was *Kamerik*.

**CANICHE** comes from the French word for poodle and implies a fabric made with a curly-face finish. Present day Poodle Cloth is a development of Caniche.

**CHAMBRAY,** one of the most popular cotton staples, originated in Cambrai. It is made of white cotton warp and colored filling and with certain variations such as stripes and novelty effects.

**CHENILLE** is the French word for caterpillar and it was used chiefly as trimming on gowns when first made. Fabric of this name today is characterized by a fluffy or fuzzy face. The name also is used for the well-known chenille rug or carpet.

An 18th Century lampas of the Louis XV era, inspired by paintings by Watteau. The combination of formal ornament, flower and wreath motifs, and figures are typical of the period.

**CHEVRON** is made from broken twill and herringbone weaves to give a chevron effect such as seen on military uniforms. The patterns have waves of popularity in men's wear suitings and coatings.

**CHIFFON** is from the French word denoting a rag of the flimsy type and has been used to signify veiling and sheer fabrics of diaphanous type known for high yarn twist to give strength.

**CORDUROY** made its debut during the reigns of the Kings Louis' of France and means "cord of the king," a fabric much used by the outdoor servants and lackeys in the halcyon days of France. Noted for its rugged construction and good wear, the material is very popular at present. (See ENGLAND: *Bedford Cord*.)

**COUPURE** comes from the French verb which means to cut through. The term is applied to pile fabrics of several types which have been cut and clipped to give a desired effect.

**CREPE** signifies crimping or creping by means of a hot iron. The cloth is always a staple in the trade and there are many types, most of which are made in the so-called crepe weave which is a variation of the plain weave. Yarn twist is also important in crepe materials since it helps to provide the crepe, granite, or pebbled effect for which these fabrics are noted.

**CRETONNE** is named for a village in Normandy. The fabric is made from Osnaburg grey goods, is strong, unglazed in finish, and may be plain or printed on one or both sides.

**DELAINE** in French means of wool. Wool by this name signifies that the stock is of the merino type, the finest wool obtained anywhere in the world. Delaine wool, in this country, originates in Ohio.

**DENIM** was first made in Nimes or *de Nimes*. This rugged, compact cotton fabric gives excellent service and is popular today for all types of garments from work clothing to evening wear. It is made with right-hand or left-hand twill constructions, usually in the latter weave, which affords quick recognition from the face of the fabric.

**DRAP D'ETE** means cloth of summer and is a lightweight fabric of several types on the order of tropical worsteds

An excellent specimen of Toile de Jouy.

or blended fabrics comparable with tropicals. It is used chiefly by the clergy for warm weather wear.

**EPINGLE,** from the word for pin, was developed by the French who made it a distinctive fabric about four centuries ago. First made of silk yarn and now made of acetate, rayon, or worsted, this fine, corded dress goods with alternating large and small ribs gives an effect of pinpoints in its pebbled effect which is aided by the use of contrasting or harmonizing yarns.

**EPONGE** is the French word for sponge. The term is applied to a group of cloths which are soft or spongy in feel and used to some extent for women's dress goods. Fabrics of this name are usually rather porous in texture, which makes them ideal for summer wear.

**ETAMINE** is a bolting fabric or sifting cloth, whose name implies a dress goods material which has porous areas in it, such as noted in leno or doup fabrics, mock leno cloths and "cloth that breathes," a term popular in advertising goods of this character. Etamine, comparable with éponge, is usually lighter in weight.

**FOULARD** means silk handkerchief and the fabric still serves this purpose as well as being popular in the manufacture of neckwear, dress goods, and scarves.

**FOULE** is the term given to fabrics which have been shrunken in the finishing operations. The verb form means to full or to shrink; hence the English term *fuller*, one who fulls or shrinks textile fabric.

**FRIEZE** is from the verb *friser*, which means to curl. The cloth has a curled-face effect and is much used in the upholstery trade, since it has an intricate pile construction which affords good wear on furniture. Fabric of the same name is popular at times for women's coatings.

**GAUFRE** means puffed or waffled and is suggestive of honeycomb or waffle material that is in demand for women's summer dress goods of cotton and man-made yarns.

**GRENADINE,** while of Italian and Spanish origin, was developed on a large scale by the French weavers in Lyons. Originally the meaning implied an outer covering, cape, or cloak made

French, late 17th Century needlepoint lace, Point de France,
depicts hunting scenes and royal crown.

on bell-shaped lines. Present-day grenadine is a dress fabric made with open
gauze weave from hard-twisted yarn.
Stripes and checks may be obtained by
cramming the yarn in some places and
skipping reed dents in other areas to
give the gauzy effect. It is made from
most of the textile fibers.

**GROSGRAIN** originated in the Middle
Ages and gained popularity in France
when silk yarn was used to make the
fabric noted for its pronounced filling-
rib effect. The term implies a heavy or
thick grain line in the cross-wise direction of the goods; grosgrain is said to
be "bengaline cut to ribbon width."

**HONEYCOMB,** also called waffle
cloth, received its name from the French
*nid d'abeilles*, a bees' nest; hence its application to the raised portions observed
in the·fabric. The high point on the one
side of the honeycomb is the low point
on the reverse of the material.

**JACONET** is a thin cotton fabric somewhat heavier than cambric; the face of
the material is given a glazing treatment

to produce high luster. East Indian in
origin, the French developed the material by making stripe and check motifs
in the goods, an improvement over the
original fabric.

**JACQUARD** is the name given to
fabrics in which elaborate motifs are
woven into such goods as brocades,
brocatelles, damasks, tapestries, napery
fabrics, neckwear, dress goods, and so
on. It is named for the inventor of the
loom which weaves the cloth—Joseph-
Marie Jacquard (1752-1834), who invented and perfected these looms between the years 1801-1810. Jacquard,
considered one of the greatest benefac-
tors of the textile world of all time, was
a friend of Napoleon, and the latter pen-
sioned him for his contributions to
French textiles.

**JEAN** is a twill-woven cotton with an
undressed finish, a lining cloth first
made in Caen. It is made with a 3-
harness twill in warp-effect or filling-
effect, some right-hand twill and some
left-hand in direction. Both types are

popular staples in the trade and are usually dyed in solid shades with a wide
variance in finish with respect to luster
and surface effect.

**LAWN** comes from the city of Laon, a
few miles from the textile center of
Rheims. Originally used for garments
worn by the clergy, present-day lawn is
a lightweight cotton or linen fabric of
the better grade, usually made of
combed cotton yarn.

**LENO,** also known as doup-woven
cloth, is known for its open-work face
which resembles lace. The term is applied to fabrics which are constructed
on the principle of cross-weaving, in
which two sets of harnesses—standard
and skeleton—are used to make the warp
ends cross each other in weaving. Marquisette is an example of doup-woven
fabric. This method of weaving is supposed to have originated in or near Laon
and the material, in some circles, has
been called a cross-woven lawn when
yarns such as those used to make lawn
are used.

**LISLE** is a fine, hard-twisted cotton or linen yarn or thread used in hosiery. Lisle was the former name for the textile center of Lille.

**LONGCLOTH** is a corruption of lawn and is thought to have been the first fabric made in a definite length in France; the original length is supposed to have been 36 yards. Made with carded or combed yarns today, the material belongs in the cambric-nainsook group of cottons, but it is more closely woven and somewhat heavier than either of these.

**LOUISINE** was named for Louis XIV. It is a distinctive silk cloth with twice as many ends as picks in the construction, since each pick crosses the warp ends at once to form a small rib effect.

**MARSEILLES** is a popular cotton summer bed covering named for this French city. It comes in several widths and weights and is bleached to white or enhanced by the use of yarn-dyeing on white.

**MATELASSE** is a bed covering and dress-goods fabric recognized by its padded, puffed, or pouched face effect which derives its name from the French *matelassé*, padded or stuffed.

**MISTRAL,** on the order of etamine, is made with nubbed, uneven yarn to give a wavy effect in the cloth and comes from the French term for strong northwest wind.

**MOIRE,** also known as watermarked, received its name from the verb *moirer*, to water. First seen on silk or mohair fabrics, the effect is also given to cottons, acetates, rayons, and comparable materials to enhance the surface effect.

**MONTAGNAC** is the registered trademark of E. de Montagnac et Fils, of Sedan. Made for a great many years, this luxury cloth is composed of wool and cashmere, the latter adding to its appearance, feel, and beauty. The silk-like feel of the goods is one of the chief assets of this smart, dressy overcoating which has a weight of 36 ounces per yard. The name comes from *mountain-wear*, for which the cloth is ideally suited.

**MOREEN** is another derivation of the verb *moirer*. Mohair, silk, cotton, rayon, and acetate fabrics are sometimes sold under this name when the watermark has been applied to poplin-type fabrics.

**OMBRE** means shaded in French, and fabrics with stripes of various colorings are often sold under this name.

**ONDULE** is derived from the French, for waved or shaded effects. The finish is brought about by causing the warp ends, in a series of groups, to be forced alternately by the ondulé reed to the right and then to the left.

**ORGANDY,** a plain, figured or dyed, thin muslin-type fabric noted for its stiff finish, received its name from the French *organdi*, a word used originally to mean book muslin.

**ORLEANS** is made of cotton warp and bright wool filling and first appeared in this French city. Alpaca and mohair are present-day fabrics of this type.

**PANNE** means to flatten and the term is linked with *peluche*, the French for plush, in many instances. Used also with velvet, the word signifies that the fabric has had the pile effect pressed flat in one direction; hence, panne velvet.

**PEAU DE CYGNE** was first made in France and because of its soft, appealing feel was given this name which means skin of the swan.

**PEAU DE SOIE** means skin of silk and the fabric was a staple until silk cloths began to decline with World War II.

**PIQUE** comes from the French and refers to *pike* or *that which pierces*. This popular cord, rib, or wale fabric achieves its effect in the filling or the crosswise direction of the goods, from selvage to selvage. Today, however, the term is applied to materials with wales that run in the warp or vertical direction in the goods as well. Piqué is made with two warps and two fillings and may also have stuffer threads in addition to the binder threads used to hold the cords in place. Birdseye Piqué, Waffle Piqué and Bedford Cord are kindred fabrics.

**PLUMETIS** is a lightweight fabric made of cotton or wool which shows a raised motif on a plain background to give a feathered effect.

**PLUSH** comes from the word *peluche*, which means shaggy. Pile fabrics with a pile of one-eighth of an inch or higher are known as plush; when the pile is less than this height the cloth is velvet or velveteen.

**POIRET TWILL** is named for Paul Poiret, one of the most popular cou-

French handkerchief of bobbin lace, Valenciennes type (late XIXth Century).

turiers of Paris in the 1920's. Still a staple fabric for women's worsted suitings of the better type, it is made in a steep-twill weave and has twice as many ends as picks per inch in the cloth texture.

**POPLIN** has been made for many centuries and its name comes from the Papacy. The Italians made the fabric, *papalino*, in the famous walled medieval city of Avignon. This silk or worsted fabric was used for church vestments and the French called it *popeline*. The contraction, *popli*, followed, and around 1800 the English named it *poplin* and used cotton to make the material.

**SANGLIER** means wild boar, since this fabric made of worsted and mohair or other hair fibers closely resembles the wiry, shaggy bristles and hair of this animal. Compact texture is important in weaving to obtain the effect.

**SCHAPPE** is a type of waste silk which received its name from *hacher*, which means to chop or to cut up. Schappe silk is cut into short lengths and spun into yarn on the spun-silk method of spinning; it can also be mixed or blended with other major fibers. This silk has good strength but poor, irregular luster.

**SOLEIL** is the French for sun, and many allied types of silk fabrics are given this name because they show bright satin-face effects which simulate the sun.

**SOUFFLE** means puffed, and the large designs seen in crepon and other cloths which are made with a raised or puffed motif are thus named.

**SUEDE** is the French way of saying Sweden. Fabric of this type is closely woven or knitted to produce a very soft, appealing nap on the goods; it simulates leather of this name.

**TAMISE** is a close-mesh fabric first made of silk and wool and now made of man-made yarns. The name comes from *tamis*, the French word for sieve, since the fabric is of the diaphanous type, such as marquisette.

**TERRY CLOTH** received its name from the verb *tirer*, meaning to pull out. Turkish toweling is the original fabric and the pile is made so that the loops are drawn through a foundation and remain uncut. The pile effect may be on one or both sides.

**TOWEL** is derived from the word *touaille*, a roller-towel of linen. The cloth of today is still made from linen, but much cotton toweling is also made.

**TRICOT** means knitting and the fabric can be woven or knitted according to the demands of fashion. Fine, vertical lines are seen on the face, while crosswise ribs are noted on the back of the material.

**TULLE,** first made in Toul, is a fine, soft, machine-made net. Hexagonal meshes are a feature of the material, which is used for veils and bridal gowns. Silk and nylon fabric of this type, despite its open-mesh construction, is strong, and gives excellent service.

**VELOUR** is the French term for velvet. The term today has a double meaning—it may be cut-pile cotton fabric on the order of cotton velvet, or a material with a raised or napped finish. Velour is also used broadly to imply pile fabrics.

## Germany

**BUNTING** comes from the German *bunt*, and means variegated or gay colored, a characteristic of bunting cloth.

**FELT** is derived from the rolling and pressing of a pulpy mass of wool fibers, hair fibers, or fur fibers into a mat-like form. The term means to mix and press into shape, a contraction of the German *falzen*. Felt is said to have been known to wandering tribes who evolved the art of making it long before spinning and weaving were invented. The patron saint of the felt industry is St. Feutre of Caen, France. While on long trips, he placed wool in his sandals to relieve foot pain. He noticed that the serrations or scales peculiar only to wool fibers, aided by heat, pressure and moisture, interlocked and formed a matted layer of wool fabric. Thus felt, as we know it today, was born.

**HUCKABACK,** also called *huck,* is a strong cloth of linen or cotton. The name comes from the German *hukkebak,* meaning pedlar's wares.

**OSNABURG,** the base fabric from which cretonne is made, is named for Osnabrück, in Germany.

**SAXONY** is a broad term today, but was first applied to the merino wool of Germany, one of the best wools obtainable anywhere. It also is the name for a quality knitting yarn and a luxury-type men's overcoating fabric. Named for the province in Germany, Saxony is a popular name to designate fabrics such as Saxony flannel, Saxony carpet, etc.

**WOOL** comes from *wolle,* the German word for wool fleece. Incidentally, Vilna on the Baltic Sea received its name several centuries ago because it grew as a center and clearing house for wool.

GREEK VASE

## Greece

**DIMITY** comes from the word *dimitos,* meaning a double thread. This lightweight staple cotton comes in plain construction or may be made in a variation of the plain weave in which bars, cords, or stripes are used to aid appearance.

**EOLIENNE** takes its name from the Greek *Æolus,* the god of the winds. The cloth is a lightweight zephyr fabric and may be classed as a very fine poplin. First made of silk warp and worsted filling, it is now made with acetate, rayon, or cotton.

**GALATEA** is a left-hand cotton twill fabric used in children's sailor suits and play clothes, an old standby for many years. The name comes from the sea nymph of Greek mythology.

**ZEPHYR** originally was a lightweight worsted yarn of good quality. Fabric made of the yarn was also known as zephyr. Today, many lightweight cottons and man-made fabrics are advertised as zephyr to attract attention to the sheerness or lightness of the material. From *Zephyrus,* implying west wind.

## India

**BANDANNA** means to tie or to bind. Cloth of this name was colored by the Indian natives by dip dyeing or by tie dyeing to produce a mottled effect. The fabric, at present, is usually dyed by the resist method or the discharge method of printing, while some of the goods, in accordance with the motif, is direct-printed. Bandanna prints may or may not be clear and clean in pattern and looks.

**BENGAL STRIPES,** named for the province in India, are distinctive stripe effects in which several colors are observed. Neckties, ribbons, dress goods and regimental stripes are some examples of these stripe effects.

**BENGALINE** was first made in India by the use of silk yarn in the warp and cotton yarn for the cross-rib effect to produce the cord. It is now made from all major textile fibers.

**CALICO,** one of the oldest staple fabrics known to mankind, was first made in Calicut, the seaport town in the southwest area of Madras province in India.

**CASHMERE** is the name for several soft-feeling fabrics which have the texture or hand of the fleece of the Cashmere (Kashmir) goats found in the vales of the Himalaya Mountains. Incidentally, many fabrics of this and similar names have little or none of the valuable goat hair in them. It also means the fine, soft, downy hair fibers which grow as an undercoat on Cashmere goats.

**CHALLIS** comes from a word meaning soft to the touch. The fabric is made from cotton or worsted and is particularly popular when made from the latter. Worsted challis is one of the very few animal fiber cloths that is printed by the direct, resist, or discharge methods.

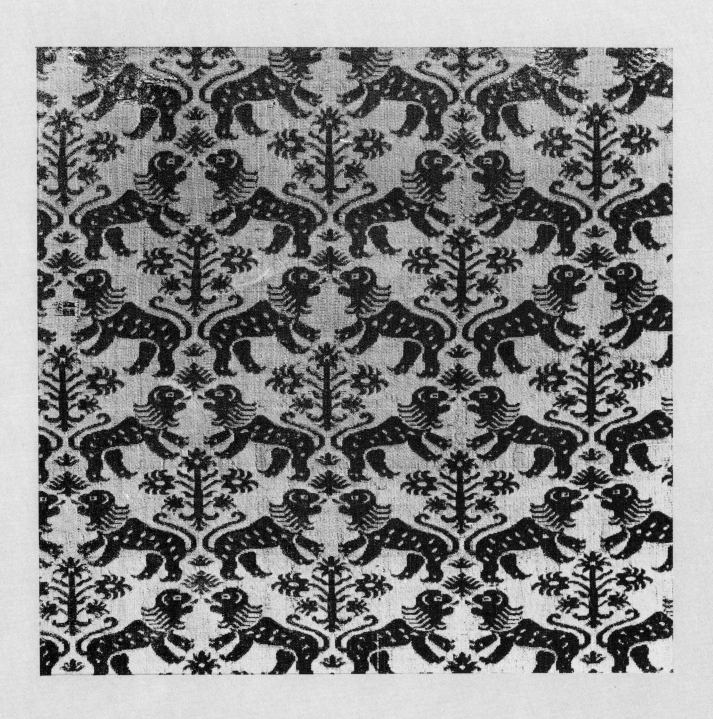

A silk brocade damask of Spanish origin, of the XVIth Century.

**CHINTZ** comes from the word meaning spotted. This cloth was colored by staining or painting the motif onto the goods. The fabrics were made to give a multicolored effect that might be bizarre or conservative, characteristics still true of this plain-woven cotton cloth which varies considerably in texture, weight and price.

**CHUDAH,** a plain-weave cotton, is named for the Indian plant noted for its brilliant green colorings. The color today is popularly known as Kelly green, a vivid shade.

**COTTON** was first known in India about 3,000 B.C., and was considered very rare and precious. In the 7th Century, the plant was classed as a garden flower. Cotton is referred to as King in America today, the universal textile fiber.

**DORIAN** was originally a striped muslin first made in India, and is still a staple in many world centers.

**INDIA LAWN,** also known as Indian linen at times, has been made in India for over 4,000 years. Fabrics of this name are seen in museums and are noted for their particularly fine yarn counts, evenness of weaving, and zephyr weight.

**KHAKI,** known by armed forces the world over, means dust-colored.

**MADRAS,** one of the most popular of shirting fabrics, originated in this Indian province. The fabrics were made with the varied stripe effects which make the cloth ideal for shirtings.

**MULL** means soft or pliable, and the cloth of this name is a type of lightweight muslin, now overshadowed by lawn, cambric, and voile.

**SURAH:** This twill silk was named after Surat, India.

## Ireland

**BALBRIGGAN** in Ireland is where the first bleached hosiery was made. Also used for other purposes today, the fabric is a lightweight, plain-stitch knitted cotton cloth with a napped back.

**BREECHES** comes from the word *briges*, a loose, trouser-like garment worn by the peasant folk of Ireland, which was a forerunner of the knickers of a later age.

## Italy

**CRASH** comes from the Latin *crassus* and means coarse. The rough, irregular surface caused by the use of thick, uneven yarns is typical of the material of today. Osnaburg is the grey goods for crash made of cotton; other types are of acetate or rayon staple stock, and linen.

**DOUPPIONI,** when applied to silk cocoons, implies that two or more of them have nested together so that when they have been reeled, an irregular, coarse, double filament results. The Italians have been very adept in the manipulation of this yarn which can be used in present-day fabrics such as nankeen, pongee, shantung and other cloths which use irregular, slub-type yarn. Douppioni silk yarn is now simulated in acetate and rayon yarns made from the staple fibers.

**FLORENTINE TWILL** received its name from this Italian city. It was first made as a silk fabric for dress goods with an eight-end satin weave in a twill effect arrangement. Plain, figured, or striped effects were used to give contrast in the material which, in addition to its use in dress goods, found favor in vestments and vesting fabrics. Cotton warp

and mohair filling were used in the lower qualities.

**ITALIAN CLOTH,** a broad term and one which signifies a smooth lining material, was known during the Middle Ages. It is made of all cotton with a 5-shaft filling-effect weave in either a satin or twill weave. Usually piece-dyed black or brown, the fabric is now made of acetate or rayon yarn, in addition to a cotton cloth for which there is still demand in the apparel trade.

**LACE** comes from the Latin *laqueos*, which means to make a knot, snare, or noose and was corrupted into the present term. Real or handmade lace is produced either by a needle, when it is known as point or needlepoint lace, or on a pillow with bobbins or pins, as in the case of bobbin or pillow lace, or, at times, by crocheting or by knotting or tatting. Machine-made lace manipulates the threads to produce the effects of real lace.

**LINEN** is from the Latin *linum*, and refers broadly to any yarn or fabric made from flax fibers. Italy was known for its linens during the Renaissance, since much had been learned of the manipulation of flax into linen fabric from extant linen fabrics which were made in Egypt.

**MESSALINE** was named for the wife of the Emperor Claudius, Messalina. This fine silk fabric was compactly woven and noted for its high sheen. The cloth was made on a 5-end satin weave and had all the characteristics of Peau de Cygne which was made on an 8-shaft weave. Both fabrics were popular in the silk trade from the turn of the century until World War II, when acetate and rayon fabrics replaced them.

**MILANESE** fabric is known as a warp-loom knit cloth made on the Milanese

Below: Wild ducks from XVIIth Century Japanese wood block engraving.

loom, usually from acetate, nylon, rayon, or silk yarns. This very fine fabric is named for the city of Milan.

**ORGANZINE** comes from the Italian and means twisted silk—the term for the silk-warp yarn in a material.

**SERGE** comes from the word *serica*, which means silk; the Spanish term is *xerga*. Originally made in Italy and Spain, the cloth was made with a small twill weave, usually a 2-up and 2-down right-hand twill construction. Serge of today is a light-to-medium-weight worsted fabric of good texture, even yarn and clear face finish.

**SICILIAN** was first made on the island of Sicily. Cotton warp and mohair filling were used for this lining fabric which is still popular at present when made from these or other yarn combinations. Another fabric of the same name, used for dress goods and also made in Sicily, used silk warp and woolen filling in which the rather bulky crosswise threads formed a rib effect in the material.

**TARLATAN,** first made from linen warp and wool filling, was a coarse, stiff, heavily sized cloth named from *Tarlatana*, a Milanese term for fabrics of this type. It resembles buckram and crinoline.

**VELVET** was originally made with a short, dense pile woven with silk warp. At present the term is applied to cloths made partly from silk, acetate, or rayon and partly of other materials, as well as to goods made entirely of other yarns. Velveteen is a filling-pile fabric and is often confused or mistaken for velvet, a warp-pile effect material. Incidentally corduroy is a filling-pile effect weave cloth. Velvet received its name from *velluto*, which implies a wooly feel to the touch. The use of silk warp and woolen filling improved the hand of the goods, and cloth of this type was made from time to time.

**VELVETEEN** is a simulation of true velvet and it may be made of acetate, rayon, or cotton with a plain-weave construction on the back. The cloth may be wax-treated to improve the luster and the finished product may be piece-dyed or printed on a dyed background.

**VENETIAN,** named for the city of Venice, is a warp-faced sateen which is stronger and heavier than ordinary sateen cloth, which is always made of cotton yarn. Eight-end satin weaves are used to make this lining material which closely resembles Italian cloth used in linings. Venetian is given a mercerized or a schreinerized finish for increased luster.

**VOILE** is a corruption of the word *vela*, which implies a covering, curtain, or sail. This staple is now made of silk, cotton, acetate, nylon, rayon, or worsted yarns.

## Japan

**HABUTAI:** Is made of Japanese silk waste stock that can be twisted or thrown very little or not at all. Habutai is used for dresses, coats, shirting, office coats.

**KIMONO SILK:** A type of cloth, most often silk but frequently a fine quality of lustrous cotton, which is used for kimonos.

**NARA:** Dates back to about the 8th Century A.D. It is named after this period. Many original Nara designs still exist in the museum at Nara, and supply constant inspiration even to modern textile designers.

**NISHIZIN:** A very tightly woven fabric, mainly silk, which originated in the Kyoto district of Japan.

## Malaya

**GINGHAM** comes from the word *gin gan*, which signified a cotton fabric of the East Indies made with stripes, cross-stripes, or barred effects—a variegated cloth. Still a most popular fabric, it is now made from woolen, worsted, and man-made yarns as well, in addition to cotton.

## Mesopotamia

**MUSLIN** was first made in this homeland area of the Turkish peoples. *Mosul* or *muslin* is now a generic term which covers a host of cotton cloths, from sheers to heavy sheetings. It is also a pure starched or back-filled finish material with a dull, thready, or clothy effect.

## Netherlands

**DUCK** is derived from the name *Doek*, which was given to cotton fabric used for sailors' summer wear, particularly pantaloons and caps.

## Palestine

**GAUZE,** first made as a veiling or netting, was given to the world by the city of Gaza. The present-day cloth is of open mesh, loose construction, and plain or doup weaves are resorted to in order to make the goods. Cheesecloth and tobacco cloth are examples of gauze.

## Panama

**PANAMA** is the name sometimes given to small basket weaves such as a 2-2, 3-3, 4-4. Some embroidery canvas, a cloth made for many years on hand looms in Panama and other Central American countries, is known by this term. The name is also given to the straw plaiting used by the makers of Panama hats which, curiously enough, are not made in Panama but in Ecuador.

## Persia (Iran)

**PERCALE** comes from the word *pargalah*, which described a cotton cloth made in Persia for many centuries noted for its fine texture, smooth finish, and small printed motif. This staple is probably the most popular cotton print goods on the market today. Sheeting of percale is also exceedingly popular at present.

**SEERSUCKER** comes from the word *shirushakar*, a puckered or blistered surface. The fabric is made with set stripes alternating with plain or crepe ground weaves. The base ends in the fabric are under ordinary loom tension, while the ends that give the puckered effect are woven with a slack tension. Another method of obtaining the effect is to print the cloth in stripes with a preparation that will resist the action of caustic soda. Thus, when the goods are passed through the concentrated caustic soda solution, the imprinted stripe areas will shrink to give the appearance of puckered or blistered stripes.

**TAFFETA** is one of the oldest fabrics known to man; originally made of silk and noted for its smooth surface, even texture, and slight crosswise rib, the Persians called it *taftah*. The plain weave used to make it is still, in some circles, called the tabby weave. Taffeta was being made in the 14th Century in England, and France was making the material prior to this time and called it taffetas. Its first use was for lining rich, luxurious mantles; later it was produced

209

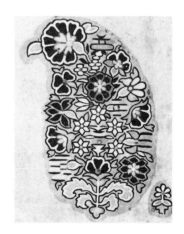

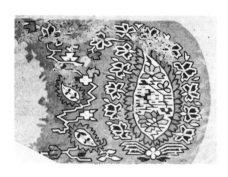

for dresses and was worn in court circles. The goods are now made from about all of the major textile fibers. Much of the present-day taffeta is moiréd.

## Russia

**ASTRAKHAN,** spelled in a number of ways, is a curly-faced pile fabric, knitted or woven, to simulate the pelt of Persian sheep of this name, a grade of Karakul-type lambskins.

**BUCKRAM** received its name from Bokhara, in Southern Russia, where it was first made. It is a stiff, firmly starched cotton fabric such as scrim, cheesecloth, or tobacco cloth, but heavier than crinoline. It is used for belt and skirt lining, in the millinery trade, and in bookbinding.

**CARACUL** is merely one of the ways of spelling Karakul, a broadtail sheep of unknown origin found in Bokhara in Southern Russia. The glossy, black fur is taken from the young lambs known as Persian lamb, Broadtail, Astrakhan, Karakul. Fabric of this name is a simulation of the fur and may be knitted or woven.

**MOSCOW** is a heavy, stiff, boardy, cumbersome overcoating peculiar to Russia and is a bulky frieze fabric that is most difficult to use in cut-fit-trim. It is named for this Russian city.

**SEBASTOPOL** is a twill-faced, heavy overcoating which originated in this well-known Crimean city.

## Scotland

**BANNOCKBURN** was first made as a cheviot-type material on a 2-up and 2-down twill weave in which there was an alternate arrangement of two-ply and single-ply yarns in both warp and filling, with the ply yarn being made of single yarns of different colors twisted together to provide a mottled effect in the goods. Always a staple in the trade, the fabric at times is a leader in both men's wear and women's wear suiting and light topcoating. It is named for the famous battle fought in June, 1314, when the Scots defeated the English.

**CHEVIOT** is a popular cloth of the homespun-tweed group and is named for the sheep that graze in the Cheviot Hills which separate England from Scotland.

This loosely woven, shaggy surface-effect tweed is now made in a wide range of quality, weight, texture, and feel. Most of the fabric is noted, however, for its distinctive feel and it does not necessarily have to be made from cheviot wool.

**MELROSE** was first made as a silk and wool dress cloth named for this town on the Tweed River, Scotland. Little of the fabric is seen today.

**PAISLEY** was first made as a worsted fabric in which scroll motifs were woven into the goods in colors of red to brown. Named for this venerable city in Scotland, the Paisley pattern is a derivation of the Indian pine-cone figure. In the Eastern world, the famous cashmere shawls of India, made for many centuries before the Scotch revived the motifs, were often constructed with the pine-cone designs.

**SCRIM** is a low-textured cotton which received its name from the fact that the reduced texture in the goods caused the material to become scrimpy or skimpy; hence, the contraction into scrim. It is used for curtains, bunting, and buckram. Cheesecloth, when bleached and given a heavy starching, is known as scrim.

**SHETLAND** is a suiting fabric made wholly or in part from shetland wool. It was first made on the Shetland Islands off the coast of Scotland and in the northern area of the mainland of the same country. Recognized by its raised finish and soft handle, the fabric is ideal for sportscoats, topcoating, and men's wear.

**TWEED** was first made on hand looms in the vicinity of the Tweed River which separates Scotland from England. This very popular suiting and coating material is now made on power looms as well as on hand looms. The latter type is much in demand and commands a good price. Two or more colors feature the goods; and while some of the fabrics are made of plain weave—the homespun weave—most of the product is made on a 2-up and 2-down twill design.

Tweed was originally known as twill cloth and there is a story to the effect that an invoice for the shipment of some of this twill material became wet and was blotted, thereby making it difficult to read the wording. The draper who received the cloth read the term as *tweed* and, thinking it appropriate since he lived in this area, began to call the fabric by the name of tweed; the name has remained for this distinctive woolen goods.

## South America

**ALPACA** is a long, white or colored smooth hair obtained from the Auchenia paco of South America, found chiefly in the Andes Mountains. The original alpaca cloth was made with a cotton warp and alpaca filling for use as a lining material. Other goods which have some content of the fiber are luster dress goods, silk-warp alpaca, alpaca mixtures, mohair linings, and sweater fabrics. The term is now used very broadly, even for materials in which none of the fiber is to be found, such as rayon alpaca, for example.

**VICUNA** provides the finest hair fiber to be found anywhere in the world; it is half as fine as the finest merino wool fiber. It belongs to the camel family and is a native of southern Peru, which still protects the animal by law so that it will not become extinct. Found in small flocks in the almost inaccessible mountain areas of Peru, the animals thrive best in an altitude of about 10,000 feet. It is necessary to kill the animal to obtain the fleece and a very limited supply is available at all times. Vicuna cloth is very expensive.

## Spain

**BAIZE** has been made for several centuries in Spain. It is named for the town of Baza and is a solid-color woven goods used for table and wall coverings.

**CHINCHILLA** fabric simulates the fur of the animal of this name, a rodent native to Spain as well as to the Andes Mountains. The fabric is made from two warps and with two, three or four fillings to obtain a spongy effect in the material. A special rubbing machine is used to obtain a distinctive curly nub effect on the face of the goods.

**GABARDINE** goes back to the Middle Ages when the Spanish called it *gabardina,* meaning protection against the elements. The first fabric known as gabardine was a cloak, cassock, or mantle which was loose fitting. The cloth of today is firmly woven, clear in finish, and

has a high texture made possible by the use of steep-twill weaves, although some of the cloth is still made with a 45-degree twill angle. Ideal for suiting, slacks, and dress goods, the cloth is now made from practically any or all of the major textile fibers.

**GRANADA,** also spelled Grenada, was first made in the city of this name in Spain. A five-shaft twill weave of 3-up and 2-down was and still is used to make this black-dyed cotton warp and alpaca, mohair, or luster wool filling cloth. It is interesting to note that the weave used in this material is arranged as a filling twill in order to give the effect of a 27-degree weave, one of the reclining-twill constructions seen occasionally in the textile trade.

SPANISH LADY SPINNING
—EL GRECO (*detail*)

**TARTAN** comes from the Spanish *tiritana,* a cloth with a small check. The Scottish Highlanders have developed these colored checks into their distinctive clan dress plaids. A twill weave is used to make the plaids and tartans which are used in the manufacture of coats, kilts, and shawls.

Incidentally, in the true sense of the word, a *tartan* is a pattern or design, while a *plaid* is a blanket-like mantle folded in several ways and joined at the left shoulder by a brooch. The two words *tartan* and *plaid* are often erroneously used interchangeably.

## Switzerland

**SWISS; DOTTED SWISS** is the permanent finish given to some cotton fabrics, organdy in particular. While a crisp, stiff finish is applied to these sheer cottons, there is a lack of luster which adds to the appearance of the cloths. The method originated in St. Gall.

## Tibet

**TIBET** fabric has been made for several centuries by the peasants. The cloth is a very heavy, coarse material made from goat hair and wool. There is another fabric of this name on the market today—a coating cloth made with various types of hair fibers and wool for use in the women's coating trade. Tibet shawls are likewise made of hair fibers and much of this fabric is in the luxury class of textile materials.

## Turkey

**OTTOMAN** is one of the most popular of cross-ribs in the trade. It was first made over 500 years ago and was constructed in a manner different from the cloth we know by this name today. The original weave was a 12-harness, 75-degree left-hand twill. This produced a flatter rib than that found in *faille Francaise.* Fabric made with this construction eliminated the extra binder warp for the rib effect.

Ottoman in the present market is merely a rib construction with a broad, flat rib definitely pronounced in the cloth. Soleil is the name for the small rib effect; ottoman has a slightly larger and heavier rib, while ottoman cord has ribs of different sizes, arranged in alternating order. All three types, however, are known as Ottoman in the trade today. Ottoman is made from silk, acetate, rayon, and cotton. The cord yarns are usually cotton since they do not show on the face or the back of the goods because they are covered by the warp threads.

**SULTANE,** named for the first wife of a Sultan, is a very old textile. It was made of silk warp and wool filling on a twill weave and given a rough finish without any shearing or singeing. It is used for dress goods, shawls, mantle cloths, and cloakings.

*In the following section will be found a collection of classical fabric examples intended to serve as a source equally for the student and professional designer.*

# MASTERPIECES OF
# TEXTILE DESIGN

Egyptian—dynastic

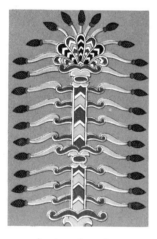

Ancient Assyrian

Etruscan

# Design Evolution in Textiles

*For the textile designer a study of ancient fabrics shows the development of timeless themes through the course of centuries.*

THE EARLIEST known textiles are those found in Egyptian tombs and at Peruvian sites. Since the grave cloths which have survived were generally of plain linen, relatively little is known of the fabric designs of ancient Egypt, although at least one example of woven ornament from the 13th century B.C. has survived—a girdle of Rameses II. But there are still in existence Egyptian paintings which show fabrics ornamented with stripes, spots and zigzags, which may have been either woven or painted.

## Coptic Fabrics

There is evidence of tapestry weaving in linen in early Egypt and it may be inferred from the very richness of Coptic fabrics in the beginning of the Christian era that their designs derive from earlier tapestry traditions. This view finds support in the discovery of graves in the Crimea containing fabrics woven by emigrated Greek weavers of the fourth and third centuries B.C., of which the themes include figures on horseback, chariots, animals, birds, flowers, scrolls and stripes.

The early Christian period, prior to the domination of Islam in Egypt, is particularly rich in fine fabrics, and the motifs seen in these Coptic textiles include human figures, cherubs, birds and animals, flowers and trees, as well as geometric ornament, treated in natural and formal fashion. A great variety of themes appears, and these continue to be used, with changes in treatment and style, in textile ornamentation for many centuries.

At Alexandria, the center of Coptic textile activity, linen was the fiber principally used, varied at times by the use of wool or silk as a filling. The use of wool in this way probably came from Syria where it was the predominant fiber and its use and dyeing were well understood. Silk had arrived from China by way of Syria which held the key position at the western end of the silk trade route.

In Syria, Antioch was the center of the weaving industry, and Syrian motifs closely parallel Coptic themes. They include those using palmettes, roses and human figures as decoration, and there are patterns formed by repeating themes of men hunting on horseback with dogs, and lions, antelopes and other game. The style of these fabrics indicates the presence of Persian influences.

The spread of the Islamic religion through Persia and Syria, Palestine and Egypt, and across North Africa, is marked by an increase in the use of silk and by the elimination of the human form,—representation of which was forbidden by Islamic law,—and frequently by the use of Kufic lettering. In early times, significant stories, such as that of Adam and Eve, had given

214

illustrative interest to textile design and, since this was impossible under Arab rule, inscriptions were introduced, replacing the literary representations. The tradition of decoration formed by Kufic lettering continued across North Africa into Spain and finally is found, changed almost beyond recognition, in German textiles after the Renaissance.

## Persian Textiles

The earliest known fabrics of Persia are silks of the Sassanian period. They carry such design themes as cocks and dragons which derive from ancient Assyrian and Babylonian decoration. Even after the Islamic domination the Sassanian style with representation of human figures continues in such themes as princes, mounted on griffins, hunting animals; or leopards attacking hunters armed with bows. And there are elephants and camels derived from Eastern sources. Christian influences appear in scenes from the life of St. Joseph or representations of the Nativity.

Persian weaving later turned to representations of scenes from the poets and perhaps also drew inspiration from miniature painting. In the 16th Century under the Safavid Dynasty, Persians produced some of the most remarkable textiles ever woven. They made velvets and brocades which portrayed human figures in historical scenes as well as birds and animals and flowers. These Persian fabrics with flower designs are recognized as being among the most beautiful ever created.

Sassanian influences appear in the fabrics of the Byzantine Empire. Silk had come to Byzantium in the 1st Century and the secrets of its cultivation in the 6th; later there were established imperial textile schools and imperial mills. In Byzantine fabrics, which are of extremely fine workmanship, there appear formalized eagles and winged horses, griffins, lions, tigers and elephants. These were often placed within medallions and used with circular, diamond or pointed ogival forms repeated to form a regular design. A noted example is a cloth from the tomb of Charlemagne at Aix-la-Chapelle in which the pattern is formed by elephants in roundels.

## Byzantine Influences

The textile influences of the vast Byzantine Empire spread across Europe, as is witnessed by the many examples preserved in vestments in cathedrals in western Europe today. But it was in Sicily that the meeting of Byzantine and Arab influences established the main current of European textile art.

Fine silk fabrics were already being woven in Sicily in the 10th Century under the Islamic rulers. After the conquest by the Normans during the 11th Century, Christian themes became intermingled with the Arabic and biblical scenes were combined with Arabic inscriptions and interlacing bands. Horsemen, deer, birds and serpents also appear in these fabrics. Roger II brought Greek weavers with their Byzantine traditions to the Palermitan mills, and thus joined two great streams of textile tradition. Later, in the 13th Century, the weavers left Palermo for Italy and settled in Lucca and Pisa, from where their art spread to Florence, Venice, Genoa and many other Italian cities.

In Italy during the great centuries of the Renaissance, the traditions which had come through Sicily blossomed into marvellous silken fabrics laden with gold which were commissioned by the great patrons of the day and by the Church. The animals, fruit, flowers and vegetation, which had been used

Primitive—Polynesian

Chinese—18th Century

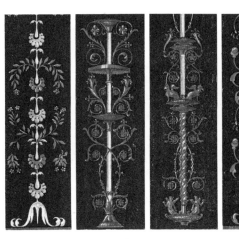

Pompeian

215

formally for so long, took on a new life and adorned damasks, brocades and velvets in amazing variety and profusion. Especially characteristic of these textiles is the pomegranate motif, still widely used in decorative fabrics.

Parallel with the growth of Italian weaving was the development of a textile industry in Spain. Silk weaving had been introduced there in the 9th Century under Islamic rule and until the 14th Century the themes favored in Arabic fabrics predominated. But, at the end of the 15th Century, with a return of Christian rulers, the influence of Italian textiles became paramount, interpreted with restrained formality and with a richness which reflected the vigor of Spanish expansion into the New World.

Agencies in France had been established by the Italian weavers and, with the recession of Italian influence, the French industry began to assume the importance which it later possessed. In France the vogue for tapestries grew, as wall paintings disappeared, with the conversion of the castle into the dwelling house. This brought gifted artists into the field of textile design who had been previously employed in mural and easel painting. Under their influence new plastic and realistic qualities were added to the formal traditional themes. New elements, such as ribbons, festoons, temples and chinoiserie gradually were added to the textile design repertory.

The subsequent invention of printing textiles by the use of engraved copper rollers opened new markets for textiles and new design possibilities.

## English Industry

The English industry, developed on a wool basis, followed French fashions and taste. The Scottish Clan Tartans, most notable contribution of the British to textile design themes, are said to have originated in France. Nevertheless the silk industry of Spitalfields became famous for its products and, with the growth of the cotton industry in the 19th Century, the fine striped Lancashire poplins become known throughout the world.

In India, cotton fabrics discovered at Mohenjo-Daro can probably be ascribed to the third millennium B.C. Conditions in India, until the Mogul emperors brought Persian influences, from the 16th Century on, were too unsettled to allow of the growth of an important textile tradition. Since that time the use of gold and silver in brocades from Swat, the woolen and silken "Paisley" shawls from Kashmir, and the growth of handcrafted blockprinted cotton textiles have made a contribution of richness and color to the current of textile design.

In the Far East there is evidence of the influences of Sassanian fabrics in China in the early centuries of the present era. In Chinese textiles until the 7th Century the warp was used to form the pattern; after the 7th Century

Italian—18th Century.

Persian—17th Century.

the filling forms the pattern as in the West, and this also indicates the extent of Western influences. After the Middle Ages, about which little is known, the themes were dragons, clouds, trees, flowers and mountains, done in both naturalistic and formal styles; gold and silver thread were increasingly used to embellish the fabrics. After the 16th Century, trade connections, established by the Portuguese, led to the development of "chinoiserie" for export to the West; here the themes were dragons, symbolic lions, phoenixes, waves, rocks and houses or temples.

In Japan the early influences were Chinese, but from the 16th Century European influences began to be felt. The Japanese tradition embodies an acute perception and appreciation of natural forms, and trees, blossoms, birds and animals, streams and bridges, are all portrayed with a delicate sense of color and design which is unrivalled.

## New World

In the New World the earliest fabrics known are those found in Peru—cotton tapestries which go back at least to 2500 B.C. These fabrics combine the technical means with the concept of design more closely than any other. Geometrically stylized animals, birds, trees and formal designs of later Peruvian fabrics, with their very rich use of color, undoubtedly exercise an important influence on textile designers today.

In North America the traditional designs which were in use among the Navajo Indians and other tribes have been joined to a great body of design material from other archaeological sources and together they constitute an American design tradition. The scope of the ideas derived from European textiles has been vastly broadened by an era of communication. The influences of Japan, Thailand and India are no less important in North American textile design of the 20th Century than those of France and Italy.

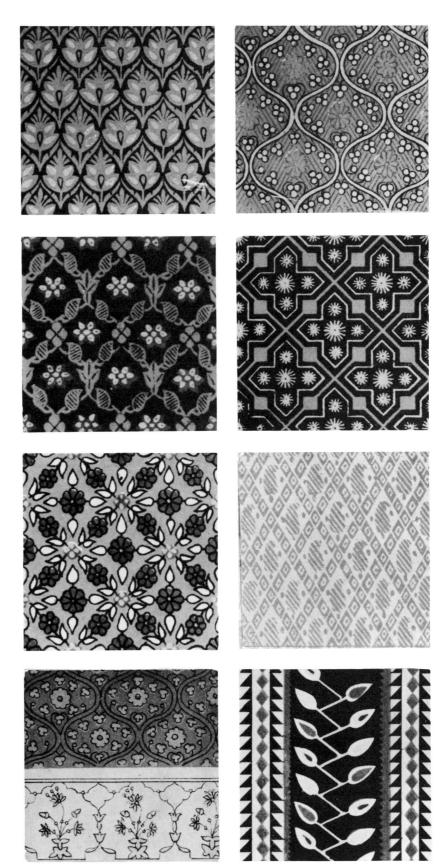

Some classic design motifs.

Star shaped panel with design of grape leaves and
braids.  Graeco-Roman  period . . . 3rd  Century.

Indian cotton fabric. Painted design shows details of Indian life.

Early 19th Century Pennsylvania Dutch design. Bird,
tree and flower motifs frequently used on toleware.

Persian gold brocade, 17th Century—Safavid period.

Italian, Venetian brocaded silk, 15th Century.

20th Century French tapestry designed by Jean Lurçat.

Contemporary satin chiné, inspired by old Persian illuminated manuscript, from Paris.

(*Opposite*) Rug, early 16th Century.
Probably from Tabriz, Northwest Persia.

225

Middle 19th Century American coverlet with twenty-five
original design motifs of embroidered cotton and wool.

American coverlet design.

Graeco-Roman tapestry, 3rd—4th Century.

Coptic tapestry panel, 6th—7th Century.

18th Century scarves woven in Poland.

(*Opposite*) Silver brocade woven with silk
and metal thread. 17th Century Persian.

Ancient bird design on glazed pottery.

(*Opposite*) Indian cotton with peacock and floral motif.

Carpet from the Mosque at Ardabil, Persia, dated 1539, knotted in woolen pile on a silk warp. The ground is deep glowing indigo, and other colors are a golden yellow, soft red, pale green, and black. The main design consists of a yellow medallion centering on a lotus-strewn pool, the both symbolizing the two principal sources of vitality. From the medallion issues a rich and complicated floral system. Pendant mosque lamps indicate the religious character of the whole work.

Imperial Court Robe with design of dragon's clouds, waves and mountains. Embroidered on raw silk . . . Chinese 18th Century.

Pre-Inca design.
Figures on alternating squares.

Shirt and sash in geometric designs
. . . Peruvian 11th-15th Century.

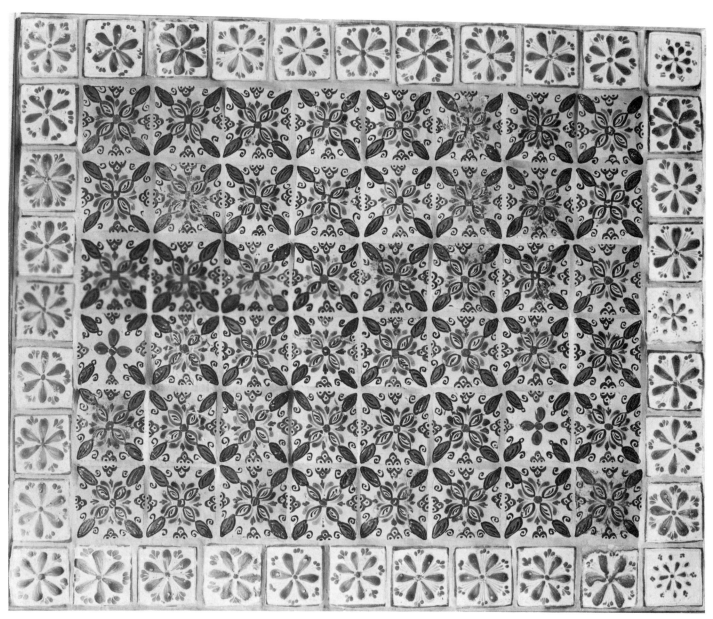

Tile Design.

(*Opposite*) The Dancing Dervishes . . . Persian 16th Century.

The Sufis, by means of dances requiring great concentration and attention, often obtained spiritual ecstasies which could never be attained by any amount of mere outward austerities.

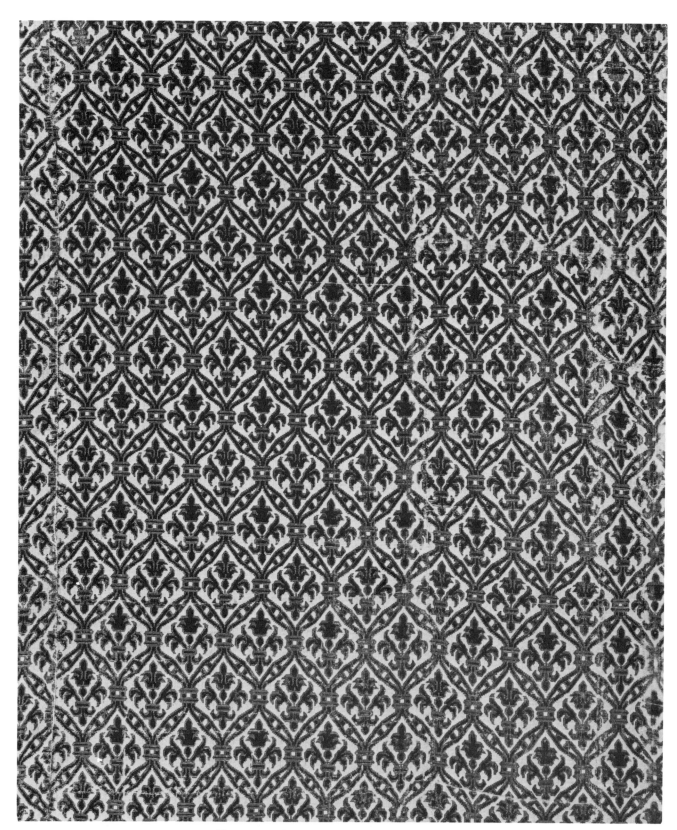

Florentine velvet. Late 16th or early 17th Century.

Printed Toile de Jouy, showing various processes in the dyeing and printing of textiles in France during the 18th Century.

La Tranquille . . . 18th Century French
design . . . showing Chinese influence.

Caswell carpet—American. Initialed and dated 1835. Signed
Z.H.G. (Zeruah Higley Guernsey), later Mrs. Caswell of Vermont.

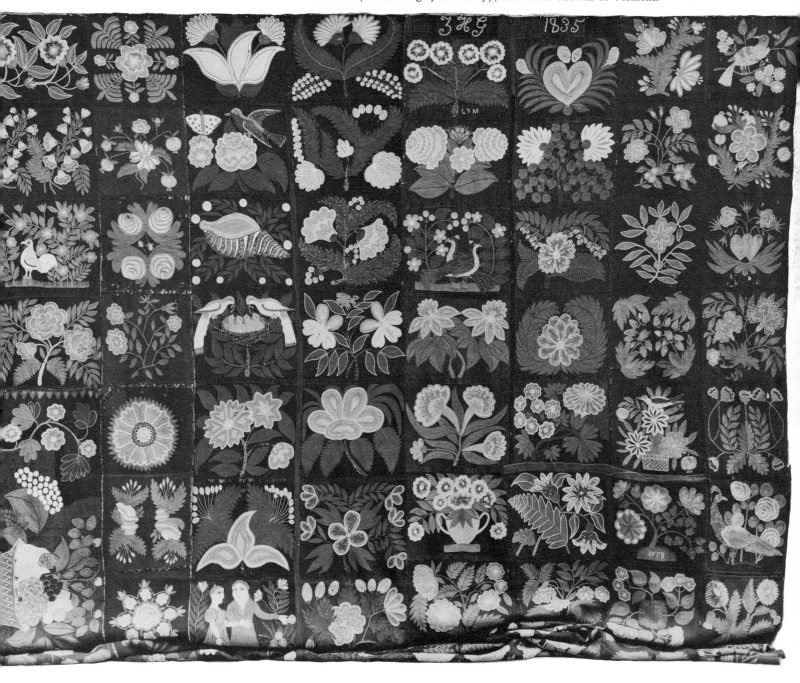

Wool prayer rug—Turkish, early 19th Century.

Design from Houquier's Book of Designs (Chinese influence).

Floral geometric design in Early American quilting.

Spanish (region of Valencia or Catalonia)
. . . 17th Century. Design painted on deep dish.

Linen embroidered sampler in brightly
colored silks . . . English 17th Century.

(*Opposite*) Contemporary 20th Century cotton. Printed paisley design.

(*Left*) Brocaded satin from the tomb of Kuo Ch'in Wang, Chinese 17th Century.

(*Opposite*) Fragment of Japanese silk woven in Meiji period . . . 19th Century.

(*Below*) Portuguese embroidery with floral entwined design.

Contemporary conversation print on linen ground, from Sweden.

Pre-Inca man and bird design.

Indian painted cotton with graceful intertwining florals.

Detail of woven Kashmir shawl. The birds are dark blue,
feet and accents are in red . . . 18th or 19th Century.

Verdure wool tapestry designed by William Morris and J. H. Dearle, from Merton Abbey, England.

Prayer curtain from the synagogue of Uherski Ostroh . . . 18th Century.

Richly embroidered ecclesiastical chasuble showing detail of the Adoration of the Magi . . . English 14th Century.

(*Opposite*) Contemporary screen print
design with stylized animal heads.

Modern printed textile design.

Fish design detailed from brocaded Peruvian textile, pre-Inca period . . . 10th-14th Century.

# Peruvian Textiles

*Weaving was the outstanding craft of ancient Peru and all techniques known to hand-loom weavers in the world, and some unknown elsewhere, were practiced by these people.*

In any study of historical textile designing and production there can be no doubt of the eminence of those textiles produced by the pre-Columbian civilizations of the Andean area. The term Peru is apt to be misleading, for what is now known as Peru was then part of a much larger area, which during the Inca Empire covered some 350,000 square miles and stretched from the mountain and coastal area of the southern border of Colombia to Central Chile.

Information regarding the many advanced civilizations that were built up in the highland Andes and the coastal Pacific plains is derived from the evidence of archeological investigation and to a certain extent from the folklore or folk-memory current among the ruling classes at the time of the Spanish Conquest. These people were distinct from their distant kinsmen of Mexico and Central America in not having any form of writing. Consequently, in recording events in their history, they relied upon human memory, which is greatly strengthened, collectively, by the absence of writing. As a result, the invading Spanish had access to a vital folk-memory ready to be set down in writing, which constitutes an invaluable mass of historical data. A reliable chronology has not yet been established owing to lack of any recorded calendars and also to this same lack of writing. Therefore all dates, though generally accepted, are approximate.

The beginning date of this era, heralded by a developed agriculture, herding, ceramics, weaving, metallurgy and building, is considered to be about 1200 B.C. The terminal date is usually considered to be 1532 A.D., which marked the onset of the Spanish Conquest.

Some of the earliest specimens of textiles have been found at Paracas, where the remains of two cultures have been distinguished. The first, Paracas Cavernas, is dated approximately 400 B.C. to 400 A.D. The Cavernas graves contained great quantities of textiles woven by different techniques. These examples show that the characteristic style of dress of the Central Andes region had been developed by that time.

The second culture, known as Paracas Necropolis, approximately 400-1000 A.D., is extraordinarily rich in examples of beautiful textiles. These had been used as wrappings for mummy bundles found in subterranean rooms, and also as part of the clothing and accoutrements of the deceased. Ponchos, shirts, shawls and turbans are not only superbly woven, but decorated with the finest over-all embroidery. The designs are elaborate and stylized forms of cat-demons, birds and anthropomorphized figures. The amount of time required to spin, dye, weave and embroider any one of these large textiles must be estimated in years. The craft standards for the weaving are consistently high and though there is such a great quantity of material it is difficult to point to one example of finer or poorer quality than the rest.

From this period, 400-1000 A.D., have come specimens of the Nazca culture, found in the valleys of Nazca and Ica. Nazcas, like the people of Necropolis, emphasized fine weaving. The over-all embroidery, so characteristic of Necropolis, is found in Nazca specimens, but brocade, warp and weft stripes, gauze and painted cloth are also prominent among the various techniques used by the Nazcas. A three-dimensional knitting needle to finish textile borders was common to both cultures.

## Design Symbols

Both Paracas and early Nazca designs are concerned with many-colored signs and symbols which are highly esoteric in character. In this connection it is interesting to note a comment by Lilly de Jongh Osborne on contemporary Indian weaving, in which she says, "There is no doubt in my mind that many of the Indian textiles still retain signs and symbols which are understood by very few, just as in prehistoric times, when all the Indian kingdoms were a well-organized flourishing whole, not everyone knew, or was allowed to know, the key to the secret of the clans. Only the learned priests and highest officials were in the secret. Perhaps this holds true today, and certain 'brujos,' 'Shamans' and 'zahoris,' or an occasional high-caste Indian, may still hold the key to the mystery. In a few years from now, all this will have disappeared from Indian lore, and another step

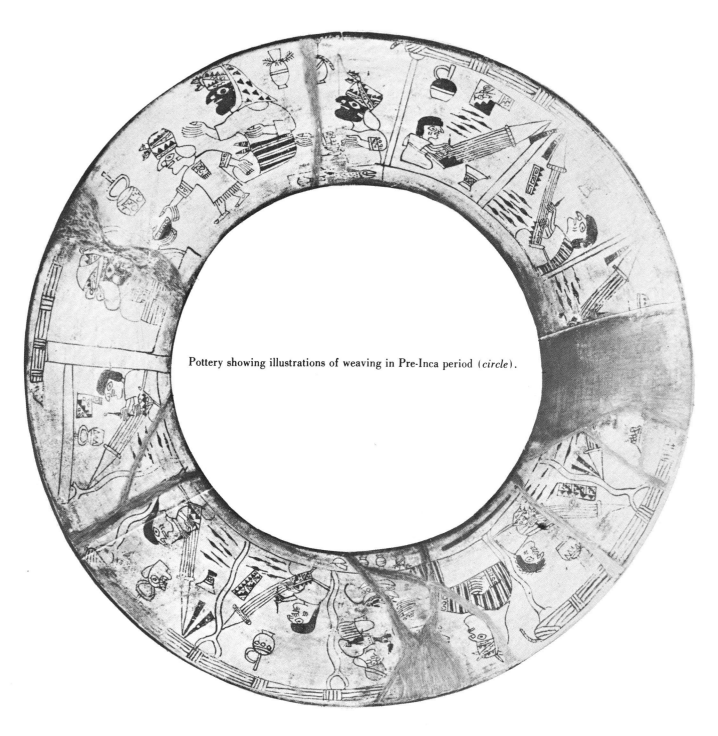

Pottery showing illustrations of weaving in Pre-Inca period (*circle*).

will have been taken in the complete downfall of this interesting race."

A constantly recurring symbol in the designs of these people is a feline, with prominent incisors, which is used in carvings, metal work, pottery and textiles from Chile to Southern Central America. Nazca symbols include a spotted cat, purely animal in character, sometimes conventionalized but almost always bear-ing in the front paws leaves or pods. It has been called "Bringer of the Means of Life" and appears to be a benevolent creature. In contrast to this symbol is the Cat Demon, a creature of ferocious appearance which sometimes has human and sometimes bird-like attributes. This creature generally carries the heads, or sometimes the whole bodies, of its victims. It is interesting to compare these dual aspects of the same deity, portrayed in these early Peruvian

263

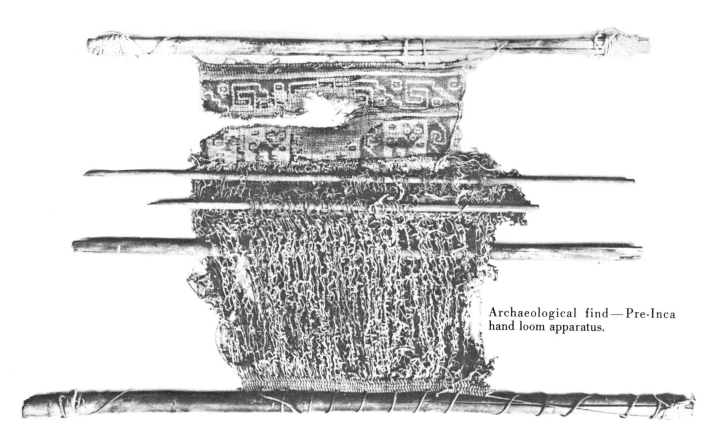

Archaeological find—Pre-Inca hand loom apparatus.

art forms, with the same duality expressed in the carvings and various memorials of the Hindu pantheon. The records of the early religions of both these peoples show an extremely realistic and unsentimental approach to the mysteries of life which the priests, and perhaps the artists themselves, were attempting to penetrate and express.

The Bird Demon is less realistically portrayed, has no human characteristics, and has to be studied with care in order to understand the design. It leaves no doubt in the mind as to the dangers and horrors attendant upon man's existence. This multiple-headed God consists of two or more unlifelike faces joined together in lines, each face having curling protuberances that spring out around it. The feet, legs, hands and arms are more realistic.

The fish motive, which has played a prominent part in the religions of many peoples, was much used as a symbol by the people of the coastal region. Painted representations of fish are found on the coarser, outer coverings of the mummy bundles. Interlocked fish designs in a step form are found in woven fabrics.

Though there seems to be difficulty in dating the Tiahuanaco cultures (Means divides Tiahuanaco into two periods, the earlier dates at approximately A.D. 600 and the later at approximately A.D. 600-

900. Wendell C. Bennett dates Tiahuanaco as approximately 1000-1300 A.D.), there is no doubt that the Tiahuanaco site, which lies on the Bolivian side of the Titicaca basin, is the most elaborate and purest manifestation of these cultures yet found. Only the area around the lake, situated at 12,500 ft. altitude, is habitable. It appears that a high archaic culture received a stimulating touch from outside, probably by the means of trade, which made it develop into a civilization in which mastery over tools and materials prevailed.

## Cultural Exchanges

Side by side with the mutual importation and exportation of Cotton from the lowlands and Wool from the highlands, must have gone a stimulating exchange of ideas in many fields, including those of decorative art. This fructifying exchange led to an extremely advanced civilization whose peculiar aesthetic style is summed up in the frieze carved on the monolithic gateway at Tiahuanaco. The central element and theme expressed in the art of Tiahuanaco is the worship of a Creator God who was known to the Incas as Virachoca.

The textiles of the period found in graves along the coastal Tiahuanaco area exhibit the same figures

A piece of poncho (robe), tapestry woven with llama wool.
Pre-Inca period.

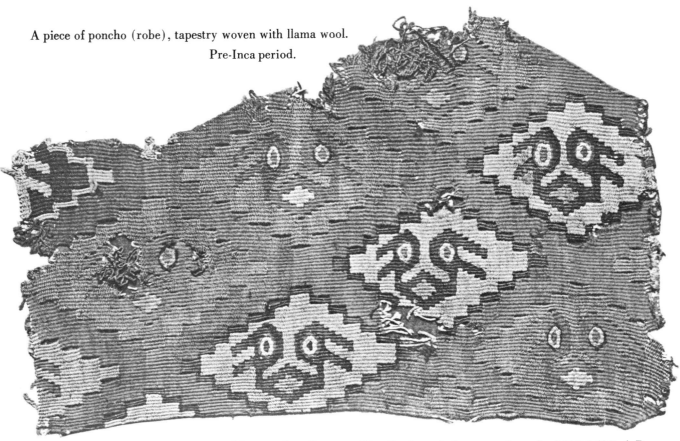

as are found in the stone carvings. Mummy bundles contain fine wrappings of brocade, double-cloth, painted fabrics, tie-and-dye and pile knot or velvet techniques. But the polychrome tapestries are the most characteristic. Some of these portray a highly-stylized feline design. Hats showing a skillful use of feathers in mosaic designs are found, as are some very freely and vigorously executed examples of painted cloth.

The growth of the Tiahuanaco culture was accompanied by a strong geographical expansion. The ceremonial nature of the ruins on the Bolivian site prove this, and the "Gateway of the Sun" is the acme of religious symbolism designed for a wide following of people.

Following this expansion, regional cultures re-emerged, approximately 1300-1438 A.D. On the north coast the Chimu culture represented a partial re-emergence of the earlier Mochica, modified by Tiahuanaco influence. The Chimu are noted for their large city units, the garrison towns and the ceremonial cities. The weavers produced great quantities of textiles, excellent in quality but not outstanding in design. Like the Ica culture which emerged on the south coast at this period, the traditional interest in weaving was continued but the design units were reduced to small geometric elements repeated over and over again.

The final period, approximately 1438-1532 A.D., was the Inca. These people appear to have been a loosely organized group in the Cuzco basin, who grew, in a comparatively short time, to be the only truly organized political state of the New World in pre-Columbian times. Its fame had spread to Panama and through the plains of Argentina to the mouth of the river Plata. The Spaniards first attempted to reach it via Paraguay and Argentina.

This vast territory of Empire (some 350,000 square miles) was welded into a political state by the power of military conquest. The Empire was based on agriculture, herding of domesticated animals, llamas and alpacas, and fishing. Hunting was reserved for the privileged as a sport. Though technology was advanced, especially in ceramics, metal crafts, for making tools and ornaments, weaving and architecture, no special innovation can be attributed to the Incas themselves; they inherited the techniques of the earlier cultures. Their great genius was for organization, and it was from this that they built and maintained an Empire.

Class distinctions were sharp in the Empire, the privileged ones having fine clothing, exclusive rights to ornament, better homes, and many other amenities denied to the lower classes. Specialists were numerous. Architects, military leaders, priests and teachers were drawn from the aristocracy; others,

Tapestry of wool, linen (?), and metal. Peruvian, 17th Century.

like specialized weavers and metal workers, were selected from commoners and supported by the State.

Inca weaving was mostly for clothing; the costume consisted of breech-clouts, wrap-around skirts, slit-neck ponchos, waist bands, head bands and carrying bags. Blankets and wall hangings were also woven, as was a great deal of cloth for mummy wrappings. The designs are largely geometric. It is characteristic for slit-neck poncho shirts to have a tapestry decoration which incorporates many small geometric elements. Examples of fine feather cloaks, wool veiling in many colors, gauzes and checkerboard designs are numerous.

Although there are no actual specimens of textiles which date from the earliest period, painting and modeling on pottery of the period depicts richly-clad men dressed in fine tunics, elaborate head-dresses and long mantles. In the British Museum there is a vase of this period, painted around the rim with a series of pictures depicting a weaving shop.

Probably the direct ancestor of tapestry in Peru was embroidery or net-work. According to Means, "the decisive step in the evolution of textile production for these people came with the omission of the weft of the net-work, and this step was taken early in the Tiahuanaco II period."

Plain webs embroidered, and plain webs painted, or even perhaps printed, are very old techniques in Peru. It has been established that in the case of painted cloths the design was applied after it left the loom. Braided and knitted work was much used in early Nazca times, as well as plain weaves decorated with embroidery, painting and printing, gauzes and voiles and a cord type of frieze also date from this period.

From Tiahuanaco came tapestry and rep weaves as well as fine examples of plain weaves, double-cloth, gauze, voile, net-work, braided and knitted fabrics and reticulated meshes and fringes.

During the Chimu period, the techniques for tapestries of all kinds, plain webs of all kinds, double-cloth, feather-work, gauzes and voiles and net-works were all well known and used.

## Materials

The two chief materials used for textile production in pre-Columbian times were Cotton and Wool from llamas and alpacas. There is occasional use of bast fibers and human hair. The cottons had as many as six natural colors and wool was of several shades of brown as well as black and white. The pre-Columbian weaver took great advantage of the use of these natural colors. Vegetable, mineral and some animal dyes (notably cochineal for red dyes) were used, and up to as many as 190 hues have been distinguished.

Slender spindle shafts were used for spinning the fibers, generally by hand-twisting, though the drop-spindle method may also have been used. Compared with modern measurements, the resulting threads are of uncommon fineness. M. D. C. Crawford measured samples of Peruvian threads against the modern scale of 840 yd. hanks to the pound. Modern Peruvian machine-spun threads range from Nos. 50 to 70; many ancient fibers are as high as 150-250. The same standard of fineness is also true of the wools, which measured two to three times the fineness of modern machine-spun wools. Although single threads were used, it was general practice to twist two or three together before weaving.

Ancient Peruvian in ceremonial dress.

The commonest form of loom was the back-strap. This loom had two bars, one of which was attached to a post, the other to the weaver's back by means of a belt, thus enabling the wrap threads to be controlled. Loom equipment was very simple, a cylindrical rod separated one shed of alternate warps, and a simple heel rod or heddle the other. Spindles served as bobbins and the weft was beaten up with a weave sword or short bone dagger. Smaller looms were used for belts and bands. Since some of the fabrics are too wide to have been woven on the back-strap type loom, it seems that a frame loom was also used.

The weaving of ancient textiles in Peru served not only utilitarian and aesthetic ends, but owing to the direct connection between the designs and the religion of the people, carried within it, from generation to generation, the story of very vital beliefs concerning the creative and destructive forces to which man is subject. It is this direct connection between the designs and their religion (it is still customary among the weavers of Central America to offer a prayer to the God of their crafts before beginning a new piece of weaving) that accounts for the forceful impact made upon the observer of these well-planned, patiently executed, vigorous designs. Above all, it is in the source of their inspiration that these historical textiles are a challenge to the inertia and superficiality of much that passes for textile designing today.

# TEXTILES IN THE NEW WORLD

*Explorers and colonists greatly enlarged the textile world as they discovered and settled the New World*

THE HUMAN RECORD of the development of fabrics in the New World is truly the history of America. It is curious to speculate what might have happened had the ancients realized the true wealth indigenous to this hemisphere in their early days of conquest, rather than seeking for gold.

When Columbus reached the shores of the Bahamas he saw cotton growing on the land. This convinced him that he had indeed arrived in India, and so he returned to Spain with great elation. Had Isabella and her advisors been blessed with a crystal ball, they would have had foreknowledge that Columbus had actually discovered a treasure-house which would eventually produce the world's greatest wealth in textiles.

## The Early Foundations

The weaving, dyeing, and embellishment of fine fabrics were well advanced in the New World many centuries before they were discovered by Europeans. Lack of knowledge by European exploiters caused them to lose far more than they had gained by usurpation and rapine. The story of American fabrics (without divergence along the main paths that history could have taken) is one that is a story of world changes. For example, the Portuguese da Gama opened a water route to India in 1497 to secure the cotton trade for his Emperor. Britain, in the 18th Century (with the aid of a half dozen mechanics) wrested the cotton empire from the East within

a short generation by inventions. Yet all these epic-making events were destroyed by a single American invention which shifted the area of cotton cultivation in America to the territorial limits of the United States. The early growth of New England is truly the story of mill building and operation. The early development of the South is the story of fabulous cotton plantations and international commerce in the fabric with its attendant latent explosive—slavery. Today, by paradox, the mills of the South far exceed the mills of the East.

This is how it was in the beginning. About twenty-five years after the first Massachusetts Bay Colony was settled in New England, there appeared this God-fearing and poignant appeal:

"Forasmuch as woollen cloth is so useful a commodity, without wch wee cannot so comfortably subsist in these pts by reason of could winters, it being also at psent very scarce & deare amongst us, & is likely shortly so to be in all these pts from whenc wee can expect it, by reason of ye warrs in Europe destroying, in a great measure, ye flocks of sheepe amongst ym, & also ye trade & meanes itselfe of making woollen cloaths & stuffs, be ye killing & othrwise hindring of such psons whose skill & labors tended to yt end, & whereas, through ye want of woollen cloaths & stuffs, many pore people have suffered much could & hardship, to ye impairing of some of yir healths, & ye hazarding of some of yir lives, & such who have bene able to pvide for yir childrn cloathing of cotton cloth (not being able to get othr) have, by yt meanes, had some of yir children much scorched wth fire, yea, divers burnt to death, this Cort—doth desire all ye townes—seriously to weigh ye pmises, &—indeavor ye pservation & increase of such sheepe as they have already, as also to pcure more—it is desired yt such as have an opportunity to write to any of their friends in England, who are minded to come unto us, to advize ym to bring as many sheep from thence as conveniently they can, wch, being carefully indeavored, wee leave ye surcease to God."

## Needs Dictate Character of Fabrics

This was the nature of the manufacture of American textiles in America in 1645. The fabrics of that time were created out of necessity—a frantic need for clothing for household use. So it is not surprising that American fabrics of the Colonial era did not approach the skill and sophistication of foreign materials. They were utilitarian in character, admirably adapted to the primitive surroundings in which they were created, and they tell of the strangest economic conditions under which they were developed.

The British Government never contemplated the establishment of a textile industry in the American Colonies. In fact, the Tory Party adopted the attitude that the Colonies were merely dependencies whose sole function it was to absorb British manufacture and to furnish Great Britain with whatever raw materials she might need. For example, the growing of flax, hemp, and silk was encouraged so that they could supply British mills, but Colonial manufacture was frowned upon since it might lead into competition or even economic independence, which had no place in British Colonial policy. For many years such occupations as spinning and weaving were known to the early settlers of New England, but this industry was not encouraged as long as British ships continued to dump their woven stuffs. In 1645, however, when shipping virtually ceased, a Massachusetts court issued what is thought to be the first order for Colonial cloth-making. Legislative records say that there was a need for domestic industry since New England was hampered by a lack of commodities to exchange for English goods.

## Power Politics and Industry Development

On the other hand, the South had enormous tobacco plantations, and tobacco could be shipped to Britain for articles of European manufacture. Thus the planter who had observed the balance of trade found no necessity of clothing himself with cloth of his own making, so he turned his efforts from the silk vineyards and mulberry trees that were the original concerns of the early founders to tobacco. When overproduction of tobacco and the bounty system attracted individuals to the manufacture of textiles, England kept her bulldog eyes on Colonial activities and Colonial governors were required to file lengthy and constant reports on manufacture. As long as fabric manufacture was confined to the needs of the individual household, such industry was tolerated by the British Government, but when it grew to such

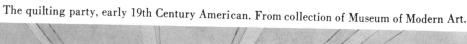

The quilting party, early 19th Century American. From collection of Museum of Modern Art.

proportions as to menace Colonial trade (as it did toward the end of the 17th Century) England immediately established measures restricting its further growth.

It is natural that with such a background of rigid restrictions, not much in the way of sophisticated industry could be looked for. However, with the release from British control in 1776, the tremendous growth of American fabrics as a world commodity came into birth. Today it is fully incorporated in the economic life of America. Our ingenious mechanisms turn out materials practical in nature and still add decorative and sophisticated character wherever and whenever needed.

It is interesting to note that among the restrictive acts that Great Britain passed to stifle American textile industry, was the Wool Act of 1699, whereby wool of any kind was forbidden exportation from the Colonies. Lord Cornbury, who had an eye to the future, stated in 1705:

> "Besides the want of wherewithall to make return to England, puts them upon a Trade which, I am sure, will hurt England in a little time; for I am well informed that upon Long Island and Connecticut they are setting upon a woollen Manufacture, and I myself have seen Serge made upon Long Island that any man may wear. Now, if they begin to make Serge, they will, in time, make coarse Cloth, and then fine;—how far this will be for the service of England, I submit to better judgments; but, I hope I may be pardoned if I declare my opinion to be that all these Colloneys which are but twigs belonging to the main Tree (England) ought to be kept entirely dependent upon and subservient to England, and that can never be, if they are suffered to goe on in the notions they have, that, as they are Englishmen, soe they may set up the same manufactures here as people may doe in England; for the consequence will be, if once they can see they can cloathe themselves, not only comfortably, but handsomely too, without the help of England, they, who are already not very fond of submitting to government, would soon think of putting in execution designs they had long harbourd in their breasts. This will not seem strange, when you consider what sort of people this country is inhabited by."

So much for the hampering political restrictions of early days. However, our inquisitive ancestors, in their first century of Colonial life, seized every opportunity to experiment with all the growing things they found which looked as if they could be useful—especially in spinning, weaving, and dyeing. Sheep

and flax were originally imported from overseas, for the finished cloth was costly. The women planted Bouncing-Bet and plucked scouring-rush for soap, and made dyes out of goldenrod, sumac, blond root, mapleback, pohweed, and other native plants. From Indian women they learned the formulas used in making dyes for quill work and basketry. However, they could not make a red dye that equaled lac or cochineal, nor could they obtain a blue as fine as that from indigo or French Pastel. So they were forced to journey to seaports to obtain this material for the making of better fabrics. Wool was the first fabric fiber to be spun and woven into fabrics. Farms that were scarcely cleared came to be used to graze sheep, while flax and cotton were carefully planted. In early Virginia, the Assembly encouraged manufacture of woolen cloths by offering a bounty of six pounds of tobacco to anyone who brought to the County Courthouse a yard of woolen stuff made in his own house.

## Early Weaving For Apparel

Since tobacco, at that time, was often used for money, miniature woolen mills flourished. However, our early law givers stated that five children under thirteen years of age could spin and weave only enough cloth to keep thirty persons clothed. Since a suit of clothing lasted from three to five years and fewer garments were worn then, it can be readily seen that child labor was not encouraged in those days.

The first commercial mill in America was founded by Master Ezekiel Rogers at Raleigh, Mass., in 1638. Ezekiel paid passage for more than twenty families of Yorkshire weavers who made fustians or "thickset" as it was sometimes called (thickset is a heavy corduroy), twill jeans from French cotton, and linsey-woolsey, a mixture of linen and wool (which might be a distant cousin of our present Palm Beach Cloth).

A second mill was started by William Penn, who sought to encourage industry in Pennsylvania. So vital was the wool industry to the fabric-starved Colonists that laws were passed in which no sheep less than two years old was to be killed and the meat sold. If a man's dog killed a sheep, the dog's owner must pay for the slaughtered animal and must kill the dog. Every family was required to have at least one spinner, and girls in those days learned to spin just as they learned to sew and cook, as matters of necessity.

The early spinners and weavers were of two categories. Entire families from cloth-making towns of Europe emigrated with the knowledge of the industry and settled in America with the idea of becoming mill men and clothiers in the new settlements. Second classification came from Scotch sheep farms, North Irish hamlets, English villages, German, Swedish, and Welsh homes, who had worked fabrics for generations. The wives wove, cut, and made the clothing for their entire families. These people showed such thrift in industry that men with money invested it, hoping to improve our fabric manufacture so that we would not depend on England even for fine linens and woolens. There was a fulling mill in Massachusetts in 1654 and (as Lord Cornbury remarked) "there was fine serge in Long Island" from 1705. Fulling was generally done by beating the cloth with heavy wooden mallets. Fuller's earth, a peculiar mineral, was used to take the oil or grease from the cloth, the object being to shrink the cloth and make it firm by heat and moisture. Originally the word was French, "*fouler*" meaning to trample, and it was done by the bare feet of the workers. The surnames "Fuller" and "Walker" are derived from it.

## Early Fulling of Cloth

Imagine a pioneer home where the home-mother came from some Gaelic croft. She would show the girls of the family how to comb, sort, and spin the wool, how to make home-made dyes, how to weave and "wauk" it. She might well do this singing the Oran Iutalk, an ancient Gaelic song that girls sang while "wauking" the cloth. Imagine, then, taking the newly woven fabric to a rushing mountain stream—they washed it by trampling the cloths with their bare feet in tubs of hot soapsuds perched over heated stones. Then eight or ten of them sit on the ground in two lines facing each other, the wet cloth stretched between them on a long hurdle. They toss it and trample it skillfully between their feet, singing the song until the work is done. A continental traveler coming upon such a company of girls singing and "wauking" with all their might would well think them crazy, but that is what the Lizbeths and Anns of America did before fulling mills were built.

Another task which had to be done by strong hands out of the home was "teaselling." This process raised the fibers to an even nap by scratching all over with weaver's thistles. It was then dyed and spread on the tenterfield and caught on "tenter-hooks." Today we use the expression "caught on tenter-hooks" which means to be in suspense or under a strain.

American fabric manufacture was given a further surging impetus by the embargo of the War of 1812. New England Colonists were forced to manufacture goods they could not buy. As a result, an increase of constant and varied home industries developed im-

portant character in the boys and girls of that period. They learned to make things with their hands and find all sorts of interest in varied subjects. This youth movement affected North and South alike. This generality may be exemplified in the story of Eliza Lucas. . . .

Eliza Lucas was a girl of sixteen who took complete charge of her father's plantation, "Wappoo," in Charleston, S.C., while he was absent as Governor of Antigua. Her mother was an invalid and could not live in the tropics so Eliza stayed home and ran the plantation according to letters her father sent her. The agriculture of the South, at that time, was based upon its export for cash money. Rice was raised on the coast where it was damp and warm, and rice could stand a long sea voyage, but rice would not grow on the uplands. Neither would cotton—that is, cotton of a grade which could be acceptable for manufacture. So Governor Lucas thought that indigo might be raised there. Indigo was practically worth its weight in pearls.

One day Elizabeth Lucas received a tiny package of indigo seeds, together with a letter giving her instructions for its planting and growing from her gubernatorial father who sent them from Antigua, one of the few places in the world where indigo was raised. The first tiny crop did well and yielded seed. The young mistress of Wappoo gave seeds to any planter who promised to cultivate it by spring. Since indigo sold for $50 a bushel (about $300 in value today) quite a few planters were interested.

After three years enough indigo was raised to begin making dye. Lucas engaged two brothers by the name of Cromwell, native Antiguans, to take over the dye-making. They built vats, cut the leaves at the right time and set them to soak, and watched the liquid froth and ferment day and night so that exactly at the right time it could be strained into a second vat and beaten with paddles until thick. It was then redistilled and dried in the shade and molded into tiny tablets for commercial use, but the dye proved to be a failure.

Nicholas Cromwell claimed the trouble came from the climate. He made all sorts of excuses, but Eliza was ready with cross-examinations and when he contradicted himself several times she fired him on the spot. With her own helpers she made a second batch of dye which was a perfect success! After the success was proven, Cromwell admitted being privately paid by British planters in Antigua to keep South Carolina indigo out of the market. Indigo became so successful that the first free school in South Carolina was established and maintained out of the profits of this trade. As a point of human interest, Elizabeth Lucas married a Mr. Pinckney and mothered

271

Charles Cotesworth Pinckney, who is remembered for his famous American saying, "Millions for defense, but not one cent for tribute." Our ancestors could thank Eliza Lucas Pinckney for her contribution to American fabrics.

In 1768, enraged by England's policy of keeping the Colonies from making or exporting anything but raw material, the graduating class of Harvard College agreed to graduate in homespun suits. About this time, a young officer in the French and Indian War, called George Washington, declared his militia men must be camouflaged in homespun uniforms rather than the gaudy red coats of Braddock's Regulars. For his own garments, he even carved the horn buttons which fastened them.

## American Inventions in Full Swing

With the conclusion of the Revolution, American inventive genius came into full swing. The most famous of these inventors, of course, was Eli Whitney, who invented the cotton gin. Prior to his invention even expert workers could not clean cotton fast enough to make it a profitable crop. But when Whitney created his Cotton Engine or "gin," cotton cultivation in the South became the most important item of its economic system.

George Washington had an aide-de-camp and close friend in one David Humphreys, a Connecticut Yankee, who firmly believed he could create a factory for weaving American broadcloth as fine as that of England. While he was Ambassador to Spain he imported merino sheep from that country to crossbreed with American sheep and thus improve the fleece. He returned to this country, founded the village of Humphreysville in Connecticut and built a factory there. In this factory the cloth was woven for the coat which President Madison wore at his inauguration in 1809.

Humphreys was a progressive and abhorred the dreadful conditions existing in the weaving cities of Europe. He hated child labor and believed in the rights of the working man as a human being. Accordingly, he founded a school for the children of his employees and hired fine teachers for them. He and some friends put through Connecticut legislation providing that every child of school age must attend school a certain number of days in the year. His friendly competitors saw the wisdom of his plans and followed them. As a result, a single generation later we find that Connecticut had more textile mills in proportion to her population than any other state and had a literacy record of only one illiterate adult out of 568, a greater literacy average

than is maintained in the United States at the present time.

Events in the manufacture of American fabrics moved with haste and precision after this time. Samuel Slater, a young Englishman of 22, came to America in 1789 looking for capital in the new republic to invest in cotton spinning. He linked up with Moses Brown of Providence, who had been experimenting with cotton-making machinery. Brown had met with little success because England would not permit machinery or models used in cotton manufacture to leave the mother country. Slater told Brown that he could build a machine from memory and he did, one of the important details which he could not remember coming back to him in a dream! Together they built the first mill at Pawtucket, R.I., where a waterfall of fifty feet gave them good power. Since most traffic was by water, the fact that Pawtucket was near the sea was equally important.

## Cotton, Linen, and Wool in New England

Three years later the first linen mill was built at Fall River. Although there was little mention in the records, these are the fabrics that were turned out in the early part of the 19th Century: native printed cottons in dotted patterns were turned out in Rhode Island; Massachusetts duck and canvas were woven at Boston, Haverhill, Salem, and Springfield; wool was manufactured at Byfield. In 1803 the first cotton factory was built in New Hampshire at New Ipswich. Cottons, linens, and woolen cloths were being spun and woven in the homes or by local weavers in all of the thirteen original states. However, in the lower counties of Georgia planters began early to buy clothing from Northern factories for their slaves. New Hampshire wove "tow-cloth" for this market. When the tumult and the hubbub of the War of 1812 ceased, a new clamor arose for power factories using water power for the manufacturing of fabrics. Where a swift rush of water was assured there was a good mill site. Legislative measures appeared to further the new and growing industry.

Contrary to popular belief, when Calhoun and Clay promoted a protective tariff in 1816 it was opposed in New England. Webster orated against it and as late as 1840 Southern Congressmen attacked New Hampshire for favoring free trade. The people of New England were of the opinion that a mushroom growth of manufacturing cities would not be good for this country. Many of the population of these towns were scarcely generations away from the prevalent abuses of English manufacturing towns and did not want this system to get a toehold in America. All admitted it would be a marvelous idea

Jackson or Indian Head Mills, from Fox History, 1842.

if factory towns could be built and directed with the following things eliminated: in England men worked in cotton mills for sixty-nine hours a week and were paid about $2.75 a week. Women worked for $2.00 to $2.25 for the same number of hours and children for less. A factory girl never had a hat or coat—wore a shawl instead. Her shoes were wooden-soled leather clogs, and over her skirt she wore a long linen apron tied with tapes from her chin to her ankles. Whole families had to labor in order to pay rent and buy food and clothing and they had to live within walking distance of the mill in order to exist.

## Child Labor in Early 19th Century

In what is termed a "humane factory act," William IV signed a bill in 1837 which forbade children under eighteen to work more than twelve hours a day or to work between 8:30 at night and 5:30. Children under nine could not work at any mill except a silk mill.

It was this sort of slave-labor market in which Amer-

ica had to compete, but men like Lowell, Appleton, Lawrence, and Humphreys believed in the future of American fabric manufacture and sought to make it come true. By contrast, in 1840 an American could bring up a family and save money on less than $2.00 a day, which he did earn. No city was so big that he could not walk to work and still have a house, a garden, a cow, a horse and chickens. Immigrants who worked in the old country for less than ten cents an hour were paid $9.00 a week or more in America. Since his total board and lodging amounted to $2.00 a week, he found America the land of golden opportunity.

Girls working in American mills lived on a plane that amazed Charles Dickens. In his "American Notes" he says that if any of his readers think these girls are living above their station, he would like to know what their station is. Some of the things that Dickens found almost unbelievable were the facts that he saw factory windows full of growing plants and vines; pianos, harps, and other musical instruments; circulating libraries; free hospitals; and savings banks

(*Below*) Wooden step bearing, from water wheel at Nashua Mill. Put in, 1853. Taken out, 1875. (*Right*) Regulations for employees of mills of Nashua Mfg. Co.

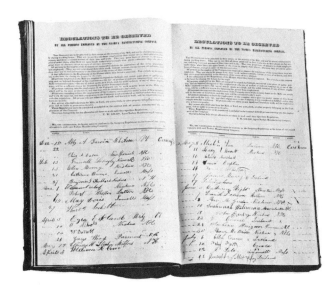

showing thousands of mill girls as their depositors with accounts averaging better than $100.

## As the Authors Saw the Situation

Dickens later goes on to say if their station is to work, they *did* work twelve hours a day. In violent contrast, Frances Hodgson Burnett, who came from Manchester, gave us a vivid portrayal of the British manufacturing city as it was in those days. "All the human framework of the great, dirty city was built around the cotton trade. All the working classes depended on it for bread. All the middle classes for employment, all the rich for luxury. The very poor, being awakened at four in the morning by the factory bells, flocked to the buildings over which huge chimneys towered and rolled their volume of black smoke; the responsible fathers of families spent their days in counting-rooms or different departments of the big warehouses; the men of wealth lived their lives among cotton, buying, selling, speculating, gaining or losing in COTTON, COTTON, COTTON."

## The Wave of Immigration

Word had spread through England and the Continent that America was the land of golden opportunity. Between 1840 and 1850, while over a million and a half immigrants tried to become absorbed in her population of about seventeen million, nearly twice as many came to these shores. The Scandinavians and Teutonic immigrants went West, giving rise to a vast cattle and sheep industry, but those from the British Isles drifted by the thousands into growing mill cities. Machinery was so simple unskilled labor could handle it. Problems arose, but with the advent of mass immigration and steam power the picture changed.

This time a greater unrest was irking the nation as a whole. The political views and the convictions of the North and the South were at loggerheads.

It is important, however, to correct an impression erroneously planted in our minds in early school days. This impression was that before the Civil War, cotton manufacture was the main source of revenue in New England, and it has been said that New England states were dependent on the slave-raised cotton. Statistics prove this idea far from true. In 1860, when more New Englanders were employed in factory work than ever before, less than half a million of the New England population of over three million were thus employed. At that time there were more cotton mills in Massachusetts than any other state in the country. Yet less than two per cent of her

people were engaged in the manufacture of cotton goods, and a similar proportion of her capital was invested in this industry. Wool and worsted manufacture amounted to approximately the same percentage. A state certainly cannot be called "dependent" upon any industry in which only two per cent of the people are occupied.

## "Shoddy" Comes into Being

As was previously stated, the immigrant mill workers coming to America in hordes changed the factory picture completely. Statistics of 1875 show that the English family in a mill town earned about $250 a year and was unable to save a penny. Going to Massachusetts, he earned $475 and found better living conditions than he ever dreamed possible. Naturally, his relatives in the old country heard about it and so the lemmings started to overrun New England towns. These immigrants could not farm, their wives and daughters knew little of cooking, mending, and even cleaning. The usual meal of the mill worker was bread, meat, and tea. As more and more unskilled labor saturated the market, the eastern states became largely overrun. After the Civil War, the demand for manufactured products was so great that any man with a few dollars could start a factory and get rich. Unscrupulous management in the woolen mills used this cheap labor to weave old rags, old carpets, and discarded war-time uniforms into a bastard cloth which was not worth even the cheap price at which it sold.

This cloth was known as "shoddy." The word has remained to stigmatize anything cheap and worthless. Today, the magic of our laboratories has enabled us to create regenerated fibers into superlative fabrics, but this knowledge was missing in Lincoln's time.

With the supply of labor many times greater than the demand, the employer, motivated solely by greed, could say "you take what I offer in pay or I get somebody who will." These owners were of a different breed than those who had originally founded the textile industry in the United States. The advent of power-driven machinery necessitated vast expenditures and investment of capital. This capital came from large cities like New York, Boston, and Philadelphia. Practically all of the investors had never seen a factory nor visited a mill town. Theirs was strictly a matter of impersonal investment with no concern for the mill workers.

## Mill Situation Worsens

This exploitation of labor led to a great discontent among the native mill workers, who objected to the degenerate standard of living that occurred among the new type of factory immigrants. Prosperous towns became squalid settlements with hastily built tenements, or old mansions or other buildings turned into tenements. Whole families lived in one or two rooms. They breakfasted on bread, molasses, and strong tea—at noon this was leavened with a slice of stringy beef or strong cheese. In order to earn more money they evaded child labor laws and put their children in the mills as early as they could. Soon an endless vicious cycle formed. The ignorant made the slum, the slum kept them ignorant and ill-paid.

This condition made the former factory worker, who had hopes of opening his own home and finding social security in factory work, seek other fields of endeavor. It also drove women out of the factory. These women drifted into needle trades, shop keeping, and even did home work.

"Bertha the Sewing Machine Girl" became a figure of song and legend. Some farsighted people who had studied English conditions realized what was happening in America. They enacted labor laws, child labor laws, sanitary laws and building laws, but these were avoided by the workers, who figured that it was a waste of time and a bother. Disease became rife in many communities where factories polluted the source of drinking water.

All during this time great studies were being made in improving machinery and systems of operation. At first nobody realized what would happen as a result of this progress, but suddenly farmers, housewives, and mechanics who were working more than ten hours a day saw no reason why factory hands should not do likewise and since children worked on the farm, why not children in factories. They would not favor social legislation. They did not realize that *their* work was controlled solely by their own movements and desires and that the worker at a power machine had every movement dictated by that machine. They could not understand the tax on nerves, the noise, the vibration and other hazards that made for occupational diseases. They did not realize that they were breathing pure, clean air, while the factory worker, even in a well-managed factory, breathed in dust, lint, fluff, and the vapors of hot oil in a temperature that sometimes stood all day at about 110 degrees.

## Capital and Labor

At the beginning of the 20th Century, capital seemed to realize that it was responsible as a class for the well-being of their employees . . . thus the American ideal was reborn.

While machinery and methods were improved, the human element was hard put to take care of itself. However, the American working men had one advantage over those of other nations. They could vote! It took a long time for them to realize the power of their ballot. On the other hand, even under benign conditions, many workers did not or could not take advantage of the devices put in for their comfort and protection. Birth certificates were falsified so that children could work in the factory. Workmen neglected safety devices because they were a bother. It took a great catastrophe to make the forces of law and order apply to both capital and labor, as well. This tragedy was the dreadful fire in the Triangle Blouse Factory in New York. A cigarette stub, carelessly dropped into a pile of waste under a cutting table, started a raging blaze in the upper two floors of a ten-story building. Hundreds of people were immolated in the fire trap. It took this dreadful event to make insurance companies put a clause in policies against smoking in workrooms. It made legislators pass laws against locking doors at the foot of stairs or having them open inward. At this time American labor unions began to make themselves heard in a really big way.

## Effects of Fashion Changes

At first labor had a difficult time of it because most of the factory hands were women and children for whom employment was only temporary and these had no desire to join unions. Next, French-Canadians replaced Irish and British in many of these mills. These workers had only one aim—to earn a nest-egg and return to Canada. Naturally they were not interested in joining unions. However, the vagaries of conditions where neither employee nor employer could tell when lay-off time came gave impetus to the union movement. Taking a leaf from the early English trade unions, organized labor was able to inform its cohorts of conditions elsewhere in the country when lay-off time occurred, so that the itinerant workers did not have to spend all their savings trying to get work elsewhere.

One of the peculiar phenomena that brought about this migration of workers was the rapid change of fashion. Fashions changed so quickly that entire plants were shut down over night when a style changed. For instance, paper collars were in vogue for a year—then suddenly they disappeared. A single New York factory employed over 800 workers and turned out two million a day. When the vogue died, these people were out of work and the machinery, invented to produce paper collars, was discarded. When a dressmaker made a gown of fine

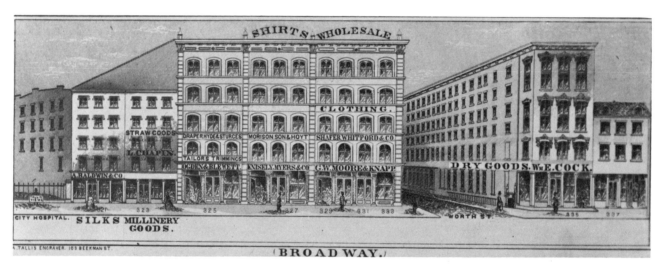

(*Top*) Worth Street from Broadway to Church Street,
1864. (*Bottom*) Broadway at Worth Street, about 1860.

silk or wool with rows of pleated flounces draped over the skirt and a pleated under skirt, it was fashion. But as soon as the costume was copied in cheap alpaca or imitation challis, which looked ridiculous, a new style had to be created immediately.

These changes affected the entire population because machinery was not adaptable and had to be discarded when new styles came into vogue. For example, hoop skirts vanished in a season, the braided bottoms of skirts became obsolete over night, laces on neck and wrist, which had been painstakingly made by hand and worn for many seasons, were discarded for ruching which was worn once and then

thrown away. All branches of clothing manufacture were in a constant state of uncertainty. Hand work and peasant skills were too costly for the mass market and thus the worker, who was constantly thrown out of work or poverty-stricken by a cut in wages, demanded cheap, ready-made goods which wore out quickly and were not worth mending.

The change of the century brought about the change of thinking. Men of integrity and intelligence studied these problems and found solutions to them. Enforced modern educational methods changed the habits and thinking of all classes. It emancipated women and so did away with freakish styles and worthless goods. Girls went in for sports, they participated in many things formerly barred to them. The simple tailor-made suit, the shirtwaist and other items of this nature that were worth making came into being.

The advent of electricity eliminated dirt and dust that made mill work a nightmare, and soon light, airy and healthy factories and shops arose. It also created manufacturing centers in the South and West. Legislation was passed in many states that raised the child labor age from fourteen to sixteen. Capital found it did not lose money by this legislation since they got more efficient work and better protection out of more mature labor.

## Capital and Labor Together

The stress and strain caused by vibration and other occupational factors were somewhat alleviated by diversions such as social clubs, bands, bowling teams, and other recreations that relieved the mental stress and strain of the factory hand, made him less likely to drop into a corner saloon to get a "tonic" for his nerves. Capital met with organized labor and came to the conclusion that the factory worker was a human being entitled to humane consideration and thus a new era was born.

This continued progress kept pace with the growth of our country. It opened a field of exploitation to the chemist who sought to create new materials in the laboratory. For example, until 1875 there was no real waterproof clothing—people wore great coats of heavy cloth or shawls in bad weather, but nothing was devised to keep clothing dry in a very bad storm. Goodyear succeeded in making overshoes of rubber, but the first rubber raincoat did not appear until 1890, when the mackintosh, a rubber-treated cloth coat, was invented. While this was a heavy, cumbersome affair, it became a forerunner of the gossamer-weight rainwear of today. Silkworm fiber was studied and re-created in the laboratories as rayon, nylon, and other synthetics which are commonplace today.

## The Age of Man-Made Fibers

From the turn of the century on, textile developments have been dominated by the laboratory. Since rayon first caused a sensation when displayed at the 1889 World Exhibition in Paris, man-made fiber developments have transformed the textile industry and the modern world.

Rayon was first produced in this country by American Viscose at the American Viscose plant in Marcus Hook, Pennsylvania, in 1910. Acetate, its companion cellulosic fiber, was first produced by Celanese Corporation of America on Christmas Day, 1924, at Cumberland, Maryland. Technical exploration continued to bring a host of new man-made fibers from the American laboratories and pilot plants during the next half-century. Nylon, the first non-cellulosic man-made fiber, was first produced commercially by Du Pont in 1939. It soon became a major factor in every major textile category, from cordage and carpeting to high fashion apparel. Acrylic, the second non-cellulosic man-made fiber, was also first commercially produced by Du Pont in 1950. Originally considered merely a "wool substitute," it has since developed into a major fiber in its own right. Polyester was first produced commercially by Du Pont in 1953. Since that time, polyester has become the most dramatic growth fiber of the era, quintupling production around the world during 1962–68, from 500 million to 2.5 billion pounds.

These were the major man-made fibers developed in the 20th century, but there have been a number of other important man-made fibers and variants developed for specialized markets. Triacetate was first produced by Celanese Corporation of America in 1954 as a women's fashion fiber. Polypropylene was first commercially marketed by Hercules in 1961 and has since become a major carpet fiber. Important stretch fibers such as Spandex and anidex were also developed during this period. Other man-made variants, developed from chemical changes and changes in cross-section, produced nylons and polyesters which were flame-resistant, soil-cloaking, loftier, more reflective, stronger, pill-resistant, etc., than these fibers in their unchanged form.

Other technical developments since the end of World War II have transformed American consumer expectations as to fabic wear and fabic care. Permanent-press garments, which emerged during the mid-1960's, have created a whole new dimension of wearability in many types of men's, women's and children's apparel. By 1970 the U.S. textile industry had come a long way from Worth Street.

Storage tank for acetate solution.

# FIBER TO FINISHED FABRIC

# SPINNING
# of
# YARNS

- Basic Principles

- History of Spinning

- Methods of Spinning

- Spindle-Less Spinning

- Fiber Blending

- Textured Yarns

- Stretch Fabrics

- Yarn Count and Denier

Modern spinning machinery permitting maximum working speeds is used by textile spinners throughout the world.

# Spinning

*The process by which the mass of the original fiber is gradually converted into the yarn which can be made into the cloth. In modern mill production, spinning is a series of progressive and interesting steps.*

From a wall painting in Egypt, *circa* 1900 B.C.

SPINNING is the process by which short fibers are converted cohesively into continuous yarns so they can be woven into cloth. Most fibers are neither long enough nor strong enough in their raw state to be used for weaving. They must therefore be drawn, and twisted together to make a continuous, strong, uniform, and workable strand. This continuous strand is called yarn.

## A Simple Principle

The principle involved is easily demonstrated. Take a piece of ordinary absorbent cotton and detach from it one thin layer. Notice that this layer is made up of many short fiber strands laid more or less parallel to each other, loosely held together by friction, and easily pulled apart. Now pull away a narrow ribbon of cotton and twist it between your fingers. Immediately it becomes a fairly strong yarn and the tighter you twist it the stronger it becomes. You can now no longer pull it apart with ease. What you have done is "spun" some cotton fibers into cotton yarn. If you wish to make the yarn even stronger and thicker you may cut the yarn in two and twist the two pieces together. You have now *doubled* and *plied* the yarn.

The reverse operation will also demonstrate the process of spinning. Take an ordinary piece of cotton sewing thread and examine it carefully. Notice that small hairy fibers protrude from the core of the thread all along its length. The yarn is quite strong and if you try to break it you must apply strength. But now untwist the yarn. It is made up of several fine strands and these in turn are made up of many short fibers. If you take out one of the fine strands you will find it pulls apart without much pressure. You are back to the absorbent cotton.

## Origin of Homespuns

The yarn you produced with your fingers was fairly rough and irregular and could not compare with the fine, uniform thread produced by modern mechanical methods. However, even allowing for your inexperience, this was the kind of yarn produced by primitive peoples long before recorded history. The yarn thus produced was uneven and "primitive"; its very irregularity gave to the woven cloth an interesting "homespun" texture which we can duplicate today by mechanical means.

## Which Fibers Are Spun?

Not all fibers need to be spun but all *short* fibers must be spun in order to make a continuous yarn. Silk in its natural state is already a continuous filament spun by the silkworm. It needs only to be thrown (twisted) together for strength and thickness. All man-made fibers are also continuous filaments, mechanically spun through the holes of a spinneret. However, in the case of silk, the so-called waste fibers are not continuous and these must be spun. In the case of the man-made fibers they are often deliberately chopped into short staple lengths and then spun just like cotton, wool, flax, etc. This is done to give the yarns a rougher, more hairy hand, and the resultant cloth a bulkier, drier and less slick surface more akin to wool or cotton.

"When Adam delved and Eve Span"—women have been the spinners of the human race since the dawn of civilization. (*Left to right*) Archaic Greek; 18th Century British: Modern Navajo Indian.

# History of Spinning

SPINNING is much older than recorded history. It parallels the development of man as a social creature who organized himself into groups for his self-preservation.

The first men—or women—undoubtedly spun the fibers of flax and wool much as we have described the experiment with absorbent cotton. As time went on implements were invented to make the work easier. The first of these was probably the *spindle* and its companion tool, the *distaff*.

## How the Spindle Worked

The distaff was the stick to which the loose mass of fibers was tied. The spindle was a short stick, perhaps a foot long. It was notched at one end and pointed at the other. Near the pointed end was attached a large washer or *whorl*, usually made of clay. Holding the distaff under her arm in order to leave both hands free, the spinner attached the fibers to the spindle notch and allowed the weight of the whorled spindle to pull the fibers downward in a twirling or spinning motion. As the spindle descended, she drew out the fibers and formed them into a thread with her fingers, while the whirling spindle twisted them into a tight strand. When the spindle neared the ground the spinner took it up, wound the finished thread around it and caught it in the notch. The motion was then repeated.

## From Stone Age Man On

This type of spinning was common to all early peoples. The remains of Stone Age Man in the Swiss Lake Dwellings revealed examples of spindles, clay whorls, and even prepared thread. Ancient Egyptian wall paintings show spinners at work more than 6000 years ago. The Bible and other ancient writings have many poetic references to the distaff and the spindle. Rome's great lyric poet Catullus (54 B.C.) wrote an accurate and detailed description of spinning. An early English translation reads in part:

"The loaded distaff in the left hand placed,
  With spongy coils of snow-white wool was graced;
From these the right hand lengthy fibres drew,
  Which into thread 'neath nimble fingers grew.
At intervals a gentle touch was given,
  By which the twirling whorl was onward driven;
Then, when the sinking spindle reached the
    ground,
The new-made thread around the spire was wound,
Until the clasp within the nipping cleft
Held fast the newly finished length of weft."

## Primitive but Wonderful

The results of such hand spinning were not necessarily crude. Some showed refinements which have not been equalled by the most complicated modern machinery. The famous Dacca muslins of India were made of thread so fine that one pound of raw cotton produced a yarn 253 miles long. The thread was so fine and delicate that it could not withstand the weight of a traditional suspended spindle. Instead, a bamboo needle lightly weighted with clay was rotated while resting on a shell.

Cloth woven of this thread was so fine that when spread over grass it was invisible, since it was difficult to distinguish from the dew.

The basic principles of converting coarse fibers or strands into finer yarns by twisting, twirling, down-pulling or spinning are still followed by modern industry.

## Leonardo's Flyer

The spindle and the distaff were the only ways known to make thread for many centuries. The spinners of India were the first to introduce the mechanical improvement of the spinning wheel but it was not until at least the 14th Century that this became known in Europe, and it was not until 1533 that the Saxony Wheel with its foot-operated treadle was invented in Nuremberg. It incorporated the use of a *flyer*, originally invented by Leonardo da Vinci about 1519. This was a wishbone-shaped device which is often described as the first continuous movement in industry. It made it possible to twist the yarn before winding it on the bobbin, and to distribute it evenly along the whole length of the bobbin.

## How the Spinning Wheel Works

The Saxony Wheel is often associated with the Colonial period in American history. It is still used in many parts of the world where handicraft prevails. Basically, it is a method of turning the spindle, twisting and winding the thread by mechanical means. Instead of being suspended as in the primitive method, the spindle is held horizontally in a frame within the U-shape of the flyer. The distaff holding the fiber is rigidly fixed in an upright position. Fiber is fed by hand from the distaff, through the eye of the spindle, then through the flyer, and finally to a bobbin on which it is wound. The spindle resembles an axle on which the bobbin is a wheel. Both spindle and bobbin are connected to the big spinning wheel by separate bands so that they revolve at different speeds—the spindle slightly faster than the bobbin. This makes it possible to twist and wind the yarn at the same time. The big wheel, of course, is operated by a foot treadle.

## An Inventive Era

The Saxony wheel was used for over two hundred years. It was not until the beginnings of the Industrial Revolution in England, and the resultant need for speed in production, that modern mechanical spinning inventions appeared. They came in a floodtide of effort. Within the short space of 40 years, from 1738 to 1779, spinning changed from a handicraft into an industrial giant. The important dates and events in this shift can be summarized as follows:

**1737.** The Englishman Lewis Paul, with the collaboration of John Wyatt, invented the *roller method* of spinning. By this method the carded slivers of fiber were fed into rollers which drew them out into long strands ready for spinning. The method was not commercially successful but laid the foundation for later efforts.

**1764.** James Hargreaves, a carpenter from Blackburn, England, made his first *spinning Jenny* and named it after his wife. It was able to manipulate eight spindles at the same time. By 1766 he had perfected the device so that it could operate 100 spindles at once.

**1769-1775.** Richard Arkwright, a barber from Preston, England, developed his *water-twist frame*, so-called because it was driven by water power. It

Model of the Arkwright spinning frame patented in 1769.

combined the roller method of Paul with the spindle, flyer and bobbin from the Saxony wheel.

**1779.** Samuel Crompton, another Englishman, developed his *spinning mule*. It combined the inventions of Hargreaves and Arkwright. He sold the device for 106 pounds. Later, in 1812, the British Government awarded him 5000 pounds. His device had by then provided work for 70,000 spinners and 150,000 weavers; Britain was operating 5 million spindles and all by steam as a result of the invention of the steam engine by the Scotsman James Wyatt in 1785.

*These four Englishmen—Paul, Arkwright, Hargreaves and Crompton—are responsible for the basic inventions upon which all modern spinning is achieved. The principles they developed have not changed with the years.*

**1828.** Charles Danforth of Paterson, N. J., invented the cap-spinning frame.

**1828.** John Thorpe of Providence, R. I., took out a patent on his ring-spinning device.

## The Four Methods of Spinning

Arranged chronologically, the four types of spinning are: *flyer, mule, cap,* and *ring*. These are all common to the woolen and worsted industry. Most cottons at the present time are spun on either the mule or the ring frame. In this country practically all our cotton yarn is spun on the ring frame, while in Europe the mule is still by far the more common.

1. FLYER SPINDLE. The earliest spinning frame employed the flyer spindle, which resembles the flyer

Roving (*photo at left*) the drawing out of the fiber into a finer strand and slightly twisting it, is the step before spinning, which is illustrated at right.

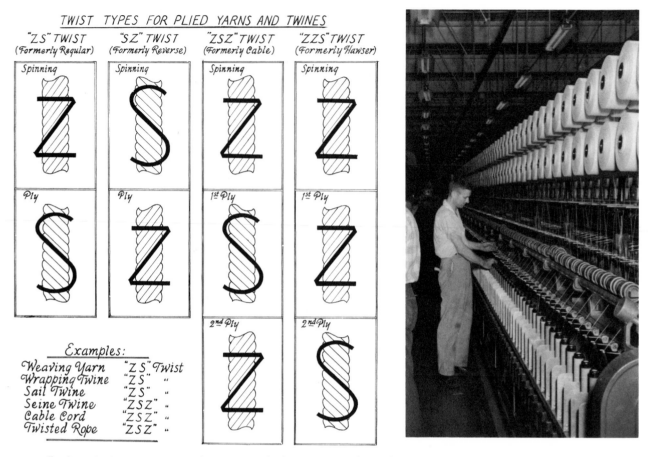

### TWIST TYPES FOR PLIED YARNS AND TWINES

**"ZS" TWIST** (Formerly Regular)    **"SZ" TWIST** (Formerly Reverse)    **"ZSZ" TWIST** (Formerly Cable)    **"ZZS" TWIST** (Formerly Hawser)

Examples:

| Weaving Yarn | "Z S" Twist |
| Wrapping Twine | "Z S" " |
| Sail Twine | "Z S" " |
| Seine Twine | "Z S Z" " |
| Cable Cord | "Z S Z" " |
| Twisted Rope | "Z S Z" " |

In the spinning process, it is the twisting which gives strength to the yarns. Twist types are shown in the diagram above. Twist "S" and "Z"—the letters S and Z are used to clarify the methods of twist given to yarn under varying conditions of ply. The process of twisting yarns as desired is done by modern, high-speed machinery (*photo above right*).

of the present-day roving frame. The yarn was drawn from the front delivery roll down to the top of the flyer; it was then twisted around the flyer leg, through an eye, to the bobbin. As these frames ran at a low speed (up to 3,000 r.p.m.) the yarn that was produced was quite smooth and free of beard. The difficulties with this method was the low production and the strain put on the yarn by the bobbin drag.

2. Mule Spinning allows the use of the free spindle and thereby offers a means of increasing production. The process is not continuous, since there are three distinct stages of operation, namely: drafting and drawing, twisting, and finally winding. The system allows spinning yarns of extreme fineness, and also with very low turns of twist per inch.

3. Cap Spinning is a continuous process. In place of the flyer, a cap or bonnet is substituted. The

bobbin, in cap spinning, is driven by a spindle-banding; the bobbin rises and falls within the inverted cap. The yarn comes from the delivery roll and drags over the lower edge of the cap. Here the bobbin may revolve up to 7,000 r.p.m. Since the bobbin is driven, there is only slight tension in the yarn at any time. Because of the higher spindle speed, the yarn may be a bit fuzzy. Much worsted yarn is spun on this type of frame.

4. Ring Spinning is a more recent development. Spindle speeds are high and the process is continuous. The use of the ring and the traveler subjects the yarn to some strain and also reduces the extensibility of the yarn to some degree, but this is not a serious factor. The bulk of yarn is spun on this system, since it allows increased production per unit of floor space. However, the dominance of ring spinning has now been challenged by the spindleless spinner, whose description follows shortly.

Automatic mixers blend the fiber.

## Steps in Commercial Spinning

In modern mill production, spinning is a long series of progressive operations by which the mass of fiber is gradually converted into finer and stronger yarns. The effect of the various steps is cumulative until it reaches a point where the yarn is ready to be woven into cloth. Slightly different methods have been evolved for treating the different fibers and these are briefly discussed elsewhere under each fiber heading. (See WOOL, COTTON, FLAX, etc.) However, the basic steps are essentially the same. In the following outline, the example used is cotton:

1. *Opening.* The bales of raw fiber are broken open.

2. *Blending.* Different grades and types of fiber from several bales are blended together for different end uses. The machine used is called a blending feeder.

3. *Picking and Lapping.* Lumps of fiber are loosened, separated, and cleaned of heavier impurities and formed into laps or rolls.

4. *Carding.* Laps of fiber are fed into carding machines which begin the proces of straightening out the tangled mass. This is done by drawing it over revolving cylinders which are fitted with wire teeth. The fibers are formed into *slivers,* or rope-like strands.

5. *Combing.* For higher-grade and finer yarns this same process is continued in the combing machine. The teeth are finer and only fibers of the same length remain in the combed sliver.

6. *Drawing.* Several slivers are combined and drawn out into a longer, thinner strand.

7. *Roving.* This is usually a series of operations, the first of which is known as a *slubber.* The result of the roving process is to draw out the sliver into an even finer strand and to twist it slightly. The product is known as roving.

8. *Spinning.* The spinning process proper takes the thick strands of roving and converts them into thinner strands of yarn which have been twisted sufficiently for strength and wound onto bobbins or tubes.

9. *Twisting and Winding.* Yarns used for the filling (crosswise) threads of cloth can usually be used in the state they emerge from the spinning frame. However, warp (lengthwise) yarns undergo more tension and must be made stronger. This is often done by twisting or plying two or more yarns together and then winding them on spools.

Automatic hopper feeders and double scutchers with automatic lap changers.

Carding machines automatically straighten out the laps or rolls into rope-like strands. Modern carding machines are equipped with automatic can changers.

The roving process is shown alongside. The combed slivers are drawn into comparatively fine strands, twisted slightly, and made ready for spinning into still thinner yarns.

View of preparatory and spinning sections (at rear) of a modern mill. Carding, drawing, and roving frames are shown.

*Packaging the yarns.* After spinning of the yarns is completed, they must be put up in a form suitable for shipping to the customer and this will vary with the yarn type and the customer's needs. It may range from sewing thread put up on tiny wooden reels to huge warp beams ready for the loom. *Above left,* Bemberg yarn being put up in skeins ready for dyeing; *above right,* asbestos yarn being wound on cones after being spun from mineral fiber; *below,* worsted yarn being wound in packages. After winding in appropriate form the yarn is packed and shipped.

Yarns intended for use in the warp of fabric are often shipped in the form of a warp beam; that is, a large cylindrical package of yarns of the correct length and type grouped in the right order for the particular cloth to be woven. These yarns are first drawn from a creel, *above left*, and then dressed or slashed with size, *above right*, to protect them from fraying during the weaving process and lubricate them on the loom. When dressed, or in certain cases direct from the creel, the yarns are wound parallel and at even tension on the beam, *below*, ready for the loom.

Wool carding, combing, spinning and weaving in a mediaeval castle.
Detail from a XIV century miniature painting in the British Museum.

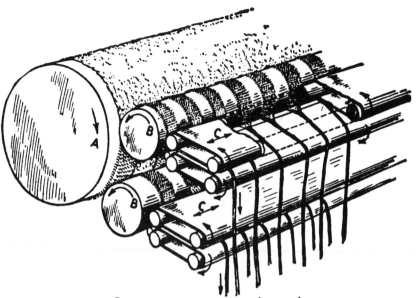

CARD DELIVERY OF ROVING for woolen yarn spinning is accomplished by two smaller rollers (B) which lift the fibers in ribbon like sections by alternate strips of wire clothing and pass them on to rub aprons (C). These, by sideways motion impart mock twist and condense the ribbons into strands of roving.

GILLING. Two slivers (A) are drawn and combined to make one small sliver (B) The fallers (C) move forward through the fibers faster than the slivers are fed forward by the feed rolls (D), but slower than the fibers are drawn by the delivery rolls (E). This reduces the sliver strand.

MULE SPINNING. Here the carriage (V) on which spindles are mounted, moves to and from main spinning frame that holds the feed rollers (J). On outward trip the spindles idle, and it draws out the roving (R). At the end of this motion the feed rollers (J) stop; the spindles (W) revolve, allowing the roving (R) to slip over the spindle top (X) thus twisting it into yarn. On the inward trip the yarn is wound onto the bobbin (Z) by the continued revolving of the spindle (W).

## Novelty Yarns

This term covers a whole category of yarns which are irregular rather than smooth in structure. Such irregularities may take the form of *slubs* of thick and thin places in the yarn. Another effect is achieved with *flake, nub* and *seed* yarns, where different types of yarn are plied together so that they form flakes, nubs, or seeds on the surface of the fabric after it is woven. *Bouclé, ratiné* and *snarl* yarns produce similar effects with raised loops and kinks on the surface. These types of yarns have traditional uses in textured fabrics, especially in heavier cloths used for draperies and upholstery.

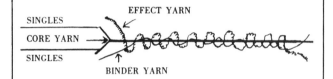

Ratiné ply yarn is sketched above
and bouclé ply yarn is below.

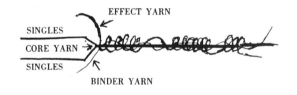

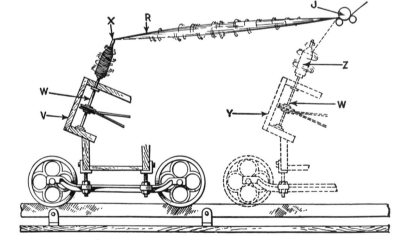

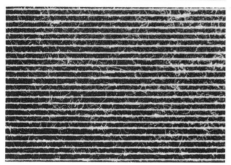

Top left: Close-up of yarn from a conventional spinning machine. Bottom: The same cotton yarn from a spindleless spinner. Right: The world's first spindleless spinning mill in Czechoslovakia, with 2,000 spinning units.

The sliver is at the bottom of the spindleless spinner; the crosswound package, ready for the loom, is at the top. In between is the unit containing the thinning and spinning mechanism that can be tilted forward for easy access. The white circles above the numbers are lights that signal yarn breakage.

# Spindleless Spinning

Late in 1967 the world's first spindleless spinner was introduced at a textile machinery fair in Europe. The "open end spinning frame," known as BD 200, was produced in Czechoslovakia by Elitex Textile Machine Co. Thus, the spindle, one of man's earliest textile tools, was challenged by a new spinning technology said to almost triple production and require less than half the manpower of conventional spinning. It also reduces floor space by one-third. The Czechoslovak unit achieves this by combining the work of the roving, spinning and cross-winding. It is said to produce yarns with more bulk and greater regularity, resembling combed cotton yarns.

### How It Works

The "open end spinning frame" spins cotton, viscose or blended yarns directly from two or three pass slivers by using a spinning chamber with a velocity of 30,000 rpm as compared with the conventional spindle-ring-traveler system of 15,000 rpm maximum.

The traditional direction of the spinning process is reversed: the supply bobbins of sliver are located at the bottom and are unwound by the feed roller of a thinning mechanism which separates, parallelizes and thins the fibers. These are sucked into a spinning mechanism in which no metallic moving parts come in contact with the yarn. The spun yarn is drawn upward and crosswound onto bobbins at the top of the frame. The final crosswound package is then ready for processing on most weaving looms.

# Fiber Blending

*The blending of fibers gives fabrics special functions, styling and wearing qualities.*

Blending of fibers is an old textile art, known and practiced for years. Different grades of wool and of cotton are often blended for different textures and uses; and wool/cotton, wool/silk, cotton/silk, are blended for the same reason. The man-made fibers, however, have added new dimensions to fiber blending. This involves a knowledge of science and technology as well as of design, and it has fostered revolutionary changes in textile production. The rapid pace of new fiber development has been matched by widespread expansion of the blend concept so that fabric blends are a dominant factor in every branch and on every level of the fabric-forming industries.

In research and development, in machinery and plant construction, in yarn production, weaving and knitting, in chemistry for dyeing and finishing, in dyeing and printing procedures, in designing and marketing activities, fabric blends have been a strong force in bringing change and growth to textiles.

It is the very nature of the man-made fibers that they are in perpetual evolution, responding to evolving needs and tastes. Thus, in every season's new developments in the man-mades, of major significance are the new blends created for superior performance and aesthetics.

## Blends and Mixtures

It is important to distinguish between *blends,* in which two or more different fibers are blended together before being spun into yarn, and *mixtures,* in which yarns spun of different fibers are combined

## MELTING POT OF THE FIBERS

"The future of the textile industry as a whole must be built on cooperative effort between the natural and the man-made fibers. The acceptance and success of the man-made fibers is based on our modern way of life, on the organization of modern industry, and it is geared to the advancing frontiers of mankind. Cooperation between the natural and the man-made fibers must be directed:

- To provide for the totality of the world's textile needs.
- To provide for such needs progressively, as they develop.
- To provide for such needs at prices that will make them available to all.

It was this kind of thinking that gave birth to the first man-made fibers sixty-odd years ago. It continues to be the philosophical base and the justification for their future growth. And it provides the background for what is perhaps their outstanding achievement: namely, the re-vitalization of the textile industry, the opening up of new textile horizons, the re-orientation of the whole industry in the direction of progress and creative experimentation.

Thus, one outstanding fact governs the textile picture of today: the stage of competition between natural and man-made fibers is now past. No longer do we speak of the pre-eminence of one fiber over another. Today a new textile reality is emerging from the gigantic melting pot of the fibers."

Automatic fiber-blending from bin, an ancient art gone modern.

by weaving or knitting into a single fabric. When we speak of a *blend,* we generally mean an *intimate blend* of fibers in a fabric; more specifically, a fabric in which exact proportions of different fibers by weight are intimately blended together at the starting point of the textile process—before spinning. Thus, the yarn blend may contain exact percentages of two, three or more fibers and can be made of:

1. NATURAL WITH MAN-MADE FIBERS, such as polyester/cotton, or acrylic/wool.

2. MAN-MADE WITH MAN-MADE FIBERS, such as acrylic/rayon, or acrylic/polyester.

3. NATURAL WITH NATURAL FIBERS, such as wool /cotton or cotton/silk.

A *mixture yarn* is less *intimate* than a blend yarn in that the blending is done *after* spinning, by twisting together two or more strands of spun yarn or of continuous filament.

A *mixture fabric* is constructed with one of the following:

1. Mixture yarns, or

2. Different single-component yarns laid side by side, or

3. Warp yarns of one fiber and filling yarns of another. This method was the one generally used in making the *mixture* or *union* fabrics of the past. An example of such a cloth was "linsey-woolsey" which was woven with a flax warp and wool filling.

A *chemical blend* of man-made fibers is achieved at the fiber-producing level. Known as "bi-component spinning," it was developed to create a textured filament yarn. Here, two chemical polymers with different ratios of shrinkage are extruded through the spinneret to form a single filament. As one shrinks more than the other, the whole yarn is pulled into a crimped formation. (See "Textured Yarns.")

## New Concepts of Design

Fabric blends provide new concepts in design—materials new in both content and form. Some of the most successful fabrics achieve their success not because of design or pattern or even texture, but rather because of hand-plus-performance developed through the combination of different fiber components which form a blend.

The interest generated by such fabrics thus comes from an interior structure rather than from surface patterning created through traditional design. Such

Pre-industrial mixture fabric.

new concepts of design, in consequence, call for a new kind of designer—one who combines the artist and the fiber technologist, who chooses a combination from many possible fibers, considering the properties of each to obtain a desired effect. The designer thus makes use of the individual properties of each component in the most effective way. Basically, many of the man-made fibers have similar characteristics, but, in addition, each has its own outstanding properties which contribute special qualities to the final fabric.

## Functions Assigned to the Man-Mades

While the man-made fibers have great versatility and can be tailored to fit a wide range of end uses, in actual practice the textile industry, in creating blended fabrics, considers each fiber in terms of its performance characteristics. In a general way, the industry is inclined to assign the following functions to the major man-made fibers:

NYLON is used for strength, abrasion resistance and as an aid in weaving. It is often used as a core yarn. It also provides fabric durability, dimensional stability and press retention.

POLYESTER is used for overall wash-wear performance, for resistance to wrinkling and for press

295

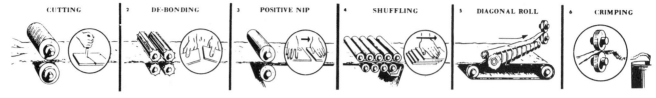

| 1 CUTTING | 2 DE-BONDING | 3 POSITIVE NIP | 4 SHUFFLING | 5 DIAGONAL ROLL | 6 CRIMPING |

Flow chart of Pacific Convertor which cuts and combines man-made fibers with other man-made or natural fibers, forming a blended and crimped sliver.

retention. It, too, adds strength and abrasion resistance to blended fabrics.

ACRYLIC is used to create bulk without weight and for versatility in surface texture. It, too, provides dimensional stability.

RAYON is used for its "natural" hand, for ease in processing and for decorative effects.

## Modern Blending Is . . .

. . . the combination of different fibers into a mass in which the components are proportionately distributed by pre-determined percentages in any given cross section of the mass. The component parts may be different types of fiber, different thicknesses of fiber, different staple lengths and different colors. This results in a yarn which has the same percentage of each component as did the original blend.

There are four basic methods for blending:

1. HAND FEEDING from behind the hopper line. This method involves a good deal of guesswork.

2. SLIVER BLENDING, which combines slivers of different fibers by doubling and drafting.

3. MANUAL BLENDING. The different components are weighed by hand, spread out in layers and fed into the hoppers from the cross sections.

4. AUTOMATIC BLENDING. Essentially the same approach as No. 3, except that all procedures are automatically controlled.

## The Range of Modern Blends

Each season brings new blends into the market. This results not only from the continuing experimentation with different basic fiber combinations, but also from the different proportions of these basic fibers used to create specific effects. They are variously used to achieve ease of care, texture, coloration, structural strength, durability and decorative effects.

The list which follows includes the fiber blends which are most widely used in textile products.

WITH POLYESTER: Cotton, High Wet Modulus Rayon (HWM), Rayon, Triacetate, Acrylic, Silk, Worsted, Flax, Mohair, Nylon/Cotton, Rayon/Cotton.

WITH ACRYLIC: Wool, Cotton, Rayon, Polyester, Rayon/Nylon/Acetate.

WITH NYLON: Wool, Wool/Cotton, Wool/Rayon, Polyester/Cotton, Cotton.

WITH RAYON: Polyester, Acrylic, Wool/Cotton, Wool/Nylon.

WITH POLYNOSIC (High Wet Modulus Rayon): Polyester, Carded Cotton, Acetate.

WITH TRIACETATE: Polyester.

WITH SPANDEX: Polyester/Cotton, Cotton, Rayon/Acetate/Nylon, Acrylic/Rayon/Acetate, Acrylic/Wool/Rayon.

A three-picker distributor for automatic blending of cotton, wool, man-made and asbestos fibers.

**Flow Chart for High-Bulk Blends of Orlon Acrylic.**

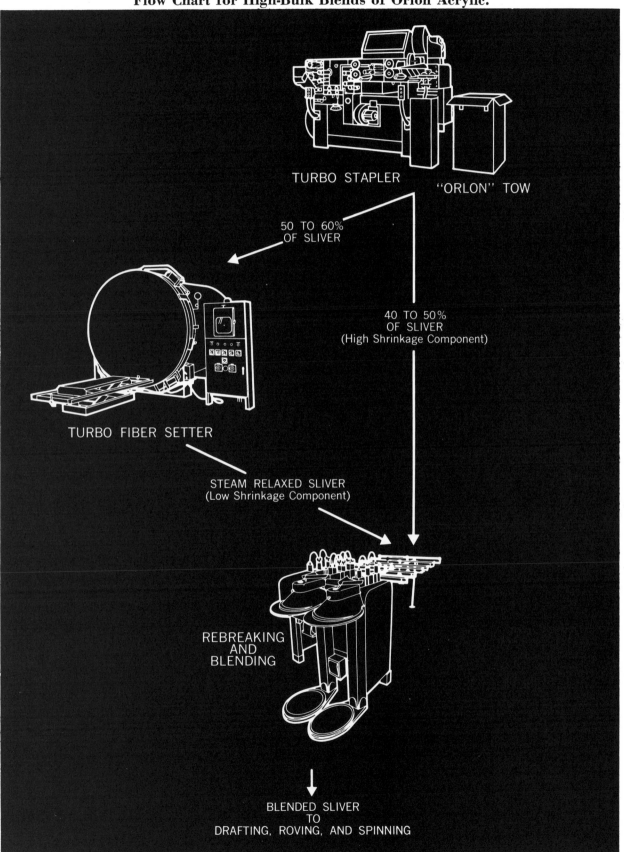

TURBO STAPLER

"ORLON" TOW

50 TO 60% OF SLIVER

40 TO 50% OF SLIVER (High Shrinkage Component)

TURBO FIBER SETTER

STEAM RELAXED SLIVER (Low Shrinkage Component)

REBREAKING AND BLENDING

BLENDED SLIVER TO DRAFTING, ROVING, AND SPINNING

A typical set-up for processing Orlon tow on the Turbo Stapler and related equipment.

Untextured yarn.

Textured yarn.

# Textured Yarns

*Broadly categorized, textured yarns may be divided into groups of which the filaments are crimped, coiled, curled or looped.*

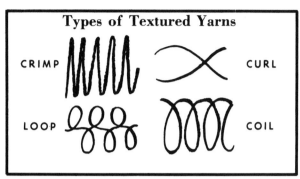

**Types of Textured Yarns**

CRIMP · CURL · LOOP · COIL

Textured yarns and the fabrics they form—yarns and fabrics made with chemical fibers—represent a significant achievement and advance in the march of progress by the man-made fibers since their emergence from the chemical laboratories. Textured yarns, because they are made from chemical fibers, came into being on the basis of the man-made fibers' ability to undergo modification through the application of heat.

## Background of Texturing

The chemical fiber, in its liquid or molten state, is forced through the holes of a spinneret and emerges as a long, smooth, rodlike filament. In this form it finds wide use in such areas as lingerie tricot, active sportswear and industrial applications. But it lacks that special character which tradition has accustomed us to associate with textiles of wool, cotton or linen.

In order to overcome this lack, the man-made filament originally was chopped into short lengths (staple fiber) corresponding to natural fiber lengths, so that it could again be processed into continuous yarns on existing conventional machinery. Later, when the value of natural crimp had been scientifically extablished, research was begun to solve the problem of giving continuous filament yarn the properties and advantages of yarns made from natural crimped fibers.

## Crimped, Bulked and Textured Yarns

The idea for crimped yarns arose from the research of a leading carpet manufacturer who was investigating the reason for the great superiority of Indian wools costing about 42¢ a pound over South American wool staple costing approximately 18¢ a pound. Research teams investigating the two types of wool determined that chemically they were identical, but came to the unexpected conclusion that the main difference lay in the crimp which the Indian wool possesses, the South American wool being almost straight. They were able to prove that the difference in properties between crimped and uncrimped wool was greater than the difference between wool and cotton.

Experiments with crimped fiber showed that the crimp serves to give resilience, higher abrasion resistance, warmth and insulation because of the air retained among the fibers. It also provides improved moisture absorption and comfort in wear because crimped fiber does not lie flat and this segregates

  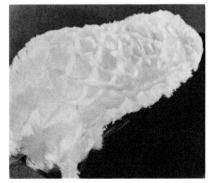

How surface area increases through transformation from filament yarns and bulked yarns . . . (1) A demonstration cone of filament yarns is cut through with a sharp knife or razor and immediately (2) Releases the life inherent in the yarn by (3) Increasing its bulk and the surface areas.

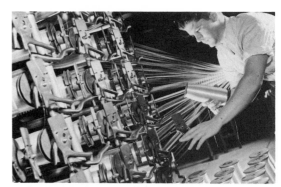

Left: Cutting man-made fiber into staple. In making staple, yarn is drawn into rope, cut into tow.

sweat droplets and maintains porosity.

The texture "revolution" began when research was started to solve the problem of giving continuous filament yarn the properties and advantages of yarns made from natural crimped fibers.

Knowing that chemical fibers are thermoplastic—that is, that heat can change their "character" by making them malleable—textile chemists found they could deform the rodlike textile filament by twisting or crimping it along its length, and then permanently set or fix the crimp by applying heat. This is the basic concept and principle of yarn texturing.

The result is to give these fibers bulk, dimension, hand—qualities which offset the stamp of the machine and give them a character more closely resembling that of natural fibers.

## Benefits of Textured Yarns

Among other special advantages obtained in textured yarns, the following are the more obvious ones:

1. They produce loft and/or stretch in a fabric.

2. They provide opacity; therefore, greater yield.

3. They give fabrics a dry and friendly hand, without slickness.

4. Textured yarn fabrics have more porosity and are therefore more comfortable to wear.

5. Fabrics made of textured yarns do not pill.

6. Strong but extremely lightweight fabrics can be knitted from textured yarns because the coverage of crimped yarn, weight for weight, is high.

The overall outcome in the use of textured yarns is to offer fabrics of equal performance at lighter and lighter weights, in which the wear factors of non-pilling and increased abrasion resistance are extremely important.

To these advantages one should add the processing logic of texturing—which is to take advantage of the filament form in which fibers are made rather than to chop them up and then reform them by spinning.

TEXTURE. The word derives from the Latin *textura*. The verb is *texere*, meaning *to weave*, and from this root comes the word *textile*. Etymologically, therefore, *texture* refers to a woven fabric, a web, the connecting of threads in a woven fabric. Today we have generalized the meaning to cover the substance or structure of an object or a condition. We speak of the *texture* of fruit, of meat, of wood, of a painting, of life itself. As related to textiles we have also narrowed the meaning to describe the surface conformations and irregularities of a fabric. Yet, when we speak of the texture of a fabric, we also evoke these other levels of meaning.

## The Difference Between Set-Textured and Stretch

The same basic false-twist process produces both a stretch and a set yarn. The difference, however, is essentially this: the stretch yarn passes through three stages—twist, set and untwist; the set yarn passes through four stages—twist, set, untwist, stabilize. In the fourth stage the stretch or torque is destroyed either by fixing the yarn in an autoclave or by passing it through an additional heater box. Thus, though one might imagine stretch yarn to be more difficult to make than set yarn, the opposite is true.

## Basic Methods of Texturing Yarn

3-STAGE. The original method used to produce stretch yarn, 3-Stage is also referred to as the "classical" method and was developed by the Heberlein Co. of Switzerland, producers of Helanca yarn.

The three stages of production are: (1) twisting the

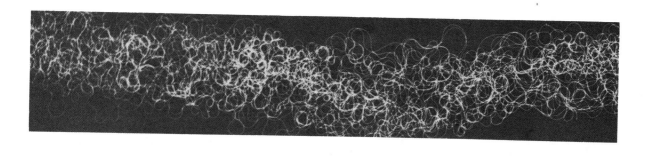

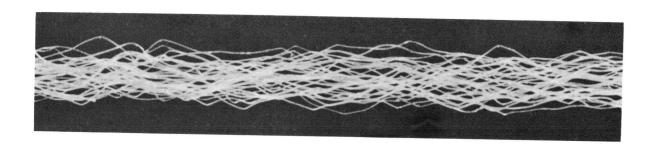

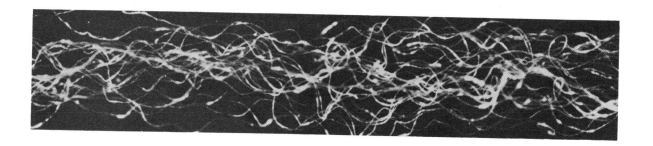

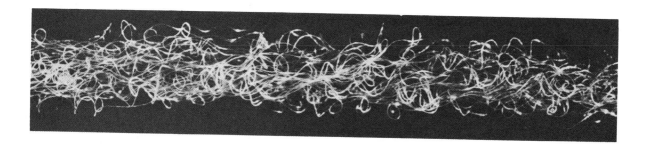

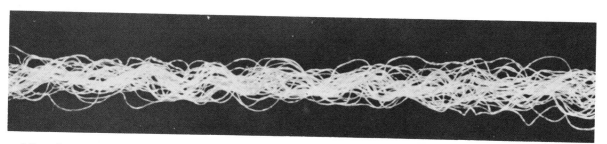

Microphotographs of various types of textured yarns in which the filament configurations are contrasted.

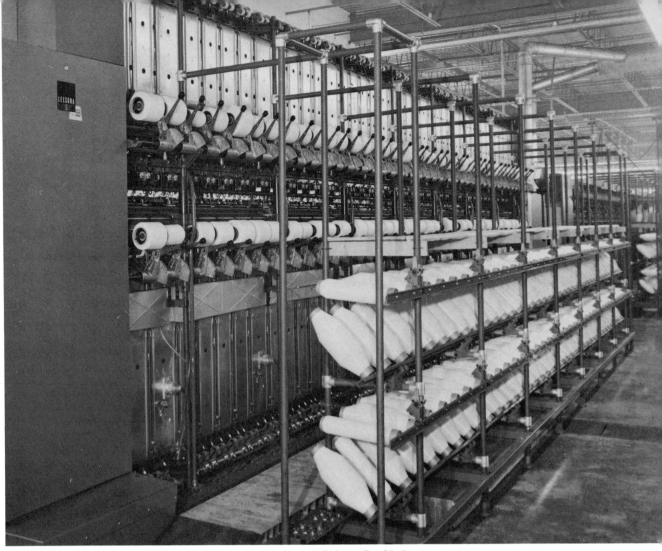

Above: A false-twist texturing machine with double-heater. Below: Double-heater texturing equipment.

**1.** **2.** **3.**

yarn; (2) "setting" the yarn by heat application; (3) untwisting the yarn. At this point it is a *stretch* yarn with a permanent torque or twist. To produce a non-stretch *set* yarn, it must go through an additional heating stage during which the torque is eliminated and the yarn becomes stable. Though the yarn has now been stabilized or "set," it still retains a memory of its twisted shape and its effort to return to that form gives it bulk and loftiness. It also retains a 10–15% of stretch, but it no longer has the bounce and recovery characteristic of stretch yarn. The result is a fluffy bundle of fibers as shown here.

False Twist.

**FALSE TWIST.** Basically the same as the 3-Stage process but refined to be continuous in operation. Twist—set—untwist are all performed in one machine and are predominantly achieved through the use of a false twist spindle and a heater box. Also added is a fourth stage providing a second heater to stabilize the yarn.

False Twist is the dominant process in use throughout the world and it appears in many variations with new refinements constantly added. The yarn bundle looks the same as the 3-Stage process.

Stuffer Box.

**STUFFER BOX.** This method takes its name from the literal stuffing of the straight filaments into one end of a heated box and withdrawing them from the other end in crimped form. In the box the yarn takes on a sawtooth conformation which is then set by the heat. Since the process does not produce a stretch yarn, it does not need to pass through an additional stabilizing stage. It achieves a bulk with loft.

This is the method used in making "Textralized" yarns which are licensed by Joseph Bancroft & Sons Co. It is one of the earliest methods for producing textured yarn and has long been an important factor in knitted dresses, pullovers and men's knitted sport shirts. The characteristic sawtooth configuration of the individual filaments is illustrated here.

**KNIT-DE-KNIT.** Anyone who has watched the unraveling of a sweater will understand the meaning of the term "Knit-de-Knit." There are three stages: (1) yarn is knitted in the form of a fabric tube; (2) the fabric is heat-set; (3) the fabric is unraveled and the resulting yarn takes on the characteristic shape of knitting. The three stages are performed in one continuous process and the yarn is rewound at the same time.

Knit-de-Knit yarn achieves a crepe or bouclé effect when knitted into a fabric. The size of crimp and its frequency can be varied by the machine gauge and stitch size. A variation of the knitting technique has been developed by Heathcoat in England. Knitting sinkers and a heated head are used, but no needles and hence no unraveling.

The characteristic form of a Knit-de-Knit yarn is illustrated here.

Knit-de-Knit.

**EDGE CRIMP.** This term is an exact description of the process. The heated thermoplastic yarn is drawn over a razor-sharp knife edge that gives it a curl formation. This process is chiefly associated with "Agilon" yarn, licensed by Deering Milliken. It has found its main application in women's nylon hosiery because of the high strength and resistance to abrasion inherent in the process. Another effect of the method is to give the yarn a bi-component quality since the side which has been drawn over the knife edge is shorter.

The process itself also develops a degree of stretch in the yarn which further recommends it for women's hosiery. The characteristic curl and reverse formation of edge-crimped yarn is illustrated here.

Edge Crimp.

**AIR JET.** This is the process dveloped by Du Pont and licensed under the name "Taslan." The process achieves bulk by subjecting the fibers to jets of air under high pressure. This disarranges their regular formation and flings them into random loopings which gives the yarn its high loft. The degree to which the fibers are disarranged can be controlled by the degree of tension in the yarn, by the speed of processing and degree of air pressure. The resulting yarns have a broad range of end uses, from shoelaces to men's shirtings and women's wear.

The Air Jet process is simple, but its use has been somewhat limited due to a factor which may seem improbable to the layman: air, under pressure, is a costly ingredient for industrial applications. The looped formation of "Taslan" yarn is shown here.

Air Jet.

GEAR CRIMP. The filament yarn passes between the teeth of two heated gears which mesh and so give the yarn the same configuration as the gear teeth. This is a sawtooth crimp formation and the process is used with nylon. A schematic illustration of the process and the resulting crimp is shown here.

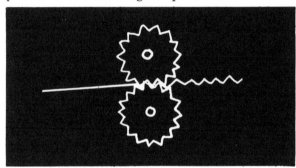

Gear Crimp.

DUO-TWIST. This process is a special development of the Turbo Machine Co. It achieves an effect similar to False Twist, but with somewhat lower twist and torque. It uses no spindle. Two yarns are twisted together and set by passing them over the surface of a heated tube. The two yarns are then separated and wound on individual cones.

Warp Crimp.

STEVETEX. This is the trademarked name of a patented texturing process developed by J. P. Stevens & Co. Inc. It is unique in that, instead of texturing a single end of yarn, it textures multiple ends arranged in warp formation. The crimping process thus achieves uniformity along the warp length and is free of torque. The number of "crimps" per inch can be reduced or increased according to end use.

A skein of 70 denier nylon yarn, (*at left*) before processing to give texture and, (*at right*) the same skein after texture has been produced by processing.

CHEMICAL TEXTURING. The processes described above are mechanical methods which depend on the application of heat. There are, however, other methods by which fibers and yarns can be textured and these have generally been referred to as "producer-textured," meaning that such yarns are textured at the source. As such, in many cases, the texturing process is chemical, not mechanical.

An example of this is a bi-component yarn. Two different components are joined together in one fiber at the processing stage. Their different characteristics, acting on each other, produce either an immediate or a latent crimp. Most such yarns are composed of two polymers with different ratios of shrinkage. When heat is applied, one polymer shrinks more than the other, thus pulling the whole yarn into a crimped formation. An example of this yarn type is "Cantrece," made by Du Pont. Most bulked carpet yarns are also textured by the fiber producer. The illustration shows a bi-component yarn.

TWO OTHER WAYS TO TEXTURE. In addition to all the foregoing methods for texturing filament fibers, there are at least two other methods in use for creating texture in fabric. One is *Compacting*, in which fabrics made from non-textured thermoplastic fibers can be given texture after the fabric is made. This is done through compacting the fabric by subjecting it to heat. Bancroft's "microcreping" process is an example of this technique. The other is *Spun Texture* in which spun yarns (as opposed to filament yarns) can be textured by false twisting.

# SOME EXAMPLES OF TEXTURED YARNS

Coiled

Peaked crimp effect

Rounded crimp effect

Curled

Curled over
heated blade

Heated gears pro-
vide the crimp

High bulk—stretched
and relaxed principle

High twist—not
highly elastic

Lofted effect from
use of air jet

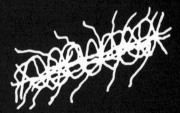

Stretch core—re-
tains good elasticity

Synfoam—twist and
untwist method

Stuffing box used
for crimp

## Effects of Fiber Variation

The form of the fiber affects the aesthetics of fabrics made with textured yarns. Fibers are either round, tri-lobal (three-sided) or penta-lobal (five-sided). Another variable is the chemical difference between a homo-polymer (all one type) and a co-polymer (two types combined). Combining these variables we find: (1) homo-polymer round has little luster; (2) homo tri- and penta-lobal give more luster and brighter colors; (3) co-polymer round gives bright color without luster; (4) co-polymer tri-lobal gives luster and color.

## Texturing Equipment

Increases in production speed, processing made continuous and automatic from start to windup, more exact electronic heat controls—these and other improvements emerge in a continuous stream from the producers of yarn texturing equipment in the U.S., the United Kingdom, France, Germany, Italy and Japan. The machines are large, complicated and expensive. Their function, in all cases, is to convert continuous filaments of man-made thermoplastic fiber from smooth to irregular conformations. How they approach this task is what distinguishes one machine from another.

## Major Textured Yarns Today

Following are some of the major end uses for the various textured yarns:

NYLON. Stretch knits in hosiery for men and women; pantyhose; leotards; swimwear; women's slacks. Stretch wovens in warpstretch ski pants; filling stretch denims. Set knits in men's and women's pullovers, turtlenecks and sweaters; printed tricot dresses. Carpeting in different types.

ACETATE AND TRIACETATE. Textured and set doubleknit dresses; striped tricot dresses. A growing trend is textured knitting yarns which combine acetate with nylon, since the nylon strengthens the yarn and makes it easier to process.

POLYESTER. Textured and set doubleknit dresses; stretch knits for women's pants and swimwear.

## Growth of Yarn Throwing Industry

The "texture revolution" has created an everwidening role for the yarn throwster (the word comes from the Anglo Saxon word *thrawan*, meaning to twist or revolve). In textile terminology the word "throwing" therefore harks back to its original Anglo Saxon meaning and describes the act of twisting together two or more continuous filaments to form one thread. A throwster is therefore one who performs this operation. With the development of man-made fibers, and then of stretch yarns, it was the throwster who logically undertook to process them.

Before the advent of man-made fibers, "throwing" was generally associated with silk as distinct from other such natural fibers as cotton, wool and flax. That is because yarns of the latter fibers are formed by drawing out or attenuating a thick rope-like structure of short staple fibers. Since silk fibers are continuous filaments (as are the man-mades), they require no drawing-out, but can simply be twisted together, or *thrown*, to form a yarn.

In the process of texturing yarn the throwster is a vital link between fiber producer, mill and cutter. As such, the yarn throwing industry grew from a volume of $10-million in 1953, to some $500-million fifteen years later.

Blend of high and non-shrinking fibers. High-shrinking fibers cause non-shrinking to buckle and bulk.

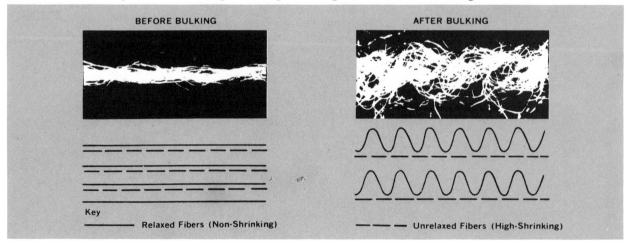

BEFORE BULKING    AFTER BULKING

Key

——————— Relaxed Fibers (Non-Shrinking)    — — — — Unrelaxed Fibers (High-Shrinking)

**FABRICS THAT BREATHE.** Increased surface areas of textured yarns result in fabrics that almost literally breathe. Air pockets are multiplied, making for warmth in cold weather, while the extra absorbency resulting from greater evaporation makes for cooler, warm-weather fabrics.

←———Sheets of paper laid flat together tend to minimize circulation of air.

The same sheets of paper, when ———→ crumpled, retain more air and permit more circulation because of greatly increased surface areas.

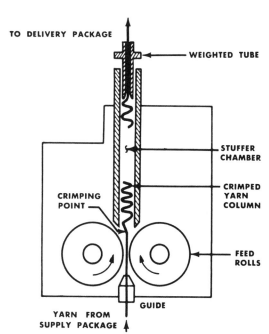

*Above:* Flow chart of stuffer box texturing used to make "Textralized" yarns for products in Ban-Lon Program.

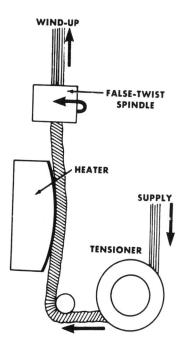

Flow chart of false twist texturing, leading method used today.

Left: Anidex fabric shown in exhibit of stretch characteristics. Right: Stretch fiber in women's dress.

Right: Men's stretch pants and jacket display the comfort and convenience of stretch fabric.

# Stretch Fabrics and Fibers

## Definition

A stretch fabric can be either knitted or woven. Its distinguishing characteristic is an ability to be stretched beyond its original dimension and then recover its original dimension when released.

In its broad concept, "stretch" might be defined as the comfort factor in textile products. In specific textile applications, the technology of stretch relates to fibers, yarns and fabrics, and the extent of its presence in textile products is a matter of its functional advantage for a particular end use.

Stretch technology became one of the major textile developments of the 1960's, with a great deal of research and experimentation behind it. It filled a need—both the physical need of fashions, geared to a fast-paced, informal, democratic way of life, and the technical need of a society and an economy where disappearing hand skills of tailor and seamstress were being replaced by automation.

## Stretch Beginnings

Fabrics that stretch have a long history. Girdles, for example, have been made of fabrics which were stretchable. This was accomplished by making yarns in which a core thread of rubber was wrapped or wound with textile threads. And it is self-evident that hosiery and knitted fabrics, by the nature of the construction, are stretchable. The concept, therefore, was not new.

The important difference between the old and the new stretch fabrics springs from new yarn-making technology and is summed up in the word *recovery*. To already stretchable knitted fabrics, modern stretch yarn techniques add the key factor of quick recovery. To previously rigid woven fabrics they add both stretchability *and* recovery.

Equally important is the fact that modern stretch yarns are produced quickly and economically as compared with the more complicated process of winding a rigid fiber around an elastic rubber core.

Credit for the development of modern stretch yarn technology goes to the Swiss firm of Heberlein & Co. Their research in this field went back to the early 1930's when the firm's object was to simulate wool, then in short supply, by putting a crimp in continuous filament man-made fibers. They deformed the filament by mechanical means and made the de-formation permanent by setting it with heat. The first experiments were conducted with viscose rayon. By crimping the cellulosic fiber, it was possible to achieve some of the dimensional properties of wool.

After World War II, when market interest in nylon began to expand, Heberlein's researchers adapted the process to nylon. From crimping rayon yarn it was a short step to the idea of twisting nylon yarn, setting the twist with heat, and then twisting in the opposite direction so that the continuous filament took on the properties of a spring. And so, by 1947, Heberlein introduced the first nylon stretch yarns under the internationally known "Helanca" trademark.

It was logical, at the beginning, for the stretch concept to find its most important end use in ski pants worn by skiers in Switzerland. European producers became famous for the quality of their stretch ski clothes made with Helanca yarns, and the interest in stretch nylon gradually spread around the world. The fabrics used in such garments were chiefly woven stretch.

Thus, it was the success of European stretch ski clothes which helped to lay the groundwork for what turned out one of the important fashion inaugurations of the era—the introduction by Pucci of Rome of his sportswear and leisurewear collections in silk and nylon stretch fabrics. It was a huge success. Pucci's influence spread, and from this auspicious beginning the interest in stretch fabrics gathered momentum.

By 1965 woven stretch fabrics appeared in almost every category of apparel for men, women and children, with an expanding market in products for the home such as stretch slip covers and upholstery. In almost all of these developments the stretch factor

Stretch wear for ballet dancers.

was incorporated into the filling (horizontal) direction as contrasted with the earlier ski fabrics and Pucci's garments, where the stretch was in the warp (vertical) direction. Few, if any, woven fabrics were made with two-way stretch, which describes a cloth that stretches both vertically and horizontally, as do most of the fabrics used in foundation garments.

Among the advantages of stretch fabrics are the following:

1. Greater comfort.
2. Better fit.
3. More shape retention.
4. Longer wear.
5. Improved wrinkle resistance.
6. Greater surface interest.
7. Reduced seam pucker.
8. Fewer sizes and alterations.
9. More design flexibility.
10. Less tailoring to shape.

## Two Basic Categories of Stretch

There are two categories of stretch fabrics based on the degree of stretchability. They are: (1) Power or Action Stretch and (2) Comfort Stretch.

*Power Stretch,* or *Action Stretch,* as the names imply, provides a fabric with a high degree of extensibility and quick recovery. The stretch factor generally ranges from at least 30 to 50 percent or more with no more than 5 to 6 percent loss in recovery. Such stretch fabrics are best adapted to skiwear, foundation garments, swimwear, athletic clothing and professional types of active sportswear.

*Comfort Stretch* applies to fabrics with less than a 30 percent stretch factor and no more than 2 to 5 percent loss in recovery. Such fabrics are used in clothing for everyday wear which needs only a moderate degree of elasticity. This category covers a wide range of end uses in both apparel and in the home, as well as in transportation upholstery.

## Techniques for Producing Stretch Fabrics

There are three basic approaches to stretch.

1. PIECEGOODS STRETCH. The stretchability is imparted after the fabric has been woven. This is often referred to as mechanical stretch. It can be applied in either the warp or filling direction, but has chiefly been used in the U.S. for filling stretch. It is logically the simplest and least expensive method for making a woven stretch fabric, but it achieves only limited stretchability — about 10-15 percent.

Two methods are used in developing piecegoods stretch. One is known as *Slack Mercerization.* It is applied to fabrics in which cellulosic fibers predominate and involves a physical alteration of the fabric by chemical means. The other process is known as *Crimp Interchange.* It is applied to fabrics in which thermoplastic fibers predominate and involves a physical alteration of the fabric by thermal means. Descriptions of the two processes follow:

*Slack Mercerization* was developed by the U. S. Department of Agriculture. Essentially, it involves the shrinking of the cotton fabric without tension (slack) in a mercerizing bath of sodium hydroxide solution. The amount of shrinkage, and the consequent amount of stretch imparted, are determined by the concentration and temperature of the caustic solution, as well as by the density and weave of the fabric. When only filling stretch is desired, the warp is held under tension during further chemical treatment and is set in that state.

*Crimp Interchange.* In this method the warp is stretched to the point where the width of the fabric is narrowed. As a result, the normal weaving crimp which existed in the warp is transferred to the filling. In that stretched position the fabric is set by heat. This generally results in a filling stretch of 10%.

2. HEAT-SET YARN STRETCH. This is the most widely used approach for making stretch fabric. Essentially it is the technique developed by Heberlein in its pioneer work on Helanca. It uses manmade yarns which have been crimped and made stretchable through de-formation and heat setting (see processes in section on Textured Yarns). These stretch yarns can be used in either the filling or the warp of a woven fabric to develop stretchability in either or both directions, and they can be used also with a wide range of other rigid fibers, both natural and man-made. They are also the dominant factor in knitted stretch where their major use has been in 100% constructions.

3. ELASTOMERIC YARN STRETCH. This is based on the use of man-made elastomeric fibers such as Spandex and anidex (see section on Spandex) which owe their stretchability to a chemical or molecular structure and not to a mechanically imparted configuration of the filament, as with heat-set stretch yarns. In this respect it is similar to a rubber band and can be extended to over five hundred percent of its length without breaking.

This method makes it possible to achieve the aesthetics and tactile qualities of a spun fiber, since the spun fibers remain on the surface of the yarn while the elastomer spandex is buried in its core. It is an economical way to get the benefits of stretch because even less than 5% elastomer provides ef-

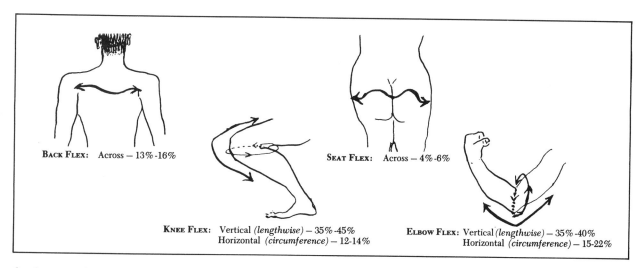

**Back Flex:** Across — 13%-16%

**Seat Flex:** Across — 4%-6%

**Knee Flex:** Vertical *(lengthwise)* — 35%-45%
Horizontal *(circumference)* — 12-14%

**Elbow Flex:** Vertical *(lengthwise)* — 35%-40%
Horizontal *(circumference)* — 15-22%

fective stretch in a fabric. Its first use was in woven outerwear, but it has been extended into a variety of knits such as socks, sweaters and children's apparel.

In addition to the above three *basic* techniques for producing stretch fabrics, there can be added a number of other variations to summarize stretch technology. These are:

4. CORETWIST ELASTOMER STRETCH. This is a later development in stretch technology, originating in Europe. It achieves a high degree of stretch and superior recovery so that it has been chiefly used for active skiwear, in warp stretch fabrics.

The original development of coretwist stretch was made and patented by the French firm of Sebac and is known as "Champalex." The technique involved pre-twisting the spandex core yarn and covering it at high speeds with one or two layers of nylon yarn which lock into position on the corrugated conformation of the core yarn.

Still another approach to the coretwist method was developed by Heberlein. It combines untwisted spandex with a wrap of Helanca stretch nylon.

5. CORESPUN NYLON STRETCH. This is the same method as No. 3 except that the elastomer is replaced by a core yarn of false-twist stretch nylon. The outside sheath can be composed of either natural or man-made yarns. This method has been used chiefly for knits since it does not develop as high a degree of stretchability as corespun elastomer.

6. BARE ELASTOMER STRETCH. Like natural rubber, elastomeric yarn can also be used bare, and in this form has been used chiefly in knits for foundation garments, support hosiery and swimwear. It is generally combined with stretch nylon yarn and is inserted into the construction at fixed intervals to produce a fabric with two-way stretch.

7. COVERED ELASTOMER STRETCH. This is the original method used to make covered elastic yarns for foundation garments. The elastic thread is literally covered with other yarns by wrapping. Natural rubber had been used for this purpose, but elastomer has gradually taken over. This type of fabric develops a high degre of stretch power.

8. BLENDED STRETCH FIBERS. These combine cut elastomer with cut staple or tow. This type of yarn blend is made at the fiber producer level, delivered to the weaver or knitter ready for manufacturing into fabric. The method has been called "Intimate Blend Spinning."

9. BI-COMPONENT STRETCH. Another process is based on "Bi-Component" fibers. This means that a filament of two components is extruded through the spinneret—two types of nylon, for example. One type shrinks more than the other and, as it shrinks, pulls the whole filament into a crimped configuration. The resulting crimped singles yarn is free of torque. Such a yarn is Du Pont's "Cantrece."

10. ALL-COTTON STRETCH. In addition to the above methods described for man-made yarns, two similar methods have been developed for producing all-cotton stretch yarns. These techniques were evolved experimentally by the U.S. Dept. of Agriculture and are described as "Back-Twisting" and "Crimping." In Back-Twisting, the cotton yarn is treated with cellulose cross-linking chemicals or resins (dimethylol ethyleneurea, etc.) similar to those used in producing wash/wear fabrics. It is then twisted, the twist is set with heat, and it is then re-twisted in the opposite direction. In Crimping, the yarn is treated with one of several chemicals (acrylonitrile, acetate anhydride, etc.) to give it thermoplastic properties (the ability to become pliable under heat). The chemically modified yarn is then heated and crimped in the same way as thermoplastic man-made fibers.

Comfort: chief appeal of stretch fabrics.

11. ALL-WOOL STRETCH (DUBBELSTRETCH). This is a special type of stretch fabric developed by the Swedish firm of Saxylle-Kilsund and originally made of 100 percent worsted.

The firm's patented process involves special techniques in yarn production, weaving and finishing, and results in a stretch factor of 9–10 percent in the warp and 12–13 percent in the filling. This produces a bias stretch of about 30 percent.

Other virtues of the DubbelStretch fabric include practically 100 percent recovery from stretch, resistance to wrinkles and retention of pleats and creases. DubbelStretch fabrics are also made in blends of polyester and wool.

## Stretch versus Set

The same basic false twist process (see description in section on Textured Yarns) produces both a stretch and a set yarn. The difference is that the stretch yarn passes through three stages—twist, set, untwist; the set yarn passes through four stages—twist, set, untwist, stabilize. In the fourth stage the stretch or torque is destroyed either by fixing the yarn in an autoclave or by passing it through an additional heater box. Thus, though one might think that stretch yarn is more difficult to make than set yarn, the opposite is true.

## Knit Stretch and Woven Stretch

Knitted fabrics, by the nature of the knitting process, are stretchable fabrics. Woven fabrics, by the nature of the weaving process, are rigid fabrics.

When knitted fabrics are made with stretch yarns, their stretch factor is improved, since the yarn itself, as well as the construction, contributes to their stretchability. However, more important than stretchability is the factor of recovery. Good stretch yarns recover quickly and thus enable the knitted fabric to return rapidly to its original shape with little or no sign of distortion.

When woven fabrics are made with stretch yarns, or are otherwise processed for stretchability, they take on a hidden stretch dimension without changing the traditional appearance of a woven cloth. They simply lose their rigidity and become stretchable in either filling or warp. And, as with knit fabrics, they are able to recover quickly after being stretched out of shape.

## Stretch Advances in Techniques and Function

STRETCH PLUS PERMANENT PRESS. The technology of permanent press has been successfully combined with stretch, bringing together two signal achievements in textiles. A wide range of fabrics is now available in this category, including the following:

Rayon/nylon warp stretch, either pre- or post-cured.

Denim filling stretch of cotton/nylon with cotton in both directions. Also with spandex in the filling.

Resin-treated for pre- or post-cured processing.

Rayon/nylon/elastomer filling stretch—post-cured.

Acrylic/nylon warp stretch—pre-cured.

Polyester/cotton/elastomer poplin and batiste—post-cured.

Polyester/rayon/elastomer—post-cured.

STRETCH PRINTS. The successful printing of stretch fabrics was a notable attainment in the stretch technology because it had at first been difficult to keep the colors in register on a stretchable fabric. The fact that the problems were solved opened up a broad volume market in women's sportswear and children's wear.

NEW TEXTURES, NEW BLENDS. A wide range of textures and patterns were added to the original plain or twill weave constructions with stretch. Likewise, the range of fiber blends for stretch fabrics was vastly increased. In addition to those listed in the permanent press category, the following became successful in fashion categories: nylon/polyester stretch for lingerie; cotton/spandex sailcloth stretch; acetate/nylon/spandex; nylon/spandex in raschel knits; acrylic/spandex in bulky sweater knits; 100 percent stretch polyester doubleknits.

The overall effect of these developments has been to lift stretch from its purely functional category and move it into the broader area of fashion.

Models display stretch properties of Anim/8 anidex fiber, an elastomeric fiber introduced in 1969.

**ACTION STRETCH:** Another term for "Power Stretch."

**BACK TWISTING:** Re-twisting a yarn in the opposite direction to the twist previously set.

**BI-COMPONENT FIBERS:** Continuous filament man-made fibers made up of two related components, each having a different rate of shrinkage. This difference creates a crimped configuration in the filament, making it stretchable.

**BODY FLEX:** The degree of bending in different parts of the body. This is used as a guide in determining degree of fabric stretch required in any given garment.

**CHEMICAL STRETCH:** The type of stretch which is imparted to a fabric through the use of chemicals in the finishing process, after the fabric has been woven. This is generally a filling stretch since the fabric is shrunk horizontally and then permanently set in this state. Also referred to as "Mechanical Stretch" and "Slack Mercerization."

**COIL, CRIMP, CURL:** Terms used to describe the type of configuration given to a yarn (nylon, polyester) in order to make it stretchable.

**COMFORT STRETCH:** One of the two basic categories into which stretch fabrics have been divided in order to describe the degree of stretch required for specific end uses. The other category is "Power" or "Action" stretch. The term "Comfort Stretch" describes stretch fabric which goes into clothing for everyday use with a stretch factor of up to 30%.

**CORE SPINNING:** A yarn spinning process by which an elastic filament under pre-determined tension is enrobed in a sheath of staple fibers. When tension is removed, the sheath fibers are pulled into a more compact formation. The yarn thus becomes stretchable to the extent of the pre-determined tension of the elastic core filament.

**DOUBLING:** Joining together an "S" twist yarn with a "Z" twist yarn to create a plied or doubled yarn free from torque.

**ELASTOMERIC:** This term refers to a substance which owes its stretchability to its chemical or molecular structure. Natural rubber is such a substance. So is synthetic rubber. So is spandex.

**FALSE TWIST:** When a heat-set stretch yarn is processed it passes through a heater box and then through a "false twist" spindle. Entering the spindle, the yarn is twisted. Emerging from the spindle, the twist is automatically removed. That is why it is referred to as a *false* twist. However, the yarn retains a "memory" of its twisted position (torque) and seeks to return to that position. It is therefore wound or taken up under tension to prevent it from curling. Later this torque in the yarn is balanced by doubling it with another yarn whose remembered twist moves in the opposite direction. ("S" twist with "Z" twist.)

**FATIGUE FACTOR:** This refers to the weakening of a stretch yarn so that it loses some of its ability to recover after it has been stretched. It becomes tired. Stretch yarn fatigue can result from twisting the yarn at speeds (RPM)

which are too high for the length of the heater box which sets the twist configuration.

**FILLING STRETCH:** This means that the stretch factor has been imparted only in the filling direction of the fabric while the warp remains rigid. Also referred to as "Horizontal Stretch" and "East/West Stretch."

**HEAT-SET STRETCH YARN:** A yarn which has been given an irregular configuration and then fixed in this position by heat. Usually, this is applied to thermoplastic man-made fibers but it can also be applied to natural fibers which have been made thermoplastic through chemical treatment.

**INTIMATE BLEND SPINNING:** The blending of cut spandex with cut staple or tow to produce a stretch yarn at the fiber producer level.

**KNITTED STRETCH:** The construction of a stretch fabric by the knitting process, using stretch yarns. All knitted fabrics are stretchable but the difference between regular knit and stretch knit is that the stretch knit will recover more rapidly and have greater holding power due to the use of stretch yarns.

**MECHANICAL STRETCH:** Another name for "Chemical Stretch" and "Slack Mercerization." This is the type of stretch imparted to the fabric after it has been woven.

**PIECE GOODS STRETCH:** This is an umbrella term to describe the various types of stretch fabrics in which the stretch factor has been imparted to the fabric after it has been woven, rather than to the yarn before weaving.

Stretch fibers have made a vital comfort contribution to many end-uses, including sportswear and swimwear.

**PLUS X:** This is a patented process of J. P. Stevens for imparting stretch to all-wool and wool-blend fabrics. It puts a permanent, accordion-like crimp into the fabric before dyeing and finishing.

**POWER STRETCH:** One of the two basic categories into which stretch fabrics have been divided in order to describe the degree of stretch required for specific end uses. The other category is "Comfort Stretch." The term "Action Stretch" describes stretch fabrics which have more snap and muscle power, more extensibility and quicker recovery. The stretch factor here generally ranges from 30% to 50% and is best adapted to skiwear, foundation garments, swimwear, athletic clothing and the more professional types of active sportswear.

**RECOVERY:** The ability of a stretch yarn or fabric to recover its original position after having been stretched.

**RESTORA:** This is a patented process of Burlington Mills for imparting stretch to all-wool fabrics without a chemical change in the wool fiber's molecular structure. It provides elasticity in both warp and filling.

**RIGID FIBER OR FABRIC:** This refers to a fiber or a fabric which is not stretchable.

**SHEATH FIBERS:** These are the fibers which form a sheath around the elastomeric fiber used in core-spinning.

**SLACK MERCERIZATION:** This process was first developed for all-cotton stretch fabrics but can also be applied to blends of cotton with man-made fibers. It involves the shrinking of the fabric without tension (slack) in a mercerizing bath of sodium hydroxide solution. It is most often used in making filling or horizontal stretch fabrics.

**SPANDEX:** An elastomeric fiber which owes its stretchability to its chemical or molecular structure. It is made up of at least 85% segmented polyurethane, which is the same chemical substance now widely used as a foam in seating, bedding and laminated fabrics.

**STABILIZATION:** The process of stabilizing or setting the dimensions of a "mechanical" stretch fabric after it has been shrunk. This is achieved by the use of appropriate chemicals and heat.

**"S" TWIST:** Term used to describe a yarn which has been twisted to the left, following the direction of the letter "S."

# The Vocabulary of Stretch

A COMPILATION OF TERMS FREQUENTLY USED IN DISCUSSING STRETCH FABRICS

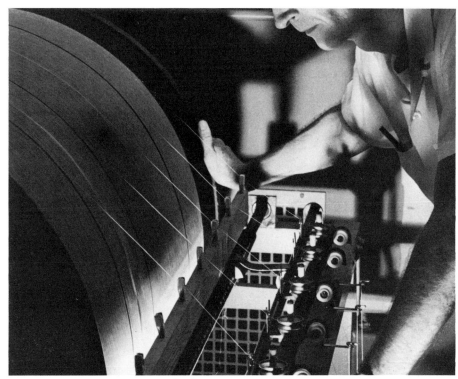

Checking spandex yarn.

**SULPHONE CHEMICALS:** Chemicals which alter the molecular structure of cotton fiber by cross-linking. They are used to give permanent stability to a mechanical stretch fabric.

**TEXTURING:** The process by which a smooth continuous filament man-made fiber is given a new and permanent configuration. This results in a textural surface interest on the fabric woven with such yarns.

**THERMOPLASTIC:** The ability of a yarn to become pliable when subjected to heat.

**THROWING:** This describes the act of twisting together two or more continuous filaments to form one thread. Originally associated with silk, which is a continuous filament, it later was applied to continuous filament man-made fibers, and to the process of texturizing such fibers. A company which performs this function is a *throwster*.

**TORQUE:** The twisting force or torsion of a yarn which has been twisted in either the "S" or the "Z" direction. This must be offset by doubling or other means to balance the yarn for easy processing.

**WARP STRETCH:** This means that the stretch factor has been imparted only in the warp or vertical direction of the fabric, while the filling remains rigid. Also referred to as "Vertical Stretch" and "North/South Stretch."

**WOVEN STRETCH:** The construction of a stretch fabric by the weaving process, using stretch yarns. Normally, all woven fabrics are rigid but the use of stretch yarns gives stretchability to the rigid construction.

**YARN CONFIGURATION:** The shaping of a smooth, continuous filament man-made fiber so that it takes on coil, curl or crimp and thus becomes stretchable yarn.

**"Z" TWIST:** Term used to describe a yarn which has been twisted to the right, following the direction of the letter "Z."

315

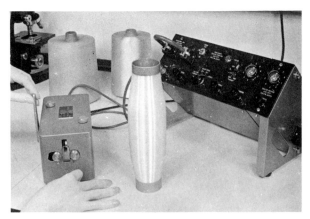

Electronic yarn filament counter.

# Yarn count and denier

To take a filament count of a yarn, it is necessary to remove all twist from the specimen being tested. When the yarn does not contain any machine twist, the filaments can be made to spread apart by rubbing with a pick needle or manipulation with the fingers. Secure the yarn to a suitable background. Place a pick glass on the prepared specimen. With the aid of two pick needles, count the filaments one by one.

```
    SINGLES
                        2 PLY
    SINGLES
```

### Yarn Ply

A singles yarn will, upon removal of the twist, fall apart under slight pressure, if composed of staple fiber. If it is a continuous filament yarn, after removal of the twist the individual filaments will be seen to fan open on application of slight finger pressure.

A yarn or thread which is composed of two or more constituent parts, each of which is found when untwisted to be singles yarn, is called a plied yarn or thread. It is known as 2, 3 (or more) ply yarn or thread according to the number of singles threads present.

The size of all common spun yarns such as cotton, wool, worsted, spun rayon, spun nylon, etc., is based upon the length contained in a definite weight of yarn. Therefore, in determining yarn count (also known as yarn size and yarn number) two facts are necessary: the known length and the known weight of the yarn.

When a test sample is in skein or spool form, it is a relatively easy matter to wind a known length (60 to 120 yards) upon a measuring reel. This measured specimen is weighed in grains. From the known length and known weight, the yarn count is calculated.

A quick method of calculating the yarn number for cotton or spun rayon, based on the cotton system, is as follows:

$$\frac{8.33 \text{ x yards taken}}{\text{weight in grains}} = \text{cotton count}$$

For worsted yarn, or any spun yarn on the worsted system, the formula is:

$$\frac{12.5 \text{ x yards taken}}{\text{weight in grains}} = \text{worsted count}$$

For woolen yarns, or any spun yarns on the woolen system, the formula is:

$$\frac{23.33 \text{ x yards taken}}{\text{weight in grains}} = \text{woolen count (cut system)}$$

The formula for linen is the same as that for woolen yarn. If a yarn is two ply or three ply, convert to single yarn size by multiplying by the number of plies, except in the case of spun silk. Indicate the ply along with the single yarn number.

For example, 20/2 cotton indicates a yarn composed of two threads of No. 20 cotton yarn.

In numbering spun silks the size of the single equivalent of the plied yarn is written before the diagonal line, followed by the number of plies.

### What the Denier Means

The denier is the old silk-filament yarn standard established in France in the sixteenth century, the standard known as the denier.

A pound of yarn of a 1-denier size would measure about 4½ million yards in length. The exact figure is 4,464,528 yards which is obtained in the following manner:

492.13 standard length yds. $\times$ 7,000 grains in one lb.

.771618, standard grain weight of one denier

Thus, one pound of a 1-denier yarn or filament would average about 2,530 miles or the distance from New York City to Phoenix, Arizona. As the size or the number of the denier yarn increases, the yardage per pound will decrease. To find the number of yards of yarn in one pound of a 15-denier yarn, merely divide 15 into 4,464,528. This will reveal that there are about 300,000 yards of the yarn in one pound. Women's stockings are bought and sold according to a particular denier size. For example, a 20-denier is finer and sheerer than a 30-denier and a 15-denier is finer than a 20-denier.

## How It Came About

The denarius, or denier as it is known today, was originally a coin used before and during the time of Julius Caesar. Of small value, it was first made of silver but copper and gold were also used to mint the coins later on. Incidentally, the English coin, "pence" (d) and the American penny are descendants of the original denarii. The coin was first used outside Rome during Caesar's Gallic Wars in what is now France. The value of the coin was 1/12 of the old French sou. Its size is about that of the middle fingernail of a man. The coin today has little monetary value but is a genuine collector's item among numismatists. One in superb condition, face and obverse, may cost up to fifty dollars. Used and worn coins may run as high as twenty dollars.

Caesar, of course, lived for posterity, but his denier lapsed into oblivion soon after his death in 44 B.C. Little was heard of the coin again until the time of Francis I (King of France, 1515-1547) known in history as the Father of the Silk Industry.

Up to about this time the old method used for measurement was the ell or aune, taken originally as a length-measure from the human arm. This length was forty-five inches in England, 46.69 inches in France, and 37.2 inches in Scotland.

When Francis came to power in France one of his first acts was to establish the silk industry in Lyons, Paris, St. Etienne, and other centers. He abolished the old method of measuring silk, which was to use eighty skeins of 120-aunes for a total length of 9,600 aunes. Its weight was now to be found in terms of the denier, i.e., the number of denier coins or weights necessary to balance the silk in question. The denier weight standard was 0.0531 grams or 8.33 grams. The procedure used today to figure denier in terms of grams is to find the weight in grams of 9,000 meters or 9,846 yards of yarn. For example, if 9,000 meters of filament weigh 100 grams the filament is known as a 100-denier yarn. A gram weighs approximately one twenty-eighth of one ounce or 1/450th of one pound. Since there are 492.13 yards used as a standard length and there are 7,000 grains in one pound, the length of a 1-denier is found by multiplying these two numbers for the total of 4,464,528 yards.

The International Yarn Numbering Congress at its meeting held in Vienna, Austria, in 1873 spent a great deal of time on the subject of denier. It was decreed finally that the denier should be defined as the weight in grams of 10,000 meters of filament silk. The basis today in England and the United States for the sizing of thrown silk filament is the weight in drams of 1,000 yards of the filament. To convert this weight into deniers it is necessary to multiply by the factor used, 33.36.

Thus, if 1,000 yards of filament weigh three drams, it would be the equivalent of 33.36 times three or a 100.8-denier yarn.

With the legal denier in use today of 0.05 grams for a length of 450 meters or 492.13 yards (often used in calculations as 492.2 yards) it is possible to convert to ounces by multiplying the grammage by 0.0353.

The present-day method to find the number of yards of yarn is shown in the following problem:

How many yards in one pound of a 150-denier yarn?

150 into 4,464,528 equals 29,763.5 yards, or 30,000 yards for calculations.

A new method which originated in France and seems to be finding favor elsewhere is to base the yarn numbering on the weight of 1,000 meters-unit per kilogram. Thus, a 60s yarn would have 60,000 meters per kilogram, which is equal to 2.2 pounds. This method may supplant others in due course of time in figuring these yarns.

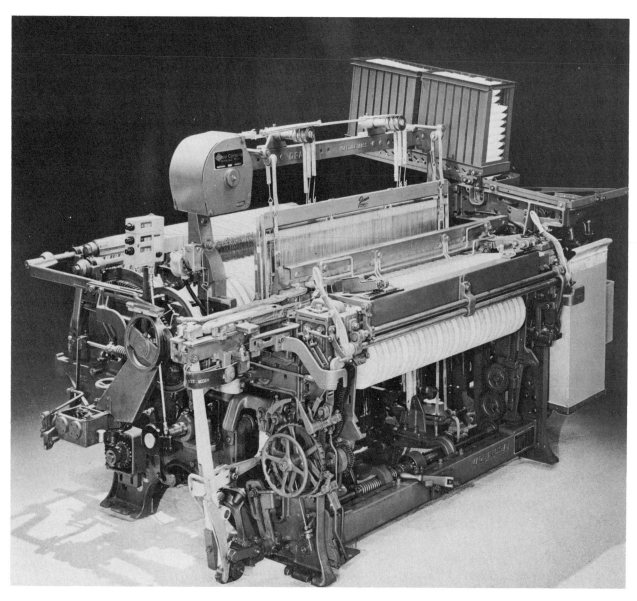

A Draper Textile weaving loom.

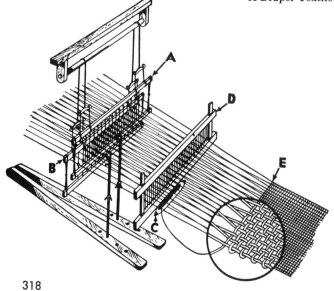

LOOM AND WEAVING: A loom is a machine, hand or power driven, to weave cloth. It consists essentially of parts that make it possible to have two systems of thread or yarn, called warp and filling, interlace at right angles.

Analysis of Plain Weave in Simplified Sketch: Harness (A) controls the odd warp ends. Harness (B) controls the even warp ends. When harness (A) raises the odd ends, harness (B) lowers the even ends to form a shed. The shuttle (C) is shot through this shed, leaving a pick in its wake. Harness (A) and (B) return to center point and the reed (D) swinging forward in the lay pushes the pick up to the fell (E) of the cloth. For the next pick, harness (A) will go down and harness (B) will rise.

# WEAVING . . .
## and the BASIC WEAVES

*The technique of weaving is fundamentally the interlacing of one strand of thread with another. Upon this basic principle the textile industry has built an enormous technology capable of supplying the requirements of Earth's two billion people.*

## Definition

Weaving is the interlacing of two systems of yarn which interlace at right angles to each other. The lengthwise threads are called warp; individually, they are known as ends. The crosswise threads are called filling, or weft; individually, they are called picks. Weaving is done on a loom which makes it possible to interlace the warp and filling threads according to a pre-arranged plan or design. The lengthwise edges of the fabric are called the selvage, raw edge, self-edge, or listing.

## How Weaving Is Done

A simplified explanation of the weaving process involves the following steps:

1. The warp yarn is wound on a beam. All the threads are arranged parallel to each other. Often they are sized to give them strength.

2. From the warp beam the threads are led over a whip roll, under and over the lease rods, through the eyes of the heddles, and then through the splits or dents of the reed. This makes it possible to manipulate the various warp threads according to a pre-arranged design plan.

3. As the warp yarns are manipulated, they separate into two layers, creating an opening called a shed. Through this shed a shuttle carries the filling yarn.

4. After the filling yarn has passed through the shed it is beaten into place by the reed, which has a to-and-fro action.

5. As the fabric is woven it is wound around a cloth roller.

A more detailed analysis of the motions of the loom follows:

## Chief Motions of the Loom

There are six chief motions on a loom. The principal motions are shedding, picking, beating-up; the auxiliary motions are take-up, let-off, pattern. The first three motions are linked together as follows:

1. *Shedding Motion:* The separating of the warp ends into an upper and lower system of threads to permit the shuttle to pass through the space that has been formed. The warp ends are drawn through heddle eyes in the correct manner and in the turning-over of the crankshaft of the loom, a shed is formed with each turn.

2. *Picking Motion:* The actual passing of the shuttle through the shed of the loom. The shuttle passes over the lowered ends of the shed and under its raised ends. The shed allows the shuttle to pass through it and thereby makes it possible for the shuttle to deposit the pick or filling yarn.

3. *Beating-Up:* The actual beating into place of the loose pick that was placed in the shed of the loom

in the picking motion. Beating-up makes each and every deposited yarn a component part of the woven cloth. The reed beats this pick into place with each consecutive turn of the crankshaft.

The auxiliary motions are as follows:

1. *Take-Up Motion:* The motion is positive when the sand roller moves a fractional part of an inch in direct ratio to the take-up wheel. The motion is semi-positive when the sand roller is not definitely controlled.

2. *Let-Off Motion:* The motion is frictional when there is a definite amount of warp allowed to leave the warp beam according to the beating-up of the lay of the loom. It is positive when the lay and the let-off work in two ratios, taking up just as much as is let off.

3. *Pattern Motion:* Not found on all looms, but generally used on machines where more than one color is desired. It is found in the following ratios:
A. From a 2 x 1 box loom to a 6 x 1 gingham loom.
B. From a 2 x 2 box loom controlling three colors.
C. From a 4 x 4 box loom controlling seven colors, pick and pick type.

## The Ten Parts of a Loom

To perform the operations outlined above, a loom has many individual parts. While their names are often unfamiliar, their operations are relatively

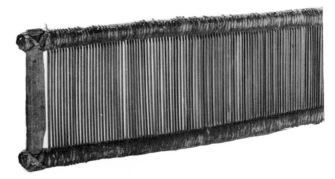

Picture of an old-time wooden reed used in looms on which Indian Head was woven about the time of the Civil War. Note the cord arrangement which causes the wooden reed splits to be firmly secured in the top and bottom bases.

simple and basically the same as those used by primitive peoples. The difference lies in their application to mechanical operation. Here are the parts of a loom:

1. *Warp Beam.* This is the roll or cylinder around which the warp threads or ends are wound in a uniform and parallel arrangement. The unwinding of the yarn from the warp beam is known as the let-off motion.

2. *Whip Roll.* This is a guide roller which directs the warp threads on their way to the lease rods and heddles.

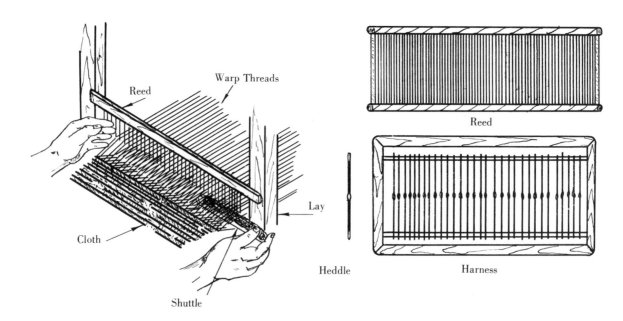

Sketch showing how reed keeps the warp threads even and parallel.

3. *Lease Rods*. Another guiding device for the warp yarns. These are two wooden or glass rods set between the whip roll and the heddles. Alternating warp threads can be kept separate by passing over and under these rods.

4. *Heddles*. The heddles control the warp threads like puppets. They are short steel wires set vertically into the harness frame. Each heddle bar controls one warp thread which is threaded through an eye in the center of the heddle.

5. *Harness*. This is the wooden frame which holds the heddles. In a simple loom there will be two harness frames, each controlling alternating threads in the warp. As the harness frames are raised and lowered they produce the shed or space between the warp threads so the filling yarn can be passed through. This is called the shedding motion.

6. *Bobbin and Shuttle*. The filling thread is wound on a bobbin which sets into a shuttle or bobbin container. As the shuttle passes back and forth through the warp shed, it releases thread from the bobbin and so forms the filling of the cloth.

7. *Reed*. This is essentially a comb made up of steel wire rods set vertically into a frame. The spaces between the wires are called splits or dents. The warp threads pass through these reed dents and so are kept even and parallel. This is the first function of the reed. Its second function is to beat in the filling thread into position. To do this it has a back-and-forth motion.

8. *Temples*. Devices at the edge of the cloth which help to maintain fixed dimensions in width.

9. *Breast Beam*. This is the bar at the front of the loom over which the cloth passes on its way to the cloth roller.

10. *Cloth Roller*. The roller on which the cloth is wound as it is woven. It is controlled by the take-up motion, and is the last stage in the weaving process.

## Background for modern weaving

The first weavers were probably basket makers. They may also have woven mats. Their materials were grasses or rushes, but the technique they used, of interlacing one strand with another, involved the basic principle of weaving.

By the time man arrived at the stage of the Swiss Lake Dwellers in the Later Stone Age he was al-

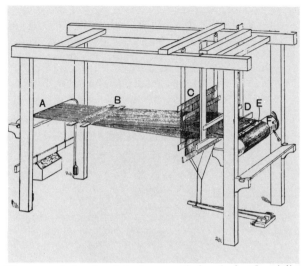

Diagram of simple plain loom with hand shuttle. (*A*) Warp beam. (*B*) Lease rods. (*C*) Heddles. (*D*) Batten and reed. (*E*) Temple. (*F*) Cloth beam.

Loom, *circa* 1895; Northrop loom with automatic filled bobbin changer at right.

Draper shuttleless loom, among newest weaving concepts.

321

## The Manufacture of Looms

Throughout history, man has built looms of all sizes, shapes and descriptions. Paintings and drawings of looms have come down to us from every period. Every culture contributed its share to the technique of loom making.

Prehistoric Greek. The sketch shows a reconstruction of an ancient loom, early Greek period.

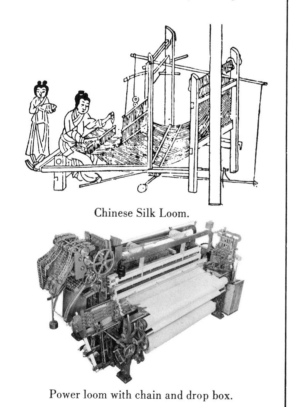

Chinese Silk Loom.

Power loom with chain and drop box.

ready weaving primitive fabrics of prepared flax. Fragments of such cloth and parts of primitive looms have been found in the diggings at Robenhausen in Switzerland.

The early Egyptians—6000 or 7000 years ago—were expert weavers and all the techniques of their craft were carefully illustrated in the wall paintings which come down to us from their first dynasties.

### Chinese Silk and Greek Vases

At least 4000 years ago the Chinese were adding improvements to their simple looms so they could weave the fine filaments of the silkworm. The principle of the draw loom was their contribution. The weavers of India developed the foot treadle at an early stage in their history and later produced the magnificent Dacca muslins.

These technical improvements in the loom spread through the East, were later carried to Europe, and eventually appeared in beautifully articulated paintings on Greek vases as early as 600 B.C. In the Western world the ancient culture of Peru produced magnificent weavers as early as 400 B.C. Their graves have yielded brilliantly colored and patterned fabrics which have rarely been equalled by any people and which indicate a textile tradition dating back to 2500 B.C.

### The Vertical Loom

The earliest looms of which we have knowledge provided a means of hanging one set of threads in a vertical position through which the crossing threads were interlaced. Apparently the first improvement consisted of a means to tighten these threads, either by hanging weights at the bottom end or by joining their two ends in such a way so as to form a loop over horizontal, parallel bars.

### From Simple Origins

Horizontal looms were used by the early Egyptians and other civilizations in early world history. In the simplest form, this type of loom provided for the tethering of a bar that carried the lengthwise warp ends to a stake in the ground. A bar at the farther end was secured to the person of the weaver, who had a straight set of warp threads through which it was possible to cross or interlace the filling yarns.

Primitive weavers improvised from simple materials a plain device or arrangement called a heddle or heald. This device enabled the alternate warp

India. 19th Century: an Indian weaver at work on a blanket of cloth is shown throwing the shuttle.

threads to be raised. Thus a shed was formed—an opening between the raised and un-raised or lowered threads or groups, through which the crossing or filling picks could be more easily passed.

## Warp Beam and Spool

At an uncertain date prior to the Middle Ages, some tribes, in what is now Great Britain, improved the apparatus by adding a frame—a warp beam. This beam was used to hold the warp ends and another beam was installed to take care of the woven cloth as it came from the loom—the cloth beam or roller.

The filling or pick that was originally conveyed across in the form of a ball, or wrapped around a twig, was now placed in a spool. This was torpedo or boat-shaped and today is known as a shuttle. The spindle upon which the filling was wound fitted into the shuttle.

## The Two Kays

It was not until 1733—at the beginning of the Industrial Revolution—that the first major modern improvement on the hand loom was made. This was the fly shuttle of the Englishman John Kay. It was a revolutionary improvement because it increased the productivity of the loom by about eight times. In 1760 his son Robert Kay added the second major modern improvement. He invented a drop box loom which made it possible for one weaver to manipulate several shuttles.

These two inventions led to the need for devices which would spin yarns as fast as the looms could now weave them. They resulted in the great spinning inventions of this period. But it remained for Joseph-Marie Jacquard (1752-1834) to contribute the greatest improvement of all to the loom. The story of the JACQUARD LOOM receives separate treatment in this section.

## Weaving of Cloth

The basic principles used in weaving cloth on looms have remained unchanged since the earliest times. Modern power looms and primitive hand looms follow the fundamental principle of interlacing warp threads with weft threads.

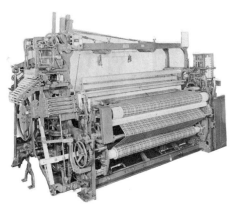

Power loom weaving plaid fabric.

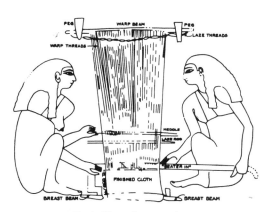

Early Egyptian weaving.

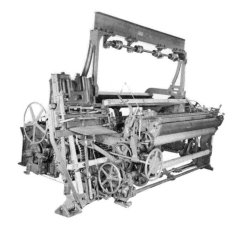

Shuttle changing medium duck loom.

Figure I

THE PLAIN WEAVE

This is the simplest form of interlacing the vertical threads (the warp, as shown in black) with the horizontal threads (the filling, as shown in grey).

In these diagrams of the three basic weaves, the black lines represent the warp and the grey interlacing lines represent the weft (woof) or filling.

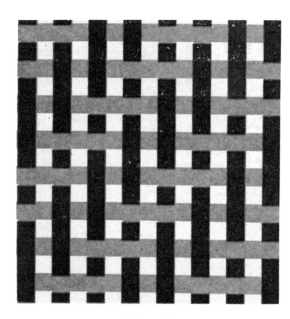

Figure II

THE TWILL WEAVE

Magnified to show interlacing of warp and filling threads in an even-sided twill with both warp and filling given equal importance.

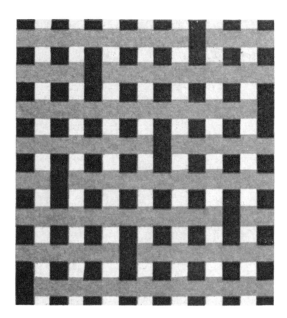

Figure III

THE SATIN WEAVE

Note the long floats (threads skipping over or under a number of other threads) which, lying parallel to one another, give the fabric its sheen.

324

# The Three Basic Weaves

*Three weaves are basic to all woven fabrics.*
*These weaves are the Plain Weave, the Twill Weave,*
*and the Satin Weave. Every woven textile must be one of*
*these weaves or a variation thereof.*

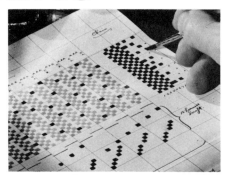

Plotting a weave.

## The Plain Weave

THE PLAIN WEAVE is the most common of all weaves. It accounts for a significant percent of all woven goods. It is also the strongest of all weaves, since its threads are interlaced the tightest. There is only one plain weave, but the number of possibilities in twill and satin weave constructions is almost limitless.

The plain weave is the simplest form of interlacing the warp and filling. To make this weave, the odd-numbered ends are raised over the first pick and the even-numbered ends are raised over the second pick. Figure 1 is a magnified picture of the plain weave illustrating this point.

REPRESENTATIVE PLAIN WEAVE MATERIALS . . . *Made from cotton:* batiste, broadcloth, cambric, chambray, dimity, flannel, lawn, muslin, nainsook, organdy, poplin, voile, sheeting. *Made from linen:* crash, dress linen, handkerchief linen, butcher's linen, art and pillowcase linens. *Made from woolens and worsteds:* albatross, balmacaan, broadcloth, challis, flannel, homespun. *Made from silk, rayon, acetate and other man-made fibers:* broadcloth, chiffon, china silk, habutai, mogadore, moiré, ninon, radium, shantung, taffeta, some plaids and novelties.

## The Twill Weave

THE TWILL WEAVE is a popular construction which is widely used in woven goods. Its tensile strength is considered next to that of the plain weave. The interlacing of the threads in a twill weave is not as tight as in the plain weave. About eighty-five percent of all twill-woven fabrics is made with a right-hand twill effect. The twill lines on the face of these goods run from the lower left-hand corner of the material to the upper right-hand corner of the cloth. Among the variations of the twill weave are the left-hand twill, the herringbone twill, broken twill, en-

twining twill, braided twill, pointed twill, zigzag twill, etc.

The twill weave is formed by interlacing the warp and filling threads so that diagonal lines show on the face of the fabric. They may be from lower left to upper right (right-hand twill) or from upper left to lower right (left-hand twill). Twills may have a predominance of either warp or filling on the face, or in many cases, be even-sided twills. Figure 2 is a magnification of a fabric in an even-sided twill in which both the warp and the filling are given equal importance.

REPRESENTATIVE TWILL WEAVE MATERIALS . . . *Made from cotton:* (right-hand twills) some doeskin, drill, twillcloth, some denim, gabardine, lining fabric; (left-hand twills) galatea, denim, jean cloth, uniform goods, institution fabric. *Made from linen:* (right-hand twills) some birdseye, ticking, toweling; (left-hand twills) some novelty linen material, ticking. *Made from woolens and worsteds:* (right-hand twills) cassimere, cavalry twill, cheviot, covert, doeskin, elastique, flannel, gabardine, gun-club checks, serge, shetland, tricotine, tweed, whipcord, novelty outerwear cloth; (left-hand twills) a few novelty dress goods. *From silk and man-made fibers:* (right-hand twills) foulard, gabardine, plaid cloths, silk serges, surah, tartan silk; (left-hand twills) some novelty goods.

## The Satin Weave

THE SATIN WEAVE and all remaining types are found in a minor percentage of all woven goods. It is the weakest of the three basic weaves since its threads are more widely spaced when compared with the plain or twill constructions.

This weave consists of threads not raised consecutively, as they are in a twill, but with a prevalence of long floats in either warp or filling. A float means

Graph paper.

Warp threads (dark).

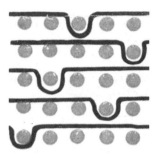

The float.

that a thread *floats* or skips over or under a definite number of other threads running in the opposite direction.

REPRESENTATIVE SATIN WEAVE MATERIALS . . . *Made from silk, rayon, acetate rayons:* brocade, brocatelle, cape or cloak fabric, cottonback sateen, coverings, curtain material, damask, dress silk, duvetyn, fancies and novelties, furniture fabric, Jacquard fabrics of many types, runners, slipper satin, sport fabrics made of silk or man-made fibers, striping effect in some materials, tablecloth and napkin material, tapestry, tie fabrics, upholstery fabrics. Cotton and linen yarns are used to make damask tablecloths and napkins.

## Designing the Weaves

The following charts and descriptions illustrate the methods used in planning different weaves.

GRAPH PAPER. Textile designers use graph paper to plot out fabric weave designs. The vertical squares are used to represent the warp ends. The horizontal squares represent the filling picks. The weave is indicated by marking the squares where the warp ends are raised over the filling picks. The illustration shows graph paper painted for a plain weave.

THE RAISER. This is a painted-in or blocked-in square on the design paper. It indicates that the warp end is raised over the filling pick at the point of interlacing. This is illustrated by the black squares on the design paper. The raisers in the

figure indicate a 2-up and 2-down twill weave pattern.

THE SINKER. This is a blank square on the design paper. It indicates that the filling pick is raised over the warp end at the point of interlacing. This is illustrated by the colored squares in the illustration. The arrangement of the sinkers and raisers in the figure indicates a plain weave.

THE FLOAT. The crossing of a thread over or under the opposite system of threads. The illustration shows a float of four in an eye-level cross-section of a five-end, filling-effect satin weave with a base or counter of three. Each colored space, for four blocks in the filling direction indicates that the single warp end interlaces with the filling once in every fifth thread, and then floats underneath or on the back of the fabric for four consecutive filling picks before again interlacing and becoming a raiser in the cloth.

THE REPEAT. This is just what its name signifies. A pattern is complete when the threads in a design begin to repeat themselves. In the illustration is a design with one full repeat of the pattern covered in the square formed by the first four boxes up and sideways from the left hand corner. The figure illustrates a 2-up and 2-down right-hand twill. The weave is painted two repeats high and two repeats wide.

## Typical Twills

Five types of widely used twill and satin weaves are illustrated and described in the following charts:

Plain weave.

Right hand twill.

Left hand twill.

Even-sided twills.

Filling-faced twills.

How iridescence is woven into a satin fabric. Seen from one side, the dark thread shows. Seen from the other side, the light thread shows.

**EVEN-SIDED TWILLS.** These are twill fabric weaves in which there is no predominance of either warp ends or filling picks on the face of the goods. Note in the illustration that the amount of the warp and filling as shown on the design paper is equal. The design shown is two repeats high by two repeats wide.

**FILLING-FACE TWILLS.** These are twill fabric weaves in which there is a predominance of filling picks on the face of the goods. Note the illustration in which the filling picks as shown by the blank squares predominate. The weave is a 1-up, 2-down, left-hand twill, filling-effect; 3 repeats for a total of 9 ends and 9 picks.

**WARP-FACE TWILLS.** These are twill fabric weaves in which there is a predominance of warp ends on the face of the goods. Note the illustration in which the warp ends as shown by the black squares predominate. This is a right-hand twill because the diagonal twill line goes from lower left to upper right. The weave is a 2-up, 1-down right-hand twill, warp-effect; 3 repeats for a total of 9 ends and 9 picks.

## Satin Weaves

**WARP-FACED SATIN.** This is a satin weave in which there is a predominance of warp ends on the face. The illustration shows a warp-face satin (note the predominance of the raisers), complete on eight ends and eight picks using a base or counter of three. The long float of seven gives satin fabrics a rich, surface effect.

**FILLING-FACE SATIN.** This is a satin weave in which there is a predominance of filling picks on the face. The illustration shows a filling-face satin complete on eight ends and eight picks using a base or counter of three. Satin weave fabrics cannot withstand friction and chafing when compared with plain and twill woven materials; the floats cause this lessened tensile strength and weakness in abrasion.

## Variations of the Basic Weaves

Among the variations of the plain, twill, and satin weaves are the following:

*Basket Weave.* A variation of the plain weave. It produces a loosely woven cloth (such as monk's cloth and hopsacking) with two or more filling yarns and two or more warp yarns.

*Rib Weave.* Also a plain weave variation. Fabrics like grosgrain, Ottoman, and some webbing are made by this method. The rib effect may be either in the length of the fabric (filling rib) or in the width (warp rib). They are achieved by grouping together a number of yarns in one direction before they are crossed by yarns moving in the other direction.

*Bedford Cord Weave.* A lengthwise cord effect is formed by allowing the filling yarns to float under and over definite warp threads, thus forming a rib.

Warp-faced twills.

Warp-faced satin.

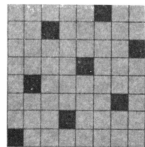

Filling-face satin.

*Mesh Fabric:* Woven or knitted fabrics made to present an open texture and effect.

*Oxford:* Shirting or suiting fabric made on a plain weave derivative or small basket construction such as a 1-2, 2-2 weave.

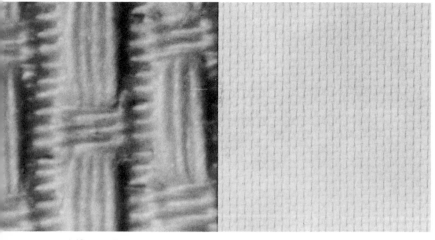

*(Above) Fancy Basket Weave:* One in which the "squares" in the weave are not all the same, in order to give a varied effect. *(Below) Bedford Cord:* Derived from the rib weave, it presents vertical or warp-wise effect on the face of the goods. Stuffer yarns are used to accentuate the cord effect.

*Piqué Weave.* Constructed very much like the Bedford cord except that the ribs are formed crosswise. The fabric is generally used with the cord running vertically.

*Bird's-eye Weave.* Diamond shaped designs are formed by floating filling yarns over warp threads in a set formation.

*Huckaback Weave.* Lengthwise but interrupted ridges are formed by floats of warp threads on the surface of the cloth.

*Waffle Weave.* Square or oblong-shaped box formations appear on both the face and back of the fabric, by allowing both warp and filling yarns to float at fixed intervals.

*Lappet Weave.* This uses an extra warp, woven in zigzag formation. The lappet warp floats on the surface of the goods and is then automatically cut to create a dotted swiss or sprig effect. Only one color may be used in the extra warp.

*Swivel Weave.* The effect of the swivel weave is usually the same as the lappet. It uses an extra filling and a series of small shuttles or swivels to create the novelty appearance.

*Clip Spot Weave.* The clip spot weave also uses an extra filling which appears on the surface of the cloth. These long floats are afterwards cut to create the design.

*Double Cloth Weaves.* This type of weave involves the joining of two cloths by the use of an extra binder in either filling or warp. At least five sets of yarn are therefore used: (1) Face warp. (2) Face filling. (3) Back warp. (4) Back filling. (5) Binder threads.

*Backed Cloth Weave.* A reversible fabric is achieved by using one warp and two fillings or two warps and one filling. No binder yarn is used. Also known as French back.

*Pile Weaves.* By the use of either extra warps or extra fillings, loops are formed on the surface of the fabric. The loops are either cut or left uncut. Corduroy and velveteen are *filling* pile fabrics, since the filling loops have been cut. Velvet is a *warp* pile fabric because the warp loops have been cut. Many rugs are woven by this pile method. So is terry cloth.

*Leno Weave.* A porous weave used for curtains and summer shirtings. The filling threads are locked in position by a crossing and twisting of the warp threads over the filling picks.

*Plain Weave:* The simplest, commonest, and strongest of all basic weaves. Each warp yarn passes successively over and under each filling pick.

*Satin:* Derived from the twill, satins do not show to the naked eye a marked twill or diagonal line, but appear solid and glossy on the face of the fabric.

# Weaving Cloth

*The application of power to loom operation is making possible continual advances in productivity and control.*

## Power Added for Speed

The power loom of today is substantially the hand loom adapted to rotary driving. The frame is iron instead of wood; the sley or oscillating frame is pivoted below and driven by a crank; and the picking arm is actuated by a cone that turns on a vertical rod. The lift of the heddle shafts or harnesses is controlled by tappets or cams.

The motions are timed accurately in order to give a high rate of speed and production. The weaver, free from supplying power, has merely to apply the filling threads, sometimes known as weft, to the shuttle. He must watch for warp-yarn breakage and for blemishes and defects in the weaving of the cloth. He must also be able to care for several looms, depending on the type and nature of the work being performed.

From time to time various improvements have been added. There are warp drop wires that cause the loom to stop or knock-off as soon as an end happens to break. Feeler wires that are set in the raceplate of the loom cause the loom to knock-off if the pick does not go all the way through the shed. There are automatic let-offs for the warp as the cloth is woven, and take-off motions for the warp beam and the cloth roller respectively.

## Power Looms in Use Today:

1. *Plain Loom:* Built for simple or plain weaving of cloth with the addition of an automatic shuttle device to change the filling as it runs out. This type of loom makes for production. The machine does not stop while the new filling bobbin is set in to replace the one that has just run out. With suitable organization of labor, one weaver may take care of several of these looms. He may care for as many as 48 or more looms at one time.

2. *Box Looms:* Box looms have parts that are additional to those found on plain looms. Stripes of color are arranged for in the warping, but the crossing stripes to form checks and plaids are put into

the cloth by the filling bobbin in the shuttle. There must be as many shuttles as there are colors of filling to be used in the cloth design. The shuttles are placed in boxes at the end of the sley or warp, and the mechanism provides that the particular box shall be in position at the instant or exact time required.

Dobby weaving.

3. *Dobby Loom:* Weaves fancy materials. The dobby loom is built so that it can take care of many harnesses. Some looms have from 24 to 30 frames in them. A particular heddle can be lifted at a given moment by means of metal projections that engage the holes in strips or bars of metal plates which are successively present in endless chain form. This is called the draft chain or pattern chain.

Small, fancy, and geometrical or symmetrical figures or designs may be woven on this type of loom which may be said to be a simpler version of the Jacquard loom.

4. *Double Cylinder Dobby Loom:* If it is desired to weave a pattern that contains a great many picks in the repeat, a large number of bars must be built for the pattern picks since, even on the double index dobby, one bar represents only two picks. When patterns of several hundred picks are woven, this becomes a matter of considerable importance as a long chain always requires much time in building.

To overcome the difficulty of building long pattern chains, the double cylinder dobby is largely used. The pattern chain for one weave is placed on one of the cylinders while the pattern chain for the other weave is placed on the second cylinder. Since it is

(*Above*) Power-looming an old Habitant hand-woven bedspread design.

(*Below*) A contemporary American power loom.

The above photograph shows Type A felt loom.

C-4 blanket loom weaving a cotton blanket.

possible to send either cylinder around as many times as there are repeats of the weave before changing onto the other cylinder, it is possible to build only one repeat for each weave, providing that the number of bars in one repeat is sufficient to go around the cylinder; if the repeat has fewer bars, a sufficient number of repeats must be built to encircle the cylinder.

Dobby motions are built with a capacity from 16 to 24 up to 30 harnesses. The 16-harness motions are used the most, whereas 20- and 30-harness motions are used for the more complicated weaves and novelty effects.

5. *Jacquard Loom:* Provides for the lifting or raising of individual warp ends without reference to adjacent warp threads. The loom is a development of the power loom. In the Jacquard head-motion there are perforated cards and the needles of the cylinder in this head stock select the required warp end or group of ends. They raise these ends, which are lifted by means of hooks and form the top part of the shed of the warp in order to admit the passage of the filling pick through the opening formed.

6. *Leno or Doup Loom:* Weaves cloth in such a way that certain warp threads twist or cross half

way around or over other warp ends. There are two sets of harnesses used, standard and skeleton. This loom is used for marquisette, curtains, draperies, novelty, and fancy perforated effects in cloth.

7. *Lappet Loom:* Uses an extra warp to produce small fancy effects in cloth. There is a base warp, and a lappet warp takes care of placing the figured design in the material. Few of these looms are now in use.

8. *Swivel or Clip-Spot Loom:* Makes small designs or effects on cloth by means of an extra filling or swivel. The results are the same as those noted on a lappet loom. Few of these looms are now in use.

9. *Pile Fabric Loom:* Material from this type of loom is made with an extra set or sets of yarns that are looped on the face of the cloth. The fabric may be cut or uncut to give the pile effect. Cutting or looping is done by means of rods which, if they are tipped at the one end with a blade, will give a cut pile effect; if there is no blade at the one end of the wire, the material will become an uncut pile fabric. Plushes of all types are made on these looms.

10. *Indian Type Loom:* Also called the *inkle* or *belt* loom, provided with frames for loopers, tapestry; or upright looms in hand weaving.

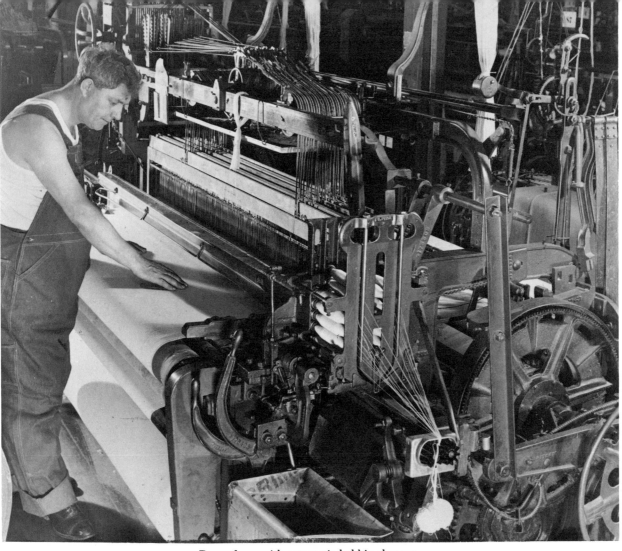

Power loom with automatic bobbin changer.

Modern loom, 650″ between swords.

# The Shuttleless Loom

As weaving has felt the competitive pressures of other fabric-forming techniques in recent years, particularly knitting, it has responded with a host of improvements among which one of the most dramatic is the shuttleless loom.

Speed and economy were the main factors behind the birth of the shuttleless loom, which first came into prominence after the mid 1940's. New textile trends also had their effect, particularly the pressure for wider fabrics. The popularity of queen- and king-size bedspreads, for example, created a demand for looms with 138-inch reed space.

Shutterless looms are either air- or water-jet. The water-jet loom, which is considerably faster than its shuttle counterpart, shows possibilities for producing fabrics at up to twice or more the conventional speeds of fly-shuttle equipment, while some industry experts envision speeds of 400 to 600 picks per minute with air-jet looms. Present maximum speeds with conventional machinery are in the range of 260 picks per minute.

However, the water-jets confine their use to filament yarns and fibers that are non-absorbent and do not deteriorate in water. Rayon, for example, would not qualify for water-jet looms.

In the meantime, fly-shuttle equipment remains dominant in the industry because of its widespread installation, dependability, versatility and sheer volume production controlled by one operator. Leading machine makers have made vast improvements in the fly-shuttle loom, concentrating on automation, width and speed.

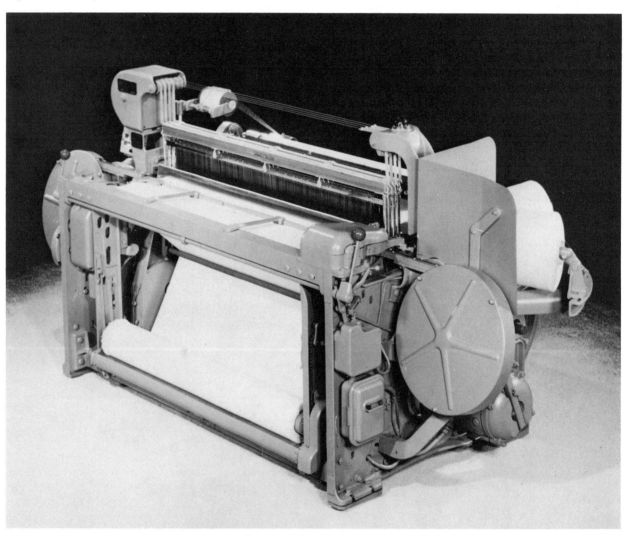

A Draper shuttleless loom with clock-spring top.

# Jacquard Weaving...
## a milestone in textiles

Jacquard loom for weaving damask. Jacquard cards, punched to control lifting of warp threads, are used to create damask patterns.

The Jacquard invention replaced the old-time drawboy by an arrangement of rods which lifted the figure harnesses in sequence.

## The Story of Jacquard Weaving

The ancient draw-loom was the first known attempt at figure weaving. Tradition points to its early European use in France and Holland in the 15th Century. This lumbering, cumbersome type of loom necessitated two operators. The draw boy raised the specified leashes or cords on the loom and also had to attend to lowering them as well. When the warp shed was formed, the rest of the weaving operation was performed by the actual weaver. He also chose the colors he desired, dyed his own yarn, made his motif or design, and developed his own color pattern.

As time progressed there was more and more demand for varied materials. It became apparent that present conditions would not suffice and that some mechanical means would have to be devised to meet these demands. Thus, if the draw boy were to be able to work faster, the weaver would have to be relieved of his many trying burdens.

The famous Jacquard Loom was the answer to these early-day difficulties.

Jacquard's head-motion was a masterpiece of perfection in the textile world, and could reproduce practically anything into fabric. Before discussing the wonders of Jacquard and his loom, it might be well to list the important dates in the textile history of so-called figure weaving. These happenings, collectively, gave Jacquard food for thought and finally brought forth from his efforts his loom for perfection in design, motif, pattern, and weaving of intricate fabric. They are a prelude to the Jacquard era.

**1455:** Silk spinning and throwing introduced into England.

**1480:** Silk manufacturing introduced in France by many skilled Italian silk workers. Francis I, King of France, is the Father of the Silk Industry there and his influence is still felt. He had spent his early life in northern Italy and saw what was being done there in sericulture and silk weaving. When he came to the throne, one of his first acts was to organize the silk industry, in all phases, on a firm basis.

**1510:** Tapestry weaving, which had lapsed in England, was re-introduced by Thomas Sheldon.

**1662:** Tapestries were being made in Paris by the famous Gobelin family.

**1725:** Bouchon invented the perforated paper or card idea for working the draw loom to give figure fabrics.

**1728:** Falcon employed a chain of cards instead of the paper-roll plan of Bouchon. His cards were made to operate on a square block or prism. Incidentally, this plan is still in use today on modern Jacquard looms, the cards controlling the needles.

**1745:** Vaucanson applied a griffe to the Falcon machine and placed the apparatus on the top of the loom as a head-motion.

**1790:** Joseph-Marie Jacquard became known as the "fixer" for the machines made by his predecessors. He began his experimental work on the looms and from this work, in time, he became the inventor of the machine that bears his name today.

**1801:** Jacquard showed his machine and for his efforts received a medal at the Paris Exposition. His machine, however, was still not too practicable.

**1820:** The Jacquard machine was now an actuality and functioning in some textile centers. Stephen Wilson, English silk manufacturer, received a patent for a reading machine and for a punching machine to punch out the cards used in Jacquard weaving, the "piano-machine" of today.

**1823:** Coventry, England, was to become a center for Jacquard weaving. At this time there were five Jacquard looms there. By 1832, there were about 600 of the looms being used. In 1838, over 2,200 Jacquards were in use in Coventry.

**1824:** The first Jacquard machine to be used in this country was bought and operated by the William H. Horstmann Company, Philadelphia, Pa. It was used for making trimmings and novelty fabrics.

**1834:** Joseph-Marie Jacquard died in Oullins, near Lyons, France.

**1842:** A Jacquard machine with a separate cylinder motion which was operated from the crankshaft of the loom, was invented by J. Bellough.

**1849:** Alfred Barlow invented the important double Jacquard.

Double-lift, double-cylinder Jacquard mechanism.

J. M. C. Jacquard.

## Joseph-Marie Charles Jacquard (1752-1834)

Joseph-Marie Jacquard was born July 7th, 1752 in Lyons, France. His father was a weaver and his mother was a patternmaker. He was destined to make the last great invention of the Industrial Revolution following the French Revolution, the American Revolution and the War of 1812.

Jacquard had a very stern father who allowed the boy little formal education, and his youth was none too pleasant. His father died when the lad was twenty. The father left a small house and a hand loom as his worldly possessions. The boy began to take deep interest in the hand loom and did some experimentation with it, but his interest soon waned. He became a plasterer, cutler, type founder, and then, in time, not showing too much liking for these vocations, he once more became interested in weaving fabric.

He was a soldier during the French Revolution. His son, also a soldier, was killed in the defense of Lyons against the Army of the Convention. Since he was known as a weaver, the Council of Lyons, after hostilities ceased, gave him a loom on which he was to do experimental work in the Palace of Fine Arts, with the proviso that he teach some of the students how to weave fabric. Jacquard evinced great inter-

18th Century hand-weaving loom, from a contemporary engraving.

est in his new task, his absorption constantly taking on impetus with the result that he showed much progress in his experimental labors.

In time, he went to London where he worked for the Society of Arts, which offered a reward for a machine that would make fish nets. On February 2nd, 1804, Jacquard received 3,000 francs and a gold medal from the London Society; he made the machine that was selected by the Commission. It was displayed in the Conservatorium of Arts and Trades and attracted much interest. He was now on his way to greater things.

Napoleon and Carnot, his Minister, heard of Joseph-Marie Jacquard and his work. Jacquard was summoned to appear before them. At the meeting, Napoleon addressed him with—"Are you the man who can do what God Almighty cannot do—tie a knot in a taut string?" The classic answer to this was—"I cannot do what God cannot, but what God has taught me to do." As a result of the meeting, Napoleon gave him the commission of assignment to the Conservatorium of Arts where he was allowed to work on the looms there and study the efforts and work of his predecessors—Bouchon, Falcon and Vaucanson, an interesting triumvirate.

## Vaucanson . . . a Mechanical Genius

Vaucanson, particularly, was an interesting individual. He had several machines in the Conserva-

torium, as well as automatons of many sorts. He had a duck, for example, that "could waddle, quack, swim, eat and digest food—all by mechanical process." Jacquard obtained many ideas from Vaucanson's findings and experimentation. He now began to work with vigor on what was in time to be the Jacquard Loom. By the end of 1804, he was back in his beloved Lyons and his loom was beginning to take shape. He combined the best ideas of his predecessors, improved upon them and finally constructed a loom that would perform practical figure weaving.

The loom was set up with weighted cords or strings which passed over a pulley and fell into perforated cards. Each motion or turnover of the loom changed the position of the cords and allowed some of them to go through the holes and draw up the warp thread so that it was skipped by the weft; others would strike the card and leave their ends in place to be woven in the regular manner. Thus, the weaver, could now pass his threads over, under or through the warp as the pattern required.

## Napoleon and the Inventor

Napoleon kept constant eye and interest on the progress being made by the inventor. Pleased with his efforts, the Emperor ordered that an annuity of 3,000 francs be awarded Jacquard. This was in 1806 and the award carried the proviso that Jac-

Mechanism of modern Jacquard showing punch cards and rods above, which operate heddles.

Weaver refilling shuttle of a Jacquard loom; patterned material is seen below shuttle.

quard should transfer all his efforts and inventions to the city of Lyons. The Jacquard loom was now a practical actuality.

Like other great inventors of the Industrial Revolution, however, Jacquard and his looms encountered violent opposition. And, like many another genius of the time, he had to flee for his life. As time passed and saner folks began to see the possibilities of the loom for the greater glory of Lyons, Paris and all France, they began to take things into their own hands and see what could be done to calm the enraged textile workers who had feared that the loom sealed their doom. Each loom, it was estimated, did away with the work of a hundred or so persons.

Gradually the looms began to meet with favor and as a result Lyons and its superb fabrics began their fabric reign.

Joseph-Marie Jacquard lived to see over 30,000 Jacquard looms being used in and around the Lyons textile area alone. At 82, he died in Oullins, France, August 7th, 1834.

## The Jacquard Machine

The Jacquard machine is a special mechanism situated over a hand or power loom and is called a Jacquard head-motion. The motion is used in the production of figured fabrics and in materials of high, compact texture with a pattern, motif, or weave that exceeds the capacity of a harness loom. The Jacquard head-motion usually replaces the head-motion of a dobby loom, in which the dobby-motion controls the harness frames in the loom.

The chief advantage of a Jacquard is in its ability to govern individual warp threads in each repeat of pattern. It may be used in conjunction with a head-motion with or without a limited number of harness frames, thereby creating additional possibilities for the designer to combine simple harness effects with the Jacquard. For this reason, the designer is allowed more freedom and expression in producing fancy figured effects. In fact, there is no limit to the possibilities of the design insofar as the machine is concerned.

A very wide range of fabrics can be made on the Jacquard loom, which may be changed over to a regular harness loom by raising the Jacquard harness and by replacing the harness frames which will be operated by the dobby head-motion. These fabrics may include blankets, brocade, brocatelle, carpets and rugs, coat lining, coatings, damask, drapery fabric, dress materials, furniture covering, handkerchiefs, labels of all types and other narrow fabrics, napkins, necktie or cravat fabric, shirting, tablecloths and table covers, loomed tapestry, Turkish toweling. Most Jacquard fabrics are woven face down to save wear and tear on the cloth.

# Hand Loom Weaving

*Dating back five thousand years, hand weaving remains today one of the most lively of all the textile arts, serving both as the inspirational source for many power-loom products and as the production means for a great variety of woven items.*

The quality and appearance of any handwoven cloth very much depends upon the individual weaver. It is the integration and balance of fiber, yarn, color and design that distinguishes any textile, whether it is an ancient piece or a modern fabric. The technical possibilities of handloom weaving are comparatively limited. For this reason the weaver must know the mechanical construction and the possibilities of his loom thoroughly. He must be able to construct new drafts, as well as adapt those of master weavers of the past to present day requirements.

He must know the qualities and relationships of the

Hand loom weaving equipment in the United States.

various fibers: flax and other members of the bast family, wool, silk, cotton and man-made types. He must understand the properties and relationships of the three basic weaves — Plain, Twill and Satin. Only then can he create new color schemes, plays of texture, and original designs in such a way as to produce the beauty and quality which belong to hand woven fabrics.

## The Principal Weaves

The classification of weaves most frequently used by weavers today is based upon the weave and not upon the material, design or color of the fabric. But fabrics may be divided roughly into those in which the pattern provides the richness through the manner of threading the heddles of the loom, and those in which the interest is in the color, texture or applied design.

The *plain weave* or cloth weave is the most ancient and universal, and probably developed from the primitive interlacing of rushes, cane and similar fibers. It is found in all ancient textiles, including those from the Swiss lake dwellers, the ancient Peruvians and the Egyptian linen weavers of prehistoric times; it is also found in the silks of the Han dynasty in China. This weave consists in the alternate under-and-over interlacing of both warp and filling threads.

The *twill weave* produces diagonal lines on the face of the goods, as well as herringbones and other variants of the basic diagonal line. The simplest that can be made is based on the alternate under and over interlacing of three warp ends and three filling picks. There are many varieties such as two up and one down, one up and two down and so on. These produce a diagonal rib which runs at a different angle according to the construction, which may be two, three, four or more ends up for one down, and these varieties give, besides 45-degree twills, 63-degree,

Handweaving of blankets is an important industry among the Navaho Indians in New Mexico.

Above is an old-time two harness hand loom which has been used by several generations of weavers.

70-degree, 75-degree twills and others.

*Satin weaves* do not have any distinguishable line on the face of the fabric, since the picks or ends which float on the surface, according to the filling or warp construction, overlap sufficiently to produce a quite even surface which, in the case of silk, has a characteristic sheen. Here a single end floats over 5, 6, 7 or more picks.

The hand weaver should choose his shuttle with great care, for it will affect the appearance of the material as well as the speed with which he can work. If too heavy it will tend to fly out of the warp, and if too light to be drawn out of its course by the drag of the thread.

## Preparing the Warp

*Threading a Loom* from the front.

1. After the warp chain is made, secure it to the front of the loom, spreading the warp-ends in the securing-cross-string.

2. With a reed hook, draw ends through the spaces (Dents) of the Reed, according to a plan decided upon earlier. Draw in Single, Double or Half-sley. (If desired, the threads may be removed from the securing cross-string during this operation as it has served its purpose to keep the warp-ends in a parallel order.) Sley

Many modern textile firms use hand looms to weave trial ideas which will later be duplicated on the power looms.

## Some steps preliminary to weaving:

1. The yarn which comes in skeins is first put on the yarn binder and is then crossed on the warping board or reel.

2. When it is taken off the board it is braided to keep it from becoming disarranged.

3. It is then separated on the comb to get the warp even on the loom before warping.

4. The warp is then set up on the loom and knotted.

5. The new warp is tied to the old warp on the heddles.

6. The warp is hooked to the reed and is then tied to the apron ready for weaving.

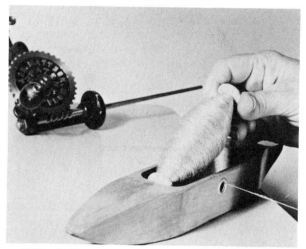

Filling bobbin in boat shuttle preliminary to getting ready for weaving.

heavier at edges for Selvages.

3. Enter each thread into an eye of the heddles according to a draft previously decided upon.

4. Check for mistakes as small units are drawn in, and tie loosely in small groups until entire warp is entered into heddles.

5. Carefully even-up ends in small groups and tie each group to the rod on the apron of the warp beam. (Place the group over and around the batten, separate in halves, bring each half up and tie a bow square knot over the top.)

6. Pull the entire warp chain forward, holding it tightly a short distance from the reed.

7. Shift the harnesses and put in the leash sticks, tying to both back and upright side beams.

*Rolling Warp on to Loom.* The longer the warp, the more care is necessary.

1. Unchain a reasonable length of warp, about three yards.

2. Hold it securely at this length, or at its end if it is short.

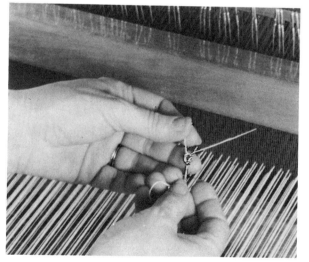

*Above left:* Tieing the weaver's knot. *Above right:* Cutting the cloth from the loom.

3. Shake out the apparent tangle, pulling entire warp (which now is firmly secured to warp-beam). This will straighten out all loose ends. If care has been taken in evening-up ends before tying, no combing will be necessary.

4. If Combing is necessary, start at far end of warp, working toward the loom until all warp ends lie parallel and are of the same tension.

5. Hold securely as the rolling-on takes place. (This may require four hands, each spaced in correct relationship with the position of the warp in the reed.)

6. Start winding (one revolution of the warp beam). Insert a piece of pliable cardboard or hard paper (Manila tag) cut to the full width of the warp, and roll on with the warp to insure a firm, uniform cylinder.

7. Hold warp slightly slack as rolling takes place and pull up very firmly after each one or two revolutions. (Assistants must regulate tension according to each other.) Watch for slack threads, snarls, and knots likely to be caught in the reed or in the heddles.

8. Continue rolling up and supplying widths of hard paper until ends are within tying distance of the reed.

9. Tie in small groups to the rod of the apron of the cloth beam, using the same method as on the warp beam, but tying only half of the square knot at *this* time.

10. Harness-up loom, if it needs it at this time, attaching heddles, treadles, levers, lams, etc. according to the loom involved.

## Starting to Weave

Start weaving to test for mistakes. Then tighten up each group of warp threads uniformly and tie the other half of the square knot or a bow. Insure an even tension throughout the entire warp.

Put in several shots of coarse weft, using the plain weave shifts, *beating in place only after two or three shots have been inserted,* so that the open spaces made by the group tying will quickly close and allow the piece of weaving to be begun against a firm start without wasting an undue amount of warp.

After the weaving is started a few inches and before it has been rolled up beyond the breast beam, hemstitch to put a firm finish to the article. This will, in many cases, be preferable to knotting where a fringe is desired. The same may be done at the other end while the material is still on the loom.

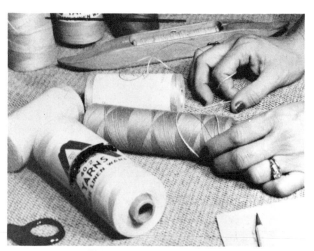

Choosing the warp threads.

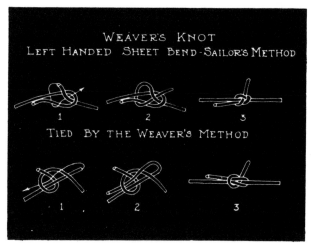

The weaver's knot (left-handed sheet bend) as tied by the sailor's method, and the weaver's knot tied by the weaver's method.

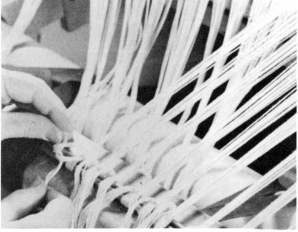

Drawing in warp and tieing to cloth roller apron.

(*Above*) Hand weaving of linen fabric on a hand loom. (*Below*) Winding the bobbin; *at left,* making two mountains at ends with valley between: *at right,* building up to one mountain at center. This prevents troublesome "waggle-tail."

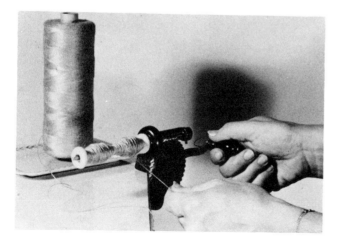
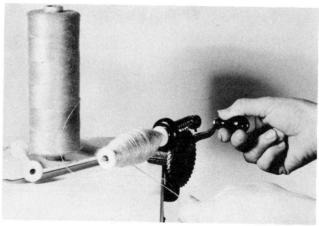

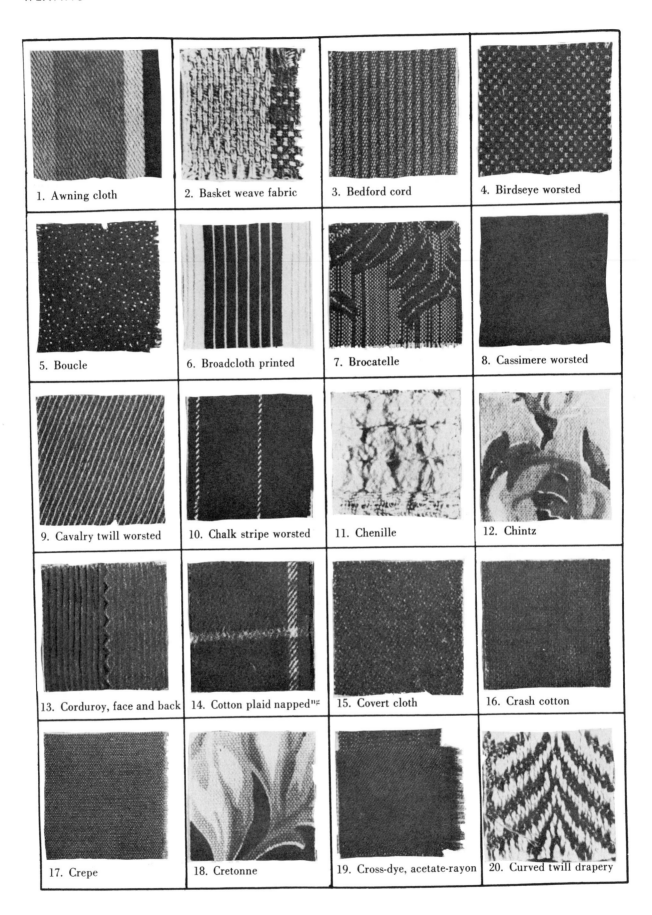

| | | | |
|---|---|---|---|
| 1. Awning cloth | 2. Basket weave fabric | 3. Bedford cord | 4. Birdseye worsted |
| 5. Boucle | 6. Broadcloth printed | 7. Brocatelle | 8. Cassimere worsted |
| 9. Cavalry twill worsted | 10. Chalk stripe worsted | 11. Chenille | 12. Chintz |
| 13. Corduroy, face and back | 14. Cotton plaid napped | 15. Covert cloth | 16. Crash cotton |
| 17. Crepe | 18. Cretonne | 19. Cross-dye, acetate-rayon | 20. Curved twill drapery |

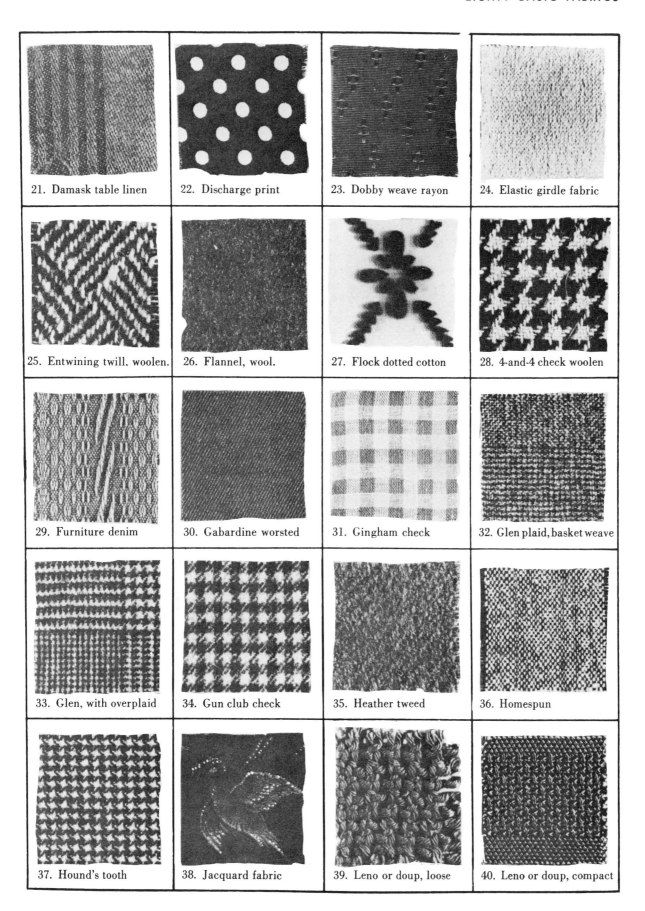

21. Damask table linen    22. Discharge print    23. Dobby weave rayon    24. Elastic girdle fabric

25. Entwining twill, woolen.    26. Flannel, wool.    27. Flock dotted cotton    28. 4-and-4 check woolen

29. Furniture denim    30. Gabardine worsted    31. Gingham check    32. Glen plaid, basket weave

33. Glen, with overplaid    34. Gun club check    35. Heather tweed    36. Homespun

37. Hound's tooth    38. Jacquard fabric    39. Leno or doup, loose    40. Leno or doup, compact

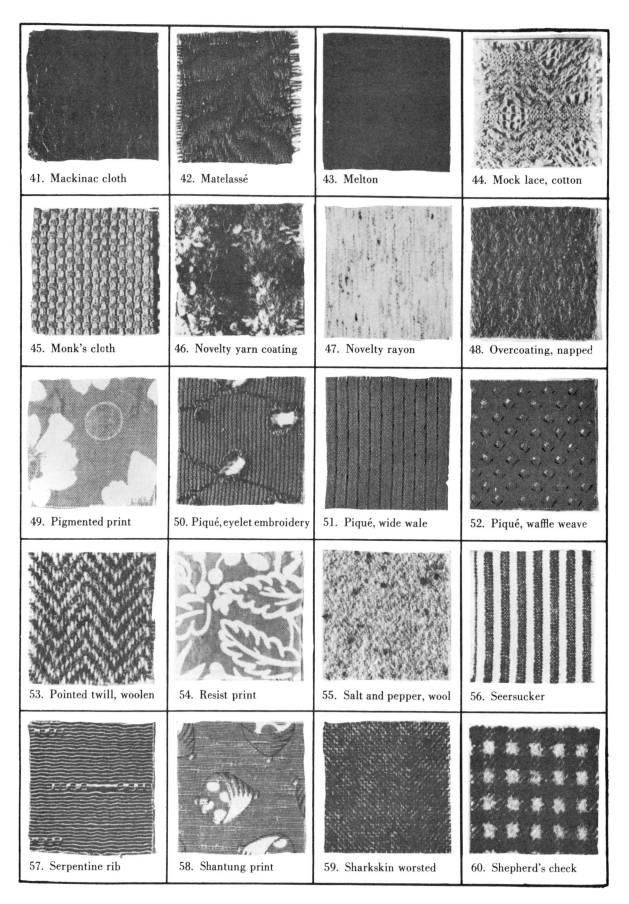

| | | | |
|---|---|---|---|
| 41. Mackinac cloth | 42. Matelassé | 43. Melton | 44. Mock lace, cotton |
| 45. Monk's cloth | 46. Novelty yarn coating | 47. Novelty rayon | 48. Overcoating, napped |
| 49. Pigmented print | 50. Piqué, eyelet embroidery | 51. Piqué, wide wale | 52. Piqué, waffle weave |
| 53. Pointed twill, woolen | 54. Resist print | 55. Salt and pepper, wool | 56. Seersucker |
| 57. Serpentine rib | 58. Shantung print | 59. Sharkskin worsted | 60. Shepherd's check |

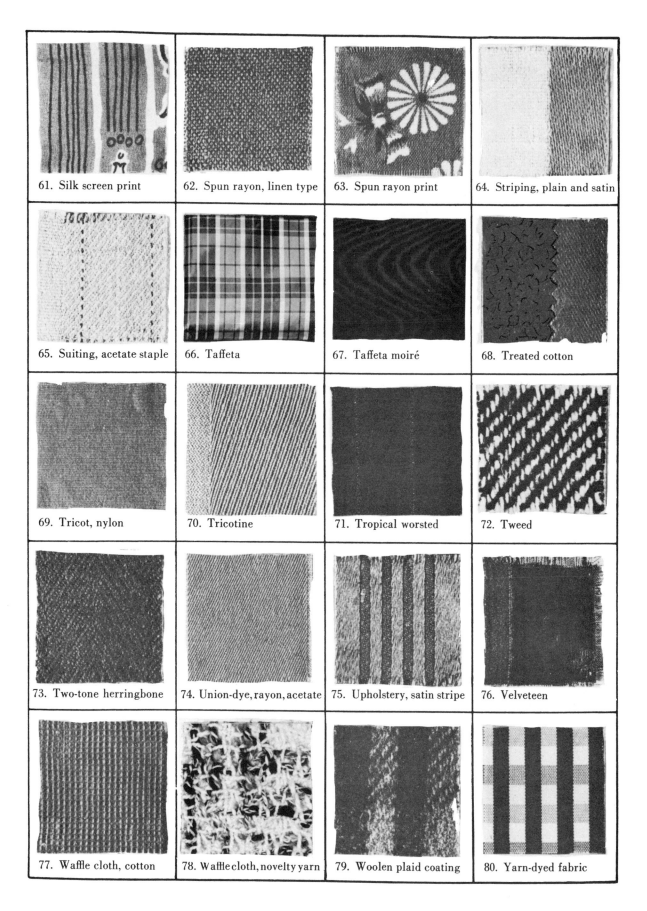

| | | | |
|---|---|---|---|
| 61. Silk screen print | 62. Spun rayon, linen type | 63. Spun rayon print | 64. Striping, plain and satin |
| 65. Suiting, acetate staple | 66. Taffeta | 67. Taffeta moiré | 68. Treated cotton |
| 69. Tricot, nylon | 70. Tricotine | 71. Tropical worsted | 72. Tweed |
| 73. Two-tone herringbone | 74. Union-dye, rayon, acetate | 75. Upholstery, satin stripe | 76. Velveteen |
| 77. Waffle cloth, cotton | 78. Waffle cloth, novelty yarn | 79. Woolen plaid coating | 80. Yarn-dyed fabric |

# What you should know about the
# *BASIC KNIT MACHINES*

### JERSEY — FLAT
The basic knitting stitch; the jersey flatbed produces full-fashioned sweaters, among many other types.

### JERSEY — CIRCULAR
The industry "workhorse," producing underwear, seamless hosiery, piece goods, other high-volume items.

### RIB — CIRCULAR
One example is the classic doubleknit, the fastest growing knitting machine category, now for men's wear.

### RIB — FLAT
A complex machine, capable of stitch transfer & widening out, expert at trim and cuffs and collars.

### PURL — FLAT
The famous links-links machine, fine for making pullovers and cardigans —and the classic golf or tennis sweater.

### PURL — CIRCULAR
The high-volume purl machine, as shown by its output: cut & sewn sweaters, dresswear and men's socks.

### TRICOT
A warp-knit machine producing fine vertical wales on the face; crosswise ribs on the back. The innerwear king, now going outerwear.

### RASCHEL
A warp-knit machine which can stitch or lay-in yarn, make open or lacy fabrics, rigid or stretchy; a fashion powerhouse, now blossoming.

# KNITTING AND KNIT FABRICS

*Modern developments in machinery, fibers and constructions, together with versatility and flexibility in manufacturing and styling, have vastly broadened the scope of machine knitting from its original use in hosiery.*

 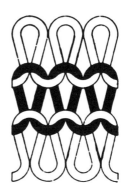

The basic structure in knitting is the plain jersey stitch. The loops are formed in one direction so that face and back of the fabric appear to be different.

## Definition

Knitting is the process of making cloth with a single yarn or a set of yarns moving in only one direction. Instead of two sets of yarns crossing each other as in weaving, the single knitting yarn is looped through itself to make a chain of stitches. These chains or rows are connected side by side and thus produce the knit cloth.

## How Knitting Is Done

When knitting is done by hand with long needles, each loop is made separately to form a row of stitches across the width of the cloth. This row is then connected with the next row as the knitter moves along. However, in machine knitting a whole row is made at one time by having one needle for each loop. The needles are controlled by cams, which move them into and out of position.

The row of loops which runs across the cloth is called a "course." This corresponds to the filling in woven fabric. The lengthwise chain of loops is called the "wale" and corresponds to the warp. The

number of stitches or loops in each square inch determines the denseness of the cloth, which can be either tight or loose depending on the end use.

## History of Knitting

Historically, knitting is usually considered to be one of the most recent methods of making fabrics. Actually, however, its principles stretch far back to prehistoric times. The making of fish nets (knotting) was basically a form of knitting used by almost all primitive peoples. The Bible refers to "a sheet knit at the four corners." The oldest extant piece of knitted fabric was found in archeological excavations at Dura-Europos (Syria) by Yale University and the French Academy of Inscriptions and Letters. It is a woolen fabric in what is called the Crossed Eastern Stitch pattern, and has been dated at 256 A.D.

Hand knitting was most likely introduced into Europe by the Arabs, and there is abundant evidence, from the latter centuries of the first millennium A.D. up to the sixteenth century, of the craft's widespread practice and development throughout western and

349

1770 stocking frame.

## Key Dates in History of Knitting

| 1745 | an Irishman | tuck presser |
|------|-------------|--------------|
| 1758 | J. Strutt | rib frame |
| 1769 | S. Wise | rotary drive |
| 1775 | Crane | warp knitting |
| 1798 | Decroix | plain circular frame |
| 1816 | Brunel | circular knitting |
| 1847 | Townshend | latch needle |
| 1849 | Mellor | loop wheel |
| 1857 | Barton | narrowing |
| 1860 | McNary | seamless hose |
| 1863 | Lamb | flat rib machine |
| 1864 | Cotton | vertical needle bar |
| 1890 | Scott & Williams | seamless hose |
| 1907 | Hemphill | revolving cylinder |

12th Century Madonna.

northern Europe. In the Viking tombs in Scandinavia there are knitted fragments which testify to the early technique practiced in the north of Europe over a thousand years ago. In the Ashmolean Museum of Eastern Art at Oxford there is an example of a Spanish altar piece which was knitted in the ninth century. At first glance, this appears to have been made from a brocade fabric, but on examination it is seen to have been knitted in "crossed stitch" following the Arab tradition. By the eleventh century hand-knitted garments were popular in England.

### The Inventive Curate

The history of the modern knitting machine has a definite beginning. The year was 1589 and the man responsible was a curate—the Reverend William Lee, M.A. of St. John's College, Cambridge, and a native of Calverton, England. In an age when mechanical inventions were a rarity, he invented and constructed a machine to knit stockings.

Lee's invention was completely original, without precedent, and remained substantially as he designed it for almost two hundred years. It was a flat-bed machine and used needles which we call the "spring-beard" type because they had a long flexible hook ending in a sharp point. Lee's assistant, Ashton, added some small improvements, but it was not until 1758 that Jedediah Strutt developed a device which would produce ribbing in knit cloths. The invention of Strutt was known as the Derby Rib Hosiery Frame.

### Improvements and Power

Thereafter, improvements in machine knitting came more rapidly. Before the end of the 18th century the rotary frame and the warp frame appeared; in 1816 Marc Brunel invented the circular knitting machine which was later improved by Peter Claussen in 1845. In 1847, Matthew Townshend patented his "latch" needle. Instead of using a barb on the needle hook, he made a half hook which was opened and closed by a swinging latch.

By 1864 William Cotton of Loughborough had perfected a power-driven knitting machine which would shape the fabric as it was knitted, and this was the basis of our modern full-fashioned machine.

### The Two Basic Machines

There are only two basic types of knitting machine: (1) flat needle-bar type and (2) circular type.

The flat knitting machine has its needles arranged in a straight line, held on a flat needle bed. The stitches move from side to side or up and down on the needles to make the cloth. It produces a flat fabric, as the loom does. One such type of machine is the full-fashioned knitting frame, which automatically adds or drops stitches to shape the fabric according to a predetermined plan. The shaped pieces must later be attached together to form a garment. It is slower than the circular type of machine.

The circular knitting machine has its needles arranged in a circle on a rotating cylinder. As the machine revolves, the needles knit the rows of loops and the cloth emerges as a circular tube. The tube can be knitted to a definite diameter and is often used as such for undershirts and garments which have no seams. More often it is slit, laid out flat, and then cut up like any other fabric.

The following section presents, in outline form, all of the basic factors of knitting technology, including construction categories, stitch formations, machines and special equipment, fabric types and uses.

# A CAPSULE OUTLINE OF KNITTING TECHNOLOGY

Tricot structure

Links-links structure

Raschel structures.

Eightlock construction.

Milanese structure.

Jersey structure

**FULL FASHIONED (Flat)**
**PILE KNITS (Circular)**
**VELOUR (Circular)**

All these
fall into
this category

## THERE ARE TWO BASIC CATEGORIES OF KNITTING:

**1. Warp Knitting.** Works with multiple yarns running vertically and parallel to each other. The fabric is constructed by manipulating these warp yarns simultaneously into loops which are interconnected.

**2. Weft Knitting.** Works with one yarn at a time running in a horizontal direction. The fabric is constructed by manipulating the needle to form loops in horizontal courses built on top of each other. Hand knitting is done by the weft method.

Within the two knitting categories, there are different methods and different machines, each producing a different construction.

There are also the two basic types of needles, described earlier: (1) the latch needle (2) the spring-beard needle. The latch needle is generally used to make the heavier or coarser knit fabrics of low gauge. The spring-beard is used to make finer knit fabrics of high gauge, such as women's stockings and lingerie fabrics.

## TYPES OF WARP KNITTING

Warp knits are made on flat bed machines and the parallel lines of yarn are arranged like the warp in a woven fabric. Each yarn is controlled by a separate needle which loops it onto itself. The yarns are connected to the next vertical row by moving back and forth from side to side, directed by metal guides.

Warp knit fabrics are generally tighter, flatter and less elastic than weft knits. They have little or no stretch in the vertical direction. They are also stronger and do not ravel.

Following are the different constructions produced and the specific equipment required.

### Tricot

*Definition:* A warp knit fabric is characterized by fine vertical wales on the face and crosswise underlaps on the back. The word comes from the French verb *tricoter* (to knit) though the tricot machine was actually invented by an Englishman named Crane in 1775. The fabric is run-resistant and hard to unravel. It has good stability and elasticity, is

351

resilient, crease resistant, and has high tear strength. It is widely used for lingerie, dresses, blouses and as a lining, or backing, in bonding. More recently its application has been extended to a broad range of outerwear through the use of both spun and textured yarns.

*Equipment Used:* Spring-beard needles and F.N.F. (Flying Needle Frame) compound needles. One needle bar. One to 18 guide bars. *Special Attachments:* Cut presser and knock-off lap. The terms "2-Bar" and "3-Bar" tricot are widely used as descriptive terms for knit fabrics, referring to the two or more guide bars which control the movement of the warp yarns and in turn determine the fabric characteristics.

## Raschel

*Definition:* The raschel machine is a versatile warp knitting machine which has the ability to stitch and lay-in yarns through the use of multiple bars. By using selected machines and attachments, the raschel process can produce lacy, open-work fabrics of great variety and can make them either stable or elastic, as required.

Dense fabrics, both textured and patterned, can also be made, again either rigid or with stretch. Also plush fabrics in the same variations. Also carpeting and rugs.

All types of yarns are adaptable to the process—from fine to coarse, smooth to slubbed, rigid to elastic. There are some 3,500 raschel machines in the U.S. and the major proportion of these are used to make lace and powernet fabrics.

*Equipment Used:* Latch needles. One or two needle bars. One to 48 guide bars.

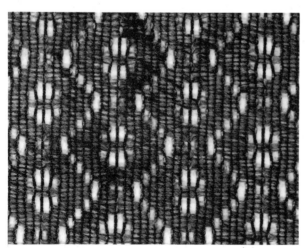

A raschel knit fabric.

## Special Types

Milanese: A warp knit fabric made with two sets of yarns knitted opposite each other in a diagonal formation. It is characterized by a fine rib on the face and a diagonal structure on the back. The fabric is used for gloves and lingerie. It uses spring-beard needles and one needle bar. There is also a faster model of the Milanese machine which is circular and uses latch needles. Both models use one needle bar, one guide bar and two warps.

Simplex: A warp knit fabric made on a Simplex knitting machine which is cousin to the tricot machine. It uses spring-beard needles, two needle bars and two guide bars. It produces double-faced fabrics used chiefly for gloves.

"Chaine" Raschel: This knits and tucks for a set number of courses and then reverses, to create an alternating surface design.

The Marrati: This produces a tubular milanese fabric.

The Cidega: This produces a fancy curtain or rug-type fabric.

The Kayloom: Like a raschel machine, it has weft-inlay attachments added.

The Jacquard Raschel: This is a raschel machine equipped with a jacquard attachment that permits intricate eyelet stitch patterns to be knitted.

The F.N.F.: This is a high speed tricot machine with a pipe type of compound needle.

THE LINK-CHAIN SYSTEM

### BASIC PATTERN SYSTEM FOR WARP KNITTING

This is the Link-Chain System. Chains with variable-height links control the movement of the guide bars. The height of the link transfers a motion to the guide bars which set the yarn in position over a group of needles, thus determining the structure of the pattern.

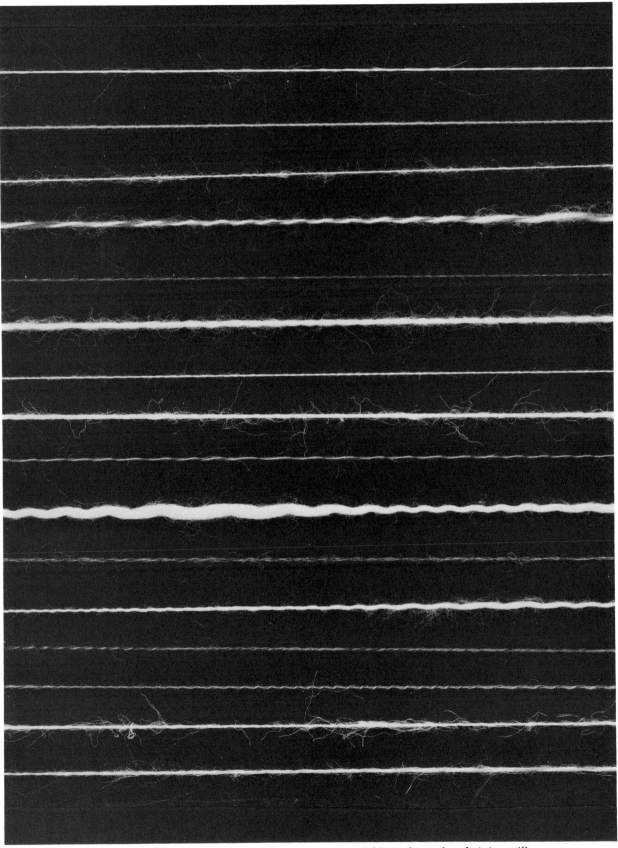

A sampling of the large variety of knitting yarns available to the modern knitting mill.

A knitted collar from a rib flat machine, noted for its knit versatility.

## TYPES OF WEFT KNITTING

The largest proportion of knitted fabrics used today are weft knits. Weft knits are made on either flat or circular machines. Following are the three basic types of stitches used—plain, purl, rib—and the specific equipment required:

### Plain (Jersey) Stitch

*Definition:* The plain jersey stitch is the most basic structure in all knitting. It is made on both circular and flat machines. Since the loops are formed in one direction only, the two sides of the fabric have a different appearance. The name is derived from one of the Channel Islands, and in England the word also describes a knit pullover shirt or sweater as well as a knitted fabric.

There are many popular variations of the jersey construction, some of which are: Full-Fashioned (Flat), Sliver (Pile) Knits (Circular), Velour (Circular).

*Equipment Used:* Spring-beard needles or latch needles. One needle bed. One set of needles. Multi-feeders are used.

### Variations of the Jersey Stitch

Straight Bar. Full-fashioning machines, plain and rib, using spring-beard needles, 1–2 sets of needles, 1–2 needle beds.

V-Bed Flat. A machine using latch needles, 2 needle beds and 2 sets of needles.

### Purl

*Definition:* This is a type of stitch produced on either a flat or circular knitting machine. It is also known as "Links-Links," a name taken from the German words, *links* (leftward), since the mechanism always moves to the left. The machine produces fancy knit fabrics with interlooping stitches in which the reverse and the face of jersey knit appear in alternate courses. The fabric is the same on both sides. It approximates the character of hand knitting and is widely used for sweaters.

*Equipment Used:* Double-headed latch needles. Two needle beds. One set of needles.

### Rib

*Definition:* A rib knit fabric is charcterized by lengthwise ribs formed by wales alternating on the face and back of the cloth. If every other wale alternates from face to back it is known as a 1 x 1 rib. If every two wales alternate it is called a 2 x 2 rib. Rib knits are made on both circular and flat machines. Such fabrics have excellent elasticity in the width and do not curl at the edges. A doubleknit fabric is made on a rib knit machine; so is an Eightlock and an Interlock fabric.

*Equipment Used:* Latch needles. Two needle beds—dial and cylinder. Two sets of needles. Multi-feeders.

The Eightlock construction—a form of doubleknit—is illustrated here. It shows a cross-section of fabric with two long needles opposite two short needles. Knitting moves back and forth from long to long and short to short.

## Formation of Stitch on Latch Needle

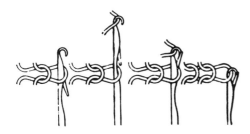

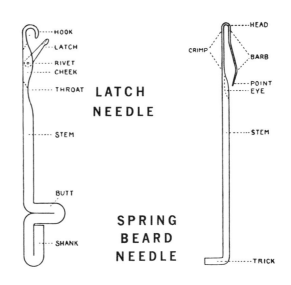

### STITCH FORMATION ON LATCH NEEDLE

The latch closes the hook automatically due to the pressure of the previous loop on the needle as it rises. When the latch is closed the needle carrying the yarn is drawn through a loop to form stitches in a continuing chain.

## Formation of Stitch on Spring Beard Needle

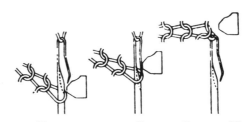

### STITCH FORMATION ON SPRING-BEARD NEEDLE

It has a flexible, spring-tensioned hook which resembles a beard. It is used together with a sinker which forms the loop and with a presser which closes the beard, thus allowing the loop to pass over the spring and form a new stitch.

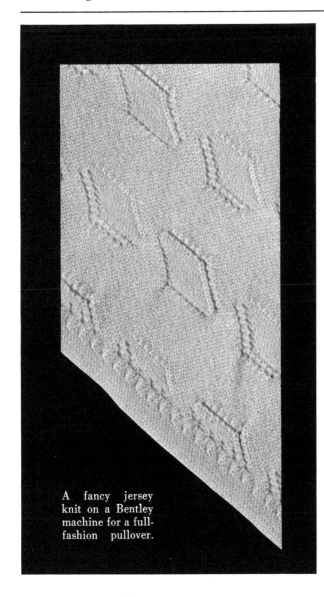

A fancy jersey knit on a Bentley machine for a full-fashion pullover.

### Major Products of Weft Knit Machines

CIRCULAR:
1. Hosiery
2. Sliver Knit: High Pile Coats and Lining
3. Jersey: Piecegoods, Underwear, T-Shirts
4. Interlock: Dresses, Tailored Apparel
5. Doubleknit: Dresses, Tailored Apparel

FLAT KNITTING:
1. Sweater Strip: Sweaters, Suits
2. V-Bed Flat: Trims
3. Links-Links: Sweaters, Infants' Outerwear
4. Full-Fashioned: Sweaters, Sport Shirts, Dresses

A purl circular fabric.

A lightweight doubleknit fabric.

## BASIC PATTERN SYSTEMS FOR WEFT KNITTING

There are four systems—with variations—which are used with all types of weft knitting machines. They are as follows:

### 1. NEEDLE BUTT (CAM CONTROL)

A pattern can be made by moving the needle butts in pre-arranged formation so that selected needles knit, tuck, welt, etc. The cam activates the needle butts in this way.

### 2. PATTERN WHEEL

A pattern wheel is a circular device with a slotted rim. Jacks are inserted in the slots to control needle positions by activating the butts to create a jacquard-like patterning.

### 3. PATTERN DRUM

A pattern drum is another method of activating the needles to create a patterned knit fabric. The one shown here stores ten patterns and is manually controlled.

### 4. JACQUARD

This is a continuous programming tape which controls a series of slotted drums. Each drum has automatic levers and each lever controls actions of a needle.

A jersey circular fabric.

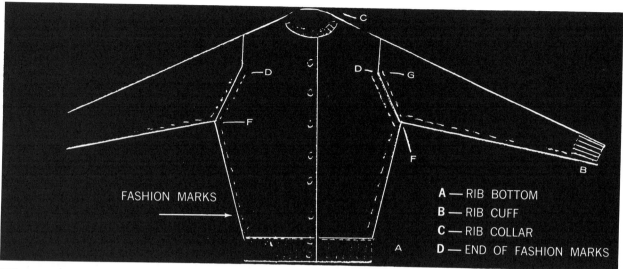

FASHION MARKS

A — RIB BOTTOM
B — RIB CUFF
C — RIB COLLAR
D — END OF FASHION MARKS

## What Is Meant by Full-Fashioned Knitting?

A garment is full-fashioned if it is fully or completely fashioned on the knitting machine and is not cut or shaped by altering stitch tension and blocking to shape. When the Rev. Lee invented the stocking-frame machine in England in 1589, he was thus inventing both the first knitting machine and the first machine used for full-fashioned knitting.

This machine comes down to us almost unchanged as today's hand-knitting machine. Operated by one person, the hand-knitting machine makes garments in sections—a front, back, and two sleeves—each being shaped or fashioned by hand manipulation of needles and stitches.

The second type of full-fashioned machine is the high-powered cotton-patent machine, invented in England in 1864. This has undergone refinements in 100 years, though the operating principle remains unchanged. It forms loops faster than the eye can see, knitting from four to thirty sections at one time, and shaping the fabric automatically.

Whether by hand-knitting or cotton-patent machine, full-fashioning remains the same. If stitches are transferred outward, thus increasing their number, the process is called widening. If stitches are transferred inward, the process is called narrowing.

Lee made full-fashioned stockings of very coarse construction on his machine, and they remained the staple product of his stocking-frame machine for more than 200 years. At the beginning of the 19th century, however, the hose-making companies turned to making underwear on the machine—first men's, then women's—with fibers such as Egyptian cotton, silk and wool, spun silk, and even cashmere. With the 20th century, came full-fashioned sweaters with fitted waists and sleeves.

## THE FULL-FASHIONED SWEATER

The best illustration of full-fashioned knitting is the sweater. Following are the four basic steps in knitting a classic cardigan on a cotton-patent machine.

1. Rib bottoms, cuffs and collars are made on different machines; ribs are made separately in string form, separated by cotton strips for better handling. Ribs are then separated and put on topping bars stitch by stitch so they can be transferred onto the cotton-patent machine's knitting needles.

2. Knitting starts, going crosswise from left to right, then right to left (see diagram). Widening starts at Point A and continues up to Point F, at the armholes. At certain set sequences, points come down at the selvages into the fabric, remove loops and transfer the stitches outward one needle at a time. From Point F to Point D, the fabric is narrowed by altering the sequence: the same fashion points descend into the fabric and transfer stitches inward, thus narrowing the fabric. Then the machine knits straight up to Point E, finishing the piece off with a few rows of knitted cotton for handling.

3. The back and sleeves are full-fashioned by the same technique. The back follows the front sequence, except that at Point E knitting and further narrowing is continued for shaping shoulders up to the collar area C. Once again, the operation stops after the knitting of a few cotton rows for handling. The sleeves start at cuff B, are widened to Point F (the underarm), then narrowed to Point G. At line GE, a few cotton rows finish off the operation.

4. The front, back and sleeves are joined and seamed together on separate machines. The nearly complete cardigan is then washed to remove spinning and machine oils, dyed (if necessary), blocked to shape, and finally cut and trimmed at the collar.

## Knitting Gauge

The knitting gauge is a term used to describe the closeness or openness of a knit fabric. It is actually a unit of measurement which indicates the number of needles in 1½ inches of space on the needle bed or cylinder and is based on the thickness of the needles. The higher the gauge, the finer will be the needles, and so the finer the texture of the knitted fabric.

In knitting nylon stockings, for instance, a 45-gauge knit (30 needles to the inch) will use a 30–40 denier yarn. A 51- and 60-gauge knit will use a 20- or 15-denier yarn. The higher the gauge number, the lower the denier number, and therefore the finer and sheerer the hosiery.

A well constructed fabric consists of the "proper thread-for-gauge" that is best suited for the machine and the courses-per-inch to produce the proper weight of fabric for the end use for which it is intended.

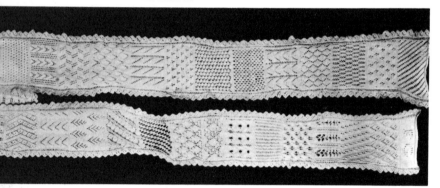

German knitted wool sampler, 19th Century.

## The Problem of Barré

Quality control has probably no more perfect illustration in today's textile manufacturing processes than that posed by the problems of barré; more specifically, barré as it appears in doubleknit fabrics of set-textured polyester yarn.

Barré has been a continuing hazard in the circular knit industry and the problems are increased when the yarn used is filament rather than spun. With polyester doubleknits the difficulties are further increased by the combination of advanced machinery and technologies, expanded end uses and the modifications required of a relatively new fiber such as textured polyester.

The term barré, as used in the knit trade, refers to horizontal lines appearing in a repeat pattern throughout the fabric, or an appreciable portion of it. These lines appear either darker or lighter than the basic fabric color, or as thicker or thinner yarn. With false-twist, set-textured polyester doubleknits, these deviations primarily reflect differences in dyestuff absorbency by yarn, generally traceable to the yarn's thermo history and tensioning.

It is useful to review the operations to understand the complexity of the problem, since without required improvements or compensations in all stages of manufacturing, knitters would be forced to limit polyester fabrics to those knit constructions which so break up the surface that barré is either diminished or eliminated.

Four basic steps are used in producing set-textured polyester doubleknits: (1) making fiber and yarn; (2) throwing or texturing the yarn; (3) knitting the fabric; (4) dyeing and finishing the fabric. In all these processes the control of temperature and tension is crucial in avoiding barré. Thus, the fiber manufacturing process may be the prime creator of barré, in turn confronting the subsequent operations with built-in problems.

When polyester is made, the polymer is extruded into filament yarn and drawn under tension to its size on multiple position machines passing hot pins. This is the critical fiber point for both heat and tension. The throwster then subjects the yarn to heat and tensioning during false twisting, and this again exposes the yarn to stress conditions for setting the false twist. Subsequently, the yarn is wound onto knitting cones, another operation involving tension which affects the knitting performance. During knitting, uneven tensioning of yarn can also create barré, which becomes apparent only after dyeing. Although often it is only the dyeing and finishing process that reveals the faults of the previous operations, it is also possible for the dyeing to minimize or even eliminate the earlier faults, since dyeing temperatures exceed any previous processing temperatures.

The barré problem, therefore, requires quality control at every stage of each operation. The fiber producer must seek polymers stable to heat variation, with minimum sensitivity to tensioning. The throwster needs machinery and controls to provide uniformity from heater zone to heater zone, as well as superior winding. Knitters need machines sufficiently similar to one another to produce uniform quality in the product units. Dyers need kettles that afford temperature, pressure and chemicals for the desired formulas, with the aim of diminishing barré tendencies that may have been formed earlier. All this involves not only close daily controls in each operation, but continued search for new materials, machines and techniques which ultimately penetrate each of the multiple operations.

**Knitting Machines in Place
1968**

Warp Machines: 8000 (approx.)

Weft Machines: 177,000 (approx.)
of which 127,000 were for men's
and women's hosiery

The world-renowned Shetland shawl, a knitted masterpiece, from the Shetland islands off the northeast tip of Scotland. The skill of making wool shawls like this one is handed down from mother to daughter. The shawl's beautiful structure is based on traditional patterns, each of which has a symbolic meaning rooted in the crofter culture of the isles.

# BASIC KNIT MACHINES

*The eight basic knitting machines commonly in use around the world. They produce everything from hosiery to dresswear to collars.*

William Lee, English inventor of mechanical knitting, made first knitted stocking in 1592.

Jersey circular machine.

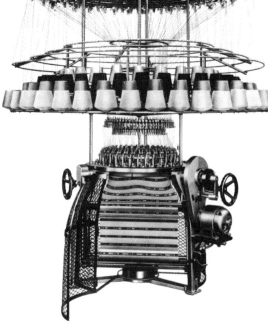

Jersey flat machine.

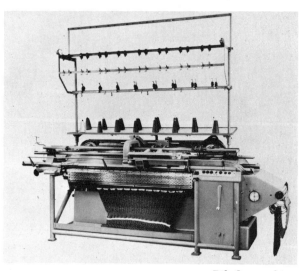

Rib flat machine.

Purl flat machine.

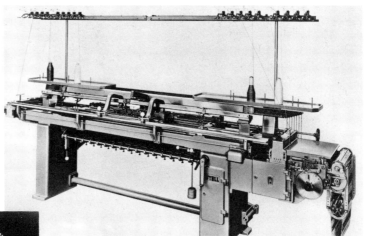

Rib circular machine.

Purl circular machine.

Raschel machine.

Tricot machine.

## Expanding Horizons for Knit Fabrics

In the latter half of the 1960's, a new sense of excitement permeated the knit industry. There was an awareness of general expansion—on the part of knitting machinery manufacturers, fiber processors, apparel designers and producers, and retailers—and this was reflected in the acceptance and increasing demand for knit fashionwear on the part of the consumer.

Great changes in knitwear had taken place in the post-World War II period. As it became evident that more people would have more time to wear leisure clothes, there was a concerted effort among all concerned to conceive and develop fresh ideas that would bring vitality and broadened applications to the knit markets.

Styling of fabrics took on as great importance in the attitude of the knitwear industry as the matter of count and construction. This encouraged many creators in the field, particularly those that knew the capabilities of knitting equipment, to try new permutations and combinations.

In men's, women's and children's wear, knitted fabrics therefore climbed steadily in popularity and volume as the industry responded to the needs and tastes of the fashion-consuming public. In an active-wear era, it was obvious that knitted fabrics, being practical and comfortable, should have a strong following. But although such advantages were inherent, it was not until the knitters came forward with more interesting constructions and used the newer yarns (especially the textured yarns) that public preference exerted itself strongly.

In evaluating the remarkable rise in knit fashions, in the burgeoning of all knit goods—fashion as well as staple items—the causes were fundamental. There are at least five significant reasons for the upsurge of knits:

1. Ease-of-care performance adapted to modern living.

2. Speed and flexibility of production as compared with weaving.

3. Unique properties of man-made fibers, applicable to knits.

4. Year-round wearability of knits.

5. Special adaptability for travel.

## Shift from Small to Big Mill

The small family knitting firms, each with a few machines producing goods, dominated the knit industry in the past. This is no longer the standard for knitgoods operations. The knit producer is now often part of a large mill management which does not regard itself as either a knitting or a weaving mill, but rather as a producer of all types of fabrics, without regard to the production method. The mill today manufactures what the market calls for and acquires facilities considered by the mill to be in line with growth potential.

These big mills began by acquiring small knitting companies, but the later tendency became that of setting up their own knitting facilities and sending weaving technicians abroad to study knitting technology. As far as the big mills were concerned, the problem was not equipment, but technological training for the anticipated expansion in knitting as new improved knit fabrics were created.

## Geared to Changing Fashions

For the fashion apparel manufacturer, knitting offers speed and flexibility—the ability to move quickly with new fashion trends. For example, from the point of the original idea to the point of consumer sale, a knitted garment can be turned out in sixty days or less. The same process generally takes at least six months via weaving.

In addition to speed, knits have made possible new categories of clothing whose simplicity and comfort suit the current era. In the women's field, this is far more than a passing fashion trend. It represents a basic approach to clothing which has become established as an integral facet of apparel production. In menswear, the growth of knits is one of the phenomena of the whole textile industry.

Knit fabrics were estimated to account for 33 percent of all apparel fabrics in 1968. The 1975 estimate is that they may be up as high as 50 percent.

## Fashion Extension of the Sweater

Once a humble garment worn by fishermen, the sweater has become the focal point—the dynamic centerpiece—and the very symbol of the expanding knitwear technology. In the versatile age of the 1960's it became probably the most versatile garment of fashion. Knitted long, it was transformed into dresses, suits, even evening gowns. Knitted short, it was a "brief," with halter or turtleneck top.

The sweater, as we know it, was in the background of fashion for centuries. At best, it was referred to as a "bridal shirt" presented to bridegrooms by their brides in British fishing towns, each town having its distinctive stitch, pattern and colors.

Fine hosiery knitting became an art recognized and appreciated by royalty, and the Knitters Guild of Paris looked upon the knitting of a carpet in designs and colors, or a pair of woolen socks with clocking, as an art form. But sweater knitting remained merely a craft, for the purpose of producing garments like "spensers" or "vesquettes" to keep out drafts in poorly heated houses. The designation *sweater* appeared later to describe a long-sleeved, turtle-necked wool garment worn by male athletes to prevent chills after exercise. Again, its derivation from the word "sweat" was typically humble.

Women finally brought the sweater out of its workaday obscurity. They began to wear the cardigan early in the 20th century, and the "shaker" sweater, with its shawl collar and warm woolen construction, became popular for driving in the early open cars. Real styling, however, transformed the sweater in the 1920's when Paris couturiers and Hollywood stars together raised its status and a variety of sweater types brought it into the mainstream of fashion. The technological development in knitting has kept the sweater on the fashion front ever since. Developments in fibers, in doubleknitting, in stitch and pattern ingenuity, in printing and other design techniques, have turned the sweater into a total fashion wardrobe.

## Modern Advances in Machinery

In large part, the astonishing increase in the market for knitted fabrics is due to the advances which have been made in knitting machines and techniques. Warp knitting machines, for example, without having undergone basic modifications since power-drive was introduced over a hundred years ago, have been improved and developed to the point where working speeds have increased from 150 to 1000 courses per minute in the last twenty years alone. Similarly, the "cut," or number of needles per inch in weft machines has been greatly increased.

The progress of knitting production might be most dramatically illustrated by comparing it with the following figures of textile output: A hand knitter may form approximately 100 stitches per minute; the Reverend Lee's knitting machine started with 600 stitches per minute; a modern automatic knitting machine produces over 4 million stitches per minute. And, comparing modern machine knitting with modern commerical weaving, the knitted output is 20 times faster than the weaving loom's output. Knitwear has, in fact, made inroads in areas heretofore dominated by woven goods, ranging from lightweight to heavy materials.

## Breakthrough

In the late 1960's a veritable machine breakthrough took place. Knits became both promising and demanding so that a whole new dimension opened up in the machine area to accommodate and spur the knit growth.

THE RASCHEL MACHINE. In the area of pattern and design, this versatile warp knitting machine produces fabrics from finest lingerie materials and trimming laces to heavy industrial goods. It has the ability to stitch and lay-in yarns through the use of multiple bars. By using selected machines and attachments, the process can produce openwork fabrics of great variety and can make them either stable or elastic, as required. Dense fabrics, both textured and patterned, can also be made, again either rigid or with stretch, and the same is true of plush fabrics and carpeting in the same variations. All types of yarns are adaptable to the process—from fine to coarse, smooth to slubbed, rigid to elastic.

CO-WE-NIT. The name is an abbreviation of the words "Combination-Weaving-Knitting" and it describes a fabric which combines the characteristics of a woven and a knit fabric. This is achieved by inserting warp threads between the knitted wales and then locking in the warp threads by means of an inlay yarn. It is done on a modified raschel machine and the result is a fabric of good thread density and tight construction, since the guide bars can insert up to four warp threads between every two wales. Co-We-Nit fabrics are quite stable and almost rigid, but can be engineered with a small degree of stretch in the width direction.

ELECTRONIC KNITTING MACHINE. Electronic controls bring increasing automation and flexibility to knitting mechanisms and production. Typical of the sophisticated developments in this area is a jacquard purl circular knitting machine which operates with an electronic pattern system instead of with traditional pattern drums. It can knit the patterned body of a sweater, as well as the ribbed bottom, in one continuous process and at considerably higher speeds than previously possible. This is achieved through the use of a punched electrotape which allows light from photoelectric cells to pass through at predetermined points and activate the mechanism of the machine. It makes pattern changing simple and allows full-length garments to be knitted from a single tape without pattern repeat.

22- AND 24-CUT DOUBLEKNIT MACHINE. In the area of doubleknits, the 18-cut machine has been the standard for women's doubleknits. One of the newer knitting developments was the introduction of the 22- and 24-cut doubleknit machines, designed for finer gauge men's suitings as well as women's wear.

Tricot's chief market is intimate apparel.

2-BAR, 3-BAR, 4-BAR TRICOT. These terms are widely used as descriptive terms for knit fabrics, but they actually relate to warp knitting mechanisms. A "bar" is a guide bar on a tricot or raschel machine, both of which make fabric from warp threads by meshing together the loops formed from individual yarns. The guide bar controls the movement of the warp yarns around the needles and this movement determines the characteristics of the fabric.

All warp knitting machines must have at least one guide bar, but a single bar machine is not commercially practical. Most warp knit equipment, therefore, has two or more guide bars which give the warp knitter design freedom. Thus, two-bar machines are generally used for plain fabrics. Three-bar machines achieve three-dimensional effects, and four-bar equipment can make ornamental fabrics. Commercial tricot machines can have up to 18 bars, and raschel machines up to 48 bars. Such multi-bar equipment is generally used only for lace work.

The advantage of tricot and raschel machines is that they can come close to the characteristics of woven fabrics, with fine gauges, good pattern definition, dimensional stability and light weight. A limited degree of stretch can also be engineered into such fabrics.

## Tricot for Outerwear

The effect of the new tricot machine technology has been to give tricot great versatility for end uses far different from the earlier lingerie and underwear fabrics. In this connection, credit must be given to the textured filament yarns which are particularly adapted to the tricot machine. They make possible fabrics with aesthetics quite different from those of lingerie fabrics. The use of coarse gauge yarns is another factor in moving tricot into outerwear. Both these developments are the result of the refinements of 3- and 4-bar mechanisms which provide design flexibility.

---

### Major Products of Warp Knit Machines

TRICOT: Lingerie, Linings (bonded) Dresses, Shirts

SIMPLEX: Gloves, Automotive Upholstery

MILANESE: Dresses, Lamp Covers

RASCHEL: Lace, Powernet, Outerwear

---

A modern tricot knitting machine, capable of high speed production.

Above: Dyeing area for computerized dyehouse. Below: Control panel of computer dyeing system.

## Role of the New Fibers

Of equal importance with the advances in knitting technology have been the developments in man-made fibers, whose properties have extended the range of end uses for knitted fabrics; for example, fibers and yarns which make the most of their elasticity and texture in knitgoods.

Basic to the growth of the entire knitwear industry has been the development of textured filament yarn, which is perhaps the prime mover in both warp and weft knitting and which has opened up new end uses and markets which had not previously existed for knit goods.

Much the same can be said for blends of man-made fibers, and such yarn blends as polyester/cotton, worsted/nylon and worsted/polyester—all of particular interest in tricot production for men's summer clothing fabrics.

## Scope of the New Knits

The strides in knitting technology, in application of new fibers, in yarns and patterning inventiveness, in fabric-to-fabric bonding—all key factors in the widespread utilization of knitted fabrics—have led to a sales rise that is nothing short of spectacular. In the first six years of the '60 decade, overall volume of business more than tripled. At the end of the decade this astounding growth rate continued at an increasing pace.

It is illuminating to cite a few statistics which reflect the position of knitgoods by the end of the 1960's. The number of doubleknit machines nearly quadrupled in the six years from 1962 to 1968—from a figure of 1,214 to an estimated 4,230.

An expansion in knitgoods production, during the same period, from 830 million pounds in 1963 to approxiamtley 1.5 billion pounds in 1967, represents an 82 percent growth. The various fibers are represented in these totals as follows:

## Men's Tailored Wear Knits

In the area of knitted fashionwear, the knitted busi-ness suit for men became a reality in 1968—a practical commercial idea with obvious advantages in comfort, ease of care and travel rightness.

The men's tailored clothing industry is especially interested in the new tricots, which have proved so versatile a fabric construction, and which come close to the characteristics of traditional woven fabrics for men's clothing. Doubleknits, too, offer a practical medium for the men's knitted suit. Chief fiber for these is textured polyester, but other fibers play a role in blends for specific applications.

Important, too, in the whole area of knitted outerwear for men is the use of bonding techniques which overcome problems of cutting and tailoring and give knitted fabrics the stability of woven goods (see Fabric-to-Fabric Bonding).

Knit sports jackets and knit slacks are growing in volume season by season. The same is true of men's knitted dress shirts, which have experienced both fashion acceptance and sales volume. Some few years earlier men's knit sport shorts had made major inroads into the traditional woven sportshirt.

## Knits and Bonding

Bonded knits, generally speaking, became an important category of fabric in the late 1960's. Standard practice was to bond single knit face fabrics to acetate or nylon tricot. A later trend was to extend the use of the bonding technique to lightweight doubleknits, with all the advantages that accrue in stability, weight, economy of cutting and sewing.

Both acetate and nylon tricot have been recognized as an ideal medium for the lining or backing fabric in bonding. The reasons are tricot's properties of stability, elasticity, resiliency, crease resistance, drapability, high tear strength and abrasion resistance, non-raveling qualities, as well as its wearing comfort and softness to touch. Above all, tricot bonded to lacy or other openwork knit fabrics makes a workable fabric out of what was previously an unstable and impractical structure.

# KNIT FUTURE

| FIBERS IN KNITS | 1968 Millons of Pounds | | | | 1972 Millons of Pounds | | | | |
|---|---|---|---|---|---|---|---|---|---|
| | Apparel | Home | Industrial | TOTAL | Apparel | Home | Industrial | TOTAL | % DIF. |
| Cotton | 547 | 23 | 35 | 605 | 560 | 25 | 50 | 635 | +5 |
| Nylon | 264 | 5 | 6 | 275 | 351 | 7 | 12 | 404 | +47 |
| Acetate | 213 | — | — | 213 | 289 | — | — | 289 | +36 |
| Acrylic | 211 | 3 | — | 214 | 470 | 5 | — | 475 | +122 |
| Wool | 113 | 2 | — | 115 | 105 | 3 | — | 108 | −6 |
| Polyester | 70 | — | 2 | 72 | 179 | 25 | 12 | 216 | +200 |
| Rayon | 23 | 5 | — | 28 | 25 | 6 | — | 31 | +10 |
| **TOTAL** | **1,441** | **38** | **43** | **1,522** | **1,979** | **71** | **74** | **2,158** | |

## Education for Knitting

One significant indication of the recognition given to knitwear's current and evolutionary importance is the new role it plays in textile colleges.

Schools like the Philadelphia College of Textiles, the North Carolina College of Textiles and the Fashion Institute of Technology have become responsive to the needs of the knitting industry for trained technologists and have adapted their curricula with the objective of "education for knitting."

Close-up of doubleknit needle.

## New Frontiers for Knitting

A number of recent developments have potential historic significance in knit technology and, consequently, in the entire fabric-fashion industry. Following are some of the more important:

FULL-FASHIONING WITH HIGH SPEED. This involves a machine patent by John Carr Doughty that combines the two distinct systems of full-fashioned knitting and high-speed multi-feed circular knitting. Knitted garments made by this equipment would possess all the characteristics of high quality full-fashioned garments without any evidence of its high-speed construction.

KNITTED VINYL—A BREATHABLE PLASTIC. Knitted vinyl is now being used in auto seats. Its advantage over sheet vinyl is that it allows air to circulate through the seat cushions, thus avoiding clamminess in summer and chill in winter. Practical production was made possible by the invention of Ronald Marx, who has developed a continuous process for slitting sheet vinyl and knitting it on conventional circular knitting machines.

In appearance the fabric has the characteristic structure of knitting, but is so stable that the structure seems almost to be embossed and the holes punched into a flat sheet of vinyl. It is, however, actually knitted and involves the following procedure:

Flat sheets of vinyl are sliced into narrow ribbons of from 1/32 to 1/4 inch in width. These ribbons of vinyl are then combined with a 200 denier nylon filament (for strength) and the combined yarn is fed into a circular knitting machine. It emerges as a tube of knitted vinyl, is then slit open, stretched and given a stabilizing coating which locks in the structure. Finished fabric is 66 inches wide.

Knitted vinyl is an obvious medium for furniture seating, as well as for various types of apparel, accessories and industrial products.

KNITTED DRAPERY AND UPHOLSTERY FABRICS. Another category due for exploitation by the knitting industry is the whole area of knitted fabrics for the home—draperies, upholstery, sheets, towels, etc. Curtains and slip covers were early forerunners in this area, but the area of upholstery promises to have the widest application for knitgoods because the possibilities for controlled stretch and recovery offer advantages of simplified tailoring and better fit. In the past, lack of fabric stability had been a deterrent to the use of knits for draperies, but the newer fibers, blends and finishing techniques overcome problems in almost every type of knit construction, especially in warp knitting.

BEDSPREADS. This is another area highly susceptible as a medium for knitted fabrics, especially in recognition of a product which calls for wide goods. And knitted bedspreads offer novel, attractive possibilities in knit designs at prices entirely competitive with woven bedspreads.

KNITTED CARPETS. Knitted carpets made on raschel machines have some advantage over tufted carpets in their greater utilization of the yarn. In tufted carpets anywhere from 20 to 30 percent of the yarn lies on the back of the carpet and is thus unused for either aesthetic or wear advantages. In the knitted carpet almost 100 percent of the yarn does duty in aesthetics and wear. However, the dominance of tufted carpets has so far prevented the knitted version from finding an important niche in the market. With future advances in knit technology, this picture may change.

KNITTED SHIPPING SACKS. Knitted constructions are a potential boon for shippers who have traditionally used woven burlap bags. Knitted fabrics offer a desirable form for these products, particularly since circular knits could be made in exactly the diameters required for bags and thus eliminate much cutting and sewing.

KNITTED BLANKETS. Blankets are equally susceptible to the knit construction, especially the thermal blankets which are so increasingly popular. They are likely to follow the reputation of thermal underwear which has for some time been manufactured on raschel machines. Moreover, the open constructions used in thermal blankets can be effectively handled under knitting construction techniques.

# Dictionary of Knitting Terms

**ALPACA STITCH:** Purl links stitch in vertical arrangement of the courses.

**ARGYLE:** Diamond-shaped design in a knit, patterned in different colors.

**ATLAS:** A tricot fabric that appears to have crosswise stripes on the back. This effect is produced by the movement of two sets of warp ends in opposite directions which, after a number of knitted courses, reverse their movement. The fabric is used primarily for cut-and-sewn gloves.

**BARRE:** A defect in the wale of a knitted fabric caused by uneven tension, defective yarn or needle action, or other mechanical factor.

**BEAM:** In warp knitting, a device which feeds the yarn to guides and needles. The device rests on a beam shaft.

**BED, NEEDLE BED:** The slotted metal piece in the flat-knitting machine in which the needles move up and down.

**BIRD'S EYE (Twill Back):** A salt-and-pepper effect on the back of knitted fabric produced by knitting every other needle on the dial but all needles on the cylinder. The result is a scrambling of the colors used on the face design of the fabric.

**BONDED KNIT:** A knitted fabric with a backing or lining of another fabric joined to it in permanent union through bonding by a wet adhesive or foam. As a result of bonding, knitted fabrics are provided with many possibilities for combining constructions, colors and textures, as well as extending their performance and range of end uses.

**BOUCLE:** Many types of this yarn are used for knitted fabrics. The word comes from the French, meaning buckle, or ringlet. Characteristically, the effect is a closed loop which projects from the fabric body at intervals.

**BOURRELET:** In doubleknit fabrics, a ripple stitch or corded effect created by loops raised on the fabric's surface. Bourrelet knit is produced by knitting and tucking or knitting and welting.

**BRUSHED PILE:** See "Pile Knit."

**BULKY RIB:** A coarse rib knit produced by all-over tucking with cardigan or half-cardigan stitch. Can be produced on flat or circular rib machines.

**CABLE STITCH:** A knitting stitch in which small groups of plain wales are plaited with one another. Often it involves two groups of three wales each, or six needles. At regular operating intervals, the groups interchange their action of stitches or needles.

**CAM:** A knitting machine device that actuates the needles by operating on the needle butts or jacks, thus achieving desired knitting, tucking, welting effects.

**CARDIGAN STITCH:** A form of the rib knitting stitch, modified by tucking on one or both sets of needles. For half cardigan stitch, tucking is on one set; for full cardigan, tucking is on both sets of needles. Tucking thickens the fabric.

**CARRIER ROD:** The device on which yarn carriers are mounted in a full-fashioning machine.

**CAST-OFF POSITION:** The position at which the needle is at its lowest retraction point, permitting the new loop to be drawn through the preceding loop and casting it over the needle hook.

**CATCH BAR:** Full-fashioning machine device for moving dividers forward simultaneously after the sinkers have been moved forward.

**CHOPPER BAR:** In raschel knitting machines, a steel bar placed between the guide bars and swinging with them in up-and-down action. Its function permits the incorporation of certain threads in the fabric without being actually knitted in.

**CIRCULAR KNIT:** Fabrics or garments knitted in tubular form on a circular knitting machine in continuous operation so that they are seamless. Later a garment may be shaped by cutting, by simulated seams, or by tightening or stretching stitches.

**COTTON FRAME:** Knitting frame named for William Cotton who in 1863 invented a power-driven machine which shaped fabric as it was knitted. The cotton frame was designed to knit fine, full-fashioned hosiery, pullovers and cardigans. It has automatic mechanisms for narrowing and widening.

**COURSE:** The row of stitches or loops that runs crosswise in knitted fabric, corresponding to the filling in woven fabrics.

**CROCHET:** A hand or machine method, by use of a special hook, of working interlocking loops or stitches which are thrown off and finished successively. Differentiated from knitting in which an entire series of loops is retained while a new course is formed. Crochet knit describes a knitted fabric patterned to resemble crochet.

**CUT:** The number of needles to the inch in a knitting machine.

**CUT PRESSER:** Device on a spring-beard needle machine, in both warp and weft types, designed to close certain needle hooks.

**CYLINDER:** A slotted section in a circular knitting machine for holding needles. The number of slots per inch around the cylinder determines the cut of the machine or the number of needles per inch. Sizes of cylinders vary; as few as four needles per inch are possible in small diameter machines for producing knitted tubing.

**DECKER:** A device like a comb used in manually operated knitting machines to move stitches from one set of needles to another; in narrowing, for example.

**DIAL:** A circular steel plate with slots arranged radially. In rib knit production, the needles operate in these slots in conjunction with the cylinder needles and therefore the number of slots is usually equal in both dial and cylinder.

**DIVIDER:** Device used with sinkers to establish loops in full-fashioned hosiery knitting. The divider has been discarded in full-fashioned sweater frames because it is not necessary to stitch formation and its elimination allows faster, smoother machine operation.

**DOGS:** Mechanism that maintains correct relation between dial and cylinder in circular knitting machines. Any malfunction of dogs causes so-called "dog lines" on the fabric. The trend in knitting machine design today is to obviate the need for this unit.

**DOUBLEKNIT:** Though not a standard technical term, doubleknit describes any of the numerous fine rib knits that appear to have been knitted twice. The effect is produced by two-needle construction which, in effect, is two single fabrics interlocked into one. By reason of its structure, a doubleknit has greater dimensional stability than single knit jersey.

**DOUBLE LOCK MACHINE:** A V-bed flat machine with two sets of locks fitted on the carriage so that two courses can be laid in one passage across the needle bed.

**DOUBLE PIQUE:** A doubleknit with honeycomb effect produced by knitting and welting. There are two types of double piqué—French and Swiss—each of which is produced by a different action of the needles. See "Double Piqué, French" and "Swiss."

**DOUBLE PIQUE, FRENCH:** Produced by a four-feed action with the cylinder needles welting at odd feeds and knitting at even, while the long and short dial needles alternate after each two feeds. By this action only short needles are in place in the cylinder.

**DOUBLE PIQUE, SWISS:** Produced when the cylinder needles knit at odd feeds and welt at even feeds, while the long dial needles knit at first two feeds and the short dial needles at next two feeds. This action results when the cylinder is fitted only with long needles.

**DROP STITCH (or Dropped Stitch):** A defect resulting from faulty stitch setting, or a defective needle, or other malfunction. Drop stitches may be introduced in a fabric by design to achieve a desired pattern effect.

**EIGHTLOCK:** One of the classical knit constructions. It produces an interlocked doubleknit rib fabric through the action of the alternate long and short cylinder and dial needles aligned on a 2 x 2 rib basis. Thus, instead of single short and long needles in the two needle housings alternately knitting and welting, each two consecutive short and long needles operate on the interlock principle.

**ELASTIC, KNITTING IN:** Use of elastic yarn in knitted fabric by knitting.

On single needle machines the elastic may be knitted in at every second or third course. On rib machines, the elastic is knitted on selected needles at specific intervals, or on a 1 x 1 rib basis. See "Elastic, Laying In."

**ELASTIC, LAYING IN:** Introduction of rubber yarn or synthetic elastomer in a knitted fabric other than by knitting in (see above). On single needle machines, the elastic yarn is laid in on the back of the fabric by means of alternate tucks and floats. On rib machines, the elastic is laid in as weft threads between the rib and plain wales.

**EYELET STITCH:** A rib stitch produced by transferring needle loops to adjacent pairs of needles, resulting in an open work effect.

**FASHIONING MARKS:** Marks characterizing a full-fashioned garment which are the result of selvage loops transferred over one or two needles. Such a mark is left each time a needle is left with a double loop on it.

**FILLER POINT:** A mechanism on full-fashioning machines which picks up one or more loops to cover a needle hole resulting from the widening operation. See "Widening."

**FLAKE YARN:** Soft, thick tufts of slub somewhat elongated in size introduced into a yarn at desired intervals.

**FLAT KNIT:** Fabric produced, in flat form, on a flat-bed knitting machine, as distinguished from tubular fabric which is produced on a circular machine. Flat knitting permits full-fashioning.

English fern stitch.

**FLAT STITCH:** Similar to the plain or jersey stitch. In flat-stitch knitting the right side of the fabric shows a series of lengthwise ribs; the reverse side shows only the crosswise loops.

**FULL-FASHIONED:** A term which describes a knitted fabric or garment made on a flat knitting machine, with shaped form achieved by adding or reducing the number of stitches at predetermined points.

**GAUGE:** Indicates fineness of knit texture, referring to the number of needles in a given width. For example, in full-fashioned hosiery the number of needles per 1½″ represents the gauge; in circular knit hosiery, it is the number of needles per 1″. The higher the gauge number, the finer the fabric texture.

**GUIDE:** In tricot and raschel machines, a device which guides the yarn to the needles. Both these warp machines can knit a wide range of patterns depending on the number of thread guide bars in the machine.

**HENKELPLUSH:** Knitted cotton velour fabric produced on a French sinker wheel machine. See "Knitted Velour."

**INTARSIA KNIT:** Derived from the Italian word for *inlay*, intarsia refers to a decorative colored motif knitted into a solid color fabric. A flat, single-bed latch-needle machine is used for this inlaid effect which requires considerable hand work.

**INTERLOCK:** A knit construction on a machine with alternate units of long and short needles. An interlock fabric is a double 1 x 1 rib characterized by good lengthwise elasticity and firm texture. It is thicker than plain rib knit and has less tendency to curl at the edges.

**INTERLOOPING:** The form of thread looping or intertwining taken by any one of the basic knitting stitches.

**JACQUARD KNIT:** Fabric with designs in pattern and color achieved by jacquard attachments which automatically select colors and needles on the knitting machine. The jacquard mechanism regulates each needle to be used for each knitting course. Jacquard attachments can be used on both circular and flat knitting machines, but the range of design size is limited on the circular machines.

**JACQUARD RASCHEL:** A raschel machine equipped with a jacquard attachment that permits intricate eyelet stitch patterns to be knitted.

**JERSEY:** The most common type of knitted fabric, jersey knit is done with a single set of needles. It may be plain or ribbed and made on flat-bed or circular rib machines.

**KNITTED VELOUR:** A sheared knitted fabric with smooth, napped finish resembling velvet or suede. It is knitted on either French sinker wheel machines or circular latch-needle machines. See also "Pile Knit, Velour."

**KNITTING:** The process of making cloth with a single yarn or set of yarns moving in one direction. Instead of two sets of yarns crossing each other as in weaving, the single knitting yarn is looped through itself to make a chain of stitches that intermesh horizontally and vertically. The widthwise loops are called "courses"; the vertical loops are called "wales."

**KNOCKING OVER:** The action which causes a set of loops to slide off the ends of the needles onto the newly drawn yarn, thus completing the formation of new loops.

**LAP:** A roll of fiber in the pre-carding stage. In knitting, *lap* refers also to the horizontal rows of floats, or laps, on the reverse side of tricot knit fabric.

**LATCH NEEDLE:** One of the two basic types of knitting machine needles (the other is the spring or spring-beard needle). It has a half-hook which opens and closes by a swinging latch. The latch needle is generally used to make heavier or coarser knit fabrics of low gauge.

**LINKS-LINKS:** Flat or circular knitting machines which produce interlooping stitches typical of purl or fancy knit fabrics. By means of links-links, a needle can be transferred from one needle bed to the opposite one in order to produce novelty effects. The name is taken from the German word, *links*, meaning "left," since the mechanism always moves to the left.

**LINK-CHAIN PATTERNING:** Basic pattern system for warp knitting. Chains with variable-height links control motion of guide bars which set yarn in position over pre-fixed needles to create the patterning.

**LOOP:** The basic unit of construction in knitted fabric, interconnected and arranged in a succession of rows. The series of loops intermesh horizontally and vertically to form the knit fabric.

**LOOP FABRIC:** This is formed by two yarns for each loop—a ground yarn and a yarn which is pulled out from the knitted ground by a special device which produces the looped or fancy effect.

**LOOPING:** A process in sweater production by which separate parts of the garments, previously knitted or cut to shape, are joined together to simulate the effect of uninterrupted knitting. Looping is used in both cut-and-sewn and full-fashioned sweaters, for joining collars and shoulder parts.

**LOOP YARN:** A slack twisted strand forming loops. The strand is held in place by binder yarn or yarns.

**MERROWING:** Refers to the Merrow machine operation, which produces smooth results in joining seams or finishing edges of knitted garments by oversewing.

**MILANESE:** Warp knit fabric made with sets of yarns knit in diagonal effect. Milanese is characterized by a fine rib on the face and a diagonal effect on the reverse side. Highly run-resistant, it is used for gloves and women's lingerie. There are two basic types of Milanese machines—a straight bar model which uses spring-beard needles, and a circular machine which uses latch needles.

**NEEDLE BED:** The flat, slotted section of the machine in which the needles function. The number of slots to the inch in the needle bed represents the gauge (or cut). The machine itself is referred to as an 8-cut machine, for example, when its needle bed has eight slots to the inch. See "Cut."

**OTTOMAN RIB:** A doubleknit with pronounced course-wise ribs or rolls. This structure is produced by knitting more stitches per unit length on one side of the fabric than on the other.

**PATTERN SYSTEMS:** The different ways of making a patterned fabric on a knitting machine. The most important techniques involve the following feeding mechanisms: 2 and 3 position cams; needle butt (long and short); pattern wheels; trick wheels; sinker wheels; loop wheels; pattern drums; pegs; paper punched cards; jacquard attachments; metal punched film; electronics.

**PATTERN WHEEL:** A device in the circular knitting machine to control the needles' movement. On a jersey machine, the pattern wheel permits some needles to tuck or welt while others knit. The mechanism is also used on rib knit machines to select cylinder needles.

**PATTERNING WITH METAL CARDS:** Perforated metal cards, used primarily in V-bed flat and flat-bed links and links equipment, fit on a rotating bar. The cards automatically adjust to as many as twelve slots depending on the jacquard pattern. Needle controls serve to knit or welt depending on whether the slots are left open or are covered.

**PATTERNING WITH METAL RIBBON:** A needle-selection unit perforated according to a laid-out design. The metal ribbon is housed in a circular unit on the side of the machine and activates jacks in the pattern wheel.

**PATTERNING WITH PAPER ROLLS:** These resemble player piano rolls, the holes punched by special machines according to designs previously laid out on cross-section paper. The rolls are placed on jacquard mechanisms around the machine, each section controlling a given number of needles.

**PILE KNIT, VELOUR:** Pile knit fabrics are produced in three ways: (1) on circular machines, the loops intermeshed with a plain knit base stitch and cut open or sheared; (2) pile may be formed with a sliver which is locked into a plain knit fabric used as a base; the pile depth is determined by the length of the sliver fibers; (3) pile may be produced by brushing.

**PLAIN KNIT:** The simplest of knit structures, as in hosiery and jersey cloth. It consists of vertical rows (wales) on the fabric face and crosswise lines (courses) on back.

**PLATING:** Knitting design techniques involving production of a two-yarn loop, one appearing on the face and the other on the back of the fabric. Plating varies from simple structural forms to more intricate techniques for pattern design purposes.

**PURL KNIT:** See "Links-Links."

**RACKING:** Movement of the needle beds in relation to each other. If the needle bed is racked to the right, the front bed shifts to the right and the back bed to the left. Racking to the left reverses the procedure.

**RASCHEL:** A warp knitting machine which uses latch needles set in one or two needle beds and employing multi-guide bars. Many types of lacy and net-like effects as well as surface patterns are produced on the raschel machine.

**RASCHEL LACE:** Lace produced on a raschel warp knitting machine. For lace production, these machines are available in widths of 75, 100 and 124 inches.

**RATINE:** Refers to a plain-woven fabric with a rough, nubby surface finish. One heavy and two fine yarns are twisted together at various tensions to form a curly, knotty ply yarn.

**RIB KNIT:** Knit fabric with lengthwise ribs formed by wales alternating on right and wrong sides. If every other wale alternates between right and wrong side it is called 1 x 1 rib. If two wales alternate it is called 2 x 2 rib. Rib knit fabric is more elastic than plain knit and is more form-fitting.

**SIMPLEX:** A warp knitting machine with spring-beard needles which produces double-faced fabrics.

**SINGLE KNIT:** As distinct from a doubleknit, the single knit fabric is knitted on a single needle machine, made by interlooping the yarn, a loop within a loop.

**SINKER:** A divider blade which moves or pushes the yarn alternately between the needles. The sinker holds down the fabric, permitting the needle to function, and acts as a loop-forming or holding mechanism in conjunction with the needle.

**SKEIN:** A length of yarn wound onto a reel, usually about 120 yards long. A skein varies from 44 to 54 inches in circumference.

**SLIVER KNIT:** The process by which groups of staple fibers are locked into a high-pile position by a backing yarn set up in a jersey ground structure. The process utilizes plain jersey backing yarn intermingled with carded staple. See "Pile Knit."

**SPIRAL YARN:** Made of two yarns—a fine, hard-twisted yarn and a bulky slack-twisted yarn. The fine yarn forms a core around which the bulky yarn is wound spirally.

**SPRING-BEARD NEEDLE:** One of the two basic types of knitting machine needles (the other is the latch needle) which has a long, flexible spring-beard or hook. Warp knitting machines fitted with spring-beard needles make finer knit fabrics of high gauge, such as women's hosiery and lingerie.

**STABILITY:** There are a number of different processes for stabilizing warp knit fabrics to control their stretch. Synthetic resins have also been used to control the dimensional stability of these fabrics.

**STITCH:** The basic element in knitting is the stitch, composed of a complete needle loop, a sinker loop and two connecting loop parts which join the needle loop to the one preceding.

**STRETCH KNIT:** Construction of a stretch fabric in the knitting operation, using stretch yarns. Though all knitted fabrics are stretchable, the stretch knit will recover more rapidly and have greater holding power due to the use of stretch yarns.

**STRIP DYEING:** Refers to the dyeing of sweater sections before they are sewed into finished garments.

**TAKE-UP:** The mechanism which draws off fabric from the machine as it is knitted. It serves as a "pull" on the cloth to assure proper cast-off of loops and on some machines rolls up the fabric for easy removal.

**TEXTURED YARNS:** Man-made filament yarns into which coils, crimps or loops are set. The process of texturing changes the hand and appearance of the fabric and increases the covering power.

**TRICOT:** See "Warp Knit." The word is French, from the verb *tricoter* (to knit).

**TRICOT MACHINE:** A warp knitting machine which uses spring-beard needles and operates with one needle bar and one to three guide bars.

**TUBULAR KNITTING:** Fabric knitted in tube form, usually on a circular machine, with no seams, such as seamless hosiery and underwear. Tubular knitting may be done on a flat machine by special arrangement of the cams for needle operation.

**TUCK BAR:** A device which permits a pattern or stripe in circular jersey knitting to be placed where desired.

**TUCK STITCH:** Formed by the needle holding one loop while taking on one or more loops and then casting all onto another loop. Tuck stitch is a variation of a basic stitch in weft knitting designed for novelty effects.

**VELOUR:** See "Pile Knit."

**WALE:** The series of loops, formed by one needle, which run lengthwise in a knit fabric. The word is derived from the Anglo-Saxon word *walu*, meaning to mark with stripes.

**WARP KNIT:** Knitted fabric in which yarns run lengthwise and are arranged parallel on a warp beam like the warp in woven fabric. Each yarn is controlled by a separate needle which loops it onto itself. The yarns are connected by guides to the next vertical row by moving back and forth from side to side. Warp knits are generally tighter, flatter and less elastic than weft knits.

**WEFT KNIT:** One of the two basic types of knitted fabrics (the other is warp knit). Hand-knitting is done by the weft method. The stitches move from side to side of the cloth, the stretch, therefore, being chiefly sidewise. Weft-knit fabrics can be made on either flat or circular machines.

**WELT:** Edge on the rib knit used in forming the end of a sleeve or waistband to prevent raveling or rolling.

**WELT STITCH:** Actually not a stitch, it is an effect produced when the needle misknits or fails to receive the fed yarn for the space of a loop. The missed yarn thus remains on the reverse side in un-looped form.

**WIDENING:** In full-fashioning equipment, the operation that shapes the fabric by moving wale loops outward to the selvage.

**YIELD:** In woolen manufacture, yield refers to the amount of actual fiber after scouring. Yield runs from 35 to 65 percent after scouring; the better the grade of wool, the lower the yield.

Deep, shaggy pile knitted from modacrylic fiber.

# Fake Furs

## Definition

Fake fur is the term given to a large class of pile fabrics which have been engineered to achieve the appearance, luxury and warmth of animal furs. The fabrics may be woven, tufted or knitted (both sliver knit and circular loop knit) and they lend themselves to dyeing, printing and special finishes which have resulted in unusual design effects and consequent wide fashion acceptance. Various fibers and blends are used in the construction.

Today the word *fake*—which implies a certain bravado and fun approach—is something of a misnomer, since these fabrics have achieved a legitimacy of their own as a separate category of textiles.

## Fashion Beginnings

Fake furs first appeared on the market in 1929 in a number of women's coats. Geared to an economy of mounting depression, the fabrics were relatively low-end plush cloths—often of alpaca—which attempted to simulate furs. The coats had little fashion flair and colors were generally grey or tan, but they were warm and the fabric became a market staple in the ensuing years. Interest in alpaca pile continued to rise and the fabrics, woven on the basic principle of pile fabric weaving construction (see "Fake Fur Through Weaving," below), showed some technical advances through more furry hand, a denser look and better abrasion resistance. New colors were introduced and the fabric began to take on more fashion interest.

A significant advance in pile fabrics came in the 1940's with the first *knit* pile fabrics, which afforded greater density and furriness of pile, as well as greater pliability. This and other technical advances furthered the progress of high pile fabrics, along with extensive experimentation with the new and emerging man-made fibers. Above all, the man-made fibers produced fabrics of bulk without weight and the visual appearance of real fur.

## Fake Fur Production Systems

FAKE FUR THROUGH WEAVING. Basic principles of textile weaving form this system, with the use of an additional filling or warp yarn (the pile yarn) which is interlaced with the backing fabric to form a loop or pile surface. Depending on the effect desired, the pile is subsequently cut or left uncut as loop pile (in Persian lamb or karakul types, for example). When the pile is cut, the surface is worked to remove the twist, with subsequent polishing ("fur ironing"), shearing, shrinking, embossing, etc. for desired finishes.

Weaving is the oldest method in the production of pile fabrics, and is a fairly slow process requiring a high degree of skill. It results in a large range of cloths and effects.

With the increasing use of continuous filament yarns for man-made fur fabrics, less extensive finishing procedures are required than in the case of spun pile yarns.

FAKE FUR THROUGH TUFTING. This system also involves a pile yarn with a backing fabric, but the tufting technique forms a loop similar in appearance (although somewhat coarser) to a terry loop. Tufting, which produces pile material at a high rate of speed, bears a resemblance to the sewing technique. Most tufted fake furs are piece-dyed and then processed through a series of napping, tigering, polishing and shearing operations to produce the end effect desired.

FAKE FUR THROUGH SLIVER KNITTING. Basically this process utilizes the same machinery used in plain jersey knitting except that the machine is altered to accommodate the pile fibers in sliver form. Thus, the construction consists of plain jersey backing yarn interlaced with carded staple. The staple, varying in length from ¾ to 2 inches, is combed into the machine to create a directional pile. The pile is then locked into the fabric construction by the looping action of the backing yarn over the knitting needle.

Height, hand, luster and color of sliver knit pile are determined by the type and length of staple and by finishing through shearing and electrification of the pile. Density of pile is determined by such mechanical factors as knitting rate, carding rate and density of the sliver itself. By the nature of the construction, the basic color of the fabric must be produced in the fiber, either through stock or solution dye processing.

In recent years most attention in the manufacture of pile fabrics has been focused on sliver knitting. This is the fastest technique for the purpose, and the most economical. Sliver knitting has undoubtedly provided the most dynamic manufacturing technique in the pile fabric sector.

FAKE FUR THROUGH CIRCULAR LOOP KNITTING. This process, while interlacing the pile with the backing, as in sliver knitting, is unlike the latter in that it uses a yarn for the pile. The backing is usually a basic jersey stitch with the pile yarns laid in and left floating over two or more wales. As with tufting, most loop knit fabrics are made with yarns and are piece-dyed, but whereas the pile yarn in tufted fabric is placed in the warp direction, the yarn in circular loop knits is laid in the filling direction. Final processing is through a series of finishing procedures, detailed under the tufting process.

## Major Fibers Used in Fake Fur Manufacture

Acrylics
Polypropylene (for backing)
Cotton          " "
Modacrylics
Mohair
Rayon
Polyester
Nylon
Blends of the above fibers

## Technical Advances

On the technical level, there is continuous experimentation with new fibers and finishes, and new adaptations of the producing equipment. Some examples of technological ingenuity: The pile may consist of a blend of shrinkable and non-shrinkable fibers to produce the long guard hair and short under-pelt, simulating mink or river otter. Also for mink effects, certain fiber combinations may be used to produce the illusion of pelts sewn together.

Where sheared beaver or mouton effects are desired, blends of fine and coarser fibers of a certain type serve to achieve a balance of "hand" and crush-resistance. In simulating karakul, wool/rayon blends are primarily used on the circular loop knit system rather than the weaving loom, as in the past. The wool fiber is made to shrink, creating the tiny tight curl of the karakul.

Pile fabrics had been produced for many years before the development and wide popular acceptance

Varied examples of pile fabrics made from modacrylic fibers to resemble animal furs.

Examples of animal designs in fake furs.

of man-made furs. The main catalyst for this development may be said to be the growth and enormous versatility of the synthetic fibers. With these fibers playing a major role in the field, and with their ever-increasing performance and quality standards, there is evidence that producers will "trade up" and sell both higher quality and higher priced materials.

## Fashion Advances

On the design and fashion level, every season simulations of animal pelts get closer and closer to the actual furs. In mink effects, for example, the later versions show great enhancement over the earlier types. While the dark ranch color has been a standard best seller, the blond shades stir greater interest among younger consumers, for whom mink effects had not created interest earlier.

Perhaps most important on the fashion level is the program of design development which has brought about a high degree of creativity in pile fabrics. By the late 1960's, fake or man-made furs came of age through printed versions of animal furs which have created fashion excitement and wide public response. Having been accepted in their own right, man-made furs also broke away from exclusively pelt designs and expanded their applications by use of color and the creation of unusual design effects.

## End Uses of Fake Furs

1. COATS FOR WOMEN AND GIRLS. These represent the most prevailing high fashion use of deep pile fabrics. Fashions with a truly remarkable luxury of hand and appearance have become available to a wide consumer group at popular prices for mass appeal.

2. MEN'S AND BOYS' WEAR. Coats, outerwear jackets—all these offer luxurious warmth and styling possibilities in a variety of male fashions.

3. COAT LININGS AND ZIP-OUT LINERS. One of the original uses, and still one of the most widespread, is the use of man-made fur fabrics for linings for men's, women's and children's coats and jackets.

4. CHILDREN'S OUTERWEAR. Hooded snow suits, coats, jackets and baby buntings provide the lightweight warmth particularly desirable for small children's wear.

5. HAT, CAP AND MILLINERY INDUSTRIES. Deep pile fabrics have become one of the mainstays of the industries for men's and women's headgear.

6. FOOTWEAR. Pile fabrics have very wide use for boot linings and slippers for men, women, children.

7. ACCESSORIES. Gloves, capes, stoles, ponchos, coat and jacket trims are some of the major accessory items manufactured of pile fabrics in a wide range of colors, pile depths and fur effects.

8. RUGS. Pile fabrics are specially engineered for floor coverings in scatter, area and accent rugs. They come in colors from pale to dark and are highly practical home decorative items since they are machine washable and long-wearing.

9. HOME FURNISHINGS. Bedspreads, pillows, couch covers, blankets—especially airline blankets—are increasingly being made of pile fabrics.

10. STUFFED TOYS. Pile fabrics, shaggy or cut, make ideal stuffed toys, treated for washability and non-allergenic surfaces.

11. COSMETIC AND MEDICAL USES. Powder puffs are one obvious end use for pile fabrics. Less apparent is their important market for bed pads, where pile fabrics have proved a boon in the greater comfort of bed patients.

Close-up of fake furs showing pile construction.

# Lace

*An open work fabric which possesses a special niche among apparel textiles, and which has received an impetus from the arrival of the synthetic fibers.*

A fine hand-made lace employing floral motifs.

LACE is an openwork, ornamental fabric strictly classed as *netting*. Like knitting, it is made by looping, tying, or twisting a single continuous strand or yarn upon itself. The word itself derives from the Latin *loquens*, which means to make a noose or snare.

Cotton, silk, wool, rayon, linen, nylon, and other man-made fibers are all used in making laces today. Spun silk, ramie, mohair, and metal thread are utilized for special types and novelty lace fabrics.

## Background for Lace

Netted fabrics were the ancestors of modern lace and were used by most primitive peoples in constructing their fish nets. As an ornamental fabric it also has a long history. The Sumerians used lace on their garments as early as 4000 B.C., and archeologists have discovered fragments of ornamental meshes dating back to 2500 B.C. The Bible and Homer both speak of nets, and the fabled Veil of Isis may also have been a netted fabric.

## A Convent Industry

Until the 7th Century A.D., lace making was purely a domestic art; but about that time convent nuns began to make articles of lace for church ceremonies and later as bridal veils and other types of adornment. Gradually the fashion spread and an industry was formed with its leading centers in the European cities of Venice, Brussels, Mechlin, Valenciennes, and Lille.

## Pillow Lace Invented

During this whole early period all laces were made by hand with either a needle or a bone pin, but in 1561 Barbara Uttmann of Annaberg, Germany, invented the *pillow* or *bobbin* method of making lace.

Instead of using a single thread and a needle she used many threads and twisted them over pins fixed into a pillow according to a set design.

## A Profitable Fashion

During the Renaissance, the quickly spreading handmade lace industry was so valuable and profitable that the Venetians were not allowed to wear lace . . . it was sent abroad, to bring gold for the coffers of the Doges.

The famous finance minister, Colbert, under Louis XIV, went to all lengths to transplant the Venetian lace industry to France. He went so far as to bribe Italian workers to emigrate to Alençon and teach the art of lace-making to workers in France. Such were the beginnings of the famous Alençon laces and the rise of the French lace industry to its position of eminence thereafter.

The lace ruffs of Elizabethan fame started a fashion which worked the early lace industry at fever pitch. Elizabeth's own ruffs grew to three-quarters of a yard deep with edges comprising twenty-five yards of lace.

### From a United States Government Brochure

Fancy lace is the aristocrat among textile fabrics; no class of textile fabric is so delicate and so difficult to make, and no other requires so long a time to acquire proficiency in the higher branches of production; none is more completely an article of voluntary consumption; none is more a creation of art, and finally no other more completely depends for consumption upon the originality, novelty, and beauty of its design.

The Leavers lace machine, built on principles discovered by John Leavers in 1813, has a complex mechanism with over 30,000 parts, almost all of them moving when the machine is operating. Taking an operator two to three weeks to thread, it will make a continuous width of lace of several yards, which may afterwards be slit into lace of various widths.

Handkerchief lace of great artistic quality. This Valenciennes lace dates from 19th Century.

Lace for fashion. The importance of lace in the fashion industries may vary according to season's taste.

Lace was so coveted that even though the Puritans preached against its use for adornment, Cromwell himself indulged in a "spot" of lace trimming.

## The Great Lace Centers

By the 17th Century, the ruff had passed its fashion zenith, but lace continued in increasing demand and production. The industry spread throughout Europe, with each community seeking to establish its own identity and leadership with pattern innovations. Today machine-made laces characteristic of the distinctive types are designated by the names of the original lace centers . . . Venetian, Burano, Alençon, Chantilly, Cluny, Valenciennes, Bruges, etc.

## The Earliest Machines

The first attempt to make a lace-like fabric by machine occurred in 1758 when Jedediah Strutt developed his stocking frame. It was not really lace, but it started a chain of developments.

From then until Napoleonic times many attempts were made to duplicate by machinery the fascinating hand work of the needlepoint and bobbin lace methods. In many quarters a rather dim view was taken of these visionaries, who seemed to be trying to make a machine do the impossible. They were frequently put into the same classification as those who sought to obtain perpetual motion.

Now we know that many of these pioneers were much more than visionaries. Important advances towards the goal of producing machine lace were being made. In 1802 Robert Brown was granted a patent for a netting machine and two years later Edward Whittaker invented something which he claimed could imitate pillow lace. The actual operation, however, did not get very far. Then in 1808, John Heathcote developed his famous bobbinet invention, which turned out to be the precursor of the Leavers machine.

## The Leavers Brothers

The manufacture of lace by machine immediately began to assume formidable stature in England's national economy. The exportation of a lace machine was punishable by banishment or death, but as soon as the Napoleonic wars were over, separate parts were smuggled into France, there to be reconstructed. The transplanted industry immediately took root on this new ground and Heathcote himself established factories on the other side of the channel, first in Paris in 1818, then in St. Quentin in 1826.

When Heathcote's patents ran out, so many textile inventors emerged that from 1823 to 1825 England was said to be suffering from an epidemic of twist-net fever. In the meantime, John Leavers with two brothers and a few nephews had already discovered the great secret of reproducing lace by machine. His first device, dating back to 1813, employed the same principles as the modern Leavers machine. That was the real start of the production of fancy lace by mechanical means. It remained only to incorporate with the Leavers machine the motion of the Jacquard loom in 1837. Everything that has been done subsequently has been in the nature of refinement and improvement rather than of basic change.

## Are Mosquito Nets Lace?

While the manufacture of lace became primarily a French industry, the manufacture of the machinery stayed in Nottingham. Lace making is still one of the great industries of France, one in which the French take an especial pride. The United States was slow in getting started. Although machine lace factories opened up in Massachusetts early in the 19th Century, the expansion of the industry towards its present scale did not start until about 1910. Because so many American soldiers had died from malaria during the Spanish American War for want of suitable mosquito netting, the Government decided to lift the duty on European lace machines and provide for the promotion and expansion of net and lace manufacture. Thus, the United States lace industry is only about fifty years old.

## A $115-Million Industry

Today there are over 500 embroidery and venise lace plants with some 1,400 schiffli embroidery machines in the United States, the vast majority of which operate in a six-mile-long strip outside New York along the Hudson River. These plants produce an annual volume of approximately $115,000,000. America, which produces the overwhelming percentage of embroideries and venise laces used in this country, does not produce the schiffli embroidery machine; they are all imported in parts from Switzerland and Germany and assembled here by experts.

## The Incredible Leavers Machine

The LEAVERS lace machine has been compared in strength with the elephant, and, in delicacy of performance. and creative ingenuity, to the spider. It is undoubtedly the most complicated and difficult piece of textile machinery the ingenious mind of man has been able to contrive.

The Leavers machine involves some 40,000 parts, practically all of them in motion, most of them built to a tolerance measured in thousandths of an inch. It is an astonishing experience to watch this mechanical wonder clanking away.

It stands nine or ten feet high. It weighs over 30,-000 pounds and costs about a dollar a pound. Some 500 square feet of floor space must be allotted to house it. Two to three weeks are required to thread-up for action. When the operator throws the starting switch, his machine may contain enough yarn to stretch half way round the world, unbelievable as it may seem.

## The Twist Hand

Where usual textile weavers and knitters generally operate a dozen or more machines, sometimes many more, there is invariably one twist-hand, or weaver, for each Leavers unit, and he is one of the best-trained and perhaps one of the highest-paid individuals in the fraternity of textile machine operators, Union rules and regular practice through the industry require a candidate for the job of Leavers operator to work, after preliminary training, as full apprentice for three years. It is only at the end of the three-year apprenticeship that he becomes a qualified Leavers operator.

## Designer to Draftsman to Jacquard

To give an idea of what it takes to develop the technicians and craftsmen who supply the machine operators with their patterns, let us start with the designer, for it is on his drawing board that each new pattern is born. Obviously he must be an artist, because he must render a realistic drawing of each new pattern in the form of a design, correct to the smallest detail. He must know the Leavers machine inside out to keep his creative thinking in a practical groove. Otherwise he might dream up designs possibly too costly or impracticable to reproduce in lace.

When the designer has done his work there is on the board a finished sketch, exact size, with the de-sign repeated sufficiently to show the flow of the pattern. At this point the draftsman comes in. He takes the design and enlarges it many times, then translates it into mathematical and mechanical terms on a highly complex chart. On this chart there is a number for every single thread. These numbers represent exactly each movement, combination and pass of every thread at every moment during the entire process.

Just as the design becomes a network of numbers that govern the mechanical motion, so the numbers now become a guide that indicates to a jacquard card puncher the position of the holes which are to be punched on the successive jacquard cards. These cards are then tied together to form a continuous band, which repeats like a piano-player roll.

## Comparison with Weaving

The jacquard motion does not make the lace; it merely governs the pattern which the Leavers machine makes into lace. The actual lace making consists of intertwisting two or more sets of threads: the warp or beam and the bobbin threads.

A comparison with other textile procedures will help in visualizing the extraordinary intricacies of the actual making of the lace. In the case of woven fabrics you have some intricate patterns like fancy brocades, which in fact employ the same types of jacquard motion as the Leavers operation. Even the most devious of these textile designs, however, are executed by one set of threads that goes lengthwise —the warp—and one that goes crosswise—the filling. They have nowhere else to go. The machine is limited to two-directional functioning: up and down or left and right. Warp knitting involves looping and knotting, but it also remains a two-directional operation. But in a Leavers machine, instead of one shuttle carrying the filling back and forth between the warp threads, there are some four thousand bobbins, each as thin as paper and spaced at nineteen to the inch, which slide to and fro between the shifting warp threads to form the lace fabric. The threads move in many directions at one time because there is no limit to the complexity of patterns which can be made on the Leavers machine.

## Two Other Ways of Making Lace

Strictly speaking, the only ways of making lace as such are by hand or with a lace machine. However, the SCHIFFLI embroidery machine does create the effect of lace by applying the design to cloth which has already been woven. In addition to this method a new procedure was recently developed for producing "lace" with weaving equipment.

The Schiffli machine originated in St. Gall, Switzerland. The word Schiffli means "little boat" and it is this little boat-like shuttle that produces lace or embroidery in widths from ten to fifteen yards and on any kind of material and in any conceivable type of design. The use of this shuttle has changed machine embroidery from a crude facsimile of handwork to a smooth finished product.

Each Schiffli machine has from 682 to 1020 needles, which make it possible to produce fine and elaborate details in appliqués and embroideries of all types on all kinds of fabrics that have the luxurious look of handwork, but without the prohibitive cost.

On lingerie versatile effects are achieved; in lace and net appliqués, combined embroidery and lace designs, net appliqués on bodices, necklines, shoulders, pockets, and skirts.

The machine also makes various types of fancy stitching and designs. New patterns are constantly developed in line with advanced fashion trends.

The Schiffli embroidery falls into two groups. One is the framework section, which makes an outstanding contribution to slips and gowns because the patterns are worked on frames and the finished pieces are then attached to the garment itself. The other type makes possible the elaborate trims which may be used in as many ways as fashion dictates. This is

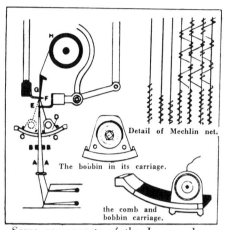

Some components of the Leavers lace machine: A, Warp threads; B, B, Guide bars; C, C, combs; E, F, points; G, guide board; H, cloth beam.

the yardage which can be made in various widths and in all fabrics, such as net, crepe, ninon, lace, and nylon; in all colors. Here, too, patterns vary from the simplest to the most elaborate.

LACE BY WEAVING is a modern development by American Silk Mills. While the process is a trade secret, it utilizes existing weaving equipment, the end result looks like lace, is offered in classic lace patterns and answers the dictionary definition of lace. While the new technique is applicable to all fibers, natural as well as synthetic, the man-made fibers are most adaptable because of their intrinsic strength and resistance to chemical finishing.

Irish needle point Lace collar.

## Murals in Lace

One of the most interesting artistic conceptions in modern lace work has been the lace constructions of Luba Krejci. Working with needle and thread as a painter might work with pencil or brush, Mrs. Krejci makes no preliminary sketches but allows her construction to grow on the frame, after first stretching a net of threads to hold her design. Her lace murals are deeply rooted in the ancient traditions of Bohemian lace making, but on this

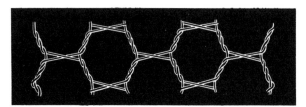

Three-twist untraversed, Brussels net when traversed.

folk craft base she has built new forms and a fresh design concept which brings her work into the main stream of modern art. As such it represents a source of design ideas for modern lace

Luba Krejci's lace constructions have been used for interior decoration, including wall hangings, both throughout Europe and in her native Czechoslovakia. She is also widely known as a leading designer of textiles, carpets, basketry, tapestries and glass laminates.

Her lace work has been exhibited at the Museum of Contempory Crafts in New York City and many other museums in Europe. They are credited

with bringing about a renewed interest in wall hangings and, to a certain extent, reviving interest in lace for apparel and openwork in casements.

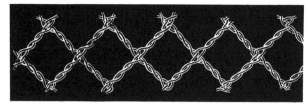

Four-twist untraversed, called square net .

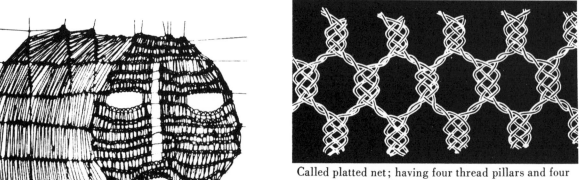

Called platted net; having four thread pillars and four sides, each of two threads, twisted but not traversed.

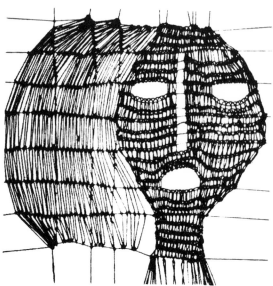

# Ribbons

*Ribbons belong to a class of woven goods known as narrow fabrics; they range in width from a quarter of an inch to about a foot; they are used in trimming and are often woven with great luxury of fiber and design.*

Aside from the completely plastic ribbons used for industrial or adornment purposes, ribbons are mainly manufactured in these types: satin, twill, taffeta, faille, grosgrain, velvet.

In order to attain fancy effects ribbon mills utilize the basic weaving constructions, but supplement them with numerous ingenious devices. Sometimes they combine various colors in one ribbon; sometimes they cross-weave, combining differing constructions; or, they use a jacquard weave in a combination of various colorings. Printing and embossing are two other broad fields, but equally usual are ribbons made of different yarn-dyed colors. One of the most interesting developments has been the use of different fibers in combination . . . silk and acetate, as an example. Each fiber takes the dye differently, so that when the two fibers are woven together a striking effect is attained.

Ribbons fall into the two main categories of woven-edge and cut-edge. The former needs no explanation, since the ribbon is woven to the required width originally. However, the cut-edge ribbon is made by slicing a wider fabric into strips with a special knife. The better cut-edge ribbon is made of an acetate fabric, and then cut with a hot knife which instantly fuses the thermo-plastic acetate and makes the edge fast and ravel-proof.

Ribbon weavers are able to use three-dimensional effects which are ordinarily denied to the weavers of broad fabrics because of prohibitive expense. Embroidery and jacquard effects are used freely in ribbons where they would be prohibitive in broad goods.

## Regimentals

A favorite ribbon theme is that associated with the colors of different crack regiments in various countries. Dating from the time when soldiers wore the armorial colors of their feudal chief, these themes have been adapted to tie-silks and other decorative apparel uses.

## The Ribbon Loom

The loom used for weaving ribbons and tapes is in fact a series of little looms, all linked together and each possessing its individual shuttle and warp. This arrangement allows of an endless variety of patterns, since each set of warps may be differently colored, and the shuttles can contain yarns in equal variety, giving great production flexibility.

In cases where the loom is fitted with a jacquard mechanism, each ribbon may be woven in the same pattern, or each may be different from the rest, weaving at the same time from six to fifty different ribbon designs. The usual number of ribbons available on a single loom is fourteen.

The ribbon loom differs from the ordinary loom in respect of the means employed for taking-up and letting-off of the warp and cloth. The warps in this loom are derived from bobbins or cheeses, and not from a warp beam as in usual loom types. Therefore, in order to maintain an even tension, each warp thread is passed over an arrangement of pulleys, among which is a pulley suspended with a weight attached to it. The weight drawing on the warp thread produces a constant tension and takes the place of usual mechanisms for regulating warp tension in other types of loom.

In the same way, after the ribbon has been woven, it is again carried round a suspended pulley before being wound or otherwise disposed of. The weight, hanging on the ribbon keeps the warp of the already woven portion at a constant tension and, when it is near the ground, the woven ribbon is wound by the operator until the weight has been again drawn up to a point where it has room to fall, as new ribbon comes off the loom.

Thus the tensions on both warp and cloth are combined with the letting-off and taking-up motion.

## Ribbon Width

Ribbon width is usually measured by the French ligne, which is one-eleventh of an inch.

# Felts and Non-Woven Fabrics

## Definition

The term "Non-Woven" refers to a category of materials made primarily of textile fibers held together by an applied bonding agent—or by the fusing of self-contained thermoplastic fibers—and not processed on conventional spindles, looms or knitting machines.

Non-woven fabrics have only a recent history, having been introduced in 1942 and developed in the wake of man-made fibers. With regard to the above definition, the editors of American Fabrics believe that a more descriptive and all-encompassing term for these products would be "web textiles," since this term reflects the essential character of these fabrics; namely, that they have a textile structure built up from a web or continuous mat of fibers without benefit of spinning.

## Basic Methods

Non-woven fabrics are made by two basic methods—the "wet process" on paper making machinery, and the "dry wet process." The majority are made by the dry method. In this process, fibers ¾ inch to several inches in length are formed into a web, either by air dispersion on a moving belt or screen, or through garnetting and carding machines by which the fibers can be oriented in longitudinal and cross directions. Then the structure is bonded by spraying with a resin or by mechanical methods such as needle-punching. Bonding can also be achieved by blending in a small proportion of a fiber with a lower melting point, and then fusing.

Still another approach is the use of continuous filaments, randomly dispersed, to form a sheet structure. Whichever way the web sheet is formed, it can be made in any thickness desired, depending on the end use envisioned.

## The Papermaking Technique

One of the significant developments in this field has been the adaptation of papermaking techniques. This is the so-called wet process and involves the use of man-made fibers ranging from one-eighth of an inch to one inch long. These fibers are relatively long by papermaking standards. Sometimes slight modification of equipment or processing techniques is required to achieve good dispersion in water and thus good sheet formation. The fibers can be bonded by addition of synthetic resin to the paper or the final sheet can be saturated with a resin and subseqently fused.

## Fibers Used in Non-Wovens

These include rayon, nylon acetate, cotton, wool, acrylic, polyester and glass, in staple or continuous filament form.

Contrary to popular belief, non-woven textiles are not produced only from waste fibers. The term "paper fabrics"—which gained public attention in the 1960's—is likewise an inaccurate description. Although some waste fibers are used, most are new. Almost any fiber, or combination of fibers, may be used in the manufacturing process; and two, three or four fibers are considered routine.

## History and Growth

Before World War II a few textile companies began experimenting with the production of loomless fabrics as an outlet for cotton waste fibers, but production of such materials on a commercial scale increased slowly during the war years. By the late 1960's, however, there were more than 160 companies throughout the world manufacturing products which could be classified as non-wovens, or web textiles.

Chief markets have been in hidden applications such as interlinings, in disposable hospital equipment, industrial uses such as wiping cloths, and household products. To these applications has been added a developing market in consumer products for apparel and the home.

Of these uses, the most important to date have been in the hospital field. Institutions of other types, such as schools, also represent a growing market. In the home, there is increasing use of "paper" curtains, bedspreads, bed linens and tablecloths, often in colorful prints.

## The Manufacturing Process

Considering that all non-wovens are made of fibers and require bonding, there are certain operations basic to all methods of manufacture. These include, in sequence:

1. Preparation of the fiber.
2. Web formation.
3. Web bonding.
4. Drying and curing.
5. Finishing techniques.

## Forming the Web

Once the choice of fiber and binder has been made, the properties of the non-woven product are vitally influenced by the method used in forming the web and applying the binder.

For web formation, there are four fundamentally different processes. The first two listed below employ techniques of the textile industry. Numbers 3 and 4 derived from paper technology; namely, production of random web by air blowing or by liquid dispersion. Still a fifth technique is the high velocity spraying of thermoplastic fibers.

1. PARALLEL-LAID WEB. In this process all the fibers run in approximately the same direction. Such a web is produced on carding machines—or cards— which are devices for combing the fibers into essentially parallel arrangement. Each carding machine delivers a thin sheet of parallel-laid fiber onto a continuous belt. Several such machines are run in series, and the thin layers produced by successive machines are superimposed on each other, running in the same direction, to form a multi-layer web. Parallel-laid web yields a product which has high strength in lengthwise direction but which is handicapped by low transverse strength. Used chiefly in disposable products.

2. CROSS-LAID WEB. In this system, the web is built up, sandwich fashion, from a sequence of layers in which the fibers run in different directions. Again the fiber is first run through a carding machine to form a thin sheet of parallel-laid fiber. However, the product of successive carding machines is delivered to the conveyor in different directions. Cross-laid web is substantially stronger in crosswise direction than is a parallel-laid web, but it is more costly to produce because of the more complicated arrangement of machinery.

3. RANDOM-LAID WEB. Whereas the other two types of web employ machinery (for fiber loosening, carding and lapping) which has been used in the textile industry for over 100 years, random-laid webs are manufactured by a process which did not reach commercial maturity until the early 1950's and which is closer to papermaking technology in its concept.

The fiber is opened up and is blown onto a rotating, perforated drum to which it adheres by internal vacuum. A heavy matte is formed and this is delivered to a high-speed rotating drum with metallic teeth which breaks up the original web structure. The resulting particles are blown onto a second vacuum drum where they form a highly uniform web, which is taken off and passed to a continuous conveyor. Thickness of the web can be varied over a wide range.

4. WET-LAY RANDOM WEB. A fourth method of web formation is known as the wet-lay random web system, or the wet process. Since this system utilizes conventional paper-making machinery, most of the development work in this area has been done by paper manufacturers. In this system the fibers are mixed with chemicals and processed through beaters and pulpers. The slurry thus formed is deposited on a wire screen where the excess liquid is drawn off leaving a web which is then processed in a manner similar to conventional non-woven fabric manufacture. A production speed many times that of the dry web system is a principal advantage of the wet process.

## First Came Felt

A distinction must be drawn between felt, which is an ancient fabric, and the modern web fabrics. Both are made without any system of yarn such as is used in weaving, knitting and lacemaking. Both are built up from a web or continuous sheet of fibers without benefit of spinning. The difference lies in the type of fibers used and in the method of bonding them together into a fabric.

Felt is made almost exclusively of wool and is based on the ability of the wool fiber to felt together naturally because of its scale structure. Heat, water and pressure are used to mat the fibers into fabric.

Non-woven fabrics, on the other hand, are produced largely from man-made fibers which do not have a natural tendency to felt together and must therefore be bonded together by adhesives or chemical action.

A large variety of non-woven products.

# Stitch-Through Textiles

The stitch-through technique is a relatively recent system offering a new approach to the forming of fabrics. Stitch-through combines some of the characteristics of both weaving and knitting. It is built around the concept of locking together either yarns or a web of fibers by the use of needles and thread. Reputedly, it was invented by a man who developed the idea after watching his wife darn a stocking.

Three systems of the stitch-through concept have been developed thus far. Following is a description, with graphic illustration, of each system.

MALIMO. This system, the first to reach commercial production, was developed in East Germany and its specialized equipment is distributed by Crompton & Knowles-Malimo Inc. of Worcester, Mass. Actually, three different machines are available, each producing a different type of fabric. They are called "Malimo," "Malipol" and "Maliwatt."

In the Malimo machine a set of warp yarns and a set of filling yarns are stitched together by needles and thread. This avoids the need to intertwine the yarns, as in weaving. The system is geared to produce fabric about twenty times faster than a conventional automatic loom. A finished Malimo fabric

Filling carrier on high-speed Malimo system.

can look like either a knit or a woven cloth, depending on the yarn counts for warp, filling and stitching. The system can also operate with a set of filling yarns only, and the stitching thread.

Its chief uses have been in tablecloths where a basic fabric is a textured Malimo cloth, and in curtain fabrics since Malimo makes possible open constructions with a locked-in structure. But Malimo fabrics are used for other furnishings items as well as apparel fabrics where their basic appeal is that they combine the appearance and texture of a knit with the stability of a woven.

The Malipol machine is used for making pile fabrics. Its system is somewhat similar to the tufting process since it stitches pile loops onto a backing fabric by a needling system.

The Maliwatt machine operates without preliminary yarns and constructs a fabric by overstitching a web of fibers with its needle and thread system.

Still a fourth machine in the Malimo system makes yarn from loose roving by stitching a thread structure around it. This machine is called "Malifil."

ARACHNE. This system in the stitch-through concept was developed in Czechoslovakia and is distributed in the U.S. by Stellamcor of New York City. In effect it is similar to the Maliwatt equipment. It utilizes a web of unspun fibers which it works into a fabric by a stitch-knit system. One of its ingenious uses has been to produce tapestries and wall coverings at a fraction of the time and cost for producing conventional woven tapestries. It allows the designer unlimited possibilities of textural combinations with threads and fabric pieces processed through the web stitcher onto a web textile backing.

KRAFTMATIC. This stitch-through technique—developed by Kintslaid Engineering in England and licensed to United Merchants and Manufacturers Inc. for the western hemisphere—forms terry, corduroy, velour, pile and plush fabrics. The process involves a knit-sew technique with certain similarities to the Malimo system. Its chief advantages are speed and fabric stability. In the case of terry cloth, the loops are locked into the fabric structure, which eliminates raveling, seam slippage and the need for overstitching in garment construction.

Early emphasis among European producers of stitch-through fabric was on utility and speed of production, with consequent cost advantages. U.S. producers, by contrast, concentrated on styling, the aim being to develop fabrics which look new and different from traditionally produced fabrics.

Technician checks material from Malimo sample machine.

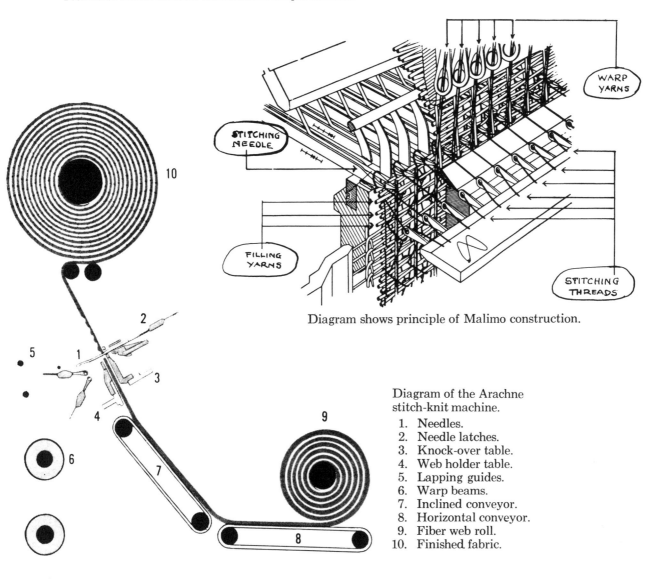

Diagram shows principle of Malimo construction.

Diagram of the Arachne
stitch-knit machine.
1. Needles.
2. Needle latches.
3. Knock-over table.
4. Web holder table.
5. Lapping guides.
6. Warp beams.
7. Inclined conveyor.
8. Horizontal conveyor.
9. Fiber web roll.
10. Finished fabric.

385

# METHODS FOR PRODUCING BONDED FABRIC

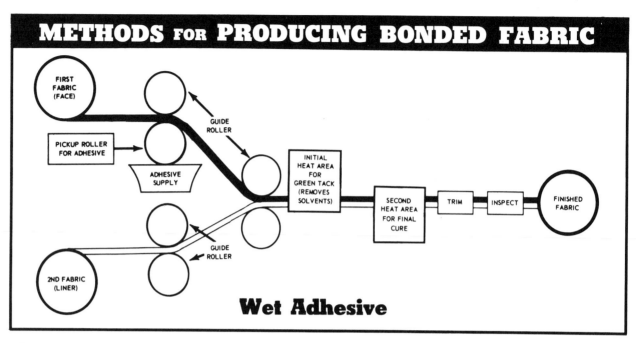

**Wet Adhesive**

FIRST FABRIC (FACE)

GUIDE ROLLER

PICKUP ROLLER FOR ADHESIVE

ADHESIVE SUPPLY

INITIAL HEAT AREA FOR GREEN TACK (REMOVES SOLVENTS)

SECOND HEAT AREA FOR FINAL CURE

TRIM

INSPECT

FINISHED FABRIC

GUIDE ROLLER

2ND FABRIC (LINER)

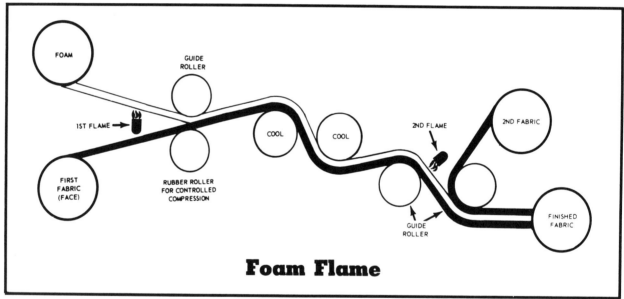

**Foam Flame**

FOAM

GUIDE ROLLER

1ST FLAME

FIRST FABRIC (FACE)

RUBBER ROLLER FOR CONTROLLED COMPRESSION

COOL

COOL

2ND FLAME

2ND FABRIC

GUIDE ROLLER

FINISHED FABRIC

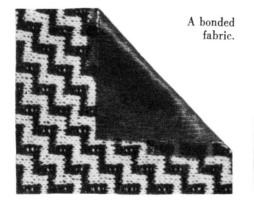

A bonded fabric.

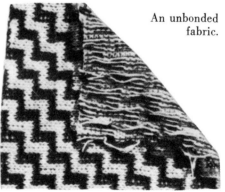

An unbonded fabric.

# Bonding Fabric-to-Fabric

*The term "bonding" generally refers to fabric-to-fabric bonding, as distinct from fabric-to-foam bonding (see definition under "Lamination"). There are two basic types, or methods, of bonding.*

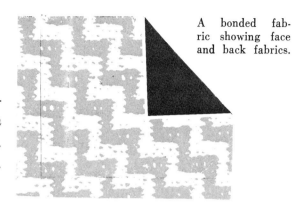

A bonded fabric showing face and back fabrics.

## The Two Basic Methods for Bonding

WET ADHESIVE BONDING. Two fabrics are bonded together through the use of a wet adhesive. The most widely used adhesive today has a water soluble acrylic base. The adhesive is applied to the underside of the face fabric which is then joined to the liner by passing through rollers. It then enters the first heat curing stage which drives out the solvents and creates a preliminary (but not permanent) bond known as a "green tack" (unripe). It then passes through a second and more critical heat curing stage which effects a permanent bond strong enough to withstand washing and dry cleaning. This second curing stage calls for exact controls to avoid any possible degeneration of the bond due either to over- or under-curing.

FOAM FLAME BONDING. Urethane foam is used as the adhesive. By applying a gas flame to the foam, it is burned off and made tacky on one side so that it adheres to the first (face) fabric as they pass through the rollers. The combination is then cooled and flame is applied to the other side of the foam which is then adhered to a second (liner) fabric. By this time the foam has been burned off from an original thickness of 40/1000 of an inch to about 15/1000 of an inch. Critical to this process is the tension control of the rollers and the control of flaming so that both sides of the foam are burned off equally. This method is often used where the face fabric is so light that it requires building up.

## History and Development

Bonded fabrics were launched late in 1962 and in the first year of production approximately 40 million yards of fabric were bonded, followed by 100 million yards the next year, with the figures continuously multiplying since that time. The bonding development has proved to be one of the most significant textile phenomena of the 1960's, along with developments in permanent press, stretch fabrics and blending.

Bonding has done more than join two fabrics together in a permanent union, and more than achieve a self-lined fabric. In the process, it created a fabric with a new dimension, whose hand and performance are substantially different from those of its component parts. And in so doing it launched a new category of textiles which presented the textile-apparel industries with a new product concept.

The development of bonding—like other significant textile achievements of the 1960's—emerged through modern chemistry and the ingenuity of modern technology. Basic to the process was the development of new adhesives—chiefly the acrylics and urethanes—which made it possible to achieve a permanent bond between two fabrics without destroying the hand or drape of the cloth, and without any adverse effect in washing and dry cleaning.

## Distinctions and Categories

It is necessary to draw a distinction between a *bonded* fabric and one which has been *laminated*. In U.S. trade terminology, the word *laminate* usually refers to a face fabric which has been backed with urethane foam (the term is interchangeable with polyurethane foam), while the British use the word *foamback* for such fabrics. Foambacks, which were launched about 1958, have developed an important place in outerwear since they provide, economically, insulation and bulk without weight.

One particular type of foamback—the foam sandwich laminate—is the prototype of fabric-to-fabric bonding since it involves a layer of foam sandwiched between two layers of fabric. The difference is that in bonded fabrics the foam is used, not as an insulator, but as an adhesive which later disappears in processing. This is known as flame-bonding. Another technique widely used is to eliminate the foam and substitute a wet adhesive. Finally, a basic difference is that bonded fabrics have drape and flexibility not generally achieved in foam sandwich laminates.

From this brief description it becomes apparent that bonding is actually a finishing process since it unites two previously constructed fabrics; we might say that the final product is "constructed" in the finishing process.

## Adapted to the Modern Era

Though the first bonded fabrics utilized two traditional textiles, each a practical construction designed for end use, some subsequent bonded fabrics were made up of face fabrics which in themselves were impractical for end use (too unstable) and were designed *only* to be bonded. Bonding, therefore, emphasizes the unlimited possibilities for combining different constructions, colors and textures to extend the performance, the appearance and the end uses of fabrics many times over.

## The Role of Tricot in Bonding

Fabric-to-fabric bonding has involved the use of tricot—both acetate and nylon tricot—as an ideal medium for the lining fabric. The reasons for this are tricot's properties which may be summarized as follows:

1. Controllable degree of stability and elasticity.
2. Great resiliency.
3. Outstanding crease resistance.
4. Excellent drapability.
5. High tear strength and abrasion resistance.
6. Comfort and softness to the touch.
7. Run-proof, non-raveling qualities.
8. Pleatability by heatsetting.

Tricot has a responsive quality which enables it to enhance the qualities of the face fabric to which it is bonded. Thus, a crease resistant fabric is made more crease resistant by combination with tricot. A fluid fabric is given increased drapability. But above all, tricot gives stability to a face fabric which might otherwise be impractical for manufacturing.

For example, an openwork wool knit cloth, which is too loosely structured to be either cut or sewn, becomes practical when bonded to tricot. Similar results are achieved with open-work lace and leno constructions. And with single knit jersey fabrics, bonding to tricot eliminates the characteristic roll which makes cutting and sewing extremely difficult.

## Special Effects and End Uses

Open weaves, laces, delicate knits are no longer subject to the traditional limitations in their wear-life. The gossamer look can be a practical reality as sheer, open, even cobwebby fabrics are endowed with strength, dyeability and durability through fabric-to-fabric bonding. As an example: sheer chantilly-type lace, bonded to a sheet of clear vinyl on the face side, becomes a fabric with stability, to be cut and sewn into umbrellas, shoes, handbags, raincoats, see-through dresses, hats, furniture coverings and tablecloths.

Reversible two-faced fabrics, heretofore in the couture class, were strictly limited. Bonding now widens the possibilities of reversible fabric combinations, with unlimited advantages in price and fabric weight. Components can be two single-knit jerseys forming a doubleknit, or two different textures or colors of tweed, or a pile with a smooth fabric, a woven with a knit, a print with a coordinated solid. Possibilities are unlimited.

Colored acetate tricot, backing a semi-sheer white or neutral colored knit fabric, projects a new color dimension on the face fabric, at the same time providing stability for garment manufacture.

Special open net backing, bonded to open crochet-type fabric, preserves the see-through quality while giving the fabric stability for construction. The open net back is an almost invisible element in the total bonded fabric.

Suiting or coating of rope tweed in thick-and-thin open construction can be backed with sheeting, offering a fabric with body and stability and obviating pressing.

Wool blended fabric, bonded to a non-woven backing which is washable or dry-cleanable and non-shrinking, provides ideal bulking and draping for a coating fabric, without affecting the surface texture.

Wool-back interlining, bonded to lightweight wool/synthetic open-weave fabric, provides an unusual fabric for suits or coats with body, stability and insulation, and results in production economies by eliminating the need for double cutting and sewing operations. Unbonded, the face fabric is not stable enough to be used as a coating or suiting.

Bonding fiberfill batting directly to a face fabric, either sheer or opaque, has functional and economic advantages. It is less costly than quilting and eliminates shifting problems during dry cleaning and washing. This type of bonding, through special adhesives and application technology, results in a wide range of uses for apparel and home furnishings.

Special bonding adhesives are available for bonding open-faced fabrics to metallic film, often with spectacular glitter-fabric effects. The metallic film is given a new dimension through bonding, making the fabric adaptable to many fashion and decorative uses in the home and industry.

Left: Urethane foam used in bonding and laminating. Right: Foam being cut for bonding.

# Foam for Bonding and Laminating

## Definition

The term refers to a family of polymers with a broad range of properties and uses, all based on the reaction products of an organic isocyanate with compounds containing a hydroxyl group.

Urethane foams used for bonding and laminating fabrics have assumed a place of importance in textile technology equal to such other milestones as permanent press.

Urethane foams (the term has gradually replaced the term polyurethane foams with which it is interchangeable) refer to a chemical family of highly complex, cross-linked polymers. These foams may be flexible or rigid. The polymeric structure of foam is formed by the reaction of isocyanate and polyol compounds. The isocyanate reacts with water, if present, to form carbon dioxide bubbles within the polymer structure, which expand the structure to the desired density.

Aside from their physical distinctions, urethane foams are generally further divided into polyether and polyester foams. In the textile industry, polyester urethane foams are used almost exclusively for both bonding and laminating.

## Uses of Foam

The flexible urethane foam used today was first produced commercially in the U.S. in the mid-1950's, but its versatility, scope and utility were not fully realized until ten years later. By the middle 1960's it found important uses in a diversity of industries and in a wide variety of applications, which include the following:

THE GARMENT INDUSTRY. Urethane foam created a whole array of new fabrics for the designer to work with, and opened up a number of new end-use possibilities for warp, circular and raschel knits, as well as woven goods. Foam is supplied to the apparel industry in a wide range of widths, thicknesses and colors, in the form of continuous roll yardgoods. By selecting the right thickness of foam—which can be peeled as thin as .024 inch (or possibly less) or as thick as .50 inch—different effects are created with the same cloths. As a labor-saving concept, foam-bonded technology permits cutting face and lining fabrics in a single operation.

FURNITURE AND INDUSTRIAL USES. Foam is used in seating and cushioning of furniture; in padding and cushioning for automobiles and aircraft; in bed mattresses, pads and pillows; in rug underlays for carpets; in packaging for the shipment of fragile products.

Other miscellaneous uses for foam include shoe innersoles, tablecloth backing, hair curlers, ironing board pads, sponges, cosmetic applicators, dish mops, clothes brushes, filters, laminations with plastic film and sheeting, and numerous other industrial and consumer products.

389

## Bonding versus Laminating

The basic difference between the two applications—foam-bonding and foam-laminating—can be summarized as follows (see also section on Fabric-to-Fabric Bonding).

Foam-bonded fabrics are two-faced or fabric-to-fabric materials, with the under, or lining, fabric usually an acetate or nylon tricot. The outer fabric may be woven or knitted, and may even be quite loosely constructed because of the stability provided by the tricot lining. The two fabrics are held together with a very thin layer of urethane foam, which serves as the bonding agent. Often the layer of foam disappears almost entirely in processing.

Foam-laminated fabrics generally consist of an outer fabric, either knitted or woven, and a backing of urethane foam. When a sandwich construction is used, involving two fabrics laminated to an in-between layer of urethane foam, the foam is thicker than that used for a bonded fabric since it is intended for insulation and light-weight bulk rather than for adhesion.

## Facts About Urethane Foam

Comes in many colors.

Is odorless and hypo-allergenic.

Washes and dries quickly and is colorfast.

Remains unharmed by dry-cleaning solvents or pressing (if the fabric to which it is bonded has this characteristic).

Is dimensionally stable and "gives" with stretch fabrics, returning to its original shape.

Provides warmth without weight, and insulation against cold.

Gives body and shape to light or loosely constructed fabrics.

Does not sag or thin out with wear, nor mat down or become lumpy.

Has drapability and is extremely wrinkle resistant.

Has good tensile strength and handles very much like fabric for cutting, sewing and stitching.

Is resistent to abrasive action because of inherent tear strength and elongation.

Does not mildew and is unaffected by shelf-aging.

Remains pliable in extremes of climate. From 22° to 270°, foam changes very little.

---

**ADHESIVE:** Chemical "glue" used to bond two fabrics together. Adhesives are usually of the water based acrylic type or solvent based urethane type.

**BACKING FABRIC:** The fabric—usually acetate tricote—that is bonded or laminated to the reverse side of a face fabric.

**BONDED FABRIC:** A fabric structure formed by combining an outer, face fabric with a backing fabric using an adhesive or thin foam system.

---

**BONDING:** Generally refers to fabric-to-fabric bonding, as distinct from fabric-to-foam bonding. (See "Lamination.") There are two basic types of fabric-to-fabric bonding: (1) "Wet Adhesive" and (2) "Foam Flame." These are named for the two types of adhesive used in the processes.

**BURN OFF:** The difference between starting and finishing thicknesses of foam after flame lamination.

**COMPATIBLE SHRINKAGE:** In bonding, this refers to the need for face fabric and liner to have the same or closely similar shrinkage ratios so that there will be no puckering in the bond.

**CURING:** High temperature treatment that is used to "set" the adhesive used in bonding. Curing is essential for permanent bonding of fabrics.

**DELAMINATION:** The undesirable separation of the components of bonded or laminated fabrics.

**DENIER:** A unit which measures the fineness of yarns in terms of weight. (A denier was an old French coin.) One denier equals .05 grams which is the equivalent of 492.2 yards. In one pound of No. 1 denier yarn there are 4,464,528 yards. The more denier the thicker the yarn and the less yardage to the pound. Thus, a 55 denier acetate yarn runs about 81,173 yards to the pound; a 40 denier nylon about 111,613 yards.

# Terms Used in Bonding

**DOUBLE KNIT:** A fabric knitted with a double stitch on a double needle machine so that it has double thickness and is the same on both sides. It has excellent body and stability.

**EDGE ROLL:** The characteristic roll which develops at the edges of a single knit fabric making it somewhat difficult to handle since it does not lie completely flat.

**FACE FABRIC:** The side of a bonded fabric which is used as the face of a finished garment or other textile product.

**FLAME LAMINATION:** Process used in laminating which is based on melting the surfaces of a thin sheet of urethane foam with an open flame. The face and backing fabrics are applied to the foam while the surfaces are still molten, and subsequent cooling causes them to adhere together.

**FOAMBACK:** The British name for a fabric which has been laminated to a backing of polyurethane foam.

**FOAM FLAME BONDING:** One of the two basic processes used in fabric-to-fabric bonding. The foam takes the place of an adhesive and is made tacky by heating with a gas flame. In the process the thickness of the foam is burned off from 40/1000 to about 15/1000 of an inch. This method is often used to build up face fabrics.

**GREEN TACK:** The preliminary bond created by the first stage of curing in the wet adhesive process. The bond is not yet fully cured and is "green" or unripe.

**LAMINATION:** Fusing fabric structure by combining an outer, face fabric, a thin layer of foam, and a backing fabric. The flame lamination process is most frequently used.

**LINER:** The side of a bonded fabric which is used on the inside of a finished garment as the lining. Usually a 55

denier acetate or a 40 denier nylon tricot.

**PEEL BOND STRENGTH:** This is a term for the force required to peel apart two layers of a bonded fabric. It is expressed in ounces of pull per one-inch width of bonded fabric. This is a test for quality and durability of the bond and is made on the fabric in both its wet and dry states.

**POLYESTER FOAM:** Urethane foam produced from polyester resin, primarily used in apparel bonding.

**POLYETHER FOAM:** Urethane foam produced from polyether resins, primarily used in furniture, bedding, automotive and other non-apparel fields.

**POLYURETHANE:** (See "Urethane.")

**PUCKER:** An uneven surface caused by differential shrinkage in the two layers of a bonded fabric during processing or washing and dry cleaning.

**REVERSIBLE BONDED FABRIC:** This means that two face fabrics have been bonded together so that the two sides can be used interchangeably. There are some limitations in this area. For example, it is not advisable to bond too stiff fabrics such as nylon taffeta. The stiffness would be increased by bonding. Similarly with hard-faced worsteds.

**SANDWICH LAMINATE:** A composite fabric in which a layer of polyurethane foam has been laminated between two fabrics—one a face cloth and the other a lining. Used for heavy outerwear.

**SINGLE KNIT:** As distinct from a double knit, the single knit fabric is knitted on a single needle machine. It has less body and less stability than a double knit.

**SKIN-SIDE COMFORT:** This describes one of the advantages of bonding. The lining side of the bonded fabric can be made comfortable and pleasant

next to the skin, regardless of how rough or scratchy the face fabric may be.

**STABILITY:** The property of a bonded fabric which prevents it from sagging, stretching or slipping. This makes the fabric easier to handle in manufacturing and helps it keep its shape in wear, as well as through washing and dry cleaning.

**STRETCH & RECOVERY:** Another property of a knit fabric when bonded to tricot. It develops the ability to return quickly to its original position after stretching.

**STRIKETHROUGH:** Something to be avoided in fabric-to-fabric bonding. The adhesive must not strike through the fabric.

**THERMOPLASTIC:** The ability of a fiber to become plastic under heat and thus be set in a predetermined shape.

**TREE BARK:** A rippled effect which resembles the texture of tree bark and which sometimes appears on a bonded fabric only when it is stretched in the width. It is caused by the bias tensions which result when two "skewed" or distorted fabrics are bonded.

**TRICOT:** From the French verb *tricoter* which means *to knit*. Tricot fabrics are warp knit and are characterized by columns of predominant vertical loops.

**URETHANE:** A chemical family of cross-linked polymers subject to reactions which cause foaming. The foams are used for bonding and laminating fabrics. The term has gradually replaced the term *polyurethane*.

**WET ADHESIVE BONDING:** One of the two basic processes used in fabric-to-fabric bonding. The adhesive now most widely used is a water-based acrylic compound. After application to the fabric it is cured by the use of heat. It creates a permanent bond without reducing the drape of the face fabric or affecting the softness of its hand.

**YIELD:** The number of yards of tricot or other fabric which can be made (yielded) from a pound of yarn.

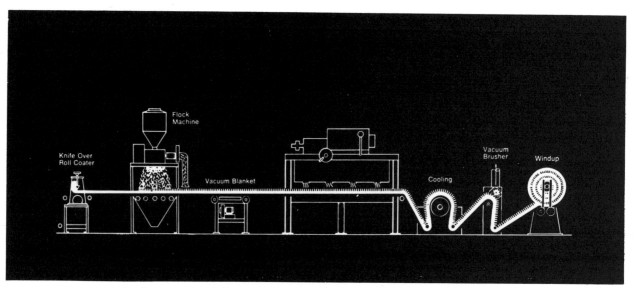

A schematic of a flocking range. Flocking is applied to a wide range of uses.

# Flocking

This technique produces design areas on any type of fabric to resemble embroidery or woven clipped figures. Applicable fabrics include even plush and carpet types. Fibers are chopped up into small lengths referred to as flocks, or flock dots. A permanent adhesive is then printed on the fabric in the desired pattern and the flocks adhere to the cloth when applied, by a blowing or spray technique.

A mechanical flocking machine.

## Electrostatic Flocking

This technique is important for fast and efficient production. It is also extremely flexible so that it can turn out a large variety of fabrics with little adjustment. Present machines permit the production of at least forty linear yards of fabric per minute. Technically, production can be geared to even faster rates, if necessary.

Though electrostatic flocking is not a new process, newly developed equipment, plus the capabilities of the man-made fibers, have amounted to a scientific breakthrough in the field of flocking.

Electrostatic flocking starts with a special coating of adhesive applied to a base material. Fibers measuring from 1.5 to 6 millimeters are specially treated to make them responsive to electrostatic activation, which makes them stand on end. Thus, the adhesive base fastens these fibers in an upright position. Nearly any synthetic fiber lends itself to the process. Among the fabrics developed are velvet-like, suede-like and plush-like texture which are both attractive and durable. Generally, manufacturers have worked with pre-dyed fibers.

The process has been applied in a wide range of uses, including: shoes, outerwear, fashion accessories such as handbags, millinery and belts; upholstery and draperies; plush toys; pool and game table covers; wall coverings; simulated fur fabrics; outdoor surface coverings for putting greens, swimming pool areas, tennis courts and playgrounds.

# Vinyl (Coated) Fabrics

A vinyl seat cover on a Lincoln Continental Mark III.

## Definition

A chemical substance designated as polyvinyl chloride (PVC), long used in the form of fiber in Europe where one of its well known trademarks is the French "Rhovyl."

After World War II vinyl sheeting began to be exploited as a substitute for leather, but in its first applications it was not found practical without a fabric backing since it lacked seam strength. It was only in the late 1950's that the vinyl coating was combined with a knit backing fabric and began to be widely used for upholstery and auto interiors.

Vinyl became attractive to the apparel industry a few years later when technological advances resulted in what became known as "expanded vinyl," a term which describes the upward expansion of the vinyl substance, similar to that of bread rising. This brought about a lightweight and flexible substance with soft, pliable hand. Its aesthetic qualities were recognized as providing an excellent replacement for leather and suede and often it was hard to distinguish the material from leather itself.

## A Big Vinyl Vogue

It was in the 1960's, however, that vinyl became an important fashion "fabric" with the introduction by Comark Plastics, a division of Cohn-Hall-Marx Co., of "patent leather" vinyl. It was a new, glossy, colorful, vinyl-coated fabric which sparked an ever-rising vogue in almost every category of apparel for women and children, and even men's wear, and for boots, shoes, bags, hats and jewelry. These new vinyls in solids and prints found a place as well in the decorative field—for wall coverings, pillows, bedspreads and curtains.

## Other Types and Varieties

In addition to the "patent" variety in bright colors and dramatic prints, other types were quickly developed, like satin vinyl in fluorescent colors; flocked vinyl with suede-like hand; gold and silver vinyl with kid finish; clear, transparent vinyl; embossed vinyl, and phosphorescent vinyl which glows in the dark. Other producers, like U.S. Rubber, Goodall and General Tire also produced their own special varieties of vinyl coated products. Du Pont's "Corfam" is still another type (not a vinyl) which uses a breathable poromeric plastic over a nonwoven substrate.

Though all PVC coated fabrics may be considered to represent the same essential concept as that long used in the production of oilcloth, linoleum and other coated fabrics, there is a vast difference between these new vinyl fabrics and their earlier counterparts due to the chemical character of the substances used and the sophistication of the production techniques. The vinyls and coated fabrics of today are no longer substitutes for other fabrics and leathers. They have established for themselves a fashion category of their own and are recognized as essentially new textile structures with important end uses in apparel and home furnishings.

*Finishing is a comprehensive term covering those processes which follow the actual construction of a fabric and are designed to give it special characteristics in accordance with the end-use to which it will be put.*

# TEXTILE FINISHING PROCESSES

- Preliminary Treatments

- Modern Finishing

- The Basic Finishing Process

- Texturizing Finishes

- Functional Finishes

- Permanent Press

- Soil Release

- Color and the Human Being

- Color and How It Works

- Color and Color Dyes

- Dyes and Dyeing Processes

- Basic Methods of Dyeing

- Differential Dyeing

- The Printing of Textiles

- Roller Printing

- Screen Printing

- Rotary Screen Printing

- Sublistatic Printing

Fabric passes through the bath in a dye jig until color sample is perfectly matched.

# The Finishing Processes

*Considered unnecessary in primitive societies, today finishing is one of the most refined arts of the textile industry. Moreover it has at its disposal the resources of basic scientific research, and of the great chemical and dye industries. These it uses to achieve fabrics adapted to their end use.*

When cloth comes off the loom it is known as *grey goods* or *greige goods*. In this loom state it is rough, full of blemishes and impurities which come either from the nature of the fibers used or were picked up in the manufacturing process. The finishing process converts such grey goods into finished cloth ready for use, and the company which undertakes this conversion is known as a converter.

There are many stages and processes involved in finishing a piece of cloth. Dyeing and printing are only two such processes, though they are very important ones. Preceding dyeing or printing, and following after them, are a host of techniques which convert the fairly inert, limp, and lifeless grey goods into the full and lustrous product known to the consumer.

With knitted fabrics, preparation for dyeing and finishing is much simpler since sizing materials are not used in yarns to be knitted. This is one of many advantages in favor of knits.

Dyeing, printing and modern finishes will be discussed in that order under separate headings in the sections which follow.

## Preliminary Treatments

Before a cloth can be either dyed, printed, or conditioned with special finishes it must go through a series of preliminary treatments. Such treatments are approximately the same for all fabrics, regardless of the fibers involved, though methods vary and fabrics of man-made fibers require less treatment. The preliminary treatments involve:

1. Inspecting and cleaning the fabric by various methods to remove lint and impurities.

2. Bleaching the fabric white.

3. Stretching (tentering) the cloth into proper width and drying it. When fabrics go into a finishing plant they are purposely wider and longer than the final finished goods because it is expected that a certain amount of shrinkage will take place. The amount can vary with the type of fiber involved and the construction of the cloth.

The following is a listing of the various types of preliminary treatment used for different fabrics.

FOR COTTON: Singeing, desizing, bleaching, tentering, drying.

FOR LINEN: Similar to cotton but no mercerizing.

FOR WOOL: Perching, burling, specking, mending, sewing, crabbing, scouring, bleaching, sometimes fulling, carbonizing, and pressing.

FOR SILK: Boiling off, bleaching, drying.

FOR CELLULOSICS: Singeing, scouring, sometimes embossing for textured effects, in acetate.

FOR OTHER MAN-MADES: Heat-setting the fibers.

FOR BLENDS: In blends of natural and synthetic fibers the preparation of fabrics and yarns is usually carried out according to the requirements of the natural fiber content present. Special attention must be given to the synthetic portion, however, to be sure that it is not degraded or otherwise affected. The reason many of these preliminary treatments are necessary is to make sure that the dyeing, printing and/or finishing are acceptable, predictable and reproducible. The impurities present—either natural or man-introduced—must be removed and the material rendered absorbent and receptive in a uniform way.

(*Above*) Application of a special finish in liquid form to a length of fabric. (*Below*)　Calendering.

# Modern Finishing

*The transition from grey goods to the finished goods employs a miracle of modern technology and chemistry.*

In some areas of the world people use the raw woven or knitted cloth just as it comes off the loom or the knitting machine. Its sole purpose is to fill a functional need, or there may exist no facilities for finishing. In either case the fabric in the grey stage is used and accepted as being satisfactory. But in most populated areas, even including so-called primitive places, fabric goes through one or more finishing steps before it is used for apparel or in the home.

For example, even today in some countries, after fabric is woven it is frequently washed in a running stream to remove certain surface impurities. Modern machinery achieves the same results in a large mill operation, and also permits controls and the use of other finishing processes at the same time. Were it not for the development of these processes, and of highly specialized finishing equipment, the world of textiles would not approach its present size or radiate so much excitement. By the same token, the task of the apparel designer would be much more difficult if he were limited to cloth in the raw state.

Furthermore, the force of obsolescence now generated by the newer finishing processes undoubtedly has a strong effect on the sale of textiles for every purpose from personal to industrial uses. Some of these facets are explained in this chapter, illuminating the important contribution which is made by modern finishing processes.

To finish a piece of cloth involves subjecting it to many treatments which will give it special appeal. As already noted, when cloth comes off the loom as grey goods it may have many imperfections. In many cases the layman would not recognize it as the fabric it will become after finishing. Truly, "fabrics are made in the finishing."

Today there are very few fabrics which are *not* given some special treatment before they are put on sale. It has been estimated that at least 500 trademarked and branded finishes are now on the market and new ones appear every day. Some finishes resist abrasion; others reduce static and are antiseptic; there are finishes for color-fastness, crease resistance, and crease retention; for crispness of hand and dryness; for flame resistance and against fading; for fastness to light, for luster and for the elimination of lint; finishes which protect fabrics against moths, mildew, rot, perspiration, shrinkage and stains; finishes to control stretching and sagging; finishes for washfastness, wash-wear and water-repellency; finishes which insulate fabric and many others which are variations on similar themes. Most important are the new treatments for Permanent Press and Soil Release.

For purposes of clarification this host of finishes can be broken down into three basic categories:

1. BASIC FINISHES which are traditional in the processing of fabrics.
2. TEXTURIZING FINISHES which change the texture of the cloth.
3. FUNCTIONAL FINISHES which extend the function of the cloth, usually by chemical treatment.

Piece dyeing, checking uniformity of shade.

Boiling off to remove natural gums.

Tentering to ensure regular width.

# The Basic Finishing Processes

## Boiling

Cotton, linen and silk are all boiled to remove the natural gums as one of the first steps in finishing. In the case of cotton the process is continuous with desizing, mercerizing, scouring, bleaching, drying.

## Bleaching

A great many fabrics are bleached to a pure white before dyeing or printing. Before the advent of modern chemical bleaching, this was usually done by spreading the cloth on the ground and letting the sun do the work. Today it is done mechanically with such chemicals as chlorine or peroxide, the latter being "more" generally used for almost all fibers. Bleaching is necessary since most fabrics are never pure white in their grey-goods state. In addition, bleaching increases the ability of the fabric to absorb dyestuffs uniformly. It also dissolves warp sizing on the yarns, natural pectins and waxes, and small particles of foreign matter. In the continuous bleaching process used for cotton, automatic machines pass the fabric through the solution at the rate of 200 yards a minute.

## Tentering

Because of the rough treatment cloth is subjected to in many finishing processes, it is pulled out of shape and becomes irregular in width. To straighten and restore it to its proper dimensions it is processed through a tentering machine. This is a long frame along each side of which is a continuous chain equipped with tenter clips which grasp the cloth at the selvages, stretch it to shape and carry it over gas flames or through hot-air drying chambers. Since the cloth usually enters the machine moist and is dried under tension, the heat sets the weave to its proper width. The process can be used with all types of woven fabrics.

## Shearing

Shearing or cropping accomplishes the same purpose as singeing, but with more control. It reduces the nap on a cloth to a predetermined height. The shearing machine operates on the principle of the lawn mower and with the same effect. It may have from one to six blades which can be adjusted to the 32nd part of an inch. Shearing is now less widely used except in a few high quality fabrics and for surface design on terry, velour and velveteen.

## Singeing

This is literally a process of singeing the cloth by passing it over gas jets or white-hot metal plates to burn off the fuzz of protruding fibers and give the fabric a smooth hand. In finishing cotton cloth, this is usually the first process, and is a preparation for further treatment, since the fuzzy nap might otherwise interfere with the even distribution of dye. Immediately after it is singed, the cloth is immersed in water to prevent it from catching fire. The water bath contains an enzyme which, while the wet cloth is piled in bins, converts into soluble sugars all the insoluble starchy material present so they can be removed by the wet treatments which follow.

## Sizing

Sizing means filling the cloth with sizing compounds to give it strength and weight. Many cottons and some rayons are starched in varying degrees to give them a basic finish, often as a preparation for further processing. The cloth is either passed through a size bath or through rollers which resemble the mangle on a washing machine. Sizing compounds contain such substances as starch, glue, tallow and synthetic compounds such as polyvinyl alcohol and other film formers. Starches are not permanent and can be washed out.

## Calendering

The calender is one of the most important of the finishing machines. It is basically an ironing machine on a factory level and consists of a series of heavy heated steel rollers through which the cloth passes at a pressure of up to 2000 pounds per square inch. There may be from two to seven rollers on the calender frame, depending on what type of finish is required, and as the cloth passes between them it is given a smooth and even luster.

Different types of calender rolls produce different effects on the cloth:

EMBOSSED effects are achieved by engraving a design on one steel roller and using hard, fiber-covered rollers in the rest of the machine.

MOIRÉ or watermarking effects are achieved in a similar way.

SCHREINER calendering creates a series of extremely fine ridges on the cloth by the use of a roller on which very fine lines have been engraved.

Singeing to remove protruding fibers.

Since such fine lines reflect light the cloth achieves a subdued luster, a mechanical simulation of mercerizing.

PALMER calendering is usually applied to such fabrics as satins, taffetas, and twills to give them a mellow hand. Steam heated rollers are covered with papermaker's felt, which gives the cloth a smooth, appealing finish.

FRICTION calenders produce a glazed finish. Cloth-covered and steel rollers are combined; the steel

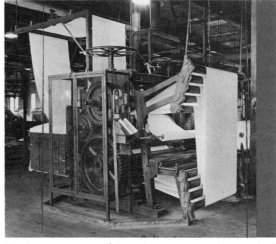

Chasing treatment which gives cotton a deep-grained luster without flattening threads.

rollers move at a faster rate of speed than the cloth-covered ones, and thus create a friction pull which provides the glaze. Early chintz was produced by this method but the finish was not permanent and has been replaced by the durable resin finish.

## Beetling

The beetling process achieves effects similar to calendering and was formerly used for linens and cottons. Instead of passing between rollers, the cloth is beaten by steel or wooden hammers, or fallers, which flatten it and fill the spaces between warp and filling. The result is a thready finish with high sheen.

## Shrinkage Control

Today cotton, linen, rayon, and wool are all pre-shrunk at the mill level by a variety of finishing processes.

PRE-SHRUNK COTTON does not shrink naturally. It is modern high-speed production which makes cotton shrink. If it were spun, woven, and otherwise processed entirely by hand there would be very

little, if any, shrinkage. The whole process of manufacture, from initial ginning to final calendering, subjects the fibers to constant stretching. Shrinkage control is therefore basically a method of taking out the stretch. It is really stretch control.

This is accomplished by what is known as compressive shrinking. The process consists of washing a sample piece, measuring the shrinkage, and then mechanically compressing the fabric back to the dimensions it would have had if it had not been stretched during manufacture. This is done by bringing the damp cloth into firm contact with a thick endless blanket which is stretched over a roller. When the blanket contracts, the cloth contracts with it and is later set by heat.

PRE-SHRUNK RAYON. Rayons are generally pre-shrunk today by a process involving impregnation of the fibers with chemicals. The process is similar to mercerization, since a solution of caustic soda is used to swell the fibers permanently and fix the yarns in the weave formation.

Chemical methods are also employed on cotton knit fabrics. Thermosetting resins are used to obtain dimensional stability.

Sanforized machines, which finish cotton fabrics by the compressive shrinking process so that they have a residual shrinkage of less than one percent, are used in more than forty-two countries throughout the world.

Adjusting compressive shrinking machine.

Checking shrinkage on a sample of cloth.

PRE-SHRUNK WOOL. Wool (like cotton, linen, and rayon) is stretched in the manufacturing process. When all these fibers are washed, they relax and produce shrinkage. Quite apart from this, the nature of the wool fiber, with its structure of overlapping scales and its native resiliency, has an additional tendency to shrink. Since wool fibers naturally felt, this also causes shrinkage. The problem of controlling shrinkage in wool is therefore more complicated than in any other fiber.

Today, a number of different processes are available for controlling wool shrinkage, each based on widely varying theories and procedures. One method, the wet-chlorination process, changes the surface of the fibers, alters their frictional properties, and so prevents them from migrating and felting. Other processes call for the use of some kind of additive, generally a resin or rubber derivative. This involves impregnating or coating the fiber and has been described as resembling spot welding. There are also mechanical methods, such as the compacting machine, and the cold-water method of London shrinking.

One of the newer chemical processes controls shrink-age by applying a skin of polymer to the wool fiber.

STABILIZING WARP KNITS. While this cannot be considered a shrinking process as such, it is a method for controlling the shrinkage of warp knit fabrics like tricot, especially nylon tricot. It uses dry heat up to 400 degrees to lock the dimensions of the knit permanently into place. The method is also used on such fabrics as net and tulle. Synthetic resins have also been used to control the dimensional stability of warp knit fabrics.

## Decating

Decating is a finishing process which uses steam to improve the appearance and luster of a cloth so that it will not be destroyed in succeeding operations. It takes two forms—dry decating and wet decating. The dry process may be used on either wool, cotton, rayon, or silk. The wet process is usually applied only to wool. In the dry process the cloth is wound on a perforated drum equipped with a steaming and vacuum system. In the wet process the cloth is wound on a roller and treated in a hot water or steam boiler which also has a vacuum system. Decating is not much used today.

403

## Mercerizing

The process of mercerizing cotton is named after John Mercer, a great English scientist and chemist, who did much to advance the finishing of cotton fabrics. It was Mercer whose observations in 1844 first suggested the use of caustic soda for obtaining cottons of improved strength and dyeing properties. The discovery of permanent luster did not come until more than fifty years later. It was not until 1889 that H. Lowe developed and patented the technique of producing a permanent luster as the result of treating cotton yarns and fabrics under tension with caustic soda.

THE MICROSCOPE SHOWS that mercerizing makes changes in cotton fibers. Before mercerizing, the individual cotton fiber looks somewhat crinkly, like a deflated length of hose, sunk in the center. When subjected to tension and treated with caustic soda, the individual cotton fiber loses a good deal of its natural twist and becomes round, more like an inflated hose. In its final full mercerized form, the individual cotton fiber looks very much like the silk fiber, and this is generally assumed to be the explanation of the unique luster imparted by the mercerization process.

There are two entirely different kinds of mercerization. The first is not a finishing process at all, but has to do with mercerizing in the yarn. The famous nationally advertised sewing threads, as well as Durene yarns, owe their characteristic luster to mercerization.

MERCERIZING IN THE PIECE is something else again. It is necessary to improve and make uniform the acceptance of dyes in both dyeing and printing. Mercerization reduces differences between the various kinds of cotton used as the raw material for making cloth. It also alters immature or "dead" fiber which, unless this treatment is carried out, takes dyes in a drastically different way. Mercerization makes colors deeper and brighter and saves on dye cost.

It should be pointed out here that if lustrous finishes are needed they can also be readily obtained through resin finishing followed by an appropriate calendaring treatment similar to Bancroft's "Everglaze" process and other, more recent ones.

## Special Wool Finishes

In addition to the range of finishes which may be applied to many fibers, wool cloth is subjected to certain special treatments. The main ones are:

PERCHING. The cloth is carefully examined for defects and blemishes by running it over a perch. This is simply a roller set horizontally into two uprights. Imperfections are marked and remedied in later operations.

BURLING. Loose threads and knots are removed with tweezers called burling irons.

SPECKING. Loose specks, burrs, and motes are also removed by the same method.

MENDING. Some of the defects are actually mended or darned by hand.

SEWING. More serious defects such as missing threads are sewn in or woven by experienced operators.

CRABBING. This process sets the weave and the yarn twist permanently by immersing the cloth in alter-

Burling and mending woolen fabrics, which are passed over lighted glass panels to facilitate inspection.

Carbonizing the cloth by passing through bath of dilute sulphuric acid to dissolve small impurities.

nate baths of hot and cold water while it is held under tension.

FULLING. The fabric is pounded and twisted in warm, soapy water to make the fibers interlock more closely. This is also known as milling or felting, and is performed in the fulling mill. Cold water is used in the rinse process which follows immediately after.

CARBONIZING. Impurities like dried grass, burrs, and straw are carbonized out of the wool by immersing it in a dilute solution of sulfuric acid followed by drying and baking. This reduces the vegetable matter to carbon, which can be dusted out of the cloth.

SCOURING. This is simply washing the wool fabric to remove yolk, suint, dirt, and any other impurities. It may be done with soaps and alkalies, or with chemical solvents.

PRESSING. As a final step in processing, wool cloth is pressed by passing it through hot calender rolls.

# Texturizing Finishes

The processes used for changing the texture of a cloth after it leaves the loom may be divided into two classes:

1. Texture treatments which are traditional and have been applied for many years by such methods as brushing, puckering and calendering.

2. Textures based on the use of synthetic resins.

## Traditional Textures

PLISSE. Cotton plissé is a classic fabric which simulates the effect of woven seersucker cloth. It converts a flat fabric into one with a crinkled surface. This is done by printing the cloth with highly concentrated caustic soda by means of a roller. The caustic soda causes the printed parts of the cloth to shrink. Since the unprinted parts do not shrink they are forced to crinkle.

NAPPING. This is also a classic process referred to by various names such as brushing, gigging, raising, teaseling, sueding. The napping operation involves running the cloth through a series of rollers which are covered either with wire brushes or teasels, which are plant burrs or thistles. This brushing operation raises the fibers so that they form a nap on the surface of the cloth. It affects the filling yarns more than the warp yarns which are more tightly twisted. Cotton flannel and brushed rayon are made in this way. So is sueded fabric, except that the brushes are set in a different manner. Napping may also be applied to both sides of a fabric.

CORDUROY is cut after coming from the loom since the fabric, as woven, has long filling floats but is without pile. To achieve the parallel piles the floats are cut and the resulting pile is repeatedly brushed and then treated with waxes and oils to set the corduroy luster.

## Synthetic Resin Textures

The development of synthetic resins for finishing

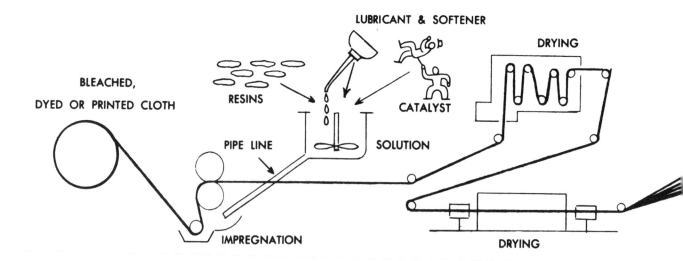

Chart illustrating resin application and embossing processes for production of textured effects.

was launched by the Everglaze process for making a durable chintz, introduced by Joseph Bancroft and Sons in 1938. Since that time the Everglaze process, and many other trademarked processes, have introduced such a host of synthetic resin finishes that the effect has been described as the "resin revolution" in textiles. Some of these finishes will be discussed under the head of functional finishes in the succeeding section. Here, we are concerned with those resin finishes which change the texture of the cloth and make this change durable.

## How the Resin Finish Is Applied

Resins are applied to the cloth from a water solution. This solution also contains a catalyst, a chemical which stimualtes the resin chemical to polymerize as described later. This solution can also contain softeners, lubricants and other materials which impart desirable physical properties to the fabric.

This is done by means of rollers, or, more properly, calenders as were the pre-resin finishes. The surface of the calender determines the final surface of the cloth. Smooth calenders are used for polishing glossy fabrics. Schreiner calenders, with barely visible fine lines (some 200 to the inch), impart a subdued luster and a soft, natural hand. Elaborately embossed textures require *male* and *female* calenders with the hills of one fitting into the valleys of the other, and vice versa.

With calendering, the new texture has been applied, but it is not durable. It would wear and wash out in no time. Durability is achieved by curing with heat and a catalyst, resulting in a reaction called polymerization, which makes the texture durable for the duration of the fabric. The resins which have been impregnated into the fiber are locked so that they cannot separate from the fiber again. In other words, the actual physical structure of the fabric is changed by a chemical reaction of the resins themselves and possible further reaction between the resins and the fibers. The individual molecules, through polymerization, are linked into chains and cross chains. In this girder-like network they are durably locked, or bonded.

## Types of Resin Textures

The number of textural effects made possible by the synthetic resin treatment is almost limitless. Cotton can be made to look like satin, linen, leather, or wallpaper. Plain constructions can be transformed into replicas of piqué, seersucker, heavy cord, thick-and-thin effects, crepes, moirés. Intricately sculptured patterns can be produced on velvets, corduroys, jerseys, and tricots of both natural and man-made fibers. Durable embossed effects of all types can be achieved and color can be added to the resin to achieve tonal nuances in the embossed areas. In addition the resin treatment adds dimensional stabilization, crispness, and resistance to wrinkles and stains.

## Do the Resin Finishes Affect the Fiber?

Yes. Sometimes beneficially, sometimes adversely. To understand why, it is first necessary to start with the woven goods. The ideal construction of any fabric, from the point of wear and service, would be a

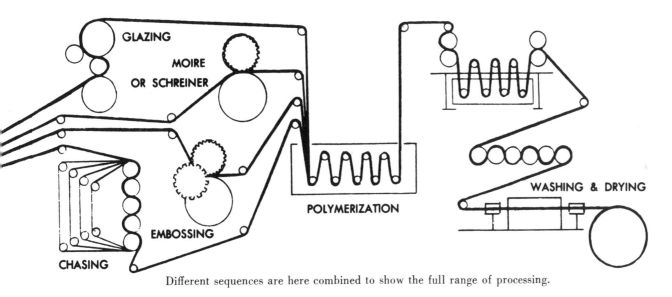

GLAZING

MOIRE
OR SCHREINER

POLYMERIZATION

EMBOSSING

CHASING

WASHING & DRYING

Different sequences are here combined to show the full range of processing.

perfect square. A cloth woven with 80 threads vertically and 80 horizontally (known as an 80-square) will deliver greater durability than, for example, a broadcloth weave with a 128 x 60 construction. The amount of strain in different directions results in a lessening of tensile strength where less threads are woven. This is assuming, of course, that the threads running both ways have the identical thickness and strength.

Insofar as the resin finish affects the fiber itself, this depends on (a) the quality of the grey goods (b) the quality of the finishing chemicals and (c) the care and technique devoted to the application to the fabric. Degradation of the fiber or fabric, often accompanied by yellowing, comes from chlorine retention of the resin selected; at other times some yellowing results from the retention of iron, fatty acids, and soap.

All resins known today weaken the fiber strength to a certain degree; the extent again depends upon the selection of the resin and the technique of its application.

### How Resin Is Used . . . What It Does

Resin is an adhesive synthetic substance. When properly applied and cured, resin should be as insoluble on the fiber as possible, or it may wash out.

When applied to a piece of cloth the resin, after oven curing, adheres not only to the actual fibers but also remains between them; thus, whereas the untreated fabric would have tiny holes or pores, the resin-treated cloth is a tighter-knit product. The main purpose of a resin finish is to so coat a hydro-

philic fiber (or even some of the chemical fibers which are classed as hydrophobic) that moisture will skid off the surface rather than be soaked up; with less moisture adhering to the fabric surface, obviously the garment will dry faster.

The danger comes when either a low-grade resin compound is applied, or when poor technique is used in the finishing process. If either of these conditions prevails, then the finish on the fabric will wash out very soon. But another danger exists: even a good finish tends to stiffen the fibers so that they are subject to fraying and abrasion more extensively than the natural soft fiber. Resin sometimes brittle-izes the fiber, just as the use of too much starch will harshen and stiffen a shirt collar, for instance; so, when the collar is folded over and over, the individual fibers will crack.

## Functional Finishes

The functional finishes represent a large group of chemical treatments which extend the function of a fabric by making it resist creasing, water, stains, rot, mildew, moths, bacteria, etc. Such finishes are generally applied to the older natural fibers like cotton in an effort to give them competitive stature with the newer, man-made fibers by fortifying them against the faults inherent in their nature. Dimensional stabilization (shrink control) is technically a functional finish though it has been discussed under the basic finishes. The so-called wash-wear finish, which makes it possible to drip-dry cotton garments and wear them with little or no ironing, is a functional finish.

Most such treatments are relatively recent. New processes are constantly being developed and no analysis can hope to be complete. What follows is a brief rundown of earlier functional finishes, followed by detailed discussions of more recent finishing developments in Permanent Press, Soil Release, Bonding and Flocking.

## Crease-Resistant Finishes

Most crease-resistant finishes are achieved by treating the fabric with synthetic resins. In the great majority of cases such finishes do not so much *resist* creasing as they facilitate *recovery* from creases and wrinkles.

Chemically, the molecules of the impregnating resin are cross-linked with the molecules of the fiber in a permanent way. Such cross links act like the spring on a screen door: they pull back when the stress is removed. Hence, wrinkle recovery. Conversely, just as the spring makes it harder to open the screen door, so the cross links resist distortion and make it harder for the wrinkles to lodge in the first place.

## Water-Repellent Finishes

Water-repellent finishes have been developed as a result of the dissatisfaction with the comfort and draping properties of the old water-proofed fabrics which were treated with linseed oil and later with rubber and still later with synthetic resins.

The breathability of a fabric which is water repellent is a much needed property in order to make a garment so treated tolerable to wear for any length of time.

Early treatments consisted of impregnating the fabrics with insoluble soaps, like aluminum stearate, and later with solutions or dispersions of waxes. With the advent of more sophisticated products like the silicones and other synthetic materials, water repellent treatments can now stand repeated washings or dry cleanings, or both, depending on the particular process used.

The soap processes are too old to be trademarked and, like many of the wax treatments which came along later, were not durable. Garments made from fabrics so treated required retreatment to retain water repellency.

The latest processes not only provide water repellency but are successful in repelling other oily fluids as well.

## Flame Resistant Finishes

Man's concern with the hazards of combustible materials, including textiles, paper and wood, has been continuous ever since he learned how to make and use fire for his own benefit. The Chinese recognized the need for noncombustible products when they used asbestos fibers to make false sleeves which were cleaned by burning the food stains from them. Charlemagne, who lived in the eighth century, owned an asbestos tablecloth which he cleaned in the same way.

Cellulosic materials such as wood, paper, or cotton, for example, cannot be made fireproof in the sense that glass, or asbestos fibers are fireproof. But they can be made "flame retardant" or "flame resistant" in that they will not support combustion after the source of ignition is removed.

Early efforts to make cotton resistant to burning involved the use of water-soluble salts. Borax, boric acid, and ammonium salts were used to impart flame resistance. But the results were not durable because the salts washed out when the fabric was laundered. However, such treatments can be and are being used for such products as draperies, throw rugs, and upholstery where temporary flame resistance is adequate and can be restored periodically by the consumer.

Since World War II, scientists at the Southern Utilization Research and Development Division of the U.S. Dept. of Agriculture have been conducting research to develop durable flame-resistant finishes for cotton products. A theory was evolved which explained the chemical changes which take place when cotton fabric burns. This information led to the preparation of new and more efficient chemicals, and the proper techniques for applying them to cotton textiles. The result was an end product, with significantly improved fire resistance, and good durability to many laundering cycles.

The early studies also disclosed that the glowing characteristic inherent in burning fabric plays a significant role in developing an efficient flame retardant. For instance, the temperature of the glow is nearly twice as hot as the active flame. So, in order for a flame resistant finish to be useful, the treated fabric must not continue to support the afterglow once the source of ignition is removed. It is also necessary that the chemicals that are used must not cause dermatitis, nor be toxic to the person wearing the treated garment.

Many factors are involved in developing a satisfactory flame retardant. The construction of the fabric has a significant bearing on the type of finish, as well as the quantity of chemicals neces-

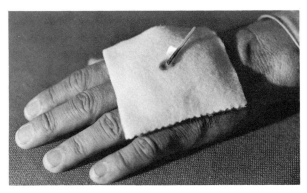

Above: Flame-retardant-treated napped baby blanket resists burning match. Below: Charred flame-retardant fabric forms barrier between blow torch and match.

sary to achieve the desired retardancy. Lightweight, loose-weave fabrics usually burn faster than heavier weight fabrics. Therefore fire-retardant chemicals efficient at lower addons, but presently more expensive, must be used. If a less efficient chemical is used, a larger quantity is required to impart adequate resistance to burning. This stiffens the lighter weight fabric and reduces its tensile and tear strength. Other important considerations involve the aesthetic properties of the fabric—its hand, its drapability, and its breathability. Perhaps no one flame retardant could be called best for cotton. The end use of the cotton product has a great influence on the type of flame retardant best suited for the purpose.

Scientists at the Southern Utilization Research and Development Division of the U.S. Department of Agriculture have developed several formulations that meet many of the requirements of adequate flame resistance. Two of them are highly effective for fabric weighing six ounces or more per square yard, and are of considerable interest to industry for certain end products. The essential ingredient is tetrakis (hydroxymethyl) phosphonium chloride, commonly referred to as THPC. Application is a simple process, and utilizes the finishing equipment commonly available in textile finishing plants. The treated fabric is somewhat stiffer, and tensile and tear strength is reduced somewhat. The degree varies, dependent on fabric weight and construction.

Quite recently Southern Division scientists developed an improved flame retardant finish for cotton based on THPC and caustic. Even lightweight fabric can be rendered fire resistant with virtually no significant change in hand or tensile strength of the fabric. Studies at the laboratory indicate that the finish continues to impart good flame retardancy to the fabric even after 30 home laundering cycles.

Just how do garments fabricated from flame resistant fabric protect their wearer? In addition to resisting burning, the fabrics treated with THPC chemicals possess the remarkable property of forming a tough, black char when burned. This char retains the fabric structure and some strength, and not only protects but insulates the wearer from excessively hot temperatures. Treated garments have afforded protection to workers even from molten steel that was splashed on them.

## "Bacteriostatic" or "Hygienic" Finish

The effect of the finish is obtained by subjecting a fabric to treatment which involves the use of chemicals classified as hygienic additives. Such additives inhibit the growth of bacteria in the cloth. They claim to prevent odors, prolong the life of the fabric, and also combat mildew and mold. Such treatments have been applied to shoe linings, coat linings, lingerie and underwear fabrics, luggage, surgical supplies, rugs, and upholstery cloths.

## Mildew-Resistant Finishes

Mildew, mold, fungus, and rot are all formed on fabrics by exposure to warm, moist atmosphere, or by soaps and sizings used in processing, which become food for vegetable organisms. The growth of such organisms can be inhibited by treating the fabric with toxic compounds which are not harmful to humans but which destroy the growths. Metallic compounds of copper, chromium, and mercury are generally used as well as chlorinated phenol followed by metallic soaps. A fabric which has been waterproofed is also generally mildewproof.

## Moth-Proof Finishes

Mothproofing of wool and other animal fibers is effectively achieved today by impregnating the fibers with chemicals which make them unfit as food for the moth larva. Chemicals such as silico-fluoride and chromium-fluoride are used, but each of the various trademarked processes utilizes different compounds.

# Permanent Press

*The development of permanent press meant final realization
of the promise implied by "wash-wear" textile products.*

"Permanent press" is a term used to describe a fabric or garment which will retain its original shape through wear and laundering and need no ironing. That means it will resist wrinkling and will retain creases and pleats indefinitely. It also means seams will be flat and free from puckering and the fabric will have a smooth surface appearance. The term is often used interchangeably with the phrase "durable press."

### Creases Versus Wrinkles

A *crease* or *pleat* is something added deliberately to a fabric or garment for reasons of fashion, utility and ease-of-care. It is therefore desirable. A *wrinkle* is something added unintentionally to a fabric or garment. It serves no useful purpose and is therefore undesirable. Creases and pleats are made by pressing. They are removed by washing and wearing the garment. Wrinkles, on the contrary, are made by wearing and washing a garment and are removed by pressing. Thus, the whole approach to permanent press clothing was built on the idea of treating a fabric to prevent both the *removal of creases* and the *formation of wrinkles* during the wearing and washing of a garment.

### The Principle of Permanent Press

Basically, the method for achieving permanent press is to treat the fabric with a cross-linking chemical or reactant which is then cured (or fixed) by the application of heat. This sets the smooth, flat shape given to the fabric during finishing. Imparted to the fabric, then, is a "memory" of its flat, finished state.

But this, the first applied method of permanent press finishing, presented a problem with some types of apparel. Having been cured as a flat fabric —designated as *pre-cured*—the garment of which the fabric was made had a tendency to return to that smooth, flat state. Furthermore, the built-in wrinkle resistance prevented the attainment of sharp creases (in slacks) or pleats (in dresses) that would be permanent to laundering. For the same reason, seams could not lie smooth and flat and puckering tended to develop along pockets and seams.

The solution of this particular problem—for garments where shape formations, creases or pleats were desired—involved the development of methods that would give "memory" to the shape of garments in their *made-up form*. This led to *post-cured* permanent press—meaning that the curing or fixing of the cross-linking chemical in the fabric is deferred until after the garment is made and pressed. Instead of giving "memory" to the flat fabric, "memory" is given to the shape of the garment in made-up form.

### How Permanent Press Started

The idea for permanent press garments, brought to

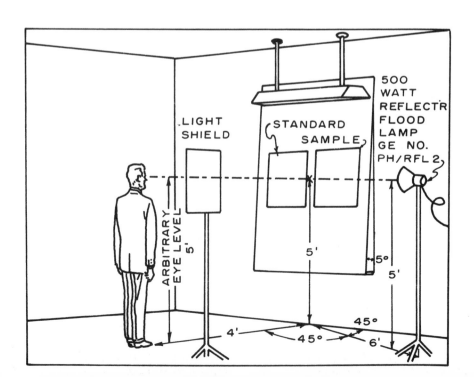

The lighting and viewing arrangement for the AATCC test method for evaluating the retention of pressed-in creases in wash and wear fabrics. This method also has application to the evaluation of creases in finished garments.

AATCC Test for evaluating crease retention after laundering.   Test garment is compared with photo and rated .

fruition through the post-cure process, was conceived and developed by Koret of California, the women's sportswear house in San Francisco. The reasoning was that if a flat fabric could be chemically treated and cured for crease retention and wrinkle resistance (the wash-wear concept), why not a made-up garment? In 1961 Koret was granted a U.S. patent (No. 2,974,432) for its deferred cure process and the Koratron Company was formed to market and license the process.

Other groups had also worked independently on the idea of permanent press apparel, notably the National Cotton Council, the U.S. Department of Agriculture, and a number of leading U.S. textile mills. But it was the Koratron Company's patented process which sparked commercial acceptance and development of permanent press.

## Breakthrough in Consumer Goods

The first application was in men's and boys' pants, introduced to the consumer in 1964, mainly owing to the vision, foresight and vigor of two firms—Levi Strauss and McCampbell Graniteville Co. Together these two firms nurtured the development of Koratron's process in men's wear.

However, it was only a matter of months before the permanent press concept was rapidly and widely extended to men's sport and dress shirts, to women's pants, blouses, dresses and skirts, to many other types of sportswear, to children's clothing and, finally, to no-iron fabrics for the home.

## Problems and Solutions in Permanent Press

Years of experimentation preceded the success of permanent press as a technological phenomenon in textile finishing. Many problems were encountered in production and much trial and testing went into their solution. Serious but successfully resolved obstacles included the following: Unpleasant odor resulted from thermosetting resins and had to be countered by developing other cross-linking chemicals to eliminate the problem. The sensitized fabric had a tendency to cure itself spontaneously, in advance of garment manufacture, and this was solved by the use of chemicals which made it possible to store treated fabric for a year or more without danger of premature curing. The shrinkage problem was resolved by compensation in garment sizing. Over-curing and under-curing were settled by constant experimentation. Modification and improvement of permanent press equipment went on continuously.

The first demonstration of permanent press—achievement of a permanent crease for pants—was a dramatic one. But basic to the concept, and more important as a major breakthrough in fabric finishing technology, was the implication for apparel development—in which shape and fit can be fixed permanently for the life of a garment without the need ever to be ironed. Permanent press also opened up design concepts such as stretchable fabrics which can be shaped and fitted with minimum cutting and sewing.

The Ameriset vapor-treatment process. This twenty-minute process produces permanent-press garments.

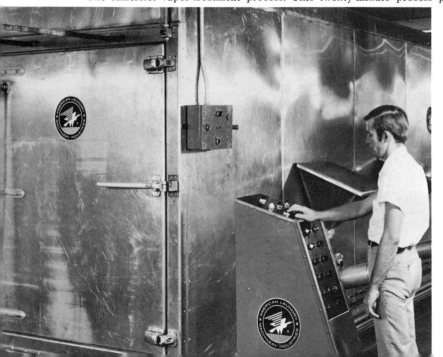

## The Four Ways to Permanent Press

1. PRE-CURE. The fabric is impregnated with a cross-linking chemical finish which reacts only with the cellulosic component of the fabric. It is fully cured in the flat state at the mill before delivery to the garment manufacturer. It is then cut, sewn and generally pressed with a hot head press which applies enough heat and pressure to shape it in garment form. The press chiefly sets the non-cellulosic thermoplastic fiber component since the cellulosic component has already been cured and set in the flat fabric state.

Pre-cured fabric provides good performance in permanent press items such as plain dresses and blouses, curtains, bed and table linens and draperies. All permanent press fabrics sold as piece-goods in retail stores are, of course, pre-cured. The most important pre-cured fabrics to date have been polyester/cotton blends and stretch blends of 75–25 cotton/nylon, chiefly stretch denims.

2. POST-CURE. Dominant use of the post-cure method to date has been on polyester/cotton fabrics of the 65/35 and 50/50 blend levels. It has also been successfully applied to stretch denims with stretch nylon warp and cotton filling, as well as to stretch blends of polyester/cotton/spandex. The fabric is impregnated with a cross-linking chemical (thermosetting resin) finish at the mill or finishing plant. This treatment reacts only with the cellulosic component. The fabric is dried at low temperatures so that only a minimum of cross-linking occurs, and becomes cured only when subjected to certain temperatures. The fabric is thus "sensitized" and the temperatures required for curing are applied after the garment has been cut, sewn and pressed. That is why the process is sometimes called "deferred curing."

The whole finished garment is cured in a baking oven which subjects it to temperatures of 300–340 degrees F. for from 4 to 18 minutes, depending on the fabric and the finish. This curing fixes or sets the garment permanently in the shape it was given by sewing and pressing before the oven.

As noted above, in this post-cure process it is the cellulosic fiber component (cotton or rayon) which is affected by the chemical treatment. Non-cellulosics are not affected but, being thermoplastic, they respond to the heat applied during pressing and curing. The non-cellulosic fiber reinforces the cotton or rayon since these lose strength and abrasion resistance in the curing treatment and require the man-made fiber for adequate wear life.

3. RE-CURE. This process represents an advance in permanent press chemistry. The method uses a special cross-linking reactant and a special catalyst with which the fabric can be almost, but not completely, pre-cured at the fabric mill level. By this method up to 85% of the cross-linking action takes place. Later, when the garment is pressed, some of the cross-links formed in the pre-curing stage can be broken in the presence of steam from pressing. They are then re-formed or set either in press or oven.

In effect, the system calls for a pre-cured fabric to be temporarily un-cured and then fully re-cured. This means that the cellulosic, as well as the thermoplastic component of a pre-cured fabric, can be shape-set by heat. The advantage of the process is that the fabric, being pre-cured and washed, is stable.

4. NO-CURE. This permanent press method uses fabrics made up of thermoplastic (heat-settable) fibers. They can be pressed into shape at temperatures of 300 to 400 F. and the process does not depend on chemical treatment, though some of the fabrics have a regular crease resistant finish. Chiefly, these fabrics have been blends of polyester/acrylic or polyester/nylon, though they may also be 100% polyester.

The No-Cure method produces satisfactory creases in pants, but there has been some feeling that it does not produce quite as effective wrinkle resistance as the other three methods. This is due to the tendency of thermoplastic fibers, under heat-setting, to make the fibers somewhat inflexible in their set position. However, such fabrics are mainly in the higher price brackets of worsted-like fabrics and removed from the traditional wash-wear category. They do have the significant advantage of being alterable in garment form, which is not practical with the other processes described.

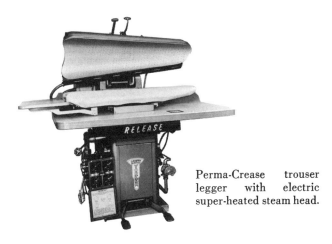

Perma-Crease trouser legger with electric super-heated steam head.

## Permanent Press in Knits

It might seem that knitted fabrics have little need of permanent press treatment since they are generally wrinkle resistant by the nature of the knitting construction. However, there are several hidden but important advantages to permanent press in knitted garments and both pre-cure and post-cure treatments are applicable. Chief advantage is a substantial gain in stability of the fabric, since shrinkage has always been a problem with knitted fabrics. In the case of blends of polyester/cotton, permanent press finishing gives increased clarity to the stitch which results from a decrease in fuzzing of the cotton fiber. And, from a fashion point of view, such knit fabrics open up many possibilities for permanently pleated feminine apparel.

## Leading Fibers for Permanent Press Fabrics

Among the numerous blends of fibers which form the bulk of permanent press fabrics, each of the man-made fibers plays a role, some more important than others. Most important have been polyester and nylon, in that order. The acrylics also are increasingly important in blends and a number of mills produce successful blends for permanent press fabrics with the high strength rayons (high-wet-modulus) as well as with acetate and spandex.

POLYESTER is used in the widest range of permanent press constructions—both in 100% constructions for no-cure process fabrics (which do not require chemical treatment) or, more often, in blends with cotton or high strength rayon for many uses and in both pre-cure and post-cure finishing.

NYLON is used in filament form for permanent press stretch fabrics and in staple form to blend with cotton/rayon and rayon/acetate. For effective performance a minimum of 15% nylon is needed in both warp and filling for fabrics of 8½ ounces or more. For lighter weight fabrics, the proportion of nylon must be increased. Permanent press nylon blends are treated both by post-cure and pre-cure methods.

ACRYLIC fibers are used in 50/50 blends with rayon for post-cure treatment and perform satisfactorily in cross-dyes. They are popular for slacks and sportswear. The acrylics are also used for no-cure permanent press fabrics in blends with polyester. The heat-setting property of such blends does the job without chemical treatment of the fabric.

SPANDEX fiber has shown good results in stretch fabrics of polyester/cotton treated for post-cure processing.

## Blends in PP Fabrics

The following list records the chief blends, with their proportions, available to manufacturers of permanent press garments:

Polyester/Cotton 75/25 65/35 50/50
Polyester/HWM* Rayon 65/35 55/45 50/50
Polyester/Acrylic 75/25 50/50
Polyester/Cotton/Spandex (Stretch)
Polyester interlinings 100%
50 HWM* Rayon/35 Acetate/15 Nylon
70 HWM* Rayon/30 Nylon (Stretch)
Acrylic/HWM* Rayon/Acetate Various proportions
55 Acrylic/45 Nylon (Stretch)
50 Acrylic/50 Rayon
100% Cotton
85 Cotton/15 Nylon
Cotton/Nylon (Stretch) 75/25 71/29 54/46
55 Cotton/30 HWM*Rayon/15 Nylon
100% Cotton interlinings
Non-woven interlinings in different blends
* HWM—High Wet Modulus

## M-S Process for All-Cotton Permanent Press

A mechanical process introduced by the Swiss firm of Radunder imparts increased strength to all-cotton fabrics under permanent press treatment. The process, licensed by The Sanforized Co., is known as "M-S"—for micro-stretch.

The first permanent press fabrics of 100% cotton were found to undergo loss of strength as high as 50% due to the heavy concentration of resins needed for the permanent press treatment. To offset this loss in strength, it became the practice to blend cotton with man-made fibers, chiefly polyester and nylon. However, the M-S processes make it possible to reduce the man-made fiber component or even to dispense with it for some end uses.

The micro-stretch process stretches the fabric in the filling direction and increases the strength of the cloth by 30–40%, at the same time increasing the fabric width by 5–15%. Tests have shown that strength losses of cotton during permanent press finishing can be cut by half or more by the M-S process.

The machines which do the job are about the size of an upright piano and operate at the rate of about 100 yards a minute.

## The Curing Ovens

The use of post-cure ovens means a considerable investment on the part of the garment manufacturer. An installation capable of processing fifty dozen pairs of permanent press pants an hour, for example, cost approximately $50,000 for the oven, press and other equipment in 1965. While some ovens are designed to cure one batch of garments at a time, the larger installations are designed for continuous operation on a moving line.

A great deal of engineering and research has gone into the curing ovens since it is necessary to generate accurately controlled and evenly distributed heat. Otherwise garments may be either over-cured or unevenly cured in different parts of the oven. The concentrations of resins or other chemicals are greater than for conventional wash-wear procedures, so that over-curing can deteriorate the fabric and under-curing result in poor shape retention.

The entire post-curing process, in view of these technical and cost factors, has resulted in a new kind of business—commission baking. Smaller manufacturers, who were unable to invest in the equipment and the technical skills needed for the post-cure operation, welcomed the arrival of the commission baker or curer who processes garments for a number of manufacturers. Pressing and baking are all done on his premises and the manufacturer benefits from his superior knowledge and experience in handling many different types of fabric and garments on a round-the-clock basis. A number of such commission curing firms operate in different parts of the country, solving a difficult situation for the smaller manufacturing firm.

## Automated Conveyor System

The conveyor system curing oven for permanent press garments is made from a welded steel framework enclosed with steel panels that encase glass batt insulation 4″ thick. A 2″ insulation protects the floor. The physical dimensions vary in accordance with the desired capacity in dozens of garments per hour.

It is recommended that a conveyor type curing oven be considered if production requirement is in excess of 25 dozen garments per hour. Depending upon the particular system, curing times vary from 4 to 5 minutes and 15 to 18 minutes at 300° to 340° F. Fabrics used vary from 100% cotton to assorted blends in different weights and constructions. All these factors are considered when selecting the proper curing conditions.

A circulating fan designed for high temperature operation discharges air into an overhead chamber with special baffles that distribute the air evenly through the garments as they pass through the oven. Air circulation is critical in this process as the current must be strong enough to give penetration for good curing, but not so strong as to distort garments during the curing cycle. The air, after passing over the garments, returns to the circulating fan by means of a special duct which directs the air through the gas burner section where it is reheated to the proper curing temperature. Each gas burner is regulated through a modulating temperature controller, allowing curing temperatures to be regulated from 250° to 400° F. The gas burner system is engineered with safety valves, regulators and flame safeguards. An oven heater may utilize natural or propane gas, or a dual gas system, or electricity.

The oven itself must be designed for explosion-proof construction with access doors to provide easy entry for maintenance. It features interior lights, indicating thermometers and an alarm system for alert if the curing temperature falls below a pre-designated point, and to insure against any failure in the curing process.

Attached to the gas section is the airlock-cooler section, where the conveyor enters and leaves the oven. This is equipped with a high capacity exhaust

A permanent-press reaction gas chamber, this one used in the Ameriset vapor treatment process.

fan to expel hot air and fumes from the oven to out-of-doors, thereby presenting an effective barrier to keep the hot air and fumes from the room. On the discharge, or cooler side, air is taken from the room and directed up or down through the garments, thereby cooling them off for handling immediately upon leaving the oven.

Depending on the size, an oven requires 15 to 20 hp to run fan motors and conveyor, and consumes from 400 to 1,000 cubic feet of gas per hour. Variable speed offers the option of running the conveyor at different speeds to suit the particular operation. A welding jig is used to align the track on initial installation, and may be used to change the conveyor arrangement at any time.

The conveyor itself may be suspended from the ceiling by numerous means. Since many different garments as well as sizes are processed, several methods of suspension are available. The number of hangers required for an installation depends upon the oven size and the length of the conveyor.

The conveyor type oven is popular because: (1) It does not require additional help to operate. (2) It provides for consistent curing operation in that the curing temperature and dwell-time in the oven (speed of conveyor) may be set and held for any length of time to suit the conditions. (3) Since conditions in the oven do not change, all garments are subjected to the same curing cycle and result in consistent quality. (4) Maintenance is low and requires only periodic lubrication of the chain and changing of the air filter. (5) The oven may be operated around the clock for days if desired.

Diagram showing the typical permanent-press operation in textiles, particularly the extensive curing ovens.

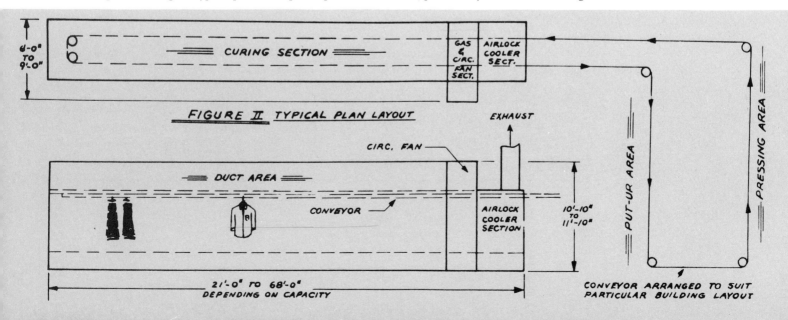

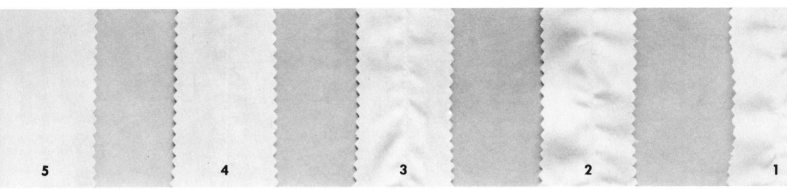

AATCC Test for evaluating seam puckering after laundering in single needle constructions. Number 5 is the top rating.

## Permanent Press Standards

To the textile testing scientist, the word "quality" is a descriptive and analytical term used to rate both good and bad quality. The rating assigned to a fabric is a specific number or percentage based on tests universally accepted by the industry.

The American Standards Association has defined essential performance qualities of fabrics for 75 different end-uses, setting minimum standards of fabric performance in wearing apparel and home furnishings. The standards cover breaking strength, shrinkage, odor, chlorine retention, wrinkle resistance, crease and pleat retention, colorfastness, hand and appearance after washing and/or dry

cleaning, resistance to staining, and other factors.

Similar preliminary standards and test procedures have been established by the big mills and finishers for permanent press fabrics.

But the shell fabric is not the whole performance story. Sewing techniques must be adapted to the permanent press approach, and these relate to linings, pocketings, waistbands, facings, zippers, sewing thread and other findings. Additionally, with post-cure fabrics, there is the problem of proper curing at the garment manufacturing level to avoid fabric deterioration.

This chart was prepared by Chicopee Mills to show the standards it sets for its post-cured all-cotton interlinings.

| QUALITY STANDARDS * * * ALL-COTTON WOVEN INTERLININGS (Post-Cured) | | | | | | |
|---|---|---|---|---|---|---|
| Fabric | Tensile Before Curing | Tear Before Curing | Wrinkle Recovery After Curing Warp & Filling | Shrinkage A 5 HBW After Curing* | Fabric Appearance After Laundering | Crease Appearance After Laundering |
| 2.5 oz./sq. yd. and under | 15 lbs. uncured | 2.0 lbs. uncured | 250 (Degrees) | 1.5/1.5 (Warp/Filling) | 4 | 4 |
| 2.5 to 4.0 oz./sq. yd. | 25 uncured | 1.5 uncured | 250 | 1.5/1.5 | 4 | 4 |
| 4.0 oz./sq. yd. and over | 35 uncured | 2.0 uncured | 250 | 1.5/1.5 | 4 | 4 |
| Method | ASTM D1682-59T | ASTM D1424-59T | ASTM D1295-60T | AATCC 88A-1964AT III-C-2 | AATCC 88A-1964T (Modified) | AATCC 88C-1964T |

*A 5 HBW - After 5 Hot Bendix Washings

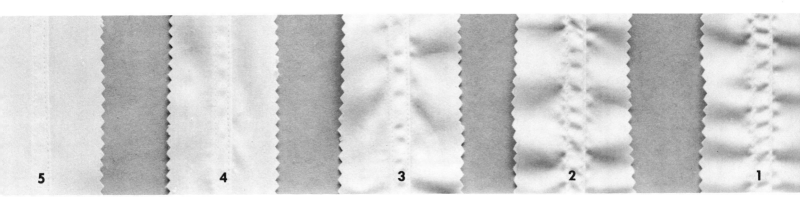

This is the same test but applied to double needle constructions. Again, class 5 shows virtually no seam puckering.

## Keeping Faith with the Consumer

Though there is no universally accepted set of performance standards for all the different types of permanent press garments produced, there are satisfactory criteria in the provisions of the American Standards Association for wash-wear fabrics. These standards, developed by the American Association of Textile Chemists and Colorists, cover surface smoothness, crease retention and seam puckering in wash-wear garments.

## Permanent Press Plus Stretch

The technology of permanent press has been successfully combined with stretch, bringing together two signal achievements in textiles. A wide range of fabrics is available in this category, including rayon/nylon warp stretch, denim filling stretch of cotton/nylon, acrylic/nylon warp stretch, rayon/nylon/spandex filling stretch, and other examples. (See also "Stretch Advances.")

Closed curing oven for permanent-press wear.

Sussman curing oven for permanent-press garments.

417

# Terms Used in Permanent Press Finishing

**ABRASION RESISTANCE:** The degree to which a fabric resists wear and tear. In relation to PP, a test for abrasion resistance would indicate the degree to which wash-wear chemicals have weakened the fabric.

**BATCH CURE:** One of two procedures used in curing PP garments. By this method one batch of garments at a time is put into the oven. The other method is continuous.

**CATALYST:** A substance which accelerates a chemical reaction. In the case of Deferred Cure, it is a chemical which helps to achieve cross-linking and is therefore added to the padding solution.

**CHLORINE RESISTANT:** Some chemical finishes retain some of the chlorine used in laundering. This is described as *Chlorine Retention*, and produces yellowing of white fabrics. When no yellowing results, the finish is described as *Chlorine Resistant*.

**COLOR SUBLIMATION:** The migration of a dyestuff on a fabric when subjected to high degrees of heat.

**COMPATIBLE SHRINKAGE:** This refers to linings and other findings which have the same shrinkage ratio as the shell fabric.

**COMPRESSIVE SHRINKING:** Shrinking a fabric with pressure and steam to give it dimensional stability against further shrinkage.

**CONTINUOUS CURE:** One of two methods used in curing PP garments. The other is a batch cure. The continuous method uses a moving conveyor system to carry garments in a continuous line from the pressing machine into and out of the curing oven.

**CREASES VS. WRINKLES:** Technically speaking, a crease is a deformation of the fabric intentionally formed by pressing. It is removed by washing and wearing. By contrast, a *wrinkle* is formed unintentionally by washing and wearing. It is removed by pressing. But when fabrics are treated for PP, the crease is not removable and wrinkles do not form.

**CROSS-LINKING AGENT:** A resin or chemical which reacts with the chemical structure of a fiber so as to form an indissoluble bond. When cured in the fabric, it gives the fabric a memory of its cured form.

**CURING:** The use of heat to fix chemicals permanently in the fabric so that they will not change. It has much the same meaning as *curing* of meat or fish.

**DEFERRED CURE:** Another term for Post-Cure.

**DIMENSIONAL STABILITY:** The ability of a fabric to retain the dimensions given it initially. This usually refers to its ability to resist shrinkage.

**DURABLE CREASE:** While this term is often used interchangeably with the term *Permanent Press*, it is more limiting in meaning since it refers only to the property of crease retention. *Permanent Press* refers to the shape-retaining properties of the whole garment.

**FABRIC MEMORY:** The property of a fabric which causes it to have a "memory" of its original form and so always return to that form. Some fibers —like wool and certain man-made fibers—have a native "memory." In the case of Deferred Cure fabrics the "memory" is induced with chemical finishes.

**FIBRILLATION:** This refers to the lightening of shade in Deferred Cure garments after repeated washing. It occurs especially along the crease line and particularly with dark colors. It is partly due to the fact that the crease line is more exposed to abrasion and this teases out to the surface some of the fibrils in the cloth.

**FINDINGS:** The supplementary fabrics used in making a garment—pocketing, waistband, zipper tapes, lining, etc. In PP garments it is important that these be chemically treated the same as the shell fabric.

**FLAT CURING:** The process of curing a fabric in the flat piece at the mill level.

**HAND BUILDER:** A finishing chemical used to improve the hand or tactile properties of a fabric.

**HOT HEAD PRESS:** A newly developed type of pressing machine designed for processing PP garments. It generates greater heat (450° to 500° F) and pressure (to 6 tons) at the head and is generally equipped with precision automatic controls.

**IMIDAZOLIDONE:** A chemical compound, one derivative of which is used in the Deferred Cure process. It was developed by Sun Chemical and is trademarked Permafresh 183.

**IMPREGNATION:** Process of treating a fabric with a finishing compound.

**PADDING SOLUTION:** The chemical solution, usually applied by padding the cloth, which is used in Deferred Cure treatments. A suitable padding solution for Deferred Cure is described by Sun Chemical as follows:

Permafresh 183—120 lbs.
Catalyst X-4—21½ lbs.
Mykon SF (polyethylene softener)—16 lbs.
Mykon WA (penetrant)—1 lb.
This produces 100 gallons of solution.

**PERMANENT PRESS:** A term which describes the ability of a garment to retain its shape-retaining properties throughout its life. This means sharp creases, flat seams, smooth surface appearance of the fabric, and seams free from puckering.

**POST-CURE:** The process by which fabrics are treated with chemical cross-linking agents which are not fixed or cured in the fabric until after the garment has been made. The fabrics remain in a sensitized condition until after the proper heat has been applied. The cure is thus deferred or delayed.

**PRE-CURE:** Another term for curing a fabric in the flat piece at the mill or finishing plant.

**PROGRESSIVE CURING:** This describes the situation when a sensitized fabric, treated for Deferred Cure, cures itself spontaneously during storage. It was one of the serious problems which had to be overcome before the Deferred Cure could become commercially feasible. It meant that sensitized fabrics had to be made up very quickly after treatment so that the fabrics would not set or cure in their flat state. The problem has been solved, and most Deferred Cure fabrics can now be safely stored for at least a year.

**PUCKERING:** The characteristic rippled appearance of the seams in conventional wash-wear garments after laundering. It is due to sewing tension and differential shrinkage of fabric and sewing thread. Quality PP garments avoid seam puckering since they are cured and fixed after being carefully pressed.

**REACTANT:** Another word for a chemical finishing compound which reacts with the fiber to form a cross-linking bond.

**RESIN:** A chemical compound used in various types of fabric finishing, especially in wash-wear treatments.

**SENSITIZED:** This refers to a fabric which has been impregnated with finishing chemicals, then dried but not cured. It therefore remains in a sensitized condition until the proper degree of heat is applied—as in the Deferred Cure process.

**SHAPE-SET:** The ability of a garment or other textile product to retain its manufactured shape as a result of permanent press treatment.

**SOFTENER:** A chemical compound used in finishing to give the fabric a soft hand.

**SPONTANEOUS CURING:** This is another way of describing progressive curing.

**STORAGE STABILITY:** The ability of a sensitized fabric to remain sensitized without curing itself spontaneously during storage.

**TEAR STRENGTH:** Related to abrasion resistance. It describes the degree to which a fabric resists tearing. In relation to PP, a test for tear strength also helps to determine how much the fabric has been weakened by chemical treatment. Sometimes a weakened fabric is described as having been *"tenderized."* This is also related to *tensile strength* which refers to the capacity for resisting longitudinal stress.

**THERMOSETTING RESIN:** A chemical compound which can be permanently set or cured through the application of heat.

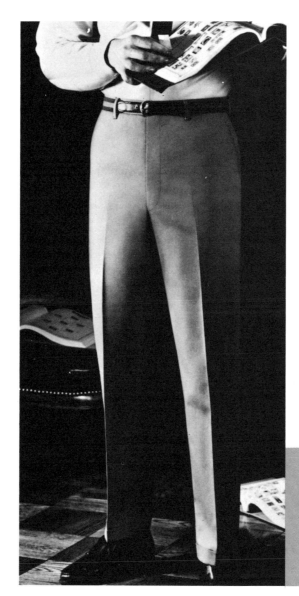

Men's pants were the bellwether for the whole permanent press development. From here the application of PP has expanded to cover virtually every category of apparel for men, women and children, along with the vast market for home furnishings.

The seams tell the story. Previous wash-wear often showed seams like those on left. With PP, seams lie flat and smooth as on right.

419

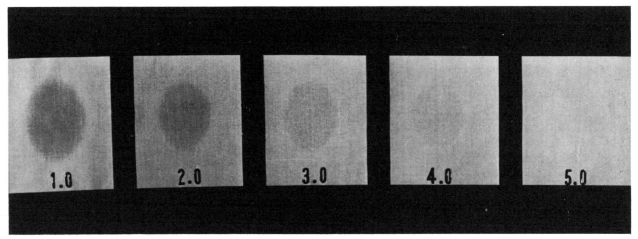

The various soil-release ratings from poor to good.

# Soil Release

### Definition

Soil release is a general term used to describe a class of textile finishes which make it possible to release stains from fabrics by ordinary washing. They were especially designed to work on polyester/cotton fabrics which have been treated for permanent press performance.

Of the many textile developments that followed one another after World War II, those relating to "easy care" fabrics have, not unnaturally, made the most direct appeal to the housewife. And among these, soil release has been welcomed with considerable enthusiasm by consumers.

To explain soil release, one must bear in mind the impact of chemistry on textiles which took a crucial turn with the advent of man-made fibers, particularly polyester. Wash/wear concepts—notably permanent press—emerged and, with them, the use of chemical resins in textile finishing.

### How Soil Release Works

Soil release fabrics made their first appearance in the summer of 1966 with Deering Milliken's "Visa" system. Like most soil release systems, it does not prevent soil from entering the fabric. It simply allows soil to leave the fabric faster. To understand this concept, one must study the nature of permanent press.

To achieve permanent press performance, chemists had to increase the amounts of resin used on the fabric. Polyester is already hydrophobic (water-resistant), and resin tends to make cotton hydrophobic too. Thus, resination imparts hydrophobia to permanent press polyester/cotton blends. Since water can't get in, soil generally can't be washed out. This, in simple terms, was why the industry developed soil release finishes and systems.

### The Four Aspects of Soil Release

Soil release is generally related to four phenomena in modern textiles, each impinging on the others but each with its own problems and solutions. These can be described as follows:

1. SOIL REPELLENCE. When soil release was introduced, it was quickly confused with soil repellence. Actually, soil repellence tends to work against soil release since the thin films used in soil repellent fabrics tend to hold stains if the wearer has mistakenly rubbed them in. If carefully dabbed off, of course, stains can be very effectively prevented from penetrating fabric by soil repellence systems.

2. SOIL REMOVAL. The chemical technology of soil release finishes is continually changing and improving, yet all soil release systems attempt to do the same thing—make the fabric hydrophilic (water accepting) and oleophobic (oil resisting)—to let water in and to keep oil out. Thus, soil release fabrics tend to resist oil-borne stains and permit water to enter for stain removal under ordinary laundering conditions. Experts recommend prespotting.

In the development of soil release, scientists developed a hierarchy of stains, ranging from the least difficult to the most difficult to remove. Mustard, dirty motor oil and grass stains generally ranked as the most difficult. Some of this controversy over stains overlooked the main point, however. The object was not necessarily to remove all stains from all fabrics under all conditions. Why, for example, would a woman want soil release finishes powerful enough to remove oil from her dress, when the finish made the dress fabric stiff? Much of this controversy has been resolved in the interests of common sense; soil release has been generally confined to permanent press garments such as work clothes, slacks and white shirts which must have it to remain viable. It has also become an important factor in expanding the use of tablecloths.

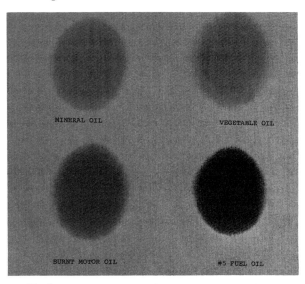

Right side of shirt is treated with soil-release.

3. SOIL REDEPOSITION. No aspect of soil release has occasioned so much controversy as soil redeposition. The problem has been most visible in yellowing or graying shirt collars made from polyester or permanent press fabrics. Many in the textile industry feel that soil redeposition will be conquered by the optical brighteners put on fabric during the finishing process or by optical brighteners introduced at the fiber stage. But many also feel that anti-soil redeposition finishes and systems are necessary in themselves. As a result, they have developed finishes which specifically attack soil redeposition.

4. ANTI-STATIC. The anti-static qualities of soil release finishes have been the least heralded properties of the finishes. Yet, since they produce a hydrophilic state, soil release finishes make polyester and polyester blend fabrics less conducive to static collection. This is a boon in such items as ladies' slips and uniforms of 100% polyester.

## Added Benefits of Soil Release

There are a number of other advantages to soil release finishes, both proven and potential, such as the following:

ANTI-PILLING AND FUZZING. Since soil release finishes make a fabric hydrophilic they almost lubricate the fabric, thus reducing fuzzing and pilling. These two problems have frequently been associated with polyester or polyester blend fabrics.

MORE WEARABLE FOR HOT WEATHER. Again, the hydrophilic quality makes any fabric more comfortable because it permits moisture absorption.

MORE DURABLE GARMENTS. Soil has always been a

Hardest to remove stains in permanent-press wear.

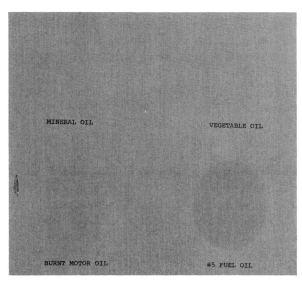

Soil-release resin permits stain removal in wash.

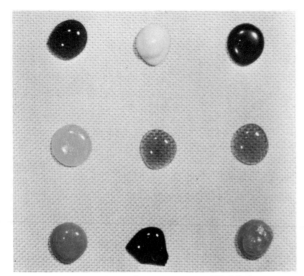

Dabs of hard-to-release stains on SR fabric.

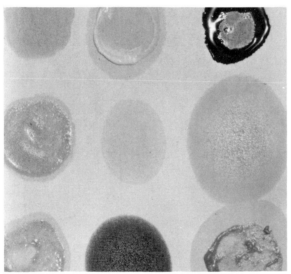

The same spots thoroughly soaked into fabric.

3-M's Scotchgard removes stains in one washing.

fabric destroyer, particularly when it remains in the fabric. Soil release systems should help to eliminate this problem.

SOFTER HAND. Once more, the transformation from hydrophobic to hydrophilic achieved by soil release makes polyester fabrics softer to the hand and, it is believed, more workable at the cutting and sewing operations.

## Finishing Problems Resolved

When soil release systems were first used, they caused criticism among a number of finishers and manufacturers. The chief objections were: dusting, which made the plant's air uncomfortable to work in; loss of permanent press qualities; harsh hand; color loss in dyeing; needle heat in manufacture; and fabric immobilization, which caused a sharp decrease in tear strength.

Many of these problems were caused by having to put permanent press fabrics through two baths at the finishing stage—one, to apply the permanent press finish, another to apply the soil release finish. Some companies which supply finishes have solved this problem by developing a single-bath finish; in other cases, the problems have been solved by reducing the amount of finishing material applied and by working out the other finishing problems through trial and error. In general, soil release finishing has become a feasible and useful process with all fabrics for which it was intended, without adding significant cost to textile producers or to the consumer.

## What Soil Release Should Do

Acceptable soil release standards should meet the following conditions (depending upon the fabric end use):

1. Remove all types of common soil in home laundering, with normal detergents.

2. Remove stains stemming from hair tonics, vaseline, deodorants and the like; remove, to a substantial degree, lipstick, liquid eye makeup and hair dye.

3. Remove all oily stains, grease, motor oil.

4. Remain effective during the reasonable life of the garment through continued home launderings.

5. Be non-yellowing and non-dulling.

6. Maintain the same hand as untreated fabrics.

7. Permit absorbency.

8. Be durable for commercial laundering.

9. Maintain all permanent press qualities.

Three PP shirts: bottom, Deering Milliken's Visa SR, worn 80 times. Untreated shirts on top worn 30 times.

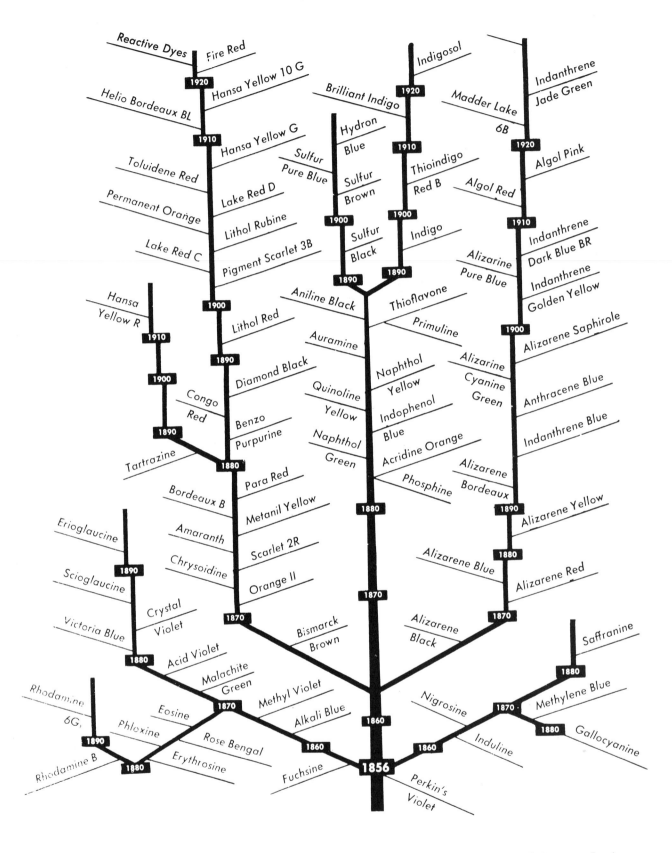

# Significant Developments in Organic Color Chemistry

424

# Color and the Human Being

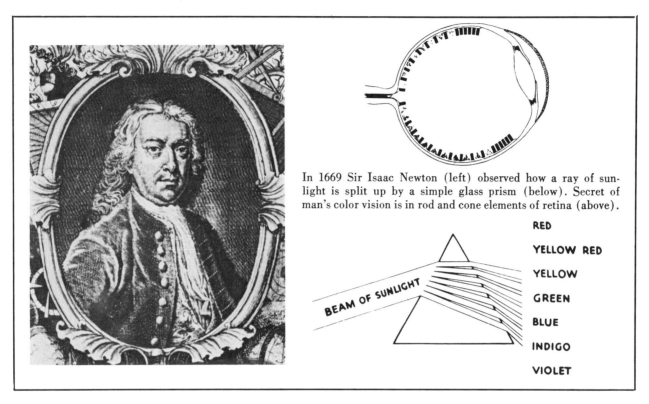

In 1669 Sir Isaac Newton (left) observed how a ray of sunlight is split up by a simple glass prism (below). Secret of man's color vision is in rod and cone elements of retina (above).

RED
YELLOW RED
YELLOW
GREEN
BLUE
INDIGO
VIOLET

BEAM OF SUNLIGHT

Color vision, one of the most marvelous of human gifts, is also one of the least explored. Nobody, not even specialists in this area of knowledge, knows much about what color is, or just how we see it, or precisely what its effects are on human well-being. Yet, no element in our sensuous natures will yield us greater or more varied pleasure than the perception of color.

Our knowledge of the physical nature of color began with Isaac Newton, who in 1666 passed a beam of white light through a glass prism and found that it was refracted into the hues of the rainbow, or spectrum—red, orange, yellow, green, blue, indigo and violet—which he called the seven primaries. He deduced that the nature of color was purely due to wave length. Goethe was a poet and philosopher. He claimed that the nature of color depends upon the observer's condition. Until recently Newton's and Goethe's were the only two concepts.

## How We See Color

To understand color it is important to know a few of the elementary facts about the way in which the eye reacts to light. Perhaps the first fact we note is

that the normal eye is largely color blind; that is, the periphery, or the outermost part of the retina, is entirely color blind; a large portion of the microscopic organs which constitute the whole of the retina are color blind; the whole of the eye is color blind in twilight (low illumination); and even the most color-sensitive parts of the eye tend to become color blind when stimulated by certain definite balanced or complementary wave lengths of light. This is an amazing fact when almost all the time we seem to be seeing color.

Another way of stating the whole situation is that only a relatively small part of the eye is color-sensitive, and this color sensitivity rests continually upon a basis of color blindness; it rests thus only precariously, so to speak, tending always to fall back toward color blindness. The normal eye has a *duplex* function, depending on two distinct kinds of light-sensitive elements, the *rods* and *cones*. Only one of these elements, the cones, ever sees color at all. The other, the rods, can never see anything but grey. With the cones we see surfaces lighted by unbalanced wave lengths as colored, but even with the cones we see surfaces lighted by balanced wave lengths as grey; of course, what the rods see is

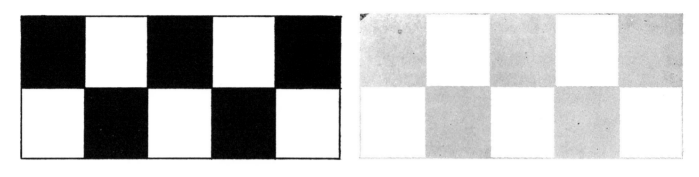

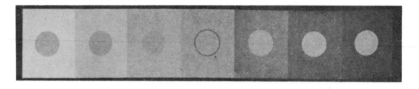

The textile designer requires a knowledge of the eye's response to varying conditions of light and shade. Some points are illustrated above: at *top left* the black and white squares look equal; *at right*, where contrast is less, the black squares appear larger than the white. In *lower strip* a circle placed against series of tonal values, itself appears to change in tone, though its value is actually constant.

---

fused in the brain with what the cones see, and the net result is a sensation which may have any quality, all the way from the purest grey to the purest color.

## Color Blindness

About eight per cent of American men are color blind, to the extent that they find considerable difficulty in distinguishing reds from greens. Color blindness is often known as Daltonism, after John Dalton, an 18th Century English chemist whose optical failings led him to attend Quaker meetings attired in drab green coat and blazing red stockings. It is transmitted from one generation to another through women who, oddly enough, are very rarely color blind.

The white races are more apt to have red and green color blindness than Africans, American Indians, and South Sea Islanders. With the exception of apes and men, practically all mammals are color blind. (A red flag doesn't disturb a bull a bit; it's the movement that infuriates him.) Birds and some fishes, however, see color very well, and some varieties of owls can see infra-red light, which humans can't. Bees can see blue or yellow, but fumble at red. Mosquitoes have a poor sight for yellow, which is the reason for their tendency to ignore porch lights which are dyed that color. Too much caffein

can make you temporarily color blind; people with jaundice see the world in a yellow light.

After viewing any color for some time, your eyes lose their sensitivity to it, and it tends to appear more grey. Sensitivity to color varies with age and, according to some scientists, with racial origin. Experiments by color psychologists show that children seem to pay most attention to yellow. Old people, on the other hand, tend to become *blue-thirsty*— they don't see enough blue. So far as is known the fluids in their eyes, normally transparent, become yellowish with age and tend to filter out some of the blue light which they would otherwise see.

Most of the retina—the photographic plate of the eye—is coated with a substance known as *visual purple*, which consists of almost pure Vitamin A. When light falls on the retina, the Vitamin A undergoes a bleaching action, and it is thought that this bleaching action stimulates the optic nerve to give it the sensation of light.

## Color, Light, and Sensation

Color is not confined to the eye. The eye merely transmits to the brain information about color sensations. The eye is probably sensitive to only three colors—red, green, blue. All colors which can be experienced can be produced by combination of these three colors. The eye is sensitive only to light, not pigment; it is sensitive only to the reflection of light on pigments. The property of all light is determined by the chemical composition of an object. In other words, color is not vested in pigment, but it is what pigment does to light. For example, yellow pigment absorbs blue and violet and reflects all other rays. Blue pigment absorbs red and yellow. Therefore, from a mixture of blue and yellow pigments you get green light.

What we know as the color of an object is simply its capacity to absorb or reflect the kind of light which illuminates it. When you look at a piece of blue cloth in white light, for example, there is nothing in the fabric which itself gives off a blue color; the dye in the material absorbs from its illuminating light, nobody knows quite how, the colors of red, orange, yellow, green, indigo, violet and some of the blue, the rest of which it reflects. In much the same way, the sky appears blue not because it is *colored* that way. According to one school of physicists it appears that way because minute particles suspended in the air, and possibly air molecules themselves, absorb from the sun a little of every other color but blue, which they reflect. And a black object absorbs all wave-lengths of colors, reflecting virtually none. Yet black is not an absence of color. Black can be readily discerned in almost any light.

There is no such thing as *the color* of an object. There are as many different colors to an object as there are kinds of light in which they can be seen. This point is readily established by holding out two pieces of especially dyed cloths under an ordinary incandescent office lamp. One can be made to appear green, the other a deep brown. But, when exposed to daylight and displayed again, both appear the identical color of green.

Incandescent light contains more red than does daylight. One piece of cloth has a higher reflectance in the red end of the spectrum than the other, and under the reddish-yellow illuminant appears brown.

Fluorescent lighting has a marked effect on colors, as illustrated in the following chart:

## Effects of Fluorescent Lighting on Colors

**Color Samples**           **Lamp Designation**

| | DAYLIGHT | STANDARD COOL WHITE | DELUXE COOL WHITE | WHITE | STANDARD WARM WHITE | DELUXE WARM WHITE | SOFT WHITE |
|---|---|---|---|---|---|---|---|
| Pink | Fair | Fair | Good | Fair | Good | Good | Enhanced |
| Red | Fair | Dulled | Good | Dulled | Good | Good | Fair |
| Maroon | Dulled | Dulled | Fair | Dulled | Fair | Enhanced | Dulled |
| Rust | Dulled | Fair | Fair | Fair | Fair | Enhanced | Fair |
| Orange | Dulled | Dulled | Fair | Fair | Fair | Enhanced | Fair |
| Brown | Dulled | Fair | Good | Good | Fair | Good | Good |
| Tan | Dulled | Fair | Good | Good | Fair | Good | Good |
| Gold | Dulled | Fair | Good | Fair | Good | Good | Fair |
| Yellow | Dulled | Fair | Fair | Good | Good | Fair | Good |
| Chartreuse | Good | Good | Good | Good | Fair | Dulled | Good |
| Olive | Good | Fair | Fair | Fair | Dulled | Dulled | Fair |
| Light Green | Good | Good | Fair | Good | Dulled | Dulled | Dulled |
| Dark Green | Enhanced | Good | Fair | Good | Dulled | Dulled | Dulled |
| Turquoise | Enhanced | Fair | Fair | Dulled | Dulled | Dulled | Dulled |
| Peacock Blue | Enhanced | Good | Fair | Dulled | Dulled | Dulled | Dulled |
| Light Blue | Enhanced | Fair | Fair | Dulled | Dulled | Dulled | Dulled |
| Royal Blue | Enhanced | Fair | Fair | Dulled | Dulled | Dulled | Dulled |
| Purple | Enhanced | Fair | Fair | Dulled | Good | Fair | Dulled |
| Lavender | Good | Good | Fair | Dulled | Good | Fair | Dulled |
| Magenta | Good | Good | Good | Fair | Enhanced | Good | Dulled |
| Grey | Good | Good | Fair | Fair | Fair | Fair | Fair |
| White | Grey | White | Dull-white | Tan-white | Yellow-white | Dull-white | Pink-white |

*Dulled*     — *Subdued from original color.*
*Fair*        — *Color less bright than under daylight of equal intensity.*
*Good*       — *Appearance as good as under daylight of equal intensity.*
*Enhanced* — *Richer in appearance. Color appears brighter than under daylight of equal intensity.*

# Color . . . and How It Works

*Primary, secondary and complementary colors, the principle of simultaneous contrast, after-image and the work of Chevreul.*

An understanding of the principles that govern the relationship of primary and secondary colors is fundamental in every practical use of color. There are three primary colors: Red, Blue, and Yellow. These are also called *simple* colors because in their pure form they are irreducible.

There are three secondary colors: Violet, Green, and Orange. These are also called *compound* colors because they are made from a mixture of two primaries. The secondary colors fall between the primaries and are thus made up of the two primary colors on either side. (See color circle.) There are infinite shadings of color between primaries.

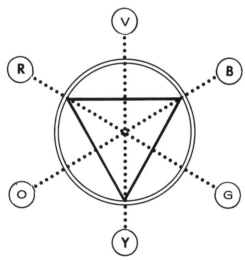

For example, starting with primary Red and moving to primary Blue, the colors gradually lose their redness as they approach Blue. At the halfway point they are Violet—an equal mixture of Red and Blue. Beyond the halfway point they turn Purple as the Blue primary begins to dominate the Red.

Thus, we speak of: a Red with either a Blue or a Yellow cast; a Blue with either a Red or a Yellow cast; a Yellow with a Red or a Blue cast . . . and so on for every shade in the color circle.

## The Complementary Colors

The word "complementary" means: "Serving to fill out or complete, mutually supplying each other's lack." This is an exact description of the scientific phenomenon we refer to as complementary colors.

This is the way the phenomenon works: Each primary color has a complementary color. This complementary color is a mixture of the other two primaries. The complementary color "completes" the primary color by supplying the lack of the two other primary colors which the eye instinctively seeks to find since light (*which is color*) is composed of all three primaries.

*Look at the color circle again:* Each primary has a complementary directly opposite it along the diameter of the circle. Each shading of color between the primaries similarly has a complementary color opposite it. Thus the complementary of Green is Red; complementary of Green-Yellow is Red-Violet, and so on around the circle.

## White Light and Black Pigment

In the light spectrum, the mixture of the three primary colors—Red, Blue and Yellow—produces white light.

In pigments, the mixture of the three primaries produces Black or Grey.

## Where Does Brown Come From?

Looking at our color circle, the color Brown seems a puzzle. It does not really fall within the continuum of the light spectrum from Red to Yellow.

But from experience we know that Brown can be made with Red and Green pigments. Looking at the color circle again, we see that Green is made up of the Blue and Yellow primaries. Thus, in effect, Brown is composed of all three primaries—Red plus Blue and Yellow which make Green. If these three were mixed in equal proportions they would produce Black. Since they are mixed unequally they produce Brown—an off-Black.

Brown can also be produced by adding Orange to Black—also achieving an off-Black.

## What Happens When You Look at Color?

When two colors are juxtaposed, each undergoes surprising changes. These changes are based in part on the scientific principle of color complementaries. It is known as *simultaneous contrast.*

The principle of *simultaneous* operates as follows: When the Red is juxtaposed with Yellow it takes on the cast of the color which is the complementary of Yellow—that is, *Violet*—which is composed of the other two primaries absent from Yellow, namely Red and Blue. (*See color circle.*)

When Red is juxtaposed with Blue it takes on the cast of the color which is the complementary of Blue—that is, *Orange*—which is composed of the other two primaries absent in Blue, namely Red and Yellow.

The principle of *simultaneous contrast* can be demonstrated to a greater or lesser degree with any combination of colors. The principle can be stated as follows:

When two colors are juxtaposed, each takes on the cast of its neighbor's complementary color. Thus, when Blue and Yellow are juxtaposed, the Blue will take on the cast of Yellow's complementary, which is Violet; and the Yellow will take on the cast of Blue's complementary, which is Orange.

It is thus most important to know the complementary of each color in order to anticipate how two colors will react with each other.

## Colors Affect Each Other

When you look concentratedly at any isolated color an after-image appears before your eyes. This is known as *successive contrast*. Each after-image will be the complementary of the original color.

Red has an after image of its complementary Green. Green has an after image of its complementary Red. Blue has an after image of its complementary Orange. Orange has an after image of its complementary Blue. Yellow has an after image of its complementary Violet. Violet has an after image of its complementary Yellow.

The after-image is not a theory. It is a fact which can easily be demonstrated. Simply place a small circle of color on a white sheet under incandescent light. Gaze steadily at it for perhaps a minute or so. After a while you will actually see another colored circle emanating from the first like a ghost figure. It will be the complementary of the original color.

What is happening is that your eyes are filling in the color needed to make white light—which is composed of Red, Blue and Yellow. Your eyes are adding the missing primaries.

Seurat's pointillist paintings were inspired by the color theories of Chevreul.

## The Interaction of Colors

The French color scientist, Michele-Eugene Chevreul (1786–1889), was perhaps the first to conduct a scientific investigation of color interaction as related to textiles.

From 1824 to 1883 Chevreul was Director of Dyeing at the famous Gobelins tapestry works in France. There, he began to receive complaints from customers who told him that some of the colors used in the Gobelin tapestries were weak. They were especially concerned about "the want of vigour" in the Blacks.

Chevreul was a chemist by profession and he made a careful scientific investigation which proved to him that the Blacks were not less vigorous than in the past but rather that their vigor was being diminished through juxtaposition with other colors then in fashion.

Carrying on his investigation in depth with the full range of colors, he recorded his experiments and came to a series of pioneering conclusions which he incorporated in a famous treatise he titled: "The Principles of Harmony and Contrast of Colours." It was published in 1835 and forms the basis for much of our present knowledge about the effects of color interaction.

# The Color Spectrum

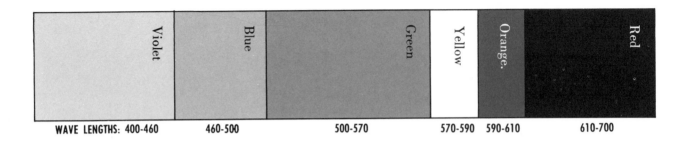

| | | | | | | |
|---|---|---|---|---|---|---|
| Violet | Blue | Green | Yellow | Orange | | Red |

WAVE LENGTHS: 400-460    460-500    500-570    570-590   590-610    610-700

The source of all color is light. It was Sir Isaac Newton who determined this conclusively in the year 1666 when he showed that if white light is directed through a glass prism it breaks down into a chain of colors ranging from Violet at one end to Red at the other.

This is the color spectrum. Today we know these colors are projected by electro-magnetic waves or waves of radiant energy which also project radio, X-ray and other waves. But while radio and X-ray waves cannot be seen, the color waves are visible to the naked eye. They can be measured and defined in millimicrons, a minute unit of measurement which equals 25 millionths of an inch.

The color spectrum (as seen in a rainbow, for instance) is an infinitely graduated series of colors which have been classified into six major divisions with corresponding wave lengths increasing from about 400 millimicrons for Violet to about 700 millimicrons for Red.

### What Makes an Object Colored?

When we see a colored object we are seeing colored light reflected from the object to our eyes.

If the object is *Red*, this means its physical and chemical composition causes it to absorb all the wave lengths of light except the *Red* ones which it reflects back. Similarly with *Blue*, *Yellow* or any other color.

If the object is *White*, this means that the full visible spectrum—from 400 to 700 wave lengths—is being reflected back. If it is *Black*, this means that all colors (*wave lengths*) in the spectrum are being absorbed by the object.

That is why it was once customary to wear *White* clothes in the summer. They reflect back the rays of light, thus reducing heat. *Black* clothes would absorb them. This scientific fact has also been offered as a partial explanation for the popularity of *White* automobiles, especially in the warm areas.

### Why Colors Change Under Lights

Different light sources are themselves differently colored and the color of the light affects and modifies the color of the object.

*For example:* the color *Yellow*, seen under incandescent electric light, takes on an *Orange* cast because the incandescent bulb has a *Reddish* hue. (*Red* + *Yellow* = *Orange*.) Under some fluorescent light the same *Yellow* takes on a *Greenish* cast because the fluorescent light often has a *Blue* hue. (*Blue* + *Yellow* = *Green*.) A similar effect also occurs under a north skylight where the light source also contains a good deal of *Blue*.

Thus, though two colors may be chemically different, they can appear to match under a specific source of light which balances them by the addition of its own color.

### The Language of Color

The language of color uses three basic and generally accepted terms—*Hue, Value* and *Chroma*.
Hue: This defines the color (*Red, Blue* etc.) in terms of its dominant wave length in the color spectrum.

Value: This refers to the *brightness* of a color, the degree of light or dark it contains. It is measured on a scale graduated from *White* to *Black*.

Chroma: This refers to the intensity or purity of the color on a scale from dull to brilliant, depending on how much or how little *Gray* the color contains.

### Here Are Some Psychological Connotations of Colors

Dark pure red—love and amiability
Medium red—health and vitality
Bright red—passion
Dark, greyed red—evil
Strong light pink—femininity, festivity
Pure medium pink—delicacy, innocence
Greyed light pink—daintiness
Greyed medium pink—frivolity
Strong dark orange—ambition
Strong medium orange—enthusiasm, zeal
Strong light orange—intensity
Dark medium brown—utility
Light medium brown—maturity
Strong light yellow—inspiration
Medium yellow—prudence, goodness
Light medium yellow—wisdom, attention
Strong light yellow—gaiety, stimulation
Dark medium yellow—love of humanity
Strong light gold—glamour, distinction
Medium gold—luxury, glory
Dark medium gold—riches
Light strong yellow-green—freshness
Light medium yellow-green—youth
Light strong yellow-green—vitality
Strong medium green—sociability
Medium green—frankness, practicality
Greyed medium green—naïveté, innocence
Strong light blue-green—restlessness
Strong dark blue-green—longing, nostalgia
Medium light blue-green—calm, repose
Greyed light blue-green—placidity
Strong medium blue—idealism
Dark medium blue—sincerity
Greyed medium blue—kindness
Light medium blue—calmness
Strong light blue-purple—sternness
Strong light purple—magnificence
Light medium purple—fragility, softness
Dark greyed purple—royalty
Medium purple—poise

# Color Dyes

Man has perceived color as long as there has been man, and perceived it with his emotions as well as his eyes. An elemental experience and part of our heritage as a race, the perception of color produces emotions as various as they are profound.

We know that primitive peoples, in whatever part of the world they lived, used color to protect themselves from the spells of evil spirits. Color, for them, had magic properties. Before they began to believe in gods, they invested their colored symbols with the values of extra-reality. Long before they began to wear clothing, they used color to adorn their naked bodies. They could tell when fruit was ripe . . . not by science, not by the calendar, but by color alone. Color served then to attract attention, it served as a mark of distinction, it served as a fomenter and warder-off of magic; it awakened, soothed and solaced the aesthetic sense of man.

Color also spoke a symbolic language. This language, made up of scores of immemorial color associations, is indelibly stamped on the pattern of our racial subconscious. Red—out of fire—means heat to us. Blue—out of the sky—means purity to us. Deep, dark black-blue—out of the cold night sky—means frigidity. Green—out of the first tender growth of spring—means freshness. Gold—out of sunlight, out of warmth—means gaiety and light.

### Symbolic Meanings

Colors by now not only have different symbolic meanings in different parts of the world, but have even upon occasion changed their symbolic meanings from era to era. Tradition, race, social convention, personal attitude, and attitude to the world all play a part in what color means to an individual. In the West, for example, people mourn in black. But the Chinese grieve for their dead in white. The social history of purple is another of color's symbolic curiosities. Purple was the favorite color of the proud and mighty in the ancient East. Alexander the Great, perpetuating the customs of the eastern empires he had conquered, established purple as the ruling caste's distinctive hallmark. In imperial Rome, Nero forbade the unauthorized wearing and even the sale of purple on pain of death. Purple as a mark of caste continued throughout the ascendancy of Byzantium. Later, however, purple gave way to scarlet, but gave way in an odd manner. For the so-called *cardinal's purple* of the medieval Church was red, in fact, and purple in name and repute only. Red then became the mark of

431

Heracles of Tyre discovered the purple Murex dye when his dog bit into a sea shell.

power. But red, as every Valentine's Day reminds us, is also the color of love.

It is not simple, then, the language that color speaks now to us and spoke then to primitive man. For color, as we have seen, is tinged again by our own emotions; its primary appeal is to our emotions. It is undoubtedly for this reason that color was linked in the mind of primitive man with magic, and that the discovery of the rarest and most precious dye, that self-same purple, was considered by the ancients so miraculous that they attributed its finding to a demigod, Heracles.

## In the Beginning

The knowledge and use of color began with the dawn of civilization. In the beginning man utilized the colors he found in the earth and in the products of the earth. It is probable that the earliest dyes were discovered by accident, by-product stains from berries, fruits or nuts used as food. Later, as these were seen to serve their purposes, blossoms, leaves, stems, roots of shrubs, bark, and twigs of trees were tried and found by primitive man to be practical as dyestuffs.

The art of using dyes seems to have developed independently, and been practiced independently, by different primitive peoples in almost every region of the earth. Their technique was simple. They roamed the woods and fields collecting known dye plants or roots which they then boiled in hot water. The range of colors they were able to achieve was limited: red, blue, yellow, green, brown, and black, with slight variations in shade and tone.

Their technique may have been simple, but the achievement if one stops to examine it was, after all, tremendous. It is common practice today to treat the discoveries of science and technology with awe and respect, and to waste no thought on the naive discoveries of our prehistoric ancestors. But the discoveries of science and technology are no more than the sum of patient, conscientious obser-

vation, an understanding of natural laws and a skillful intelligence. The unknown, unsung, prehistoric man who discovered the first dyestuff undoubtedly had more than his fair share of luck. But the generations upon generations of primitive men who followed him, so that eventually more than one thousand different plants, vines, shrubs and trees were used for extracting dyes, were as much scientists for their time as their modern counterparts. For they too observed nature painstakingly; they too, in their primitive way, understood natural laws; and they too were capable of translating their observation and understanding into creative action.

## The Search for Brighter Colors

As the generations succeeded each other, and primitive society gave way to ancient civilization, man was increasingly successful in his untiring search for better colors, brighter colors and more varied colors. At the dawn of history, indigo, the most important of all dyestuffs, was obtained from a plant in Asia. And who is to say which discovery was greater—the discovery of natural indigo or Kekule's representation in the last century of the benzene molecule as a ring structure, which contributed so largely to the synthesis of dyestuffs? For the solution to the problem of extracting the deep blue dye from the green leaves of the indigo plant was by no means either self-evident or easy. The processes of fermenting the leaves, reducing the dye and reoxidizing are complicated. They demand a discerning eye, a quick brain and the power to exercise both deductive and inductive reasoning.

A red dye, too, was extracted from the root of the madder plant. Madder, also used today as a dyestuff, was known from an antiquity so remote that it is not possible to say when or in which country the dye first originated. It was used very early in India, we know, but it seems to have been equally well known to the ancient Persians and Egyptians, for red cloth, very evidently madder-dyed, has been found on Egyptian mummies of a pre-dynastic era.

## Origin of Woad

The leaves of the woad, a plant thought to have originated in southern Europe, provided, like indigo, a blue dye. It was early discovered that young leaves gave a light blue dye, mature leaves a darker blue, and fully ripe leaves a bluish-black pigment. Woad was grown in ancient China in order to provide the blue dye. It was undoubtedly also cultivated in pre-dynastic Egypt. And William F. Leggett in his book *Ancient and Medieval Dyes* tells us that Julius Caesar encountered woad in Britain 2,000 years ago. He writes:

> Caesar found that the aboriginal inhabitants, an ancient Celtic race that had invaded the country after the Stone Age, and who were called *Picts* or painted people, had long punctured their skin with flint tools, and into the abrasion had rubbed anil of the woad plant, and thus formed various designs.

Caesar himself wrote in his Commentaries: "All Britons stain themselves with woad which grows wild and produces a blue color which gives them a terrible appearance in battle." (Blue apparently did not suggest purity to Caesar!)

Prior to the introduction of indigo from India, which did not take place until the 16th Century, woad was the only blue dye used in western Europe, and it was used more, incidentally, than all the other dyes combined. The earliest plant to be cultivated for its pigment content, its preparation was complex. The pulp was crushed, placed in small heaps to drain and, when sufficiently dry, kneaded into balls three to five inches in diameter, and each about five pounds in weight. These were spread on wicker trays to dry for four weeks, then put away in storage until the whole crop had been gathered and processed. When the crop was in, it was all subjected to a process of fermentation. For this, each ball was ground into a fine powder, spread on the

Long after the dark ages, woad, precursor of indigo, was almost universally used as a blue dyestuff. This illustration from the 18th Century shows woad cultivation.

floor of an open shed and sprinkled frequently with water, which reduced it to a paste. For nine weeks the hot, fermenting mass of paste was turned and watered. This fermentation process had to be watched very carefully. If it went too slowly, too bulky a product resulted. If it went too quickly, the dye was impaired. When the right fermentation was finally complete and the stiff paste sufficiently cooled, it was packed into casks ready for the market, one part by weight of finished pigment being obtained from nine parts of woad leaves.

## Saffron and Other Dyes

The ancient Greeks and Romans extracted saffron, their principal yellow dyestuff, from the pistils of the *Crocus sativus*, a fall-flowering crocus. The plant had long been cultivated in Persia and from there had found its way with the Mongol nomads into China, where it was at one time used in the dyeing of carpets. In Rome, the streets were strewn with saffron whenever the Emperor returned with his army to the city. In Greece, it provided at one time the official color. Later, in the Middle Ages, it became one of the principal articles of dawning trade, for it was used not only as a dye but as a spice and drug as well. It even gave its name to a war, the *Saffron War of 1374*, during which a consignment of 800 pounds of saffron was seized as booty.

It would be tedious to go through the entire list of plants ancient men utilized for color. There were hundreds of others, many of them with histories as ancient and interesting as those already discussed. The lore of indigo, for example, is full of fascination. It was anciently classified as an astringent medicine; it was one of the prides of Venetian commercial artistry; and the American Indians who often tinged their birthday suits a blue-violet color used for this purpose a local plant closely resembling the indigo plant of Asia.

Ancient man used trees as well as smaller plants for his dyestuffs. Nine varieties of Brazilwood, for example, were utilized at various times in various countries. These medium-size redwood trees were cut into small, regular sections, after which the units were rasped to coarse powder, moistened with water and fermented for five or six weeks, in order to increase the coloring properties of the wood. Brazilwood gave all kinds of fabrics, except silk, a bright red color.

Logwood, still important today despite the advent of synthetic dyestuffs, is used principally now as a black cotton dye. In its heyday it provided purple for wool dyeing, blue and black for cotton and wool, and black and violet for silk.

## Ancient Animal Dyes

While ancient man was successfully exploiting the vegetable kingdom for his color, he did not neglect the animal world. The development of a purple dye from the purpura shellfish of the Mediterranean is one of the most interesting chapters in the annals of dyestuffs. Legend, perpetuated on the coins of Tyre, has it that Hercules' sheepdog when biting into a shellfish stained his jaws bright red. The dog's master, the story goes, noticing this, immediately ordered a gown to be dyed with the newly found color. Fact, based on the records of historians and archaeologists, tells us that Tyrian purple dye was made in Crete as early as 1600 B.C. and brought prosperity to Tyre, through its distribution by the sea-faring Phoenicians.

Purple is not the oldest color known to man, but from the day it was first manufactured in the ancient factories at Tyre, Tarentum, and Palermo, it had its identity as the rarest and most costly color with which man could adorn himself and his property. During Diocletian's reign it was so rare that wool dyed with it is said to have cost $350 a pound. We know this because the plaint of an irate husband whose wife treated herself to some purple wool is recorded by an ancient historian. Perhaps this is the first recorded instance of a husband complaining about the cost of his wife's shopping jaunts.

Not only shellfish but insects were pressed into service for making dyes. The oldest of all insect dyestuffs comes from *kermes*, an Oriental field louse living on the leaves and stems of low, shrubby trees with prickly leaves. Kermes, processed, provided a deep, bright, red dye. From cochineal insects, too, was obtained a rich, red crimson. And other dyes were made from minerals, ores, and mineral earth substances.

## Artistry in Color

The modern art of color had its beginnings in the great periods of Egyptian, Grecian, Roman, Gothic, and Renaissance art and architecture.

The early Egyptians had a penchant for brilliant colors, living as they did, in the full glare of the sun. The sun beat down upon them all day, its brilliance rarely interrupted by rain. For protection against the heat, homes were built virtually win-

dowless. Still, wishing to live in coolness, the Egyptians did not desire to live in dull gloom. So they ornamented the walls of their homes with strong, bright colors, the use of which their life in perpetual sunlight had taught them.

Because of the absence of rain in the Nile valley, the brilliance of the original wall colors has been retained for centuries. Strong, bright colors, of course, reflect light best, and there is evidence dating back as far as 4000 B.C. to show that the Egyptians were aware of this and were the first known appreciators of color's ability to reflect light. To this day, vivid ceiling hues, cool colored walls and glowing rugs turn heavy shadows into rich bloom. Much of our present-day knowledge and use of color in dark places owes its success to the lessons learned and handed down from early Egyptian colorists.

Beyond this the Egyptians did little to develop the art of color, for they were content to repeat their traditional color associations through the centuries.

## Early Standardization

It is to the Greeks that we owe the origin of color standardization. They set up definite color conventions, among them the practice that no two adjoining architectural members or parts of a figure should be the same color. For example, a blue cornice and a blue gutter could not be used together. One or the other of these members had to be in an alternate color. Color realism, harmony, balance, and rhythm also originated with the Greek colorists. Their contributions have played a basic role in the progress of color artistry. While Rome in its turn contributed the concept of order and efficiency to color art, it is to the religions of all ages that we owe ideas expressed in color in temples, decorations, vestments, and religious objects of all kinds.

Among the ancients, the Persians and Chinese are regarded as the world's finest colorists. Their palettes included such notable and delicate hues as powder blue, a background color used chiefly for ornamental patterns; and mazarine, a blue not unlike Nankin, favored as a base for design accents. The Chinese prized greens, particularly apple green. Today, Chinese tints are still favored for modern wall decorations and woodwork. The delicate colorings of the early Ming and Sung porcelains, notable examples of color art at its best; the dainty transparent quality of the bluish-green-greys of Fenching ware dating back to 1000 A.D.; fine buffs, biscuit colors and creamy whites—these are all widely used to this day.

## Through the Ages

Man used color through the ages as the breath of the life of the spirit. But much of the knowledge and art of color, and most of the technique of the dyer, were lost during the barbaric ages that followed the downfall of Rome. It was the Venetian merchants of the 13th Century, those same merchants who did so much to revive ancient arts of all kinds and transmute them into the stuff of commerce, who imported Oriental dyes and gave the impetus for the rebirth of color in goods, in art, in clothing, and architecture.

From that time on, the palette grew, dye-plants began to be cultivated all over western Europe, and chemists beginning their experiments in the 17th Century started to investigate intensively the nature of color and the dyeing process. Between 1700 and 1825, six French chemists rendered yeoman service to the art of color by investigating the chemical properties of dyeing, by publishing accounts of the various processes in use, by examining the nature and properties of known dyestuffs, and by explaining what they knew of the phenomena of dyeing. During the 18th Century, very rapid progress was made. Modern chemistry had been born and certain chemical products and processes were seized upon by the dyer. Prussian Blue was developed in 1710, Saxony Blue or Indigo Extract in 1740, and before the end of the century sulphuric acid, murexide, picric acid, carbonate of soda and bleaching powder had all been added to the dyer's technique.

## Vegetable, Animal, Mineral

Down to the middle of the 19th Century, the dyer was dependent, with but rare exceptions, on natural dyestuffs, on the products of the earth—vegetable, animal, and mineral—with which prehistoric, primitive, and ancient man had worked. Then, in 1834, the German chemist Runge noticed that aniline, one of the products resulting from the distillation of coal-tar, became a bright blue when bleaching powder was added. Twenty-two years later, in

Dyeing with vegetable dyes.

1856, the English chemist Sir W. H. Perkin turned his observation to practical use. He prepared the first aniline dye—mauve—a color so celebrated that it gave its name to an era.

But more than giving its name to an era, the first aniline dye provided the basis for a gigantic new industry—the synthetic dyestuff industry, which has done so much to revolutionize the way we look and our habits of living. The story of the coal-tar derivatives, and the development of the synthetic dye industry, is a chapter in itself. For its story is the story of color's coming of age.

## Color Comes of Age

As we now know, treasures built up over the ages by the sun's light lie hidden in many forms beneath the surface of the earth. Ordinary lumps of coal are the transformed products of generations of colorful plant life engulfed in the course of elemental catastrophes.

At first, coal served no purpose other than to warm. Later, in the steam age, it was used to produce mechanical power. Still later, the gas coal gave off, when heated, was used to provide a source of light. But not until the middle of the 19th Century was it discovered that the semi-liquid tars and residues left over in the industrial production of coal gas were usable, too. It was this discovery that gave birth to the world-wide synthetic dyestuffs industry. It was this discovery that released color from its place among the rich and privileged few to become not only the delight but the servant of the many.

In actual fact, the birth of the synthetic dyes should be called a rebirth. Just as coal gives off the sun's energy stored in plants countless aeons ago, in the form of heat and light, so coal gives up the sun's stored color to the knowing. (Alchemy? Well, it sounds like it.) All that man needed were the tools with which to liberate these colors from their dark and unlikely-looking prison. The 19th Century supplied the tools.

### Discovery of Coal-Tar Colors

The history of synthetic coal-tar dyes started in 1856 when Perkin, the English chemist, discovered mauveine. Nothing was further from Perkin's mind than the production of a synthetic dyestuff. He was trying to synthesize quinine, which was then as now, an important drug. The brownish black, tarry substance he turned up promised little. But patiently Perkin purified the unpleasant-looking sludge. Finally it yielded a powder with a pleasing color.

Did Perkin appreciate the significance of the phenomenon? Whether he recognized its implications we do not know. We do know that something impelled him to dip a piece of silk into a solution of the powder. History was made at that moment by accident; the dyer and printer had been shown the way into nature's storehouse of color.

Perkin's success set the ball rolling. Another chemist, like Perkin not a color chemist, discovered the extensive range of azo dyes. It was this brewery chemist, Griess, who first applied the nitrogenous compounds to wool and silk. Thereafter, laws of dye formation were rapidly formulated. By the end of the century, the dyer and printer had dyestuffs at their disposal which were suitable for all the textile fibers then in use. Most natural dyes had been ousted by the overwhelming numbers of basic, acid, direct, sulphur and insoluble azo dyes formed on the fiber.

## Laboratory Replaces Plough

The outcome of the struggle was finally decided when the centuries-old dyes, indigo and madder, revealed their inner structure to the chemist, making possible their synthesis by chemical process.

The cultivation of madder had reached a peak when the chemists Graebe and Liebermann succeeded in extracting alizarine, a dye contained in rubiaceous plants, from a distillation product of coal tar. France alone, at the time, was exporting twenty-five million francs' worth of madder. In an attempt to save its madder industry, the French army decreed that its soldiers be clothed in bright red trousers dyed with madder extract—a step comparable to the Dutch boy's attempt to stop the flow of water through the dike with his thumb. But as with many technological advances, benefit to the many brought want to the few. Less than ten years later, France's madder fields lay fallow. Shortly before the turn of the century, Baeyer's discovery of the structure of indigo led to the synthesis of the blue dye and, in the same way, this brought about the ruin of the Indian indigo growers. In the 1880's, 1,400,000 acres had been devoted to indigo raising in India. By 1912, this had shrunk to 214,000.

## The Road to Perfection

Dyers of the 19th Century bent their efforts to emulating nature. The 20th Century dyer has set himself the task of outdoing her. A large percentage of the dyestuffs synthesized up to the turn of the century were simple in application and bright in color. But their degree of fastness to light and washing was something less than good. Stuffs dyed with natural madder and natural indigo had withstood the wear of centuries. But the first stuffs dyed with the new synthetic dyestuffs refused to remain fast. It looked as if sunlight, the source of color, was as intent on taking away as it was on giving.

But again the retort and test-tube proved their power. The discovery of sulphur dyestuffs yielded dyes much faster to washing and sunlight. The development of dyestuffs on the fiber improved color-fastness because they were insoluble in water.

## Indigo Is Synthesized

Then, at the turn of the century, came a most important development. Indigo, the king of natural dyes, and the only vat dye then surviving, encountered its first rival. Synthetists had worked for many years to dethrone natural indigo. Now in a substance derived from anthraquinone, a compound which had hitherto been used in the synthesis of alizarine, they found the answer. By 1905, chemists working for the Swiss firm Ciba had opened the gateway to a whole new realm of vat dyes—based on variants of indigo—from which it was possible to obtain a range of colors throughout the whole visible spectrum. These vat dyes, built upon a basis of anthraquinone and a few other substances, showed fastness properties surpassing those of natural indigo in many respects.

## Twentieth-Century Research

But they were insoluble in water, and were therefore complicated in their application to materials. Researchers of the 20th Century set themselves the task of overcoming this bug. By 1924, the first good vat dye, which was also soluble in water, was developed. The printer who had had to struggle with the old vat dyes was able with this stabilized leuco form of dye greatly to simplify his procedures.

Twentieth Century research has also solved other problems. It had, for example, been known for a long time that the quality of certain natural dyes like madder, logwood, and cochineal depended on the use of metallic mordants. The 19th Century applied this knowledge to a large number of direct cotton and acid dyes by using metallic salts for their fixation, these being added to the fiber either before or after dyeing. The 20th Century has carried this further in order to simplify application—by incorporating the metal in the dyestuff molecule. Substantive dyestuffs of this kind, like the cuprous Chlorentine Fast colors, have solved the problem of producing direct dyeings on cotton and rayon which are fast to light.

The 20th Century has also produced direct cotton dyes fast to light and washing, such as the Corpantine colors. And the fast dyeing of wool was greatly simplified by the development in the 1920's of the chrome-complex Neolan dyestuffs.

The last fundamental dyestuff discovery and one which had been sought for more than a generation was announced in 1956 with the introduction of fiber reactive dyestuffs. For the first time it was possible to attach a dye to a fiber by chemical bonds far stronger than the physical means previously used.

The dyestuffs industry in the U.S. now makes more than 400,000,000 lbs. of dyes a year. The manufacture of dyes is probably the most difficult industrial process of its size because of the complex nature of the process.

Dyes can take from two to ten months to make and are most difficult to make correctly in shade and strength because they have to satisfy that most critical of sensitive instruments, the human eye.

A Ciba-Geigy dyestuffs plant.

## New Problems to Solve

By no means have all the problems in this manufacture been overcome or settled. Industry still keeps the dyestuff chemist in the universities and in the manufacturing fields working hard. First, both the fastness properties of many dyes and the completeness of overall color ranges leave much to be desired. Second, the form in which the dyestuff is delivered to the user still offers a number of difficulties. For example, acetate could not at first be dyed with the usual dyestuffs. Had the dyestuff not been converted into a very fine dispersion so that the

fiber could retain it, printed acetate, as we know it, would not have been possible.

Pigments, both organic and inorganic, are playing an increasingly important part in modern dyeworks. And the new man-made fibers are also greatly multiplying the dyer's problems. Add to this the progressive advances made in the technology of dyeing and printing, which in the case of continuous dyeing methods involve the special preparation of pigments. Today a large part of the research work done in connection with these problems is carried out by the dyestuffs manufacturers themselves, working in close contact with the dyers and printers.

## Color and Industry

We take for granted the miracle of cheap, effective color today, as we take for granted so many other modern miracles. It is only when we stop to examine the miracle that we realize what modern production of color means to us.

Our clothing, homes, automobiles. furnishings, books and magazines, and our business practices have all been revolutionized by the ready availability of synthetic colors. Changes wrought in our clothing and our homes are by this time a familiar story, but if we look back only a few decades to our business practices, we can see that there too change has taken place under our very eyes.

With the War and after, in the release it gave, color began to come into its own. Manufacturers began to invest surplus profits in color experimentation. The response on the part of the buying public was overwhelming. Business jumped on the bandwagon in every possible way, but many businessmen then still felt that color was a fad which was bound to go the way of all fads. No one bothered to concern himself with the scientific aspects of color—to suit the color to the product, to the preferences of the buyers, to the environment for which it was destined.

As soon, however, as industrial leaders realized that color had come to stay, that it represented a logical step forward in the artistic development of the people, the consideration of pleasing combinations of color began to enter into practically every phase of industrial enterprise.

Color, at last, is recognized for something more substantial than its surface value. Its power to arouse emotion, to stimulate buying, to provide the background for the proper display of merchandise and to decrease fatigue and eyestrain is increasingly understood with each passing year.

In a modern dye manufacturing plant: (*above*) dye vats on an upper floor; (*below*) testing in the quality control laboratory.

# Dyes and Dyeing Processes

*The technology of dyeing, developed from a simple vat in which cloth was immersed in a vegetable extract, today covers the chemical synthesis of a host of dyes for special applications.*

Most synthetic dyestuffs today are made from coal-tar derivatives. Their manufacture is a highly complicated technical operation and one which is constantly changing to meet the needs of the man-made fiber industry. Different fibers respond to different dyestuffs and even the same fibers do not always produce a full range of colors with a particular type of dye. No discussion of this complicated field can hope to be complete today but a simplified breakdown by categories can be achieved in a historical progression.

## The Basic Dyes

This group was the first of the synthetic type to be made out of coal-tar derivatives. As textile dyes, they were largely replaced by later developments, but are still used in discharge printing, and for coloring leather, paper, wood, and straw. More recently they have been successfully used with some of the newer man-made fibers. The name *basic* derives from the fact that these are dyes with an organic base which is soluble in a simple acid. Basic dyes were originally used to color wool, silk, linen, hemp, jute, ramie, etc., without the use of a mordant, or binding agent. With a mordant like tannic acid they were used on cotton and rayon. While basic dyes produce brilliant colors they have poor fastness to light and have a tendency to crock or smudge off, due to inadequate fixing or penetration of the color.

Today basic dyes are no longer used to any great extent on cotton or linen and seldom on wool or silk. Because they are cheap, however, they are still used for hemp, jute and similar fibers.

Their most important use today is on acrylics. They can also be used on basic-dyeable variants of nylon and polyester.

## The Direct Dyes

Historically, the direct dyes followed the basic dyes and were widely hailed because they made it unnecessary to use a mordant or binder in dyeing cotton. The colors are not as brilliant as those in the basic dyes but they have better fastness to light and washing, and such fastness can be measurably improved by after-treatments (diazotized and developed). Direct dyes can be used on cotton, linen, rayon, wool, silk, and nylon.

## The Acid Dyes

This is a very large and important group of dyestuffs. While an acid dye is a salt—as is a basic dye—the color here comes from the acid, while in the basic dye it comes from the organic base. The first acid dyes were combinations of basic dyes with sulphuric or nitric acid.

Colorfastness of acid dyes generally has been increased by adding metallic salts—especially chrome—to the dyestuff in an after-treatment. Acid dyes cannot be used for wool tops but are widely used in dyeing wool piece goods, silk, nylon, and some of the other man-made fibers. If a mordant is used they will successfully dye cotton and linen, though this is seldom done today. The ordinary type of acid dye is reserved largely for apparel fabrics and for knitting and rug yarns. A great deal of it is used on nylon carpeting.

The chemist Adolf von Baeyer, who first achieved the synthesis of indigo dye, leading to many new colors.

Closed pressure filter for solvent containing dye slurries; in foreground, plate and frame filter press.

## The Sulphur Dyes

The sulphur dyes have excellent resistance to washing but poor resistance to sunlight. They will dye cotton, linen, and rayon, but the colors are not very bright. One of the problems with sulphur dyes—especially the black colors—is that they make the fabric tender, or weaken its structure, so that it breaks easily. Sulphur dyed fabrics therefore usually must be treated with alkalis to neutralize the acids which have formed.

## Azoic Dyes

These dyes are used primarily for bright red shades in dyeing and printing since most other classes of fast dyes are lacking in good red dyes. Azoic dyes, called Naphthols in the industry, are actually manufactured in the fabric by applying one half of the dye. The other half is then put on and they combine to form the finished color. Unless they are carefully applied and well washed, they have poor fastness to rubbing. Many of them tend to bleed in dry cleaning solvents.

The word, azo, in a general sense, means compounds which contain nitrogen. Specifically, the word means compounds in which nitrogen is substituted for another substance. In a particular sense, the word azo refers to compounds derived from the aromatic hydrocarbons, which contained nitrogen combined in a peculiar way, thereby constituting the azo and the diazo compounds, better known as the azo-derivatives. Thus, the word, azoic, of Greek origin, means a substance that does not possess any organic trace or traces, or no trace of life.

## The Vat Dyes

These are perhaps the best known group of dyes in use today because of their all-round fastness to both washing and sunlight.

The term vat comes from the old indigo method of dyeing in a vat: indigo had to be reduced to liquid form. Vat colors also have to be reduced chemically to a soluble substance and, like indigo, the vat solution is not the same color as the original dye but reverts back to its original color when applied to the fabric.

Vat dyes are made from indigo, anthraquinone and carbazol. They are successfully used on cotton, linen, rayon, wool, silk, and sometimes nylon.

Vat dyes are also used in the continuous piece goods dyeing process sometimes called the pigment application process. In this method the dyes are not reduced before application, but after they have been introduced into the fabric. This makes for a dyeing of superior appearance and economy. There are no bright red vat dyes.

## Reactive Dyes

Reactives are the latest dyestuff discovery and because they react chemically with cotton, viscose, linen, wool and silk they are very fast to washing treatments. They can be dyed and printed by many methods and, for the first time, the whole spectrum of color can be put onto cloth using just one class of dyes.

Production of yellow dye on Nap Isle, Micronesia. Roots are crushed to powder, mixed with water and strained.

The madder plant which has been for centuries the source of a bright and lasting red dye, now replaced by alizarin.

## Dyes for Man-Made Fibers

Dyeing man-made fibers such as acetate, the polyamides, polyesters and acrylics, etc., has proved to be a challenge to dyers. Each new fiber, as it emerges from the laboratory, must be carefully analyzed and tested for its reaction to different dyestuffs. The process has been one of continual experimentation with new developments turning up constantly.

To date both basic and acid dyes have been used as well as what is known as *disperse colors*. A dispersed dye may be any one of a number of insoluble dyestuffs dispersed, or held in suspension, in the dye bath. Perhaps the best known example is the dispersed dye method for coloring acetate, which cannot be dyed by any other technique. For acetate dyes, the dye substance is derived mainly from anthraquinone. It is ground in a colloid mill. When dispersed in the dye bath (colloidal suspension), the particles are microscopic and cannot be detected by the naked eye. They may be from 1 to 100 millicrons in size and in this suspended form they are absorbed by the fibers.

## Other Textile Dyes

*Acetate Dyes.* These are used to color cellulose acetate. They are insoluble but are dispersed with a soap solution. Acetate dyes produce brilliant colors and are the most commonly used dyes for acetates. These dyes are also effective on the newer manmade or synthetic fibers. They are now the major class of dyes used for polyester.

*Alizarin Dyes.* These are vegetable dyes, originally derived from the madder plant and now produced synthetically. They are used on wool and sometimes on cotton. They produce a brilliant turkey red, among other colors.

*Aniline Black.* They are produced from the chemical aniline, and are usually associated with the color black. Aniline black is a fast black, much used on cottons, and is developed by oxidizing the aniline on the fiber. It is very fast to light, washing, and chlorine.

*Chrome Dyes.* These are a special type of acid dyes and they are used to color animal fibers, especially woolens and worsteds. They will react well on a fabric with metals such as chromium. The process, however, tends to dull the color brilliance but does provide high lightfastness and washfastness.

*Soluble Vats.* These are water-soluble preparations of vat dyes.

*Neutral Dyes.* These are metal-containing acid dyes and the metal is added in manufacture.

*Indigo.* The oldest known vat dyestuff, formerly made from the indigo plant, but now made synthetically.

The name Indigo is derived from the word INDIC, meaning *of India,* where it was an important agricultural product for centuries. Even as late as the year 1880, some 1,400,000 acres of land in India were devoted to raising the Indigo plant.

441

DYES FROM PLANTS, MAJOR NATURAL: Many of these have been known for centuries and several of them are still in use today:

1. ANNATO is from the pulpy part of the seeds of Indian plant. *Bixa orellana;* fugitive orange-red color.
2. BRAZILWOOD is from wood of the tree, *Caesalpinia echinata;* bright red color.
3. CUDBEAR comes from the lichen, *Lecanora tartarea;* lilac color dye.
4. CUTCH is obtained from boiling the wood of *Acacia catechu,* native to India; rich brown color.
5. FUSTIC, OLD: Obtained from wood of tropical American tree, *Chlorophora tinctoria;* gold to yellow in color and still popular on wool.
6. FUSTIC, YOUNG OR ZANTE: Comes from the powdered wood of the *Rhus cotinus,* a shrub-size tree of the cashew family; yellow to dark olive in color.
7. INDIGO is obtained from the plant, *Indigofera tinctoria;* blue color.
8. KERMES is extracted from bodies of tiny insect, *Coccus arborum;* red dye.
9. LAC is obtained by boiling tree incrustation produced by tiny lac insect, *Tachardia lacca;* bright red color.
10. LOGWOOD comes from a Central American tree, *Haematoxylon campechium;* gives purple on wool, blue and black on cotton, violet and black in silk.
11. MADDER comes from the roots of the plant, *Rubia tinctorum;* red color.
12. ORSEILLE is obtained from the lichen, *Lichen Rocella tinctoria,* found on rocks of the Mediterranean islands; reddish-purple color.
13. QUERCITRON comes chiefly from the inner bark of the black oak, *Quercus nigra;* brown to yellow colors.

DYES FROM PLANTS, MINOR NATURAL:

1. BENGAL KINO TREE, *Butea monosperma.*
2. BABUL TREE, *Acacia scorpioides.*
3. BAEL TREE, *Aegle mermelos.*
4. INDIAN MADDER, *Rubia cordifolia.*
5. HENNA PLANT, *Lawsonia inermis.*
6. MONKEY-FACE TREE, *Malotus phillippinensis.*
7. POMEGRANATE, *Punica granatum.*
8. RED SANDLEWOOD, *Pterocarpus santalinus.*
9. SYRIAN RUE, *Peganum harmala.*
10. TAMARIND TREE, *Tamarindus indica.*
11. TULIP TREE, *Thespesia populnea.*

The power room of a modern dyestuffs plant.

(*Above*) The shellfish *Murex trunculus*, from which the ancient royal purple dye was extracted in ancient times.

(*Left*) Frontispiece of "Plictho de Larte de Tentori," a book on dyeing printed in Venice in the year 1540.

(*Above*) Traditional and time-honored rule of thumb has been replaced by scientific calculation and laboratory precision in formulating dye preparations. (*Below*) View of a cloth dyeing shop in the 18th Century, from Diderot's Encyclopedia.

The receiving end of a vat-dyeing unit—can drying.

Fabric passing in a continuous band through the dye solution. Note how machine is development of more primitive method with wooden poles.

# Basic Methods of Dyeing

There are five basic methods of dyeing cloth, determined by the various stages of textile production. They are: (1) stock dyeing, (2) solution dyeing, (3) top dyeing, (4) yarn dyeing, and (5) piece dyeing.

### Stock Dyeing

By this method the fibers (or stock) are dyed before they have been spun or blended. It is often used for producing mixtures, heathers, and fancy cloths. The expression "dyed in the wool" had its origin in this method of dyeing and is a good reflection of the depth of color penetration achieved.

Early methods of stock dyeing called for immersing the fiber mass in a tub heated by a steam pipe. The fibers were manipulated by hand with long poles. Later this method was improved by using a mechanism very much like a coffee percolator, which eliminated hand poling. Modern stock dyeing machines generally involve the principle of a rotary drum holding the fibers and turning them in a bath of dye. Some methods keep the fibers stationary and circulate the dye liquid with precision pumps.

### Solution Dyeing

Man-made fibers can be dyed while they are still in liquid state (solution) and before they have been extruded through the spinneret. Color is simply added to the solution. The advantage of this method is that it offers guaranteed uniformity of color, as against traditional methods where different dye lots

may have shadings which vary slightly from the standard.

### Top Dyeing

This method is generally associated with worsted cloths. The fiber is combed into slivers and wound into cheese-shaped tops. In this state the tops are placed in cans which rest in a tank through which the dye solution is pumped. After dyeing, the tops may be blended together before further processing in order to produce special color effects.

### Yarn Dyeing

The ancient method of yarn-dyeing was to hang the skeins on poles and turn them in a tank of dye solution. Today, machines very much like a Ferris

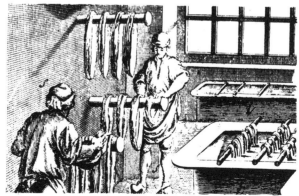

Skein dyeing in traditional style.

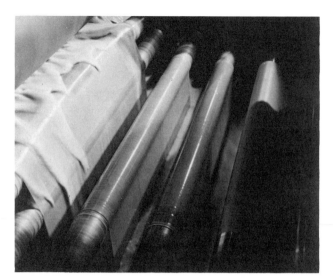

(*At left*) Continuous boil off and scour preparatory to dyeing piece goods. (*Right*) Stock dyeing of scoured wool in a vat. (*Below*) Piece dyeing goods in a jig.

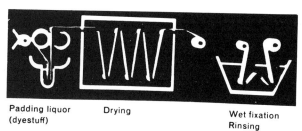

Padding liquor    Drying      Wet fixation
(dyestuff)                      Rinsing

Diagrammatic representation of the pad-jig method.

wheel do the turning. Another technique—called the package method—winds the yarn on perforated spools through which the dye is forced in and out. The warp or beam method also involves winding the yarn on perforated beams through which the dye solution is forced.

*Color space-dyeing* is a form of yarn dyeing which is again coming into use. It is an ancient craft to which different local names, such as *tie-dyeing*, have been applied. It refers to the coloring of yarns at intervals spaced along the yarn length.

In Malaya and Madagascar, in Arabia and Persia, and in many other countries of the Orient, this form of dyeing arose spontaneously and became a part of the textile craft tradition. In many places, tie-dyeing methods were the only ones used to create pattern in a fabric. The Japanese, for instance until fairly recently used tie-dyed yarns for the warp and weft of fabrics to produce a diversity of interesting and popular designs. Color space-dyeing flourished during the 17th and 18th Centuries in Europe.

*Developments in technique.* In this country, with its genius for production techniques, mechanized methods have replaced the ancient laborious ones of applying color space-dyeing. The processes today employ many variants of customary techniques, which result in the achievement of complete dye penetration, fast color, washability, etc., whether applied

Early piece dyeing in open vats.

to coarse or fine twisted yarns. The product is often referred to as *multi-colored, cycle-dyed,* or *ombré* yarn. The new techniques can be used for dyeing yarns in skein or in warp form and can even be applied to yarn packages. The process has now assumed new importance for tufted carpets.

## Piece-Dyeing

Dyeing the fabric in the piece after it has been woven is the most common method in use today, since it is the most economical. Converters prefer it because they do not have to commit themselves to such big yardages as in yarn-dyed fabrics and can therefore adjust themselves more flexibly to fashion changes in color.

*Beck dyeing* is usually a continuous process by which the cloth is passed through the dye bath in rope form. The ropes of cloth move over a rail, then onto a reel which immerses them in the dye and then draws them back to the front of the machine. Since this is a continuous process, it can be repeated as often as necessary to produce the correct intensity of color.

*Jig-dyeing* involves the same basic procedure except that the cloth is held at full width throughout the process instead of being passed through in rope form.

*Padding* is another method of piece-dyeing the fabric at full width. The cloth is run through a color box, then through squeeze rolls which force in the dye and remove the excess liquid. Padding is the basis for all continuous dyeing processes.

It is possible to achieve two or more color effects in piece dyeing by either the *union* or *cross-dyeing* methods.

*Union-dyeing.* Some fabrics are woven from a union of different fibers or yarns, say acetate and rayon. Dyeing is done in a one-bath process by which the same color can be imparted to the different fibers.

*Cross-dyeing* is another form of union-dyeing. It is also based on the different reactions of two or more fibers to the same dye. An example would be a fabric woven with viscose and acetate yarns. When passed through certain blue dyes, for instance, only the acetate absorbs the blue color. The viscose remains white. If the cloth is then passed through a second dye bath—say, red—only the viscose absorbs the red color. The acetate remains blue. The result would be a two-color red and blue pattern without yarn-dyeing. Can also be dyed in a one-bath process to achieve a two-color effect.

# Differential Dyeing

*Each of the man-made fibers tends to have an affinity for one class of dyestuff—and often only one. This scientific fact of life has evolved into a sophisticated science of multi-color dyeing via a single dye bath.*

Each of the man-made fibers tends to have an affinity for one class of dyestuff—and often only one. This scientific reality has brought into being a corollary science of multi-color dyeing via a single dye bath. The technology has important advantages for textile producers since it achieves yarn-dye effects through simple piece dyeing. For textile designers it is a new approach to color which expands the range of design possibilities in piece-dyed fabrics.

The process can be described by the term "fiber-mix dyeing," since this precisely describes the technology and points up its relationship to the development of fabric blends. Technicians also refer to the process as "differential dyeing."

## Fiber Response to Dyes

The concept and procedure are based on the fact that each fiber used in a fabric blend responds differently to different classes of dyestuff. Some reject one class of dyestuff and accept another. As an example: In a fabric blended of fiber "A" and fiber "B", fiber "A" absorbs dyestuff "X" and rejects all others, while fiber "B" absorbs dyestuff "Y" and rejects all others. Thus, if we put the two dyestuffs into the same dye bath, each forms a chemical bond with the fiber for which it has an affinity. The percentage of each dyestuff used in the solution determines the color intensity. When all the dyestuff has been absorbed by the fibers, the dye bath solution is left virtually clear of color.

The result of this procedure is a two-color fabric from one dye bath and the distribution of color depends on how the different fibers have been distributed during weaving or knitting. In all cases, the effect is that of yarn-dye patterns and colorings made through piece-dyeing.

The concept itself is not new since it has long been known that different fibers either absorbed or rejected different types of dyestuff. Traditional cross dyeing and union dyeing were based on this knowledge. The ancient blends of linen/wool and silk/wool, for example, were often treated in this way. But modern chemistry has so refined the concept that it may be regarded as a new technology.

## Advantages in Fabric Production

As compared with yarn-dyeing, fiber-mix dyeing has the advantages of speed, economy and flexibility. The first two are obvious since it is logically faster and cheaper to produce piece-dyed fabrics than yarn-dyes.

The advantage of flexibility is of even greater significance in today's fabric-fashion industries, where the pace of change becomes faster with each season and success often depends on the ability of a fabric producer to shift quickly as the wind of fashion changes. In the area of color, this is often critical.

And that is where fiber-mix dyeing has a major advantage. The fabric converter and the garment maker need commit themselves only to greige goods and have the goods dyed only as they are needed. In this way colors can be changed within the same season or from season to season. They are thus able to avoid losses which might result from stockpiling unsalable colors, as might occur in yarn-dyeing. Also, the fabric producer has the opportunity of coordinating solid colors with patterns throughout his collection. Modern chemistry has thus given him variety and flexibility within the framework of the mass production system.

## Fiber/Dye Affinities

Following are major fibers listed with the class of dyestuff for which each has an affinity:

| | |
|---|---|
| Acetate | Disperse Dyes |
| Acrylic | Basic Dyes |
| Acrylic (Modified) | Acid Dyes |
| Cotton | Direct Dyes |
| Nylon | Acid Dyes |
| Polyester | Disperse Dyes |
| Polyester (Modified) | Cationic and Disperse |
| Rayon | Direct Dyes |
| Rayon (Modified) | Acid Dyes |
| Wool | Acid Dyes |

### I   THREE-COLOR WOVEN PLAID

| Fabric Blend | Dyebath Contains | Effect |
|---|---|---|
| Polyester | Blue Disperse Dye | Polyester takes Blue Disperse |
| Acrylic | | Acrylic takes Yellow Basic |
| Polyester (modified) | Yellow Basic Dye | Modified polyester takes both Blue Disperse and Yellow Basic for green |

*Result: three-color woven plaid of Blue/ Yellow/Green—piece-dyed.*

This four-color circular knit stripe was constructed with four different fibers and colored by piece dyeing in a single dye bath.

### II   FOUR-COLOR STRIPE

| | | |
|---|---|---|
| Nylon | Blue Acid Dye | Nylon takes Acid Blue |
| Rayon | Yellow Direct Dye | Rayon takes Direct Yellow |
| Acrylic | Red Basic Dye | Acrylic takes Basic Red |
| Polyester | | Polyester rejects all three and remains white |

*Result: four-color stripe—through piece-dyeing. A fifth color could be added by using solution-dyed Black yarn.*

### III   TONE-ON-TONE

Tone-on-tone dyeing can be achieved by using two different types of polyester. Both types accept Disperse dyes, but one has a greater affinity for the dye and accepts a greater percentage than the other, its coloring resulting in greater intensity. A tone-on-tone effect is thus produced.

FIBER IDENTIFICATION: Since all fibers used are white before piece-dyeing, they are generally tinted in different shades for purposes of identification during weaving or knitting. This gives the woven or knitted pattern a temporary and visible definition in the greige state. Tints are later washed out.

This 100% polyester doubleknit contains three different types of polyester and was the result of many experimental dyeings.

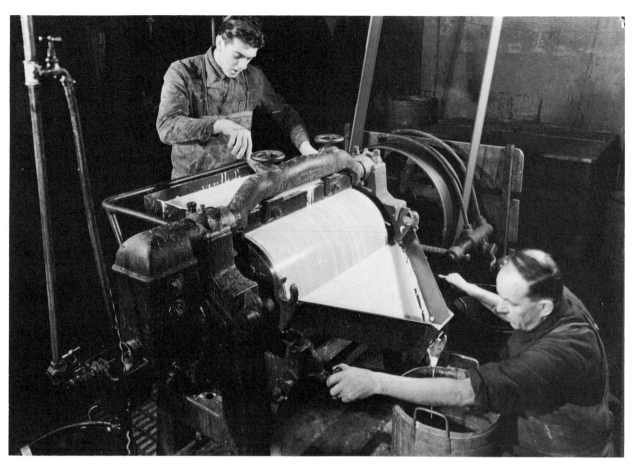

Preparing color for textile printing.

Application print.

Discharge print.

## The Application and Discharge Methods of Printing

A design may be printed on either white cloth or cloth already dyed. When the color is applied directly to white cloth it is known as *direct* or *application* printing. When the color is applied to cloth previously dyed, the dye color must often be destroyed or discharged out before the design colors will show. This method is therefore known as *discharge* printing. Application printing may also be applied to dyed grounds where the print color is darker than the dyed ground, or where an opaque pigment or metallic color like gold is used. In such cases it is known as an *overprint*.

450

# The Printing of Textiles

The printing of textiles is not unlike the process of dyeing. Instead of being applied to the whole cloth, as in dyeing, print color is applied only to specific areas of the cloth to achieve a planned design. Printing has often been referred to as localized dyeing. The same dyestuffs are used in both processes, but dye baths use liquid, and printing techniques start with a paste. The application techniques, of course, differ.

## History of Textile Printing

The history of textile printing is the developing story of the many different methods used from earliest times in applying colored designs to the surface of cloth. Many of the origins are vague, lost with the civilizations which produced them. Archeological investigation has not been too fruitful, since colors are destroyed with time and few actual samples of prehistoric textile prints have been discovered.

## Resist Prints Came First

However, certain broad developments can be traced. It is known that the early Egyptians used printed fabrics. Wall paintings on the tomb of Beni Hassan (2100 B.C.) show costumes decorated with what appear to be printed designs. The early cultures of India were familiar with the technique of resist-dyeing and this may well have been the first form of textile printing. Resist-printing of wools was also used by the peoples who lived in the region of the Caspian Sea as early as 600-500 B.C. The early peoples of Indonesia, Java, and Peru are also known to have produced resist prints.

## Printing with Mordants

Mordant painting, the foundation of modern madder printing, was used on very early Indian calicoes, as was Ikat or warp-printing. By the 5th Century B.C. the Greek historian Herodotus was able to describe printed garments worn by inhabitants of the Caucasus; during the 1st Century A.D. the Roman author Pliny wrote a detailed description of the mordant paint-and-dye method of printing used in Egypt.

## Wood Blocks and Stencils

The use of wood blocks for printing either books or textiles is generally credited to the Chinese at some time during the 8th Century A.D. but there is also evidence that the Egyptians used printing blocks as early as 400 A.D. The technique later appeared in the Mediterranean countries, especially Italy, in the 12th Century and from there spread to the great printing centers of Europe.

China at a very early date, and later Japan, developed stencil printing into a fine art and thus laid the foundation for modern screen printing.

## From Paper to Cloth

By the 13th and 14th Centuries, block printing was being expertly used by Rhenish monks in Germany to produce the initial letters on their illuminated manuscripts. From paper or vellum the process was easily transferred to textiles, and Germany became the center for an industry which simulated in print the rich and elaborate designs of woven textiles. By the 17th Century Augsburg in Germany was famous for its printed linens; competitive industries sprang up in Holland, Switzerland, Spain, France, and England.

## The Vogue for Indiennes

The development of printed fabrics in modern times really began with the importations of Indian cot-

451

Indian flowering tree fabric, late 18th Century.

Hand-blocked English cotton of late 18th Century.

tons by the East India Company in the early 17th Century.

The demand for these Indian prints, known as *palampores, Indiennes,* or *toiles peinte,* was so immediate and so great that the European manufacturers of woolens and other fabrics insisted upon governmental prohibition of their importation. By 1686 in France, the edict of kings not only imposed restrictions on importation and domestic manufacture but even private use of printed cottons was banned.

## France Takes the Lead

With every prohibition the demand increased. Smuggling and secret manufacture of Indian imitations throughout France merely added to their glamour. Ladies continued to turn out in their calicoes in spite of severe sentences; the least of which was a public stripping by the gendarmerie. (In 1717 persons found with Indiennes in their possession were condemned to the galleys.)

As England, Holland, Spain, and Switzerland found their trade with India and their local "counterfeiting" of the Indiennes highly profitable, French commercial interests withdrew their support of the embargoes. By the middle of the 18th Century all edicts were removed and printing of cottons in France began to reflect the artistic imprint of the Romantic Age.

With the establishment of the famous Oberkampf factory at Jouy in 1759 the great era really began. The genius of Christophe Philippe Oberkampf elevated textile printing to a fine art and made it a leading industry of France. Born in 1738, of Bavarian parents, he lived most of his life in France.

His earliest experiences in textile manufacture were as his father's employee in Wisenbach. There he experimented in dye work and colorfasting by the use of mordants. By the time the manufacturing bans were lifted, he was ready to start his own business. On May 1, 1760, the first Toile de Jouy, designed, printed and dyed there, was ready.

## The Toiles de Jouy

Toiles de Jouy were an immediate success. A man of artistic perception as well as an inventive and competent businessman, Oberkampf attracted and hired artists of high caliber to design his textiles. By 1783 his factory had won such high favor that it was designated a Royal Manufactory. Ladies of the court demanded toiles designs from Jouy for housefurnishings as well as wearing apparel. To meet this market the simple flower patterns and decorative motifs inspired by the Indiennes gave way to more elaborate designs which show little restriction as to subject.

## Series of Famous Designs

The factory at Jouy, and its imitators in other parts of France and England, depended heavily upon events of local or national interest to provide inspiration for design, and to keep their goods at the fashionable level. There are many examples of stock patterns which had a center motif replaceable at a moment's notice with a newsworthy item. Perhaps the most famous of these is the "Balloon Ascension," in which a dog motif was replaced by the rising balloon to commemorate the first ascension in Paris in 1783. Oberkampf showed his genius

Toile de Jouy, French roller printed fabric, 1785.

Resist dyed painted cotton, Japanese, 19th Century.

not only in being a good news editor, but in maintaining the fashionable level of his goods, as evidenced by their continued popularity through the numerous changes of regime from Louis XVI through Napoleon. It was the economic disorganization following the Napoleonic Wars, and the death of Oberkampf fifteen years earlier, which brought about the dissolution of the Jouy factory in 1830.

## Roller Printing Sets New Pace

Oberkampf is sometimes credited with having originated roller printing but the first successful roller print operation was set up by a Scotsman named Bell, who had earlier (1770) invented a flatbed method of printing textiles from engraved copper plates. In 1785 Bell had a roller print machine working at Monsey, near Preston, England. That same year, Adam Parkinson of Manchester added improvements to Bell's machine so that it would accurately register several colors. Almost immediately, the firm of Livesey, Hargreaves, Hall & Co. was in production at Preston turning out calicoes simultaneously printed in six colors by the roller method. Since that time roller printing has been so perfected and mechanized that today

Engraving copper rollers for textile printing.

modern machinery can produce printed fabrics in as many as 16 colors at a rate of up to 200 yards a minute.

## Screen Printing Most Recent

Screen printing—which uses the same principle as the ancient Chinese stencil print—is historically the most recent method of printing textiles. Lyons, France, seems to have been the first city to industrialize the technique, about 1850. By 1870 screen prints were being made in both Switzerland and Germany. During the early 1900's several attempts were made in England and the United States to put screen printing on a paying basis but it was not until the 1920's that it began to develop the stature of an industry. By 1926 France, Switzerland, Germany, Great Britain, and the United States were all producing commercially successful screen prints. More recently, this traditional hand operation was revolutionized by the invention of a Swiss machine which prints the screens automatically.

## Printing Methods, Past and Present

Most of the methods listed in the historical development of printing are still in use today in various parts of the world. The older and more laborious techniques are now used only in the simpler, nonindustrialized cultures where handicraft is still practiced. The overwhelming proportion of the world's printed textiles today are produced by the roller machine method and a smaller proportion by the screen method. All techniques, however, both ancient and modern, produce beautiful textiles.

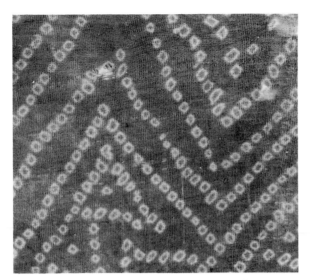

Tie-dyed cotton from Peru, 10th to 15th Century.

Batik sarong cloth, cotton, Java, 19th Century.

Copper-plate printed cotton, French, about 1820.

Roller printed cotton, French, 18th Century.

Double Ikat silk fabric from India, 19th Century.

Resist-printed cotton, Japanese, 20th Century.

454

Contemporary French screen prints show trend to free design motifs.

Cotton cloth ornamented with a combination of tie-and-dye and stitch-resist, Nigeria.

Cotton cloth with a design in batik; note the crackled effect from wax resist, Java.

## Tie and Dye (Resist)

This is one of the earliest methods of decorating cloth, developed in the Far East. It is sometimes called Plangi and is based on the *resist* principle by which certain areas of the cloth are covered with wax which resists the coloring dye. When the wax is removed the design appears on the white ground of the cloth. In the Plangi method, small puffs of cloth were tied very tightly with wax threads. When the cloth was dipped into the dye bath, the wax-tied areas resisted the color and produced roughly circular white designs on a colored ground.

## Stitch Resist

This was a form of tie and dye but more complicated designs could be achieved because the design areas were stitched rather than tied.

## Wax Resist (Batik)

This is the basic resist technique still used by the craftsmen of Java in producing their elaborately colored batik prints. The designs are applied in wax, the cloth is dipped in dye, and the wax is then removed by boiling or using a solvent like benzene. The removal of the wax leaves a white design while the rest of the cloth is colored. This process must be repeated for each color used and there are examples of batiks using as many as 16 different colors to achieve the final design.

When the wax is applied by hand it is called *Tjainting* and uses a tiny spouted pitcher mounted on a pen. When blocks are used to apply the wax it is called *Tjap* printing. The blocks are made by inserting small strips of copper into wood to produce a raised design. The blocks are then dipped into hot wax and applied to the cloth.

In the European countries pastes made of rice or other vegetable matter were generally used instead of wax.

## Warp Print

The Indonesians call this *Ikat*. In Japan it is known as *Kasuri*. It was the origin of modern color space-dyeing of warp yarns. The warp threads are tie-dyed before being warped on the loom. Sometimes the filling threads are also tie-dyed. When the cloth is woven the colored areas appear at fixed intervals, creating a planned design.

Today warp printing is done either by the roller method or the drum method. The roller method prints the yarns after they have been wound on the warp beam and in the same way as woven cloth is printed. The designs may be just as elaborate and they achieve a subtle effect by being broken up with the unprinted filling yarns as the cloth is woven.

The drum method is sometimes used for printing

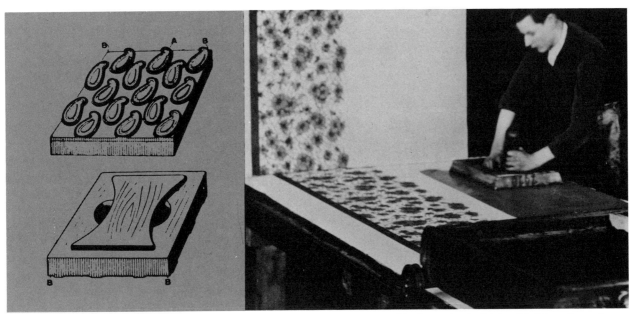

Block printing by hand. At left, front and back of traditional printing block—at back the hand-hold, at front the design. At right, the printer inks the block by pressing on inked pad, before application.

the pile warp yarns in velvet tapestry rugs. The yarns are wound onto a huge drum and printed with all the colors to be used in the pattern. The drum has 576 squares or guides for registering the color areas so that when the yarn is fed into the loom the design appears as it is woven.

*Vigoureux printing* is a variation of warp printing used for wool. Instead of the color being applied to the warp yarns, it is applied to the wool tops or slubbings while they are in rope form and before they have been spun. The designs are usually horizontal or cross stripes laid on by a variation of the roller method. When the tops are later spun and woven the stripes are broken up and appear as color flecks in the finished cloth. Also called *melange*.

## Painted and Dyed

This technique is also referred to as mordant printing. It was used in Egypt at the beginnings of the Christian era but is more associated with India, where it was traditional for many centuries. The so-called Indian "chintzes" were forerunners of Europe's 18th Century block-printed designs and the more modern madder prints were produced by the same basic principle.

The technique originally consisted of painting the cloth with mordants or binders rather than with color. Several different mordants were used and since each mordant reacted differently to the same dye bath, different colors could be produced on

the same cloth with only one dye bath. For even more complicated colorings the mordant process was combined with the wax-resist process.

*Madder printing,* usually associated with British tie silks of deep, subtle coloring and bloom, is a modern extension of the mordant-printing technique. It is so named because madder was originally used for the dye coloring, though it has since been replaced by *alizarine.* It involved the same process of printing with mordants and then developing different colors from a single dye bath. To fix the colors after dyeing, a primitive but still very effective method was used until quite recently: the cloth was passed through a solution whose chief ingredient was cow dung. The method is known as dunging.

## Wood Block Printing

Printing by the use of wood blocks is usually associated with the Chinese and was developed into an exacting craft by the British printers of hand-blocked neckwear fabrics and dress silks. It is a hand operation and consists simply of applying the design to the cloth by the use of a wooden block. One side of the block has the design either cut out in relief or produced by embedded copper strips as in Tjap printing. Usually the end grain of pearwood or sycamore is used and the blocks are about 18" square and 3" thick. The printer inks the block from a pad or color holder and then presses it onto the surface of the cloth which is stretched on a

Typical hand-block print from India; at left the color mass, at right the outline in contrasting color.

padded table. He is able to register the design accurately by the small guide points on the blocks which are outside the design area and which leave marks on the cloth. The process is very slow and laborious, and has largely been replaced today by faster methods. It takes almost 700 pressings of the block to cover a piece of cloth 28 yards long by 30 inches wide with only one color. A four-color print would take four times the number of pressings.

*Perrotine and Surface Printing.* In an effort to speed up the block-printing process different machines were invented. The best known is the Perrotine, invented by Perrot of Rouen in 1834. It used three large blocks, each 3 feet long by 3 to 5 inches wide, which were mechanically inked by brushes and applied to the cloth in sequence. The cloth moved underneath the blocks on a special

table. The *surface* or *peg printing* machine is another device which prints from a raised design in the form of a cylinder rather than a block. The design cylinder is inked from a continuous blanket which carries the color.

## Copper Plate Printing

Copper plate printing was the forerunner of modern roller printing and was developed by the same man, the Scotsman Bell, in 1770. The method has been generally abandoned today and is only of historical interest. In effect it operated very much like the flat-bed letterpress machine except that incised or engraved copper plates were used instead of type.

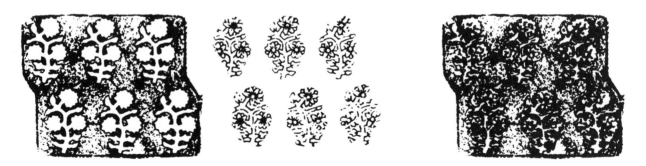

How the color mass and outline, on separate blocks at left, are combined in the finished print, at right.

A Japanese fabric printing stencil with a rich use of natural plant and butterfly motifs; note the net of human hairs which holds the design together while allowing the color to pass through it.

## Stencil Printing from Japan

Printing with cut-out stencils was the forerunner of modern screen printing and was developed by the Japanese into an impressive art form at an early stage of their cultural history. Design areas were knife-cut in a sheet of paper, laying the paper on the cloth in much the same way as block printing, and then applying the color to the stencilled areas with a brush. The Japanese *Yuzi* style was achieved in this way. Later, thin metal sheets were used, or paper stencils were coated with oil or varnish to keep them from softening and disintegrating under the inks. The difficulty with the process was that the design areas had to be connected together with ties to keep them from falling apart, and these ties produced interruptions in the design. To offset this, the Japanese craftsmen developed unbelievably fine ties made of either human hair or raw silk so that they were able to produce a stencil with more open areas than closed, and the ties were so fine that they were practically invisible.

The next step in the process of development was to dispense with the paper stencil and to attach the web of human hair to a wooden frame. From this to the use of silk gauze was an easy step.

Today stencil printing is used in several minor forms of textile decoration. Generally an air brush or a spray gun applies the color through the cut-out parts. Screens are also used for this method. Another method is called *flocking*, and involves the application of loose fibers to design areas which have been stencil-printed with an adhesive.

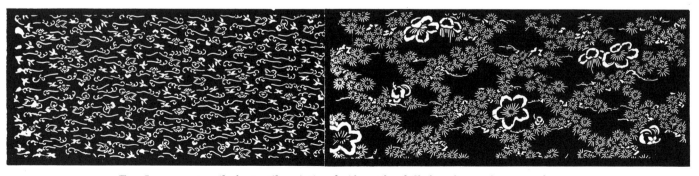

Two Japanese stencils for textile printing, knife-cut by skilled craftsmen from waxed paper.

Hand engraving roller direct from the design.

# Roller Printing

The vast majority of printed fabrics today are done by the roller printing method invented by Bell in 1785. This process combines the developments of engraving and color printing of the type you see in colored advertisements in any magazine, with modifications and developments necessitated by the substitution of fabric for paper. In essence, the process calls for transferring the original design onto copper rollers; the rollers are covered with dye, and as the fabric and rollers meet, the design is transferred to the fabric.

Because the quality of the finished print is dependent upon many separate operations in preparation and execution, the process is here given step by step as it is used in modern production.

Making the Sketch. The original artist's drawing is made into a *repeat* so that it will be reproduced over and over as the roller strikes the fabric, without the loss of continuity.

A roller printing machine at work; at the rear the cloth can be seen going up to the after-treatment stages.

Photographing the Design. An overhead camera photographs every design element representing a single color onto one sensitized copper plate; each color requires a different plate, and as many as 14

## Roller Printing Machine

Invention of a roller printing machine, on the principle shown in the diagram at right, speeded printing from a few hundred yards of fabric to thousands per day. In this method a series of engraved copper rollers, up to sixteen generally, marked "A" in the diagram, are held in stands arranged through the front and bottom circumference of the platen or main drum. For each print roller, which represents one color, there is a color trough, color roller, and doctor blade for the removal of excess paste. All the colors including the ground color are applied continuously at a rapid speed. Depending· on whether the applied color was direct or developed, the processed cloth then proceeds to the steaming, ageing and other after-treatment operations.

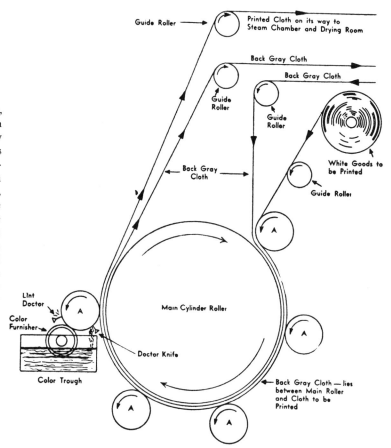

**Seven Steps**

**in**

**Roller Printing**

1. Engraving the artist's design on a metal plate.

2. The design is transferred to roller by pantograph.

3. Chemical resistant is applied by brush or air-brush.

plates may have to be made according to the number of colors to be used.

The Plate Is Painted. An artist paints in the pattern from the traced outline of the original drawing.

Transfer to Roller. Using a pantograph, the engraver traces the lines of the design which appear on the flat plate, and they are automatically transferred to the curved surface of the roller.

Painting the Roller. A chemical resistant is painted over the color areas of the design on the roller.

Etching the Roller. Wherever the chemical resistant has been applied, the lines are protected; everywhere else, acid etches away the copper surface and leaves hollow indentations which cannot be reached by the dye when the roller is locked into the printing machine.

Photoengraving. Rollers may also be engraved by

a photo-chemical process which reproduces all the detail and shading of a photograph.

Hand Engraving. Using a needle-sharp awl, the engraver tools out tiny flecks of copper which might mar the perfect lines of the design.

Finishing the Roller. The entire surface is polished to a uniform smoothness removing microscopic bumps, so that the dye will spread evenly on all protruding areas and lines.

The individual copper roller may have a circumference of anywhere from 14 to 36 inches, and a length of from 46 to 60 inches. It is hollow, and steel mandrils are pressed into the hollow to hold each roller in position accurately and to turn it at the right speed.

When the roller is locked into the printing machine, a set of turnscrews is adjusted to obtain the precise pressure necessary between the surface of the roller and the cloth as they make contact. Each roller,

4. Etching leaves design in relief on the roller.

5. Polishing roller to secure smooth contact with cloth.

6. Mixing the colors which will finally appear on cloth.

7. Placing the color in feed trough of roller, above.

which imprints one repeat of the design in one color, is inked from a color-trough (or color-pan) and, as it spins around, a doctor-knife continually scrapes away any excess dye.

Behind the cloth which is to be printed there is a cotton- or paper-back grey cloth which absorbs excess color; and a rubber or felt blanket, as well as a linen-and-wool lapping cloth, are used as a cushion so that fabric and roller meet with steady pressure.

ACTUAL PRINTING OF THE FABRIC: The cloth passes in turn between the various rollers (each of which deposits a single color impression) and comes out at the end with the completed print pattern clearly transferred. How clearly and sharply this is done depends entirely on the care and skill with which all the preparatory work has been done, and on the quality of the actual printing. The machine can print up to 16 colors at one time at the rate of 150 to 200 yards a minute.

The ingenuity and accuracy of the process is such that the ground or *blotch* color can be printed at the same time as the design or *head* colors and all will be registered so closely as to appear like a discharge print from a dyed ground. The only visible difference is the back of the cloth, where the blotch color has not penetrated and which therefore has a greyed-over look. However, by a process known as duplex printing, both the face and the back of the cloth can be printed at the same time with the same design and with such accuracy of registration that the fabric at first glance appears to be yarn dyed and woven.

AGING THE PRINTED CLOTH: When all of the colors have been printed on the fabric, it goes through a steam-heated machine which firmly sets the colors to prevent running or fading.

WASHING THE FABRIC: In this process any excess compounds left on the surface are neutralized and scoured off to leave a uniformly smooth effect.

View in screen-printing workshop. The fabric is laid out on table, and the screen is moved along it, reproducing repeats of pattern. For each color a different screen is used.

# Screen Printing

The screen printing method in textiles is basically a stencil process. A wooden or metal frame is covered with a bolting cloth, which may be made of silk, fine metal thread, or nylon. The fabric is covered with a film and the design areas are cut out of the film just as in stencil making. The frame is then laid on the fabric and color is brushed or squeezed through the open areas of the film by the use of a big rubber knife or squeegee.

Originally, the design was cut out of film and then adhered to the screen. Today the cutting is done mechanically by a photo-chemical process which reproduces the design exactly as it was painted in the art which is being reproduced.

In printing, one screen is used for each color and these are accurately registered one on the other by the use of fixed stops attached to an iron rail running the length of the table. The length of the table determines the number of yards which can be printed at one laying; this varies depending on the available space, though 30 yards is considered the smallest space which is practical for economic production.

## Electronic Aids

*Automatic screen printing.* Until recently, screen printing was a slow process, almost as laborious as block printing. It involved carefully laying out the fabric on padded tables, pinning or gumming it flat and regular, then laying on the screens one color at a time, hand-forcing the color through with the squeegee, and, finally, lifting the printed cloth from the table and drying it on overhead racks.

This whole series of operations has been revolutionized within the past decade through the invention of an automatic screen printing machine by the Swiss firm of Fritz Buser Engineering. Several variations of this machine are now available but the principle in all is about the same. It is a continuous production method which uses electronic devices to control both pattern and dyes. It is from 5 to 7 times as fast as the hand screen method and enables two men to do the work formerly done by at least 15 men.

## How Automatic Screen Printing Works

The new operation, made possible by the Buser machinery, is a continuous process in which the cloth moves along a table, the application of the screens being automatic and electrically controlled. The colors are applied by an automatic squeegee operation also electronically controlled. The entry of the cloth into the machine is held straight to fine tolerances by the same type of electronic controls.

The machine is built with eight frames, each of which can apply a different color if required, and the operation of each of which can be adjusted for pressure, rate of lowering and raising and so on, separately. When the machine is running, all frames operate simultaneously, and the cloth moves forward one frame-width between each application of color. The process therefore is equivalent to continuous printing of up to eight colors at one time. Height of design repeats can be up to 80 inches.

As the fabric leaves the last frame it passes into a drying box, from which it emerges dry and ready for aging.

## Advantages of Screen Printing

While screen printing, either by hand or machine, is a slower and more expensive process than roller printing, it has several virtues. From the point of view of design, pattern repeats can be much larger than in roller printing. Also, since the process is slower, pigment colors can be laid on in heavy layers to produce a handicraft effect. From an economic point of view, it does not require as large an investment as roller printing because the runs can be shorter, especially in the hand operation. This has encouraged smaller converters to adopt the screen method and to experiment more with design than they would be able to do in the roller method, where they would be required to contract for a minimum of about 8000 yards per pattern.

## Steps in preparation for screen printing:

1. Opaquing the color tracing where the resisting medium will be applied to the screen.

2. Photography is used to copy the completed design on clear acetate sheets.

3. The opaque negative obtained from camera is used in contact printing on screens.

4. The completed screen in place, color is poured on, ready for printing to begin.

## Steps in Making
## a Screen Print

The first step in the creation of a screen printed fabric is transferring the designer's sketch or drawing. It is carefully traced for each separate color, to provide the outline of that area of color. Next the different screens, each representing a separate color, have the area outlined by the tracing, opaqued. The area which is not opaqued will become the colored area when the ink is forced through the screen mesh onto the fabric below.

When screens are made by photographic method, the design is photographed and the negative is used for the opaquing process, using a specially sensitized screen.

The colors are mixed in bulk precisely to the artist's indicated samples and transferred to smaller containers, as required, for use. From the small container they are poured onto the corresponding screens and forced through the screen mesh onto the fabric by squeegee.

The fabric is stretched out on long tables, and one screen is printed at a time. The screen is laid on it in successive positions corresponding to the repeat. When one color has been completed the next is printed.

After the colors have all been printed the fabric is treated with steam heat to set them, then finally given decatizing or other finishing treatments for fullness and texture.

*The printing screen:* the screen itself was formerly made of silk and the name *silk-screen process* is still used in the trade. Screens today are largely made of synthetics, and the material is securely stretched over a heavy wooden frame. as shown above. The design to be reproduced is transferred to the screen by photography by placing a special sensitized coating over the screen. A separate screen is used for each color.

Fox Talbot, Father of Photography, whose work made present day silk-screen printing possible.

Special cameras are used to make color separations from the artist's designs.

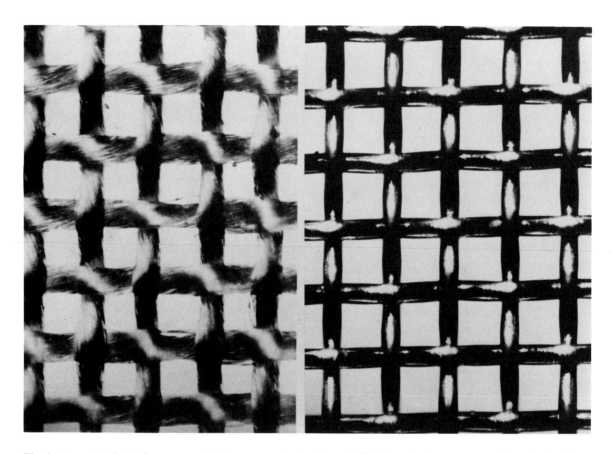

The basic principle in the screen printing process is forcing a thick dye solution, or paste, through the fine mesh of a stencil screen (*above:* two types of mesh, greatly enlarged) onto the cloth with the aid of a heavy rubber blade or squeegee (*below*). By blocking the mesh with a coating where color is not desired, the dye is allowed to pass through the design onto the cloth. The cloth is laid out on a long table and by moving the screen, repeats are produced and a continuous pattern achieved.

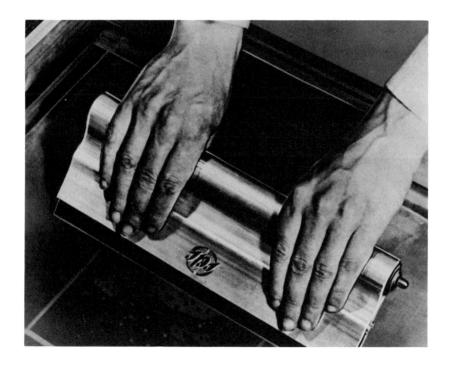

The cloth which is to be screen printed is held in place on sixty-yard-long tables with a tacky wax, while the printer operates the screen (*above*). After printing, the cloth is suspended for drying from racks placed above the tables (*below*).

Fully automatic multi-color screen printing machines ensure faultless printing of the most complicated designs. All fabrics from the finest silks to the heaviest linens can be printed with neatness and precision, and the designs can run to as many as eight colors. Change over is rapid, and the machine can accommodate repeats ranging from 16 to 80 inches. Two men using this machine can print from 250 to 450 yards of fabric per hour.

# Automatic Screen Printing

*The screen process for printing textiles, while producing the highest quality work, has been essentially a hand process. The introduction of an automatic screen printing machine by Buser of Switzerland greatly speeds up the output of screen print production.*

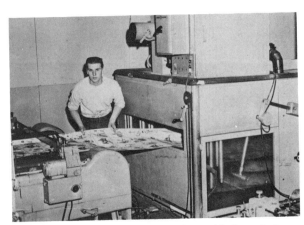

The drying chamber: hot air plant with forced circulation dries fabrics as they leave machine.

Semi-automatic printing: the cloth is moved automatically but color is applied by hand.

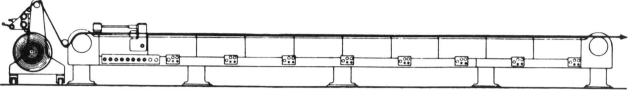

Diagrammatic drawing of an automatic screen printing machine.

When the screen printing is done on these new machines five-hundred-yard rolls of cloth are used instead of sixty-yard pieces as in the hand process. As the roll enters the machine, it is coated on the back with a gum-arabic solution which causes it to adhere to the continuous rubber belt that serves as the table top for the printing. The belt, bearing the fabric, advances to the first printing position and stops. The screen then automatically lowers to the cloth and a chain-driven squeegee moves across the screen, as is done by hand in the other room.

The pressure of the squeegee on the screen and the number of passes it makes back and forth across the frame are adjustable and may be pre-set to suit the requirements of the particular dye and fabric being used. The machine will accommodate eight different screens, and the squeegee mechanism for each operates individually. Thus, if one color needs more passes with the squeegee than another, the belt waits for the operation to be completed before moving the cloth forward to the next position.

The forward movement of the cloth is adjustable to 1/256 inch, to insure perfect register of colors. Electronic speed controls enable the belt to start slow, speed up for most of the travel distance, and then slow down again to the stop, so that the cloth will not be stretched in the passage from frame to frame. Similar precision devices regulate the operation of the squeegees, which are of double-bladed design. One rubber blade carries the dye paste one direction across the screen and then lifts, allowing the other to bring it back.

Another feature of the machine is the continuous belt cleaner. As the rubber belt returns to starting position, having discharged the cloth into the drying oven, it passes through a wash and dry cycle which puts it in condition to again receive the gum-arabic-treated cloth as it enters the machine.

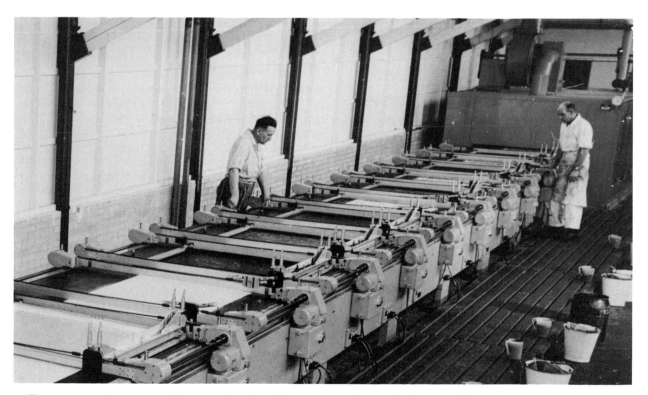

Buser automatic screen printing machine in which the controls are all electronically operated to achieve a high degree of precision in registration combined with rapid operation for commercial output.

# Other Printing Methods

*Sublistic and rotary screen printing represent two new printing methods which permit faster rates of production than earlier flat screen methods. They constitute major advances in speed, design flexibility and clarity.*

The sublistatic machine made by David Gessner.

## Sublistatic Printing

Sublistatic printing is a dry printing process which was introduced in the late 1960's. This system employs a pre-prepared pattern paper from which a design can be transferred to nearly any fabric by a simple, hot-transfer or calendering operation. After printing, no subsequent treatment of the fabric such as scouring or steaming is required.

During the hot-transfer operation, the temperature of the fabric is raised to 200° C (424° F). The main advantages of the sublistatic system are ease of application, clarity of reproduction, flexibility in design choice and wide range of design size. Patterns can be transferred onto a wide variety of fabric constructions and weights, including wovens, knits, non-wovens, stretch covers, fur fabrics and even carpets. Because of the easy changeover capability of the system, it permits short runs and a reduction in the amount of printed fabric which is desirable to be held in stock. The sublistatic print papers are prepared by a photo-lithographic process and can reproduce nearly any pattern or a painting of any size in the graphic world.

## Rotary Screen Printing

Rotary screen printing, as the term implies, combines some of the advantages of both roller printing and screen printing. The rotary screens, which are made from metal foil rather than fabric, are extremely lightweight and are also considerably less costly than copper rollers. Though the rotary screen printer is used for small repeats only, it can achieve the same color depth associated with flat screens.

Rotary printing is continuous, just as is roller printing, and thus its rate of production is higher than that attained by the flat screen method, which necessitates stopping and starting again at intervals. Though rotary screen printing does not achieve the production speed of roller printing, its down-time during pattern changeover is less than that of roller printing.

The similarity of rotary screen printing to flat-bed screen printing lies in the fact that in both instances fabric is fed into a conveyor belt where it is pasted in place and run under the cylinder screens—one run for each color—before being fed into a dryer.

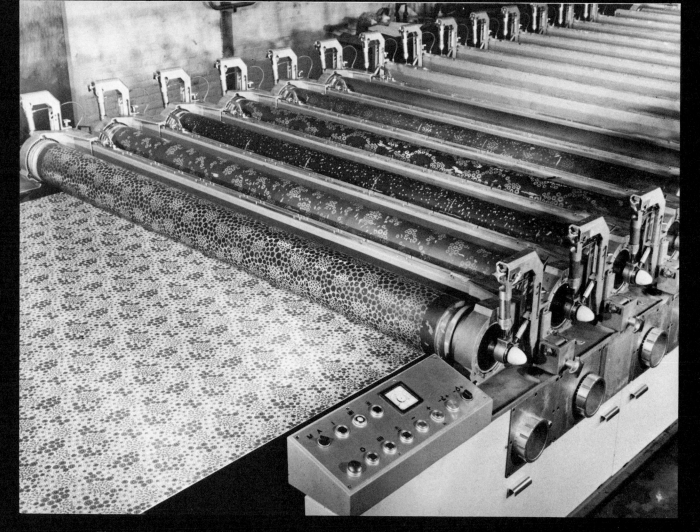

The rotary screen printing machine combines advantages of roller printing and screen printing.

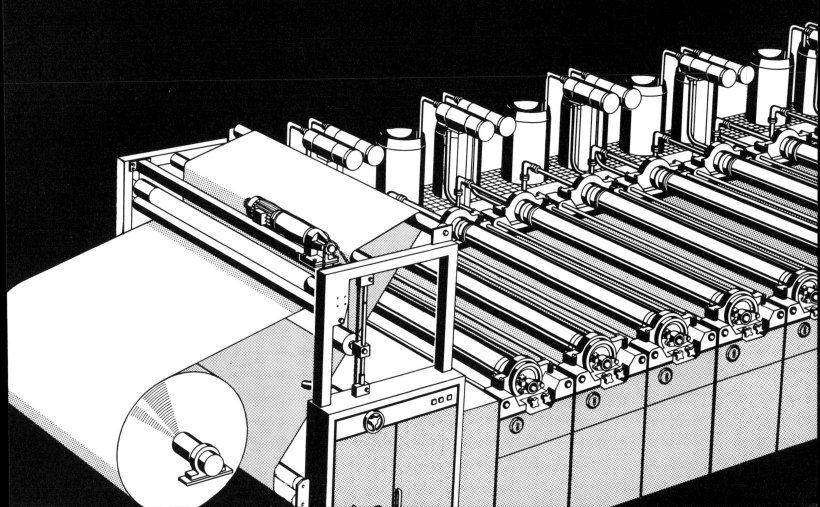

Reception room of a business suite with glass fiber draperies.

# Curtains and Draperies

*An important item in domestic textile applications
are the fabrics used to exclude or diffuse light,
especially in present-day architectural settings.*

A 500-year-old dictionary would have defined curtains approximately like this:

"Curtains are lengths of cloth designed to cover cold walls, hang across open doorways and generally keep heat in a room."

In later editions the definition would have appeared slightly changed and the word window would have been mentioned for the first time.

From wall adornment to window framing was a process of slow inchings, and almost until the Machine Age of the last century was considered by the great majority of under-waged people a needless luxury. They quite uniformly used wooden and later metal inside shutters which kept out glare and wind whenever, as was often the case, there was no glass or paper in the windows.

In India and China there are records of windows being draped in temples and palaces as far back as the 6th Century, but it wasn't until the late Gothic era of Europe that the West began curtaining any-thing but walls and doorways, nor was the custom widely accepted even by royalty and merchant kings until the Renaissance was well under way.

## Draperies and Architecture

As was to be expected, the development of draperies is bound closely to that of architecture, and especially windows. In the early days, window glass was only as large as the glass blower's lung capacity, and it was thick and bubbly; or, more often, oiled linen filled the frame. It was difficult enough for the light to get through, and certainly no outside eye could penetrate.

In the fortress-like castles of the Dark Ages, for reasons of defense the windows were small and irregularly placed about, but with the rise of states over feudal princes and relative stabilization of society and, more especially, the introduction of gunpowder which outmoded feudal defenses, the style of architecture changed from moated castles to chateaus . . . and windows came into fashion.

474

## Drapery Designs During the Renaissance

At first these were very simple with just one piece of material to draw across the window and, hung by big iron rings, they slipped across ornate metal rods. When not in use they rested against the wall beyond the end of a window, still decorating more wall than window.

The textiles were as brilliant and striking as the style was simple. There were barbaric velvets and fiery brocades brought by merchants from the East, or from the eighty-five textile work-shops which flourished in Florence alone by the mid 1400's.

The Louis XIV era was marked by grandiose patterns, and a breaking away from the tight medallions and over-stylized conception of nature with which Eastern weavers had so long filled Europe. Instead, Louis insisted that his weavers model their florals after those in his Garden of Versailles of which he was so proud; and when he founded the lace factories he recommended that weavers incorporate patterns of lace in their fabrics.

## Development of Cotton Prints

In England, as was repeatedly the case, the style . . . almost identical with the French . . . was slightly larger and without the French lightness of touch. For their dark, formal rooms the English clung closely to the wooden-based valance covered by fabric matching the curtains. This was especially true in the reign of Queen Anne, whose unostentatious personality tempered all designs of the time. Later the Dutch style of double-hung curtains,

"Creation of the World," showing detail of embroidered border. Italy, 17th Century.

each pair only half the length of a window, found lasting favor in England. England's claim to nationalistic difference lay only in her greater use of cotton print and chintz from India. While France used some at the time, it wasn't until she conquered Annam and Tonkin that cotton prints became more the fashion than the exception.

In the natural course of events during the Louis XIV reign of 72 years, styles changed and where under LeBrun the straight, classic line of early Quatorze became a never-again equalled blending of curve and line, under his successor, Pierre Mignard, the curves began besting the lines and soon rolled themselves into the rococo; it is this style which has been identified in history as Louis XV.

## The Rococo Style

The curtains became irregular and sinuous like everything else in the Rococo Age. Billowing in

(*At left*) Crewel embroidery on curtain. Cotton worked in wool. England, 17th Century. (*Center*) "The Goose Hangs High," Chinoiserie fantasy cotton. France, 18th Century. (*At right*) Detail of embroidered bed cover, silk on cotton. India, 17th Century.

great profusion, they cascaded and frilled at every opportunity, and everything was lavishly trimmed. There were two favorite styles . . . one which offered no valance but was caught back in several places in generous loops and drapings, and the other which had deeply scalloped and generously overlaid valances, fastidiously avoiding repetitious curves.

There was no formal balance in the drapery; rather, it was based on rhythm and an evening up of mass and detail. Curtains were restless like the Court itself, and balance was boring. Caprice ruled decoration; trimmings were used without restraint . . . great excesses of lace and ribbons, yards and yards of heavy fringes, tassels and figured galloons.

It was the Age of the Boudoir, and things were decorated accordingly. Measured balance in the chambers of Mesdames Pompadour and duBarry were impossible to imagine, and who would have them restrained? The King's mistresses were always redecorating their apartments and encouraged or ruined styles at the whim of a moment. In one instance, the minister of finance, in order to nurture the newly begun factory of toile de Jouy, ordered contraband and illegal chintz from India. Immediately, Pompadour decorated an entire apartment in the material and created such a demand for it that riots and street fighting ensued all over France.

## Influence of Chippendale

Textile patterns were smaller, rounder and more broken-lined than those of the starched era of Louis XIV. They were gay and extravagant like the age they represented . . . elegant ladies, amorous and playful gods, delightful landscapes, lush flowers, nymphs, rocks and shells, plumes and feathers. There were many irregular lines and broken diagonals; and under the influence of England's Thomas Chippendale, as well as the newly acquired Indo-China, France became flooded with Chinese-type designs, freely translated by the weavers.

Chippendale also influenced European decorating with his elaborate, Oriental-style cornices of gilt or japanned wood. It added many ornate curves to what had formerly been bare wall, and carried the restless eye higher. It exactly fitted the decadent charm of Louis XVth's court.

Bold pomegranates, artichokes, animals, large bands and medallions were woven into almost all the material at first; then local weavers worked in Hellenistic motifs. There was gold cloth everywhere, and heavy fringes of gold, silver or strong colors on

almost all drapery material, especially in England's contemporary Tudor houses. As the Renaissance progressed, materials became smoother and more feminine.

## France the Center of Drapery Fashions

While the Latins were amusing themselves with the labyrinth of twists and curls, the decorating style center moved north to a vigorous France where it remained, at least in the realm of curtains, until Napoleon exhausted his decorators in his attempts to glorify himself; but from Louis XIV until that time, a period of approximately two hundred years, the world copied, with few modifications, the curtains of France.

The king who said, *I am the State,* a man almost unequalled in history by his vaunted idea of self-importance, would certainly have demanded that he be sole arbiter in even so unpolitical a question as the style of curtains; and at first he approved the type which was almost architectural, it was so heavy and full. The materials were usually heavy, but where lighter silks and taffetas were used, they had to be lined and interlined with canton flannel. This precedent lasted through all the Louis kings in diminishing degree.

About 1660, when Charles LeBrun became decorating advisor to the Sun King, curtains grew more voluminous in tribute to the king's exorbitant wealth, and there were great masses of rich and always regal decoration. Never under LeBrun did either ornamentation or draping become redundant or immoderate.

## Fringes, Tassels, Draw Curtains

Lambrequins, either plain or cut in dentils, were greatly favored, and they were trimmed with galloon or other rich bands, and the fringes and tassels on the long curtains were justly proportioned. Perfection dominated the execution of every detail in both curtain and fabric.

At first the fashion was for a single glass curtain to drape the entire window, but about 1673 it was split in two and draw cords were introduced. The outer drapes were caught back low with ornamental tie-backs, and at first were of plain, bright-colored velvets; then, with the development of the Lyons factory, silk became the favorite material. The king and LeBrun did much to promote weaving and all the arts in France, and were generous patrons.

Reversing the Renaissance's color-style relationship, 18th Century France foiled delicate pastels against vivid style; and in a room there was never a sharp contrast of color. Typical of the time was a shade like duBarry's Blushing Rose Pink. The fabrics were smooth, elegant silks, which were all made in France by that time . . . damasks and frivolous brocades. Then in 1759 there was toile de Jouy, with its partridges and fashionable hunting scenes. Another innovation for the court and very wealthy outsiders was the lace curtain . . . not the patterned, heavy curtains of later ages, but very soft, almost gossamer material which replaced muslin and silk as inner curtains.

## Revolt Against Rococo

Although the king had promised his court that things would go on that way until his death, the over-taxed people of France had begun the rebellion which was to culminate a few years later in revolution, and court designers thought it wise to temper the lavish show of wealth; thus Louis XV lived to see the Revolt against the Rococo, as the reign of his grandson, Louis XVI, is called.

Curtains were among the first to feel the reform. Lambrequins were skimped and straightened. Some still retained shallow curves, but became so measuredly balanced that it seemed each thread was counted. Often curtains hung from simple cornice boards and, having no valance, were festooned for daytime use.

The long draperies became less bouffant and, influenced by the recent uncovering of ancient Pompeii and Herculaneum from the ashes of Vesuvius, became classic in tenor. Grace and suppleness replaced the lavish bloom of the past, and everything, even tassels and fringes, became smaller.

## Smaller Provincial Designs

Patterns in the fabric indeed became miniature and stiff . . . little croisillons, sprigs, classic urns, garlands and torches, prim florals, cameos, petite pastorals, bows and quivers, and everywhere dainty stripes and ribbons. There was a feeling of space and separateness, instead of the disorder of the Quinze.

The trimming was flat and classically restrained; and the silks became lighter and less expensive, with taffeta as favorite. Cottons were also extensively used, and for the first time average homes were widely curtained. Although French Provincial is usually dated from 1700 to 1800, their curtains were more XVIth style than XVth, very simplified, or course, and leaning heavily toward a quilted valance board and full draw-curtains of toile, checked gingham and other cottons, and home-made textiles of the region; although in the best rooms, they often used cheaper-grade silks, especially a striped satin.

Much of the design and style of the period were inspired by the simple tastes of Marie Antoinette, who was never happier than when playing milkmaid at the miniature farm she and the king set up near the Petite Trianon. It was a most feminine period dedicated to home life and chastity, but the revolutionists were not assuaged and finally set up business with Madame la Guillotine and beheaded the Bourbons.

## Directoire and Related Periods

The government changed hands many times during the next few years; but to decorators it doesn't matter whether the Jacobins or Encyclopedists were at Versailles; the period is known as Directoire, and the classic trend started by the last Louis was continued and intensified. Draperies became mere Greek pillars of material with a few box-plaits and the merest suggestion of *eased* material. A delicate swag was draped over a metal pole or pulled through large brass rings, ending high up on the window in a graceful cascade or flat jabot.

In the beginning, there were seldom any inner window curtains, as the extra curtains suggested wealth and reminded people of royal extravagance. While the mob ruled, those with money felt it safer not to call attention to themselves; and designers also were influenced by the austere writings of Diderot, Rousseau, and Voltaire which vaunted Reason and Logic over decadent Luxury. This period in France was copied in England by *Regency* and in America by *Federal*; although both foreign periods continued in France's *Empire* period and are identified with it. In this era it is interesting to note that venetian blinds were first introduced into America.

The colors of the Directoire were strong and brilliant with much deep yellow, bright red, green, black and white. The patterns were formal and mostly of classic motif, and everywhere there were draperies of narrow, highly contrasting stripes.

Directoire is often dismissed as mere transition between Louis XVIth and Empire, but this is only because of the shortness of time (15 years), not because of indefiniteness of style. It is true that it gradually became the heavier, more Roman *Empire* period, but that is to be expected when a classic style has been refined to its most supple form, and when . . . due to outside reasons . . . it cannot turn to the Rococo.

Detail from an 18th Century fabric.

## Influence of the Empire Era

Napoleon's own egomania and confusion of himself with Julius Caesar helped to give the style its direction; as for Empire curtains, they were slung like togas over ornate poles which were usually made like spears, staffs, or eagle heads which caught the cloth in their beaks. There was a sense of agitated movement in the draping, and though it was supposed to look careless, only the most skilled workmen could cut and hang the material properly.

As the Empire progressed, lambrequins were crossed and criss-crossed so often, and materials were pitted against each other in such complication, that only the most daring and competent drapers survived.

In many informal rooms there was much use of calico, unsymmetrically crossed and gathered in generous folds, but in the drawing and formal rooms they chose heavy material which fell in impressive folds . . . elegant satins, heavy silks, moirés and embroidered velvets. Most often, at one window there would be three sets of draperies in contrasting colors, such as red, green and gold; or the more startling blue, orange and pink. Colors were always bold and usually harsh. Under-curtains were usually of fine lawn or batiste with generous festoons and ball fringes.

## Napoleonic Motifs

The watchword was Stiff Massiveness and everything about the draperies suited, even the heavy bullion fringes and tassels which hung several inches long, and the gigantic metal rosettes which caught back the draperies.

There were no masses of flowers or light-hearted designs woven into the material . . . that had belonged to Royalty, and Napoleon's dynastic soul longed for his own symbols; so he appropriated from ancient Rome the laurel wreath (in which his N was always centered), Roman eagles, lion heads, torches, urns, griffons, strong circles, and always stripes . . . thick, heavy stripes of stark colors. Red, gold, and black were often used.

When he conquered Rome, Napoleon adopted the bee as his own trademark, signifying the subjection of the leading family of Italy, the Barberini, whose symbol was the bee. Then, after defeating Egypt, he decreed that there be sphinx heads and lotus leaves throughout decorated France. And it was about this time that the famous jacquard power loom began.

Because of the desire to impress with massiveness, decorators often treated two somewhat adjoining windows as one, including the wall in their sweep and giving a unity as never before; and they went in strongly for hanging or painting drapery on the walls.

## England Becomes the Style Hub

When Napoleon went to Saint Helena the *raison* of all Empire decorating went with him. How meaningless the laurel leaves, N's and flaming torches looked when another Bourbon sat on the throne, even though Louis Philippe was not the one to inspire new styles. There apparently was no place to go in decorating, and Napoleon had thoroughly exhausted his designers with demands that they glorify him; so for the first time, at least in curtain history, England became the style hub. Interestingly enough, Victorian curtains were nothing more than Empire drapes with the characteristic English stamp of larger and heavier; and it apparently didn't bother them that they were developing a style created to glorify their enemy.

In any event, there are few who will say that Victorian draperies glorified anything. With fantastic loops and swags and matching ponderous drapes, their main functions were apparently privacy and the exclusion of any ray of sunlight which might fade the new, patent furniture.

Fabrics were as heavy as the style . . . richly colored damask or velvet, usually of dark red or gold. They were fringed and tasseled in equal ostentation.

There was much use of shaped and low-hanging valance boards which were usually covered with heavy damask and brocatelle; and where swags were used . . . mostly of satin . . . they often hung way below the middle of the window. This weightiness was felt most strongly when Victorian England was under the Oriental influence, which came after the opium wars and the establishment of trade with China.

## Changing Styles of the Last Century

Like any long period, the Victorian era went through many phases of style, but the curtains we generally associate with the name came after Industrialism was well under way, and those who dominated the style, even more than the court, were the insecure *nouveaux riches* who decorated on the theory that if something was big and there was lots of it, then it must be good. In America, where society was even more insecure, the theory still more strongly pressed; and curtains of Victorian America were on the whole more lavish than those of England.

It was the age of machine-made cloth, including the lace which hung at every window from the palace to the tenement flat, and for the first time in history even the poor could afford draperies. Indoor shutters continued to be used in England and America, however, until very recently, but it was habit more than economics which kept them on.

In France the drapery *croiseé* of the Second Empire became so heavy and complicated from 1860 on that almost no sunlight could get in. It contributed nothing to curtain development, except that around 1900 some French designers tried to introduce *L'Art Nouveau*, which would have draped both doors and windows even more heavily than

Resist-print cotton plain cloth. Probably New England, 18th Century.

Victorian was already doing; and probably would have influenced fabric designs with its emphasis on naturalistic principles. The movement, fortunately, didn't find much favor in either Europe or America.

## Beginnings of Modern Style

Between Victorian and Modern periods, there were many fads and changes of style, following the eclectic architecture of the age. Draperies were made of every fabric imaginable and copied from every style, until somewhere around the 1920's, the idea of treating a window and wall as a single flat-plane surface was declared *modern;* and the past principle of framing the window was discarded.

The practice of pulling a curtain back against the wall for daytime and treating that side of the room as a one-fabric unit at night, might thus be said to most nearly approach the pre-Renaissance concept of curtains. It is thus we complete a first cycle of drapery history: Wall to window . . . window to wall.

# The MODERN MOVEMENT in DECORATIVE FABRICS

During the period immediately following World War II, there began a unique chapter in the American fabric industry. In an industry that has always been geared to volume output and committed to designs that satisfied the largest possible number of buyers, there began to be signs of another idea in fabric production. This idea attracted little or no attention from the large producers, with one or two notable exceptions, and even today when it has grown to respectable proportions its portent is not widely recognized or understood.

## To Fill a Need

As is often the case with the growth of a new concept, it develops to fill a need either unrecognized or ignored. In this case the need was adequate printed and woven fabrics to satisfy the drapery and upholstery requirements of a small but growing group of modern designers and architects. Before World War II the modern movement in architecture and design, although it was already over fifty years old, was still considered something strange and remote and certainly very far from anything that could be considered seriously by a volume-conscious industry. There had been sporadic efforts during the pre-war years to produce a so-called Modern design, usually influenced by early Viennese, German, Swedish or French efforts, but it can be safely said that there were no well-designed modern fabrics available in any quantity or at reasonable prices that satisfied the rather demanding needs of the new designers. This could be said of almost everything in the modern furnishing line; there was no modern furniture available at that time either.

The war seemed to bring release to modern design. Ideas that had existed for years were eagerly grasped by young people everywhere. Most of the large producers of drapery and upholstery fabrics had little experience with the principles inherent in modern design. They were usually unable to visualize any potential market for such fabrics and generally left the development of this new field to small and often inexperienced firms and individuals.

## The Organic Design Exhibit

Perhaps the most important single event shaping the direction of modern American fabric design, outside of European influences, was the Organic Design Exhibition organized by the Museum of Modern Art in New York. This was an international contest in furniture, lamps and fabric design, with plans for the manufacture in quantity of the winning entries. The vitality and validity of this effort are demonstrated by the fact that several of the best pieces of modern furniture available today trace their direct outgrowth to this exhibition and contest. This is also true of the fabrics.

## Use of Unexpected Materials

A very important attitude differentiated the early modern fabric producers from the larger concerns. Designs were never planned for specific or seasonal markets. They were always planned to satisfy some specific, need in modern interior design and some have done this so well that they continue to sell five years after their first introduction. The best modern fabrics, like the best modern furniture, have never been planned to satisfy a preconceived notion of what the public wants, but rather to satisfy personal ideas of validity in relation to the whole growth of modern design. Another idea common to the pioneers was the use of fabrics usually thought of only as cheap or utility fabrics. Turning away from the lush and expensive brocades, satins, and

silks so beloved by the traditional interior decorator and so well supplied by the large fabric producers, the modern designers explored, discovered, and exploited kinds of modest utility and industrial cloths never before thought of as appropriate for interior design use. These modest fabrics as a background for printed designs gave an air of freshness of color and design that could not be achieved with the more traditional materials.

## Screen Prints and Small Production

An extremely potent factor in this entire development was the perfection of silk-screen printing on fabrics. It was possible with a very small outlay of capital to be in the fabric printing business. And because the investment in a new screen was so small, it was possible to produce designs that would probably interest only a small segment of the public. Even though the investment in screen-printing equipment was small, a surprising number of the producers made no effort to own their own equipment but commonly shared printers that were set up for their type of operation. None of the concerns keep any large stock on hand, as most of them are prepared to provide special colors.

## Unorthodox Merchandising Methods

In all of the modern furnishing business, the merchandising methods have often been as unique and unorthodox as the designs themselves. Most modern furniture and fabrics have been sold to the architects and designers and they in turn have sold these to their clients. Not until quite recently was it possible for the general public to go into a department store and purchase good modern furniture and fabrics. At first glance this technique would seem to provide an almost microscopic market, but the astonishing fact is the growth of this market in the last few years. Aside from the educational and propagandizing efforts of the designers, a series of new publications and the development nationally of small shops specializing in contemporary furnishings have helped to develop and extend this originally small market. The personalities of the designers of furniture and fabrics were usually given a kind of publicity that was rare in the traditional field. The anonymous design, purchased for a small sum from some fabric studio, was not the method of the modern producer. Every design was the work of a personality usually with an already established reputation in some area of design. Aside from the emphasis on personality, the remuneration was usually considerably higher than in the traditional field.

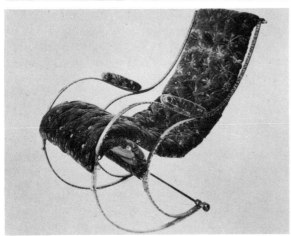

(*Above*) Design for a "Confidente" by Lalonde, about 1770. (*Below*) Steel rocking chair with plush upholstery, designed by Peter Cooper about 1855. (*At right*) 20th Century domestic interior with glass fabrics and vinyl-coated upholstery.

## Modern vs. Traditional

What are some of the characteristics distinguishing a modern from a traditional fabric? Perhaps the single largest difference is not the character of the pattern or texture, but the use to which it is put. In a modern interior, drapery fabric is used as a part of the architecture and functions as a plane of color or texture rather than as panels to hang on either side of a hole cut in the wall. In modern architecture the windows are organized into more compact and usually larger areas than in traditional architecture. The quantity of fabric used is usually considerably more than in traditional use. Whole walls of soft fabric act as foils for walls of wood or stone and become much more than devices to screen windows. Often one will find drape hanging as a partition and acting as a screen partially to divide one area from another. Such an approach naturally affects the character of the pattern. The better designs keep the pattern small in scale and closely knit in character, so that the unity of the fabric is maintained and its character as a textural wall is not destroyed. The large, insistent patterns of the past

obviously would not work for this approach. Sometimes the fabric is conceived more as a wall hanging and then larger patterns will work. Some of the designs by modern painters work best when they are used more as tapestries than as quiet elements of an architectural ensemble.

## New Fibers for Modern Needs

Just as modern curtains and draperies have developed sharp new geometric forms and patterns, they have also demanded new materials to express this change. Among these materials are vinyl, glass and untextured filament fibers. Glass fibers tended to have poor draping quality when first introduced, but new technologies have improved their hand, drape and texture. Untextured polyester filament began to make significant headway in ninon, batiste and marquisette sheer curtains. These curtains, because of their ease-of-care and no-wrinkle qualities, have made great inroads into markets once held by cotton and rayon fibers, which once were very prominent in curtains and draperies.

481

# Sheets and Quilts

Early American design used for modern linen.

In ancient times the Egyptians wound their revered dead in a coarse heavy type of sheeting known as mummy cloth. . . . Up to a relatively late period in the world's history most people took to their blankets, and the sheet of silk or linen was the prerogative of royalty or great wealth. . . . The great textile revolution which set in in this country before the death of Washington and raised cotton from a minor textile fiber to a pre-eminent position in a brief span of years, cleared the way for sheets of cotton. . . . Heavy and coarse narrow sheetings, probably counting about 44 threads per inch in the warp and 40 in the filling, were among the earliest products of the infant industry in this country.

## Beginnings in 1839

The development of the business in real cotton bed linens began around the year 1839 when the Dwight Manufacturing Company at Chicopee, Mass., made such a cloth, and the Pequot Mills at Salem, Mass., went into production. Until 1892 the housewife bought sheeting from bolts of cloth and, after long hours of patient needlework, converted it into hemmed sheets. The ready-made sheet of Fruit of the Loom muslin was born in 1892 in a factory in Port Chester, New York. Even then Mr. Jordan, of the Jordan Marsh Company in Boston, first to market the ready-made sheet, said women never would buy them. In 1902 Mr. Joseph W. Simons patented a machine to hemstitch sheets after the threads were drawn by hand. Pepperell Manufacturing Company is reported to have made up 64 square muslin sheets with plain hems at Lewiston, Maine, in 1894,

and hemstitched sheets in 1895. Utica and Mohawk also were among the first of the leading mills in this field. Dan River Mills, then known as Riverside and Dan River Cotton Mills, were making finished hemstitched sheets by 1910. After World War I, the rise of great chain and mail order distribution brought labor-saving ready-made sheets within the reach of all, even in the rural areas.

## Minimum Specifications

Leading members of the industry several years ago met and arrived at minimum specifications for different constructions of sheets to protect the consumer in buying. Constructions were named by type numbers, the type indicating the total number of threads in both warp and filling woven to the square inch before bleaching. These different constructions are Type 112 for economy, such as camp sheets; Type 128 for home muslin utility; Type 140 for luxury muslin; Type 180 for combed percale; in the very finest construction there are the combed percales with 200 threads to the square inch. On Types 128 and 140 the Government has adopted specifications that parallel those in the industry. To protect the public, four inferior grades were labeled as *irregulars, second quality, second selection*, or simply *seconds*, plainly marked on the face of each article.

Still another development was the 108-inch sheet, introduced in the early 1930's. Several states have laws specifying the 108-inch length as minimum for sheets used in hotels and public institutions. Colored sheets first appeared in the late 1920's in imported items, but the industry here quickly seized upon and improved them, making both solid color and colored-border sheets to match home decorative colors. Today printed sheets in both stripes and patterns, are also being manufactured.

Mills have experimented with rayon and also nylon tricot sheets, the manufacture of electrically heated sheets, and have successfully produced the contour sheet to fit the mattress. Mills have been in the forefront of labeling their individual sheets so that the buyer may have every pertinent detail as to the quality and usefulness of the product. The linen supply industry, providing freshly laundered sheets weekly to those who rent rather than purchase their bed linens, is a growing development in the field.

Fifteen or twenty years ago, in the United States, 20 to 25 million people did not use sheets. Today the number of non-sheet users has been reduced by more than half.

Candlewick spread, 18th Century American.

## Patchwork Quilts and Bedspreads

An important social as well as economic fabric in early Americana, the patchwork bedspread has contributed to the development of an important trend in textiles for home interiors. Patching and quilting, along with knitting, have never relinquished the place they held in women's hearts early in the 18th Century.

The women of a house would save up odd-shaped bits and pieces of cloth and when an important occasion arose, such as a wedding or a christening, the neighbors would gather for an evening and each would be given a square or other shape of calico, gingham, or chintz to piece together. Talk and refreshments would be the order, and thus a tedious task grew into a social pastime.

Later the patches were gathered, sewn into the final pattern, stretched on a quilting frame, and finished. The quilting itself, which served to hold together the patterned top, the filling, and the bottom, ranged from the simplest to the most intricate stitching. Modern textiles often reproduce quilts, bedspreads, and even fashion ideas, based on the original patching and quilting designs of old.

## New Developments in Domestics

The sheet has undergone considerable change, both as a fashion and functional item, in the last 20 years. The chief developments involve the contour construction, prints, tricot fabric and permanent-press. The contour construction became a household standby, while prints, in everything from the Baroque to the comic, have become another staple of the sheet market. Tricot fabric has also made some headway in a field more given to change than at any other time in its history. But the biggest single development has been the permanent-press sheet, which became immediately popular upon its introduction in the mid 1960's. A polyester/cotton blend, the permanent-press sheet provided long-sought, ease-of-care properties.

(*Above*) A 15-foot Jacquard or Wilton loom employing up to 4860 cards in the weaving of a 36-inch section of a carpet design. (*Below*) Old technique is applied to modern carpets; expert technicians "hand-carve" designs in new tufted carpets using electric shears. The method of hand-carving has been used for centuries in Chinese and Oriental rugs.

# Rugs and Carpets

*The traditional methods of ancient rug and carpet weaving have been assimilated and perfected by modern looming techniques.*

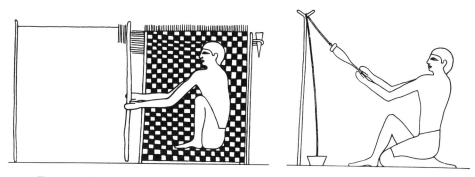

From a wall painting in the tomb of Khety at Beni Hasan (about 2000-1788 B.C.).

## Legendary and Early Rugs

The finest fabric ever invented for use under foot was the creation of nomads who had neither houses nor artificial floors. This fabric, although more durable under wear than any other, was never trodden upon with shoes and indeed, in nomadic tent dwellings, was often used as decoration on walls and ceilings and for warmth. Made of a heavy woven base and finished with knotted threads to form a pile surface, the rug became both a functional article and the principal art-form of the Levant and of the countries of the Near East.

Legend has given credence to the great antiquity of the origin of the rug, but the earliest historical evidences of its existence are some fragments found in Turkestan by Sir Aurel Stein which, it is said, do not antedate the Christian era. Thus the myths of Solomon and his flying carpet and of Cleopatra and her fabled rug must refer to tapestries, which were made as far back as 1500 B.C. Tapestries are structurally similar to cloth weaving, whereas true rugs are knotted.

Authorities claim that the carpet and rug as we know them had their inception at the end of the 15th Century and reached their peak of craftsmanship a century later. The mosque of Ala-ed-Din at Konia has a piece dating from the early 13th Century, but this and other isolated exhibits may be exceptions. The later Crusades and the invasion of the Turks under Suleiman into Europe introduced the rug maker's art to western peoples. The Polish rug industry is said to owe its origin to captured Persians who became transplanted artisans of this Slavic country, thus introducing their craft.

## Rug and Carpet-Making Technique

Both rugs and carpets are textile products of the loom. The modern method of power looming of certain types of rugs and carpets (Axminsters) differs only in degree from the antique, hand-crafted creations of the gifted Oriental nomads and shepherds.

The earliest method employed in the East consisted of a loom made of four poles joined together in the size that the rug was to be woven. A set of threads (the warp) was then stretched between two rollers or beams in a vertical position. These were interlaced with another set of threads (the weft), each weft thread passing alternately over and under the warp threads. In the finish, the weft and warp, usually of wool, are only on the back, the pattern on front being created by tufts of wool inserted and tied in knots, forming a design which is the individual choice of the weaver or one established by tradition.

One or more weavers work on the same rug under the rigid auspices of the khaidi or head weaver,

Still following old traditions. The photo shows a number of hand-weavers in the Orient at work on a single carpet.

who pins a pattern chart to the center of the loom and from it reads off the colors and patterns to be used. He chants in a sing-song voice and his co-workers, often women and children, orchestrate his instructions in brilliantly colored wools. Seldom looking at their work, they rapidly loop the yarn which forms the pile around two warp threads and knot it. After each row is completed it is knocked down tightly against its fellows with a heavy metal comb and the ends of the pile are rough-trimmed with a knife or shears. When all of the knotting is finished an expert clips the pile to a desired, even height. This brings out the gem-like quality of the true Oriental design and finish. The closer and more even the shearing, the cleaner and crisper the design appears in the finished rug.

## Shepherds Were the Originators

This method of rug making was a natural result of conserving the wool crop surplus by the wandering shepherds of the Near East. Sparse grazing lands, rugged, rocky hills and climatic extremes all tended to create a type of fleece that was thick and admirably adapted for rug making. In fact, in modern rug manufacture in the United States, practically all the wools used are imported to a great extent from the countries of the Near East, which breed sheep with coarse wool suited for carpet yarns.

The shepherds accomplished the development of the rug. Since their music was rudimentary and pictures were more perishable, it was inevitable that this craft should develop into a fine art. Caliphs and sultans, sheiks and khans covered their floors, walls, and ceilings with fine rugs. Shepherds traded their woven products for grain, swords and other wealth. The rise of Islam also encouraged the development

of this art, since the man of means wanted his own personal prayer rug which he used five times daily in his genuflections toward Mecca. So the rug became a symbol of wealth and piety and was prized and valued by all.

## Rug Design

The rug design must be pleasing at a short distance from which detail cannot be clearly seen. From this developed a scheme of composition upon which the design masses are based. Usually it starts with the running edge or border divided into two or more parallel bands. Inside of this border is the field, a tonal construction which bears shaped panels in a variety of combinations. More often than not there is a prominent central medallion which may be associated with four quarter panels in each corner of the design.

Motifs seemingly of obscure symbolic significance are often variations of designs whose meanings are lost in antiquity. In floral forms can be recognized the date palm (and its conventional form the *palmette*), rose, jasmine, willow, and cypress, but others are unrecognizable except as generic flower forms. The cloud band is of Chinese origin and probably is an abstraction of the great snake or dragon idiom. Over-all patterns which include the *herati* (diamonds and flowers) and the *mina khani* are not comparable with natural flora.

## Western Rugs

The British started early (with hemp warp and weft) to imitate the spoils of war brought home by their seafaring adventurers in the East. Captive Moslems had taught 16th Century artisans their skills and the use of the Ghiordes knot.

Early designs show patterns resembling embroidery including heraldic devices and often dates. The earliest known piece of this type is the Verulam carpet, which dates from 1570. The second type resembles early Turkish carpets and, known as *Turkey-work*, were used for chair and sofa coverings.

In more recent times, the British gave great impetus to power-loomed carpet manufacture, and the design of rugs was much influenced by William Morris. The persistence of British technical efforts to solve rug-making problems is attested by the common names given to our present-day floor coverings such as Axminster, Kidderminster, and Wilton, the names of English manufacturing towns. In 1839 James Templeton of Glasgow invented a device for

 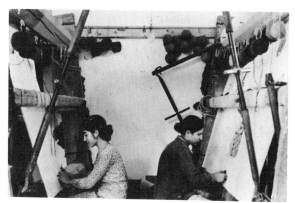

(*Left*) Wool being dried on racks out in the sun in Baghdad, Iraq. High wooden poles support ropes on which the wool is hung. (*Right*) Two women weaving carpets on primitive upright looms.

the manufacture of chenille carpets, employing a two-fold weaving process.

## Rugs of the United States

At the close of the 18th Century, Philadelphia, responsible for many innovations, was the city which gave birth to the first carpet factory in America. W. P. Sprague started his establishment in this city in 1791, and the United States thence evolved carpet-making machinery.

The *chef d'oeuvre* of Sprague's factory was an Axminster carpet bearing the arms and achievements of the infant United States. Alexander Hamilton was so impressed with this work, and with the possibilities it offered to American workmen, that he recommended tariffs on imported rugs and carpets to protect the homegrown product and its future.

In the early days, looms were imported from Great Britain and the Continent. Before long the jacquard pattern machine for carpet weaving was introduced into America almost as soon as it was invented.

In 1825 a Scottish immigrant named Alexander Wright founded a mill for making ingrain carpet at Medway, Mass., near Boston, later going into partnership with Henry S. Burdett, a Boston merchant. This mill was purchased in 1828 by the Lowell Manufacturing Company which moved the equipment to Lowell, Mass. It was here, eleven years later, that the United States made its first major contribution to the carpet-weaving industry when Erastus B. Bigelow invented the first power loom ever used for making carpets. This loom first turned out ingrained carpet, but in 1848 Bigelow's genius led to the perfection of the Brussels power

Old prayer rug in the Cartozian Collection. This royal blue wool rug, made in 1292, by Persian weavers, has the sheen of velvet, still retaining its original lustre.

Modern hand rug weaving is still being done in the United States. Weaver is shown using steel comb to beat down rows of weft and nap knotted on cotton warp.

(*At left*) The work of Heriz weavers, this silk rug has from 650 to 700 knots to the square inch. (*Right*) Collector Cartozian with a prized example of rug weaving.

loom, which with slight modification also made possible the manufacture of Wilton carpets.

Somewhat later in the century an English emigrant, named Johnson, opened a plant in Newark, N.J., for the making of tapestry and velvet woven rugs. His method consisted of printing the pattern with dyestuffs on the individual strands of wool.

And so the industry grew. In 1867, Halcyon Skinner invented the spool Axminster from an idea originating with Alexander Smith of Yonkers, N.Y. Another Philadelphian, James Dunlap, developed a process for printing tapestry and velvet carpeting. The latter part of the 19th Century saw a rise in factories making imitation Smyrna rugs. These were the double-faced Axminsters.

At this time 27-inch widths completely dominated power-loomed carpets. Rugs were made by sewing the strips together. But at the turn of the 20th Century the invention of the broad loom or wide-width loom gave rise to large one-piece carpeting which is so popular today. The majority of modern looms turn out carpet ranging from 9-feet to 18-feet wide, and the chenille loom can produce a 30-foot width.

The Brussels, tapestry, Smyrna, and ingrain carpets, which were popular weaves in the 19th Century, are no longer produced in the United States. Several of these weaves have evolved into the modern Wiltons, velvets, and Axminsters used today. Developments in carpet-making since the turn of the century concentrated on refinements and improvements in the specialized carpet looms, permitting increased output and many new variations in texture and design.

The most significant carpet-manufacturing development in the 20th Century was the creation of a completely new construction process—tufting.

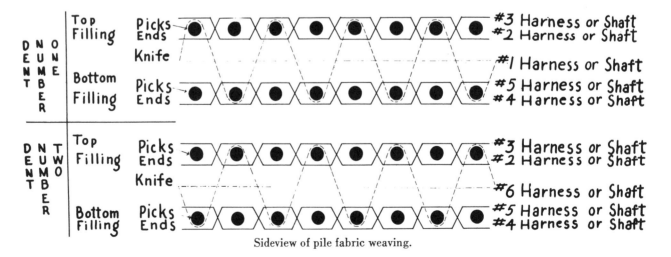

Sideview of pile fabric weaving.

# Tufted Carpets

In twenty years of dramatic growth, tufting has become the nearly universal way to manufacture carpets (see definition and method under "Tufting"). In 1951 tufting accounted for only 9.4 percent of all carpets made, yet within two decades the figure rose to over 90 percent.

Tufting has largely replaced weaving in carpet manufacture because of speed; as a process it is generally considered to be eight times faster than weaving. In addition to its high production rate, tufting has demonstrated its versatility and high rate of technological development.

With the creation of wide, multi-needle machines, which were introduced after World War II, the tufted carpet industry began its rapid ascent to top position in the manufacture of rugs and carpets. Room-size rugs, wall-to-wall carpeting and expanding uses for commercial carpeting began to be produced in volume around 1951.

## How Tufting Is Done

Basically, a modern tufting machine is a giant sewing machine with hundreds of needles. Multiple ends of yarn are fed to a bank of heavy needles with a standard span of 12 to 15 feet. The actual tufting process begins with a previously constructed primary or backing fabric of either natural or synthetic fibers, which passes under the needles and anchors each stitch. The pile yarn is stitched into the backing fabric, leaving loops which form the carpet pile.

Synthetic textured yarns yield excellent tufting results, with loop pile, cut pile or cut-and-loop pile used in a wide variety of patterns, gauges and colors.

## Two Basic Constructions

These are (1) loop pile and (2) cut pile. Each can best be understood by following the action of a single needle.

LOOP PILE (*see diagram*). In stage 1, the needle descends as the looper starts to pull back from the previously inserted loop of yarn. In stage 2, the needle passes the yarn through the fabric backing, while the looper has begun its forward motion toward the newly inserted loop. In stage 3, the looper has entered the new loop and will remain there until the needle reaches the top of its course. The two are synchronized so that they never interfere with each other's motion.

In designing a carpet, a charcoal sketch is made in scale. From this, the design is reproduced in full color on checked paper, each check representing one tuft or loop.

Following the hand-painted design, this woman is punching out the Jacquard cards that form the pattern in Wilton carpets by selecting the necessary colored yarns.

Looking at the check paper design on the drum, these carpet workers are "setting" the frames for an Axminster loom. Here the pattern is set, as each frame represents a row of tufts in the design.

489

Cut Pile (*see diagram*). In stage 1, the looper holds two loops while the knife cuts the third against the sharpened edge of the looper. After cutting, the knife moves down, while the looper moves forward to enter the next loop. In stage 2, the needle has descended through the fabric backing with the correct amount of yarn for the looper. The looper enters this new loop while the knife moves away from the cutting edge to allow the next uncut loop to enter the cutting area. In stage 3, the needle moves upward, having left the loop on the looper. The knife moves upward to cut the third, previously inserted loop.

On modern tufting machines cut pile and loop pile can often be introduced simultaneously in the carpet by pushing off certain loops from the hook before they are cut. In this and other ways of varying the settings, a wide range of design effects can be achieved on a single machine.

## Controlling the Pile Effects

The height of a carpet pile is determined by the rate at which a patterning device or the friction rolls draw the yarn from the creel to the needles. Pile height is determined by two factors: (1) the distance between the backing fabric and the loop-retaining hooks, and (2) the rate at which the yarn is fed to the needles. Both these factors are interrelated, however, so that in order to change pile height they are both involved in making the desired adjustments.

Generally speaking, there is less pile height variation in commercial carpeting than in carpets for home use.

Density of pile is a major factor in carpet value and carpet durability—of almost equal importance with the choice of fiber and yarn. With a given face yarn, the tufting machine gauge and the stitch rate determine the density of the pile, since density is achieved in proportion to the number of tufts per square inch.

## Versatility of Tufting

A modern tufting machine can make carpets in widths of 9, 12, 15 or even 18 feet. They can be made with level piles, in many patterns and colors. Tufting machines have many hundreds of needles, usually arranged in a line but sometimes staggered. A machine for tufting carpets 15 feet wide may have as many as 1,188 needles.

An embossed pattern with a high and low loop is achieved with special attachments which vary the quantity of yarn delivered to each needle. One of the most popular types is the Scroll Type Pattern attachment, comprising two groups of rolls revolving at speeds with an approximate ratio of 2 to 1.

The pattern system also has a translucent drum surfaced with acetate film; the pattern to be made is inked on this drum. Light from the interior of the drum is received through the translucent acetate film by a photo-electric cell, thus engaging the slow roll supplying yarn to the needles and making a low pile loop. When the light strikes the inked pattern on the acetate, however, the photo-electric cell is not activated. Thus, the fast roll is activated and a high pile loop results.

Numerous different styling effects are also made possible by the choice of yarns and their combinations, as well as by the variations in looper twist. For example, combinations of left-hand and right-hand loops with yarns textured by various twist methods, allow for various surface effects in a

Other construction methods which have gained popularity during the last decade are needlepunch, flocking and knitting. Needlepunch carpets became popular as indoor/outdoor carpets, then as do-it-your-self indoor carpets. Flocked carpets provide more variety as design items and knitted carpets offer a more economical construction method in terms of volume of yarn used. Carpets have also been used for wall coverings.

## Use of New Carpet Fibers

Another dramatic innovation in the carpet industry has been the development and introduction of new carpet fibers to supplement the increasing demand for carpet wools. Because of the diminishing sources of good carpet wools, the U.S. carpet industry began to experiment with man-made fibers in the late 1930's. Since 1950, a wide variety of new man-made fibers have been introduced in all constructions. These include rayon, acetate, nylon, acrylics, polypropylene and polyester. Today, the dominant man-made fibers are nylon, acrylics and polyester.

Backing materials are generally made from jute, cotton or synthetic fibers, with jute accounting for the greatest proportion among the natural fibers. Man-made fibers, however, are making steady inroads into this application, with polypropylene, in both woven and non-woven form, becoming more and more widely used for carpet backings

An example of polypropylene used for primary backing in tufted carpets is the spun-bonded "Typar" made by Du Pont, which is a non-woven polypropylene primary backing.

## CONSTRUCTION FEATURES

### of the

### MAJOR CARPET WEAVES

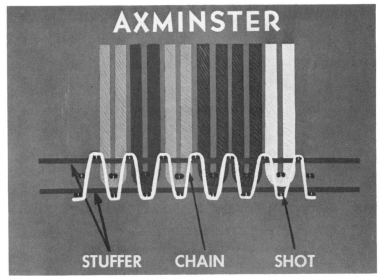

STUFFER     CHAIN     SHOT

In the Axminster weave, each pile yarn is inserted independently, as in the hand-tufted carpets of the Orient. This permits infinite variation of color and pattern.

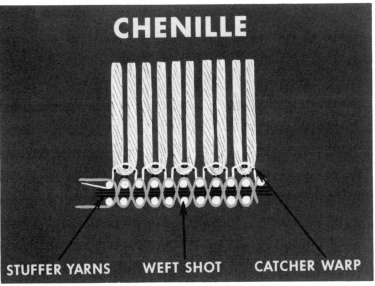

STUFFER YARNS     WEFT SHOT     CATCHER WARP

Chenille Carpet is thick and soft. It can be woven in a range of patterns and in any color, shape or size up to 30 feet wide, and is often custom made.

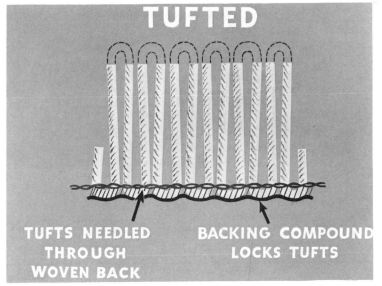

TUFTS NEEDLED THROUGH WOVEN BACK     BACKING COMPOUND LOCKS TUFTS

In the Tufting construction, the pile yarn is needled through a pre-woven backing fabric, usually of jute, then firmly locked by a latex backing compound.

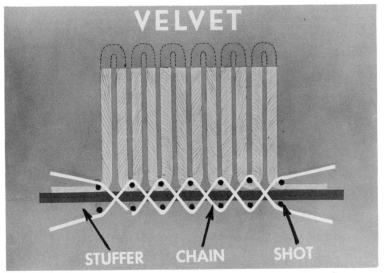

STUFFER     CHAIN     SHOT

In the Velvet weave the pile yarns can be cut or looped. A variety of textural effects, including tight frieze, pebbly surface, and multi-looped textures, are possible.

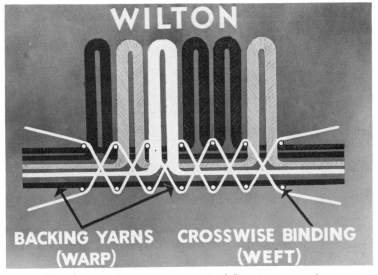

BACKING YARNS (WARP)     CROSSWISE BINDING (WEFT)

The Wilton loom uses up to six different yarns to form the pile. These yarns are buried deep in the body of the carpet and give it a luxurious feel.

491

## TUFTING

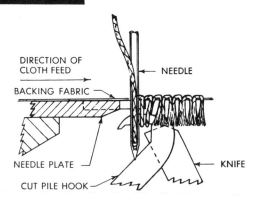

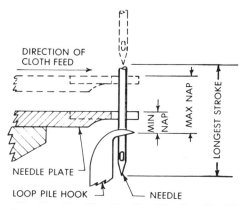

Cut Pile: Loop cannot get off needle unless cut. Cutting resembles action of shears.

Loop Pile: Needles insert loops through backing fabric where hooks pick up loops.

## NEEDLEPUNCH

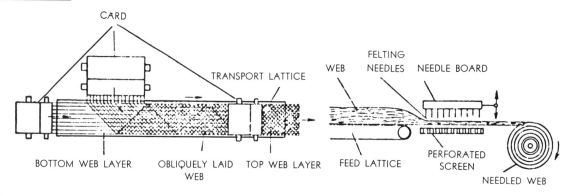

Needle Punch: Webs are first cross-layed to produce material with adequate strength. Needled fabric is produced by mechanically entangling fibers as the barbed needles pass through web. In indoor/outdoor, web is punched into backing, latexed.

## FLOCKING

Mechanical Flocking: Beater bars under substrate cause upright fiber adhesion.

Electrostatic Flocking: Electrical field under substrate causes fibers to stand.

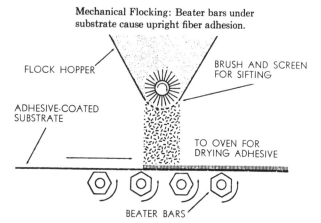

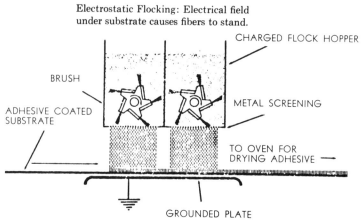

Design details from Oriental rugs.

# Oriental Rugs and Rug Weaving

There are two styles of weaving oriental rugs.

a. The rectilinear—or straight lines—used by tribal or village rug weavers and more recently in town weaving.

b. The curvilinear—or curved lines—used by the town rug weavers in fine floral, medallion and animal designs of rugs and carpets.

An Oriental rug is made up of individual knots tied and cut on the warp of the rug loom, and, the two types of knots used are: the Persian knot, made by the Persians and sometimes called "Senna" knot; the Turkish knot or Ghiordes knot, made by the Turks or the Persians of Turkish tribes.

Three basic forms of design dominate in Oriental rugs. They are the medallion center-well covered field; the medallion center-open field and the all over designed rug. Interspersed between these forms we have a medallion center-semi-open field and plain ground with border. Within these basic forms a number of well-known designs may be employed.

Oriental rugs are usually named after the town or village in which they are woven. Each town or village has a certain characteristic of weave, design and color which makes the rug easily identifiable. A few of the more abundant types with some of their characteristics are as follows:

## KERMAN

Kerman is a well-known city in Southern Persia (Iran). All rugs woven within the city itself and in towns and villages in the proximity of the city are named Kermans. Their designs are usually composed of floral forms, frequently roses, bound together with roaming tendrils and sprays that make an exquisitely graceful and elaborate decoration. The colors are one of the outstanding achievements in Kerman rugs. Fine highland Persian wool permits of pastel shades in green, soft rose, red, rich gold, ivory, sky and deep blue. This unusual, different kind of wool is endowed by nature with qualities that make it ideal for this purpose, combining silky softness with remarkable durability. The knotting is generally fine and compact and of contract quality.

## SAROUK

The rugs known as "Sarouk" are likewise named after a town in the western part of Iran. Thick napped and solidly woven, the modern Sarouk is characterized by floral designs placed on a deep rose or blue background. A few are woven with an ivory or beige ground. The rugs are heavy and durable; many of them weigh more than 100 pounds in the nine-by-twelve-foot size. Two of the main design motifs in Sarouks are the Cypress Tree and the Vase. The former represents to Persians the Tree of Life, which symbolizes eternal life. The Vase is a relic of the love of the old Persian Shahs for Chinese vases. The floral designs are formed in colors of gold, green, and blue, blended to attain maximum harmony.

## KAZVIN

The contemporary Kazvins are woven in the town of Hamadan (Iran). They offer a high pile with good wool, good weave and, in the main, an attractive medallion- and corner-design.

### HAMADAN

The Hamadan area is the most prolific carpet-weaving center in all Iran. From all points of the compass, in close proximity to the city of Hamadan, rugs and carpets are woven in hamlets and villages and brought for sale to the bazaars of Hamadan.

The following weaves are to be found in this area:

| | | | |
|---|---|---|---|
| Dergazine | Bibicabad | Bijar | Borchalou |
| Kapoutrang | Housenabad | Joozan | Mehriban |
| Senneh | Genjtepe | Enjillas | and others |

Rosette

### KASHAN

The Kashan has often been called the most "heavenly" of rugs. They are chiefly woven in the city of Kashan. It would seem that the weavers incorporate in their rugs their dreams of a fair and lovely place in which to live. The designs are usually foliage motifs. This motif may be repeated in a dignified all-over arrangement. The background color is commonly a deep rich rose or blue. Contemporary Kashans also appear in a beige ground although they are an anomaly. It is not uncommon for a good Kashan to have as many as 40,000 to 50,000 knots in every square foot.

Palmette

### HEREZ, SERAPI, GOREVAN, MEHREVAN

These four weaves emanate from the Herez area in the northwestern district of Iran. They have attractive, imposing designs usually containing a medallion and rectilinear corner decorations. The designs are geometric, bold, and yet present a graceful, desirable appearance. They are extremely durable.

Palm leaf

### TABRIZ

The city of Tabriz in northwestern Iran is the home of this famous weave, specimens of which include both medallion and all-over designs. It is the site of the famous Blue Mosque and in the 16th Century was the Iranian capital and a prominent rug-weaving center. Contemporary weaves include some of the finest weave-count found in any type carpet.

Guli Hennai design

Latch hook

### MESHED

Magenta and blue colorings are most popular in these rugs which originate in and around Meshed in Khorassan, East Iran. Thousands of devout Mohammedans come each year to pray at the shrine of Ali Riza, regarded as a saint.

### TEHERAN

This rug is woven in the city of Teheran, progressive and dynamic capital of Iran. The city is in the shadow of 18,000 foot Mount Demavend, which, Iranians declare, is where Noah's Ark came to rest. Teheran rugs are compactly woven with pile clipped short to give clear definition to intricate designs.

### ISPAHAN

This rug is woven in one of the most sumptous cities of Iran. Here are to be found gorgeous mosques and famous palaces. Across the river and connected by a bridge is the Armenian city of Julfa, inhabited by descendants of Armenian artisans brought here forcibly by Shah-Abbas in the 16th Century from the Caucasus. . . . Ispahan is the market place of several types of rugs woven in the surrounding country.

### SHIRAZ

Woven by nomad tribes in southwestern Iran, Shiraz rugs display bold medallion designs done in bright reds and blues. Here is the birthplace of the famous poet Hafiz.

### SARABAND

In rugs of this type, the field is always covered with a design consisting of rows of pears, the stems of which alternate from right to left in each succeeding row.

### YEZD

These rugs come from the city of Yezd. They favor the Herati design and their colors are quiet and refreshing, mellow brown, clear blues, ivory whites. Marco Polo, on his historic journey to the Far East, made an extended note of Yezd in his diary, wherein he wrote, "Yezd is a city of considerable traffic where a species of cloth of silk and gold is manufactured."

Persian knot

Ghiordes knot

Weavers' tools

# Industrial Fabrics

*A large and important group of textiles which includes woven and non-woven cloths vital to many industries, ranging from primitive agriculture to jet transportation*

Above: Air-structure warehouse of Dacron and elastomeric coating withstands the worst weather.

Industrial fabrics are largely specification fabrics, since they are produced to specifications set by the large corporations, institutions, or government agencies which buy them. Such fabrics may be roughly divided into four categories:

DIRECT USES. This group includes specification cloths which are used directly for end products, such as boat sails, baggings, coverings, tentings, beltings, webbing, book bindings, etc. Also included are rugs, upholstery, and drapery fabrics produced to specification for automobiles, airplanes, railroad cars, buses, and institutions.

INDIRECT USES. These include textiles which go into the composition of other products: shoe linings, tire fabric, typewriter ribbons, coated materials, plastics.

PRODUCTION USES. A wide variety of specially constructed textiles are used by industry during the course of production or processing for such purposes as buffing, insulating, filtering, ventilating, laundering.

WORK CLOTHING. Fabric used for work clothing is also classified as an industrial material. Special types of cloth are used for industrial uniforms worn by gas station attendants, bottling plant employees, delivery men, hotel and hospital personnel, soldiers, policemen, firemen, as well as protective clothing used by workers in various industries.

## Scope of Industrial Textiles

Industrial fabrics represent a vast and varied field of textile production relatively unknown to the layman. Some indication of its scope can be obtained from the following list of fabric types in use:

FOR THE MECHANICAL RUBBER TRADE:

| | |
|---|---|
| Army duck | Lawncloths |
| Balloon fabrics | Leno or doup fabrics |
| Belting duck | Napped fabrics |
| Bootleg duck | Osnaburgs |
| Chafer fabric | Sateens |
| Drills and twills, wide | Sheeting, |
| Enameling ducks | narrow and wide |
| Hose duck | Tire fabrics |

FOR THE SYNTHETIC RUBBER, VINYL, ETC. COATING TRADE:

| | |
|---|---|
| Wide drills and twills | Wide sateens and |
| Wide moleskins—chafers | broken twills |
| Wide printcloths | Wide sheeting |

FOR THE SHOE TRADE:

| | |
|---|---|
| 37″ Army duck | Enameling duck |
| 37″ drills | 30″ Gem duck |
| 37″ four-leaf twills | Leno or doup |
| | specialties |

FOR THE USE OF FILTERING MEDIA—Chemical and paint manufacturers, oil refiners, soap manufacturers, sugar refiners, etc.:

| | |
|---|---|
| Chain cloths | Drills |
| Duck | Twills |
| Felt | |

FOR THE LAUNDRY SUPPLY TRADE:

| | |
|---|---|
| Laundry apron ducks | 36″—3.50 Sheeting for |
| Laundry nets and tubing | ironing boards |
| Roll cover duck | 40″—3.15 Sheeting for |
| Roll cover sheeting | ironing boards |
| Twills, etc., for rental | |
| laundry | |

495

For the Converting Trade:

| | |
|---|---|
| Army duck, waterproofed for various purposes | Sheeting |
| Drills | Single and double filling duck |
| Enameling duck—38″ to 100″ inclusive | Twills |
| Gabardine | Wagon cover duck |
| Moleskin | Wide duck, waterproofed |
| Sateens | Printcloths |

For the Tent and Awning Trade:

| | |
|---|---|
| Army duck | Numbered duck |
| Awning stripe | Nonwovens |
| Double filling duck | Single filling duck |
| Mineral khaki duck | Waterproof duck |

For Specialty Manufacturers:

| | |
|---|---|
| Advertising specialties— duck, drill, printcloth, sheeting | Napped fabrics |
| | Vat dyed fabrics |
| | Window shades—sheeting, printcloth, enameling duck |
| Fireproof material | |
| Golf bag duck | |

For Dry Goods Jobbers and Chain Stores:

| | |
|---|---|
| Crash | Single filling duck |
| Denim | Turkish toweling |
| Double filling duck | Wide duck |
| Huck toweling | 30″—2.50-2.85 drill |
| Printcloth | |

For Flag Manufacturers:

| | |
|---|---|
| Government type—all wool, acrylic, nylon | Single filling duck |
| | Printcloth |
| Navy type—all wool | 30″—2.50 and 2.85 drill |
| Commercial— nylon | |
| Sheeting | |

For the Work-Clothing Trade:

| | |
|---|---|
| Army duck in plain and water repellent finish | Grey drill, duck, twill |
| | Indigo blue denim |
| Bedford cord, gabardine, jean, moleskin, sateen, suede, suiting fabric | Khakis, drapery fabrics, drill, herringbone, jean, twill, upholstery fabric |
| Corduroys for men's wear and women's wear | Single filling and double filling duck |
| Express, hickory and fancy stripes | |

Unbleached Sheeting—in standard constructions:

| | |
|---|---|
| 36″—3.50—64 x 68 | 36″—5.00—48 x 48 |
| 36″—3.75—64 x 64 | 36″—5.50—44 x 44 |
| 36″—4.00—56 x 60 | 36″—6.50—40 x 40 |
| 36″—4.25—56 x 56 | 40″—3.15—64 x 68 |
| 36″—4.50—56 x 52 | 40″—3.60—56 x 60 |
| 36″—4.70—48 x 52 | |

For Miscellaneous Industries:

Abrasive Industry: Drill, jean, double filling duck
Army and Navy:
   Ballistic Cloth: Nylon
   Boat Covers: Army duck, Numbered duck, tarpaulins
   Gun Covers: Army duck
   Sandbags: Acrylic, Polypropylene, nonwovens

   Tents: Army duck, shelter tent duck
   Wagon and Truck Covers: Numbered duck
Automobile Industry, Headlinings: Broken twills, sateen, sheeting
Bakelite and Synthetic Resins: Duck
Buffing Wheel Manufacturers: Naught duck and sheeting
Railroads: Cab curtains and ceilings for refrigerator
   (Cars use Numbered duck)
Shipping Covers: Fabric to suit particular use
Spring Covers: Double filling duck
Upholstery for auto, aviation
Wallcovering (usually coated): Scrims, Nonwovens are now chiefly man-made fibers or coated cotton.

## Automotive Textiles

At least ten yards of different types of fabric are used in most cars which come off the production line today. Interior upholstery for a car includes sidewalls, seat cushions and cushion backs which are made of wool, mohair, cotton, rayon, nylon, and other man-made fibers or combinations of several fibers.

Fabrics are also used for floor carpeting, shelf material, along the bottoms of doors, headlinings, and certain decorative purposes. Through the years almost everything that could be called automobile upholstery has been tried. Today, because of the great strides made by the textile industry in fabric development, the car manufacturer has easy access to a great many proved fabrics in either flat or pile weave in an almost unlimited assortment of patterns and colors.

In the use of trim material in today's car, those responsible for their selection must keep in mind that the quality should be excellent and that the car owner is entitled to reasonable satisfaction in wear and continued good appearance. To this end a great many tests are performed by laboratories on specialized *torture* equipment and the results are care-

Assessing automobile fabric in design studios; at rear is seen color chip screen indicating paintwork shades.

fully observed and evaluated by a staff of highly trained technicians.

## How Specifications Are Set

Before new interior trim is introduced, stylists, engineers, laboratory experts, and sales executives spend many months of work selecting and testing the fabrics.

First step in the process starts with the styling section, through which manufacturers present their fabrics. The styling section reviews literally thousands of samples for each fabric to be selected. In most cases the fabrics are presented by the manufacturers after a brief explanation as to what is sought in the particular fabric. In many cases stylists will sketch out a design and suggest that something similar is desired.

When thousands of blanket samples are gathered, all are considered together by the styling section. Anywhere from several to a dozen may be selected and orders put through to hand-trim them in special bodies. When the trimmed bodies are ready for presentation, engineers and sales executives are called in and with the stylists make the decision as to the fabric to be used.

## Analysis and Testing of Fabrics

Before production is started on a new order for fabrics, rigid specifications are given the manufacturer. They include specifications as to fiber content, weight, thread crossings, color fastness, strength, and finish.

When new fabrics are considered, samples of them are sent to the engineering laboratory for exhaustive analysis by trained technicians there.

Wear testing of the materials is done on an abraser, which in a matter of less than an hour will create as much wear on the material as it would undergo in years of use in an automobile.

Another method of condensing a test into hours is in the use of a fabric friction tester. This device has an oscillating drum which rubs against three half-moon arms. A typical suit fabric is placed on the drum while samples of seat fabrics are placed on the arms. Results of this demonstrate how well a fabric will hold up against clothing, and, also, how much it will or will not wear on the clothing itself.

Among other tests conducted by the laboratory are a tensile strength test to determine the tearing point of materials, fiber analysis, stretch tests, and thread counts.

Results of all testing are dispatched by the laboratory to the trim department, where results of the examinations are matched against the specifications set up in advance as to what standard the materials must meet to be considered for use.

After the months of preparatory work are out of the way and the final fabrics have been selected, orders are placed with the manufacturers for the materials. When received at the body fabricating plants, they are matched against the master samples from which they were selected, and additional cuts of the fabrics are tested to insure that they meet the specifications.

The upholstery of cars has come a long way since the days when velour and plush were the vogue. These materials were hot, heavy, hard to clean, and difficult to move on. The next fabric phase was that of finished broadcloth and whipcords, which were better looking and lent themselves to greater versatility in design. Then, as cars became lower and running boards were eliminated, there developed an increased desire for fabrics that held one in position and also permitted one to slide on them.

## Use of New Fibers

Following World War II, man-made fibers began to be used in automobiles in addition to the natural fibers, cotton and wool. The progress of man-made fibers has been meteoric. Within recent years, blends and combinations have been resorted to such as a fabric of nylon warp and cotton filling. This structure is lower in cost than an all-nylon fabric, static is reduced, and more comfort is afforded the rider. Two-tone effects are made with blends and combinations of various fibers but cost requests, however, must be met. Nylon has become the major factor in auto upholstery, with vinyl as a covering fabric and metallics as a decorative element. Cotton's place is chiefly as a backing fabric.

Great progress has been made in color effects made possible from yarn combinations. For example, a four-color effect may be obtained by the use of solution-dyed black viscose rayon, Mylar metallic yarn, nylon dyed red, and acetate yarn dyed blue.

Nylon is in greatest use since it has strength, cleanability, and provides very long wear and service and has met with public acceptance.

Vinyl is much used in many fabrications and styles in which it is necessary that the color be achieved by pigmentation during extrusion, so that the color-fastness is very good, and over long periods of time color change is negligible. Since it is a plastic, it does not absorb moisture, which makes for ease of cleaning.

A modern car interior showing the use of vinyl-coated fabrics on seat and side door panels.

## Five Specifications

Automobile fabric demands, in order of their importance, are: 1. Ease of cleaning; 2. Durability; 3. Slidability; 4. Color fastness; 5. Wrinkle-resistance. Many cars feature foam-back carpet, a new type of carpeting that has foam rubber backing which is an integral part of the carpeting itself. This new process of integrating foam rubber with the carpeting has many advantages: water will not penetrate the rug, thus offering quicker drying; and dirt and dust cannot infiltrate the carpeting, making easy vacuuming possible. Furthermore, tests have shown that carpeting is more durable when placed over foam rubber. No binding of edges is necessary with this new process, and, since color can be incorporated in the foam rubber to match the carpet, no unsightly edges appear.

Vinyl became widely used in the late 1950's as an upholstery fabric in autos, because it was discovered at that time that vinyl coating combined with a knit backing fabric was very attractive, durable, cleanable and fashionable. Since then, vinyl has been used in many different constructions and in lighter and lighter weights in order to make vinyl-coated upholstery fabrics more breathable and comfortable to the human body. Knitted vinyl fabrics became quite popular in the late 1960's.

## Keeping Pace with Style

From the moment the interior decorators began to use bold and brilliant colors, the bell began to toll for drab automobile interiors. The old rule for automotive upholstery used to be: any color so long as it is either grey or taupe, and any pattern so long as it is a stripe. With this old style went interiors that were poorly lit, providing dark corners where the fabric was unnoticed.

Naturally the automobile manufacturer has been influenced in his choice of colors and fabrics by the increasing use of high shades and unusual colors in furniture upholstery and in decorative fabrics. Naturally, too, the emphasis on texture interest, that has been one of the dominant factors in fashion trends and in apparel fabrics, has carried over into the modern living room on wheels, which our best automobile interiors have become, to all intents and purposes.

## Style Plus Slide

The evolution of automobile upholstery fabrics has shown the way to combine these two trends. The use of nylon facing, for instance, and the development of special weaves and styling, has made it possible to build into the same fabric the quality of *slidability*, demanded by the consumer, with a pattern that displays both refined coloring and three-dimensional texture interest. In addition, this fabric has good tailoring ability and long-wear life.

By all odds, however, the greatest influence in the automotive color revolution is the hard-top convertible. With this has come a two-tone color scheme and an increase in the glass area, which has finally done away with ill-lit interiors. Result: the fabrics—and not only the upholstery, but the side-wall and floor covering fabrics—are clearly visible from inside and the body character of the interior is also easily seen from the outside, as a part of the whole styling of the car.

In this new development there is both a stricter limitation and a greater freedom for the fabric designer. The limitation demands that the fabric shall be styled as part of a whole scheme, including a two-tone exterior, and this has led to the package concept of color schemes replacing the choice of upholstery colors. The freedom lies in this, that by upgrading the whole overall styling, bright colors and materials that would have looked gaudy or garish in the old days today look rich and beautiful, because they have become a part of a harmonious whole.

# Tire Cord

To grasp the quality of the problems facing the modern automotive tire engineer, it is helpful to visualize an architect working with flexible steel and elastic and plastic concrete to develop a building which could, without damage, bend to the ground under the force of a hurricane and withstand, without melting, the concentrated heat of the tropical sun.

The earliest rubber tires were solid tires of natural rubber; when pneumatic tires were introduced makers often used steel studs on the tread to give a longer wear life. In those days the life might be no more than two hundred miles. Nevertheless, as long as speeds and mileages remained low, the natural materials of rubber and fiber served their purpose very well.

It was with the coming of higher speeds and heavier loads at the end of World War I that a new factor —the internally generated heat caused by flexing and pounding on road—entered the picture. Thus the need arose for a tire both lighter and thinner, which could disperse the heat more rapidly, remain

cooler in running, and last longer.

In 1929 an idea for a new solution to the problem occurred at almost the same time to the tire manufacturers and the makers of rayon. This was that the newly developed man-made rayon fiber might provide the strength necessary for a lighter build.

As research was begun and progressed, the problems to be faced became clear; and they were many. Among them were: the manufacture of a cord of high tensile strength, the satisfactory bonding of yarns with rubber, and how to render the cord tough enough to stand constant flexing and to resist fatigue.

## First Commercial Production

A number of years passed before these problems, and others which arose, were overcome sufficiently for a rayon cord tire to be placed commercially on the market.

By that time loads and operating speeds had once again risen; it was claimed, however, that the new tires gave fully adequate performance under existing conditions. By the outbreak of World War II in Europe, a number of rayon producers were in the tire cord business, making high-tenacity yarns to be incorporated in the tires for heavy goods and passenger transport vehicles. At that moment this activity assumed a new and vital significance.

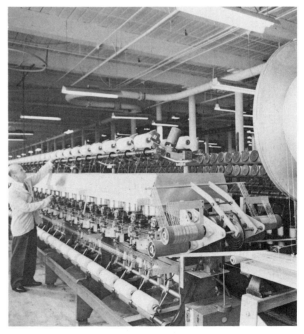

Clarkson cord former which forms and winds tire cord (left) and beams it (right).

During the period between the outbreak of war in 1939 and the entry of the United States into hostilities, further advances were made. The ability to build lightweight but tough tires led to the use of rayon in landing-wheel tires for military aircraft. Its gradually increasing use also spread to passenger cars. It was recognized that in time of war rayon had a vital defense role.

## Synthetic Rubber and Rayon

When America entered World War II, it was immediately cut off from all supplies of natural rubber. Though heavily stockpiled, rubber became a most precious defense material, and the development of synthetic rubber manufacture mushroomed.

In order to make possible the use of the highest obtainable percentage of synthetic rubber in tires, the problem of cool running had once again to be confronted. Heat standards which were satisfactory with natural rubber were not valid with synthetic products, and it was therefore necessary to again revise ideas about tire structure. The walls would have to be made thinner than ever and yet stronger, for the rough usage of war service.

The key to this situation lay with the fiber manufacturers, for only man-made fibers could provide yarns with the necessary tenacity and resilience in the quantities which expanded programs demanded.

Initially the War Production Board figured its requirement at fifty million pounds a year, divided among five producing companies. This estimate proved to be just the starting point of a vast expansion program. By 1945, in addition to greatly increased production capacity, much of the textile rayon yarn production had been converted to high-tenacity output. With the existing high-tenacity plants they were able to give an annual output of almost three hundred million pounds.

Tremendous as was the war-time achievement of the rayon industry, on the cessation of hostilities even greater efforts were called for. Tires made for war purposes had advanced technically beyond any that had been made before the war. With the switch to civilian production, the automobile industry demanded tires in tremendous volume, incorporating all the latest improvements. It appeared that a further increase of rayon producing capacity would be justified.

In the course of the next six years, the output of high-tenacity rayon again doubled. The introduction of nylon cord in tire manufacture made pos-

Dried chips of polyester being fed into extruders to form yarn, to be spun into tire cord.

Polyester fiber produced at Goodyear's Point Pleasant, W.Va., plant goes into cord for bias/belted tires.

Spools of polyester yarn for use in tire cord. Each spool has enough yarn to reinforce six tires.

Hundreds of individual cords of polyester are tied to a loom to be woven into fabric for tire plies.

sible further improvements in tire construction, on account of its superior tensile strength and heat resistance.

During the 1950's and 1960's there has been a three-way struggle among rayon, nylon and polyester for predominance in the tire cord field. Until the mid-1960's, rayon was the major fiber in the original equipment market for cars, while nylon was the major fiber for replacement tires. In the heavy-duty bus and truck market, and in the aircraft and off-road, heavy-equipment market, nylon was virtually alone.

Polyester began to invade the tire cord market at that time and by the end of the decade had become the biggest fiber in the original equipment market for passenger cars, followed by rayon, and had become the second largest fiber in the replacement tire market, behind nylon. Nylon maintained its predominance in the heavy duty truck and airplane market because of its high stability under high temperatures.

Untextured polyester filament actually goes into the carcass or air-holding envelope of the tire, not the bias-belted tread area. There, glass fiber is used very widely because of its high strength. Thus the most popular fiber structure in original equipment tires is the polyglass structure, and many industry experts expect this to remain so for the better part of the 1970's. In 1970, the tire-yarn poundage relationship was as follows: nylon, polyester, rayon and glass.

## Aviation Fabrics

The development of aviation fabrics is an American contribution which involved special engineering, design, and styling for the unique and exacting requirements of service many thousand feet in the air. Aviation fabrics must be extremely fast to sunlight because actinic rays are stronger at high altitudes and over water. Furthermore, the exigencies of transcontinental and transoceanic flights call for flame-retardant fabrics right across the board, not to mention a degree of lightness far beyond anything needed on the ground. Reduction in weight must be achieved without sacrifice of durability, and must be combined with resistance to soiling and easy-cleaning properties.

Styling problems are correspondingly complicated and difficult. Passengers see fabric more than anything else in the interior of a plane and today competitive factors demand colors which are skilfully blended with pleasing harmonies.

### Lighter in Weight

The first aviation fabrics built to specification were developed in 1941 by the firm of Collins & Aikman in cooperation with Douglas Aircraft Company. Up to that point traditional carpeting and upholstery materials had been used, and these were not only far too heavy but were not designed to fit the needs of the aviation industry. As a result, Collins & Aikman began a research and development program which resulted in a carpeting reduced from 64 to 44 ounces per square yard by means of finer cotton backing stiffened with latex. Similarly, they developed a worsted-faced Bedford cord upholstery fabric to replace a wool-faced cloth, and reduced the weight from 22 to 13 ounces per square yard.

The weight saving in both the carpet and upholstery fabrics turned out to be an enormous contribution to military transport by air during World War II. That is why these fabrics were immediately adopted by both the Army and Navy. The armed forces standardized olive drab seat coverings and luggage tan curtain fabrics, together with green carpetings. Thus Government aircraft became the proving ground for modern aviation fabrics.

### How the Post-War Shift Was Made

Upon the termination of hostilities and the transfer of Army and Navy planes to commercial airlines, it became imperative to obtain interior fabrics and carpets quickly, to replace equipment requisitioned for war use. One hundred percent olive drab walls and seats would not do. On the other hand, how could new civilian fabrics be developed overnight? Collins & Aikman found a way. They made up 5,000 yards in the grey of each of the four basic aviation materials: carpeting, seat cover material, curtain cloth, and wall covering. It was then pointed out to the various commercial airlines that by the use of individual color combinations, these basic proven interior materials could be used and still maintain individuality of interior appearance. It would also make possible the conversion of this replaced equipment in weeks instead of months. Nonflammability and low-smoke-generation are critical in aircraft upholstery and other interior fabric uses. Therefore, tightly-woven wool and Du Pont's Nomex (nonflammable) nylon have become big factors in airplane upholstery. Other man-made fibers which maintain a position in airplane fabric are nylon, vinyl and polyester.

## Beltings

Beltings are of two types—flat belting, both rubberized and non-rubberized, and V-beltings. Such belts are used for power transmission or for handling and conveying materials.

The original belting was made of cotton, then succeeded by rayon, which in turn has been superseded by nylon and polyester, with Nomex nylon becoming a large factor in v-belts.

### Flat Belting

Flat belting may either be built up from two or more plies of plain duck stitched together, and combined with plies of wrapper fabric where desired, or it may be woven directly. In this case the fabric may be of special construction, having from one to twelve sets of warp yarns, held together by a complex system of filling threads. Stitched belting is usually made from 33 to 39 oz. cotton duck, or from an equivalent lighter fabric of man-made fiber. Both types are generally impregnated with oil or wax, bituminous material or latex, or other material in order to give improved durability and serviceability, under conditions which produce heating, abrasion, or where chemicals are present.

Where flat belting is used for direct power transmission the resistance or sensitiveness of the fabric to strains imposed at the fastening point of the metallic belt fasteners, generally used to join belts, is important. Here some man-made fibers are found to perform better than cotton.

Where flat belting is used for conveying materials such as ore and coal in mining or heavy items in factories, the qualities of impact resistance, troughability, long flex life and resistance to edge wear

Boeing's 747 has interior walls of Nomex nylon.

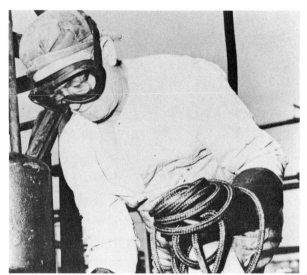

Man-made fibers used by technical services.

Conveyor belt of high-strength rayon.

are the prime considerations. For this reason special constructions employing appropriate man-made fibers either in the filling alone, or in both warp and filling, are being used increasingly in handling and conveying applications.

Heat resistance is important in such fields as foundry work, and resistance to chemical degradation in some industrial uses; mildew and rot resistance are vital in hot and humid conditions, especially where belting stands idle for long intervals. Polyester is the most important man-made fiber in this area, with some nylon being used and a considerable amount of Nomex, wherever heat-resistance is imperative.

In the manufacture of paper and corrugated board special belting fabrics are used which serve to carry the paper or board over heat and which must be porous enough to permit the ready escape of mois-

ture during drying.

In extreme applications belting may be faced with asbestos to protect the fibers of the belting.

## V-Belts

The use of reinforced rubber V-belting for power transmission was introduced in 1921 and is presently rapidly increasing. It has been calculated that in the United States alone over 15 million pounds of fiber are used in its manufacture; again, polyester is the main fiber with nylon and Nomex being used in special areas.

Small V-belts such as those used in automobiles and on small auxiliary power units, are generally constructed with cord as the reinforcement; in heavier industrial V-belting a cord fabric is employed for reinforcing the belt. In addition to reinforcement

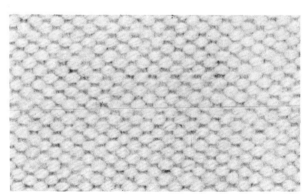

Cotton duck for belting, magnified twice.

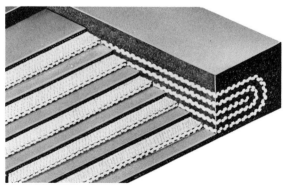

Belt construction: cross-section.

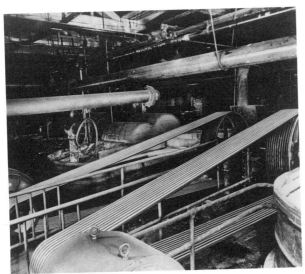

Dacron-reinforced V-belts driving pulp-beaters.

Plate and frame filter press showing filter cloths.

there may be a protective cotton wrapper on the outside of the belt.

As with flat belting the qualities of heat resistance, stretch resistance and low moisture absorption are important and in this field belts with nylon fiber reinforcement are gaining ground despite higher initial cost.

Their greater strength results in lighter constructions for delivery of the same power output, with less heating and longer wear-life; or where equally heavy units are used, fewer are necessary to deliver a particular load, as compared with traditional cotton reinforced beltings.

## Filter Media

Industrial filtration of gases and liquids is an important application of textile fibers and fabrics. It is particularly important where strength and non-corrosibility are required. In this area, acrylic, nylon and polyester are the important man-made fibers. Acetate tow is the major man-made fiber used to make cigarette filters.

Woven fabrics, non-woven fabrics and random fibers are all used in filtering. Practically every industry employs filtration in some form, either to cleanse liquids or gases, or else for recovery of valuable wastes in dust or sediment. Among the industries which employ filter media most extensively are: petroleum, chemicals, dyes, pigments, soap, plastics, food, beverage, metals, rubber, coal products.

Man-made fibers are used exclusively in the applications where heat or chemicals are involved—for example, in filtration of hot concentrated acids which would not be possible with any natural fiber except perhaps asbestos. Glass fibers are extensively used in air filtration for domestic purposes, their freedom from organic contamination being an asset. In instances where bacterial rotting is a consideration, for example in sewage filtration, man-made fibers are found to give approximately five times longer service than wool fibers.

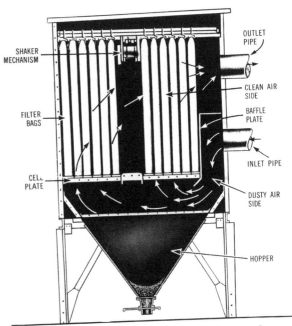

An automatic shaker-type of dust collector, showing fabric dust bags.

Workmen's overalls of synthetic fiber resist acids and abrasion and dry quickly.

Nylon fiber is excellent for cordage.

The type of textile used in a particular filter varies with the type of filtration required. For dust filtration fabrics may be woven of spun yarn or, if woven from filament yarns, they may be napped to give higher dust retention. For recovery of solids in liquid filtration, a fabric woven from filament yarns without any nap offers easier cake release; where clear filtrate is the aim, spun yarn fabrics offer advantages.

In cases where elevated temperatures are employed, correct finishing of the fabric is of importance, to avoid shrinkage in position resulting in loss of efficiency. This special finishing consists in relaxation of the fibers under suitable conditions to encourage shrinking of the fabric and tightening of the weave before installation.

Terylene tow-ropes are used for towing in sub-zero temperatures.

These are the advantages and disadvantages of the most-used fibers:

Nylon: For its excellent filter quality under alkali, mild acid, abrasiveness, high flex, or quick cake-release conditions. Nomex used in high-temperature and acid-exposure filtration.

Acrylic: Orlon, the first fiber to operate continuously in the range of 275°F., and to resist highly acidic fumes. Dogbone cross-section makes it highly desirable for filter purposes. Only Orlon staple fiber is used in pneumatic tires now.

Modacrylic: Dynel, resistant to both alkaline and acidic conditions, and flame-resistant. But temperature can only go to 180°F. in its limitation.

Polyester: In wide use for liquid filtration, not much in high temperature applications.

Teflon: Fantastic in its chemical resistance, even sustaining no damage in boiling aqua regia. The chemical resistance properties of Teflon have given it a significant application in liquid and gas filtration.

Glass Fibers: Very successful in reverse air-flow filters where very little flex is required. Used in filament form, it has to be treated with a silicone or

Nylon nets which provide light weight, long-term service and easy care in use.

A five hundred foot length of four-inch hose which has no splice in it.

Teflon resin finish to be practical. Withstands temperatures of well over 425°F., a point in favor of its expanded use.

## Fishing Nets and Twine

The fish net and twine industry in the United States is dominated by commercial fishing gear made from polyester and nylon. This is because of their high tensile strength and low moisture absorption in operation, as well as its rot resistance. A nylon tuna seine in use in the Pacific is 2460 feet long and weighs 10,000 lbs. It has a dry weight advantage of 2400 pounds over cotton net, and when wet the weight differential is much greater. These factors represent economy in rapid setting and recovery and data indicate that, due to resistance to rotting, such a net will far outlast one of natural fiber in service.

## Hose

Hose may be manufactured by weaving, braiding or wrapping; in the latter case a rubber hose is wrapped with fabric and, where necessary, with wire

reinforcement. The hose industry in the United States uses asbestos, polyester, glass and nylon.

Industrial hose, fire hose and automotive hose are major users; the automotive industry alone, for example, uses the following types of hose: for fuel and oil lines; for radiators; for heaters; for hydraulic brakes; for windshield wipers; for defrosters; for air conditioning; for power steering; for automatic transmission coolant; and some other applications.

The industrial uses of hose are innumerable and

Light weight of fire hose is an important factor in action, where lives may be at stake.

New man-made fibers allow manufacture of hose in lighter weights with less bulk, an important storage factor.

cotton is being increasingly supplemented by man-made fibers to give special qualities such as: higher burst strength, higher flex resistance and abrasion resistance, rot resistance, ease of handling, which may be connected with low moisture absorption, greater flexibility, and weight reduction due to using high-tenacity fiber.

Among the industries using special types of hose are: the oil industry, chemical plants, paper and pulp mills, steel manufacturers.

## Coated Fabrics

Fabrics may be coated with a variety of substances in order to render them impervious to water and other liquids. The coating materials include oil, pyroxylin, rubber, resins, and various plastics. Applications range from bookbinder's cloths to inflatable warehouses.

This field has made rapid advances as a result of continuing technological advances both in coating materials and in the construction of fabrics for coating. For example a truck cover, traditionally woven of cotton and impregnated with oils, can now be obtained woven from nylon and coated with neoprene or other weather-resistant plastic material. The product is lighter, stronger and more durable in use than the traditional cover, since a 16-18 oz. nylon fabric is approximately equivalent in use to a conventional No. 8 cotton duck tarpaulin and weighs about half as much.

Among important uses of coated fabrics are: agriculture, for machinery protection, for bunker silos, for temporary grain storage bins, for irrigation, for livestock protection; marine uses, including hatch covers, deck awnings, lifeboat covers and equipment coverings; oil industry uses, including covers for well-drilling rigs; construction applications, various protective coverings; recreational uses, especially athletic field covers, swimming pool linings; military uses, including tents, storage, transportation coverings, and special structures for protection or warehousing in various climates.

Among the latter an impulse has been given to coated fabrics by the invention of frameless inflatable structures for many types of use.

Radome instrument housing which is constructed from coated nylon and air supported.

Air-supported swimming pool dome of transparent plastic combined with coated nylon fabric.

507

Nylon cordage and sails are light, strong and non-absorbent in use.

## Sailcloth

This canvas or comparable fabric is strong and has to be able to withstand the elements in all kinds of weather and wear. Polyester has captured nearly 100% of the market for mainsails, jibs, etc., while nylon is predominant in spinnakers. Polyester fiber has excellent strength resistance, is uniform and smooth, has no striations, and has excellent recovery. One type of sailcloth is on the order of balloon and typewriter fabrics and it is often used for spinnakers and head sails. Finished at 40-inches, the texture is about 184-square and its weight is about six yards to the pound. Nylon fabric is liked for use on some racing boats. Boatsail drill that is made of Egyptian cotton, or the best of the cottons raised in the United States, is made in a plain weave and has a high, compact texture and structure of around 148 x 60, or higher pickage. This fabric has very high strength and good wind resistance.

## Laundry Textiles

Laundries are substantial consumers of textiles in the form of apron ducks, cover cloths, feed ribbons and special paddings for flatwork ironers; cover cloths, flannel and padding on presses; wash-nets and other items.

Calender sheeting which is used in modern power laundry equipment.

Man-made fibers contribute satisfactory service in the hot, acid conditions of the metals industry.

Generator rotor is manufactured with the aid of tape woven from high-insulation fiber.

Some advances in the technique of construction of press cover materials and flatwork ironer covers have been made through the increasing use of man-made fibers, some of which have higher heat resistance and abrasion resistance than natural fibers. Biggest advance has been in wash-nets, where these qualities combined with low moisture absorption and high resistance to alkaline bleaching materials have resulted in an improved product.

Nylon used in practically all cases, except for the use of Dynel and nylon in dry-cleaning press covers, and dry nets are made solely from Orlon. Arnel is used in press felt, in addition to nylon.

## Military Uses

Military requirements have always played a large part in industrial fabric manufacture. Today there is a premium on strength and light weight and the traditional "Army ducks," conventionally made of cotton fiber, are now increasingly being made of polyester or polyester blends. Other related applications such as space wear have employed nearly all of the man-made fibers, including polyester, nylon, Nomex and metallic fibers.

Inflatable air structures use man-made fibers because of their strength, resiliency and resistance to wear.

A nylon woven fabric which combines density with high tensile strength.

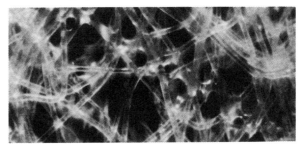

Non-woven fabric of nylon is based on heat bonding of the individual filaments.

In heavy industry handling-cords which are stretch and rot resistant are at a premium.

## Ropes

Ropemaking is a dual-twisting operation in which the yarns are first plied or formed into strands, and then three or more of these strands are laid with backturn into the rope. In the strand-forming operation, it is most important that the yarns be arranged in properly patterned concentric layers as they are twisted to form the strand so as to develop optimum strength and simultaneous compression. When the strands are being twisted together, they are kept at proper tension to make sure that compactness of structure is achieved.

Since these structures are large, the physical attributes can be easily measured. Turn, measured as the spiral pitch of a strand, designates the degree of twist in a rope of a given size.

When multifilament or monofilament polymer fibers are processed into rope, the conventional methods used for natural-grown fibers have to be modified to cope with the man-made fibers. The twisted structures are often heated in steam, hot water, or hot air, inducing shrinkage and thus making the structure compact.

Nylon is used because of its high strength and stretching quality, suitable for shock tension loading service. Ideal for harpoon lines, towing and mooring lines. A rope or cord must have three basic stresses—tensile pull; friction associated with bending and flexing; and surface friction that contributes to abrasion. Nylon stands up very well under these conditions.

Polyester and polypropylene are coming to the fore in this field. When wet, natural fiber ropes, such as manila and comparable fibers, will shrink and thus can be stretched more when the tension is applied to the wet rope. Nylon cordage, under these wet conditions, will show even greater wet elonga-

tion. However, cordage made from polyester fibers is generally not affected by wetting and shows no changes in stretchability when wet. However, if the man-made polymer fiber cordage is kept under tension when it is heat set, much residual stretch will be eliminated and elongation under tension will be reduced. Cordage with low stretch is known as high modulus cordage; cordage used in V-belting is so treated.

Polyester, nylon and polypropylene make rope handling easier than is the case with ropes made from natural fibers such as manila, abaca, henequen, sisal, etc. There is an absence of adverse effects such as the wetting deterioration and increased stretchability when ropes used are made of polyester, nylon and polypropylene.

Nylon rope is considered best to use where variable loads are present, such as climbing ropes, drive and marine ropes. Outlasts cotton 7 to 1.

Polyester is better for applications where stretch is not desired and load control is desired. Polyester cordage needs little care and can be stowed away when wet, without degradation.

Polypropylene comes closest to the properties observed in natural fiber rope. The use of an antioxidant stabilizer improves the weather performance of this type of rope. It has an added advantage in that it will not sink in most constructions.

## Summary

The foregoing paragraphs deal with a number of the principal fields where textiles and textile fibers are of importance to industry.

In the century which elapsed between the early years of the industrial era and World War II, cotton was the principal fiber in industry. Today the man-made fibers have substantially replaced cotton in many applications, because they possess or can be endowed with special qualities for the demanding industrial market. The trend has been toward a constant search for perfection. Therefore the history of industrial applications has been dominated first by cotton, then in some instances by rayon, but most recently by nylon, polyester and polypropylene.

It may therefore be said that the man-made fibers are destined in some cases to supplement and in others to replace the natural fibers in industry, and to occupy a primary place in certain specialized fields. In addition, new techniques of fabric manufacture including bonding, coating and foam techniques, are continually modifying and affecting the industrial uses of textiles.

Sewing shoes with acid-resistant thread to meet conditions found in certain industries.

Coiling nylon hawser which, because lighter than hemp rope, is more pliable and handles better.

Special resistant threads are used for sack closures in the chemicals industries.

High-tenacity yarn gives better service for bag closure in the agricultural industry.

- Over 3,000 commonly used textile terms and definitions

- Scores of pointed, explanatory art adornments

- Many ancient textile terms, their origins and adaptations

- Terms covering phases of textiles down through the ages

- Fibers, fabrics, machines, and processes are described

- Many archaic words are included, with modern interpretations

- Alphabetically listed terms in easy-to-find rotation

# DICTIONARY

## OF

# TEXTILE TERMS

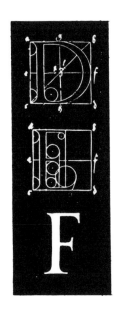

# HOW TO USE THE DICTIONARY
## OF TEXTILE TERMS

IN ALL MAJOR RESPECTS this Textile Dictionary can serve the same basic function as any good dictionary for the English language. The major difference is that here, instead of listing and defining words of common usage in the English language, the Editors have concentrated the contents on words of both common and rare usage in the textile industry.

Quite frequently, through usage, a word grows to attain a meaning which is not quite accurate; this often stems from a misuse in one quarter and then the felony is compounded over and over again until the original and true meaning has become lost.

FOR QUICK AND EASY REFERENCE in connection with any important word used in textiles, you will find well over 3,000 words alphabetically listed here; each has a completely accurate definition (sometimes accompanied by a helpful illustration). If you require still more detailed information as to a particular word or operation, by referring to the General Index you will find the pages where you will find a more detailed explanation—usually profusely illustrated.

In general, consider the Dictionary as your first simple source for information; the Encyclopedia as the place to gain really full knowledge of every important subject.

# DICTIONARY OF TEXTILE TERMS

## A

**ABA:** A wool, hair fiber, or combination-stock material used by the peasants in southern Europe and Asia. The fabric is coarse, thick, and has considerable felting applied in the finishing.

**ABACA:** See Manila Hemp

**ABRADED YARNS:** Continuous filament rayon yarns in which filaments have been cut or abraded at intervals and given added twist to bring about a certain degree of hairiness. Abraded yarns are usually plied or twisted with other yarns before using.

**ABRASION RESISTANCE:** The degree to which a fabric is able to withstand surface wear and rubbing.

**ABRASION TESTER:** An instrument that tests a fabric's resistance to surface wear and friction.

**ABSORBENT COTTON:** See COTTON.

**ABSORBENT FINISH:** A chemical treatment of fabrics to enable them to absorb water more readily.

**ACALA:** Native Mexican cotton; also grown in Arkansas, Texas, Oklahoma.

**ACCA:** A cloth used in British Isles for formal, regal, and conventional purposes. Vestment cloth is made from Acca. It is a richly brocaded silk material often interspersed with animal or pastoral designs to enrich its appearance.

**ACETATE:** A manufactured fiber in which the fiber-forming substance is cellulose acetate. Where not less than 92" of the hydroxyl groups are acetylated, the term triacetate may be used as a generic description of the fiber. Has different physical and chemical properties from rayons, especially in its reaction to dyes, and a whole new set of dyes had to be developed for it. The principal developmental work was done by two brothers, Camille and Henri Dreyfus of Basle, Switzerland.

**ACETATE AND RAYON RULES:** The following trade-practice rules on the use and the identification of acetate and rayon were announced on December 11th, 1951 and became effective on February 11th, 1952: The Federal Trade Commission has decreed that *rayon* is to be used for man-made textile fibers and filament composed of regenerated cellulose; and yarn, thread, or textile fabric made of such fibers and filaments. The term *acetate* is to be used for man-made textile fibers and filaments composed of cellulose acetate; and yarn, thread, and textile fabric made of such fibers.

**ACETYLATION:** The chemical reaction whereby cellulose is changed into cellulose acetate. The cellulose linters (cotton) are treated with a solution of acetic anhydride in glacial acetic acid. It is possible to partially acetylate cotton to increase its heat and rot resistance. Fully acetylated cotton has been developed experimentally. It looks like untreated cotton, has improved heat and rot resistance, and other good qualities of ordinary cotton.

**ACID:** A chemical compound which will neutralize an alkali. Acids have a sour taste, pungent odor and are widely used in bleaching, dyeing and printing.

**ACID DYE:** A type of dye used on animal fibers. Acid dyes on cotton and linen require mordant, a substance that fixes the dye. See DYES.

**ACID RESISTANCE:** A term describing a fabric that will resist any acids it would encounter in normal use. The type of acid should be stated, i.e., organic or inorganic.

**ACRILAN:** A fiber spun from a copolymer of acrylonitrile with vinyl derivatives. Product of Monsanto.

**ACRYLIC:** A manufactured fiber in which the fiber-forming substance is any long chain synthetic polymer composed of at least 85% by weight of acrylonitrile units $(-CH_2-CH-)$.
CN

**ADELAIDE WOOL:** Obtained in and around this city in Australia, the wool is a high merino quality which is slightly lower in quality when compared with Port Philip and Sydney wools raised in Australia. It can spin to 60s worsted counts and finds use in high-quality worsteds made from very fine, choice fibers.

**ADMIRALTY CLOTH:** 1. Slang expression for melton cloth used for officers' uniforms and coats in the British navy.

2. General term for heavyweight pea jackets and officers' coats used in the American naval service.

**AEROPHANE:** Thin silk gauze used as trimming on dresses and headgear; made on doup weave.

**AFFINITY:** The attraction between fiber and dyestuff. If the dye takes readily, it is said to have good affinity for the fiber. Some dyes do not take very well on certain fibers and they are classed as having little or no affinity for these particular fibers.

**AFGHAN:** A knitted or crocheted wool blanket or robe made with a series of stripes, zigzag effects, or squares varying in size and vivid colorings; gives great warmth.

**AFRICAN WOOLS:** Refers chiefly to wools from the Union of South Africa—Orange River Colony, Natal, Transvaal, Rhodesia. These very soft, fine, white merino wools are much sought for by woolen and worsted mills all over the world. Native breeds of sheep furnish much of the annual yield of African wools and it should be borne in mind that this stock is apart from the merino-type wool. Low yield and inferior quality, along with careless handling, mark the characteristic of wool from the native sheep.

**AFTER-IMAGE:** The complementary color image which appears after looking concentratedly at a color area.

515

**AFTERTREATING:** A comprehensive term referring to any treatment following actual dye application. It may be color-fixative, resin application, neutralization, washes, or other.

**AGAR-AGAR:** A vegetable fiber used experimentally in England; makes a gauze type of fabric.

**AGEING:** Refers to the process used in developing colors in yarn or cloth. Usually achieved in a steam bath.

**AGILON:** Trademark of Deering Milliken Research Trust for its stretch yarns made from elasticized thermoplastic filaments and their combinations with other textile fibers. Versatility of hand ranges from one of soft silkiness to any desirable degree of firm or crisp texture. This stretch nylon filament yarn has good strength, durability, affinity for dyestuffs, possesses ease of washing and drying.

Agilon is adaptable to women's hosiery, men's and boys' hosiery, body-knit fabrics, tricot materials, and woven cloths.

**AGRA GAUZE:** A strong, transparent, gauze-like silk fabric; given a stiff finish.

**AILANTHUS SILK:** Wild silk or tussah, from India; produced by the large moth *Attacus atlas*. Also called Atlas Silk.

**AIR BRUSHING:** Blowing color on the fabric with a mechanized air brush.

**AIR CONDITIONING:** A chemical process that seals the short fuzzy fibers into the yarn, thus making the fabric more porous. Porous fabrics are cooler because they allow circulation of air.

**AIR PERMEABILITY:** The warmth or coolness of a fabric is measured by its porosity, or the ease with which air passes through it. Air permeability determines the wind-resistance of sailcloth, the warmth of blankets, etc.

**AJIJI:** Cotton muslin from India; usually made with colored stripes in rayon or silk.

**ALASKA YARN:** Mixture yarn of about two-thirds cotton and one-third combined wool stocks; popular in knitting and hand-weaving circles.

**ALBATROSS:** Soft, loosely woven, twill material, dyed in the piece, and usually made of worsted stock. Cotton may be used. The cloth is not popular but seems to return to favor periodically in the cycle of cloths.

**ALBERT CLOTH:** Double cloth, woolen overcoating of the dressy type. The double-cloth construction gives added weight, texture, and warmth. A velvet collar adds much to nattiness of garment.

**ALCOHOLS:** Chemical compounds consisting of one or more hydroxyl (OH) grouping attached to a hydrocarbon. The three most widely used are methyl or wood alcohol, ethyl or grain alcohol, and glycerol or glycerine.

**ALENCON LACE:** See LACE.

**ALENCONNES:** A linen fabric incompletely bleached; has many domestic uses in France.

**ALGIL:** A man-made fiber with a polystyrene base, usually made into batting and used as a substitute for kapok.

**ALGIN:** A product obtained from certain marine algae. It may be extracted from kelp or seaweed and has been spun into filaments on a commercial basis. Also used in printing pastes and as a dressing material.

**ALGINATE FIBERS:** They are produced by extruding alginate solution through spinnerets into solution of beryllium sulphate or other chemicals. Various alginates differ in their properties; several are supposed to have good resistance to mildew. Beryllium alginate is said to be resistant to alkalies. The chief uses of the fibers are for experimenting in garnishing camouflage and netting.

**ALIZARIN DYES:** See DYES.

**ALKALI:** A strong base such as caustic soda. An alkali will act to neutralize an acid.

**ALLOVERS:** Relating to the design which covers a net, distinguished from motifs of borders. See LACE.

**ALL-WOOL:** A material of any description whose yarns are all wool, understood to be the wool of sheep. The term has to be weighed carefully, since it includes, in addition to the pure, new fibers, other stocks, such as shoddy, mungo, extract wool, reused wool, remanufactured wool, etc. All-wool is often misunderstood in the trade when purchasing fabrics or garments and the consumer may be the loser. Cotton, for example, may cost more per pound than some of these aforementioned fibers that go into an all-wool fabric. Very often an all-wool fabric may not mean too much where quality is considered. Distributive and consumer education can do much to alleviate these possible misunderstandings which, at times, may befuddle the purchaser.

**ALMA:** A mourning fabric which has been known among the Egyptians for centuries, is made from cotton or linen and dyed black or purple.

**ALOE LACE:** A form of bobbin lace made of the fibers of the aloe plant. See LACE.

**ALPACA:** Raised in the Andes Mountains, the fleeces are usually obtained after a two-year growth. The fiber diameter is about 1/800 inches. The fiber is lustrous, soft to touch, strong, wavy; the fleece will weigh about ten pounds.

Fine alpaca is from 4½ inches to 8 inches in length; medium alpaca is 5½ inches to 9 inches long; coarse alpaca is from 7 to 11 inches in staple length.

In color, alpaca fibers range from white to brown or black. The two types of fibers obtained from the 180-pound animal are: 1. Soft wool-like hair.

2. Stiff beard hair.

Alpaca is coarser than camel or vicuna.

**ALPACA CREPE:** Made of two-ply yarn, the fabric simulates woolen cloth of that name.

**ALTAR CLOTH:** Fine, sheer linen with wiry yarns to give a crisp hand. Used in cloth for altars.

**ALTAR LACES:** Used for altar decoration; of medieval character, darned, drawn, or cut-work.

**ALUM:** Used as a mordant in dyeing; also as an agent with alizarin for printing woolens. A colorless crystal which is soluble in water.

**AMERICAN COTTON:** See COTTON.

**AMERICAN PEELER COTTON:** See COTTON.

**AMERICAN PIMA COTTON:** See COTTON.

**AMIENS:** Originated in city of that name in France. Material is a hardtwisted worsted cloth made of a twill weave in solid colors or novelty patterns.

**AMUNO:** A chemical compound used in treating animal fibers to preserve them against moths and carpet beetles.

**ANDALUSIANS:** Made from Spanish merino wool and comparable grades, these fine worsted dress goods made in England come in a variety of twill constructions and fabric weights.

**ANGOLA CLOTH:** A twill-weave overcoating, usually dyed red and heavily napped.

**ANGORA:** 1. Goat hair; the white fleece of long, fine fibers; when manufactured is called mohair. Because of its smoothness and softness, it must be combined with other fibers in weaving.

2. Rabbit hair; Angora rabbits possess an exceptionally fine hair that is very light in weight and furnishes much warmth to the wearer of garments thus made. This fiber is often blended and mixed with wool to lower the price of the finished article and to obtain fancy or novelty effects in weaving. Must be designated as Angora rabbit hair.

3. A highly finished, plain-woven fabric made of cotton warp and mohair filling.

4. A twill-woven overcoating with a shaggy, fuzzy surface effect.

5. A soft yarn used for knitting purposes. Genuine Angora knitting yarn is scarce in this country and the center of the industry is France.

6. The well-known, highly cherished Angora shawl. This luxury, heirloom article gives excellent wear for many years.

**ANGUILLA COTTON:** The original source of Sea Island cotton. The first seeds came from the island of Anguilla in about 1780.

**ANIDEX:** A generic elastomeric fiber launched in 1969 by Rohm and Haas under the trademark, Anim/8. This fiber was declared a generic fiber by the Federal Trade Commission in 1970. It is equally adaptable to weaving and knitting and can be used in corespun, covered, plied or bare yarns. It takes both permanent-press and soil-release finishes, and it retains its elasticity after washing and dry cleaning. If bleached with chlorine, Anim/8 remains white, not graying or yellowing.

**ANILINE DYE:** A coal-tar derivative and an important factor in the dyeing process. For instance, Aniline Black is a very intense black and has excellent colorfast qualities.

**ANIMAL FIBERS AND FILAMENTS:** Obtained from an animal for purposes of weaving, knitting, or felting into fabric; some animal fibers are alpaca, angora goat hair, camel hair, cashmere, cow hair, extract wool, fur, horse hair, llama, mohair, mungo, noil, shoddy, silk, spun silk, tussah or wild silk, vicuna, wool, worsted, worsted top.

**ANTI-BACTERIAL FINISH:** Treatment applied to fabric to make it resistant to attack by micro-organisms.

**ANTI-CREASE FINISH:** A process for treating fabrics with a synthetic resin or chemical that helps them resist and recover from wrinkling. Used on cotton, rayon, linen and combination fabrics. Silk and wool have a natural resistance to wrinkling.

**ANTIMACASSAR:** Originally a doily type of covering placed on chairs to protect them against Macassar oil, which was once a popular hair dressing.

**ANTIQUE LACE:** See LACE.

**ANTIQUE SATIN:** A furniture or evening wear fabric made to resemble silk satin of an earlier century.

**ANTIQUE TAFFETA:** See TAFFETA.

**APPAREL WOOL:** Broad term used chiefly for tariff purposes, which embraces all wools except carpet and pulled wools. Apparel wool finds much use in blankets, felt, upholstery, and similar materials.

**APPLICATION PRINTING:** The printing onto white goods irrespective of the type of material involved; a term rather popular in printing of rayons and silks. There is no discharge- or resist-printing procedure involved in application printing, which is sometimes also known as *direct* printing.

**APPLIQUE:** Surface decoration which is sewed, embroidered, or otherwise attached to the fabric.

**APPLIQUE LACE:** A lace in which the design detail is made separate from the background. Point appliqué is an application of needle-point details on net.

**ARGENTAN:** This Argentan net is firm and large; the pattern is flat, not employing a cordonnet.

**ARGYLE:** A design motif, usually knitted consisting of diamond shapes, generally based on three colors. Its name derives from the district of Argyll in the West Highlands of Scotland.

**ARKWRIGHT, SIR RICHARD:** The "Father of the Factory System" in industry. He revolutionized the art of spinning in 1768, by his invention of the spinning frame that would draw the stock into a finished, spun yarn. It was the successful application of automatic spinning. He did not receive his title for his work in textile machinery inventions, as is generally believed.

**ARMOISINE:** Taffeta-type fabric made of silk for men's and women's wear in the 18th Century and earlier.

**ARMURE:** This French term implies a fabric made with a small pattern in a pebble or embossed effect. Drapery fabric of this name is made with the small woven designs on a twill or rep background. Armure is used as a dress fabric and comes plain, striped, ribbed, or woven, with a small novelty two-color design. Any of the major fibers or fiber blends serve to make this appealing dressgoods cloth.

**ARNEL:** The name of Celanese for fibers and yarns made from its cellulose triacetate. Triacetate has a much higher proportion of acetate to cellulose than does regular acetate; together with heat setting in the finished fabric, this accounts for the good wrinkle resistance, ease of care, pleat retention, and launderability of fabric containing Arnel.

**ARRAS:** 1. Name of a city in France which for centuries has been noted for its tapestry work. Arras is so well established today that people no longer use the capital "A" when speaking of an arras or tapestry wall covering; the terms are considered synonymous.

2. Arras is the name given to certain French worsteds made in this locality.

3. This center produces a white, French bobbin lace which resembles Lille lace. Arras lace is compact, strong, and has a straight edge with the mignonette used as the basic pattern.

**ARTIFICIAL LACE:** Term applied to a lace that is not woven or embroidered, but is produced by chemical methods.

**ARTILLERY TWILL:** Another name for whipcord.

**ART LINEN:** Plain weave, cylindrical yarn, soft finish. Unbleached or bleached sheeting material may be used.

Widely used in needlework, as it is easy to "draw" the yarns. Also see LINEN.

**ASBESTOS:** The most important mineral fiber, without which it would hardly be possible to have the conveniences enjoyed today. It is found in veins of the solid rock formation of the earth's crust. Asbestos is found chiefly in the Province of Quebec, while other sources are Ontario, New York, Vermont, Arizona, South Africa, and the Savoy district in Italy. Thetford, Quebec, is the greatest asbestos center in the world.

**ASBESTOS CLOTH:** Has a wide variance of style, texture, grade, weight, and thickness. The standard width of fabric is 40 inches, although any width can be made for some desired purpose. Asbestos is woven in plain, twill, or herringbone effects and in either metallic or non-metallic construction. The fabric ranges in weight from a few ounces to several pounds per square yard. Thickness varies from .015″ to .100″ for single ply.

Asbestos ore.

Uses of asbestos fabric include the following: conveyor belting; draperies; automobile, airplane and locomotive equipment; passenger, sleeping, express, mail and freight car equipment; electrical insulation for toasters, broilers, coffee makers, sweepers, fans, refrigerators, washing machines, etc. It is also used for friction materials, fire blankets, ironing board covers, jackets for pipe insulation, laminated plastics, packings, safety clothing, welding, and theatre curtains.

**ASSAM:** East India short-staple cotton.

**ASSILI COTTON:** From Egypt. The word means thoroughbred and indicates a yarn of high tensile strength.

**ASTRAKHAN:** Luxuriant fur used in coatings, cloaks, and for a trimming for collar and cuff sets. Curly, wavy, and often having a tufted surface, the most popular shade of astrakhan is brown. It is secured from young lambs in the Astrakhan section of Russia and is much imitated in the trade.

Astrakhan fabric is woven cloth made of wool on a pile weave construction to assure curliness after the threads are cut.

Knitted astrakhan is a cheap imitation of the cloth and fur, thereby making it possible for a greater number of people to own an "astrakhan" coat.

Mohair warp adds luster and curl to the surface of the material, improvements which are brought about by steaming the mohair under tension while it is on the spindles.

**ATMOSPHERIC FADING:** Gas Fading or Fume Fading— The change of shade exhibited by some few dyes when exposed to certain gases, principally oxides of nitrogen, given off during the burning of fuels. Inhibitors may be used to counteract this tendency as well as the use of resistant dyes.

**ATTENUATION:** To diminish the diameter, as in the case of a group of fibers when they are drafted and drawn among themselves to make a smaller size roping form. In machine manipulation of fibers the stock is made into sliver form and then attenuated into slubbing, roving, and yarn.

**AUBUSSON:** A fine-pile carpet made to imitate the tapestries of that name made at the Royal French factory at Aubusson, France. Aubusson is now made in several world carpet centers. It is made in one piece and the designs show traces of the technique used by the famous East Indian needleworkers and weavers. This carpet commands a high price. Aubusson was popular in the 18th Century life of the French salon.

**AUNE:** A unit of measure once used for silk. It was 45 inches long.

**AUSTRALIAN BALE MARKINGS, NEW:** These were adopted in February, 1958 and provide for 28 classifications in medium or large clips, and 20 for smaller clips. Classifications include "AAA M" for the best and finest of merino clips, with "AA M" and "A M" being the second and third, respectively. A comeback or crossbred clip will drop the "M" for merino and will be marked "AAA" or "AAA CBK" for identification.

**AUSTRALIAN MERINO:** A very high grade, distinctive breed developed from several various strains. Australia, since the days of the famous Captain Macarthur, who was known as the father of the sheep industry in Australia, 160 years ago, has constantly improved the quality of its wool.

Sheep in this class are large in stature, thrive well in large flocks, and have the stamina to withstand drought and dry vegetation better than other breeds. The fleece is very dense and averages 8 to 10 pounds in weight. Staple length is 2½ to 4 inches. This high-quality stock can spin from 60s to 90s count.

**AUSTRIAN CLOTH:** Is one of the finest woolen and worsted fabrics to be found anywhere today. Made in Austria for many years, the fabric is produced from the highest grades of merino wool obtainable, either Austrian Silesia or Botany Bay-Australian wool. It is used for men's formal wear.

**AUSTRIAN SHADE CLOTH:** Striped cotton cloth woven with a crinkled effect produced by weaving alternating groups of slack and tight warp-ends— the slack-held ends form the crinkled stripes. Similar to seersucker with broader stripes. May also be silk or rayon. Used chiefly in hotel and store windows for shades.

**AUTOCLAVE:** A large chamber which can be sealed and filled with steam under pressure. Temperature and pressure are electronically controlled. It is used to stabilize false twist yarn.

**AUTOGENOUS BONDING:** There are two methods used in the manufacture of non-woven fabrics: 1. Bonding by means of chemically activating the surface of the fibers to an adhesive state. 2. Activating the surface of thermoplastic fibers through the application of heat.

**AVA COTTON:** Grown in India.

**AVIGNON:** A silk taffeta fabric, light in weight; used for linings.

**AVLIN:** A polyester fiber manufactured by FMC Corporation, American Viscose Division, in filament yarn and staple form.

**AWASAI:** A carpet wool grown in Mesopotamia.

**AWNING STRIPE:** Heavy firm-woven cotton duck canvas with either yarn-dyed, printed or painted stripes. Used for awnings, beach umbrellas, etc. Drills are used for inexpensive painted awning stripe fabrics. See CANVAS.

**AXMINSTER:** A cut pile woolen fabric, 7 tufts to the weft inch inserted throughout guiding tubes into cotton chain warps and bound with a heavy Kraftcord of jute weft filling and binding yarn carried by a needle thrust to weave a 3-shot construction. Unlimited in use of colors in design, the Axminster weave is identified as rollable warpwise but not weftwise.

**AZLON:** A manufactured fiber in which the fiber-forming substance is composed of any regenerated naturally occurring proteins.

**AZOIC DYE:** See NAPHTHOLS under DYES.

**BABY:** A term for narrow and light laces.

**BABY COMBING WOOL:** Fine, choice wool fiber which ranges from 1½ inches to 2½ inches in staple length. The French method of combing is used to make high-grade worsted yarn from the stock.

**BABY IRISH:** Irish crochet of delicate character.

**BACK DYEING:** See DYEING METHODS.

**BACK BEAM:** The back beam of the loom which corresponds to the breast beam at the front of the loom where the weaver works. Also known as Slabstock, Whip roll.

**BACKED CLOTH:** Single-texture material with addition of an extra warp or filling that is added for weight and warmth. The extra warp or filling may be of wool, worsted, or cotton. This type of construction is found in Frenchbacks,

vestings, worsted, dress goods, suitings, and skirtings. Satin-weave constructions, as well as twill-weaves, may be used in the designing of the cloth.

**BACK-FILLED FABRIC:** Fabric treated with an excess of sizing on the back only, to give it added weight and a better handle. This sizing dissolves readily with washing or rubbing.

**BACK FILLING:** An extra filling woven into a cloth to add weight strength, warmth, or to define a pattern such as pique, Marseilles quilting, Frenchback, overcoating, etc.

**BACKING, BACK CLOTH:** Grey goods material, usually a print cloth, used to absorb surplus dye and to re-inforce fabric on the printing machine.

**BAD:** A linen fabric used in ancient Egypt.

**BAGDAD WOOL:** Dark carpet wool from Mesopotamia; much used in this country.

**BAGHEERA:** A fine, uncut velvet, piece-dyed. See VELVET.

**BAIZE:** Coarse, long napped, woolen cloth that has been made in Great Britain for many centuries. Such materials were dyed "bay" or a brownish red color. Hence the name, which is a corruption of the plural form. Baize, at one time, was made thinner and finer in quality than modern fabric of this name and was used in clothing.

**BALDACHIN, BAUDEKIN, BODKIN, BALDOQUIN:** Costly brocades of silk interspersed throughout with gold or silver threads and often further embellished by the use of precious stones. These gorgeous fabrics, many of which are still extant, reached their greatest popularity during the Crusades, the Renaissance, and other days of chivalry. Baldachin has been or is used today for canopies, ceremonial robes, pageants, trappings, armor, etc.

**BALDOQUIN:** See BALDACHIN.

**BALE:** 1. A compressed pack of wool of a convenient form for transit, varying in weight from 150 pounds to 1,000 pounds, in the countries of production. Australian bales weigh about 300 pounds. Argentine bales, 1,000 pounds. Burlap is used as the covering.

2. Cotton bales vary much in size and weight. The American bale measures 54

x 27 x 27 inches, and weighs about 500 pounds. Other bale weights are: Sea Island, 380 pounds; Egyptian, 750 pounds; Indian, 400 pounds.

3. The average European silk bale weighs 100 kilos or 220 American pounds. Japanese and Shanghai bales average 133.33 pounds; Canton, 106.67 pounds.

**BALIBUNTAL STRAW:** See STRAW.

**BALING PRESS:** A machine for compressing bolts or cuts of cloth, or waste, into a compact bale for shipment.

**BALMORAL:** A strong, heavy, British woolen fabric made on a twill weave; stripes of red, blue, black and grey feature the material.

**BANBURY PLUSH:** An English pile fabric made with cotton warp, wool filling.

**BANDAGE:** Narrow cotton or linen cloth of plain weave and low texture. Woven in widths up to 40 inches, the gauze is split into a variety of widths for hospital purposes.

**BANDANNA:** A large cotton square printed by the resist method so that the design appears white on a colored ground. The word comes from the Hindustani and means "to tie before dyeing."

**BANI COTTON:** Probably the best cotton raised in India, mostly in Hyderabad.

**BAN-LON:** This is a trademark for garments and articles which are made primarily from "Textralized" yarn and which meet the specifications and standards of quality prescribed by Joseph Bancroft & Sons.

**BANNOCKBURN:** Name is derived from village of that name which is about twenty-five miles from Glasgow, Scotland. Obviously, this is a tweed center. Cloth should be made with alternating single- and two-ply yarn, the latter being of contrasting colors. Used for suitings and top-coatings, and always in demand. Is one of the best tweeds on the market and a typical British fabric.

**BARATHEA:** Fine-textured material of broken filling character. Made of silk or rayon warp and woolen or worsted filling. Other combinations may be used. High-quality stock is used in making this cloth. Used as mourning materials and in cravat cloth. Cloth is black as a general thing.

**BAREGE:** A sheer fabric originally made at Barèges in the Pyrenees; usually woven of wool and silk or cotton.

**BARK CREPE:** A woolen or rayon fabric that produces the effect of rough bark on trees. A crepe with much surface interest. Used in women's wear coating. See CREPE.

**BARK FIBERS:** Shredded bark of the redwood and other large trees of the West Coast can be used in blends for mackinac, ski cloth, etc. Heavy fabrics with 20 to 30% bark fiber in content meet test requirements for the trade.

**BARONET SATIN:** Satin-weave, very lustrous, cotton warp and rayon filling. Has tendency to "catch particles." Comes in white and colors and may be made with all rayon. Wears well, washes easily, and has good draping qualities. "Roughing up" in the cloth is detrimental to it.

**BARRÉ:** A French term denoting the horizontal lines appearing in a repeat pattern throughout a piece of fabric or any appreciable portion thereof. These lines, which appear in both woven and knitted fabrics, can be either darker or lighter in shade as compared with the basic color of the fabric. On occasion they may appear as thicker or thinner yarn. This fabric flaw can be caused by the following factors: uneven winding and thick-and-thin yarns at the spinning level; uneven knitting tensions and faulty machine settings at the knitting level; or poor temperature control and faulty dyestuff selection at the dyeing level.

**BARS:** Connecting threads ornamenting open spaces in lace, sometimes called *brides*.

**BARYTA:** An alkaline compound which is used in textiles as the chemical standard for 100% pure white.

**BASIC DYE:** See DYES.

**BASKET:** A fabric weave of any material which, instead of having single threads interlace at right angles, is made by having two threads or more weave alike in both warp and filling direction, conjoined in the regular order of the

plain weave. Effect noted is similar to straightly plaited cane basket work. Hopsack suiting and monk's cloth are examples.

**BAST OR SOFT FIBERS:** The flexible, long strand that comes from the inner bark of flax, ramie, hemp, jute, etc.

**BATHROBE OR BATHROBE BLANKETING:** Double-faced cotton blanketing that is thick and warm. Woven with a tightly twisted warp and two sets of soft filling yarns which can be napped to produce a soft surface. Used for bathrobes, crib blankets, bunting.

**BATIK:** A printing or dyeing method by which the design areas are covered with wax which repels the color. When the wax is later dissolved the design appears in white on the colored ground.

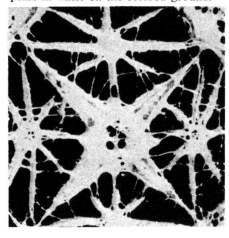

**BATISTE:** Soft, sheer cotton fabric, plain weave, textures range about 88 x 80. Mercerized and made of high-quality yarn. Comes in white, printed or in solid shades, 50s yarn or better used. Dress goods and underwear material.

Durable; launders very well; limited in use, however, because of its softness. Light in weight, 14 to 16 yards of cloth to the pound.

**BATTEN:** Part of the loom which pushes the filling yarns into place.

**BATTENBERG LACE:** Name applied to Renaissance lace when made of Battenberg braid or tape.

**BATTING:** Carded cotton or wool, sold in sheets or rolls, used for warm interlining or as a comforter stuffing.

**BAUDEKIN:** See BALDACHIN.

**BAVE:** A cocoon thread in which two filaments of silk are joined.

**BAYADÈRE:** Stripes in strongly contrasted multicolors, running crosswise in a fabric. Name derived from garment worn by dancing girls in India.

**BAYEUX TAPESTRY:** One of the world's most famous tapestries. It shows the Norman invasion of England and the Battle of Hastings, 1066. It is 214 ft. by 20 in., of linen and colored wool.

**BEACH CLOTH:** Lightweight cotton warp and mohair filling, or all cotton, to imitate linen crash. For summer clothing, nurses' uniforms, draperies, table scarfs.

**BEAD EDGE:** A series of looped threads edging a lace.

**BEADED, OR CUT VELVET:** Velvet with a cut-out pattern or velvet-pile effect. Often done on chiffon velvet. Brilliant designs and effects noted. Made on jacquard loom. Principal use is for evening wear. Other uses are for hangings, decorative material, salon furnishings. Most difficult to handle and manipulate. Drapes well, will dry clean, crushes. Wear depends on quality and type of design.

**BEAM DYEING:** See DYEING METHODS.

**BEAMING:** The process of winding the warp yarn onto the warp beam.

**BEAT-UP:** Signifies the number of tufts per inch of length in a warp row of pile in carpet weaving. The term is used in connection with Axminster, Chenille and other materials not woven over wires and is synonymous with the term 'wire' used in weaving Brussels and Wiltons.

**BEAVER:** A heavily-napped, face-finished overcoating which has the softest feel and the longest nap when compared with the other cloths in its group —melton, kersey, and broadcloth. The grade of wool used accounts for the high quality of the goods—a 64s or better of half-blood wool.

**BEDFORD CORD:** The practice of adopting English localities for the names of many cloths, not necessarily of local make, is again resorted to in naming this material. Cloth has longitudinal cords that run in the warp direction. Used for coatings, suitings, riding habit cloth, and uniform material. The original color of the cloth resembles covert cloth. Bedford cord is the sister cloth of piqués, which should have their cords in the filling direction. The corded effect is secured by having two successive ends weave in plain-weave order, thereby actually holding the fabric in place and showing the cord plainly. Bedford·cord is also made today for the trade in various major fibers. Incidentally, New Bedford, Mass., is also claimed as the home of bedford cord.

**BEETLED FINISH:** A finish with a high gloss and highlight effects, achieved by beating the cloth with hammers. This also produces the appearance of moiré.

**BEIGE:** 1. A dress-goods cloth made of cotton, worsted, or union materials, of low texture and made with a 2-up and 2-down twill weave. Piece-dyed or printed.

2. French term for natural or neutral color.

**BEMBERG RAYON:** The yarns and fabrics composed of products of the American Bemberg Corporation noted for its cuprammonium stretch system of spinning.

**BENGAL:** 1. Raw silk from Bengal, India.

2. Also a silk and hair cloth, originally made in Bengal, for women's dresses.

3. Also a printed striped imitation muslin.

**BENGALINE:** Cross-rib material, with filling yarn coarser than warp. Made of silk, cotton, rayon and wool, or of silk and wool. Comes dyed. Used in dresses, coatings, ribbons. The cloth has compact texture.

Wears well, launders well if care is taken; good draping qualities. Pronounced filling cords add much to the cloth. Widths range from ribbon size to broad goods. Used much as mourning fabric.

**BENGAL STRIPES:** Named for the province in India, are distinctive stripe effects in which several colors are observed. Neckties, ribbons, dress goods and regimental stripes are examples of these multicolored stripe effects.

**BERBER:** Is a lightweight, satin-faced fabric, made of all silk or of cotton back and silk face; it came into prominence at the turn of the present century when the famous English general, Gordon of Khartoum, defeatèd the Berber tribes in his campaign in North Africa.

**BIAZ:** Is a linen or cotton fabric used as dress goods and is still a staple fabric in many areas. Cotton cloth of this name is finished to simulate more expensive linen fabrics.

**BI-COMPONENT FIBER:** A fiber which is composed of two generically similar but chemically or physically different polymers, physically joined in a single filament. See Third-Generation Fibers.

**BI-CONSTITUENT FIBER:** A filament composed of two generically different compounds physically joined together or dispersed one within the other. See Third-Generation Fibers.

**BILLIARD CLOTH:** The highest grade of material made from the best of stock—Saxony, Silesia or Australian merino wool. Two-up and one-down twill weave is used. Cloth must have body, substance, evenness, and smoothness. Set in the reed at 144 inches and is finished at about 72 inches. Dyed green and its use is obvious.

**BINCHE:** Bobbin lace resembling Valenciennes. Origin Binche, near Flanders.

**BINDER FABRIC:** Rugged, strong cotton webbing which comes in several widths and thicknesses. Used for trunk straps and industrial mechanisms.
Used for reversible toweling, has good absorptive properties, is durable and launders well. Loosely twisted filling aids properties of absorption. Material must be free from foreign matter.

**BIRD'S-EYE:** When this term is applied to worsted cloth it implies a clear-finish, staple worsted cloth, the face of which is marked by small indentations. These are produced by the weave which suggests the eye of a bird. Simulated in cotton and rayon, and sometimes known as diaper cloth.

**BIRDSEYE LINEN:** Made of novelty twill and small diamond weaves that resemble the eyes of birds. Cloth is also known as diaper material. Texture is about 66 x 46.

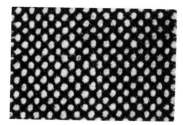
Bird's-eye worsted weave.

Bird's-eye cotton weave.

**BISSO LINEN:** Also known as altar cloth, the fabric is made of wiry yarns to give it a stiff, crisp feel. This fine, sheer linen is much used in cloth for altars.

**BLANKET:** This cloth is named in honor of the man who first used it as a covering for warmth and sleeping purposes, Thomas Blanket (Blanquette). He was a Flemish weaver who lived in Bristol, England, in the 14th Century. The cloth is made of wool, worsted, or cotton, or by combining these fibers in varying percentages in the construction. Material is heavily napped and fulled. Used for bed covering, robes, steamer rugs. An essential cloth to people in the Temperate Zone.

The word is also used in mill terminology to denote a sample warp, 6 to 20 yards in length, which shows a wide variety of colorings and crossings in one piece.

**BLEACHING:** Cloth as it comes from the loom, and as received from the weaving plant, contains motes, shives, slubs, specks and similar foreign matter, all of which would be detrimental to finished fabric since they would affect the even color of the dyes used. There are two types of general bleaching followed today:
1. CONTINUOUS PEROXIDE BLEACH. Generally believed to produce the best bleach with the minimum amount of fiber degradation. Approximately 85% of bleached cotton cloth is processed in continuous

peroxide bleaching systems.

2. KIER BLEACH. Formerly used for most cotton cloth. Has been superseded by peroxide bleach. Kier bleach process consists of a long alkaline boil-off in the kier, followed by washing, hypochlorite bleach, sour, neutralizing, and rinse.

**BLEACHING-IN-CLEAR:** An operation, usually the first rinse in a washing formula, where bleach is applied. Some plants prefer to bleach in an operation that contains little or no soap. It is felt that the bleach attacks the insoluble stains more directly if less soap is present.

**BLEEDING:** Term used to describe loss of color when wet due to improper dyeing or from the use of poor dyestuffs. Fabrics that bleed cause staining of white or other light fabrics in contact with them while wet.

**BLEND:** Two or more entirely different but compatible fibers in the same cloth, each used to lend certain characteristics. One example is the blend of 65% Dacron-35% cotton; the former contributes quick drying, the latter adds the feel and appearance of all-cotton.

**BLENDED FABRICS:** Fabrics composed of yarns made from a blend of two or more different fibers.

**BLENDED FILAMENT YARN:** A yarn made by intimate blending, i.e., twisting, interlacing or otherwise making a coherent bundle of dissimilar filaments. See Third-Generation Fibers.

**BLOCK PRINTING:** The printing of fabrics by hand, using carved wooden blocks. Distinguished from printing by screens or rollers.

**BLONDE:** Unbleached silk lace made with varying sizes of yarns. Floral designs are used in this lustrous article which appears in colors, black, and white. The original name for blonde was Nanking, the city in China where the natural, unbleached silk was raised.

**BLONDE LACE:** Bobbin lace originally cream or white silk. Later applied to silk type even when black.

**BLOOD:** A term used in connection with various fractions (½-blood, ¾-blood) to denote the percentage of merino blood in a certain sheep. In common practice today the term denotes any

wool that is of the same fineness as the wool grown on such a sheep. Full-blood merino implies that the wool comes from the offspring of a merino ram and ewe.

**BLOTCH PRINTING:** Refers to printing cloth by the direct method. This includes printing of the ground as well as the design color.

**BLUE "C":** Polyester staple made by Monsanto.

**BLUTEAU:** A silk fabric with a very fine weave, used for sifting flour.

**BOARDY:** A term used to describe the hand of fabrics when they feel stiff and hard.

**BOBBIN:** The device upon which the filling yarn is wound. It sets around the spindle shank of the bobbin, and is then set into place in the shuttle. The latter passes through the shed of the loom in order to place the loose filling pick between the raised and the lowered warp ends. A full bobbin has yarn wound on it in a snug manner, so that the filling will come off the nose of the bobbin in an easy, uniform manner.

**BOBBINET:** A net fabric in any of the basic yarns.

**BOBBIN LACE:** Originally made on a cushion by means of bobbins, the design laid out by means of pins around which the thread was interlaced.

**BOBBIN SPINNING, FILAMENT:** Filaments emerging from a bath are wound without twist onto bobbins with revolving perforated barrels. The bobbins are then placed in a pressure-type machine where purification and bleaching take place. The yarn is then dried, oiled, and twisted to a standard take-up package prior to skeining or coning. Rayon and nylon can be spun by this method. See POT SPINNING.

**BODKIN:** See BALDACHIN.

**BODY:** The compact, solid, or firm feel of a fabric.

**BOHEMIAN LACE:** Term applied to bobbin lace made in Bohemia with tape-like character.

**BOHEMIAN TICKING:** A tightly woven ticking, usually in narrow stripes on white ground. Also comes in chambray effects.

**BOLIVIA:** Cloth is usually a cut pile, with lines or ribs cut in the warp or in the diagonal direction. The height of the pile varies much. Bolivia is used for cloakings, coatings, and has appeared in suiting cloth.

**BOLL WEEVIL:** A parasite which attacks cotton wherever it is grown.

**BOLT, CUT, LENGTH OF CLOTH:** These terms are used to designate the length of the woven cloth as it comes from the loom in the grey goods state or in the finished length in the trade. Men's wear and women's wear cloth in the woolen and worsted trade will range anywhere from a 50-yard piece to a 100-yard length. The most popular cut lengths seem to be 55, 60, 72, 75, 80, 90, and 100 yards. These lengths are the most desirable for the cut-fit-and-trim trade. Cotton lengths usually run from 40 to 50 yards. Rayon and silk cloths usually range from 38 to 40 yards; however, lengths other than these are used when warranted.

**BOLTING CLOTH:** A plain woven sheer silk or nylon fabric used in flour mills for sifting flour. Now widely used by screen printers. Sign painters use it woven in a heavier texture.

**BOMBAZINE:** Name comes from the Latin *bombycinum*. It means cloth made of silken texture. One of the oldest textile materials known. Bombazine has gone through many changes through the ages. Originally it was an all-silk fabric. From time to time other fibers have been used in making the cloth. Today this cloth is made of silk warp and worsted filling. Imitations in cotton are seen on the market. When dyed black it is used in the mourning cloth trade. Can be made with rayon yarn.

**BONDING:** Generally refers to fabric-to-fabric bonding, as distinct from fabric-to-foam bonding. (See "Lamination.") There are two basic types of fabric-to-fabric bonding: (1) "Wet Adhesive" and (2) "Foam Flame." These are named for the two types of adhesive used in the processes.

**BOOKBINDER'S CLOTH:** Cloth made from several of the staple cotton cloths that is given a starching, glazing, and calendering. Used in binding books of the cheaper quality. Much filler material is used to cover up the spaces between the warp and filling in this low-textured cloth which is dyed any color. Cotton or linen fabric thus treated is also used for belts, collar stiffening, and hat crowns.

**BOOK CLOTH:** A coarse, plain-woven print cloth or sheeting. Dyed, heavily sized, often pyroxylin coated or embossed. From two to six treatments are given the material to ensure proper sizing and coating. Care has to be exercised in making the color of the filling substances match the piece-dyed goods.

**BOOK LINEN:** See LINEN.

**BOTANY YARNS:** Fine wool, rated at 60s or better in classification, is used in these high-quality worsted yarns.

**BOUCHE:** A plain weave, fine French woolen fabric left in the undyed state. Used as a shirting material, this cloth is much used by the clergy of southern France. Sometimes called Bluché.

**BOUCLÉ:** From the French and means buckle, or ringlet. Staple suiting fabric on the order of a worsted cheviot with drawn-out, looped-yarn construction. These yarns give a "ring appearance" to the face of the cloth. Also made in cottons. Bouclé yarn is very popular in the knitting trade. There are many types of this yarn to be found in this end of the textile business.

**BOURETTE:** Derives its name from the French bourré, which means hairy in appearance. The material has a hairy effect on the surface, since the yarn is interspersed with nubs.

**BOX CLOTH:** Really a coarse melton used for the overcoating trade. Cloth is very heavy. Made into the formal type of garment. Repels water.

**BOX-DYED:** Used for woven or knit fabrics which are piece-dyed in loose rope form by successive immersions in the dyebath.

**BOX LOOM:** Loom using two or more shuttles for weaving fabrics containing yarns different as to size, twist, or color. Typical fabrics made on box loom are plaids, checks, crepes, and ginghams.

**BRADFORD SPINNING:** English method of spinning wool into worsted yarn. The wool is thoroughly oiled before it is combed, which produces a smooth lustrous yarn used for worsted suitings. This is distinct from the French system, which is dry spun.

**BRAID:** A narrow textile band or tape formed by plaiting together or crossing diagonally and lengthwise several threads of any of the major textile fibers to obtain a certain width, effect, pattern, or style. Used for binding coat edges and for decoration in military uniforms.

**BRAID WOOL:** Wool grading term more or less synonymous with luster wool. Compared with merino stock, it is low in quality and is used in medium and low-quality clothing, carpets, robes, blankets, and low-priced uniform fabric.

**BREAKING LOAD:** In the test for tensile strength, it is the maximum load required to cause rupture of the fabric. The figures are read directly from the testing instrument.

**BREECHES:** Comes from the word briges, a loose, trouser-like garment worn by the peasant folk of Ireland, which was a forerunner of the knickers of a later age.

**BREECH WOOL:** See BRITCH WOOL.

**BRETON LACE:** See LACE.

**BRIGHTON WEAVE:** Achieves the effect of the honeycomb or waffle weave. Used in summer cotton dress fabrics.

**BRIGHT WOOL:** A common term applied to wool raised east of the Mississippi River, where the farm system of sheep raising is popular. Contrasted with semi-bright and Territory Wools, bright wool is light in cast, contains less dirt and other foreign matter, and is a clean type of fiber.

**BRILLIANTINE:** Smooth, fine, wiry fabric in plain or twill weave. Cotton warp, worsted, or mohair filling. Used for linings, suits.

**BRITCH WOOL, BREECH WOOL:** Wool from the lower thighs or hindquarters of the sheep, usually the coarsest type found in the fleece. It has considerable length but is very irregular and of little value. This wool is used in cheap suitings and coatings, windbreakers, ski cloth, mackinac and carpets.

**BROADCLOTH:** Originally the opposite of so-called narrow cloth and considered an inferior material. Modern broadcloth is a term used today with no particular significance and covers a host of materials. Unless made of silk, rayon, or cotton, the cloth in the woolen and worsted trade is a splendid fabric made in staple colors, has a compact weave, and receives a high, lustrous, appealing finish.

In the same group of face-finished fabrics as beaver, kersey, and melton, popular broadcloth runs from 10 to 16 ounces per yard. An ideal weave to use is a 2-up and 1-down twill, with the goods woven face down. Some of the material may be made with a plain weave. The material is set very wide in the reed of the loom to allow for great shrinkage in order to obtain the proper width. Higher qualities of the goods are form-fitting and ideal for women's wear tailored suitings, where drapiness and clinginess are essential.

**BROADLOOM:** Refers to carpets woven in widths from 54″ to 18 feet. Narrow widths are 27 inches or 36 inches.

**BROCADE:** Jacquard construction is used to give the embossed or raised effect. Face easily distinguished from back. There is a wide range in quality and price. Made from any of the major textile fibers, the material gives good service for decorative purposes or in furniture covering.

**BROCATELLE:** A fabric similar to brocade but having designs in high relief. Weave is usually a filling satin or a twill figure on plain or satin ground. Made in silk, rayon, and union fabric constructions. Used for draperies, upholstery.

**BROCHE:** A pin-stripe cloth.

**BRUSHED WOOL:** Knit or woven fabric which has been brushed, napped, or teaseled. Used in some garments, scarves, sweaters, trimmings.

**BRUSHING:** A finishing process in which circular brushes raise a nap on knitted or woven fabrics. Used on sweaters, scarves, underwear, wool broadcloth.

**BRUSSELS CARPET:** Named after this important city in Belgium, the carpet was developed after 1700, when Belgium became the rival of England in making carpets. Brussels is a staple which is made in body, border and stair carpet sizes. There are 6 to 10 piles to the inch in texture. Tapestry and Body Brussels are in this group of fabrics.

Within recent years carpeting called Brussels, made with a cut-pile structure, has found favor here. There is a wide range of carpeting under the name and the variety and color patterns vary considerably.

**BRUSSELS LACE:** A net lace with cordonnet edging the pattern in needle-point; designs made separately and appliquéd on the net. The ground is worked around the motif in very elaborate brides and toile.

**BUCKRAM:** Cheap, low-textured, cotton cloth, heavily sized. Used for linings in skirtings, in the millinery and suiting trades, and in bookbinding. Sturdy in feel, stiff and boardy.

**BUCKSKIN:** 1. A cotton cloth with a clear surface and napped back. Better grades are made with an 8-end, filling-effect satin weave, a base of three or five being used. An extra raiser is added at the top or at the right of the basic raisers in the repeat; this affords a tighter interlacing of the warp and the filling when compared with the ordinary 8-shaft satin construction. Cheaper grades of buckskin are usually made with a 5-shaft satin weave.

2. A rugged, durable, woolen fabric made on an 8-shaft, warp-effect satin weave. The cloth is heavily fulled and napped, and is then cropped so that a smooth finish results. It is used for over-coating and riding breeches.

**BUFFALO CLOTH:** Mackinac cloth has replaced this once-popular material. This cloth was heavy in weight, made from twill weave; the finished cloth had considerable nap. Found usage in the cold sections in winter.

**BULKY YARNS:** Filament yarns which have been modified in spinning to give more bulk. See TEXTURED YARN.

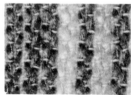

Cloth with bulky yarns

**BUNTING:** Plain-weave, loosely constructed cloth made of wool yarn. Finds use in flags and bunting. Its open texture is suggested because of the fact that the material was originally used for meal sifting or bolting. The term is a corruption of this cloth, bolting. Not used in apparel. Piece-dyed. When made of cotton, cloth is boardy in feel since a low or medium thread count prevails and the cloth may resemble cheesecloth or scrim. May be dyed or printed.

**BURL:** Remove loose threads. Hand inspectors clip and pick out knots, burrs, and surplus hanging threads from the surface of the cloth.

**BURLAP:** A coarse fabric of plain weave, usually made of jute or allied yarns. Much of the material is woven 40 inches wide and is from 6 to 14 ounces in weight per yard. Comes natural or may be dyed; when printed, finds use in curtains and hangings.

**BURNT-OUT, ETCHED-OUT FABRIC:** A material which contains two different yarns whereby the pattern effects have been produced by acid. The acid is used to treat one of the yarns in order to remove certain portions of it to create a patterned effect or motif. Basic weaves are used in the construction. Used for dress fabric and curtains.

**BURNT-OUT LACE:** Applies to lace made by Schiffli and other embroidery methods, the embroidery being of one material, the background of another.

**BURNT-OUT PRINT:** See PRINT.

**BURSTING STRENGTH:** In the ordinary sense, it is the ability of a material to resist rupture by pressure. In the specific meaning, it is the force needed to rupture a fabric by distending it with a force applied at right angles to the plane of the cloth, under specific conditions.

**BUTCHER RAYON:** A coarse rayon fabric of spun yarns made to resemble the original butcher linen used for aprons. Not permissible to call this fabric "Butcher Linen," according to F.T.C. ruling, because there is no linen content.

**BUTCHER'S LINEN:** Plain-weave, strong, stiff, heavy cotton cloth. Used for aprons and coats. Bleached to the white, calendered, and laundered. Cloth is converted from coarse sheeting material. Launders well, sheds the dirt, is durable, and gives good wear. There is no linen in this cloth. Also used to describe linen-textured rayon fabrics. See LINEN.

**CABLE YARN:** Name given to yarn of two or more ply that has been twisted together. More than two yarns are often plied together to increase the diameter of the cable effect. Cables have good twist and high tensile strength and are used for fancy yarns in suitings, coatings, and women's dress goods of novelty or fancy design. High-twisted and specially treated yarn is used for sewing thread.

**CADET CLOTH:** The standard blue, grey, or indigo and white mixture, made of woolen yarn, as decreed by the United States Military Academy at West Point, N.Y. Other public and private institutions use this or similar cloth. Heavy in weight, durable, rather boardy in feel. Is an excellent outdoor cloth. The material is a double cloth construction. The texture is very compact and fabric is heavily fulled and carefully finished.

**CAEN:** A type of wool serge in France.

**CALENDERING:** A mechanical method done by rollers to provide glaze, glossiness, hardness, luster, sheen, and even embossed designs to textile materials. Calendering is usually done to afford a special finish to fabrics; usually not permanent to washing.

**CALICO:** Cheap cotton print, of plain weave, low in texture, coarse, made of carded yarns. Small design effects when printed. Service will depend on the quality, which is determined by the texture in warp ends and filling picks.

**CAMBRIC:** Plain-woven linen or cotton cloth which is bleached or dyed in the piece. The cheaper grades have a smooth, bright finish. Used for handkerchief linen, children's dresses, slips, underwear, and nightgowns. Light in weight, well adapted for sewing work; has good body; is well sized and has a neat finish; launders well.

**CAMEL:** There are two types of camel: the Dromedary or one-hump type, and the Bactrian or two-humped type. Dromedaries, whose fibers are never used in fine fabrics, are found in Arabia, Egypt, Iran, Senegal, and Syria. Bactrians are native to all parts of Asia from the Arabian Sea to Siberia, and from Turkestan to the Steppes of Tartary, Tibet, Mongolia, and Manchuria to all parts of China. The finest fiber comes from Mongolia.

**CAMEL HAIR:** Hair obtained from camels. Wool-like in texture, its natural color varies from light tan to brownish black. This underhair of the camel is lustrous and extremely soft, and used, either by itself or combined with wool, for coats, suits, sweaters, some blankets and oriental rugs.

**CAMEL SUEDE:** A cotton cloth which resembles camel hair fabric; the cotton content in the fabric must be stipulated in accordance with ruling of the Federal Trade Commission.

**CANALE:** See CANNELE.

**CANDLEWICK:** A soft woolen dress material made in imitation of the candlewick bedspread, with tufted patterns similarly applied.

**CANDLEWICK SPREAD:** It is made of muslin sheeting with machine tufted motifs of soft, rather coarse cotton yarn called candlewicking. The yarn comes in white and all colors. Distinguished by its individually spaced tufts and dots which, taken collectively, form the designs or motifs. This is the point of demarcation from the chenille type spread recognized by its closely-spaced tufts which form continuous lines.

**CANELE:** See CANNELE.

**CANELLEE:** See CANNELE.

**CANICHE:** Cloth that has a curly face in imitation of the fur of the French poodle, *caniche.*

**CANNELE, CANALE, CANELLEE, CANELE:** When ribs are woven in the goods, the term signifies the cord effect in the warp direction, somewhat similar to the bedford cord weave. Filling effects can be made as well, and there have been instances where the term has been applied to these constructions.

Cannelé is made of silk yarn with two warps and one filling. One warp is single ply which gives body to the fabric; the other is a ply warp which makes the cord effects.

**CANTON CREPE:** Filling crepe with a pebbly surface, often made with six right-hand and then six left-hand threads in arrangement. 14/16 to 20/22 denier, if made in silk; also made with rayon. Durable, launders well, and is a sturdy silk material. Manipulated easily. White or piece-dyed.

**CANTON FLANNEL:** Cotton cloth made with a warp-faced twill with heavy, soft filling yarn and lighter warp than the filling. Has a long nap on one side only. Comes unbleached or bleached, dyed or printed. Used for men's work gloves, infants wear, linings.

**CANTON SILK:** Broad silk term for the raw silk from southern China. Despite its softness and good luster, the silk is difficult to throw because of its hairiness.

**CANVAS:** Also known as Numbered Duck, this plain-weave cloth is rugged and heavy. The ply yarns used give much strength and body to the fabric. From 2-ply to 14-ply yarns are used to make the goods. It is manufactured in the grey state or natural condition, but is also dyed olive drab or khaki for the armed services.

**CAPE WOOLS:** General name given to wool obtained in Natal, Orange River Colony, Transvaal, Rhodesia, and Cape Colony, the states which comprise the Union of South Africa. These high-quality fleeces are in great favor in this country because of their excellent working properties during manipulation; they are much sought for use in the heavier woolen materials.

**CAPROLACTAM:** See POLYMER.

**CAPROLAN:** Trade name for Allied Chemical Corporation's polycapramide nylon filament, staple fiber, and tow. This "deep-dye nylon" has excellent affinity for all classes of dyestuffs used on nylon, and is outstanding in affinity for the acid, direct, pre-metalized acid, chrome, and vat dyes.

Caracul (or Karakul) lamb.

**CARACUL:** A short, curly-haired fur distinguished by its flat, open wavy curl.

Chinese caracul is larger and lighter in weight than Russian caracul, which is naturally brown, black, and occasionally, white. Wearing qualities, good. Judged by luster of fur and pattern. Found in Russia and China. Worn for dress. Indian lamb, also in the caracul group, comes in white, black or grey—now being dyed in honey beige and brown.

**CARACUL CLOTH:** Heavy woolen fabric woven to resemble Persian lamb. Used for women's and children's coats, capes, muffs, etc. Named for the Persian lambs found in Russia.

**CARBONIZING:** Manufacturing process to free raw wool of burrs or vegetable matter. Done by using chemicals and heat. When wool is dry the carbonized matter "dusts off." A process also used on reused wool.

**CARDED YARN:** Not combed. All cotton yarns are carded, but some are given the additional process of combing. Carding machines straighten, clean, and untangle the fibers before they are spun into yarn.

**CARDIGAN:** 1. A form of the rib knitting stitch, modified for tucking on one or both sets of needles. For half cardigan, tuck on one set, for full cardigan, tuck on both sets of needles. Tucking thickens the fabric.

2. Also a sweater style usually referring to a 3-button coat sweater with either a V or a round neck. There are also cardigan jackets made of a woolen or worsted fabric.

**CARDING:** The process in yarn manufacture in which the fibers are brushed up, made more or less parallel, have considerable portions of foreign matter removed, and are put into a manageable form known as sliver. This approximates the size of a man's thumb in diameter.

Carding is done by means of rollers or flats that are clothed with fine, cylindrical, pressed-steel wire called card clothing. No fiber-twist is applied in carding operations.

**CARD WASTES, TYPES OF COTTON:**

1. CYLINDER STRIP WASTE: It is removed from the card cylinder by vacuum or roll stripping at the end of the stripping cycle. This strip is chiefly normal-length staple fiber which has become em-

bedded in the clean card clothing when the machine is started after stripping. The strip also includes short fibers and trash which accumulates during processing of the fibers.

2. DOFFER STRIP WASTE: It is obtained from the doffer roller at the end of the stripping cycle; comparable with cylinder strip stock. Cylinder and strip wastes are combined and sold as vacuum strips.

3. FLAT STRIP WASTE: Fibers and trash collected in the carding action between the cylinder and the card flats. Much usable fiber is contained in the waste which is considered to be the most valuable of all card wastes.

4. FLY WASTE: Composed of short fibers thrown out between the opening of lickerin and cylinder screens, it is light and cleaner than other card wastes. In practice, fly and motes are combined usually as one type of waste to facilitate cleaning beneath the card without attempting to separate them.

5. MOTE WASTE: This is the mass of heavier type waste found underneath the lickerin roller. Composed of leaf, lint, seed, fragments of seeds, and trash, it is removed by the opening and cleaning action of the lickerin and mote knives.

6. REWORKABLE WASTE: It comprises pieces of picker lap stock removed in starting a new lap and running out an old lap, short sliver lengths, and the soft roll of fibers formed by the doffer comb when it is started.

7. SCAVENGER OR CLEARER WASTE: This is collected by the revolving flannel-covered clearer roll at the small opening between the lickerin cover and the feed roll. It consists chiefly of rather short fibers that are carried around by the air set in motion by the lickerin roll.

8. SWEEPS WASTE: General term for all wastes collected and swept from the floor around the cards. It is composed chiefly of lint but may contain much foreign matter of vegetable and non-vegetable nature.

Reworkable and sweeps wastes is a problem of mill management wherein proper training for picker tenders and card tenders will pay off. The other six types of waste are controlled chiefly by me-chanical changes and in modifications of the card.

**CARISEL:** Coarse, plain-woven cotton or jute cloth used as foundation fabric in making carpets. Textures are low, and the cloth comes in many widths.

**CARMELITE CLOTH:** Named in honor of the Carmelite Order of the Roman Catholic Church. Plain-weave, low-texture, woolen cloth that is given considerable fulling. Somewhat resembles woolen bunting. This cloth is also used as garb.

**CARPET:** A floor covering woven from a variety of fibers, including wool, mohair, cotton, rayon, nylon, Acrilan, Verel, grass, straw, jute, fiber, and mixtures. Sold by the yard. Types of carpets include Axminster, chenille, tapestry, velvet, Wilton and rag. See BROADLOOM and RUG.

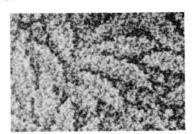
Carpeting weave.

Smooth-pile carpeting weave.

High- and low-pile carpeting weave.

**CARPET LOOM:** Machine, threaded with carpet yarns, on which carpet is woven, much as clothing fabrics are woven.

**CARRICKMACROSS:** Irish lace, either applique or guipure. The appliqué is worked upon net; the guipure is an embroidery made with fine lawn in which the design is traced around the outlines, and the centers cut away and filled with open stitches.

**CARTRIDGE CLOTH:** Made originally from silk cloth to hold powder charges for big guns; silk noil is ideal for cartridge cloth, since it burns quickly and completely.

**CARTWRIGHT, EDMUND:** In 1789, he applied power of the Watts and Bolton steam engine to the machines of Arkwright. He invented the power loom and the combing-machine—two of the greatest contributions to the textile industry. Incidentally, he was a great friend of Robert Fulton and gave the latter many valuable ideas for his steamboat.

**CASEIN FIBER:** Synthetic protein fiber made from casein, which is precipitated from skim milk. Lanital was the first casein fiber to appear in the trade, an Italian product. When cut to staple length the fiber has many of the properties of wool. Fibers are made from a base of condensed milk, evaporated milk or skimmed milk.

**CASEMENT CLOTH:** A term used to cover many curtain materials. A variety of simple basic weaves are used to make the cloth which is now made in cotton, rayon, or silk. The cloth is often écru in color.

**CASHMERE:** 1. The finest cashmere goat is raised in Tibet, the Kashmir province in Northern India, Iran, Iraq, and Southwest China. Cashmere is more like wool than any other fiber. The hair is very cylindrical, soft, strong, and silken-like. True cashmere, which is brownish in color, ranges from $1\frac{1}{4}$ to $3\frac{1}{2}$ inches in length. The long coarse outer fibers are from $3\frac{1}{2}$ to $4\frac{1}{2}$ inches long. The fiber diameter is 1/1600 inches.
2. The cloth was first made from the downy hair of goats of the Vale of Cashmere. Indian commercial cashmere cloths are found in overcoatings, suitings, and vestings. Cloth is made of fine wool that may be mixed with hair fibers. Soft finish is noted in the fabric. In all-hair fiber cloth, the material is made into the famous, well-known, highly desirable Indian shawls.

**CASKET CLOTH:** Also known as undertaker's and coffin cloth. A thin, lustrous, cheaply made material of wool, wool wastes, wool and cotton, rayon and rayon acetate. Its use is implied by the term.

**CASSIMERE:** Suiting and trousering material of various compact weaves and color effects. Popular, staple cloth. Hard-twisted yarn is employed. Often made with worsted warp and woolen filling. Can be made with a cotton warp with worsted or woolen filling. Cassimere is rather lustrous, harsh in feel, and light or medium in weight. Shines with wear. May be classed as a serge with a pattern.

**CATIONIC DYES:** Cationic dyes are another form of the basic dyes. The name "basic" derives from the fact that these are dyes with an organic base which is soluble in a simple acid. They were the first synthetic dyestuffs to be made out of coal tar derivatives. They were originally used, without a mordant or binding agent, to color wool, silk, linen and the bast fibers. With a tannic acid mordant they were also used for cotton and rayon. They produce brilliant colors.

**CAUSTIC SODA (NaOH):** Sodium hydroxide, a strong alkali. It is very useful in cotton finishing because cotton fiber does not dissolve in it (as wool does). It is used as an assistant in scouring, dyeing, and other finishing operations, especially for mercerizing.

Cavalry twill weave.

**CAVALRY TWILL:** A strong, rugged cloth made with a pronounced raised cord on a 63-degree twill weave. Woolen or worsted yarn is used. The weaves used for cavalry twill and elastique are the same and there is no set weave for either fabric. The weave may vary according to the size of the yarn used and the fabric weight per yard. Cavalry twill is the original name; elastique is a United States government term, used very likely because of the different texture of the alternating picks which give the fabric more elasticity and properties and characteristics resembling knitted fabric. Cavalry twill has the coarser rib effect when compared with elastique, which has a smoother effect and feel. The cloth is now made in spun rayon. Used for riding habits, ski wear, sportswear, uniform fabric.

**CELANESE:** The registered trademark of Celanese Corporation of America, used to designate its textile and other products. Certain characteristics set Celanese fabrics apart from others. Some of these features include retention of body in damp climates, easy application of dyestuffs, drapability, dimensional stability, and ease in care.

**CELAPERM:** A color-pigmented acetate yarn with sealed-in color. Fabrics colored with Celaperm come in a wide range of colors and are claimed to be lightfast, washable, dry cleanable, and able to withstand perspiration, gas fading, crocking, and sea water. The term is a registered trademark of Celanese Corporation.

**CELLOPHANE:** The viscose method produces the thin, smooth, transparent, and lustrous sheets of cellulose that are known as cellophane. This by-product has much commercial value because of its many unique properties. It is flexible, insulative, odorproof, greaseproof, and moistureproof. Cellophane may be made in many colors.

**CELLULOSE:** A white, shapeless or amorphous substance which forms the cell walls of plant life. It is made up of woody, fatty, or gummy substance and amounts to about 96% content of the cotton fiber whose chemical formula is $C_6H_{10}O_5$ taken "x" or "n" times. Cotton minus its water content gives cellulose, which finds use in making nitro-cellulose from which gun cotton is made, pyroxylin, Cellophane, collodion, and other commercial products. One of the greatest products made from cellulose base is the man-made fiber group of textile yarns—viscose, cuprammonium, nitro-cellulose, and acetate rayon. Cotton linters or hemlock, pine or spruce chips, all vegetable matter, are used as the base for these yarns. See POLYMER.

**CELLULOSE ACETATE:** There are three forms of acetate . . . mono-acetate, di-acetate, and tri-acetate. The recognition of this acetic acid ester of cellulose depends on the number of hydroxyl groups of cellulose replaced by the acetyl group. See ACETATE.

**CEVENNES:** The best grade of French raw silk. This white silk is used in the manufacture of silk lace made in Bayeux, Caen, and Chantilly. It was first made, however, in Cevennes.

**CHAFE MARKS:** A defect caused by abrasion during manufacture of the fabric or finishing operations. May be identified by fuzzy appearance.

**CHAIN CLOTH:** Used for filter fabric, this compact, heavyweight cotton is made with two-ply yarn in both directions. Identified by the weave used— 2-up and 2-down broken twill, 2 ends of right hand and 2 of left hand; repeats on four threads each way.

**CHAIN DYEING:** See DYEING METHODS.

**CHAIN WEAVE:** Effect noted on clear finish worsteds of staple variety. Chain breaks in cloth are purposely made in the construction of the cloth. Johann Erckens Sohns, textile manufacturer of Burtscheld, Prussia, is given credit for revealing this novelty type of design.

**CHALK STRIPE:** Popular suiting cloth for men's trade especially. Usually of light or white color, resembling a chalk line.

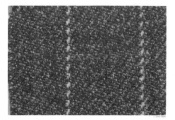

Chalk stripe weave.

**CHALLIS:** Soft, lightweight worsted cloth made of plain weave. Is of medium construction. May be dyed or printed. Used for women's and children's dress-goods, comforters, counterpanes, kimono cloth, robes, and spreads. The cloth is inexpensive. Originated in England about 1830. The cloth is made in cottons and from hair-fiber yarn. One of the most popular types of this material is made from silk warp and worsted filling.

Challis is also a spun-rayon fabric made with plain weave. Printed to simulate woolen or worsted challis. Durable, launders well, and drapes in satisfactory manner.

**CHAMBORD:** Woolen mourning cloth that may contain cotton, rayon, or silk fibers. The cloth has a ribbed appearance and the size of the ribs vary in diameter.

**CHAMBRAY:** Plain-weave, smooth, lustrous fabric made of dyed warp and white filling. Carded or combed yarns used; sometimes made with rayon. Sturdy, wears well; attractive and launders quite well, has good working properties for manipulation.

Chambray weave.

**CHAMOIS FABRIC:** Cotton cloth that has been napped, sheared, and dyed to simulate chamois leather. The material must be designated as "cotton chamois color cloth."

**CHANTILLY LACE:** Made originally in Chantilly, France, this lace is characterized by fine ground and elegant floral patterns.

**CHARDONNET, COUNT HILAIRE DE:** The Frenchman who was responsible for the development of rayon, first known as artificial silk. His first experimental fabrics of rayon fibers were displayed at the Paris Exposition of 1889.

**CHARMEUSE:** 1. Silk, cotton or rayon dress fabric with a satin weave that has a dull back and semi-lustrous surface. Used for pajamas, dresses, especially draped gowns. If not of all silk, fiber content must be declared.

2. A term used to denote a soft silk-like luster formerly widely used on fine cotton-warp sateens produced by mercerizing and schreinering.

**CHARVET SILK:** Made from a diagonal rib weave, this soft, dull tie-silk made in stripe effects drapes very well.

**CHECK:** A small pattern usually white combined with colors woven in or

Check weave.

printed on a fabric. Hound's Tooth, Shepherd, Gun Club, Gingham and Glen are all examples of checks.

**CHEESECLOTH:** A soft, plain-woven cotton of low-thread count or texture. Similar to tobacco cloth and sometimes called gauze. The coarser grades are used for dust cloths, wrapping cheese. Better quality is used for drapings, flag bunting, fancy dress costumes, innerlining. Comes white or colored.

**CHEMICAL BLEND:** A chemical blend of man-made fibers is achieved at the fiber-producing level. Known as bicomponent spinning, it was developed to create a textured filament yarn, in which two chemical polymers with different ratios of shrinkage were extruded through the spinneret to form a single filament. As one shrinks more than the other, the whole yarn is pulled into a crimped formation. See Third-Generation Fibers.

**CHEMICAL FINISHING:** Imparting special characteristics to materials by chemically modifying the material. Examples: water-repellency, glaze, crease resistance, mercerizing.

**CHENILLE:** A cotton, wool, silk, or rayon yarn which has a pile protruding all around at right angles; simulates a caterpillar. Chenille is the French word for caterpillar. The yarn is used as filling for fancies, curtains and carpets, embroidery and fringes. It is woven in gauze weave with cotton or linen warp and silk, wool, rayon, or cotton filling. The warp threads are taped in groups and the filling is beaten in very compactly. After weaving the fabric is then cut between the bunches of warps, and the latter twisted, thereby forming the chenille effect.

**CHEVIOT:** Rough woolen suiting and overcoating cloth. Similar to tweed in construction. Name is derived from the fact that hardy wool from the Cheviot Hills of Scotland is used in making the cloth.

Today the cloth is made from a plain or twill weave. Many other cloths use cheviot wool but are not classed as cheviot cloth. True cheviot is very rugged, harsh, uneven in yarn, does not hold the crease and sags with wear. It is a good "knock-about" cloth and ideal for sports wear. May be piece- or stock-dyed and has the tendency to shine with wear. In quality, material ranges from low to high, and it is made on hand or power looms. A genuine British fabric.

**CHEVIOT, TWEED AND HOMESPUN CLOTHS:** Strictly speaking, original tweed cloth showed warp and filling, stock-dyed and of the same color. There is a wide range of color used in all three cloths. While a homespun should be made with a plain weave and a cheviot with a twill weave, there is much confusion as to just what is a homespun and what is a tweed, in the trade today. Homespuns are sold for cheviots and vice versa. In the mill, however, a plain-weave cloth of the usual characteristics is called a homespun, and a twill-weave cloth would signify cheviot or tweed.

Homespun, as a tweed, is the heaviest tweed in weight per yard. It has the salient features noted in genuine tweed. In the trade today, the belief seems to be that homespun is very coarse, rather irregular and of low texture. The lighter cloths in this group are called tweeds.

The center of this cloth industry, in the olden days, was along the banks of the Tweed River which separates Scotland from England. Prior to the Industrial Revolution the material, from raw stock to finished cloth, was made in the home —shearing of the sheep, sorting, mixing, carding, spinning of yarn, dyeing, and weaving. From about 1750 the factory system began to replace the home system. The result was that most of the cloth was then made on power looms that were coming into use.

**CHEVRON:** Is made from broken twill and herringbone weaves to give a chevron effect such as seen on military uniforms. The patterns have waves of popularity in men's wear suitings and coatings.

**CHEVREUL, MICHELE-EUGENE:** A famous French color scientist (1786–1889) who was probably the first man to conduct a scientific investigation of color interaction related to textiles.

**CHIFFON:** Plain-weave, lightweight, sheer, transparent cotton, rayon, or silk fabric made with fine, highly twisted, strong yarn. Dyed or printed and often used as "drape over silk or rayon." The material is difficult to handle but drapes and wears well. This stately or conventional type of fabric is very durable despite its light weight; however, it is not for everyday wear. Must be laundered with care.

**CHIFFON VELVET:** Similar to woolen broadcloth but is lighter in weight, ranging from 7 to 10 ounces per yard. Broadcloth will run from 10 to 16 ounces or slightly more per yard. Chiffon velvet has a smooth feel, excellent finish, and is one of the better quality cloths in demand.

Another type of this fabric is made of silk or rayon in a clear-pile material which comes in many qualities. The better grades are quite expensive. Drapes well, is durable, dry cleans, and has tendency to crush. Used in evening wear and wraps. See VELVET.

**CHINA COTTON:** See COTTON.

**CHINA GRASS:** Fibers from the ramie plant used for weaving. See RAMIE.

**CHINA SILK:** A very soft, extremely lightweight silk made in a plain weave, used chiefly for linings. Irregularities of threads, are caused by the extreme lightness and softness of China silk.

**CHINCHILLA:** The name of a rodent whose fur is mixed with other textile fibers in making cloth of high quality. The cloth of today does not resemble the pelt of the animal. The knotted-face, modern overcoating takes its name from the town of Chinchilla, Spain. The present-day type of chinchilla cloth was first made here. The product is made into coatings, uniform cloth, and livery wear.

Chinchilla is made in double and triple construction. Cotton-warp yarn is used because of the property of twist that it has. This is essential because of the construction of the material. The cotton warp does not show on the face or back of the cloth, and adds to the wearing quality. The nubs found on the face of the material are made by the chinchilla machine. It attacks the face of the cloth, and causes the long floats used in the construction to be worked into nubs or minute balls. The length of the floats is usually five or seven. Chinchilla is a pile cloth and may be piece, stock, or

skein dyed. Weaves, other than the filling to be floated, are usually satins. They aid in bringing about the best possible appearance of the cloth. The fabric is one of the "cycle group" and comes into prominence about every seven or eleven years and for a year or so is a genuine leader in the trade.

**CHINO:** A cotton fabric with a plain or twill weave made popular as summer wear for the armed forces.

**CHINTZ:** Printed cloth made in bright and gay colors of flowers, birds, etc. Word means "varied." Usually of good quality and far better than cretonne. Closely woven texture, singed, sized, starched, glazed, and friction calendered. Used for dresses, curtains, boudoir chairs, hangings.

Not easily laundered, as starching or sizing is usually not permanent. Gives good wear; easy to cut and manipulate.

Chintz first became popular in the 18th Century as a wearing apparel fabric. It is shown here used in a dressing gown.

**CHLORINATED WOOL:** Chemically treated woolens whereby shrinkage is decreased and dyeing properties increased, especially in the case of fabrics that are to be printed.

**CHLORINE:** An elemental gas of the halogen family. It reacts with water to release oxygen; it plays an important part in bleaching operations.

**CHLORINE RETENTION:** The degree to which a fabric assimilates the chlorine used in washing, and does not permit it to rinse out completely. This is what causes yellowing, or a dirty grey cast.

**CHOPS, CHOP MARKS:** Used by the Chinese and Japanese when silk bales are shipped. Each reeler has his own chop mark or trade mark. By these it is possible to distinguish good silk and poor silk; most silk, however, runs fairly uniform. The neatly designed printed chops are found in all silk bales.

**CHROME DYES:** Dyestuffs which make use of chrome salts as a mordant for fixing the dye on the fiber.

**CHROMSPUN:** Trade name for Eastman's made-in-the-color acetate yarn and staple fiber. The coloring agents are introduced at the solution stage, before the fiber is actually formed.

**CHUDDAR:** Applies to billiard cloth and relates to the color, bright green. Chuddar is the name for bright green in Anglo-Hindu.

**CIRCULAR KNIT:** Fabrics or garments knitted in a circular form so that they are seamless. Later a garment may be shaped by skillful cutting. Simulated seams and fashion marks are often added. See KNITTING.

**CIRE:** Originally the term meant English shroud fabric which had been given a wax treatment. The finish is still the same as in the original and is much used on silks on which a smooth, lustrous effect and feel is desired. Used chiefly for evening wear.

**CISELE VELVET:** See VELVET.

**CLAN PLAID:** Any Scotch plaid in the true colors of some particular Scotch clan such as Cameron, Campbell, MacPhee, MacDonald, etc.

**CLAY WORSTED:** Class of staple worsted cloth, as to weave and construction, made famous by J. T. Clay of Rastrick, Yorkshire, England. The weave is a 3-up and 3-down right-hand twill. Texture is usually low. The cloth has been greatly imitated, until the term is common rather than distinctive. Imitation is the sincerest form of flattery; the imitations of the genuine cloth prove this to be true.

**CLEAN BASIS:** The price of scoured wool minus loss and charges incurred in the scouring operation.

**CLEAR FINISH:** Cloth in the woolen and worsted trade finished so that no nap or fuzz remains on the face of the goods. All protruding fibers have been removed because of the operations that the cloth is subjected to in finishing; the warp and filling are plainly seen. This finish is given to fabrics where the weave is an outstanding characteristic. Clear-finish fabrics have the tendency to shine with wear but hold the crease very well.

Examples are cassimere, charmeen, covert, diagonal worsted, gabardine, serge, poiret, tricotine, elastique, twill cloth, twillcord, whipcord.

**CLIP:** 1. Wool taken from sheep after one season's growth.

2. To cut with shears or scissors in order to separate material or to relieve tension.

**CLIP SPOTS:** See DOTTED SWISS.

**CLOKY:** Small irregularly raised figures formed in weaving, used in fancy piqués, etc. Americanized spelling of French word "cloqué," meaning blistered.

**CLOTH OF GOLD:** Cloth which through the ages has been referred to as having gold threads, strips of gold, or gold twisted with other textile fibers. Gold has been used in tapestries, brocades, brocatelles, and other silk fabrics, many of which now repose in museums.

**CLOTH, THE PARTS OF A PIECE OF:**

1. FIBER: The smallest unit in a woven, knitted, braided or felt material. Fibers are also used to make felt material.
2. FILAMENT: A long fiber that may be indefinite in length.
3. YARN: This is made up of twisted fibers or filaments and can have considerable strength and length.
4. PLY YARN: Two or more yarns that are twisted or plied together.
5. CLOTH: This is made from yarn in three ways:
   A. Woven cloth is made from two systems of yarn or thread which interlace at right angles to each other;

serge, homespun, damask.
   B. Knitted cloth is made from one system of thread or yarn which interloops, a loop within a loop; hosiery, jersey, sweater fabric.
   C. Braided or plaited material is made from an interlacing of one yarn only. The yarn may be made to interlace at any angle; lace, veiling, shoe lace.

   Felt is not made from yarn; it is made from a mass of fibers that are interlocked and made into a material by means of heat, pressure, moisture, pounding and rolling, hot water, etc.

6. THREAD: It is used in sewing materials and is a ply yarn of some special nature. This ply thread is given a high number of turns of twist per inch. It is often waxed, coated or treated in some way for a particular use in order to work smoothly and well. Ply yarn, such as automobile tire fabric, may have a ply of 9, 10 or 11.

**CLUNY:** A coarse, open, white bobbin lace. The name is derived from the Cluny Museum.

**COAL TAR:** A chemical used in making dyes. Derived from coal, it is very important to the dyestuffs industry.

**COATED FABRIC:** Any fabric which is coated, filled, impregnated, or laminated with a continuous-film-forming polymeric composition in such a manner that the weight added to the base fabric is at least 35% of the weight of the fabric before coating, filling, impregnation, or lamination. The term is often applied to fabrics not coated but rather impregnated with various chemicals and synthetic resins. See IMPREGNATED FABRIC, WATER REPELLENT, OILCLOTH.

**COBURG OR COBOURG:** A lining and dressgoods material made from a 2-up and 1-down right-hand twill. Warp is cotton, filling is worsted. May be piece-dyed or printed.

**COCHINEAL:** A brilliant red dye made from the insect *Coccus cacti*.

**COCKLE, COCKEL:** From French *coquille*, meaning cockle shell. Name is given to a distorted or shriveled effect on fancy cloths. This is result of uneven scouring and fulling in finishing. Cockling may also be caused by improper tension on yarn in weaving, or lack of uniform quality in the raw ma-

terial used. Several novel ideas have been advanced for the correction of this detriment to cloth.

**COFFIN CLOTH:** Black-dyed material made of cotton warp and wool filling for coffin interiors.

**COIR:** A fiber taken from the coconut husk. Used for both rope and fabrics.

**COLORAY:** Trade name for Courtaulds' viscose rayon staple. The color is added while the viscose is still in solution form, making for uniform color.

**COLOR FASTNESS:** The determination as to whether a color is fast in a number of standard tests used for the purpose. Yarn or fabric may be tested for fastness to color fading, spotting, or staining. Some of the tests employed include fastness to crocking, color bleeding, dry cleaning, laundering, sunlight, perspiration, ironing.

**COLOR LAKE:** The insoluble combination of a mordant and a dyestuff that has been fixed on the fiber, such as tannin with basic dyes on cotton, or chrome dyes with a mordant on wool.

**COMBED YARN:** Extra smooth, fine, and strong, due to combing machine which removes short fibers after carding.

**COMBING:** An advanced form of carding. Combing separates the long, choice, desirable fibers of the same length from the short, immature, undesirable stock that is called noil. Combing practically removes all remaining foreign matter from the fiber stock. Only the best grades of cotton, wool, and other major fibers may be combed. Combed yarns are always superior to carded yarns.

**COMMERCIAL DYE:** Applied to direct colors which, in most instances, are not fast to light and washing.

**COMMERCIAL STANDARDS:** The U. S. Bureau of Standards issues Commercial Standards which are *not* laws, but they are important as "recorded voluntary standards of the trade." These standards are usually referred to by number.

**COMPLEMENTARY COLORS:** Complementary colors are colors which serve to fill out or complete each other, mutually supplying each other's lack. Each primary color has a complementary color, which is a mixture of the other two primaries. The complementary color "completes" the primary color by supplying a lack of the two other primaries which the eye instinctively seeks to find, since light (which is color) is composed of all three primaries.

**CONDITIONING:** Process for determining the true weight of fiber by establishing the standard percentage of moisture. Also process for restoring to fibers moisture lost during manufacture.

**CONE:** 1. The bobbin upon which yarn is wound prior to weaving. 2. A package of yarn wound into a suitable or convenient shape. 3. A tapered cylinder of cardboard, metal or wood around which yarn is wound.

**CONSTRUCTION:** A fabric description. For instance, a 39 inch, 4.00 yard 80 x 80 print cloth is 39 inches wide, weighing 4 yards to the pound, with 80 warp threads to the inch and 80 widthwise filling threads per inch.

**CONTINUOUS FILAMENT:** Synthetic and regenerated fibers can be manufactured in a continuous filament, as distinguished from all natural fibers, except raw silk, which have a short staple or length.

**CONTINUOUS PEROXIDE BLEACH:** See BLEACHING.

**CONTINUOUS VAT DYEING:** See DYEING METHODS.

**CONTOUR SHEETS:** See FITTED SHEETS.

**CONVENT CLOTH:** Use is obvious. The cloth is made of crepe weave to give it a pebbled effect. Light in weight, it is made of wool warp and silk or rayon filling. A piece-dyed fabric.

**CONVERTED GOODS:** Converted or finished from grey goods ready for sale.

**CONVERTER:** The individual or concern that buys grey goods from the loom, finishes them, and then sells his wares to the trade. The converter issues instructions for bleaching, mercerizing, dyeing, printing, type of finish to be applied, etc. He must be conversant with the current trends in the trade from all angles, know the wants of his customers and prospective customers and, very often, he has to create his own markets for outlet.

**CORDELLA:** A fine net lace with raised cord outline.

**CORDONNET:** The cord outline applied to a pattern.

**CORDURA:** A rayon-process yarn with great strength, used for tire cords. As the tire heats up and drives out moisture, Cordura becomes stronger. Product of DuPont.

**CORDUROY:** A cut-filling-pile fabric made of cotton which has hard-wearing qualities. When woven with a plainweave back the fabric is called a "tabby-back" corduroy; with a twill weave back it is known as a "Genoa-back" corduroy. Corduroy is woven in about the same way as velvet, except that the pile filling picks are bound by the warp yarns to form straight lines of floats thus producing the ribbed surface.

There are several types of this material —fine reed for pinwale fabric, eight-shaft corduroy, thickset, constitutions, cables, et al. The material is often waxed and singed to remove any long protruding fibers. Corduroy, it should be noted, is made with the filling forming the pile-effect after the cutting which is a separate process after the cut of cloth has been taken from the loom.

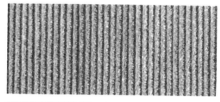

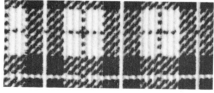

Corduroy weaves. (*Top*) Pinwale weave. (*Center*) Wideweave. (*Bottom*) Plaidprint on pinwale base.

This lengthwise wale or rib fabric has textures which range from 46 x 116 to 70 x 250.

Very strong and durable; launders well; heavy cloth; warm and rugged for outdoor wear, as in hunting cloth, aviation coats, slacks, knickers, windbreakers, sportswear.

**CORE YARN:** A yarn made by twisting fibers around a previously spun yarn, thus concealing the core. Used in blankets, socks, and to obtain novelty effects in dress fabrics.

**CORKSCREW:** Twill rib, worsted staple used in suitings, overcoatings and spat cloth. Construction is such that the warp threads appear only on face of cloth. Term is a misnomer and its derivations are doubtful. Corkscrew weaves are used to make the cloth.

**CORONIZED:** A trademark for the process of Owens-Corning Fiberglas Corp. for a heat-treating finish applied to Fiberglas cloths. It is a finish that permanently sets the weave of the fabric and releases strains in the glass yarns resulting in improved hand and drape.

**CORONATION CLOTH:** Originated in England and first seen at the coronation of King Edward VII. In wool and unfinished worsted suitings of solid-ground staple colors, it is a cloth upon which there are single-thread stripes or decorations that run lengthwise. The stripes are about one inch apart and a gold or tinsel yarn is used.

The "Queen's Mourning"—black cloth with a white hairline, was a contemporary cloth. A variation of coronation cloth was noted in this country some years ago. The fancy yarns were red, white and blue, and the fabric was known as "Inauguration Cloth."

**COTE DE CHEVAL:** This is a corded woolen or worsted cloth of France used for riding habit material and uniform cloth for officers. *Côte* means ribbed or lined, *cheval* means horse; hence, the name for the cloth. It has the grosgrain effect broken at intervals with a short stop to produce a striped appearance that is slightly rounded, which may be compared to the ribs seen on a horse.

**COTTON:** Soft fiber obtained from the seed pod of the cotton plant. Was first known in India about 3000 B.C., and was considered very rare and precious. Today it is one of America's greatest crops, and is spun into yarn and thread, woven and knitted into fabrics. Different types of cotton have different fiber lengths. Usually, the longer the fiber, the better the quality of cotton.

1. ABSORBENT—Cotton batting made highly absorbent by chemically removing the natural waxes. Used for medical purposes.

2. ACALA—Mexican variety introduced into U. S. Medium staple cotton grown in the southwestern states.

3. AMERICAN—Upland cotton grown in this country. It forms bulk of world's crop. Fiber runs from ¾" to ½".

4. AMERICAN PEELER COTTON—Longer staple (1¼") used for combed yarns and fabrics, i.e., lawns, dimities, broadcloths.

5. AMERICAN PIMA COTTON—A cross between Sea Island and Egyptian. Grown in Arizona. Brownish color. Fine strong cotton. (Averages 1⅜" to 1⅝".) Used for airplane, balloon cloths and for tire fabrics.

6. CHINA—Harsh, wiry, very short staple. Can be mixed with wool for blankets. Limited uses.

7. EGYPTIAN—Fine lustrous long-staple cotton. Several varieties—usually brown in color. (1-2/5" Average.) Used in U. S. for thread and fine fabrics.

8. INDIAN—Cotton grown in India, for many years the consistent second largest cotton producing country. The Indian cottons imported are generally of the harsh, short staple type (8/10" to 9/10") for such uses as blanket filling.

9. SEA ISLAND—Finest of all cotton. White, silky (1-3/5" Average staple), which is spun into yarns as fine as 300s for lace yarns. Originally grown on small islands off the coast of the Carolinas and in the southern lowlands along the coast.

10. S X P—Egyptian Sakellarides crossed with Pima. Lighter in color than Pima, with slightly shorter staple but greater strength. Grown largely in Arizona and New Mexico.

**COTTON, ACETYLATED (PA):** A treatment which uses acetic anhydride to improve the resistance of cotton to acids, heat and rot. Woven fabric of the product is used as covering for calender rollers, press rollers, etc.

**COTTONADE:** Generally three-har-

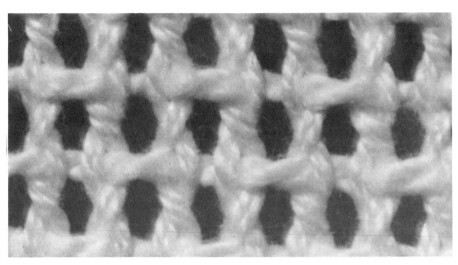

Enlarged photo of cotton leno construction.

ness, left-hand, warp-faced twill of coarse yarns. Comes mostly in dark stripes on a solid or medium-dark ground. Durable finish and used for suiting fabric in the South and in tropical climates; a very popular material.

**COTTON, AMINIZED (AM):** When cotton is treated with aminoethyl sulphuric acid greater dye receptivity and chemical reactivity become apparent. Fiber, yarn, or fabric becomes faster to light and laundering and reacts more readily with the various chemical treatments applied in processing.

**COTTON, BA:** A durable flame-resistant application to cotton in which a vinyl type monomer (bromo-alkyl allylphosphate) application is followed by heating the presence of a peroxide to cause polymerization.

**COTTON BACK SATEEN:** A cloth, made in silk or rayon mills, single in construction, and with good body. When made of a 5-shaft satin weave, it is called sateen; when made of 8-shaft satin, warp-effect, it is known as a Venetian. The fabric is finished in special widths that range from 26 to 58 inches; textures range from 64 to 190 by 48 to 72. The use of the fabric determines the texture of the goods. Cotton back is dyed in all colors.

Uses include blanket binding, comfortables, corset coverings, draperies, dressing gowns, bedspreads, brassieres, mattresses, pajamas, parasols, pillows, ribbons, shoe uppers, slips, suit linings, ticking, underwear, umbrella fabric.

**COTTON BROADCLOTH:** A fine, mercerized fabric in which the warp and filling are usually of the same size or count. Used in men's shirting, pajamas, sportswear, and for striped effects in women's dress goods. A genuine staple in the cotton trade, it comes in white, dyed or in printed effects.

The material is very strong, durable, launders well, takes the dye readily, and the mercerized, permanent finish is an outstanding feature. Textures are always high and compact.

**COTTON, CARBOXYMETHYL (CM):** Two distinct forms are taken on when cotton fiber, yarn, or fabric is carboxymethylatèd by treatment with monochloroacetic acid followed by treatment with strong sodium hydroxide. One reaction is that a modified fabric is produced which has a built-in, starched effect, increased water absorbability, and greater receptivity to crease-resistant treatments when compared with ordinary fabric.

The other result is obtained by treating with a higher concentration of monochloroacetic acid-sodium hydroxide which results in a retention of 80 to 100% of original strength, and which becomes soluble in ordinary tap water.

**COTTON CARD WASTES, TYPES OF:** See CARD WASTES, TYPES OF COTTON.

**COTTON COVERTS:** Made of single yarns mock twist (half white, half black or blue) to resemble wool covert. Used for pants, shirting, and work clothes.

**COTTON CREPES:** These include balanced, box, filling, warp, and matellasse types made into lightweight dressgoods with crinkled, crepe, granite, or pebble effect. Crepe yarn and crepe weave used. Comes in white or is printed or dyed. Wide range in price, quality, texture, and finish. These cloths are generally washable without the effect of crepiness being lost. Does not have to be ironed repeatedly.

**COTTON, CYANOETHYLATED (CN):** An acrylonitrile treatment developed and perfected in the Institute of Textile Technology, Charlottesville, Va. The product increases resistance of cotton to heat and rot, and improves receptivity of dyes to the fiber.

**COTTON, DECRYSTALLIZED:** Low crystallinity of cotton is brought about by treating it with anhydrous liquid ethylamine. The reduction in crystallinity is about thirty percent, and it improves fiber toughness, increased extensibility, higher absorbency, and higher dyeing capacity.

**COTTON FELT:** An undyed cotton cloth, heavily napped on both sides. Serves as silence and preserving cloths under table covers.

**COTTON FIBERS:** Raw cotton, as it is taken from the plants, is in fibers of various lengths. For marketing purposes these fibers are graded and classed (a) by staple length (b) by grade (c) by character. "Character" includes diameter, strength, body, maturity, smoothness, and uniformity of the fibers.

**COTTON FLANNEL, FLANNELETTE:** See FLANNEL, COTTON.

**COTTON GRADE:** Describes qualities of cotton other than staple length. Grade is composed of these factors: color, foreign matter, preparation.

**COTTON, LEAD CHROMATE TREATED:** Cotton tobacco shade cloth is treated with lead acetate and then with potassium or sodium bichromate from which a yellow chromate pigment is deposited onto the fabric. This action screens out the sun's rays and extends the life of the fabric to three times that of similar untreated cloth.

**COTTON LINTERS:** Short-fiber stock that is used to make absorbent cotton, guncotton, rayon, celluloid, and other products from cotton and its seed. Linters are not used to make cotton yarn. The fibers are obtained from secondtime ginning of the cotton. First-time ginning is done in the plantation areas at the community gins.

Linters come in a brown sheet form and cost only a few cents per pound. Their greatest use is in making acetate and rayon, for which they serve as the base. When treated with strong acids, linters form the basis for guncotton, which is used for explosives. The term should not be confused with lint.

**COTTON, PROPIOLACTONE (PL):** Dye receptivity on cotton comes as the result of treating it with propiolactone.

**COTTON SUITING:** Cotton fabric which has enough body to tailor well. Used for suits, slacks, and skirts.

**COTTON TAPESTRY:** See TAPESTRY.

**COTTON, TH PC:** A crease, flame and tor resistant applied to cottons in which a monomer of the condensation type is known as TH PC is used in conjunction with methylolmelamine.

**COTTON TWEED:** See TWEED, COTTON.

**COTTON VELVET:** See VELVET, COTTON.

**COTTON-WARP UNION:** Staple or fancy cloths made with cotton warp and animal fiber filling. "Cotton-warps" can stand more friction, chafing, and tension than animal fibers; hence, their use for some particular purpose. The use of cotton warps is an economic measure and some woolens and worsteds do not call for any yarn better.

**COTTON WASTE:** Lint and other yarn refuse which accumulate during the manufacturing process. The softer parts are used for padding and the harder, coarser pieces for paper manufacture. Waste from the carding machine is used by some mills. Varying percentages are mixed with regular cotton in making part-waste osnaburgs.

**COTTON YARN NUMBER:** Cotton yarn is measured in terms of length per unit of weight. No. 1 cotton has 840 yards per pound. No. 10 has 8,400 yards per pound. The count is inversely proportionate to the size of the yarn, therefore, No. 100 yarn is ten times finer than No. 10.

**COUNT OF CLOTH:** The number of ends and picks per inch in a woven fabric as counted by an individual. If a cloth is 64 x 60, it means that there are 64 ends and 60 picks per inch in the fabric. A cloth that has the same number of ends and picks per inch in woven goods is called a square cloth—64 x 64. Pick count is the term that is synonymous with texture and counts of cloth, in speaking of cloth construction.

**COUPURE:** French for "cut." The cloth is a cashmere, cut so that the lines cut through show the twill in the lengthwise direction of the cloth.

**COURSE:** The row of stitches across a knitted fabric. Corresponds to the filling in woven goods.

**COUTIL:** A brassiere or corset fabric that finds use in linings, bandings, and suitings in tropical climates; also much used in foundation garments. Coutil is high in texture, made from medium, highly-twisted cotton yarn on a threeharness herringbone or on a reversetwist twill construction. The cloth has a smooth finish. Designs in the fabric may vary to some degree.

Covert cloth weave.

**COVERT:** Twilled, lightweight overcoating cloth. Usually made of woolen or worsted yarn with two shades of color, say, a medium and a light brown. Cloth was first used as a hunting fabric and it is very durable. Name is derived from a similar term in connection with field sport. Covert is very rugged and stands the rigors of wearing very well. Highly desirable cloth and gives smart appearance to the wearer. The material is a staple stock-dyed fabric.

Covert is also made in cotton or rayon, spun rayon, wool, and spun acetate. The speckled effect is a characteristic of the goods. Used for coats, raincoats, riding habit cloth, sportswear, and suits.

**COVERTS, COTTON:** See COTTON COVERTS.

**CRABBING:** A wool finishing process to prevent creases or other forms of uneven shrinkage in later stages of finishing. The fabric is treated with boiling water to set or fix the yarns permanently.

**CRASH:** Term applied to fabrics having coarse uneven yarns and rough texture. Usually made in linen but also made in cotton, rayon, and wool. Plain or twill weave, or twill variations. Used for sportswear, men's, women's and children's summer suits and coats, draperies.

**CRASH TOWELING:** Usually a plain-woven fabric with a yarn-dyed striped edge, made of coarse, uneven yarns for added absorbency. Thread counts: 32 x 30 to 84 x 38. Made of linen or cotton.

**CRAVENETTE:** Registered trade name for the well-known rainproofing process for woolen and worsted fabrics and apparel. The name was coined by a Bradford, England, manufacturer named Wiley; for want of a better term he named the process for the street in which he lived—Craven Street, London.

**CREASE RESISTANCE:** The capacity of a fabric to resist wrinkles. Usually achieved by the application of synthetic resins, but man-made fibers like polyester are inherently resistant.

**CREEL:** Device used as a spool rack for winding warp. Also used to hold warp ends for a sectional beam.

**CREPE:** Lightweight fabric of silk, rayon, cotton, wool, synthetic or a combination of fibers. Characterized by a crinkling surface obtained either by use of 1. hard twist yarns, 2. chemical treatment, 3. weave, 4. embossing.

ALPACA CREPE: Soft, dull finished rayon or acetate, or silk made to resemble wool crepe.

BARK CREPE: Crepe finished with a rough texture surface that suggests the bark of a tree.

CANTON CREPE: Filling crepe with pebbly surface heavier than crepe de chine. It drapes beautifully and is widely used for dresses; originally was made of silk in Canton, China. Fiber content must be declared if not all silk.

CHARMEUSE CREPE: A rich filling, dull luster, piece-dyed silk that has glove-like smoothness. Grenadine silk is used for the warp while the filling is of crepe-twist yarn. Charmeuse clings and drapes very well. It may be dyed in all colors.

CREPE-BACK SATIN OR SATIN-BACK CREPE: Fabric that may be used on either satin or crepe side. Crepe back is obtained by alternating hard twisted yarns which give the fabric a dull finish. A silk or synthetic fabric or mixture.

CREPE DE CHINE: A very sheer silk crepe. There are two types: 1. A fabric of medium luster, woven from raw silk; the crepiness is obtained by degumming the fabric. 2. A more lustrous fabric made in Japan with a spun silk warp and a thrown silk filling. Both are used for lingerie, blouses and dresses.

CREPE GEORGETTE—A sheer, dull-textured fabric, with a crepy surface, obtained by alternating left- and right-handed yarns.

CREPE MAROCAIN—Heavier dress weight crepe similar to Canton crepe in texture.

CRINKLE CREPE (PLISSE)—Thin cotton fabric with puckered stripes or patterns or all-over blistery effect. Obtained by printing part of surface with resist and then passing fabric through caustic soda, causing untreated portion to shrink. Used for kimonos, nightgowns, lingerie, summer dresses.

FAILLE CREPE: A dress fabric made of either silk or synthetic fibers or mixtures. It is smoother, duller, richer-looking than crepe de chine. Unless all silk, fiber content must be declared.

Fine crepe weave.

Coarse crepe weave.

LINGERIE CREPE: Formerly called French crepe. Originally creped by embossing (pressing over fleece blanket). No longer embossed, so not a crepe texture. Construction from 150 x 94 to 92 x 69. Silk, rayon or nylon. Used for lingerie and inexpensive dresses.

MATELASSE CREPE: A soft, double or compound fabric with a quilted appearance which looks like two separate fabrics held together with creped threads on both sides. Named from the French verb meaning to pad or stud. Used for suits, coats, wraps, trimmings, dresses.

MOSSY CREPE: Fabric woven with a surface that gives a fine moss-like effect. Sometimes called SAND CREPE or MOSS CREPE.

MOURNING CREPE: Has dull black finished surface, pressed with hot engraved rollers.

ONE HUNDRED DENIER CREPE: Crepe made of 100 denier viscose yarn in similar construction to a flat crepe.

ROMAINE CREPE: Heavier semi-sheer crepe similar to Alpaca crepe.

ROUGH CREPE: Heavy creped texture fabric made with alternately twisted filling yarns two right and two left.

WOOL CREPE: Soft fabric made of wool with irregular surface due to slack warp yarns.

**CREPE-BACK SATIN, SATIN CREPE:** Satin weave with a crepe-twist filling is used in this silk or rayon cloth. As the fabric is reversible, interesting effects can be obtained by contrasting the surfaces. Used for dresses, blouses, linings.

**CREPE CHARMEUSE:** A rich-feeling, dull-luster, piece-dyed cloth. It has glove-like smoothness; grenadine silk is used in the warp and the filling, the latter being crepe-twisted. The cloth has stiffness and body characteristics of a satin. It clings to the form very well and drapes gracefully. It is used for dresses, waists, evening clothes.

**CREPE DE CHINE:** A very fine, lightweight silk made with a crepe weave, is usually constructed with raw-silk warp and crepe-twist silk filling, alternating with 2-S twist and 2-Z twist. Usually piece-dyed or printed.

**CREPE de LAINE:** The latter word is French for wool. The cloth is a thin lightweight dress goods fabric, made with plain weave, or a crepe weave. Material is of the sheer variety.

**CREPE MAROCAIN:** A rather heavy dress-weight crepe fabric simulating canton crepe in texture. Popular dress goods material made in rayon or silk.

**CREPE, WOOLEN:** From the Anglicized French word *crêpe*. Originally a mourning cloth that showed a crimped appearance. Popular dress-goods cloth, woven or knitted.

**CREPON:** A crepe-weave fabric but of heavier construction.

**CRESLAN:** Manufactured by American Cyanamid Company, this is a true acrylic textile fiber in that it is composed of 85% or more of acrylonitrile. Formerly known as Fiber X-54.

**CRETONNE:** Cotton plain-weave cloth, although often made with a twill weave. It has large printed patterns similar to chintz but is not glazed. Launders well; used for hangings, furniture covering, and beach wear.

**CREWELWORK:** A type of embroidery stitch used to form a ropelike design.

**CRIMP:** 1. Fiber: The waviness in fibers; e.g., certain wools and rayon staple fibers.
2. Yarn: Also curvature produced in warp or filling yarn by weaving.

**CRINKLE RESISTANT:** Material which will retain its crinkled surface after repeated washings is termed crinkle resistant. A laboratory test is required before making this claim.

**CRINOLINE:** A smooth, stiff, strong material made of cotton warp and horsehair filling. Plain, twill, or satin weaves may be used in making this interlining for hat shapes. Imitation crinoline is made with hemp and is finished with glue or varnish; comes in shades of white through grey to black.

**CROCHET LACE:** Lace introduced in Ireland imitating Venetian point. The distinguishing mark of Irish crochet is the fine stitch followed by every thread.

**CROCK:** (Etymology undetermined, but probably a simple colloquialism). That undesirable property of a dyed cloth by which the coloring matter rubs off the fabric and smudges or soils other materials with which it comes into contact. This fault is usually traceable to imperfect dyeing, either in regard to the method employed or the inadaptability of the dyestuff.

**CROCKMETER:** Is the apparatus used for testing colorfastness to crocking (rubbing). A square of bleached, unstarched, cotton cloth is held firmly over a so-called finger of the crock meter. The finger is slid back and forth over the test specimen.

**CROMPTON, SAMUEL:** He invented the mule frame in 1779 by further developing the ideas of Hargreaves and Arkwright. The mule frame today is one of the greatest and most phenomenal of all machines. It is composed of twenty to thirty thousand distinct parts and is absolutely self-acting. As many as 1,400 ends of yarn may be spun at one time.

**CROPPING:** A dry-finishing operation used on all woolen and worsted goods to cut away or level the fiber pile or nap which has previously been raised. Also called shearing.

**CROSS-BRED WOOLS:** In this country they are obtained from breeding a long-staple sheep with a short-staple one. Much cross-breeding is done all over the world. Several new types and qualities of wool have resulted from sheep crossing and there are now approximately 200 cross-breeds that have been developed from the forty distinct breeds extant.

**CROSS-DYED CLOTH:** Various animal fiber cloths that have some vegetable fibers in them are cross dyed. A cloth might have a cotton warp and a worsted filling. The cotton yarn is dyed prior to weaving and the animal fiber yarn worsted, requires a dyestuff of different chemical composition from the cotton. The cloth as it comes from the loom would show a dyed-cotton warp and an undyed-worsted filling. The cloth is then dyed in a vat and the worsted stock is colored, cross dyed. While this is the accepted definition of cross dyeing, the process need not be confined to the fibers of the order of their arrangement as here noted. The piece goods do not have to be one color. Expediency is one of the reasons for cross dyeing. Much used in blacks and solids. See DYEING

Another meaning of cross dyeing implies the multicolored effects produced in cloths whose fibers possess varying or different affinities for dyestuff. Much man-made fiber cloth is dyed this way; for example, a viscose warp and an acetate filling fabric would often be cross-dyed to obtain pleasing color effects. At present, a popular method of dyeing.

**CROWFOOT WEAVE:** A satin weave with a broken-twill effect.

**CROWSFEET:** 1. A fabric defect produced in finishing process by wrinkling or staining.
2. Irregular or random marks apparent after laundering dyed fabrics.

**CRUSH RESISTANCE:** A finish used on pile fabrics, such as corduroy or velvet, to improve the ability of the pile to spring back to its original shape after being subjected to crushing or pressure.

**CUIT:** The term means "cut" and is used to describe silk from which all the gum has been removed.

**CUPRAMMONIUM:** The second method, in historical order, of making rayon. The product is a regenerated pure cellulose. Generally referred to as Bemberg rayon.

**CURING:** Application of heat (usually 280° F. and up) to fabrics which have been treated with resin-forming or other chemicals to produce an insoluble resin or other finish on the fabric.

**CURING OVEN or CHAMBER:** Any type of drying equipment in which curing temperatures can be obtained. The chamber may be of the loop, roller or enclosed frame type.

**CUSHION DOT:** A brushlike dot in marquisette that is larger and puffier than a polka dot. Made by one or more roving yarns which are woven into the material and then cut close to the surface.

**CUT:** Used in connection with sample pieces refers to a limited yardage of a particular pattern or color to be used to make up one or a few sample garments.

**CUT-PILE FABRICS:** These have a surface of brushlike tufts which stand up from the ground of the cloth, as in corduroy and velveteen. An extra warp or filling yarn forms the pile, which is cut on a special cutting machine after weaving, exposing the free ends of the fibers.

**CUT-RUBBER YARN:** The original

core yarn cut into size from a rubber sheet form.

**CUT STAPLE:** The same as rayon-staple fiber, it is the mass of rayon filaments which have been cut to short and uniform lengths. Staple stock may be cut as short as the cotton fiber or as long as the longer wool fibers. When these short rayon fibers are spun into yarn, in the same manner as cotton or wool, the product is known as spun-rayon yarn.

**CUT VELVET:** A fabric in which the pile has been cut by the cutting knife. There are several types on the market: mirror velvet is one in which the looped pile or face filling has not been cut. In wire velvet a series of wires is used in the weaving of the cloth which has regular rows of loops across the goods. Incidentally, these loops are cut to give a cut-pile material.

**D**

**DACCA MUSLIN:** Made from the Dacca cotton of Bengal, usually about 100-square in count. Considered one of the world's finest muslins.

**DACRON:** Pronounced *Day-cron*, it is the trademark name for the synthetic polyester textile fiber produced by Du-Pont. Formerly known as Fiber V, it was first developed in England under the trademark of Terylene, and the American rights were obtained in 1946.

Dacron is a condensation polymer obtained from ethylene glycol and terephthalic acid. It is not related to or connected chemically with nylon or the acrylic fiber Orlon.

Properties include high tensile strength and high resistance to stretching, both wet and dry, good resistance to degradation by chemical bleaches and to abrasion. Fabrics made with either filament or staple fiber indicate excellent resilience and resistance to wrinkling, easy laundering and quick drying, and they can be heat-set. The fiber has good electrical insulation properties and is not weakened by fungus, mold, or mildew.

**DAMASK:** Figured fabric, originally made in silk, that came to us from China via Damascus in Asia Minor. Marco Polo, in his travels of the 13th Century, spoke of the material and gives an interesting tale about it. Damask has been made for centuries and is one of the oldest and most popular staple cloths to be found today. Damask belongs to the group embracing brocades, brocatelles, and jacquards. The cloth is made from cotton, linen, wool, worsted, silk, rayon, etc. Used for table cloths, napkins, towels, doilies, runners, interior decoration, wall coverings, furniture covering. Elaborate designs are possible and damask is made on the intricate Jacquard looms where it is possible to give vent to the whims of the designer of these cloths.

Linen or cotton single damask is made on a five-shaft satin weave, double damask is made on an eight-end satin weave. The cloth is beetled, calendered, and is usually grass bleached. Very durable, reversible fabric, sheds dirt; the firmer the texture the better is the quality. Launders well and holds high luster, particularly in the linen goods. Smaller designs give a stronger cloth than designs that have long floats in the weave formation. The price range of damask is very great, inexpensive to costly fabric. Linen damask, "the Cloth of Kings," is widely imitated and cheapened. Rayon damask has about the same uses as the silk fabric.

**DARNED LACE:** Netting darned to form a design. The modern term for this character is simply *Antique*.

**DARTMOOR:** Hardy, British mountain sheep which, however, are raised chiefly on the moorlands at present. Rather free from *kemp*, the stock is about 40s quality.

**DECATING, DECATIZING:** Wools, cottons, rayons, and fabrics made with both rayon and cotton in them are wound on a perforated drum equipped with a steaming and vacuum system. The cloth, as it winds, is laid between layers of a decating blanket. Steam is passed through the cloth from the inside to the outside layers, and then the action is reversed. The vacuum pump takes out the steam on completion of the treatment. Decating sets the material, enhances luster, and gives some assurance against shrinkage.

**DECORTICATING:** Process of removing woody matter from bast fibers, like flax, after the retting process. See RETTING.

**DEGREASING:** The process of removing foreign matter from wool by the use of naphtha.

**DEGUMMING:** The process of removing the gum from silk, the sericin from fibroin. Boiling-out of the silk in a hot soap-bath removes the gum. The amount of gum removed will be from about 10% in the poorest grades to 30% in the best qualities.

**DELAINE:** A fine grade of wool used in high-grade worsteds. The term was originally French and means "of wool."

**DELUSTER:** The process of reducing the sheen or luster on rayon and acetate fabrics. Chemicals such as titanium dioxide are used.

**DENIER:** Originally it was a coin and its weight is used as the unit in speaking of the size of a silk or synthetic filament. In the time of Caesar the denier was used for coinage. It was revived in France during the reign of Francis I, the founder of the silk industry in that country. In value it is worth about one-twelfth of a French sou. One denier weighs .05 grams.

The weight of 450 meters, or 492.2 yards of silk, is .05 grams or one denier in thickness.

There are 4,464,528 yards in one pound of a Number One Denier silk. This number is obtained by multiplying 9072, the denier in one pound, by 492.13, the metric length used in calculating the weight of the yarn in question.

To find the yards of silk in denier size, divide the size of the yarn or thread, such as a 24/26 denier, medium of 25, into the 4,464,528 yards, the standard for the Number One Denier.

25)4,464,528 = 178,581.1 yards of this silk to the pound.

To find the yards to the pound in a rayon, acetate, or similar filament, divide the denier size into the standard, 4,464,528 yards.

For example, the number of yards per pound in a 150-denier rayon would be obtained in the following manner:

150)4,464,528 = 29,763.33 yards of this rayon to the pound.

**DENIM:** Made of a small left-hand twill weave, the cotton warp is usually dyed blue or brown. The cotton filling is always white. Warp stripes are also used in denims.

Strong fabric; launders well. Used for

furniture covering, work clothing, and play suits.

**DENSITY:** A standard measurement of thickness in fabric weight. A fabric's density is rated high or compact as contrasted with low or open.

**DENT:** The space between the vertical bars of the reed through which the warp ends are drawn. The reed size is noted by the number of dents or splits to the inch.

**DESIGN PAPER:** Special paper marked off in small squares or rectangles and used to indicate weave pattern or the manner in which the warp yarns interlace with the filling yarns. Each vertical space represents a warp end, each horizontal space a filling pick. At each square a warp and a filling yarn cross each other. If the warp yarn is over and the filling under, it is usually shown by marking the square. An empty square means filling is interlacing over the warp.

**DESIZING:** A process which removes starch or sizing put on the warp previous to weaving. Acids or special enzymes are used to convert the size to a soluble form which then washes out.

**DEVONSHIRE:** Cotton fabric used for utility clothing. Yarn-dyed and strong.

**DIAGONAL:** Cloth that shows an oblique twill line that may run to the left or right on the face of the material. Most twill lines are 45 degrees and they go from the lower left-hand corner of the cloth to the upper right-hand corner. Steep twill lines may be 63, 70, or 75 degrees in angle. Diagonal cloths are easily recognized, as the twill line is prominent. Only a few diagonals are made with a left-hand twill face effect.

**DIAGONAL WEAVE:** See TWILLS.

**DIAPER:** In the Middle Ages the term meant a rich silk material first made in Ypres, Belgium. As time went on this cloth of Ypres (*d'Ypres*) took on a different meaning until today it now means the soft, absorbent, bleached cotton.

**DIAPER LINEN:** See LINEN.

**DIAZOTIZING:** An intermediate step in the process of developed dyeing. The dyed material is treated with a solution of nitrous acid which changes the amino group in the dyestuff to a diazo grouping, which can then unite chemically with a "developer" to give a new dye compound on the fiber.

**DIMENSIONAL RESTORABILITY:** Refers to the ability of some fabrics which shrink in washing to return to their original dimensions by ordinary ironing. A 2% restorability means that while a fabric may shrink more than 2% in washing, it will return to within 2% of its original dimensions when ironed at home.

**DIMENSIONAL STABILITY:** Tendency of a fabric to retain its shape and size after being subjected to wear, washing, and dry cleaning. This stability may be brought about by the kinds of fiber used in the fabric, by chemical treatments, or by mechanical means.

**DIMITY:** Thin, sheer cotton fabric with corded stripes or check effects. Similar to lawn. Comes in white, dyed, or printed.

**DIP DYEING:** See DYEING METHODS.

**DIRECT (OR COMMERCIAL) DYE:** See DYES.

**DIRECT PRINTING:** See PRINT.

**DISCHARGE OR EXTRACT PRINTING:** Printing by removal of some of the color of a previously-dyed fabric. A colored design may be imprinted at the same time during this process. See PRINT.

**DISPERSE DYES, NON-IONIC:** These are "a class of water-insoluble dyes introduced originally for the dyeing of cellulose acetate (54 to 55% acetic acid) and applied usually from fine aqueous suspensions."

Although all commercial disperse dyes are actually slightly water soluble under dyeing conditions, at least to the extent of 0.5 mg. per liter, their chemical and physical properties distinguish them from other dye classes (vats) which may be insoluble at some stage in the process.

**DISTAFF:** This staff, from which wool or flax was drawn in the early days of spinning and then manipulated with the spindle, was in use until the 17th Century. The first distaffs were fashioned like a forked twig. A cleft in the staff held the mass of carded fibers conveniently while the spinner drew out the tufts for twisting between the thumb and finger and wound the strands on the rotating spindle.

The spinning or Saxony wheel superseded the spindle and distaff method of spinning yarn.

**DOBBY:** Woven on a dobby loom. Includes material with small figures, such as dots and geometric designs; floral patterns woven in the fabric, including certain shirtings, huck towels, diaper cloth, certain dress goods, drapery and upholstery fabrics. Can be dyed, bleached, or yarn-dyed in many colors. Dobby designs may be used in cottons, rayons, silks.

**DOBBY LOOM:** A type of loom on which small, geometric figures can be woven in as regular pattern. Originally this type of loom needed a "dobby boy" who sat on top of the loom and drew up warp threads to form a pattern. Now the weaving is done entirely by machine.

**DOBBY UPHOLSTERY:** Heavy cotton woven on a dobby loom, which can weave small geometric figures in a regular pattern.

**DOCTOR BLADE:** A long steel blade used in roller printing to remove the excess color from the surface of the roller.

**DOESKIN:** Used for trousering, broadcloth coating, waistcoat cloth, and riding habit fabric. The material is of fine quality, medium weight, smooth face finish, compact, and made of wool. There are few points of similarity between this cloth and a buckskin. A five- or eight-harness satin weave is used and the yarn employed is of high count and twist. A dress finish and slight nap are features of the finished garment.

Rayon fabric of this name is a twill-woven cloth napped on one side; some of the fabric is made from a small satin-weave repeat. Used for coating, suiting, sportswear, and gives good service.

**DOFF:** To remove the beam, bobbin, or package from a textile machine. The full bobbin is usually replaced at once with an empty one.

**DOILIE:** Is a corruption of the name *Doyley*, a linen merchant of London who brought out this linen napery material in 1707-1714.

**DOMESTIC:** 1. A term applied to textiles produced in the United States, especially when they are normally, or traditionally, made here.

2. Also, a general name for household goods, such as sheets, blankets, towels.

3. English term for cotton fabrics in plain weave, but varying in quality. The average domestic is made of about 60 ends of 24s warp and about 60 picks of 36s filling. The grey cloth is finished in a number of different effects.

**DOMET FLANNEL:** Plain or twill weave. Generally white with a longer nap than outing flannel, although the names are interchangeable. Soft filled yarns of medium or light weight. Also spelled Domett. See OUTING FLANNEL.

**DONEGAL TWEED:** 1. Hand-scoured, home-spun herringbone tweed that was originally made in county of this name in Ireland. The fabric is popular rough-and-ready material which does not possess high texture.

2. Tweed made in the British Isles on power looms; Yorkshire mills provide the yarn for the material, which is dyed and finished in Donegal.

**DOPE-DYED:** Trade term for solution-dyed or spun-dyed, which means that color is put into the chemical liquid from which rayon or synthetic fibers are made before they are formed through the spinneret. The fiber is colored all through, which means colors will be fast.

**DORIAN:** Originally a striped muslin first made in India, and is still a staple in many world centers.

**DOTTED SWISS:** Made of lappet weave, it is a sheer cotton fabric with crisp finish. Woven dots made by the lappet warp are the outstanding points of the cloth; used for waistings, curtains, dress goods.

This popular cloth has woven dots which are not affected by washing and ironing. Launders very well; gives good wear. From four to twenty threads are used to make the dots. Can also be made on swivel and clip-spot looms.

**DOUBLE CLOTH:** Cloths woven with two sets of warp and one filling, one warp and two fillings, two fillings and two warps, or with a fifth set of binding yarns to unite the two cloths. This can be varied with different colors on each side, or with patterns that are reversed. Used for suits, coats, ribbons, blankets, filter cloths and some jacquard fabrics.

**DOUBLE SERGE:** Made of two warps and two fillings. Heavier than other worsted serges. Cloth is clear finished, dyed

In double cloth, two cloths woven one on top of the other are held together by stitching.

in the piece, and runs from 12 to 20 ounces in weight. The cloth is not in as much demand as formerly because people do not dress as warmly as they used to do years ago.

**DOUBLE WOVEN PILE FABRIC:** A kind of pile cloth woven as two fabrics, face to face, with interlacing ends that later are cut to form the pile. Two distinct ground fabrics are woven, one above the other, and each pile end interlaces first with one fabric and then with the other. A travelling knife that passes back and forth across the breast beam cuts the pile ends when they reach this point and separates the top and bottom fabrics into two single cloths. Double velvet and double plush are examples.

**DOUBLING:** Feeding two or more slivers, slubbings, rovings, or yarns into some textile machine. Doubling offsets drafting, as it is necessary to double-up on the feeding-in end of a machine to offset and balance this draft which draws out the fibers. Without doubling, it would be impossible to make yarn.

**DOUPION:** Silk thread made from two cocoons that have nested together. In spinning, the double thread is not separated. The yarn is uneven, irregular, and diameter is large.

It is used in cloth of this name as well as in pongee, nankeen, shantung, and other cloths where desirable.

**DOWN:** The soft, fluffy filaments grown under the feathers of ducks and other water fowl. Used for pillows, quilts, paddings.

**DOWNPROOF:** Closely woven fabric which cannot be penetrated by down is termed downproof. Materials such as pillow ticking are down resistant.

**DRAFT:** The directions for weaving, usually plotted on cross-section or design paper to give the correct threading plan to be used in drawing the ends through the heddle eyes of the respective heddles.

**DRAFTING:** The drawing of fibers, that may be in some sort of rope form, among themselves to make the stock take on more the appearance of yarn. Excess speed of the front rollers of the machine in question, over the carrier rollers and the back rollers, makes drafting of textile fibers possible.

Twist is added in drafting to sustain the fibers in their form—sliver, slubbing, roving. These forms must not be drafted to the point where the fibers will collapse and not be able to sustain themselves. Doubling-up on the stock fed into machines takes care of this end of the work.

**DRAP D' ETE:** French meaning is "cloth of summer." Used for evening wear and very popular with the clergy. Material is a thin-staple woolen or mixture fabric that has a fine-twill weave with high counts of yarn used. Is rather expensive.

**DRAPE:** A term to describe the way a fabric falls when hung. The stiffness or draping quality of material can be measured by a Drapeometer.

**DRAPER, GEORGE:** American inventor who was granted a spindle patent in 1867, and by 1887 had patent rights on twelve named-variations of spindles.

**DRAPER, IRA:** American inventor of the loom temple and an improved fly-shuttle hand loom (1816). In 1818, brought out his self-moving temple, so a weaver could handle two looms instead of one. In 1829, he made further improvements on loom temples.

**DRAPERY**: Decorative fabrics for the home. Made of cotton, silk, rayon, nylon, spun glass, Orlon, wool, mohair, and mixtures. Used 1. as hangings at the sides of windows and doors for artistic effects, 2. as inner curtains of sheer materials to hang next to the window pane; as draw curtains to insure privacy or to shut out light as sash curtains.

**DRAWING**: To hold at one end or point and pull or draw from the other end to increase the length of the mass or bulk of fibers, sliver, slubbing, roving. Drawing is closely allied with drafting and the terms may be interchangeable.

**DRAWING-IN**: The process of actually threading the warp ends through the correct heddle eyes. When these ends are drawn through the reed the procedure is known as reeding or reeding-in.

**DRESDEN POINT LACE**: See LACE.

**DRESSING**: The process of winding yarn on the warp beam. The various colored yarns are set up in the creel and the pattern is "picked." This is according to the design given to the dresser by the mill designer. The yarn is run off the various spools which have the various colored yarns on them and wound onto the dressing frame. The warp is made up in sections on the dressing frames, and as many yards as desired are run off to make the first section; the other sections will have the same yardage.

**DRILL**: A durable fabric of medium weight. Usually three-harness warp-faced twills made of carded sheeting yarns. Comes in various weights and thread counts. When dyed, known as khaki, tickings, silesia, herringbones.

**DRIP-DRY**: Refers to garments which, after laundering, will dry quickly and regain original shape without ironing.

**DROP-STITCH KNIT**: See KNITTING.

**DRUID CLOTH**: See MONK'S CLOTH.

**DRUM PRINTING**: A method by which yarns are printed on a drum before weaving. The printing is so engineered that the color design appears as planned after the fabric is woven.

**DRY CLEANING**: A process used to clean fabrics which cannot be readily laundered. Organic solvents such as carbon tetrachloride or mineral spirits, are used to remove dirt and some stains.

Other stains are removed by special methods.

**DUCHESSE**: A silk fabric made with a dense warp, very lustrous, smooth in hand, and popular for women's wear.

**DUCHESSE LACE**: An old Bruges lace of bobbin type, with a tape-like character.

**DUCK**: The name duck covers a wide range of fabrics. It is the most durable fabric made. A closely-woven heavy material. The most important fabrics in this group are known as number duck, army duck, and flat or ounce duck. Number and army ducks are always of plain weave with medium or heavy ply yarns; army ducks are the lighter. Ounce ducks always have single-warp yarns woven in pairs and single or ply filling yarns.

**DUNGAREE**: A cotton denim fabric originally used for sailors' working clothes.

**DUPLEX PRINTING**: A printing technique by which both the front and back of the fabric are printed with either the same or different designs. When the design is the same, the registration of pattern is often so accurate that it looks like a woven fabric. See PRINT.

**DUPLEX SHEETING**: A 4-end, reversible twill weave is used in this soft-filled sheeting which is finished with a heavy nap on both sides of the fabric. Used for table felt chiefly, it comes in light weights and is napped on both sides and then sheared to give a suede effect.

**DURENE**: A mercerized, combed cotton yarn whose quality standards are set and controlled by the Durene Association of America.

**DUST-RESISTANT**: Any fabric, which has been tightly woven so that it resists dust penetration. Fabric should be laboratory tested before claiming dust-resistance.

**DUVETYNE**: Used in the millinery trade and in women's wear. The six-harness irregular satin weave is used, or it is possible to use a seven- or eight-end satin construction. Originally the cloth was made of cotton warp and spun silk filling. Other combinations are used as well. Cloth ranges from ten to twenty ounces in weight in woolen duvetyne,

and is stock, skein, or piece dyed. Material is face-finished to give a smooth, plush appearance. Duvetyne has a kindly feel and comes in many shades and casts of color. When the cloth is in demand, it is often difficult to supply it to the trade. One of the better-quality cloths. Duvetyne resembles a compact velvet; wears very well, good draping effect, soft to the feel, and spots easily.

**DYED-IN-THE-WOOL**: Woolen stock dyed before blending, oiling, mixing, carding, and spinning. Considered as synonymous with stock-dyed, a popular method of dyeing woolen fabrics.

**DYEING**: A process of coloring fibers or fabrics with either natural or synthetic dyes. Dyes differ in their resistance to sunlight, perspiration, washing, gas, alkali, dust, etc., their effectiveness on different fibers, their reaction to cleaning agents, their solubility and method of application.

**DYEING METHODS**: These are the principal dyeing methods:

BACK DYEING—Known also as back chroming, this method is used in dyeing especially in the case of logwood blacks, where the material is given a treatment with a chrome mordant after dyeing for better fixation of the color.

BATIK—A resist-dyeing process in which parts of a fabric are coated with wax; only the uncovered parts take the dye. The process can be repeated so that several colors are used. Often imitated in machine printing.

BEAM DYEING—A method of dyeing warp yarns before weaving. The warps are wound on perforated beams—the dyes are forced through the perforations saturating the yarns with color.

CHAIN DYEING—A method of dyeing yarns and cloths of low tensile strength. The fabrics are tied end-to-end and run through the dye-bath in a continuous process.

CONTINUOUS VAT DYEING—A process of applying heavy shades of vat dyes in one continuous operation developed by Dan River Mills simultaneously with the beginning of World War II.

CROSS-DYEING—Different fibers react differently to dye. Cross dyeing is the

Dyeing (*left*) by hand dipping of yarns into the dye bath is still prevalent. Modern skein or yarn dyeing on a large scale production basis, done with automatic machinery, still follows the immersion principle shown in sketch at right.

process of dyeing stock (fibers), yarn or fabric with different fibers present with such dyes that some of the fibers are not colored or take different colors from other fibers in the same material.

DIP DYEING—A process of dyeing hosiery and other knit goods after knitting.

JIG DYEING—Full-width piece goods may be dyed in jigs. The cloth is passed from the feed roller through the dye bath, and by means of other rollers is given a thorough treatment in the liquor. The treatment in this open vat can be repeated until the desired shade has been obtained.

PACKAGE DYEING—A method of dyeing yarns on cones, cops, and other put-ups, or packages. The dye solution passes from the center of the package outward and then from the outside through to the center. Beamed warp yarn may be handled in this way. Most carded and combed cotton yarn used in the knitted outerwear industry is dyed in this manner.

PAD DYEING—A process of first passing the fabric through trough containing dye, then squeezing it between heavy rollers to remove excess dye.

PIECE DYEING—Dyeing woven fabrics.

PRINTING—Designs on fabrics applied by plastic dyes, used on blocks, engraved metal rollers, or screens. Process is called block printing if done by hand from carved blocks. Most printing is done by roller. For Types of Prints, see PRINTS.

RAW STOCK DYEING—Process of dyeing fibers before spinning.

SKEIN-DYED—Another name for yarn-dyed. The skeins are dyed before the yarn is woven into cloth. Skein dyeing is used considerably in dyeing rayon crepes, plaids, overplaids, stripe-effects in suitings and dress goods which have two or more colors in the pattern, etc.

SLUB DYEING—See TOP DYEING.

TIE DYEING—Designs are made by tightly tieing parts of the fabric so that those tied parts do not take the dye. Done by hand. Also called Random Dyeing.

TOP DYEING—The dyeing of fibers in top-form of sliver or slubbing which is wound into a top and resembles a cheese in shape and size. The top has been carded and combed but not spun into yarn. Following dyeing, the various colored tops may be blended together to obtain some cast, hue, tone or shade of a color. Top dyeing is much resorted to in coloring fibers that are to be spun into yarn and then woven into worsted fabric. Considerable amounts of men's wear and women's wear worsted cloth are dyed in this manner.

UNION DYEING—Term applied to fabrics that contain more that one fiber, either in blend or combination. Such fabrics are dyed in one or more baths to obtain the same color and shade on the dif-

ferent fibers.

VIGOREUX PRINTING—The printing of worsted top fibers by passing the sliver through a printing machine which has a roll with raised bars to carry the dyestuff. The sliver is impregnated with the dyestuff when it comes in contact with the revolving bars or rollers. Black is used chiefly in Vigoreux work but shades of blue, brown, and green may be printed by this method for coloring what will be finished spun-yarn, when manipulation is completed.

YARN DYEING—The dyeing of the yarn before the fabric is woven or knitted.

**DYES:** These are the principal dyes:

ACID DYE—A type of dye used on wool, other animal fibers and nylon. Seldom used on cotton or linen for then it requires mordant, a substance which acts as a binder for the dye. However, it still rates low for color resistance to washing.

ALIZARIN DYE—Vegetable dyes originally obtained from madder root; now usually obtained synthetically. Used most successfully on wool, but in some cases on cotton. For instance, the popular color "turkey red" is an example of its use on cotton. This red is brilliant and resistant to sun and washing.

ANILINE DYE—Any dye derived from aniline. A term generally used for any synthetic organic dye.

BASIC DYE—A type of dye which has a direct affinity for wool and silk. Can be uesd on cotton if mordanted. Very poor for color resistance, but produces brilliant colors.

CATIONIC DYES—The same as basic dyes, they produce brilliant colors.

DEVELOPED DYE—A type of dye in which one color may be altered by use of a developer. Used on direct dyes to make a different shade of the same color, or to increase color resistance to sun and washing.

DIRECT OR COMMERCIAL DYE—A dye with an affinity for most fibers. Used when color fastness unimportant.

FLUORESCENT DYES—They are made from inorganic dyestuffs designed to impart to textile fibers and fabrics an unusual color brightness both in daylight and under the so-called "black light" conditions.

INDANTHRENE DYE—A type of vat dye producing highly resistant colors.

INDIGO—The oldest known vat dyestuff, formerly obtained from the indigo plant. Now made synthetically. The blue shades produced by indigo cannot be obtained by any other dyestuff. They have a character brilliancy and tone which has made this dyestuff popular for ages. Has good resistance to washing and light.

NAPHTHOLS (Azoic)—Insoluble azo dyes formed on the fiber by coupling a naphthol prepared with the diasotized bases or salts of a base. Used principally to obtain fast, brilliant scarlets and reds at relatively low cost.

SULPHUR DYE—A dye derived from chemicals containing sulphur, fairly resistant to washing, but has weak resistance to sunlight.

VAT DYE—Insoluble dye which is reduced in the process of application to a soluble form, put on the fiber, and then oxidized to the original insoluble form. Vat dyes are the most resistant dyes on the market to both washing and sunlight.

**DYESTUFF:** The name given to materials, solutions, or matters that color textiles. Prior to 1850, most of the dyestuffs used were animal or vegetable matter, but with the scientific progress of today many noteworthy inventions and discoveries have been introduced in the field of textile coloring. Rapid strides in dyeing have been made chiefly in Germany, France, England, Italy, and the United States.

Dyestuffs may be classed according to their origin . . . animal, vegetable, mineral, synthetic. The chief animal dyestuff is cochineal, which is obtained from a dried insect. This dyestuff or coloring matter is much used to color Oriental rugs in Persia, Turkey, and other centers. Cochineal may be compared with the famous shellac bug, mica.

There are many vegetable coloring matters, such as logwood (used to obtain good black on silks), madder root, quercitron, fustic, sumac, and indigo.

Most dyestuffs today are made chemically from coal-tar preparations, the so-called artificial or synthetic group.

**DYNEL:** A staple fiber spun from a copolymer of acrylonitrile and vinyl chloride. The name distinguishes it from the older Vinyon yarns developed by Union Carbide Corporation. Features of this fiber include strength, warmth, and quick-drying properties, good dimensional stability, and resistance to acids and alkalies. It will not support combustion, is completely moth- and mildewproof, can be dyed with either acid- or acetate-type colors, and is easily processed on the cotton, woolen, worsted, or silk systems. Dynel has been particularly successful in the fields of wigs and fake furs, where its fire-resistant capacity is especially important.

A man's wig of Dynel fiber.

# E

**ECCLESIASTICAL LACE:** Used for church purposes. Usually heavy, and drawn or darned.

**ECRU SILK:** Silk in which only the most soluble part of the natural silk gum has been removed along with the coloring pigment found in the filament. Ecru means natural or unbleached in the textile trade. Some inexpensive odds-and-ends silk cloth is known as écru silk.

**EDGING:** Embroidery, lace, braid or fringe used as a decorative trim on the edge of garments—narrower than flouncing.

**EGGSHELL FINISH:** A full finish created by running fabric through rollers engraved with minute depressions and elevations which break up light reflections.

**EGYPTIAN COTTON:** One of the world's most important cottons, grown mainly in the Nile valley, and noted for

its long staple and high quality.

**EIDERDOWN:** 1. A lightweight warm fabric, napped either on one side or both. Is either knitted or woven. Used for infants' wear, negligees, etc.

2. Also a term for a down quilt.

**ELASTIC MATERIAL:** A fabric composed of yarn consisting of an elastomer or a covered elastomer.

**ELASTICITY:** A characteristic of fibers, yarns, woven and knit fabrics, which enables them to return to shape after being stretched.

**ELASTICIZED:** Fabrics which have elastic threads running through them, or elastic qualities. Used for girdles, garters, suspenders. Lastex is a trade name for an elastic yarn or fabric which has this quality. See LASTEX.

**ELASTIQUE:** A 63-degree right-hand twill weave is used to make this narrow and wide wale, double-diagonal line fabric. It is made of woolen or worsted yarn, and gives excellent service. See CAVALRY TWILL, TRICOTINE.

**ELL:** Once used as a measure of cloth. One ell equals 45 inches.

**ELONGATION:** Is the measurement of degree of ductility of a yarn or fabric.

**ELURA:** Monsanto's modacrylic fiber, introduced as a wig fiber in 1970.

**ELYSIAN:** A rough, napped woolen cloth of high quality with the nap laid in diagonal lines. Used for overcoating.

**EMBOSSED CREPE:** The pebble or crinkled surface produced by passing the fabric between heated rollers which impart a rough, crepe-like surface. The effect can be made permanent.

**EMBOSSING:** Any pressure process producing raised or relief figures on the surface of fabrics. Usually accomplished by means of engraved rollers and heat application. Previously embossing tended to be lost in washing, but recent methods have fixed the design with a permanent resin finish, especially in cottons, which makes the fabric washable without loss of the embossing.

**EMBROIDERY:** The word comes from the Anglo-Saxon and means a border. It was originally used to describe the ornament on ecclesiastical garments.

**EMERIZING:** A finishing operation producing a fine suede-like nap on a fabric by friction from emery-covered rollers.

**EMERY CLOTH:** Cotton or linen cloth coated with fine, powdered emery, and used for polishing.

**EMPEROR:** A lining cloth made with cotton warp and alpaca or worsted filling.

**EMPRESS CLOTH:** Hard-twisted, cotton warp and worsted filling cloth, of the rep family. Popular in the middle of last century and brought out by the ever-prominent Empress Eugènie. The cloth was fashionable during her era. Two-up and one-down twill is used on the face construction. A rib weave is used for the back structure.

**ENAMELED CLOTH:** Imitation leather material used in luggage, trimming for carriages, overnight bags, table covers, millinery trimming, etc. There are many qualities of this glazed-finish cotton material based on the sheeting, drill, or other grey goods which may be used.

**ENAMELING DUCK:** Plain-woven fabric with a laid warp and ply-yarn filling. Weight is based on a width of 46.5 inches.

**ENCRON:** American Enka's polyester fiber, which is produced as continuous filament yarn, staple and fiberfill for a variety of end-uses.

**END:** A warp yarn or thread that runs lengthwise or vertically in cloth. Ends interlace at right angles with filling yarn to make woven fabric.

**END-AND-END WARP:** A warp made from two warps by taking the ends from each warp in an alternating order when the warp dressing is done.

**END USE:** The final use to which a fiber is put in its completed state.

**ENGINEERS' CLOTH:** Broad term for denims, dungarees, heavy drills, and overalls.

**ENSIGN CLOTH:** Plain-woven cotton or linen cloth used for bunting and flags.

**EOLIENNE:** Dress material made of silk warp and cotton, rayon, or worsted filling. The cloth is light in weight, has a glossy finish, is dyed in the piece, and

the weave used forms cross ribs.

**EPINGLE:** Women's suitings and dress goods material, of woolen or worsted, that weighs from seven to ten ounces per yard. Plain weave used. Cloth is piece-dyed and given clear finish; is popular at times and is a true cycle cloth, ruled by the demands of fashion and style.

**EPONGE:** The name means "sponge." Is a woolen dress-goods cloth that is very soft and sponge-like. Texture is low, about 20 x 20. A plain warp and novelty yarn filling is used, or the reverse can be used to advantage. Cloth is bleached and dyed.

Rayon éponge is soft, loose, and spongy, somewhat simulating terry cloth. Novelty weaves are used in the fabric, which is used for coats, sportswear, and summer suits.

Cotton eponge: see RATINÉ.

**ERI SILK:** The product from silk-worms which have been reared on the leaves of the castor tree, primarily by hill tribes in the state of Assam in India.

**ESKIMO CLOTH:** A napped over-coating fabric in which most of the warp shows on the face of the cloth.

**ESTER:** An ester is formed by the replacement of the acid hydrogen of an acid, organic or inorganic, by a hydro-carbon radical. When the radical is not mentioned by name ethyl is understood, generally speaking. For example, acetic ester is ethyl acetate.

**ESTRON:** The trademark name for Eastman acetate yarn and staple fiber of one or more esters of cellulose with or without lesser amounts of non-fiber forming materials. In addition to its many uses in the apparel field, it is used industrially for electrical insulation. Plasticized Estron acetate staple offers a wide range of applications in fiber-bonded webs, and as base materials for the manufacture of oilcloth, linoleum, artificial leather, etc.

**ETAMINE:** Is a bolting fabric or sifting cloth, whose name implies a dress goods material which has porous areas in it, such as noted in leno or doup fabrics, mock leno cloths and "cloth that

breathes," a term popular in advertising goods of this character. Etamine, comparable with éponge, is usually lighter in weight.

**ETCHED-OUT FABRIC:** See BURNT-OUT FABRIC.

**EVERFAST:** Trademark of Everfast Fabrics, Inc. for large group of high-style cotton dress and drapery fabrics, all of which carry an unqualified color guarantee by Everfast Fabrics, Inc.

**EXFOLIATION:** The tendency of a filament to split into elemental fibrils especially concerning the processing of silk.

**EXHAUSTING AGENT:** A chemical which forces more of the dye out of the dyebath and on to the fabric.

**EXTRA LONG STAPLE:** Cotton whose individual fibers average $1\frac{3}{8}$ inches and longer, such as Sea Island or an American-Egyptian variety like Supima, distinguished by its extra strength and luster.

**EXTRACT PRINT:** See DISCHARGE PRINT, under PRINT.

**EXTRACT WOOL:** Waste wool which is processed by carbonizing.

**EXTRUDED LATEX:** This basis for lastex and latex is forced through a nozzle into a coagulating bath, from which the formed yarn is drawn off by a pair of rollers. This solid, round, elastic core will give about 14,000 yards to the pound in laton and about 11,000 yards in lastex. Its uses are about the same as those of lastex.

**EXTRUSION:** The forcing of a liquid through orifices in such a way as to produce a solid in the shape given by the orifice. Synthetic and man-made fibers are extruded to form continuous filaments, which are then spun into filament yarns, or cut into staples.

**EYE:** The opening or eyelet in the middle of the heddle. Sometimes called a mail.

**EYELET EMBROIDERY:** In this process small holes are punched in the fabric, after which decorative stitching is embroidered around them.

# F

**FABRIC, WEIGHT OF:** Three methods are used today to figure the weight of cloth:

1. OUNCES PER YARD: Woolens, worsteds, specialty fiber fabrics, and similar "heavy fabrics" in which man-made and/or synthetic fibers have been blended with wool or worsted, use this method. Thus, an 8-ounce worsted tropical, a 14-ounce tweed, a 22-ounce coating fabric.

2. YARDS PER POUND: This method is used considerably when finding the weight of most cotton fabrics, and those made of man-made or synthetic fibers. Some very lightweight materials may not weigh as much as one ounce per yard. Hence, the value of this method in figuring the weight of very light, sheer materials. Thus, a symbol such as Broadcloth-3.85 means that there are 3.85 yards to the pound of this particular material. Some of the cloths figured on this plan include printcloths, tobacco cloths, carded piques, poplins, broadcloths, three-leaf twills, four-leaf twills, jean cloths, sheetings, sateens, osnaburgs, drills, pebble cloths, etc.

3. OUNCES PER SQUARE YARD: This comparatively new method was introduced in France following World War II. It spread to the British Isles, other nations in Europe, then to Canada, and is now meeting with favor in the United States. Many man-made fabrics are figured this way.

Most large mills that make a wide variety of fabrics use a demarcation weight between ounces per yard and yards per pound methods. Weight demarcation limits may be four, six, or eight ounces, as a general rule.

**FACE:** That side of a fabric which is intended to be shown and by reason of weave or finish presents a better appearance. In many fabrics, especially industrial ones, there is no distinction between face and back.

**FACE-FINISHED FABRIC:** Cloths finished on the face only. Much resorted to in case of meltons, kerseys, and other overcoatings. The weaves used are such that they will permit the type of finish, notwithstanding the fact that the texture is high and the interlacings tight. Plain, twill, and satin weaves are all used jointly in proper construction of the various face finish cloths. Other face-finish cloths are bolivia, bouclé, chinchilla, montagnac, tree-bark cloths, Saxony overcoating, Whitney and Worumbo finishes.

**FACING SILK:** Light weight, closely woven fabric, now usually made of rayon. Used for linings, collar and hem facings. If made of rayon or acetate, cannot be called "silk."

**FACONNE:** French for fancy weave and implies small, jacquard-effect designs in fabrics. Materials of this type drape well and give good wear. Made with silk or rayon.

**FACONNE VELVET:** See VELVET.

**FADING, FUME:** See FUME FADING.

**FADE-OMETER:** A standard laboratory device for evaluating a color's fastness to sunlight.

**FAILLE:** Ribbed silk or rayon cloth with crosswise rib effect. Cords are stouter than the warp. Soft in feel and belongs to the grosgrain family of cloths. Used for coats, dress goods, handbags.

Difficult to launder well; good draping effects; wears well if handled carefully.

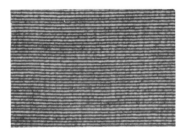

Faille weave.

**FAILLE CREPE:** See CREPE.

**FAILLE TAFFETA:** Stiff and crisp with a fine cross-ribbed appearance. Used for dresses and coats. Made in silk or rayon. See TAFFETA.

**FAKE FURS:** A whimsical or popular term for high-pile garments in a wide range of textile markets. Fake furs have simulated very successfully the furs of many animals, such as broadtail, chinchilla, ermine, French poodle, giraffe, leopard, tiger, pony, lamb and a number of other animals. Fake furs have also been created in original patterns such as diagonals, checkerboards, chevrons and stripes. The predominant fiber in this market is modacrylic since it is highly flame-resistant. Fake furs have also been used as decorative and ornamental elements on other garments. See Pile Fabric.

**FALLER:** A device used in the gilling, or carding, of worsted fibers. Each gill box has 18 fallers. They operate to straighten and parallel the fibers and clean them of foreign matter.

**FARMER'S SATIN:** Italy contributed this cloth as an imitation of the genuine silk cloth; a name for lining fabric today.

**FAST COLOR:** A color that will resist color destroying agents such as sunlight, washing, drycleaning, and rubbing.

**FAST DYE:** A dye that does not change shade appreciably during the life of the material on which it is used. Term should be qualified, i.e., fast to washing, sunlight, or other specific color destroying agent.

**FEARNAUGHT:** English overcoating of the cheviot group. Cloth is heavy in weight and the filling yarn aids in obtaining the well-known characteristic shaggy face finish of the fabric. Much shoddy and other reworked fibers are used in making the cloth.

**FEEDER:** The device which feeds stock into a textile machine.

**FELT AND FELTED MATERIALS:**
1. FELT FABRIC: A felt cloth is made with no system of threads, but is constructed by an interlocking of the fibers of stock to be used. There is a woven felt cloth, however—papermakers' felt cloth—that is used in the newspaper presses and is made of the best wool obtainable. The nature of the uses of this fabric makes it necessary that the fabric be woven.

Felt fabric is made by subjecting the stock to be used to heat, moisture, water, pressure, and in the case of derby hats and other stiff felts, shellac. The amount of shellac used depends on the desired stiffness of the finished material.

Leading felt products are felt hats, the most important felt item; banners, pennants, slippers, linings of many types, piano hammers, board erasers, insoles, etc. Any and all types of stocks, wastes, etc., find their way into felt cloth.

2. FELTED FABRIC: This type of woven material is also known as fulled or milled

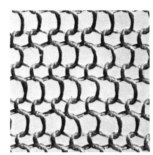

The photos above show how the structure of a felt fabric (*left*) differs from the structure of a woven fabric (*center*) and a knitted fabric (*right*).

cloth. Felting, fulling, or milling is the process resorted to in order to give woven cloth a thick, compact, substantial feel, finish, and appearance. The construction of the goods is covered up and not seen when the cloth is examined. Napping and shearing may be applied, to aid in making felted cloth. The effect may be produced on woolens and cottons.

Felted material runs from medium to heavy in weight. Most of it is used in outerwear during the cold months. Cloths that may be felted are flannel, cricket cloth, molleton or silence cloth; many types of overcoating, such as melton, kersey, beaver, and broadcloth; fleece coats, reefers, ulsters, and heavy uniform goods. Certain suiting and dress goods material, robes, and blankets are felted.

The process of fulling and felting is like that of removing a spot or stain from a cloth or garment. In rubbing the affected area the cloth has the tendency to felt or mat, and the fibers to interlock. This tends to cover up the weave construction and gives the goods a felted appearance. Soap, heat, water, friction, and proper temperatures produce the felted effect seen on woven goods. Felting covers up the spaces between the interlacings in the weave, gives compactness to the goods, and thus affords more warmth.

Felt may be made of:

   a. Camel and goat hair.
   b. China cotton.
   c. Other cottons.
   d. Cow and rabbit hair.
   e. Flocks and other mill wastes such as card strippings, shear wastes, willow wastes.
   f. Reprocessed or new wool.

   g. Reused wool.
   h. Shoddy, mungo, extract wool.
   i. Short staple wool noils, the most important fiber for felt.

**FELT, SILICONE-TREATED:** Particularly adaptable to fashion garments such as jackets and skirts, this type of felt has the following advantages over the non-treated material—silkier hand and improved draping quality in lightweight felts; improved wrinkle recovery and better sewing properties by a decrease in needle resistance; resistance to water-borne stains and water spotting in dry cleaning.

**FEUTRON METHOD IN NON-WOVEN FABRICS:** American Felt Company, Glenville, Conn., in 1955 produced the first nonwoven fabrics consisting exclusively of synthetic fibers not bonded either by resin or thermoplastically but interlocked by mechanical means of an interlocking on a needle-loom system, followed by a felting process by the use of chemicals. Uses of the product include wet and dry filtration, high temperature oil bearing seals, reinforcement for plastics, gaskets, oil wicking in high temperatures, thermal and acoustical insulation, base fabrics for special coatings and impregnants, and for high temperature moisture seals in street and airport lighting fixtures. The method is named for St. Feutre of Caen, France, the patron saint of the felt industry.

**FIBER:** An individual strand, sometimes referred to as a filament. It is a slender, fine diameter, single strand. Several fibers, however, may be combined to them ready for spinning, weaving, and knitting purposes. A fiber usually has a rather definite set length.

**FIBERFILL:** A specially prepared filling for pillows, comforters, garment and furniture padding, etc. It is generally staple fiber.

**FIBERGLAS:** Textile fibers and yarns are produced from glass, which, when drawn fine enough, can be woven into strong, flexible fabrics. The raw materials that are used to make ordinary glass are refined and shaped into glass marbles. These marbles are remelted and formed into more than a hundred glass filaments, which are simultaneously attenuated into a single yarn of minute diameter. Glass yarns have been produced as fine as 100s cotton count.

Short-staple glass fibers, ranging from 8 to 15 inches in length, are produced by striking the streams of molten glass with jets of high-pressure air or steam. This process separates the filament where required, and seals the ends of the short staple. Short-staple glass yarns have a fuzzy surface, but the continuous filament produces smooth yarns.

Fiberglas is used for fireproof clothing and is insoluble in organic solvents. It is affected only by hydrochloric and phosphoric acids, and by weak, hot solutions or strong, cold solutions of alkalies.

Fiberglas is used for fireproof clothing and draperies, for electrical insulation, and for soundproofing. It is noninflammable, nonabsorbent, moth-proof, mildewproof, and resistant to sunlight; it does not deteriorate with age. These qualities make Fiberglas a very hygienic fabric. Home-furnishing products include bedspreads, curtains, tablecloths, and shower curtains. A trademark of Owens-Corning Fiberglas Corp.

**FIBROIN:** The insoluble part of the raw-silk filament. The worm has two glands that contain the silk or fibroin which, on coming into the air, is cemented together by the silk gum or sericin.

**FILAMENT:** An individual strand that is indefinite in length. Examples are silk, which may run from 300 to 1400, 1600, and even 1800 yards in length; synthetic filaments are indefinite in length and may attain a total length of several miles. Filaments are finer in diameter than fibers. A fiber or a filament is the smallest unit in any type of cloth.

**FILATURE:** A place or establishment where silk reeling is carried on. Japan has about 3,000 of these places with more than 300,000 reeling basins. Filatures will range from 50 basins up to more than 1,000. About 350,000 people are employed in this part of the industry, and all but about 10,000 are females.

**FILATURE CLASSIFICATION IN THE YOKOHAMA MARKET:** There are six major grades in silk classification: 1. Grand double extra; 2. Double extra; 3. Extra; 4. Best number one extra; 5. Best number one; 6. Number one.

The percentages of the above grades are as follows: Grand double extra, 1%; Double extra, 6%; Extra, 8%; Best number one extra, 16%; Best number one, 37%; Number one, 32%.

**FILLED CLOTH:** Cloth in which the weave openings have been filled by a heavy sizing. Examples are buckram and bookbinding cloth.

**FILLING:** 1. An individual yarn which interlaces with warp yarn at right angles in weaving fabric. Also known as pick or filling pick. Filling usually has less twist when it is compared with warp yarn.

Irregular filling in fabric.

2. Weft, the English term for filling, is used in this country in the carpet trade. This term, at times, is rather misleading and is sometimes confused with woof, the English term for warp.

**FILLING FACE:** That weave in which the face of the fabric is formed by the filling yarns. Fabrics so woven are also called filling flush.

**FILLING PATTERN:** In a fabric composed of different filling yarns or differently colored filling yarns, the filling pattern indicates the order or arrangement of the various yarns.

**FILLINGS:** Fancy stitches employed to fill in open spaces in lace.

**FILLING-BACKED SERGE:** Serge of one-warp and two-fillings. Has same characteristics as French-back serge.

**FILLING SATEEN:** Cotton cloth made with a filling-effect satin weave on the face of the fabric.

**FILTER CLOTH:** A warp-effect, twill-weave fabric which varies much in weave, yarn count, texture, and weight. Finds much use in industry in the food, candy, paint, chemical, petroleum, and similar industries.

**FINGERING YARN:** A worsted knitting yarn in which the lower qualities are not combed, the noil being allowed to remain so as to give fullness to the thread. In many world centers for hand knitting the term fingering is considered synonymous with worsted yarn.

The origin of the term may be derived from the hand spinning days to imply a process of passing the yarn through the fingers to obtain a straighter run of the fibers. Hand knitting and finger knitting are synonymous in British Isles.

**FINGER MARK:** A fabric defect consisting of an irregular spot having a different appearance from the rest of the cloth due to localized variations in picks per inch.

**FINISH:** Treatment of a fabric to give a desired surface effect, such as napping, calendering, embossing, lacquering, or crinkling. Some finishes add luster, others give a muted dull effect. Special finishes can be applied to make a fabric waterproof or wrinkle resistant. A finish may contribute to the "feel" of a fabric, as well as to its looks and usefulness.

**FINISHED WIDTH:** The width of a fabric after it has completed the finishing operations and is ready for use.

**FINISHING:** The art and science of making materials presentable to the consuming, buying public. Cloth is converted from the grey goods state, as it comes from the loom, into a fair, medium, good, or excellent cloth ready for usage. Textile fabrics are "made in the finishing" as there has never been woven a perfect yard of cloth, free from defects of some sort. Finishing takes care of these defects in the material.

**FIREPROOFING:** Some of the methods of fireproofing fabrics are:

1. A composition, which may be ap-

plied to all kinds of fabrics without causing deterioration in any way, consists of sulphate of ammonia, two-fifths of a pound; boracic acid, three pounds; borax (pure), one-seventh of a pound; starch, two pounds; and water, 100 pounds.

The cloth to be treated is steeped in this hot solution until thorough impregnation is assured. Squeezing and drying follow.

2. Vogt method—use two parts of sublimated sal ammoniac and sulphate of zinc, one part in twenty parts of water. Squeeze and dry.

3. Siebrath method—Steep the cloth in a solution of 5% alum and 5% phosphate of ammonia. Squeeze and dry.

4. Paris Municipal Laboratory method —prepare a 2% solution of aluminum sulphate and a 5% solution of silicate of soda. Mix and immerse the material. After squeezing and drying, the aluminum silicate formed in the fabric is insoluble.

**FIRSTS:** An inspection classification for fabrics that meet established commercial standards for minimum number of defects and imperfections.

**FISHEYE:** Large diamond effect that is similar in shape to the eye of a fish. Comparable with the smaller pattern noted in bird's eye, and used for the same purposes.

Durable, has good absorptive properties, is reversible.

**FISH NET:** Wide mesh material resembling fishing nets, and used for scarfs and dress trimming.

**FITTED SHEETS:** Sheets with boxed corners to fit the mattress.

**FIXING:** The process by which colors are made permanent in dyed or printed cloth. Heat, steam, or chemical used.

**FLAKE YARN:** A novelty ply yarn in which flakes or tufts of roving appear at intervals. The tufts are not part of the single yarns, but are held by ply twist.

**FLAMEPROOF:** Applied to a fabric, this term does not mean that the fabric will completely resist all possible damage by fire, but it does mean that material so treated will not sustain combustion when removed from the source of heat. Usually flameproofing treatments are not permanent, since the flameproofing salts used are water soluble. After repeated launderings, the properties of flameproofing may disappear.

**FLAME-RESISTANT FINISHES:** Man has been concerned with the hazards of combustible materials since he first learned how to make fire for his own benefit. Early in written history the Chinese used asbestos fibers to make false sleeves which were cleaned by burning the food stains from them. Charlemagne owned an asbestos table cloth in the Eighth Century which he cleaned in the same way. Cellulosic materials such as wood, paper or cotton cannot be made fire-proof in the sense that glass or asbestos fibers are fireproof but they can be made flame-retardant in that they will not support combustion after the source of ignition is removed. Pre-World War II flame-retardant finishes for cotton involved the use of water-soluble salts. Borax, boric acid and ammonium salts were used to impart flame-resistance, but the result was not durable because the salts washed out in laundering. More recent finishes have been more successful. Their essential is tetrakis (hydroxymethyl) phosphonium chloride, commonly referred to as THPC. This has been used successfully in draperies, bedding, hospital gowns, cubicle curtains and some work clothing and military garments.

**FLAMMABILITY TEST:** The Flammable Fabrics Act provides that fabrics to be used for wearing apparel shall be tested as specified in Commercial Standard 191-53 to determine if a fabric is dangerous when worn.

**FLAMMABLE FABRIC, HIGHLY:** As decreed by the commercial standards of the U.S. Department of Commerce, a flame the size of a match is applied to a material for one second to a swatch that measures two inches by six inches. Held at an angle of 45 degrees, the spread of the flame is measured. If the flame-spread is less than four seconds, and the intensity of the flame is such that it sets the base fabric on fire in napped, pile, tufted, or flocked fabrics, the goods are classified as having a "rapid and intense" burning quality and are then considered unsuitable for clothing.

**FLAMMABLE FABRICS ACT:** A law passed by Congress and signed by President Eisenhower June 30, 1953, prohibiting the introduction or movement in interstate commerce of fabrics for clothing that are flammable enough to be dangerous when worn.

**FLANNEL:** Loosely-woven cloth of simple weave which the dull finish tends to conceal. Cloth is found in standard blue and in fancy effects, chiefly in stripe form. Material is used for suitings, uniform cloth, outing material, and in night wear. Flannel cloth originated in Wales. There is considerable variance in weight and texture in this cloth. Made of cotton, wool, or rayon.

**FLANNEL, FLANNELETTE, COTTON:** A heavy, soft material that is given a napped finish. There are many types on the market. Used for pajamas, nightgowns, pocket lining, quilts, clothing, shirting. Flannelette is made in stripes, plaids, prints.

Launders well and is easy to manipulate. Nap will come off in the cheaper qualities. Soft filling yarn is used so that a good nap may be assured.

**FLANNEL, RAYON:** There are two major fabrics under this term. Both cloths are made in 2-up, 2-down right-hand twill weave. One material is a 2/30s yarn construction while the other is with a 1/15s. The 2/30s is run usually with 70% rayon and 30% acetate. The 1/15s is run in two versions—a 50% each of acetate and rayon, or a 70% rayon and 30% acetate. This is done to obtain different color effects. Practically all these fabrics are crossdyed and a slight nap is provided in the finishing of the goods.

**FLAT CREPE:** Similar to crepe de chine but has flatter surface. Made in silk or rayon and is the smoothest crepe on the market.

**FLAT-KNIT:** A knitted fabric made on a flat, rather than a circular, machine. See PLAIN-KNIT.

**FLAX, LINEN:** An important type of bast fiber, the plant is called the flax plant and the product is called linen. Flax is obtained from the plant stalk which grows in many world areas. It is the oldest textile fiber known in the vegetable group and it may attain a length of about forty inches. The name of the plant is *Linum usitatissimum*.

The plant is raised for two purposes, the fiber and the seed. The latter is known commercially as linseed and it is used as linseed meal for animal feed, for birdseed, and in cake form in the chemical industry.

The fibers are manipulated into yarn and cloth, and the fabric is used for tablecloths, napkins, doilies, runners, crash, toweling, suiting material, twine, canvas, aprons, shoe thread, fishing tackle and nets, cigarette paper, currency and bank note paper, and similar products.

The chief flax-producing countries are Russia, which supplies 75% of the world output; Belgium, which raises the best flax in the world; Ireland, where the best workmanship is found; the United States, Holland, South Africa, France, India, Japan, China, and Asia Minor.

In this country, Oregon is the leader for fiber and seed, while Michigan, Minnesota, Wisconsin, Washington, and Kentucky are interested mainly in the seed.

Fiber flax is sown about 85 to 100 pounds to the acre. The straws grow straight to a height of 30 to 40 inches. The seed branches are seen at the top only. The Oregon fiber is high in quality and compares favorably with the well-known Belgian thread fiber known as Courtrai stock.

**FLEECE:** Heavy, compact, long-napped overcoating much in use. Interlacings well covered up by nap. Range from cheap to expensive cloths. Stock, skein, or piece dyed. From 15 to 25 ounces per yard.

Good-quality cloth, gives fine wear. Material is often cumbersome and bulky, therefore it may be difficult to manipulate. Nap wears out in time.

**FLEECED:** A napped surface, usually in knit goods. The term cannot be used for a fabric not made of wool, unless the fiber content is declared.

**FLEECE LINED:** A double-knit fabric which has floats on either one or both sides. These floats are napped, which makes the fabric warmer than an ordinary fabric. Used in eiderdown and cotton "sweat-shirts." Term also applied to sheep-lined coats.

**FLOAT:** 1. The portion of a warp or filling yarn that extends over two or more adjacent filling picks or warp ends in weaving for the purpose of forming certain designs.

2. Flaw in cloth made by a misweave.

**FLOCK DOT:** Dots or figures called flocks composed of wool (or other fibers) applied, rather than woven, to a fabric with paste, adhesive, rubber cement. They are usually washable and dry cleanable, although lacquered figures may not be durable. ·

**FLOCKING FABRIC BY SPRAY METHOD:** Viscose rayon staple may be flocked onto fabric, leather, cardboard, etc., to give plush, suede, and velvet effects. Known as Flisca Fiber Technique, the method has been developed by Societé de la Viscose of Emmenbruecke, Switzerland.

The short-staple fiber may be applied to an adhesive backing either by spray or by an electrostatic plan. The spray method uses compressed air much on the order of spraying paint. In the electrostatic method the fibers are drawn by an electromagnetic set-up onto a resin-treated surface. Suedes are developed from an 0.5 millimeter length of fiber, while velvet is simulated from a length of 1 millimeter and plush from a 1.5 millimeter length.

**FLORENTINE TWILL:** Lightweight dress goods of the lustrous type. Cloth comes in waves of popularity at times. Various weaves are used and the term holds the significance that a Florentine twill cloth must repeat on eight warp ends and eight filling picks.

**FLOUNCING:** A decorative lace or embroidery used as trimming on dresses and slips. It has one straight edge and one scalloped edge (12 x 54 inches wide).

**FLUORESCENT DYES:** Dyes which give greater brilliance to yarns and fabrics because of their ability to reflect more light than conventional types of dyes. See DYES.

**FLYER:** A device used in spinning. It sits on top of the spindle, twists the fiber, and winds the yarn on the bobbin. The first flyer was invented by Leonardo da Vinci about 1516.

**FLY SHUTTLE:** Literally, this is a shuttle that flies through the warp threads to produce the filling in the weaving process. It was invented by John Kay in 1738 and was one of the first major advances in textile production.

**FORESTRY CLOTH:** Used by the United States Government for uniform cloth, overcoatings, trouserings, knickers, shirts, blouses, etc. The cloth is olive drab in color and it is made from a twill weave. Made of worsted, wool, cotton, mixes, etc. This cloth is used essentially in the Forestry Service of the nation, but is likewise utilized by some other departments. In short, the name is nothing more than another term for khaki cloth.

**FORTREL:** The polyester fiber manufactured by Fiber Industries and marketed by the Celanese Fibers Marketing Company. It is produced as filament yarn, staple, tow, fiberfill and continuous filament fiberfill.

**FORTUNY PRINTS:** A series of rich artistic fabrics executed by a secret screen-printing process. Originated by Mariano Fortuny of Venice, the Renaissance motifs used were featured by the use of light colors on dark backgrounds. Some of the fabrics were stamped with gold or silver to give further vividness to the pattern. Twill or satin weaves are used in the plain constructions, while pile-effect weaves are used in velvets and velveteens for the more expensive materials.

**FOULARD:** A lightweight silk or rayon cloth noted for its soft finish and feel. Made with plain or twill weaves, it is usually printed with small figures on dark and light backgrounds. Suitable for dresses, robes, and scarves, foulard is always a popular staple for summer neckwear fabric.

**FOULE:** From the French verb *fouler*, to full. The cloth is made of a twill weave, is unsheared and unsinged. The face is quite uneven and rough. Much shrinking gives the finish.

**FOUR-LEAF TWILL:** A popular diagonal weave which uses no more than four harnesses in the design of the repeat. Four-leaf twills are used in such fabrics as sailcloth and uniform cloth.

**FOURTEEN POINT, FIFTEEN POINT:** The numbers indicate the openings to the inch in the machine-made lace net.

**FRAME:** A general term used to describe many types of textile machines.

**FRAY:** Wearing out of threads in a fabric as a result of rubbing or friction.

**FRENCHBACK:** A cloth with a corded twill backing of different weave than the face of the cloth, which is clear-finish in appearance. It is a staple worsted cloth. Back weave is of inferior yarn when compared with the face stock. The backing, usually of cotton, gives added weight, warmth, more texture and stability to the cloth. The interlacings are covered up better than in the average single cloth. Frenchbacks can be made with little extra cost to the cloth. Fabric is usually made of two warps and one filling. It is piece- or skein-dyed, weight ranges from 15 to 20 ounces per yard. Cloth has good feel and clingingness and may be used for formal or informal wear.

**FRENCHBACK SERGE:** Men's wear serge of two warps and one filling. Runs from 16 to 18 ounces per yard in weight, is piece-dyed, given clear or semi-finish. Used much in winter suitings. Quality and price vary considerably.

**FRENCH CREPE:** See LINGERIE CREPE under CREPE.

**FRENCH LACES:** There are three major types:

### LINGERIE LACE:

1. VALENCIENNES LACE: It is now made of long-staple cotton, nylon or rayon. It comes in varying widths but is usually narrow for use in trimming lingerie, edging, insertion-work or applique.

2. CHANTILLY-TYPE: Made in rayon or silk it comes in long bands or in flounces. Used for lingerie and smart, dressy garments.

3. ALENCON-TYPE: Manufactured in and around Lyons, it is the finest of these three types and higher in price. Used for classic silk lingerie chiefly in applique motifs inserted into the fabric.

### COUTURE LACE:

1. RE-EMBROIDERED LACE: This presents an allover motif in which the patterns are enhanced by means of an embroidery outline thread either stitched on by machine after the lace has left the machine for the fine quality laces, or woven in while the lace is being made on the frame. Of late, this lace has been made

with the re-embroidery outlined with other products than embroidery thread, such as ribbon, narrow braid, cellophane, metallic yarns and threads.

2. FINE CHANTILLY-TYPE: These have been made since the time of the well-known Madame DuBarry (Jeanne Bécu, 1746-93), a favorite of Louis XV who was guillotined during the French Revolution. The motif is outlined with a fine embroidery thread or, sometimes, worked right into the center of the pattern. This is the acme of perfection in fine fashion of today.

3. GUIPURE: This is the heaviest of the three laces, and the beauty and elegance of guipure comes from a judicious grouping of motifs. Used in couture fashions and for expensive blouses.

VEILINGS AND TULLE: Although these items are not classed as lace, generally speaking, they still come under the commercial classification of lace. They are made on machines similar to those that manufacture lace and this manufacture is governed by the same traditions that prevail throughout the entire lace industry in France today.

**FRENCH SERGE:** Very high type dress goods with a fine, lofty, springy feel. Superior to the average run of serge and one of the best cloths on the market. Warp may be singles or doubles and filling is usually single-ply worsted. Weight runs from 6 to 10 ounces per yard. Fabric is piece- or yarn-dyed. An ideal cloth for women's wear of the better sort. The yarn is cylindrical and has the best of tailoring qualities. The best of this cloth is imported from the noted textile centers of France—Arras, Lille, Roubaix, Rouen, Tourcoing, and Fontainebleau.

**FRENCH SPUN:** A soft worsted yarn, combed and spun in the French system, of short fibers. Widely used for sweaters.

**FRIARS CLOTH:** A coarse drapery fabric in a 2-2 or a 4-4 basket weave. A trade name for monk's cloth.

**FRIEZE:** Heavy woolen overcoating with a rough, fuzzy, frizzy face. Cloth is said to have originated in Friesland, Holland. Irish frieze has an established reputation. Cloth ranges from 22 to 30 or more ounces per yard. Much used in times of war as overcoating for soldiers. The grade and quality vary considerably. The average army frieze is made

of cheap stock, is stock-dyed, harsh and boardy in feel, has much flocks in it and is not any too serviceable. A composition of frieze could be 67% of three-eighths wool and 33% of shoddy and reworks. Much adulteration is given the cloth, hence the wide variance as to the quality.

Lightweight frieze is now made with a blend of spun rayon and wool. Double cloth constructions are used in the overcoating material, which gives fair to good service.

**FRIEZETTE:** A cotton fabric of lighter weight than standard frieze made of wool or wool wastes. The rib effect is the same as in frieze but the texture is not as wiry or harsh in feel. This converted fabric is piece-dyed in solid colors. The rib or rep effect is obtained by weaving alternately, one end of single or ply yarn under a regular tension, and one end of singles under a slack tension. Used for upholstery fabric. Gives good wear and comes in inviting colors.

**FRISE:** Sometimes called Cotton Frieze, the material is used in the upholstery trade. It usually has uncut loops and is sometimes styled by shearing the loops at varying heights. Some fabric of this name has appeared on the market with a rayon content in the fiber construction.

Frisé fabrics are usually woven double shuttle, single cloth, the top pick or filling end forming the loop. A wire gauge is used in each dent that runs parallel to the pile yarn. Frisé fabrics may also be woven double shuttle and double fabrics, but this gives a rib effect on the face of the cloth. Frisé fabrics are also woven on wire looms, where a round wire is thrown across the loom and the pile yarn loops over the wire. The wire forms the loop instead of a top filling end.

**F. T. C. RULES:** Rules drawn up by the Federal Trade Commission to interpret what industry must do to meet the regulations of specific federal legislation.

**FUGITIVE DYE:** A dye lacking durability to one or more of the various color destroying agents such as sunlight or washing. Often used for identification purposes because easily removed.

**FUJI:** A popular, silk-like fabric much used in women's blouses and men's sport

shirts. The smooth hand of the fabric is achieved by the use of fine, cylindrical filling yarns. Many versions of the fabric are now made in viscose and acetate.

**FULL-FASHIONED:** A term which describes a knitted fabric or garment made on a flat machine, with a shaped form achieved by adding or reducing the number of stitches at determined points.

**FULLING:** A process in the finishing of woolen cloth. The cloth is dampened and beaten under heat, which causes shrinking, increases the weight, and obscures the weave of the cloth.

**FUME FADING:** Some man-made materials, especially red, violet, blue or green dyed cellulose-derivative acetates, will react to gas fumes in the air by turning a reddish shade or hue. Found more in industrial areas where these fumes seem to prevail. May be counteracted by special resistant dyes and chemical compounds, and by frequent airings of the clothes closets. Incorrectly called, at times, gas fading.

**FUR FABRICS:** Large class of pile fabrics of spun-rayon or other fibers, imitating various furs by dyeing and special finishing. Fabric can be either woven or knitted. Any variations of basic weaves are used. The fabrics are used in popular-priced winter coatings and trimmings.

**FUR-LIKE FABRICS:** Pile fabrics made to imitate fur. The fur imitated should be named in selling. "Fur fabric" is an incorrect term (F.T.C. Ruling). See FAKE FURS.

**FUSE:** To melt with the application of heat. Nylon, orlon, dacron, and acetate are examples of thermoplastic fibers that will melt or fuse between 400° to 500° F., and therefore require lower temperatures when ironing or pressing.

**FUSED COLLARS:** Especially prepared interlinings, often made of acetate yarns, which are fused to the outer and inner lays of the collar after high temperature is applied. Collar tends to hold its shape. See TRUBENIZING.

**FUSED FABRIC:** Two layers of fabric which are bonded or fused together with a layer of cellulose by the application of heat.

**FUSED RIBBONS:** Acetate ribbon fabrics woven in wide width then cut into narrow strips with a hot knife which fuses the cut edges thereby eliminating need for selvages. Less expensive to weave than narrow goods.

**FUSTIAN:** The origin of this cloth is traced to the Egyptians and the Arabs. The walls that protected one of the Roman legions became the nucleus of the city of Cairo, Egypt. It was in the Fustat, or old Arab quarter of the city, that the cloth was supposed to have been first made. Cotton and linen were used in the fabric.

# G

**GABARDINE:** Construction is the same for wool as for cotton gabardine; a 45 or 63-degree twill. These weaves give the characteristic, single-diagonal lines noted on the face of the cloth. Material is piece-dyed and used in men's and women's wear. Combinations of yarn as to color and cast may be used, as in the case of covert cloth. In this event, the yarn should be skein-dyed. It is also possible to use the stock-dyed method. Because of the twist in the yarn and the texture, the cloth wears very well and outlasts similar materials used for the same purposes. Weight ranges from 8 to 14 ounces per yard, clear finish is given. Cotton yarn is often found as the warp structure in the cloth.

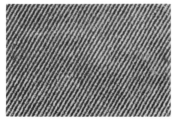
Gabardine weave.

Cotton gabardine is made with carded or combed yarn. The twill line is usually to the left if made with all single-ply yarn, and to the right when ply-warp and single-filling are used. The cloth may be mercerized, napped on the back, made water-repellent, preshrunk; usually bleached or dyed with sulphur or vat colors.

Uses include bathing trunks, raincoats, jackets, riding habit, uniform fabric, skirts, slacks, sportswear of many types.

Rayon gabardine simulates the cotton fabric and has about the same uses.

**GAGE:** See GAUGE.

**GALASHIELS:** 1. Popular Scotch tweeds made in and around this district in Scotland.

2. Scotch system for numbering woolen yarn. The standard is a cut of 300 yards, which weigh 24 ounces, so that the Number 1 yarn would have 300 yards of yarn to the pound. Also known as "gala."

**GALATEA:** Cotton fabric made with a small left-hand twill weave and occasionally with plain weave. It comes in white, plain colors, or stripes and is given a harsh, lustrous finish. This rugged material is used for nurses' uniform cloth, children's clothing, middy blouses, kindergarten fabric, and linings.

**GALLOON:** A narrow, ornamental fabric used to decorate uniforms. Often in the form of braid using metallic yarn.

**GAMSA:** A rather coarse rayon made in crepeback satin construction with twill weaves used as the base. Wears well and a good dress fabric.

**GARNETTING:** The process of recovering the fibers from hard-twisted thread wastes, rags, clippings, etc., esp. of wool. The object is to thoroughly break up the material and return it to a fluffy fibrous condition so it can be reused in blends, or in some cases alone. A garnett is used for the treatment.

**GAS FADING:** Signifies the effect of certain gases in the atmosphere which cause acetate goods that have been dyed shades of blue, violet, brown, and beige to take on a reddish shade. This condition can be overcome by the use of proper dyestuffs but, at times, at the cost of loss of light fastness, more difficult dyeing conditions, and restriction of shades. See FUME FADING.

**GASSING:** The process of burning off protruding fibers from cotton yarns and cloth by passing it over a flame or heated copper plates. This gives the fabric a smooth surface and is very necessary for fabrics to be printed and for fabrics where smooth finishes are desired. Same as singeing.

**GAUFRE:** Means puffed or waffled and is suggestive of honeycomb or waffle material that is in demand for women's summer dress goods of cotton and man-made yarns.

**GAUGE:** The gauge indicates fineness of texture in knit fabrics. It refers to the number of needles in a given width. For example, in full fashioned hosiery the number of needles per 1.5" represents the gauge; in circular knit hosiery it is the number of needles per 1". The higher the gauge-number the finer the texture of the fabric.

**GAUZE:** A sheer and usually light woven fabric made of silk, rayon, or cotton in which some of the warp ends are interlaced with each other—plain gauze, full gauze, or leno constructions. Some very sheer knitted fabric is called gauze. Rayon or silk gauze has a pronounced open, lacy effect which makes the fabric ideal for curtains.

**GEORGETTE CREPE:** The warp and filling arrangement in this silk material consists of two ends of right-hand twist and then two ends of left-hand twist yarn. Crepe weave used to enhance the pebbled effect. Harsher than crepe de chine and canton crepe. Comes in white, dyed, or printed.

Always a staple cloth. Desirable cloth to work with. Gives very good wear due to yarn twist and manner of construction. Lightweight cloth that is rugged. Has exceptional stiffness and body for a light cloth. See CREPE.

**GERMANTOWN:** A coarse, four-ply worsted knitting yarn with a slack twist. Term must not be used except to describe yarns which are made in Germantown, Pa.

**GHIORDES KNOT:** In Oriental rugs the ends of the hand-knotted pile alternate with every two threads of the warp. This produces fewer knots per inch than Senna knotting, which shows a complete loop formed by the yarn to give a pile effect from every space between the warp threads. Senna construction gives a denser, thicker, and evener pile effect on rugs than the Ghiordian knot.

(*Left*) The Ghiordes Knot. (*Right*) The Senna Knot.

**GIGGING:** The raising of nap on fabric by drawing it across rollers that contain teasels set in frames which extend the width of the machine. The bristles of the teasels "scratch-up" the surface fibers of the goods.

**GILLING:** One of the operations in the combing of fibers; gilling is an advanced form of carding which helps to separate the long, choice, desirable fibers of the same length from the remaining short, immature, or otherwise undesirable fibers. Only choice fibers may be gilled. The operation is comparable with a person combing his hair with the fine-mesh part of a comb. See FALLER, DRAWING.

**GIN:** The cotton gin was invented by Eli Whitney in 1793. It made possible the separation of cotton lint from the seeds by mechanical means.

**GINGHAM:** Cotton plain-weave material made with medium or fine yarn; comes in stripes, checks, and plaids; is yarn-dyed or printed. The weight is about 6 yards to the pound. Textures average about 64 x 66, but may vary considerably. Some ginghams are: chambray-gingham, nurses-gingham, Scotch, tissue, and zephyr.

The working properties show gingham to be strong, rather stout and substantial, in order to give good wear. Launders well. The thinner and lower textured gingham may shrink unless it has been pre-shrunk. Cloth varies from very cheap material to expensive fabric.

**GLASS:** A manufactured fiber in which the fiber-forming substance is glass.

**GLASS CURTAINS:** Sheer curtain fabrics which hang against a window pane.

**GLASS TOWELING:** A plain-weave linen cloth with highly twisted yarns arranged with red, blue, or some other color for the stripe or check effects noted in the material. Has no fuzziness or protruding fibers, launders well, and gives excellent service.

**GLAUBERS SALT:** The hydrated grade of sodium sulfate, a common assistant in dyeing.

**GLAZED CHINTZ:** Chintz and some tarlatan may be treated with glue, paraffin, shellac, or size and then run through a hot friction roller to produce a smooth, high luster. The method will not give good results, since washing will affect the chemicals used in dressing the cloth prior to roller treatment. Synthetic resins are now being used to make the glaze permanent.

The fabric is brightly colored, printed, or made with solid-color effects. Uses are for summer drapery fabric, pillows, covers.

**GLAZING:** Cotton fabrics such as chintz or tarlatan can be treated with starch, glue, paraffin or shellac, and run through a hot friction roller to give them a smooth high polish. Process is not durable to washing unless chemicals (such as synthetic resin) are baked in at high temperatures. See EVERGLAZE.

**GLEN CHECK:** A checked design similar to a shepherd's check. See CHECK.

**GLENGARRY:** 1. An English tweed cloth of the homespun and tweed group. Made from woolen yarns of the "hit-or-miss" type. This fabric often admits of the use of some so-called waste stock and low-quality fibers.

2. The Inverness or cape-overcoat.

3. A Scotch cap.

Houndstooth Glen Plaid weave.

**GLEN PLAID:** The trade interpretation shows that it is a four-and-four and a two-and-two color effect weave in both warp and filling directions. The fancy overplaid, seen in an overplaid, is missing in a glen plaid.

**GLEN URQUHART PLAID:** Woolen or worsted suiting or coating material made with the ever popular plaid or overplaid effect from two or more colors; most combinations are made of three colors at least.

**GLISSADE:** A polished satin-weave cloth made in England. Often used in cotton linings.

**GLORIA:** A very closely woven, lightweight fabric used for umbrella covering. Generally made with plain weave, but twills and satins are also used. Originally made with silk warp and fine worsted filling; also made with cotton filling, as well as all cotton.

**GLOVE SILK:** A finely knitted silk fabric made on a warp knit machine. Used mainly for gloves and underwear.

**GOBELIN TAPESTRY:** It is made by one of the greatest tapestry concerns in the world. Gobelin is known the world over and is a real institution in world culture. There are over 400 of these tapestries extant which have the old quality pattern and workmanship. Some of them are well worth over one hundred thousand dollars. Beauty in Gobelin is achieved by a clever medley of colors and skilled workmanship.

The Gobelin tapestry works was founded by Jehan Gobelin, a dyer from Rheims, and a member of a Flemish family that settled in Paris in the 15th Century. The Gobelin factory was taken over by the French government in 1662, and has been since then a national institution. The plant is located in Faubourg St. Marcel in Paris.

**GOSSAMER:** A very soft silk of the veiling variety with a pronounced gauze effect. Used for brides' veilings.

**GOTON:** Egyptian word for cotton.

**GOUT:** A fabric defect in which foreign matter such as lint or waste has been woven into the fabric by accident.

**GRAB TEST:** A method of determining the tensile strength of a fabric.

**GRAIN:** A unit of weight. 7,000 grains equal one pound. 437.5 grains equal one ounce.

**GRAM:** A metric unit of weight equal to 15.43 grains. One pound equals 453.6 grams.

**GRANADA:** From the Italian *granito* and the Latin *granum*. In English the term means "grained or grainy." The material is a fine, face-finished cloth, made of worsted stock. Often dyed black. Broken-up appearance of the weave tends to give fabric the regular granular effect noted when the cloth is examined.

**GRANITE:** An irregular, mottled, and pebbled effect in the weave produced by an irregular wide twill weave used. The weave is often used in cravat cloth.

**GRASS BLEACHING:** The bleaching of cotton or linen by spreading it on the grass and exposing it to light and air. This is a slower process than chemical bleaching. See BLEACHING.

**GRASS CLOTH:** A fabric woven from vegetable or bast fibers like jute, hemp, and ramie. The uneven texture of the weave makes it interesting as a wall decoration. Often referred to as China grass cloth because of its origins.

**GREASE WOOL:** Wool from the live sheep with yolk and suint intact.

**GRENADINE:** Curtain grenadine is a fine, loosely-woven material similar to marquisette. Is often mixed with cotton. Also, a fabric made on a jacquard loom. Uses include blouses, dresses, etc.

**GREX:** A system of numbering yarns based on the grams per 10,000 meters of yarn, or grains per 70 yards.

**GREY GOODS:** Also spelled gray, greige, griege. They are cloths, irrespective of color, that have been woven in a loom, but have received no dry or wet finishing operations. Grey goods are taken to the perch for the chalk-marking of all defects, no matter how small. These blemishes must be remedied in finishing of the cloth. Material is converted from the grey goods condition to the finished state.

Dry finishing operations may include: perching, measuring, burling, specking, mending, sewing, experienced sewing, shearing, napping, gigging, pressing,

Wet finishing operations may include: dyeing, printing, washing, fulling, milling, scouring, soaping, shrinking, crabbing, tentering, sponging, decating, London shrinking, waterproofing, mercerizing, gassing or singeing; beetling, chasing, schreinerizing, embossing, bleaching, sizing, calendering, friction calendering, Sanforized, etc.

**GRISAILLE:** French for "grey or greyish." Warp and filling have contrasting black and white threads that give greyish appearance to cloth.

**GROS DE LONDRES:** Lightweight silk or rayon dress goods with narrow and somewhat wider flat filling ribs alternating. The filling is the same size all over, only there are a larger number of picks in the wider ribs which are also covered with pairs of ends, while the narrow ribs are covered with the ends arranged alternately.

The cloth is piece-dyed or made in changeable or warp print effect. A glossy finish is applied to the goods, which are used for dresses and the millinery trade.

**GROSGRAIN:** A heavy, rather prominent ribbed silk cloth that is made from plain or rib weaves, according to various combinations. The cloth is rugged, durable, and of the formal type. Used in ribbons, vestments, in churches, and in ceremonials.

**GROUND:** The basic part of the fabric surrounding the figures or designs. In a pile fabric, it consists of the warp and the filling yarns which support the pile.

**GUANACO:** A species of wild llama from the Andes. Only the hair of the young animal, about 15 days old, is suitable for spinning.

**GUIPURE:** Large pattern in lace, held together by connecting threads called brides or bridges. The word itself derives from *guipe*, a cord around which silk is rolled.

**GUM ARABIC:** Used as a filling material in textile manufacture. It is tapped from the tree which grows in Africa and parts of Asia.

**GUNCLUB CHECKS:** Men's and women's wear dress goods used for street and sportswear. Three colors of yarn are used in making the cloth. The warp and filling make a natty combination in the cloth.

**GUNCOTTON:** A powerful explosive prepared by treating raw cotton with a mixture of nitric and sulphuric acids, or other strong acids.

# H

**HABUTAI:** Meaning soft and downy, this lightweight silk cloth, originally woven in the gum on Japanese hand looms, is now woven on power looms in the Orient. Heavier than so-called China silk, the cloth comes in the natural écru color and is used for dress goods, office coats and jackets.

**HACKLING:** A process by which flax is prepared for yarn.

**HAIRCLOTH:** Used for covers for upholstery, as interlining and stiffener. Material is made from any of the major textile fibers in the warp, while the filling is made from single horsehair stock. The width of the cloth is as wide as the length of the horsehair used in the filling.

**HAIR FIBERS:** Specialty fibers obtained from animals other than sheep. Sometimes used alone but generally blended with wool, rayon staple, or cotton and made into apparel fabrics, novelties, etc. The main one is mohair; others are alpaca, camel, cashmere, rabbit, etc.

**HAIRLINE:** Narrow striped color effect that resembles a hair. The use of stripings and fine, fancy lines sets off the wearer of the fabric by making him appear slightly taller than he or she actually is. Hairlines are usually worsted cloths and often come forth in great demand from season to season.

**HALF-BLOOD:** A theoretical American designation of wool compared in fineness with full-blooded merino wool as a standard; it is supposed to be between a ¾-blood wool and a ⅜-blood wool in classification. Half-blood is inferior in all respects to ¾-wool, but is superior to ⅜-wool.

**HAND-BLOCKED:** A hand-printing technique which uses wood, metal, or other types of blocks for the application of the design. British tie silks were formerly printed by this method. See PRINT.

**HAND, HANDLE:** The reaction of the sense of touch when fabrics are held in the hand. There are many factors which give character or individuality to a material observed through handling. A correct judgment may thus be made.

**HANDKERCHIEF LINEN:** Cambric or lawn serve best as handkerchief linen; comes plain or barred and may be in the white, dyed or printed. This plain-weave cloth is also used for dresses, infant's wear, lingerie, neckwear, table linen. See LINEN.

**HANDLE:** See HAND.

**HAND LOOM:** A weaving loom operated manually as compared to a machine-operated loom.

**HAND SPUN:** Yarns which are spun by hand, or fabrics made from such yarns. They are more interesting and more unusual than the absolutely even, smooth machine spinning.

**HAND WOVEN OR HAND LOOMED:** Fabrics which are woven on either the hand or hand-and-foot power loom. They are admired because they express the individuality of the wearer.

**HANK:** A length of yarn already reeled in the form of a skein. The term is also used to refer to the size of the roving.

**HARD FINISH:** The term usually refers to worsteds which have been sheared clean of all nap.

**HARE, OR JACKRABBIT:** One of the well-known animals in the United States, this rodent exists everywhere in the world except on the island of Madagascar. Its hair texture is wooly and of interest not only to the textile trade but also to hatters and furriers. The hare's clipped outer hairs when blended with wool before the fabric is spun give the finished goods an appearance of hairiness. When the fur fibers are used, the end fabric is soft to handle. The wooly texture of the hare's coat lends itself particularly well to felting. More than 50% of all fur fibers used in woolen clothing are selected from the hare, the angora goat, and the plain rabbit.

**HARGREAVES, JAMES:** From 1754 to 1768, Hargreaves perfected methods of spinning yarn. His spinning jenny was the first machine to spin more than one thread of yarn at a time. Tradition has it that the frame was named in honor of his wife. He came from Standhill, near Blackburn, England, and is supposed to have received the idea "from seeing a one-thread wheel, overturned on the floor, when both the wheel and the spindle continued to revolve." The spindle had thus been thrown from a horizontal position to an upright one, and, if a number of spindles were placed upright, and side by side, several threads could be spun at once.

The spinning jenny was a forerunner of the spinning mule, which was invented by Samuel Crompton in 1779 in England.

**HARNESS:** The frame upon which the heddles used in weaving cloth are placed.

Warp ends are drawn through the heddle eyes. Harnesses have an up-and-down movement in the loom which causes all the warp ends on the harness frames that are raised, to be up, and those that are lowered harnesses, to be down. This action causes the formation of the shed of the loom to make the weaving of cloth possible.

Harness frames are controlled in the machine so that, by their action, the designs in woven cloth are possible.

**HARRIS TWEED:** Under the terms of the British Board of Trade and the Federal Trade Commission, Harris Tweed refers only to woolen fabric hand-woven on the Islands of the Outer Hebrides off the Northern coast of Scotland. This includes among others the Islands of Harris and Lewis.

It has been ruled on several occasions by the Federal Trade Commission to be unfair trade practice to use the term Harris Tweed to describe fabrics not in accordance with the definition referred to. This eliminates the question of imitations inasmuch as there is only one Harris Tweed.

Harris Tweed trademark label is shown with Harris Tweed fabric.

This outstanding fabric is always hand-woven. There are two types of Harris Tweed:

1. Fabric woven from hand-spun yarn.

2. Fabric woven from machine-spun yarn.

Comparatively few of the tweeds are now woven from hand-spun yarn because to spin such yarn for a length of fabric sixty yards or more much time and labor is consumed. Today only in very rare circumstances will the crofters in the islands take the time to spin enough yarn by hand for weaving into the piece.

There are some Harris Tweeds made from machine-spun yarn and hand-spun filling. Harris Tweed made from hand-spun yarn is stamped to that effect in addition to the Harris Tweed Trade Mark. Harris Tweed is the registered trade mark of the Harris Tweed Association of London, which is a non-trading body set up under charter from the British Board of Trade to protect the article and to increase the appreciation of Harris Tweed throughout the world.

This activity is completely separate from the selling of Harris Tweed.

**HAWSER CORD YARN:** Heavy plied yarn, usually cotton, rayon, or nylon in which the plies are twisted in opposite directions.

**HEAD END:** In the textile trade this refers to a sample cut of new fabric which comes from the beginning or head of a new piece in the loom.

**HEALD:** See HEDDLE.

**HEATHCOAT, JOHN:** An Englishman who invented the bobbinet lace-making machine in 1808.

**HEATHER MIXTURE:** Named for the Scotch heather, it is a blend yarn used in the knitting trade, and in home-spun and tweed fabrics. Stock-dyed, basic-colored slivers, slubbings, and rovings are drawn, drafted, doubled, redoubled, and finally spun into a yarn which will show the shade of the color or colors which predominated in the original blending, oiling, and mixing of the stock. Used in suiting, top coating, some overcoating, cap cloth, mufflers, golf hose, socks, stockings, knitting yarns.

**HEAT SETTING:** Certain chemical fibers, when woven into fabric, can be treated with pressure under certain heats so that a crease or pleat will remain permanent through many washings and dry cleanings. This process is now also available in natural fibers when they are treated with chemicals.

**HEDDLE:** Also spelled heald, the English term. The warp ends are drawn through their respective heddle eyes according to the plan or motif in drawing in these ends. Heddles keep the warp ends under control in a uniform manner. The top and the bottom loops of the heddles fit onto the respective bars of the harness frames. Heddles are made of fine, pressed-steel wire, cord, or iron, dependent on the type of cloth to be woven.

**HEER:** A unit of measure which equals 600 yards. It is used in reckoning jute and linen.

**HELANCA:** Brandname for stretch nylon yarn which has the power to stretch as much as five times its length. Micro-photographs of the yarn show the nylon expanded into a string of soft filaments that curl in all directions. Pulled tight, it condenses into a strong solid line. Relaxed, it returns to its curls. The process uses two yarns, one highly twisted to the right and one to the left. Combined, one counterbalances the twisting tendency of the other. Any size filament yarn can be used. The first adaptation of this yarn was in France and Switzerland for use in men's socks and in gloves, which are now available in this country. Helanca is a product of Heberlein and Company of Switzerland.

**HEMP:** This is found in the Philippines, Spain, Italy, Russia, Poland, and India. Russia produces more than all the other nations combined. The best quality comes from Italy. Hemp is grown in this country in the states of Kentucky, Illinois, Missouri, Indiana, and California. In recent years Wisconsin has begun raising the fiber and excellent results have been obtained due to the mineral matter in the soil.

The fiber is difficult to bleach, a serious drawback to its progress. Like jute, the fiber comes from just inside the outer bark of the plant, which grows from six to ten feet high. Hemp is stronger than jute and withstands water better than any other textile fiber. Uses of hemp are ropes, twines, cables, and rugs.

**HENEQUIN AND SISAL:** These closely related plants are found in Mexico, chiefly in Yucatan. Fibers are obtained from the leaves, and henequin far outstrips sisal in the Mexican belt with regard to production and use. Sisal, however, is raised in British East Africa and in the Dutch Indies; it comes from the same family group as the century plant and belongs to the agave species.

Henequin and sisal are rather easily obtained from the plant and both are ideal in the manufacture of rope. Salt water, however, will quickly destroy the fiber, thereby limiting its use for maritime purposes. Binder twine, small diameter rope, and some hard-fiber twine are other uses of these two fibers. The binder twine is a favorite with workers in the grain fields since it is ideal for bundling and tying.

**HENNA:** An orange-brown textile dyestuff derived from the Oriental shrub of that name.

**HENRIETTA:** Dress goods that vary somewhat in detail. Some of the woolen or worsted material is like cashmere cloth, other cloth is of the salt-and-pepper type. One of the popular cloths of years ago and not much in use in recent years. Cloth comes in the white state or may be piece-dyed. Used in children's clothing. Weight ranges from seven to fourteen ounces.

**HERCULON:** The olefin fiber produced by Hercules as continuous multi-filament, bulked continuous multifilament, staple and tow.

**HERRINGBONE:** Used for suitings, topcoatings, overcoatings, sport coats, dress goods in men's and women's wear. The cloth gives a weave effect in fabrics that resembles the vertebral structure of the fish known as herring. The cloths are staples and always in demand. All herringbones are broken-twill weaves but all broken-twill weaves are not herringbones. The latter should balance perfectly to be called a herringbone and not a broken twill. Many types of stock, color, and weaves are used in making the cloth.

**HESSIAN:** Used for sacking purposes, it is a rough, coarse material made from the major bast fibers, alone or in combination.

**HICKORY CLOTH:** Resembles ticking somewhat, but of lighter weight and not so firm a weave. Much used as institution fabric and for work clothes.

**HIGH-BULK YARN:** Generic name for a fluffy yarn, first made from Orlon acrylic fiber, made from a combination of high and low shrinkage staple fiber.

When the combined yarn is immersed in boiling water during processing, the shrinkable fiber draws itself down to the center of the yarn causing the low shrinkage yarn to buckle or fluff up, thus producing a fluffy yarn, ideally suited for sweaters.

**HIGH-TENACITY YARNS:** These yarns have been developed for purposes where fabrics of extra strength are required: for example, tackle twill and similar specially durable fabrics required for military purposes, drapery and tire cord.

**HIGH-WET MODULUS:** The quality in a fiber which gives that fiber excellent stability in washing. It was first developed in high-performance rayon.

**HIMALAYA:** A type of cotton shantung cloth, with irregular slub formations in the filling.

**HOLLAND:** Usually a low-count cotton print cloth or high-count cheesecloth, heavily sized and glazed. Occasionally, sheeting constructions are used. Also known as shade cloth.

Holland comes in many muslin constructions; it is dyed, stretched, calendered, filled with the desired sizing, dried, wetted, and then given a second calendering to produce the smooth, brilliant finish. It may be further treated with starch, oil, or pyroxylin.

**HOLLAND FINISH:** A finish consisting of sizing and oil applied to cotton or linen to make it opaque and stiff.

**HOMESPUN:** Originally an undyed woolen cloth spun into yarn and woven in the home with the rather crude machinery used by the peasants and country folk the world over. The industry came to the fore in the British Isles and then spread to the Continent. Owing to the substantial appearance and serviceable qualities, homespun is imitated to a great extent on power looms today. Genuine homespun cloth supply is very limited, and much power-loom cloth is sold as genuine homespun. The term is much abused and the gullible buying public often is fooled when buying the cloth as some particular quality. The cloth should always be made on a plain weave. Coarse, rugged yarn is used and quality varies much. The material is coarse, rugged, and an ideal rough-and-ready type of cloth. All types and kinds of stock from the highest to the lowest go into the cloth in its wide range.

**HOMESPUNS AND TWEEDS:** Tweed is the Scotch word for twill. Tweeds are closely allied to homespuns. They should be made from a 2-up and 2-down twill weave of 45 degrees. Homespuns and tweeds can be used to show readily the difference between the plain weave and the twill weave. In tweeds, several variations of twill weaves are often used—broken twills, straight twill weave, color effects, pointed twills, twilled baskets, fancy entwining twills, braided twills, diamond weaves, ice-cream effects and combinations of these weaves taken in a group. Much variation of design and color is noted in the cloth. Some of the more prominent tweeds that have won their place in the trade are: Scotch, English, Irish, Bannockburn, Donegal, Kenmare, Linton, O'Brien, Selkirk, Cornish, Harris, Lincoln, Cheviot, Manx, etc.

There are certain cloths sold as homespuns which in reality are tweeds, and vice versa. Consequently, in the trade, it can be seen that each cloth may be made with either weave, plain or some twill, and be accepted by the public under the name given to it. Homespuns, when used as tweeds, have the heaviest weight of the cloths in question. It has the average characteristics—yarn, feel, finish, twist, body. From this it may be gleaned that in the trade today the heavy homespun is classed as a tweed. Disregarding the trade and looking at the problem from the mill and manufacturing angles, the following may prove of interest: the homespun must be made from plain weave, the tweed from a twill weave. After the cloth leaves the mill it may be called tweed or homespun to suit the whims of the public.

In many of the outlying districts of the world today both cloths are hand-loomed and the industry is on a firm footing. Many of our Southern states make quite a little of the cloth. Asheville homespuns from the Carolinas and other nearby sections are sold in the best stores in the large cities and bring high prices here and abroad. They have color backgrounds, tradition, sentiment, history, a psychological appeal and, best of all, are correctly advertised to catch the eye of the person financially situated who can afford to pay the rather high prices of these fabrics.

**HONAN:** 1. Silk pongee cloth made from wild silkworms raised in the Honan area in China. The fabric is noted for its uniformity of color, since the worms are the only wild type that give even dyeing results.

2. Also the name for a linen-textured rayon fabric which shows small checked-effects, squares or oblongs made by the flattened or wider yarns used in the material. These yarns, used in both the warp and the filling, set off the effect by contrast in diameter size with the regulation yarn used in the motif. Usually dyed a single color, the fabric finds considerable use in summer dress goods in the women's wear field.

**HONEYCOMB:** A raised effect noted on cloth made of worsted yarn. Material is used as dress goods and suiting cloth. The appearance of the fabric resembles the cellular comb of the honey bee. The material is often called "waffle cloth," in the cotton trade. The high point on the one side of the cloth is the low point on the other side.

Printed cotton honeycomb or waffle cloth weave.

Cotton honeycomb or waffle cloth is used for draperies, jackets, skirts, women's and children's dresses, and coats. Rather popular fabric.

**HONITON:** A type of English bobbin lace first made in the town of that name. Honiton lace usually has flower motifs.

**HOOKE, ROBERT:** English naturalist and scientist, who discussed in his book "Micrographia" (1664) the possibilities of making an artificial yarn by mechanical means . . . the forerunners of man-made fibers of today.

**HOPPER:** That part of a textile machine from which the stock is fed into the mechanism.

**HOPSACKING:** While the real hopsacking is a coarse plainly-woven undyed stuff made of jute or hemp fiber, otherwise known commercially as burlap and serving among the hop growers as well as general merchandise shippers as bagging, the name has been applied to a class of staple woolen apparel cloths in basket weaves which resemble the original hopsacking.

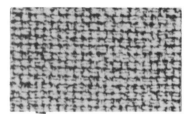

Hopsacking weave.

Cotton hopsacking is used for dresses and coatings, printed decorative fabrics, and hangings.

**HORSEHAIR:** Russia sponsors the industry. The body hair of the horse is more lustrous than cow hair. The length is from 1 cm. to 2 cm., while mane and tail stock ranges from a few inches to several feet. It is used for stuffing in upholstery and summer horsehair hats, as a shape retainer in lapels of coats, and as "filler-in" stock.

**HOUND'S TOOTH CHECK:** A medium-sized broken check often used in tweeds, clear-finish worsteds, etc. A staple in the woolen trade.

**HOWE, ELIAS:** He invented the sewing machine in 1846.

**HUCK, HUCKABACK:** This linen cloth has a honeycomb effect; the filling yarns are slackly twisted to aid absorption. Material is heavy. This toweling often has the name of a hotel, school, etc., woven through the center for recognition and to establish ownership. In white or colors.

Very absorbent, durable, serviceable for towels, and will withstand rough use. Cotton huck has a rough surface and may come bleached or with a yarn-dyed striped border to simulate genuine huck.

**HUNTER'S PINK:** Brilliant scarlet velvet cloth worn by hunters. Also name for that color used on any fabric.

**HYDROPHILIC FIBER:** The word, "hydrophilic," means water-favoring. Thus a hydrophilic fiber has a high water absorption and is moisture sensitive. Taken from the Greek, "hydro" meaning water and "philic" meaning to favor or to like. Examples of textile fibers in this category include rayon,

11%; acetate, 6.5%; cotton, 7%; worsted, 10%; wool, 15% to 16%. These absorptive powers of the fibers are given at normal condition.

**HYDROPHOBIC FIBER:** The derivation of the word, "hydrophobic," is from the Greek, "hydro" meaning water and "phobos" meaning fear. Literally the interpretation means "water fearing" or "water hating." Thus, the hydrophobic fiber is one that is relatively non-water absorptive and moisture insensitive. The amount of water that any fiber in this category will absorb under normal conditions ranges from zero to 4.5%. Examples include Dynel and Saran at zero, nylon at 4.5% of water absorption.

**HYDROSCOPIC or MOISTURE-RETAINING PROPERTY:** The ability of a fiber to absorb and retain moisture. Fibers possess this property in varying degrees.

**HYDROSTATIC TEST:** Method of ascertaining water repellent properties of a fabric.

**I**

**ICELAND WOOL:** Wool from sheep raised in Iceland. The outer hair is coarse; the underhair is fine and is used for sweaters.

**IMPERIAL:** Italian brocade embellished with gold and silver threads worked into the motif. This type of silk fabric was mentioned by Marco Polo in the 13th Century.

**IMPERIAL COATING:** A worsted fabric woven with 2-up, 2-down twill weave from fine Botany worsted yarns. The construction is about square and the threads are closely set, giving a firm, durable cloth but of a somewhat hard handle. Usually dyed navy blue and showerproofed.

**IMPREGNATED FABRIC:** A fabric whose interstices in the yarn have been completely filled with chemical compound usually to make the cloth water-repellent. Sometimes yarns are impregnated before they are woven into cloth but this method is not included in the definition. In a sized or a coated fabric the interstices in the yarn are incom-

pletely filled with the compound. See COATED FABRIC, WATER-REPELLENCY, and WATER RESISTANCE.

**INDANTHRENE DYE:** See DYES.

**INDIA LAWN:** Also known as Indian linen at times, has been made in India for over 4,000 years. Fabrics of this name are seen in museums and are noted for their particularly fine yarn counts, evenness of weaving, and zephyr weight.

**INDIAN BLANKET:** All wool, or woolen filling blankets woven with characteristic Indian designs. The term should apply only to blankets actually hand-made by the Indians, and such blankets should be so-marked. The genuine Indian hand-made blanket is more of a rug than a blanket. Today most Indian blankets are power loom woven.

**INDIAN COTTON:** See COTTON.

**INDIAN HEAD:** Trade name of one of the oldest cottons woven in America. It was first used in 1831 by Nashua Manufacturing Co.

**INDIA PRINT:** Cotton printed with a characteristic native pattern, usually hand blocked in glowing oriental colors. Most often sold as squares, runners, and bedspreads.

**INDIA SILK:** Hand-loomed plain-weave fabric that is very thin in texture and soft in feel. Made chiefly in India.

**INDIGO DYEING:** A type of blue textile dye originally made from the indigo plant but now duplicated by chemical means. It is usually associated with denim. See DYES.

**INDUSTRIAL FABRICS:** As differentiated from consumer textiles, these are textile products which are commonly used in the various manufacturing industries for factory purposes. Prominent in this group are such textile products as machine beltings, straps, pads and similar types of fabrics or yarns, both manmade and natural.

**INSERTION:** A decorative fabric trimming such as lace, embroidery or braid inserted and sewn between two cut edges of fabric as in a blouse, dress or skirt.

**INTERLINING FABRIC:** 1. A lightweight, napped, cotton, wool, or other

fabric used in tailoring for extra weight or warmth.

2. Firm stiff linen canvas for men's coats.

**INTERLOCK:** A cotton knit made on a machine with alternate units of long and short needles which produce a variety of colors and patterns in a closely knit fabric.

**INTIMATE BLEND:** A fabric in which exact proportions of different fibers by weight are intimately blended together at the starting point of the textile process—before spinning.

**IRIDESCENT:** In silk weaving the term implies a color effect made by the use of warp ends and filling picks of varying tints or hues. Properly, iridescent effects will show alternating or intermingling colors, and the term refers to any colors which seem to change when rays of light fall onto the fabric, without reference to what the colors are.

**IRISH LINEN:** A generally fine, lightweight linen woven in Ireland of Irish flax. The very best is still often woven by hand. Used for handkerchiefs, and collars. See LINENS.

**IRISH POINT:** Appliqué curtain lace, the pattern being joined to net.

**IRISH POPLIN:** The fabric originally had a silk warp and a wool filling, was first made in China and later duplicated in Ireland. Another meaning of the term is fine linen or cotton shirting made in Ireland. This type of fabric was also used for men's neckwear.

**IRISH TWEED:** Characteristically this type of tweed has a white warp and colored filling.

**ISOVYL:** See POLYVINYL CHLORIDE FIBERS.

**ISTLE, IXTLE:** Also called Tampico or Mexican fiber; little attention has been given to raising it. This yellow fiber is hard, rugged, and exceptionally stiff. Finds use in brushes and twine, and in low-grade sacks.

**ITALIAN CLOTH:** Twilled or smooth, glossy-faced cloth made of cotton and worsted. Used as garment linings. Also known as Farmer's Satin.

**IXTLE:** See ISTLE.

# J

**JACKRABBIT:** See HARE.

**JACONET:** Is a thin cotton fabric somewhat heavier than cambric; the face of the material is given a glazing treatment to produce high luster. East Indian in origin, the French developed the material by making stripe and check motifs.

**JACQUARD:** A celebrated method invented by Joseph-Marie Jacquard of Lyons, France, at the beginning of the 19th Century, and so named for producing elaborate cloth weaves in the loom by the substitution of perforated strips of cardboard punched according to intricate design for the ordinary and restricted number of heddle frames and pattern chains. These perforations, in connection with rods and cords, regulate the raising of stationary warp thread mechanisms. The jacquard motion revolutionized the weaving industry and while of limited importance in the fabrication of men's wear, it plays a very prominent part in modern tapestry, brocade, brocatelle, damask, and figured dress-goods production.

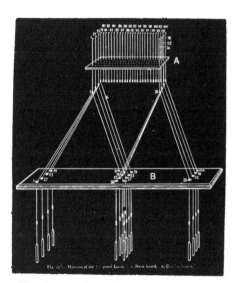

The Jacquard mechanism is essentially a hook-and-needle harness which makes fancy weaving possible. The reproduction is a simplified drawing of a Jacquard loom harness with neckboard and comber A and B.

Jacquard patterns are found in all the major textile fiber fabrics. Cotton and linen jacquard designs are much used in table cloths and napkins.

**JANUS CLOTH:** A worsted fabric with two faces, each a different color.

**JASPE:** A durable cotton cloth made with a narrow woven stripe on a dobby loom with multi-colored threads or with different shades of the same color. Has a shadow effect. Sometimes printed versions are shown on the market. Often small dots are woven into the fabric. Used for draperies and slip covers.

**JEAN:** Three-harness warp-faced twills of lightweight sheeting yarns. One warp thread goes over two or more filling threads, then under, moving one pick higher for each return filling thread. Sometimes made in chevron or herringbone versions.

Some cloth of this name is made of cotton warp and low-grade wool or shoddy filling. Often dyed some shade of grey and used for work clothes.

**JERSEY CLOTH:** Woven or knitted, popular at times, and always a staple material. Woven jersey, made of silk, is made into men's shirtings. Much of the cloth is made in woven trade for dress goods and often called jersey cloth.

Knitted jersey is plain or ribbed. Made in cotton, wool, rayon, nylon, and silk. Uses, dependent on the type of yarn used, include dress fabric, shirting, underwear, sportswear. Jersey is serviceable, drapes well, but may slip or sag.

**JET:** The spinneret used in making synthetic fibers.

**JETSPUN:** A trademark for the solution-dyed continuous filament rayon yarns made by American Enka Corp.

**JIG:** This machine is used to dye piece goods. Full-width material is passed from a roller through the dye bath in an open vat and then proceeds to another roller. The treatment is repeated until the desired shade is assured.

Jig-dyeing piece goods.

**JIG DYEING:** See DYEING METHODS.

Toile de Jouy.

**JUNGLE CLOTH:** Trade name for the strong, heavy but compactly woven cotton cloths made for the U.S. Navy. Woven with about 300 picks to the inch, the fabric gives good results in wind-swept, frigid areas.

**JOUY, TOILES DE:** The famous printed cottons made by Oberkampf at Jouy, France, about 1760. The design motifs were usually floral and approximated the feeling of woven Oriental brocades.

**JOUY PRINT:** See PRINT.

**JUTE:** This bast fiber comes from the species known as *Corchorous capsulcris*. Bengal and other parts of India, southern Asia, and tropical Africa are the centers where the fiber is raised. Bengal is the world market center. The plant grows from two to twelve feet in height and the fiber layer is quite thick. The stalk produces two to five times as much fiber as the flax plant.

The plants are rippled and retted like flax. Stream retting is the most popular treatment and it takes from three to four days to complete it. Scutching and hackling treatments are also given to the fiber.

Jute spins well and is a cheap fiber. The great disadvantage to the fiber is that water and moisture disintegrate it. When dry, jute is durable. The fiber is not very strong and much difficulty is encountered in bleaching it.

# K

**KAPOK:** Found in Borneo, Java, Sumatra, and Central America, it resembles cotton in some respects and seems to have the characteristics of silk in feel and smoothness. Kapok has been called the cotton-silk fiber despite the fact that, unlike cotton and silk, it is irregular, weak, transparent, and inconsistent. It is used for pillows, mattresses, and in upholstering furniture.

**KAPRON:** The Soviet equivalent of nylon.

**KARAKUL:** Originally an Asiatic breed of sheep, the long carpet wool obtained from the fleece has made it a favorite in Texas. Lambs of the breed, one to three days old, are skinned and called astrakhan or broadtail. Shrinkage is about 35%. The name comes from the village of Kara Kul (Black Lake) in eastern Bokhara. See CARACUL.

**KASHA CLOTH:** 1. Fabric made from the hair fibers of the Tibet goat. Very soft in feel, and napped with a slight crosswise streaked effect in the darker hairs used in the cloth. Rodier Freres, Paris, introduced the fabric several years ago. Ideal for dresses, jackets, etc.

2. A tan-colored cotton lining flannel.

3. A cotton flannel with napped face and mottled color effect bordering on tan or écru; an unbleached soft-filled sheeting.

Mixed yarns may be used with sized warp yarns that take the dye and filling yarns with natural wax that do not take the dye. When bale-dyed, the result is always mottled.

**KAY, JOHN:** English inventor of the fly shuttle for use on a loom (1738).

**KAY, ROBERT:** Son of John Kay. He invented the dropbox loom (1760).

**KEEL:** A red ochre pigment, sometimes called Indian Red, which is used in marking sheep or to mark the end of a cloth warp.

**KENAF:** A five-foot fiber is obtained from the bark of this bast fiber plant. Runs from light yellow to grey in cast and is used chiefly for cordage and twines. Sources are Africa and India. Other names used are Ambari, Da, Bimlipatam, Deccan hemp.

**KENDAL GREEN:** Name given to coarse, woolen cloth originally made by the weavers of Kendal, England. This material is noted for its distinctive green shade and is a favorite color in high-quality homespuns.

**KERATIN:** A protein substance which is the chief component of the wool fiber.

**KERMES:** Brilliant scarlet dyestuff obtained in ancient times from the oak tree insect, *Quercus coccifera*. Now replaced by cochineal, also derived from insects.

**KERSEY:** Originated in Kersey, near Hadleigh, Suffolk County, England. Present-day kersey is heavily fulled or milled, and has a rather lustrous nap and a grain face. Luster is caused by the use of luster cross-bred wools such as Lincoln, Leicester, Cotswold, Romney Marsh, etc. In southern areas of the United States there is a low-priced kersey that is a union fabric with much reused or remanufactured wool in it.

Face-finish weaves are used to make the goods so that the ultimate finish will be acceptable to the trade. When compared with beaver, kersey is often fulled more, has a shorter nap, much higher luster.

Kersey is finished like beaver and the only difference in the two fabrics seems to be the quality of the raw stocks used, the latter ranging in grade from a low, through medium, to a rather good grade of $\frac{3}{8}$-blood or $\frac{1}{2}$-blood wool.

The material gives good wear and is of the dressy, conventional type of fabric. Blues, browns, and blacks are the colors used the most. Other colors are only seasonal.

**KERSEYMERE:** A fancy woolen fabric of cassimere type. The name would tend to indicate that such fabric was a product of the mills along the waterways of Kersey, England. As there are no meres or lakes in the vicinity of this town it is more probable that the term is simply a variation of "cassimere."

**KETTLE:** A machine for dyeing piece goods in the rope form.

**KHAKI:** From Hindu, meaning dusty. Cloth is made in cotton, wool, worsted, and linen, and with combinations of these fibers. Cloth first gained prominence when it was taken as the standard color for uniform cloths of the British army in all parts of the Empire. Since then other nations have adopted the color. It is an ideal shade for field service. Fabric has limited use in civilian dress. Some trousering and riding breeches are made with that color.

**KIER BLEACH:** See BLEACHING.

**KIER BOILING:** A scouring operation performed on cotton or linen to remove wax, oil, and other foreign matter. The kier is loaded with cloth, then the chemicals are pumped through the cloth, sometimes boiling under pressure.

**KIMONO SILK:** This kimono and lining material is a soft, plain-woven, lightweight silk which is usually printed in elaborate designs.

**KIN:** This equals 1.32 pounds, and 756 kin approximate 1,000 pounds. The kin is used in quotations for raw silk . . . "yen per kin."

**KINKY FILLING:** A fabric defect with short thick places running filling-wise in which small loops in the filling are spaced at irregular intervals. The filling yarn may be looped and twisted.

**KNITTED ASTRAKHAN:** Today is in demand and much cheaper than the woven article. The cloth, as a substitute, is found in the fur trade for coatings and is popular in winter wear. People who cannot afford real Astrakhan buy the woven or knitted cloth of that name.

**KNITTING:** The process of making fabric by interlocking series of loops of one or more yarns. Originally done by hand, now turned out by machine in mass production. Hand knitting is done either on straight or round needles by slipping stitches from one needle to the other, each change making one stitch.

The eight basic knitting stitches are as follows:

JERSEY FLAT—The basic knitting stitch from the jersey flat bed machine which produces full-fashioned sweaters, pullover shirts and related items.
JERSEY CIRCULAR—The fastest method of weft knitting, producing underwear, seamless hosiery and other high-volume items.
RIB FLAT—A knitting system capable of stitch-transfer and widening-out, which makes the production of collars, cuffs

and trim possible.

RIB CIRCULAR—A very popular stitch most closely associated with the double-knit fabric which is widely used in dresses, sportswear, men's tailored wear and many other garments.

PURL FLAT—The links-links stitch, commonly used for making pullovers and cardigans.

PURL CIRCULAR—The high-volume purl stitch, used in cut and sewn sweaters, dresswear and men's socks.

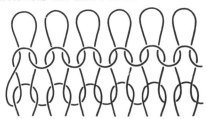

TRICOT—A high-volume, warp-knit system producing fine vertical wales on the face and crosswise ribs on the back, predominant in intimate wear.

RASCHEL—A warp-knit machine which can stitch or lay in yarn, producing open, lacy, rigid and stretch fabrics. Popular in dresswear, powernet, thermal underwear, laces, netting and carpeting.

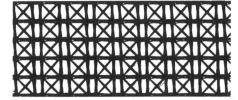

MILANESE KNIT—Type of warp knitting with several sets of yarns, knit diagonal effect. Highly run-resistant.

**KNOTTED LACE:** An approximation of old hand-made lace made by modern methods.

**KNOTTER:** A device for tying knots automatically in yarn making process.

**KODAPAK:** See CELLOPHANE.

**KODEL:** A registered Eastman trademark, and a product of the Tennessee Eastman Company. This polyester fiber is different from other fibers in this category both in chemical composition and in the internal molecular structure of the fiber. It is spun to fine counts of yarn on the cotton, woolen, or worsted systems of spinning. Properties show outstanding resistance to pilling, high resistance to heat, high crease-retention and wrinkle-resistance, excellent dimen-

sional stability even without heat setting or other special processing. This naturally white fiber has a low specific gravity of 1.22.

**KUZUMAYU:** Term used in Japanese sericulture to designate waste cocoons.

# L

**LACE:** Open-work fabric consisting of a network of threads formed into a design. Made by hand with bobbins, needles or hooks. Also done by machinery. Used for trimming on lingerie, dresses; also for entire garments, curtains and table cloths. The word "lace" is of Latin origin, meaning a noose.

ALENCON LACE—Delicate and durable lace with a solid design outlined with cord on sheer net ground.

ALL-OVER LACE—A fabric up to 36 inches wide with the pattern repeated over the entire surface.

ALOE LACE—Fragile lace made from Aloe plant fibers in the Philippines and Italy.

ANTIQUE LACE—Hand-made bobbin lace of heavy thread with large, often irregular, square knotted net on which designs are darned.

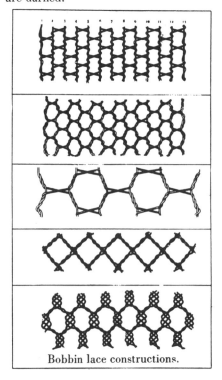

Bobbin lace constructions.

BATTENBURG LACE—A coarser form of Renaissance lace, made by hand or machine, of linen braid or tape and linen thread brought together to form various designs. Used for collars, cuffs. Machine-made for draperies.

BINCHE LACE—Flemish bobbin lace having a scroll floral pattern and a six pointed star ground sprinkled with figures like snowflakes. Used for dresses, blouses, lingerie.

BRETON LACE—Net which has designs embroidered with heavy, often colored, thread.

CHANTILLY LACE—Bobbin lace with fine ground and designs outlined by cordonnet of thick, silky threads, used for trimmings on bridal veils. Originally made in silk, now made of rayon, nylon or mercerized cotton.

CLUNY LACE—A rather heavy bobbin lace identified by a paddle wheel and/or a bat wing design. May also have a poinsettia. Used for doilies, scarfs, collars.

DRESDEN POINT LACE—Type of drawnwork with ground of fine linen with some threads drawn, and others embroidered and interlaced to form square mesh.

IRISH LACE—A variety of laces made in Ireland. The best known are crochet, net embroideries of Limerick and Carrickmacross.

LILLE LACE—Fine bobbin lace with patterns outlined with flat cordonnet. Sometimes dotted.

MALINES—One of the oldest and best known of lace, net and silk fabrics; diaphanous in nature and named for the Belgian city.

MILAN LACE—Originally made in Milan. Tape lace with needlepoint mesh and picot edging. Easily imitated by machine, but machine-made must be so described.

NEEDLEPOINT LACE—Lace made entirely with a sewing needle rather than with a bobbin. Worked with buttonhole and blanket stitches on paper pattern.

NOTTINGHAM LACE—Flat lace originally made in Nottingham, England. Now used as name for lace made anywhere on Nottingham-type machine.

RATINÉ LACE—Machine-made lace with groundwork of heavy loops similar to turkish toweling.

RENAISSANCE LACE—Woven tape motifs joined by a variety of flat stitches.

ROSE POINT LACE—Venetian needlepoint lace which has a delicate and full design of flowers, foliage and scrolls connected by string cordonnet.

SPANISH LACE—Any lace made in Spain. The most common is of silk with heavy flat floral designs held together with varying meshes.

TATTING LACE—Knotted lace worked with the fingers and a shuttle. Made in various designs, the most popular being the clover leaf and wheel.

TORCHON LACE—Sometimes called beggar's lace. Characterized by a shell design. Used on children's dresses, scarfs, doilies.

VAL LACE—See VALENCIENNES LACE below.

VALENCIENNES LACE—Flat bobbin lace worked in one piece with the same thread forming both the ground and the design. Ground is 1. round (lozenge shaped) called round mesh Val, once called German Val; 2. diamond shaped often called French Val. French Val originated in Valenciennes, France. Real Valenciennes lace is made of linen. The imitation of cotton and commonly called Val. The imitation must be so described.

VENETIAN LACE—A needlepoint lace decorated with floral motifs and designs connected with irregularly placed picot edges called brides.

**LACE EFFECT:** Refers to novelty fabrics of cotton, rayon, nylon or silk. Woven either in a leno pattern or in a heavy machine embroidery on a thin ground.

**LACQUER FINISH:** A chemical treatment which produces a thin film on the surface of cloth; may be applied in a design. Not durable against dry cleaning unless so stated.

**LACTOFIL:** A Dutch fiber in which milk casein has been mixed with latex and glue.

**LAID FABRIC:** Cloth which has no filling yarn in its construction. The warp ends are laid parallel and set into a binding material which holds the warp ends in place. Laid fabric yarn is treated and will rest on the cloth upon which it has been laid.

**LAKE:** Usually referred to as a color lake. It means the insoluble combination of a dyestuff with a mordant which has been fixed on the fiber.

**LAME:** Any textile fabric in which metallic threads are used in the warp or the filling for decorative purposes. Lamé fabrics are used chiefly in evening wear. From French *laminer*, "to flatten."

**LAMB'S WOOL:** Wool shorn from lambs up to seven months old. Soft and possessing superior spinning properties when compared with wool from older animals. Lamb's wool has a natural tip which is lost after the first or virgin clip.

**LAMINATED FABRIC:** Two or more layers of fabric which have been fused together by the use of an adhesive.

**LAMPAS:** A fabric made of two warps and one or more fillers. This type of fabric always works with the warp of the same color, so you can have a definite two-tone fabric or multicolored fabric where each flower has its own color combination with the same color in the warp.

A lampas of crimson satin. Woven at Lyons, France, about 1780-90.

**LAMP WICKING:** Wicks for lamps are made by using a flat or tubular fabric composed of coarse, soft spun, loosely twisted cotton yarn.

**LAMS:** The horizontal bars or levers which extend between the harnesses and treadles to which they are attached by cords or chains. Lams allow the harnesses to be pulled directly down from the center, although the pedal to which they are attached may be far to the right or to the left of the exact center. This, incidentally, makes for a clear, clean shed.

**LANOLIN:** A complex chemical substance, fatty in nature and chiefly a mixture of cholesterol esters obtained from grease wool. It serves as an emollient for the skin of the sheep and for its fleece.

Purified sheep grease under the name of lanolin or lanoline serves as the basis for grease paints, ointments, salves, skin creams.

**LANSDOWN:** Dress goods made of a three-leaf twill. Silk or rayon warp and worsted filling used. Light in weight and not very popular.

**LAP:** The roll of wound fiber in the early stages of processing.

**LAPPET EFFECTS:** These are obtained by the use of one or more needle bars fitted with "depending needles" which carry a series of floating threads in front of the reed. The action is such that the pattern is woven or "laid" on the surface of the woven goods. Chains of various lengths are used to determine the width and character of the motif to be woven in.

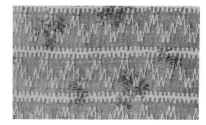

Lappet weave, made by use of an extra warp in construction.

The needle bar or bars is raised, moved to the right, and then to the left, and then lowered into position, which means that the pattern warp ends are threaded through the needles in a line with the

(*Top*) Lappet weave with unclipped floats. (*Bottom*) Lappet weave clipped.

shed of the loom. The needles are raised and kept stationary until the chain indicates and activates the needle bar for the next effect to be woven into the fabric.

**LAPPING:** The backing or cushion cloth used on printing rollers. Usually wool.

**LASTEX:** Lastex yarns combine rubber with cotton, wool, silk, or rayon yarns to produce a permanently elastic yarn that is used for a variety of purposes. Latex composes the rubber core, and any of the textile yarns may be wound around it, forming a filament whose surface is fully vulcanized.

Lastex yarn may be used as warp or filling; the woven fabric stretches in the direction of the lastex yarn. If used for both warp and filling, it is stretchable in both directions. Product of United States Rubber Company.

**LATEX:** The raw material from which rubber is made.

**LAUNDER-OMETER:** The standard laboratory device for testing a fabric's colorfastness to washing.

**LAUNDER-PROOF:** Fabrics and garments which have been laboratory-tested to withstand laundering without losing color or shrinking under normal washing conditions and length of time. This term can only be applied to fabrics which have been so tested.

**LAY:** The combination of various parts of a loom in action.

**LAWN:** Fine, sheer, crisp finish cotton or linen cloth made of plain weave. Lawn

is crisper than voile but not as crisp as organdy. High-grade, high counts of yarn used. Comes in white, dyed, or printed, and is made of combed or carded yarns.

Crisp finish is often temporary; durable, but must be starched to bring back crispness. Lawn is given a great variety of finishes. It is easy to manipulate.

**LEA:** 1. A unit of length (300 yd.) used to determine the number of linen yarn.

**LEASE:** The same as the cross in the warp. Keeps the warp ends under control at all times.

**LEASE PEGS:** The pegs on a warping frame between which the lease or cross is made.

**LEASE RODS:** The wooden or glass rods or bars used to hold the "cross of the threads" in place while the loom is being set-up and threaded. The lease rods are set in the loom when the piece is to be woven and they are set between the whip roll and the harness frames.

**LEAVERS, JOHN:** In 1813 he invented a lace-making machine whose basic principles and design are still used today.

**LEE, WILLIAM:** English minister who invented the knitting frame. For a time the frame could knit only woolen yarn. In 1598 he invented a frame for knitting silk stockings.

**LEFT-HAND TWIST:** Also known as the Z twist. Refers to yarn twisted from right to left.

(*Top*) Left-hand twill fabric. (*Bottom*) 2 x 2 left-hand twill interlacing.

**LEFT-HAND TWILL:** A twill or diagonal weave whose lines run from upper left to lower right on the face of the goods.

**LEGHORN STRAW:** See Straw.

**LEICESTER WOOLS:** In this group are also Lincoln, Cotswold, Romney Marsh, and Cheviot wools, spoken of as Long British and Long Crossbreeds and now raised throughout the world. The rams weigh from 235 to 300 pounds, ewes from 175 to 250 pounds. Fleece weight is from 7 to 16 pounds. The fiber length ranges from 4 to 16 inches, while the fiber diameter is from $\frac{1}{700}$ inch to $\frac{1}{950}$ inch; there are from 800 to 1,000 serrations per inch in the fibers. Numbered at 40s to 44s.

These hardy luster wools, which have the tendency to reflect light rays, are used in homespun, tweeds, cheviot, and shetland fabrics for outerwear.

**LENGTH OF CLOTH:** See Bolt.

**LENO:** A weave in which the warp yarns are arranged in pairs so as to twist one around the other between picks of filling yarn, as in marquisette. This manner of weaving gives firmness and strength to an open-weave cloth and prevents slipping and displacement of warp and filling yarns.

Leno weave with heavy yarns.

**LEVANTINE:** A stout twilled silk, each side finished the same but of different colors.

**LEVEL DYEING:** The dyeing of cloth to produce uniformity of color with no streaks or shaded areas.

**LIBERTY PRINTS:** The famous hand-blocked designs, usually on silk, produced by the firm of Liberty Ltd., London.

**LIBERTY SATIN:** A popular seven, eight, or ten-shaft satin cloth of raw silk warp and single, spun silk filling. It is named for the Liberty Co.

**LICKER-IN:** A toothed roller which slowly feeds the fiber stock to the main cylinder on a carding frame.

**LIGNE, LINE:** A unit of measurement used in button-making. The word originally was derived from the French but actually it refers to the "line" division on a micrometer. Each such line is .025 inches. For example, a 40-ligne button would be 40 times .025 inches, or one inch in diameter.

**LIGHT FAST:** Colors which will not fade with normal exposure to sunlight. No color is entirely fast to light, but some are more resistant than others.

**LILLE LACE:** A bobbin lace made on net ground in hexagonal or square form so that it is easily distinguished from Mechlin or Valenciennes which it otherwise resembles. See LACE.

**LINCOLN SHEEP:** Possessing the longest staple of any wool grown, this popular long-wool breed originated in Lincoln County, England. Probably the world's largest rams are Lincolns; they weigh from 300 to 375 pounds. Rich, well-watered pastures are essential for these sheep, which are much used in cross-breeding. Fleece weighs from 12 to 16 pounds.

Lincoln belongs in the luster wool group along with Leicester, Cotswold, Romney Marsh, and Cheviot.

**LINE:** Longest flax fibers. The shortest ones are called "tow."

**LINEN:** Strong lustrous yarn or fabric of smooth-surfaced flax fibers. Can be either plain weave or a damask weave for table linens. Used for wearing apparel, household articles, fancy work.

ART LINEN: Plain-woven linen, unbleached, écru, or white. Used for embroidery. Also for dresses, uniforms, table linens. Sometimes called embroidery linen.

BANDLE LINEN: Coarse Irish linen, handmade in strips about two feet wide. So called because bandle is the Irish measure of two feet.

BOOK LINEN: Firm linen with sizing to make it stiff. Used as stiffening for collars and belts, and for book binding.

BUTCHER LINEN: Type of plain woven crash, originally used for butchers' aprons, jackets. All-rayon fabric erroneously called by this name.

DIAPER LINEN: Fine figured linen fabric woven with a small diamond pattern. Used for toweling, fancy work, children's dresses. Also called diamond linen.

HANDKERCHIEF LINEN: Sheer, fine linen in plain weave.

IRISH LINEN: Fine, lightweight linen made in Ireland; often still made by hand. Used for handkerchiefs, collars.

SPUN LINEN: The finest hand-woven linen, used for handkerchiefs, neckwear.

**LINEN CAMBRIC:** Cloth may be sheer or coarse; of plain weave. Known also as handkerchief linen. Used also for dress goods.

If fairly good quality is used, fabric will give excellent wear and service. Material is sized and gives neat appearance after laundering.

Cotton cambric is made from print-cloth or lightweight sheeting construction. It is given special sizing treatment and a calender finish.

**LINEN CANVAS:** There are several fabrics in this category:

1. Open-mesh canvas is used for embroidery; made of hard-twisted yarn, the cloth is very durable; the most popular cloth in this group is known as Java canvas.

2. Close-woven canvas is made from hard-twisted yarn in plain-weave construction; comes in various weights, and finishes range from the heavily-sized varieties to soft effects.

**LINEN MESH:** Open-mesh fabric. Extremely strong and washes very easily. Used for children's clothes, men's shirts.

**LINEN TESTER:** Same as Pick Counter or Pick Glass. A magnifying glass for counting yarns and examining weaves.

**LINEN-TEXTURED RAYON:** A large and important category of rayon fabrics having the distinctive textures of linens. These range from sheer hand-kerchief-linen texture to heavier, rougher "butcher-linen" texture. Usually plain weave. Used in lighter weight for handkerchiefs, women's and children's dresses, tablecloths, towels, sheets, pillowcases; heavier weights for summer coats, suits, sportswear.

**LINGERIE CREPE:** See CREPE.

**LINKS-AND-LINKS:** A type of knitting which produces purl stitches.

**LINOLEUM:** This floor covering is made from a burlap base. Oxidized linseed is mixed with ground cork and other pigments to give the composition which is rolled over the base. Linoleum comes in plain, printed, or inlaid patterns. Plain linoleum has a single color face; the printed type has colored designs; inlaid has colored motifs which penetrate through to the burlap base.

**LINSEY:** Term used in rag sorting. Implies wool stock, yarn, or cloth that has vegetable matter in it, except in the case of carpets, dress goods, and flannels.

**LINSEY-WOOLSEY:** Cloth made of linen and woolen yarn. Cotton may be used instead of linen. Either stock is always the warp. Animal fibers always are the filling. Cloth is of loose structure, coarse, and often highly colored. It originated in England and was much in use in the Colonies at one time. It is more or less obsolete now. A little of the cloth finds use by the rural folk in outlying districts.

**LINT:** 1. A good, workable fiber used to make yarn. In this sense, it is the staple cotton fiber which will withstand machine treatment.

2. Fly that floats around mill rooms during the manipulation of stock. Another use of the term signifies the minute fibers that cling to clothing, especially blue garments.

3. The waste from the cotton ginning process. This amounts to about one-third.

Lint should not be confused with linters.

**LINT BLADE:** A blade which removes lint and other impurities from the printing rollers. Usually made of soft brass.

**LINTERS:** Short cotton fibers which adhere to the seed after the first ginning. These are cut from the seed and used as a source of cellulose for the manufacture of rayon and acetate.

**LINTON TWEED:** A distinctive range of tweed fabrics used for summer and winter coatings and for women's ensembles, is a product of Linton Tweeds, Ltd., Carlisle, England. Made for a great many years, the fabric weight runs from 8 to 18 ounces per yard with most of the cloth averaging 12 to 14 ounces. It is known for extreme softness, wide variance in design, and an appealing hand.

**LISLE:** Usually refers to a knitted fabric or garment made of lisle yarn. This is a two-ply cotton yarn of fine quality which has been mercerized and singed to give it a smooth, lustrous surface. The word is taken from the city of Lille (formerly Lisle), France.

**LLAMA:** The members of the llama family include four distinct types and two hybrid types. The distinct types are, llama, alpaca, guanaco or huanaco, and vicuna; the hybrids are huarizo, the offspring from a llama father and an alpaca mother, and paco-llama or misti, the offspring from an alpaca father and a llama mother.

Llamas are raised in Bolivia, Peru, Southern Ecuador and Northwestern Argentina. Lake Titicaca, 125 miles long and 75 miles wide, which forms a part of boundary between Bolivia and Peru, is center of llamaland.

The animal, which weighs about 250 pounds and is about one-third the size of a camel, has a natural habitat around 12,000 feet; hence, llamas are found in the Andes Mountains of the aforementioned countries. The life span of the animal is 10 to 14 years. The animal is not found north of the equator.

Full fleece-bearing capacity of the llama is not obtained until the animal is more than four years old. The fleece, obtained every two years, weighs about 5 pounds; the staple length ranges from 6 to 12 inches.

**LOADING:** Increasing the weight of fabrics by addition of various substances during finishing.

**LODEN CLOTH:** This fabric originated in Austria in the 16th Century. The peasants who first made the cloth in this mountainous district, called Loderers, loomed the material from the rough and oily wool of the mountain sheep of the area. Some camel hair, at times, is blended with the better quality fabric of this name. The fabric is a thick, fulled, soft material and is quite waterproof without being treated chemically. It is an ideal cloth for use in winter wear garments such as sports clothes, fingertip or full-length coatings throughout the world. A feature of the garment is that it is usually made in double-breasted coating to allow for free and easy movement despite the bulk of the goods used to make the garment.

**LOFT:** A term used to describe the springiness of wool as it resumes its normal position after it has been squeezed.

**LOGWOOD:** Natural dyestuffs. Also name for a reddish brown color, usually used in connection with fur.

**LONDON-SHRUNK:** The shrinkage of cloth by the cold water method which removes mill finish in order to prevent shrinkage. Cloth in the London-shrunk condition is ready for the cutting-up trade.

**LONGCLOTH:** Also known as fine-plain. A plain-weave cotton cloth, closely woven, high in pick count, fine-quality fabric. The weight is between a print cloth and lawn. Generally made of fine, high-quality combed yarns, and with more threads to the square inch than percale.

**LONG-STAPLE:** Refers to cotton fibers whose length is 1⅛ inches or over.

**LOOM:** The machine by which warp and filling threads are woven together. The basic principles of the loom are the same now as they were in prehistoric times.

**LOOM-FINISHED, LOOM-STATE:** Fabric which is used in exactly the state it comes off the loom, without any further finishing operation.

**LOOP YARN:** A slack twisted strand forming loops. This strand is held in place by binder yarn or yarns.

**LORETTE:** A brand name used by Deering, Milliken & Co. It is a blend of 55% Orlon and 45% wool; a dress-goods fabric.

**LOUISINE:** A soft, silk fabric woven to produce a small basket effect.

**LOVAT:** Was named after Lord Lovat in Scotland. It is reported that he preferred greyed-down hues; these gave his name to such tones, especially greens.

**LUMARITH:** The Celanese acetate process produces this plastic—a transparent sheeting pliable enough to wrap a powder puff but rigid enough for shaping into a lunch box. It will not stretch or shrink, and is dust-proof and resistant to moisture. Product of Celanese Corporation.

**LUMEN:** A longitudinal canal or cavity in vegetable fibers such as cotton.

**LUREX:** A metallic yarn of plastic-coated aluminum made for use in lamé fabrics. The yarn is composed of an aluminum base fiber sandwiched between two plies of specially formulated plastic film. Special processing and adhesives make the yarn impervious to tarnish, and also much lighter than ordinary metallic yarns. Lurex is used in evening wear fabrics, curtain drops, millinery, and fabrics for pageantry. Product of Dow Badische Company.

**LUSTER CLOTH:** Lining material which is made with cotton warp and mohair filling. Synthetic fibers sometimes replace the cotton, and other hair fibers replace the mohair.

**LUSTERING:** A finishing process; making luster on yarns or cloth by heat and pressure.

**LUSTER WOOL:** A group of wools which have a natural gloss. The five basic groups originated in England. They are: Lincoln, Leicester, Romney Marsh, Cotswold, and Cheviot.

**LUSTRON:** A polystyrene plastic, very light in weight, produced by Monsanto Chemical Co.

**LYCRA:** The elastic fiber made by Du Pont, used in undergarments, foundation wear, ski pants, athletic garments, bathing suits and similar apparel.

**LYONS LACE:** A lace of the malines order characterized by outlining of the design in silk or mercerized cotton.

**LYONS VELVET:** See VELVET.

**MAARAD:** An Egyptian cotton grown from American Pima cotton seeds.

**MACCLESFIELD TIE SILK:** This high-texture, hand-woven tie silk is characterized by a small all-over pattern. Ties made of this fabric give splendid wear.

**MACINTOSH:** An early waterproof coating fabric named after Charles Mac-Intosh, who developed it in 1823. It was basically a laminated cloth using crude rubber and coal-tar naphtha as the adhesive.

**MACKINAC OR MACKINAW CLOTH:** An extra-heavy cloth used in cold climates. Used as blankets, shirts, mackinacs, reefer cloth, underwear, and lumberjackets. An ordinary grade of wool is used and varying amounts of shoddy and wastes find their way to this cloth. Much of the cloth is in plaid design. The material is given a severe treatment in wet finishing and it is napped on both sides, the weave being covered up because of the rigid treatment. Cotton yarn is often used as warp. Filling is softly spun yarn so as to insure results wanted in finishing operations. The weight of the material ranges from 14 to 28 ounces or so per yard. Miners, lumbermen, hunters, fishermen, trappers, and cow-punchers use much of the fabric.

**MACRAME LACE:** One of the oldest types of lace, distinguished by knotting. Applied mainly to household purposes.

**MADDER:** A red dyestuff derived from the Asiatic plant *Rubia tinctorum.* It has been largely replaced by Alizarine but the old name is still used to describe printed fabrics with a soft bloom which use Alizarine and mordant in the dyeing process.

**MADRAS:** Originated in Madras, India. It is a plain cotton weave, usually in strongly colored plaids, stripes, and checks.

**MALABAR:** A brilliantly colored, inexpensive cotton handkerchief cloth which originated in the East Indies.

**MALINES:** Is one of the oldest and best known of lace, net, and silk fabrics diaphanous in nature, and named for this city of Belgium.

**MALINES LACE:** See LACE.

**MANILA HEMP:** Grown chiefly in the Philippine Islands, it belongs to the banana family and grows to the size of a small tree. The fiber is obtained from leaf stalks which form on the trunk of the tree. When compared with sisal, the fiber has greater diameter, is not so stiff, and is stronger. Russian hemp is the strongest; Italian is the finest in diameter. Abaca is another name for this type.

**MANIPULATED CLOTH:** While manipulated woolen and worsted cloths are not literally a hand process of preparing and combining as the term implies, they are cloths in which the yarns are part wool and part cotton. The yarn is usually made from homogeneous combinations of fibers in the carding and spinning operations. Cloths that have a small percentage of cotton in them are often spoken of, in the trade, as "commercial all-wool fabrics."

**MAN-MADE FIBERS:** An inclusive term for all textile fibers not provided by nature.

**MANX TWEED:** Tweed made on the Isle of Man.

**MARBLE SILK:** Silk material which has a mottled appearance caused by the use of multi-colored filling yarn or by warp printing prior to weaving of the cloth. This lightweight dress fabric is popular from time to time.

**MARCO POLO SHEEP:** A high-type species of the genus, this wild sheep, *Ovis poli,* comes from the Pamir Plateau and other Central Asia sheep-raising areas. The animal is large in stature and has considerable horn-spread.

**MAROCAIN:** A crepe fabric of major fibers, featured by a ribbed effect. It is used for suits of dressmaker type.

**MARQUISETTE:** Made on leno or doup weave; gauze fabric. It is light in weight. Comes in white, solid colors and novelty effects, used for curtains and dress fabrics. Made with cotton, rayon, silk, nylon, or glass fibers.

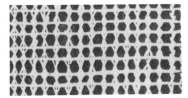

Marquisette weave.

Gives good service for a loosely-woven material; launders well. Better qualities are made of choice cotton.

**MARSEILLES:** Cotton vesting cloth made in plain and fancy designs, in plain and colored effects. Named after city in France.

**MARVELLA OR MARVELLO:** Women's wear coating cloth of high quality. It is a high-luster, pile fabric that weighs from 20 to 30 ounces per yard. Warp is usually worsted, and filling mohair and silk, although other combinations are used, dependent on the quality of cloth wanted. The material is made in the finishing; piece-dyed cloth.

**MARVESS:** The olefin fiber made by Phillips Fibers Corporation in staple, tow and filament yarn.

**MAT, MATT WEAVE:** Another name for basket or hopsack weave.

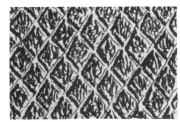

Matelassé weave.

**MATELASSE:** Figured fabric made on dobby or jacquard looms. The patterns stand out and give a "pouch" or "quilted" effect to the goods. Comes in colors and in novelty effects. Made in cotton, rayon, silk, or wool, the cloth will give good wear, drape well, but must be laundered with utmost care. Matelassé garments are very attractive and when in vogue are much in demand. Some cotton fabric used for bedspreads.

Matelassé means padded or cushioned in French, and is of Arabian derivation, meaning bed. As used in textile weaves, matelassé produces a raised effect by interlacings of the yarn which show a quilted surface on the fabric. Some of the fabric may have tinsel threads worked into the pattern.

**MATELASSE CREPE:** See CREPE.

**MATT FIBRO:** The dull type of viscose rayon staple fiber produced by Courtaulds, Ltd.

**MATTRESS DUCK:** Implies single-filling flat duck.

**MAZAMET:** Name given to a type of French melton. It is the name of the city in France where the largest wool pullery in the world is located.

**MECHLIN LACE:** The most supple of all laces. the close portions of the pattern being more filmy than Valenciennes.

**MEDIUM WOOLS:** 1. Those wools which average in length between long and short wools. Short wool ranges from 1 to 6 inches; long wool is from 6 to 12 or more inches in staple length.

2. Sometimes refers to the general quality of wool and includes wool that is high ¼-blood, ⅜-blood, and low ½-blood wool. Medium wools grade between 50s and 58s in quality.

**MEDULLA:** The central portion of an organ or tissue; e.g., the central part of a wool fiber.

**MELAMINE RESINS:** Made by reacting melamine with formaldehyde; the resulting product and some of its derivatives may be used for textile finishes to provide shrinkage control, wrinkle-resistance, crispness, soil-resistance, etc.

**MELANGE:** From French meaning "mixture." Hence a cloth that shows a mixture effect. Also used to imply printed slubbings or top of worsted stock, and the name is given to the cloth produced therefrom.

**MELROSE:** Double-twill cloth of silk and wool, named for Melrose on the Tweed River in Scotland.

**MELTON:** Originated in Mowbray, the long-popular hunting resort in England, known the world over. Originally a hunting cloth, melton is now classed with kersey, beaver, and broadcloth. Melton does not have a so-called "laid-nap." It is dull and non-lustrous and comes in many qualities, dependent on the grade of wool used.

Melton may be finished in the following manner; soaping with good quality soap, fulling for three to four hours; scouring is done with a medium consistency good grade of soap and alkali until well cleansed; hot and cold rinses are then applied, followed by carbonizing, neutralizing, washing, steaming, drying, and then shearing with three runs on the face of the goods. Steam brushing is an optional operation. There is no raising in a true melton.

The fabric is used for overcoating, uniform cloth, pea jackets, regal livery, and metropolitan cloth for the police and fire departments. The rigid construction of the fabric affords excellent wear, since

the finishing treatments cover up all interlacings of the warp and filling, thereby making a genuinely "solid" cloth.

**MELTONETTE:** Women's wear cloth of very light weight melton.

**MERCERIZING:** Named after its originator, John Mercer, this finish is extensively used for treating cotton yarns and cotton goods to increase luster and improve strength and dye affinity. The treatment consists of impregnating the fabric with cold concentrated sodium hydroxide solution. Best results are obtained on combed goods, the process being most widely used for knitted fabrics.

**MERCILINE:** A closely woven, thin, diaphanous silk fabric. See MARCELINE.

**MERINO:** (The Spanish word *merino* signified roving from pasture to pasture, said of sheep; probably from the Latin, *major*, greater.) The very fine quality of wool of the so-called merino sheep of Spanish origin. Hence a cloth of such material. The term "merino" is now applied also to knitted woolen fabrics, notably undergarments constructed of yarns with an admixture of cotton to prevent shrinkage in laundering.

**MERINOVA:** This casein fiber produced by Snia Viscosa Company of Italy has replaced the old-time Lanital casein fiber made in Italy up to the end of World War II.

**MERINO WOOL:** The highest, finest and best type of wool obtainable. The best wool in the world comes from Botany Bay and Port Philip areas of Australia. This merino stock is used for worsted cloths of the better grade. Merino wool is listed as a Class One wool, and 85% of all Australian wool is merino. Other world centers for the fleeces are Ohio, Austria, Saxony in Germany, France, Argentina, Spain, and the Union of South Africa.

**MERINO YARN:** This term has two meanings. In the woven trade it is the best yarn made. In the knitted trade the term implies the best grade used for woolen and worsted knitting. There is, however, the understanding that it may contain shoddy, mungo, cotton, re-used wool, re-manufactured wool, etc.

The yarn is comparable with a good ⅜-blood stock. Some knitted fabrics, as a general rule, do not require stock any

better than this quality when their uses are considered.

**MERVEILLEUX:** An all-silk or all-rayon, or silk and cotton mixture cloth made on a twill weave. Used as lining in men's outer apparel.

**MESH FABRICS:** Any fabric, knitted or woven, with an open mesh texture. Can be either silk, wool, cotton, linen, synthetic or combination. Fiber content must be declared.

**MESSALINE:** Named for Messalina, the wife of the Emperor Claudius, it is a 5-shaft satin-weave silk fabric which is lustrous, soft, and dressy. Two-thread organzine and three-thread tram are used in making the goods, which are usually skein-dyed. Most messaline comes in solid shades.

**METALLIC CLOTH:** Any fabric, usually silk, that has gold, silver, tinsel, or other metal threads interspersed throughout the design in the cloth. Lamé is a metallic fabric.

**METALIZED DYES:** A class of acid dyes which have a metal-complex in their molecules and which provide outstanding fastness properties.

**METALLIC FIBER:** A special fiber composed of metal, plastic-coated metal, metal-coated plastic, or a core completely covered by metal.

**MIDDY TWILL:** Twill-weave cotton cloth in which right- or left-hand twill is used. In the white, it is called middy-cloth; in colors, it is called jean cloth. Used for uniform cloth, children's wear. Very durable; easy to manipulate; launders well; gives good service and withstands wear. Cloth is mercerized or plain.

**MIGNONETTE, TRICOLETTE:** Knitted rayon or silk materials made on circular machines. Very elastic, has some porosity, comes in white, flesh, pink, and other colors. Underwear and dress cloth. Mignonette is of finer mesh and gauge.

**MIGRATION:** The movement of dye from one place to another in a newly dyed material.

**MILANESE:** A type of warp-knitted material made in silk or rayon, characterized by a distinctive diagonal cross effect. Used in glove fabric and women's underwear.

**MILANESE KNIT:** See KNITTING.

**MILAN POINT:** Heavy plaited lace with patterns usually of flowing scrolls and flowers. See LACE.

**MILAN STRAW:** See STRAW.

**MILDEW-RESISTANT:** Textiles treated to resist mildew and mold are usually processed with chlorinated phenols, mercurials, and metallic soap.

**MILIUM:** Trademark of Deering, Milliken & Co., Inc., for metal-insulated fabrics. Practically any fabric of natural or man-made fibers, or blends of these, can be metal-insulated, using as a radiant heat barrier aluminum or similar metal flakes in a resin base. These porous, metal-insulated fabrics allow the body to breathe freely, provide insulation against cold, and prevent the loss of body heat. In summer, they reflect the sun's rays, thus keeping the wearer cooler.

**MILKWEED:** A common plant whose fiber is also known as vegetable silk. Sometimes used in pillows and mattresses.

**MILL ENDS:** Remnants or short lengths of finished fabric.

**MILL FINISHED COTTON GOODS:** Yarn dyed cotton fabrics that are finished fabrics when they leave the mill.

**MINERAL DYES:** Colors produced on cotton by the precipitation of colored mineral compounds on the fiber. Most have excellent fastness properties but with very limited shade range.

**MINERAL FIBERS:** Fibers obtained from minerals in the earth, such as asbestos.

**MISTRAL:** On the order of etamine, it is made with nubbed, uneven yarn to give a wavy effect in the cloth, and comes from the French term for strong northwest wind.

**MIXED FABRICS:** Fabrics composed of two or more kinds of fibers.

**MOCK LENO:** A fabric which approximates the openwork leno construction without its weaving complications. Usually found in the form of stripes.

**MOCK SEAM:** Hose knitted in tubular form but seamed up the back to imitate seam in full-fashioned stocking. Mock fashion marks are often put on the back to make the imitation better.

**MODACRYLIC:** A manufactured fiber in which the fiber-forming substance is any long chain synthetic polymer composed of less than 85% but at least 35% by weight of acrylonitrile units ($-CH_2-CH-$).
$\qquad$ CN

**MODIFIED STAPLE FIBER:** Rayon staple or spun yarns treated to give them wool-like characteristics, such as a rough surface.

**MOGADOR:** Originally a cravat fabric made of silk but now a prime favorite when made with rayon. The cloth resembles a fine faille; plain weave is used. Mogador is used in neckties and sportswear.

**MOHAIR:** (From the Arabic *mukhayyar*, a goat's hair fabric.) Called in medieval times "mockaire." A glossy lining cloth in both plain weave and twills, in dyed or natural colors, made from the hair of the angora goat of Asia Minor. It is made of domestic fibers, also of other stock.

**MOIRE:** Cloth which has the desirable wavy or water-marked effect in the finished fabric. Taffeta and many lightweight and sheer fabrics of various fibers are given this watermarked finish.

**MOIRE TAFFETA:** See TAFFETA.

**MOISTURE CONTENT:** The amount of moisture found in a textile fabric expressed as a percentage of the original weight as determined by testing. Under normal conditions dry fabrics absorb moisture—cotton cloths normally regaining 6% of their dry weight, woolen 16%, worsted 10% and silk 11%.

**MOISTURE REGAIN, COMMERCIAL:** An arbitrary figure formally adopted as the regain to be used in calculating the commercial or legal weight of shipments or deliveries of any specific textile material.

**MOISTURE REGAIN, STANDARD:** The amount of moisture contained by a textile when conditioned or brought into equilibrium in a standard atmosphere. The equilibrium is to be approached from a state of lower regain.

**MOLESKIN CLOTH:** A one-warp, two-filling rugged cotton fabric in which there is a two-and-one face-filling arrangement—two picks of face filling to one pick of back filling. Made in satin

construction, the cloth is given a thick, soft nap on the back to simulate mole fur. Used for coat linings, semi-dress trousers, and work clothes.

**MOLLETON:** French for melton. Name also given to silence cloth in cotton goods trade. The fabric is heavily felted and napped on both sides; used as a protecting cloth under the tablecloth to absorb the rattling of dishes and to protect the finish on the table.

**MOMIE CLOTH:** A crinkled, lusterless black fabric made with cotton warp and wool filling. Used chiefly as mourning fabric.

**MOMIE WEAVE:** An irregular weave of small repeat; a granite weave is another name for this weave.

**MOMMIE:** A Japanese unit of weight used in silk production. One mommie is .13228 of an ounce. There are 120.96 mommie to the pound. The word is also used in referring to an irregular weave as well as to fabric which imitates Japanese mommie silk cloth.

**MONASTERY WOOL:** Soon after the Roman army withdrew from England, evangelizing monks erected monasteries and abbeys and ultimately became the great shepherds of England. In 1270, the abbey at Meaux had over 11,000 sheep and, in 1309, the abbey at Crowland owned over 9,000 sheep. For nearly one thousand years English abbeys supplied both the domestic and foreign markets with wool. They raised large flocks of sheep in Scotland, Ireland, Wales, and Spain, as well. From the 6th to the 16th Century, the principal raw wool producers in these countries were the monasteries. Their wool was superior in quality to that raised anywhere else in the world.

**MONK'S CLOTH:** Made of coarse cotton or linen yarns. A 4-and-4 basket or some similar basket construction is used. Hangings, couch covers, and furniture material are uses of the cloth. Not easy to sew or manipulate; yarns have a tendency to slide. Cloth may sag. It is a rough, substantial fabric.

**MONOFILAMENT:** When the viscose solution is forced through only one minute hole in a spinneret, a single filament yarn of unlimited length and resembling horsehair may be produced. The yarn is called a monofilament.

**MONTAGNAC:** One of the highest type overcoatings available. Classed as woolen fabric that is heavily fulled. Curls are seen on face of cloth. Material is piece-dyed and ranges from 20 to 36 ounces in weight per yard. Twill weaves resorted to in constructing cloth. Genuine Montagnacs have varying amounts of cashmere in them. This fiber adds greatly to the appearance and smooth feel and enhances the beauty of the fabric. The smooth, silken-like feel is one of the main assets of the material.

The cloth, when wet, loses much of the curl on the surface and this takes out, to a degree, the splendid, appealing finish. The fabric is expensive. A trademark of E. de Montagnac et Fils, France.

**MORDANT:** Any substance which, by combining with a dyestuff to form an insoluble compound or lake, serves to produce a fixed color in a textile fiber, leather, etc. Most mordants are metallic salts, although some are acidic in nature, such as tannic acid.

The formation of a mordant, for example, could be as follows: Tannic acid is soluble in water; tartar emetic is also soluble in water; however, they combine to form an insoluble mordant.

**MOREEN:** Another derivation of the verb, *moirer.* Mohair, silk, cotton, rayon, and acetate fabrics are sometimes sold under this name when the watermark has been applied to poplin-type fabrics.

**MOSCOW:** Overcoating of the shaggy, napped type, heavy in weight. Cloth gives warmth and somewhat resembles shetland cloth. Name is given because of the fact that the cloth is in favor in Soviet Russia as well as in other cold sections of the world, where it is used for winter wear. There are many types and grades of the cloth, ranging from very low quality to high, expensive materials.

**MOSQUITO NETTING:** Used for screening and netting, it is a heavily sized, plain or barred cotton or nylon cloth which is referred to in terms of meshes to-the-inch, such as 12, 18, 36, etc. The more meshes, the better the fabric. It can be bleached or dyed.

**MOSSY CREPE:** See Crepe.

**MOTES:** 1. Impurities in cotton consisting of tiny specks of seed or other fragments of the cotton plant.

2. Black spots in yarn or cloth due to presence of these impurities.

**MOTH REPELLENCY:** Chemical treatment of wool to make it resistant to moth attack. Various processes differ in their resistance to laundering.

**MOURNING CREPE:** See Crepe.

**MOUSSELINE:** Taken from *mousseline de soie,* meaning "silk muslin." Originally made in silk and now made in rayon. Firmer than chiffon, stiffer than rayon voile. A sheer, crisp, formal fabric. Plain weave. Used for evening wear, collars, cuffs, trimmings.

**MOUSSELINE DE LAINE:** "Wool muslin" in French. This dress goods cloth is of plain weave, light in weight, and made of worsted. Cloth is often printed, and qualities vary according to composition, which is often stock other than straight worsted warp and filling.

**MOUSSELINE DE SOIE:** Silk or rayon muslin on the order of chiffon with a crisp, firm finish. While cool to the wearer and popular in evening wear, the material does not launder satisfactorily. Its service to the wearer is comparatively short.

**MOUTON:** A short to medium length fur with a dense pile, the trade name for processed, sheared sheep. Usually dyed beaver color, or darker brown, beige, grey, and, occasionally, red, green, and blue. Wearing qualities, good. Judged by density of pile, softness and pliability of pelt. Found in Australia, Argentina, South Africa, and parts of America. For sports, business, and school wear.

**MOZAMBIQUE:** Named for the island off the east coast of Africa, is a staple decorative cloth of the grenadine type made with large floral effects in relief to form the motif. Originally made of silk and thus one of the more expensive materials, now available in acetate and rayon.

**MUGA SILK:** Silk obtained from the cocoon of a species of moth, *Antheraea assama.* Found in India and cultivated in Assam. Fawn or gold in color, and one of the best of the wild silks.

**MULBERRY SILK:** Silk from worms fed on the leaves of cultivated mulberry trees, as distinguished from wild silk from silkworms feeding on oak and other leaves.

**MULE:** A type of spinning frame which has an intermittent action. It draws out and twists a length of yarn then winds it in the form of a cop, repeating the cycle several times each minute. Used to a considerable extent for spinning wool but only to a limited extent, in the United States, for cotton, and then only for fine counts of yarn.

**MULL:** Means soft or pliable, and the cloth of this name is a type of light-weight muslin, now overshadowed by lawn, cambric, and voile.

**MULTIFILAMENT:** Man-made yarns composed of many fine filaments.

**MUMMIE:** A term in silk finishing which refers to the weight of fabric; thus, for 36-inch jap, mummie means 20 ounces; 4 mummie is 26 ounces, and so on. Also see Mommie.

**MUMMY CLOTH:** One which resembles crepe; made of silk warp and woolen filling in the better qualities, and with cotton warp and wool filling in the lower qualities. Used chiefly as a mourning fabric because of its lusterless face effect.

Another meaning of the term is a fine, closely woven linen material used in ancient Egypt for wrapping mummies. The best examples have a two-ply warp and single filling with the warp count in texture showing two or three times that of the filling picks. One staple type has 140 ends and 64 picks in one square inch of fabric, made of 100s linen both ways. Some of the very fine cloth has been made with as many as 540 ends per inch.

**MUSLIN:** A plain-weave substantial cotton cloth stronger and heavier than longcloth; only the poorer qualities are sized and the calender finish effect disappears after washing. Wide muslin is known as sheeting. Muslin finds much use for underwear and household purposes; comes in unbleached, semi-bleached, and full-bleach, dependent on use to be made of the goods.

A sheer, plain or printed muslin is used for dress goods.

**MYLAR:** A polyester film made from polyethylene terephthalate, the polymer formed by the condensation reaction between ethylene glycol and terephthalic acid. It has a combination of physical, electrical, and chemical properties which makes it suitable for a series of new industrial uses. Strong, tough, and durable, it has excellent insulating qualities. It retains its flexibility at very low temperatures. Mylar retains its physical and electrical properties under a wide range of heat and humidity changes. It has good resistance to attack by chemicals. A product of DuPont.

# N

**NACRE VELVET:** See VELVET.

**NAINSOOK:** Soft, fine cotton fabric, similar to batiste but made of coarser yarns. Light in weight, of plain weave, and resembles a soft-finished dimity. English nainsook has soft finish; French cloth has calendered finish.

Lacks full body due to the type of finish; wears well; rather durable; launders well and will retain finish if it has been mercerized.

**NANKEEN, RAJAH, SHANTUNG, TUSSAH:** These fabrics, all about the same, are made with silk or rayon and come in the natural tussah silk tan or écru color and in plain or twill weaves. The weight and the texture will vary with the quality.

Much of the cloth is dyed or printed. The material is durable, cool, and it withstands friction and chafing rather well. Tailors well and without wrinkles. The lightweight fabric is ideal for popular summer wear.

**NAP:** The fuzzy or protruding fibers noted on the surface of a finished material. Nap covers up to a great degree the interlacings between the warp and the filling threads. It gives added warmth to the wearer. The length of the nap will vary somewhat in the several cloths given this type of finish. Nap is applied to flannel of all kinds, cricket cloth, blanketing, baby clothes, silence cloth, molleton, some lining fabrics, overcoatings, knitted fabrics, etc.

**NAPERY:** A generic term used to describe household linen.

**NAPHTHALATING:** A process by which virgin wool is gently cleansed in three baths of naphtha and then rinsed in clean flowing water. No soap or alkaline solutions are used; raking, fork-ing, and excessive handling are eliminated. The wool retains its original life, strength, and resiliency.

The first bath removes large amounts of the grease; most of the remaining grease is removed by the second bath. The third bath removes all of the remaining grease but leaves the natural potash for further cleansing of the wool, which follows in a clear rinsing bath. Naphthalating was a patented process for scouring wools with organic solvents, owned by the now defunct Arlington Worsted Mills, Lawrence, Mass., and it has become a great help to the industry.

**NAPHTHOLS (AZOIC):** See DYES.

**NAPPING:** A finishing process that raises the fibers of a cloth to the surface by means of revolving cylinders covered with metal points or teasel burrs. A finish for such fabrics as outing flannel, wool broadcloth, knit goods, and blankets.

**NARROW GOODS:** Cloth 27 inches, or less, in width. Nine inches equal "one-quarter," hence cloth classed as narrow is known as three-quarter.

Narrow fabrics also include webbings and ribbons woven on narrow looms where it is possible to make from 96 to 144 pieces of fabric at the one time.

Woolen goods less than 52 inches wide finished.

**NAUGAHYDE:** A vinyl-resin-coated fabric produced by the United States Rubber Co. It is chiefly used for upholstery.

**NEEDLEPOINT:** Refers to needlepoint lace which is made with a needle and single thread, usually by hand.

**NEEDLEPOINT FABRIC:** A novelty wool fabric that looks like ratine and bouclé; made from curled or nubby yarns. Used chiefly for women's coats. Must be described as machine-made. Trade names are "Gros" and "Petit Point."

**NEEDLEPOINT LACE:** See LACE.

**NEEDLEPUNCH:** A fabric-forming method which is widely used in carpets. The needlepunch fabric is produced by needles which punch through a web, thereby entangling fibers.

**NEEDLE TAPESTRY:** Fabric whose pattern is embroidered to simulate a tapestry. See TAPESTRY.

**NEPS:** A defect consisting of a tiny mass or lump of tangled, short cotton fibers.

**NEUTRALIZE:** To change from either an acid or alkaline condition to a neutral condition.

**NETTING:** A lightweight or heavy open-weave, knotted fabric. The knots come at each corner of the square. Ranges in weight from very sheer to very heavy fabrics, from fine nets to fishing or laundry nets. Made in cotton, rayon, silk, vinyon, and nylon.

**NICKED SELVAGE:** Small cut made into the selvage by the folding machine (hooker).

**NINON:** Sheer rayon fabric made of plain weave. Several varieties on the market.

Washable, comes in variety of constructions and used much for curtains and portieres.

**NOILS:** The short fibers that are taken from any machine operation in the processing of textile fibers. They are obtained mostly in carding and combing operations. The stock may be high in quality but short in length, too short to admit of their being manipulated into yarn by itself. Noil is worked in with longer staple fibers to make yarn. Some noil may be of inferior quality. Silk noil is often used with other fibers to add life and luster to the resultant yarn.

**NON-CRUSHABLE LINEN:** Plain-weave cloth with highly twisted filling yarn, or finished with resin to enhance elasticity. Has about the same uses as dress linen.

Serviceable, durable, does not wrinkle, launders well.

**NON-SHATTERABLE GLASS:** The use of an acetate filler between layers of glass has produced non-shatterable glass, which serves several purposes but is an especial boon to the automobile industry.

**NONWOVEN FABRICS:** A term used to describe materials made primarily of textile fibers held together by an applied bonding agent or by the fusing of self-contained thermoplastic fibers, which are not processed on conventional spindles, looms or knitting machines. Nonwoven fabrics are textile-like structures consisting of a web or mat of fibers in which the fiber is greater than a half inch in length and the fiber content is at least 50% of the fabric weight. The fibers are held together with bonding agents which constitute at least 10% of the total fabric weight. Nonwovens are made by two methods: the wet process on paper-making machinery and the dry-web process. The majority of nonwovens are made by the dry method in this fast expanding field.

**NORFOLK SUITING:** Named for that county in England. This type of belted and pleated woolen or worsted suiting has waves of popularity, mostly in boys' clothing and in summer and golf toggery clothes.

**NORTHROP, JAMES:** Expert mechanic for Draper Corporation who perfected a loom which was better than any then in existence (1889). Known as the Northrop Loom, it is said to be first commercial loom to supply filling automatically, and to include a warp stop-motion.

**NOTTINGHAM LACE:** A machine-made lace produced in Nottingham, England and in the United States.

**NOVELTY YARNS:** Yarns produced for special effects. Usually uneven in size or colors. Flakes, nubs, and slubs are typical of novelty yarns.

**NUB YARN:** Novelty yarn containing slubs, beads, or lumps introduced for a purpose.

**NUN'S VEILING:** Used as religious garb with some call in the dress-goods trade. Cloth is all-worsted, all-silk, worsted and silk, etc. The fine, sheer types made are dyed black or brown in the piece, but other colors are given when there is a call for the material in the dress-goods trade. Fabric shines with wear. This cloth, when used by laymen, is made into dresses, cloaks, kimonos, and babies' coatings.

**NURSES CLOTH:** A stiff, firm, white cotton cloth with a linen-like finish. Used for nurses' uniforms.

**NYLON:** A manufactured fiber in which the fiber-forming substance is any long chain synthetic polyamide having recur-

ring amide groups $(-\text{C}-\text{NH}-)$ as an

integral part of the polymer chain. A versatile textile material, nylon was first introduced as bristles; and in mono-filament or single-strand form it is still used in brushes of all kinds. In flake form, melted and applied as a coating, nylon is especially suitable for electrical insulation.

**NYLON PUCKERED FABRIC:** See PUCKERED FABRIC, NYLON.

**NYTRIL:** A manufactured fiber containing at least 85% of a long chain polymer of vinylidene dinitrile $(-\text{CH}_2-\text{C(CN)}_2-)$ where the vinylidene dinitrile content is no less than every other unit in the polymer chain.

# O

**OATMEAL CLOTH:** Soft, heavy cloth with a crepe or pebbled effect that resembles oatmeal.

**OILCLOTH:** Material which is treated with linseed-oil varnish to give a patent leather effect. When used for tablecovers or shelf covering, it may be given a satin-like sheen and finish and is made in printed designs or plain colors. Also used for waterproof garments for outerwear, book bags, covers, belts, bibs, pencil cases and other containers, surgical supplies, bags, and luggage.

**OILED SILK:** Silk sheer fabrics in the gum state may be treated with linseed oil, at high temperature, then dried and made waterproof. The linseed oil oxidizes to a hard, smooth, translucent surface. This pliable cloth is used for medical supplies and raincoats.

**OILSKIN:** Cotton, linen, silk, man-made, or synthetic yarn material which has been treated with linseed oil varnish or pigment in varnish. In plain colors, the fabric is used for rainwear and sailors' clothing; in printed effects it has several household uses.

**OLEFIN:** A manufactured fiber in which the fiber-forming substance is any long chain synthetic polymer composed of at least 85% by weight of ethyl-

ene, propylene, or other olefin units.

**OMBRE:** Means shade in French, and fabrics with stripes of various colorings are often sold under this name.

**ONDE:** French dress goods of cotton warp and bright colored, wool filling. This cloth is supposed to have originated in Orleans, France. Fabric is cross-dyed, with the warp and filling therefore showing different colors in the finished garment.

**ONDULE:** Is derived from the French, for waved or shaded effects. The finish is brought about by causing the warp ends, in a series of groups, to be forced alternately by the ondulé reed to the right and then to the left.

**OPALINE:** A cotton lawn of fine quality and soft finish.

**OPEN DENT:** A fabric defect characterized by an open streak of variable length parallel with the warp.

**ORGANDY:** Sheer, stiff, transparent plain-weave cotton cloth. Textures range from 72 x 64 up to 84 x 80. Combed yarns always used. Arizona, Pima or Egyptian cotton used. White, dyed, or printed. Counts of yarn may be 150s in warp, 100s in filling.

Stiffness is permanent or temporary. Very attractive cloth, but difficult to launder and not practical for daily wear. It has more crispness than lawn, cambric, dimity, or other cloths of the same family grouping. May run twenty yards to the pound. Much of the cloth has the well-known permanent Swiss finish.

**ORGANZA:** Thin, transparent, stiff, wiry rayon fabric. Crushes or musses, but is easily pressed. Plain weave. Used for evening dresses, trimmings, neckwear.

**ORGANZINE:** A warp yarn in the silk trade. Tram is the name for filling yarn and does not require as much twist as organzine.

In organzine, the thread is made from a series of continuous filaments taken from three to eleven cocoons. The threads are given sixteen turns of twist per inch in the first-time spinning, and then two threads from the first spinning operation are taken and given fourteen turns of twist in the opposite direction. This is called second-time spinning and it will make a thread that is strong and durable.

**ORLEANS:** A dress fabric with cotton warp and wool or worsted filling.

**ORLON:** An acrylic fiber produced by Du Pont.

The raw materials which may be used for Orlon include coal, air, limestone, natural gases, petroleum, water. The product is a fiber based on a polymer of acrylonitrile and therefore is classed as an acrylic fiber.

Features of Orlon include resistance to sunlight and atmospheric gases, which makes it ideal for awnings, curtains, and other outdoor uses; stability, little or no shrinkage in fabrics, a soft, warm hand, and good drapability. The same washing techniques and ironing temperatures as used for acetate rayon and nylon apply to Orlon.

The filaments have a tensile strength which corresponds to from 60,000 to 75,000 pounds per square inch when dry, and the strength is almost as good when wet. The fibers have good elasticity and low moisture-absorption. Orlon is resistant to chemicals, chiefly acids, and it has the ability to withstand high temperatures, thereby providing suitability for various industrial uses.

Orlon, in staple form, can be used alone or blended with the major textile fibers, either natural or man-made, for suitings and blankets.

**OSNABURG:** A coarse cotton cloth, often made with part waste, of plain weave, medium to heavy in weight, and resembling crash. It is named for the city of Osnabrück, Germany, where it was first made. When sold, either the term P.W. (part-waste) or the term Clean is stated. Some of the fabric, because of the dirtiness of the waste used, is sold as Grade B Osnaburg. P.W. cloths are made with red-tinged cotton. Motes, dirt, and card wastes are found in the dingy, off-color cloths.

**OTTOMAN:** Is one of the most popular of cross-ribs in the trade. It was first made over 500 years ago and was constructed in a manner different from the cloth we know by this name today. The original weave was a 12-harness, 75-degree left-hand twill. This produced a flatter rib than that found in *faille Francaise*. Fabric made with this construction eliminated the extra binder warp for the rib effect.

Ottoman in the present market is merely a rib construction with a broad, flat rib definitely pronounced in the cloth. Soleil is the name for the small rib effect; Ottoman has a slightly larger and heavier rib, while ottoman cord has ribs of different sizes, arranged in alternating order. All three types, however, are known as Ottoman in the trade today. Ottoman is made from silk, acetate, rayon, and cotton. The cord yarns are usually cotton since they do not show on the face or the back of the goods because they are covered by the warp threads.

**OUTING CLOTH:** Cloth used for tennis, cricket, light field sports, and general outdoor recreations. The woolen or worsted material is made of plain weave, has wide range of plain colors or may be striped in pattern. The name is also applied, at times, to fancy flannels, white and cream-colored serges, and straight flannel cloth.

**OUTING FLANNEL:** Can be either plain or twill weave. Lightweight or medium-weight soft-filled single yarn with nap on both sides. Mostly yarn-dyed. Woven in stripes, plaids, or checks. Sometimes bleached or piece-dyed, and occasionally printed. Classed as cotton or spun-rayon fabric.

**OVERPLAID:** In reality a double plaid. This is a cloth in which the weave or, more often, the color effect is arranged in blocks of the same or different sizes, one over the other. Again, the cloth may show a plaid design on a checked ground construction. This effect is noted in English mufti and in golf togs, neat business woolens and worsteds in morning, lounge, and semi-formal wear. This cloth goes under the name, sometimes, of

Overplaid weave.

*Glen Urquhart*, the name of the Scottish clan that is given credit for bringing this type cloth to the fore. Urquharts are usually light or medium in weight, running from 9 to 13 ounces. Two, three, or more colors are used in designing the patterns. Overplaids are

ideal for travel as they do not show the dirt as readily as other cloths, generally speaking. Uses of the cloth as overcoating and topcoating is considerable. Overplaids are cycle cloths that come in vogue about every seven or eleven years, and when in demand, they seem to overshadow other fabrics. There are many grades and qualities found on the market as staples.

**OVERPRINT:** A print applied on top of a colored, piece dyed fabric.

**OXFORD CLOTH:** Plain, basket, or twill weaves are used in this cotton or rayon cloth. There are two yarns which travel as one in the warp, and one filling yarn equal in size to the two warp yarns. Better grades of cloth are mercerized if made of cotton yarn.

Rather heavy cloth which launders well. This shirting fabric has a tendency to soil easily; used also for jackets, shirts, skirts, and summer suiting.

Cotton oxford shirting weave.

**OXFORD GREY:** A grey color effect produced by blending white and black fibers. The percentage black is usually 80-95% so that the cloth produced is dark grey.

**OXFORD MIXTURE:** Usually a color effect in dark grey noted in woolens and worsteds. The degree of shade is governed by the mixed percentages of black and white stocks used. Mixing takes place prior to the carding and spinning of the yarn. Its reference to Oxford, England, has suggested calling the lighter weight mixture cloths by the name of Cambridge, the rival university of Oxford. Oxford and Cambridge are the two oldest universities in England and are known all over the world. The colors of the schools are dark blue and light blue respectively. Hence, the use of dark and light oxfords or greys under those two names. In this country much grey cloth is given the name of oxford.

**OXIDATION:** 1. The addition of oxygen to any chemical formula. In some dyeing processes the dye chemistry is completed by exposure to air, or to chemically generated oxygen.

2. In chemistry, the term oxidation has a broader meaning. On the basis of the electron theory, oxidation is a process in which an element loses electrons.

**OXIDIZING AGENT:** 1. Any substance which will release some of its oxygen.

2. In a restricted sense, a substance which can furnish oxygen and thereby cause oxidation of other substances. For example, sodium or hydrogen peroxide can liberate nascent oxygen, a useful reaction in bleaching.

# P

**PACKAGE DYEING:** See Dyeing Methods.

**PADDER:** A set of squeeze rollers used to impregnate any fabric with a liquid by continuous passage of the fabric through the liquid and then between the rollers.

**PADDOCK:** A worsted fabric very much like gabardine, made in England. The name probably derives from the fact that clothing made of this fabric was worn in the paddock.

**PAD DYEING:** See Dyeing Methods.

**PAISLEY CLOTH:** Used for coverings and shawls. Originated in Paisley, Scotland. This characteristic cloth of worsted has scroll designs all over the material. Colors run from red through to brown with spots of other colors noted so as to enhance the design. The medley of color in this cloth is often very attractive. Genuine Paisley is expensive.

**PAJAMA CHECK:** A fancy basket-weave fabric of print cloth yarns grouped so as to form a checked effect. Given a nainsook finish and used for men's underwear.

**PALM BEACH:** Summer suiting material ranging in weight from 7 to 10 ounces. Plain weave, cotton warp and mohair filling. Some of the better grades of cloth have choice stock in them and the price per yard of the material is somewhat high. Cloth is piece- or skein-dyed and is given a clear finish. Trademark of Palm Beach Company, Inc.

**PALMERING:** A finishing process often applied to such fabrics as twills, taffetas, and satins to give them a smooth hand.

**PANAMA:** Summer suiting that ranges from 8 to 10 ounces in weight. Piece, yarn, or skein-dyed and made of cotton warp and worsted filling, although other combinations are resorted to from time to time. Plain-weave material. Cloth appears in solid shades and mixtures.

**PANAMA STRAW:** See Straw.

**PANNE SATIN:** Silk or man-made fiber satin with an unusually high luster because of a special finish. If made of rayon or acetate, fiber content must be declared. Used chiefly for evening wear. Care must be used in handling; crushes easily.

**PANTOGRAPH:** An apparatus for copying designs to any scale within the capacity of the device. A dummy point traced over the original drawing moves a series of arms to a stylus that reproduces the traced line in larger or smaller scale. The machine is used in the printing industry for transferring the artist's design to the copper printing roller.

**PAPER TAFFETA:** See Taffeta.

**PARACHUTE CLOTH:** Fabric used in the making of parachutes. It is lightweight, closely woven, and may be made of several basic fibers.

**PARAFFIN DUCK:** Canvas or duck that has been treated with a paraffin preparation. It is stiff, heavy, and waterproof. It is used for coats and trousers by loggers, lumbermen, hunters, and fishermen. Some of the fabric is used as tent material.

**PARALLELING:** To cause strands or fibers to lie even and straight after some machine operation, such as combing or drawing.

**PASTEUR, LOUIS:** To the world of textiles Pasteur is known as the saviour of the silk industry. About 1860 the industry was threatened with disaster because of a silkworm disease. By scientific methods of selection he was able to eliminate the diseased worms and breed only healthy eggs.

**PATTERN:** Design or motif of a fabric which is either woven-in or printed on the cloth.

**PAUL, LEWIS:** Together with John Wyatt, invented (1738) drawing rollers to draft fibers so that the spinning of yarn could be done by machine. In 1748 they invented the revolving cylinder, later to become an integral part of the carding machine.

**PEASANT LACE:** Simple, inexpensive lace made by peasants.

**PEAU DE CYGNE:** Means skin of the swan. This satin fabric has a soft, lustrous feel with a very fine, appealing finish.

**PEAU DE SOIE:** Means skin of silk. This soft, good-quality, silk satin-type of cloth has a rather dull finish and a grainy appearance on the face of the goods. It is made in single face or double face and is woven with an arrangement of close rib effect. When double-faced, the cloth is, of course, classed as a reversible. Granite weaves and quarter-turn weaves are used in producing the cloth.

**PEBBLE CHEVIOT:** Overcoating material that runs from 16 to 25 ounces per yard. Made of twill weaves, and piece-dyed cloth has a shaggy, nubby, curly appearance in finished state. Wool or worsted, alone or in combination, used in making the material, which is a staple cloth and has waves of popularity.

**PEBBLE WEAVE OR TEXTURE:** A cloth with a roughened surface formed by either a special weave or highly twisted yarns which shrink when wet.

**PECTIN:** Any of a class of water soluble compounds of complex carbohydrate derivation found in various fruits and vegetables.

**PEKIN:** 1. A motif in which the white and the colored stripes are of equal width.

2. A broad-striped silk dress goods, in which broad satin strips alternate with white rep stripes of equal width.

3. Term used in the French silk industry for fabrics made with longitudinal stripes made from a variety of suitable weave constructions.

**PELLON:** The trademark for non-woven inner construction textiles produced by the Pellon Corporation.

**PENCIL STRIPES:** Suiting material of various fibers that has fine, light, white or tinted stripes running in the warp direction. Body of the material is dull or dark in color, and the contrast shows up well in the finished fabric. A staple material that in some seasons is much sought for.

**PEPPER AND SALT:** Woolen apparel material of fine, speckled effect. The appearance of the cloth suggests a mixture of salt and pepper. Cloth is made in shades of grey, brown, green, and blue. The effect is obtained by the use of two-colored twisted yarns, ordinarily in black and white, or by the intricacy of the weave with two or more solid-color yarns.

**PERCALE:** Closely-woven, plain-weave cotton fabric. Cloth resembles cambric. Cylindrical yarn is used. Comes in white or is printed. Small, geometrical figures are often seen in the designs.

Launders well, colors are very fast; finish gives a good temporary luster. Material stands up well for wear because of its compact texture.

**PERCALE SHEETS:** Smooth, fine, luxury sheets with a high thread count (90 x 90 or finer). Combed percale is finer than carded percale.

**PERCALINE:** In the lightweight, low-count cotton print cloth or lawn group, with a bright, soft finish. Usually mercerized. Made in both fine and cheap versions. Used for the lining of furs.

**PERCHING:** Examining fabric for defects by passing it over a set of uprights that support a roller over which the cloth is passed.

**PERMANENT FINISH:** A finishing process applied to various fabrics which will retain their specific properties, such as glaze on chintz, crispness on organdy, smoothness on cotton table damask, crease and crush-resistance, shrink resistance during the normal period of wear and laundering.

**PERMANENT PRESS:** A system whereby fabric is treated so as to prevent the removal of creases and the formation of wrinkles during the wearing and the machine laundering of the garment. Permanent press is achieved by the following basic method: the fabric is treated with a cross-linking chemical or reactant, which is then im-

mediately cured or fixed by the application of heat. This sets the smooth, flat shape given to the fabric during finishing. The fabric then has a "memory" for its flat finished state. This is pre-cured permanent press.

Post-cured permanent press garments are produced by treating the polyester/cotton fabric at the mill or finishing plant with a reactant for the cotton component, but not curing the fabric.

This compound is often referred to as a thermosetting resin, since it reacts to the cellulosic fiber components and becomes cured only when subjected to certain temperatures. The fabric is thus "sensitized" and the temperatures required for curing applied after the garment has been cut, sewn and pressed.

The finished garment is cured in a baking oven which subjects it to temperatures of 300–340°F. for anywhere from four to 18 minutes, depending upon the fabric and the finish.

**PERMEABILITY:** State or quality of being penetrable by fluids.

**PERSPIRATION RESISTANT:** A term applied to fabrics or dyes which will resist acid and alkaline perspiration. Should be laboratory tested before so described.

**PERUVIAN COTTON:** A type of cotton grown in Peru. It is a varied crop, some rough and some smooth. See COTTON.

**PETERSHAM:** A heavy woolen overcoating with a high nap.

**pH:** Measurement of the acidity or alkalinity of solutions. On the acid side, the pH is less than seven; on the alkaline side, the pH is more than seven.

**PHOTOGRAPHIC PRINTING:** See PRINT.

**PHOTOMICROGRAPH:** A magnified photograph of a fiber, yarn or fabric obtained by attaching a camera to a microscope.

**PICK:** A filling yarn or thread that runs crosswise in woven goods.

**PICKGLASS:** A magnifying glass with gauged aperture used for making a count of cloth. Also called pick counter.

**PICOT:** A decorative loop which projects from the edge of lace fabric.

**PICK-AND-PICK:** The throwing of single picks of different colors through the shed of the loom in weaving.

**PIECE DYEING:** The dyeing of cloth rather than raw stock or yarn. It is a continuous or semi-continuous process which takes place in a dye-beck, box, or jig, or some other form of continuous machine.

The greige cloth is scoured usually in a separate machine and is then loaded on one of the above types of dyeing machines. On jigs and continuous machines the cloth is handled in the open width, while on the dye-beck it is in rope form. See DYEING METHODS.

**PIECE GOODS:** Any fabric that has been made up for sale, usually used in reference to that sold by the yard in retail stores.

**PIGMENT DYEING:** See DYEING METHODS.

**PIGMENTED:** Delustered synthetic filaments made from a spinning solution to which minutely divided pigment (titanium dioxide) has been added. Pigment crepe and pigment taffeta are made with pigmented yarns.

**PIGMENT PRINTING:** A method of printing textiles with opaque pigments which have a tendency to lay on the surface of the cloth. Especially effective when white is the color used.

**PIGMENT TAFFETA:** See TAFFETA.

**PILE:** The cut or uncut loops which make the surface a pile fabric. Not to be confused with nap. Most pile fabrics are made by sliver knitting.

**PILE FABRIC:** A material that, to some degree, resembles fur. The cloth may be cut or uncut. It has a nap on the face of the goods, or it can be made so that there will be long loops in the uncut type of material. Pile cloth may be soft or harsh in feel, have considerable body, and an appealing appearance.

Some common pile cloths include terry toweling, furniture covering, velvet, velveteen, panne velvet, corduroy, runners, rugs and carpets.

**PILE WEAVE:** Weave in which an additional set of yarns, either warp or filling, floats on the surface and is cut to form the pile. Velvets and plushes are made with extra warp yarns; velveteens and corduroys are made of extra filling yarns. Turkish toweling is a pile-weave fabric with loops of pile on one or both sides. Loops left uncut.

**PILLING:** This may be defined as the tendency of fibers to ball or roll up on the surface of a fabric. Pilling results when loose fiber ends escape from the yarn used in making a fabric and work their way to the surface of the fabric. After working the way to the surface of the fabric these loose ends begin to collect and wherever the fabric is exposed to rubbing they form little balls of fuzz called pills. These unsightly pills are not at all new as they have always been fairly common on certain types of woolen fabrics, particularly knitted fabrics. Their appearance in wool, however, was not nearly as serious as it is in fabrics made with some of the newer synthetic fibers. The pills that appear on wool fabrics will usually work their way out and be eliminated when the fabric is cleaned. This is not generally true, however, when these pills form on some of the synthetic fiber fabrics as the great strength of the synthetic fibers causes the pills to cling permanently to the surface of the fabric. Some of the many things that determine how well a finished fabric is going to resist pilling are as follows:
1. Staple length of the fibers used.
2. The amount of twist in the yarn.
3. The degree of sheering or singeing to which the fabric is subjected.

**PILLOW-CASE LINEN:** Plain weave, high count, good texture, bleached. Yarn is very smooth and has high count of turns of twist per inch.

Launders easily and well, sheds dirt, has cool feel and appearance, is strong and durable. Very desirable cloth. Cotton fabric is made to simulate the linen fabric.

**PILOT CLOTH:** Uniform cloth that is heavy, bulky, and strongly made. Wool is the fiber used and the cloth is on the order of the average kersey. It is not as lustrous as the latter cloth. The material is drab in finish and is dyed navy blue or some dark color. An ideal cloth for seafaring men. The weight runs from 20 to 30 or more ounces.

**PIMA COTTON:** A fine quality cotton named after Pima County, Arizona, where it was raised. It is also grown in Texas, New Mexico, and California.

**PIN-CHECK:** Worsted suiting that has a small, figured effect about the size of a pin-head. Color effects are used in making the design, and the finished fabric shows a cloth studded with the minute pin-checks.

Also a fine rayon fabric made with different colored yarns. The pin-checks are very small. Gives good service.

**PINKING:** Cutting a piece of fabric so as to produce a serrated edge which prevents raveling.

**PIN STRIPES:** Very narrow stripes the width of a pin scratch. Usually associated with worsteds.

**PIN WALE:** Corduroy with a very narrow wale or rib.

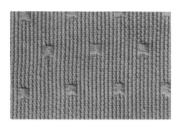

(*Top*) Piqué. (*Bottom*) Novelty piqué.

**PIQUE:** Medium-weight or heavyweight cotton cloth with raised cords that run in the warp direction. Combed or carded yarns used; used for women's and children's wear, shirts, vests, neckwear, collar and cuff sets, infants' coats and bonnets, etc.

Very durable; launders well; a rather expensive cotton cloth. This substantial cloth is made on dobby, jacquard, dropbox, and other types of looms; it will retain the rugged characteristics irrespective of the type of loom used.

**PLAID:** The crossing of lines in either a woven or printed fabric to produce a rectilinear pattern.

**PLAID-BACK:** A light, medium, or heavy overcoating made on the double cloth principle—two systems of warp

and filling, with a binder warp or filling arrangement. The underside of the cloth (often of cotton) is a plaid—a series of cross stripes that form a dull or vivid effect. Weight, warmth, and the covering up of the interlacings are features of the material. Plaid backs take the place of linings in some of the cloths used for coating material.

**PLAIN-KNIT:** The simplest of knit structures, as in hosiery and jersey cloth, consisting of vertical rows (wales) evident on the face of the fabric and crosswise lines (courses) visible on the back.

A plain weave is one in which warp and weft threads of about the same thickness pass over and under each other alternately, as illustrated above.

**PLAIN-WEAVE:** The simplest, most important and most used of all of the hundreds of weaves used in making textile cloths. Eighty percent of all cloth made each year is made on this simple construction. There is only one .plain weave, and it gives a checkerboard appearance. It is made, and repeats, on two warp ends and two filling picks, and is read as "1-up and 1-down." There are one raiser and one sinker, painted and unpainted block, on each warp thread in the repeat of the weave.

**PLASTICS, TYPES OF:** There are two types of plastics: 1. Thermoplastic Type: This type is softened by heat and hardened into definite shape by cooling. An example would be in the case of nylon. This fiber or material can be heat-set, and then on re-heating to a higher temperature it once more becomes plastic and can be reset into a different shape. Thermoplastic resins can be either "low temperature" or "high temperature" resins.

2. Thermosetting plastics are those which harden or set into permanent

572

shape when heat and pressure treatments are accorded them.

**PLATED:** Knitted fabrics which have one kind of yarn on the face of the fabric, and another on the back. A good example of plating is the heel, sole or toe of stocking where the yarn used on the back makes for greater comfort or better wear.

**PLISSE:** The effect of a woven seersucker fabric produced by chemical action. Caustic soda is used to shrink some areas of the cloth, leaving others untouched.

**PLUMETIS:** is a lightweight fabric made of cotton or wool which shows a raised motif on a plain background to give a feathered effect.

**PLUSH:** Woolen or worsted pile cloth, the pile being one-eighth of an inch or more in height. Plush has many well-known uses and is an exaggerated form of velvet. The term is from the French, *peluche*. This, in turn, is taken from the Latin, *pilus*, which means hair. The cloth is compact and bristly. Made in silk, cotton, mohair, and combinations of fibers, as well as in wool or worsted. Cotton plush has a deeper pile effect than velour or velvet. Used in capes, coats, muffs, powder puffs, and upholstery. Rayon plush simulates the cotton type and has the same uses.

**PLY:** 1. The number of individual yarns twisted together to make a composite yarn; a "six-ply sevens" would mean that six single yarns of a count of seven are plied together to give the composite yarn of 6/7s.

2. When the term is applied to cloth it means the number of layers of fabric combined to give the composite fabric. A three-ply webbing, for example, means that three single cloths are plied together in the weaving of the material on the loom by a manner of stitching or binding threads to hold the single layers in combination to produce the finished product.

**POINT:** 1. 1/100 of a cent, in quoting the price of raw cotton.

2. The ornamental stitching on the back of a glove.

3. Various stitches in hand-made lace.

**POINT A L'AIGUILLE:** French for needlepoint.

**POINT ANGLETERRE:** Originally a Brussels lace smuggled into England and so-called to avoid duty; subsequently made in England.

**POIRET TWILL:** Women's wear dress goods made of worsted yarn and one of the pronounced diagonal twill cloths. Named for Paul Poiret, deceased Parisian designer. Cloth is made on a 45-degree twill and there are twice as many ends as picks per inch in texture. A three-up and three-down, right-hand twill weave may be used and some of the cloth has been made from a steep twill of 63 degrees. High-twist counts of yarn are used and the material has a soft feel, excellent draping and clinging qualities which make it ideal in tailoring. Weight of cloth ranges from 8 to 14 ounces per yard. Material is well-balanced, has excellent finish, and comes in all shades and colors. Piece-dyed cloth, genuine staple, and very popular at times.

**POLISHED COTTON:** Generally a plain-weave cotton cloth to which a glazed finish has been mechanically applied. Originally this was achieved by friction calendering but was not permanent. Today, resin finishes, plus calendering and curing, make the process permanent.

**POLISHING CLOTH:** A square of napped cotton, 12 x 12 inches or 18 x 18 inches in size.

**POLKA DOTS:** Round dots, embroidered, printed or flock, of any size forming a surface pattern. If rather large, called coin dots.

**POLO CLOTH:** May be woven or knitted. Used for men's and women's topcoating, polo coats, cap cloth, blankets, and sportswear. Cloth is face-finished, has considerable nap. The fibers used are wool, combined with any of the major hair fibers. Quality and price range is very wide. The weight runs from 15 to 30 ounces per yard. Plain, twill, and basket weaves are used in making the fabric, which may or may not be made on a pile-weave construction.

**POLYAMIDE:** The noun, amide, means any of a group of compounds of the type formula, $R-CO-NH_2$, derived from ammonia by the substitution of a univalent acid radical for one or more hydrogen atoms. Also, amid, noun; adjective form is amic or amidic. Amido is

the combining form from amide, indicating a compound containing both the $NH_2$ radical and an acid radical.

In a broad chemical sense, polyamides (many amides) are the polymerization products of chemical compounds which contain both amino and carboxyl groups, a condensation taking place between the amino and the carboxyl groups of different molecules. Thus, from the foregoing, the natural and the man-made protein fibers, along with nylon, may be classed as polyamide fibers. Present conception, however, implies that polyamide refers to nylon-type fibers or filaments.

**POLYESTER:** A manufactured fiber in which the fiber-forming substance is any long chain synthetic polymer composed of at least 85% by weight of an ester of a dihydric alcohol and terephthalic acid (p—$HOOC-C_6H_4-COOH$).

**POLYETHYLENE:** A synthetic resin adapted to molding and casting purposes and for the extrusion of yarn and staple textile fibers. Its specific gravity of 0.92 indicates a high covering power. The product comes in the form of granules ready for the extrusion process.

**POLYMER:** Molecular chain-like structure from which synthetic fibers are derived; produced by the linking together of molecular units called "monomers." The following are representative polymers from which many synthetic textile fibers are derived: Copolymers are obtained when two or more monomer types enter into the polymer chain.

**POLYPROPYLENE FIBER:** An Italian textile fiber developed by Professor Giulio Natta, consultant to Montecatini, the largest chemical producer in Italy. The fiber may be used for satiny silk fabrics or for heavy wool-like yarns with strengths comparable with those of nylon. Terminal uses of the fiber include clothing and industrial fabrics, transparent plastic sheeting, and film.

**POLYVINYL CHLORIDE FIBERS:** In some countries, other than the United States, polyvinyl chloride fibers are referred to as vinyon fibers. These are manufactured fibers in which the fiber-forming substance is any long chain synthetic polymer composed of at least 85% by weight of vinyl chloride units.

**PONGEE:** Originally a Chinese silk cloth, tan or ecru in color, and very light in weight. Tussah silk was used and the fabric was woven on hand looms in the home; thus a rather crude, uneven textured material resulted. Pun-ki, the basic Chinese word for weaving in the home on one's own hand loom, gives rise to the present term, pongee. Also refers to a soft, plain-weave cotton cloth which is schreinerized or mercerized in finishing. It has more picks than ends, 72 x 100 is average texture. Uneven yarns are used.

**POODLE CLOTH:** A fabric usually made of mohair and wool, which resembles the fur of the poodle.

Print.

**POPLIN:** From the French, "pope-line." It is a staple, dress-goods material. The cloth resembles bombazine, and silk warp and woolen filling are used. In the higher-priced cloth, worsted filling is utilized. Filling yarn is particularly cylindrical as it tends to give the rounded form of rib line, noted in the fabric, in the horizontal direction. The cloth is also made from other major textile fibers.

Cotton poplin has a more pronounced rib filling effect than broadcloth. The filling is bulkier than the warp but there are more ends than picks per inch in the material. In the carded poplin the textures vary from 88 x 40 to 112 x 46; combed poplin ranges from 88 x 44 to 116 x 56. The cloth is mercerized and usually chased for high luster. May be bleached or dyed with vat colors; printed poplin is also popular. Heavy poplin is given water-repellent finish for outdoor use; some of the fabric is given suede finish.

Rayon and nylon poplin are also made.

**POROSITY:** A term applied to fabrics which have open spaces in the texture to admit air to pass through or to allow the heat of the body to escape. Summer fabrics, known under the heading of air-conditioned cloth, have found much favor with the public since certain chemical processes removed the protruding fibers from the goods, allowing the material to become more or less porous.

**POST-CURED GARMENTS:** See Permanent Press.

**POTTING:** A finishing process for woolens designed to produce a bright, glossy face and a soft hand. It consists of a heat and steam treatment. Same as wet decating.

**POT SPINNING:** Emerging viscose rayon filaments are led through the bath to a hook at the surface, and up to a Godet wheel, the speed of which controls the take-up of the still plastic filaments. These are then passed through a glass funnel, thence into a spinning pot which imparts a small amount of twist to them. The pot, with a speed of 8,000 to 10,000 r.p.m., also lays the filaments by centrifugal force into a "cake form." The cakes are then washed to remove the spinning bath liquor, desulphurized, bleached, rinsed, treated with an emulsion, and then dried. See BOBBIN SPINNING, FILAMENT.

**PRE-CURED FABRIC:** See Permanent Press.

**PRE-SHRUNK:** Term used to describe fabrics or garments which have been given the shrinking process before being put on the market. The percentage of residual shrinkage must be declared. See SHRINKAGE.

**PRESSURE DYEING:** Dyeing under superatmospheric pressure, primarily with the object of raising the temperature of the dye liquor above its normal boiling point.

**PRIESTLEY:** A well-known English worsted that is found in the better types of clothing stores. Made by the English manufacturer Priestley.

**PRIMARY COLORS:** Primary or simple colors are given this name because they are in their pure or irreducible form. There are three primary colors: red, blue and yellow. Secondary colors—violet, green and orange—which are also called compound colors, are made from a mixture of two primary colors.

**PRINCESSE:** A Duchesse imitation valued for its delicacy and hand-wrought appearance.

**PRINT:** General term for fabric with designs applied by means of dyes used on engraved rollers, wood blocks or screens. See also PRINTING under DYEING.

BURN-OUT PRINT—Print showing raised designs on sheer ground. Made by printing design with chemical on fabric woven of paired threads of different fibers, then burning out one of the yarns from the parts printed. Often used on velvet.

DIRECT PRINT—Colors for designs applied directly to a cloth. Synonyms—roller or application print.

DISCHARGE OR EXTRACT PRINT—Method used for dark-colored fabrics with white or colored designs. The cloth is piece-dyed and color is discharged or bleached in spots leaving white designs. When a basic color is added to discharge paste, a colored design is produced.

DUPLEX PRINT—Method of printing a pattern on the face and the back of the fabric with equal clarity. Often used on drapery fabrics. Imitates a woven design fabric.

HAND-BLOCKED PRINT—Fabrics printed by hand with either wooden or linoleum blocks.

INDIA PRINT—Muslin printed with design typical in form and color of those used in India. Genuine India prints are hand-blocked with nature patterns in glowing oriental colors. Imitations must be declared as such.

JOUY PRINT OR TOILE DE JOUY—Cotton or linen fabric printed with modern reproductions of 18th Century French prints. Often monotone landscapes or figure groups in red or blue on light or white grounds. Imitations must be indicated.

PHOTOGRAPHIC PRINTING—Application of a photographic image to cloth.

RESIST PRINT—The principle used in batik dyeing. Substances which will resist dye are applied to a fabric in designs, and then the fabric is dyed and resist removed. Then some or all white areas are direct-printed. Then the "resist" is removed. See BATIK under DYEING.

SCREEN PRINT—Method similar to a stencil. Background of designs is painted on screen (bolting cloth) with paste, and dye is printed through exposed fabric. Separate screens may be used for different colors.

SHADOW PRINT—Silk, ribbon, or cretonne, woven with printed warp yarn forming indistinct design. Reversible.

STENCIL PRINT—A type of resist printing. Portions of the design to be resisted are covered with paper or metal so those parts do not take dye.

WARP PRINT—Warp yarns are printed with the design before weaving. Fillings are either white or neutral color. Greyed effect is produced.

WEDGWOOD PRINT—Print of white design on colored ground similar to the effect of Wedgwood china.

**PRINT CLOTH:** Carded cotton cloth made with the same yarns as cheesecloth but with more warp and filling threads to the inch. Most print cloths are made in narrow widths up to 40 inches. It is given a range of finishes, thus producing cambric, muslin, lawn, longcloth, printed percales, etc.

Narrow printcloths are 27-inches to 40-inches wide with constructions varying from 64 x 60 up to 80 x 92. Yards per pound range from 3.50 to about 7.60.

Wide printcloths are 45-inches wide with textures ranging from 60 x 48 to 64 x 60. Yards per pound run from 4.65 to about 5.35.

**PROGRESSIVE SHRINKAGE:** Shrinkage that occurs on repeated washing or cleaning.

**PROTEIN FIBER:** Made from soy beans and corn meal, the latter being known as Zein. The vegetable matter is crushed and oil is extracted. Saline solution extracts the protein. A viscous solution is made and chemical treatment produces the extruded filaments through a spinneret into a coagulating bath. Winding and reeling follow to give the commercial product.

**PRUNELLA:** A dress-goods material and cloth used in children's apparel, made from a 2-up and 2-down right-hand-twill weave. Worsted yarn is used in the cloth. Light in weight, usually piece-dyed and not in vogue at present.

**PUCKERED FABRIC, NYLON:** The original nylon pucker fabric was made of preshrunk and nonshrunk nylon yarns. For example, if the designer wanted a quarter-inch pucker stripe on a 180-end

taffeta, he would preshrink half of his warp yarn, and then arrange his layout as follows: 45 ends of preshrunk nylon, 45 ends of nonshrunk nylon, repeated across entire width of the goods. All yarn would be on a single beam. After the fabric is woven, and when the goods have been boiled-off in finishing, the nylon yarn that had not been preshrunk would shrink, while the other yarn, really having no place to go, would pucker in the material.

A second method to obtain the effect is by printing with phenol. A plain taffeta which has not been heat set, when printed in floral motifs, checks, stripes, etc., with phenol paste, will pucker at the areas where the design has been printed.

A third method may be obtained through the use of different denier yarn and various weaves. For example, an arrangement of a 15 monofil nylon yarn with a 70-denier nylon yarn, using a Louisine weave (2-1 or 1-2 basket weave), will give the effect, usually in the plan of two warp ends of the 15-denier monofil yarn over one pick of the 70-denier nylon yarn. This plan allows the goods to pucker because of the difference in the takeup in weaving the cloth. The same principle may be applied for pucker effects in the filling direction of the fabric. Various small weaves are used to obtain various effects in either warp or filling direction.

Thus, in this third method, any reasonable number of ends of warp may be used of both 15-denier and 70-denier yarns. The number of ends should depend upon the width of the stripe desired. The 70-denier yarn could weave on the 2-1 basket effect while the 15-denier yarn would be drawn-in to weave in plain weave order so that different shrinkages and takeups would be realized in the finishing of the goods. For this effect one or two warp beams may be used.

**PULLED WOOL:** This is obtained from the pelts or hides of dead sheep. It is inferior in all respects to fleece wool, which it taken from live sheep. The stockyard centers produce pulled wool. However, the packing houses are interested mainly in the carcass; the wool is of secondary consideration. They dispose of all this stock to textile plants. There is more pulled wool produced per year than first-clip wool. Pulled wool is

used with better grades of fleece wool to make woolens and worsteds.

**PULLED WOOL, METHODS TO OBTAIN:** There are three ways to obtain pulled wool:

1. SWEATING PROCESS—The hides are sweated until the wool is loosened so that it may be taken from the pelts with ease. However, the hides may be affected if the work is not properly done.

2. LIME METHOD—The flesh sides of the pelts are painted with lime. This allows the wool to be removed easily after a short ageing. Hides are subject to injury and dyeing is sometimes irregular.

3. DEPILATORY METHOD—This is the best method to use. A solution of sodium sulphate will loosen the fibers. In the solution there is also sulphuric acid and an alkali made of oyster shells. The flesh side of the pelt is treated just as soon as it comes from the slaughtered animal. Ageing will last from 8 to 24 hours. The action is such, that when ageing is consummated, the fibers will leave the pelt in the same way lather may be taken from a man's face in shaving.

**PURE SILK OR PURE DYE SILK:** Silk goods which do not contain metallic weighting or finishing materials exceeding 10% (15% is allowed on black).

**PURL:** In machine knitting a stitch which shows horizontal ridges on both sides of fabric. In hand knitting, purling makes vertical wales in the fabric on the right side.

**PUSSYWILLOW:** A popular silk staple which is soft, thin, dull in appearance and gives good wear. This attractive cloth is used for dresses, waists, and lining material.

**PYROXYLIN:** A cellulose product which is used to coat cotton, rayon, or other fabrics to make a fabric waterproof, stain-resistant, etc.

**QIANA:** A silk-like nylon manufactured by Du Pont.

**QUALITY CONTROL:** Continuous testing and inspection of textile mill operations to make certain that all yarns and fabrics measure up to quality standards previously set.

**QUARTER BLOOD WOOL:** Domestic wool which constitutes the bulk of American 50s worsted stock.

**QUILLING:** 1. The last process in the long-chain system for filling yarns, in which the threads forming the chain are wound on filling bobbins, or quills, ready for the shuttle.
2. Winding filling yarn, especially of rayon or silk, on to quills.
3. A strip of lace, ribbon, or the like, fluted or folded, so as somewhat to resemble a row of quills.

**QUILT:** 1. Usually a bed covering of two thicknesses of material with wool, cotton or down batting in between for warmth.
2. Also used for jackets coatlinings.
3. Also the sewing stitch to make quilt.

**QUOTON:** As the Arabs speak of cotton, is a derivative of the Egyptian term for cotton, *goton.*

# R

**RABBIT HAIR:** Rabbit hair is used in combination with other fibers. It is soft and lustrous. In the better fabrics, enough hair may be present to justify the use of the term. Much used in varying percentages in wool and blend fabrics.

**RACK STITCH:** A knitting stitch similar to the half cardigan stitch. Gives a herringbone effect with a ribbed back.

**RADDLE:** A device for spreading the warp threads evenly as they are wound onto the beam. This is used when the loom is warped from the back to the front.

**RADIUM:** A lustrous, supple silk or rayon fabric having the drapability of crepe and the crispness of taffeta. Plain weave. Used for women's dresses, slips, negligees, blouses, linings, draperies.

**RAJAH:** A fabric much like pongee, usually made of tussah silk but also of synthetic fibers.

**RAMBOUILLET:** This breed, the largest and the strongest-bodied wool sheep, is a pure descendant of Spanish merino, imported by France in 1785. Rambouillet were brought to this country in 1840; today they constitute about 27% of all sheep here. Rams of this hardy breed weigh about 250 pounds, ewes about 140-170 pounds. A ram fleece of a year's growth will weigh 15 to 25 pounds of fine wool which will sort to 64s or higher. Fiber length is 1½ to 3 inches. Shrinkage averages about 60%. Range sheep have blood of the Rambouillet or other merino breeds.

**RAMIE:** An important bast fiber also known as Rhea or China grass. Ramie resembles flax but it is coarser, more difficult to manipulate and its uses are limited because the cost of production in making the yarn is high. The fibers are straight and from 8 to 12 inches long.

Ramie is often mixed with other fibers, and because of this finds its way into many textile materials. It is a fiber that is undergoing much experimentation since its great strength, luster, good body, and appearance warrant further research. The chief uses of ramie include fishing lines and nets, gas-mantle fabric, cordage, dress goods and shirtings, upholstery, and napery.

**RASCHEL:** A warp-knit stitch which has many end-uses: lace, power net, dresswear, netting, carpeting, etc. The raschel machine is a versatile machine which can stitch and lay-in yarn through the use of multiple bars.

**RATINE:** From the French, meaning "frizzy or fuzzy." An overcoating cloth on the order of chinchilla. Used in women's wear coatings in woolen trade.

Cotton ratiné is a loose, plain-woven cloth with a rough, nubby surface finish; one heavy and two fine yarns twisted together at various tensions form the curly, knotty ply yarn. Cheaper qualities use ordinary yarn as warp while the filling is made of ratine. Can be bleached, dyed, or printed and is given a high luster or other types of finish.

**RATINE LACE:** See LACE.

**RAW FIBERS:** Textile fibers in their natural state such as silk "in the gum" and cotton as it comes from the bale.

**RAW SILK:** Silk from the cultivated silkworm, *Bombyx mori,* before the gum or sericin has been removed.

**RAW STOCK DYEING:** See DYEING METHODS.

The process of manufacturing rayon is based on the formula: a *solid* (cellulose) is dissolved to a *liquid* and then hardened back to a *solid* (textile fiber).

**RAYON:** A manufactured fiber composed of regenerated cellulose, as well as manufactured fibers composed of regenerated cellulose in which substituents have replaced not more than 15% of the hydrogens of the hydroxyl groups. (Definition of the Textile Fiber Products Identification Act of 1960).

The cellulose base for the manufacture of rayon is obtained from wood pulp or cotton linters, which are the short brown fibers left on the cotton seed after the first-time ginning on the plantation or at the community gin. Wood pulp for rayon comes from spruce, pine, or hemlock chips.

Rayon, at present, includes yarn made from the cuprammonium, nitro-cellulose, and viscose methods.

Rayon fibers, like cotton, leave an ash when burned.

Acetate, a cellulosic derivative, has its filaments formed by a compound of cellulose and acetic acid which has coagulated. Cuprammonium filaments are made of regenerated cellulose coagulated from a solution of cellulose in ammoniacal copper oxide. Viscose filaments are made of regenerated cellulose coagulated from a solution of cellulose xanthate.

**RAYON STAPLE FIBER:** Originally referred to the waste coming from the manufacture of filament rayon. It is now specially made on a large scale comparable with that part of the rayon business given over to filament yarn. Filament is cut to staple lengths on its emergence from the spinneret in the processing. It is ideal for spinning on the cotton, woolen, worsted, and flax methods. Staple fiber comes in bright and dull effect and in varying deniers.

**RAYON STRAW:** A ribbon-like filament of viscose rayon. It is folded in spinning process, and resembles straw.

**REACTIVE DYE:** A dyestuff which combines chemically with cellulose molecules and becomes an intrinsic property of the dyed material.

**RECLAIMED WOOL:** This broad term implies wool obtained from the following sources: clippings, old and new woolen or worsted rags, tailor's clippings, reprocessed wool, remanufactured wool, shoddy, mungo, extract wool, etc.

**REDOUBLING:** In reality a form of doubling which implies the constant doubling in a series or set of textile machines. Doubling and redoubling are essential in making even, uniform yarn; without the use of either, yarn just could not be made.

**REDUCE:** To take oxygen away from any material.

**REDUCING AGENT:** A substance that is readily oxidized.

**REED:** The comb-like device through which the warp ends are drawn after leaving the harnesses and heddles. The reed prevents the warp ends from tangling or snarling. It keeps the ends under control at all times.

(*A*) shows comblike reed. (*B*) shows how reed keeps warp threads from tangling in the process of weaving.

The reed beats the loose filling pick lying in the shed of the loom into its proper place in woven fabric. The reed is parallel to the whip roll.

A Number 12 reed, for example, means that there are 12 splits or dents to the inch in the reed.

**REED MARKS:** Unwanted streaks warpwise in a fabric when caused by defective dents.

**REELED SILK:** Silk filaments wound directly from several cocoons into skeins. Result is a "raw" silk with only a slight twist. When twisted tight it is known as "thrown silk." Compare with "spun" silk.

**REELING:** The process by which yarns are drawn out in order to be wound in skeins.

**REGAIN STANDARD:** A definite percentage of moisture added to the bone-dry weight of the material being treated. Under normal conditions, the amount of regain for the various cloths are: cotton, 6%; worsted, 10%; woolen, 16%; silk, 11%, etc.

**REGENERATED CELLULOSE:** Viscose and cuprammonium rayons are examples of regenerated cellulose. In their formation cellulose is first brought into solution, as a chemical compound, but when this solution is extruded through the spinnerets into the spinning bath, cellulose is re-formed.

**REGIMENTAL STRIPES:** Stripes of various widths which represent the colors of famous British regiments.

**RELATIVE HUMIDITY:** The ratio of the water vapor present in an atmosphere to the amount present in a saturated atmosphere at the same temperature. It is generally expressed as a percentage. In a standard atmosphere the relative humidity is maintained at 65%.

**RENAISSANCE LACE:** A modern tape lace, the coarser types used for curtains. See LACE.

**REPEAT:** 1. An entire completed pattern for design and texture. Repeats vary in size considerably, depending on the weave, type of material, texture, and the use of the cloth.

2. The form which indicates the size of the weave and the number of threads that the weave contains in both the warp and filling. A weave may be repeated any reasonable number of times on paper.

**REP, REPP:** A fabric with a ribbed effect. The word is a corruption of "rib."

**REPROCESSED WOOL:** Woolen fibers obtained from woven, knitted, or manufactured goods which have never been used by the consumer.

**RESIDUAL SHRINKAGE:** The shrinkage or shrinkage properties remaining in such goods after the same have undergone a shrinking process. The residual shrinkage of unsponged or unshrunk material should be interpreted as that which would occur after the material has been subjected to a shrinking process.

**RESILIENCY:** A natural property of wool and silk which causes them to spring back when crushed in the hand. This helps prevent wrinkling of the cloth. Linen, cotton, rayon are not inherently resilient, but can be treated chemically to help them resist creasing and crushing.

**RESIN FINISH:** Cottons treated with natural or synthetic resins (frequently combinations of synthetic chemicals like formaldehyde and melamine); may be soil, water, and wrinkle resistant. They also can be finished in glazed, embossed, pleated, and sculptured surfaces to achieve a variety of textures.

**RESINS:** These are used widely to impregnate fabrics, thereby affording desirable qualities such as water repellency, wrinkle resistance, dimensional stability, spot- and stain-resistance. If impregnated fabrics are baked or "cured" by heat, the results are durable through many washings and drycleanings. Melamine resins are chlorine-retentive and some other type of bleach has to be used on the goods if bleaching is to be done to the fabric.

**RESIST DYE:** A form of "cross dye" in which the fabric is composed of one kind of stock, as worsted, for example, with part of the yarns in either warp or filling systems of threads being dyed before weaving. Such yarns are so chemically treated in the dye bath that when the cloth from the loom is piece-dyed a different shade for the ornamentation of the goods (which is often of intricate weave), they "resist" the action of subsequent coloration. This defines the principle of true resist dyeing.

**RESIST PRINTING:** The design desired is printed on the fabric with material which will resist dyeing. The fabric is then piece dyed. Washing removes the resist material in which the design is printed, leaving a white pattern. A different color may be applied in the resist paste, which reverses the process used in discharge printing. See Print.

**RETICELLA:** The earliest of needlepoint laces. It was a development of cut-work and drawn-work.

**RETTING:** A process of decomposing woody and gummy matter surrounding the bast fibers of a plant stalk. See BAST FIBERS.

**REUSED WOOL:** Fibers obtained from garments worn by consumers. The cast-off apparel finds its way to the garnetting plant where the material is returned to the fibrous stage. Shoddy and mungo are the names applied to the unfelted and felted fiber residue following the garnetting operation, which breaks up the garments and produces the fibers.

**REVERSE KNIT:** A flat or plain knit used inside out. Used often in silk hose or jersey to give a dull texture.

**REVERSIBLE FABRIC:** It is an accepted fact that many plain-woven fabrics are alike on both sides, unless napped or printed. Sometimes, cloth is printed on both sides; this is often called duplex printing. Reversible cloth is also produced by weaving a pattern on each side of the fabric. Many woolens, such as blankets, plaid-back overcoatings, robes, and steamer rugs are made in this manner.

**REVERSIBLE TWILLS:** A general term for fine, high-count, plied-yarn fabric made with combed cotton in an even-sided, four-harness twill, in which the twill line runs from lower left to upper right. The number of warp yarns per inch is about twice as many the filling yarns.

**RHEA:** Indian name for ramie or China grass.

**RHYTHM CREPE:** Rayon seersucker or plisse effect cloth. Plain-weave cloth with crimped effect running in warp direction.
Washable, drapes well and gives good wear. Imitates seersucker and cotton plisse.

**RIBBON:** Narrow fabric used as trimming, made in several widths and a variety of weaves.

**RIB CLOTH:** Fabrics which show rib lines in warp or filling because of the fact that cylindrical yarn or rib weaves were used in making the material. Cloths in this group could be poplin, rep, bedford cord, piqué, corduroy, tweeduroy, and certain fancy dress-goods materials.

**RIB KNIT:** Knit fabric with lengthwise ribs formed by wales alternating on right and wrong sides. If every other wale alternates between right and wrong side it is called 1 x 1 rib. If two wales alternate it is called 2 x 2 rib. A rib-knit fabric is more elastic than plain-knit and has form-fitting characteristics.

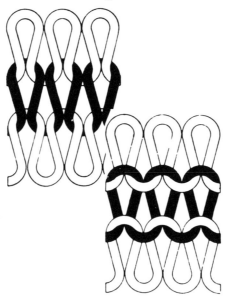

(At left) The face or front of plain stitch. (At right) The back of the fabric, showing crosswise courses.

**RIB VELVET:** Cloth of the velvet group with a lengthwise rib effect. In cotton, material is called corduroy; sometimes made with rayon.
Good draping quality, though rather difficult to handle and manipulate. Durable, must be dry cleaned, may be crushable.

**RIB WEAVES:** They are derivatives of the plain weave, and show rib lines warpwise (a filling rib weave) or crosswise (a warp weave). It should be noted that, for example, a filling rib weave will show the rib or cord effect in the opposite direction, the vertical direction in this instance. Common or simple warp ribs repeat on two warp ends, filling ribs on two picks. Thus, all even-number ends or picks in the goods will weave alike, and all odd-numbered ends or picks will weave alike. Examples of rib weaves or rib effects may include hat banding, grosgrain, bengaline, ottoman, transportation fabric, Russian cord shirting, several types of webbing, etc.

**RICKRACK:** Flat braid in zigzag form. Made of cotton, synthetic, silk, or wool in many different widths and colors. Used for trimming. See BRAID.

**RIGMEL SHRUNK:** A shrinking process by which fabrics will not shrink more than 1% in length or width. The process causes the texture of the goods to become more compact, thereby assuring greater strength and longer wear. At the same time the shrinkage can be controlled and the natural luster and handle of the goods are enhanced.

**RING SPINNING:** A method of spinning cotton and worsted roving into yarn. The roving, after it has passed between the sets of drawing rollers, is guided in a downward direction through the traveler, a small inverted U-shaped device which is flanged onto its respective ring in the ring rail of the machine. It travels around the ring at the rate of 4,000 to 12,000 revolutions per minute. As the spindle revolves to wind the yarn the latter has to pass through the traveler and carries it around on the ring at this rapid pace.

The narrower the width of the traveler, the finer is the diameter of the yarn and the higher its count or size.

The up-and-down motion of the ring rail causes the winding of the yarn onto its bobbin at the nose, body, and heel. The spindles are driven by means of cotton friction banding. One endless belt drives two spindles on each side of the frame, four in all.

**RIPPLE CLOTH:** A British fabric made from coarse woolen yarn in which the face-effect of the goods, because of the long, protruding fibers, make it possible to give the fabric a rippled or waved type of finish.

**RIPPLING:** Combing progress for removing the leaves and seeds from the dried stalks of the flax plant in preparation for retting.

**ROCKY MOUNTAIN SHEEP:** Similar to but smaller in stature than the Asiatic argali sheep, this "bighorn" type of sheep ranges over the western coast of Canada, this country, and Mexico.

**ROLLED LATEX:** Known also as Controlastic, it is first formed as a flat strip and then rolled on itself much in the same manner as one would roll paper into a tube form. Stretching straightens the molecules and adds strength. A fine-core thread results.

This fine core, which is covered with nylon, is used for foundations, bathing suits, cushions, and hosiery.

**ROLLER PRINTING:** Method of printing fabrics with engraved metal rollers. The rollers, one for each color in the pattern, are placed around the circumference of a large cylinder so that the cloth to be printed passes between the rollers and the cylinder. Each roller is provided with its own trough containing one color, all combining to produce the pattern. See PRINT.

**ROMAINE:** A semi-sheer fabric of creped yarns. Originally made of silk, now woven of synthetics or wool. Used primarily for dresses. Fiber content must be declared.

**ROMAINE CREPE:** See CREPE.

**ROMAN STRIPES:** Silks which have vivid lines of color in the warp direction. The name is applied to all cloths with prominent stripes, irrespective of the fiber or fibers used in making the goods. Silk fabric of this name is often reversible. Romans are used in dress goods, ribbon, trimming, edging, binding, and in rich silks which are often given a moiré effect to add brilliance to the fabric.

**ROMNEY MARSH:** Originating in the marshes of Kent County, England, this hardy breed of sheep is now popular in America, Australia, New Zealand, and South America. The wool is not as long nor as lustrous as Cotswold or Lincoln wool of Great Britain; however, it is denser, finer, and grades from low ¼-blood to ¼-blood. There is much variation in Romney, which shrinks 30%.

**ROPE MAKING:** In the early days of rope making, during the spinning of yarn for rope, following the hackling process, it was necessary for the operatives to do considerable walking. The walker or spinner had to back down the walk and draw out the fibers as they turned on the hooks of a wheel. The spinner often had a course that covered as much as 400 yards; he had to keep his backward pace constant with his forward pace in order to insure even rope. Today, with improved methods, the spinner rides a machine which resembles the well-known hand-car used by railroads.

**ROSE POINT LACE:** A fine type of Venetian Point. See LACE.

**ROUGH CREPE:** See CREPE.

**ROVING:** A product of the roving frame used in the manufacture of yarns made from natural fibers and man-made or synthetic staple stock which may have been mixed with them. Roving is always the last operation before spinning into yarn, one step removed from spinning. It is a continuous, soft, slight-twisted strand of fibers such as cotton, acetate staple, etc. It is obtained from sliver, slubbing, or other roving which would be greater in diameter at the feeding-in end of the particular frame. The fibers are drafted as they proceed through the machine to obtain a finer cylindrical diameter of the stock. See SLIVER, SLUBBING.

Rovings (*A*) are drawn out and twisted into the finer, smaller diameter spinning yarns (*B*).

**RUBBER:** A manufactured fiber in which the fiber-forming substance is comprised of natural or synthetic rubber.

**RUBBER SHEETING:** A plain cotton fabric with heavy coating of cured rubber on one or both sides. Used in various weights in hospitals and for baby cribs.

**RUBBERIZED FABRIC:** Any fabric with a rubberized coating on one or both sides making it waterproof, and resistant to most stains.

**RUG:** A thick, heavy fabric usually with pile and commonly made of wool, mohair, nylon, or mixtures.

**RUN RESIST:** Knitting stitches, so constructed as to make runs difficult. Used particularly on hosiery and underwear.

**RUNNING YARD:** One yard of cloth regardless of width in which it is woven.

**RUN WOOL:** The number of 1600 yard hanks of wool yarn in a pound. A 4 run wool has 4x1600 or 6400 yards in one pound.

**RUST, JOHN AND MACK:** Brothers and native Texans, they invented the automatic cotton picking machine in 1936. This mechanical picker revolutionized the industry and increased production a great deal. It is estimated that four thousand previous attempts had been made to develop the mechanical cotton picker.

# S

**S AND P COTTON:** See COTTON.

**SAILCLOTH:** 1. Canvas that is particularly strong, durable, and able to withstand the elements. Linen, cotton, nylon, and combed-yarn duck are used to make the fabric. One very popular type is on the order of balloon and typewriter ribbon and is used for spinnaker and head sails. Finished at 40 inches, the texture is around 184-square and there are about 6 yards to the pound.

2. Boatsail drill that is made of Egyptian cotton yarn in plain-weave construction. The texture is about 148 x 60 and the cloth has high strength and good wind-resistance.

**SALEMBAREE:** Heavy, plain-woven cotton used for tents in northern India. Also known as Kathee.

**SALISBURY:** Popular white English flannel; made of woolen yarn, it comes in varying widths.

**SAMITE:** A fabric which became a symbol of textile luxury in ancient times. It is still used in ornamental and ecclesiastical fabrics and is characterized by the use of metallic threads. The body of the fabric is a rich silk.

**SANDWICH BLENDING:** The result of spreading in two or more horizontal layers, fibers from different package units, lots, or of different characteristics; the strata weight being proportional to the percentage of each element used. Thus, all elements are present in the proper proportion when vertical sections are cut from top to bottom for feeding to the next machine in the manufacture of yarn.

**SANFORIZED:** A checked measure of shrinkage. The trademark is applied to fabrics that have been shrunk by the compressive shrinkage process and indicates that the residual shrinkage of the fabric is less than 1% and that the tests have been made by the trademark owner to ensure that the shrinkage conforms to the 1% standard.

The trademark owners, Cluett, Peabody and Co., Inc., permit the use of the Sanforized label on compressive pre-shrunk fabrics wherever the following conditions have been met: 1. The residual shrinkage in the fabric, that is, the amount of shrinkage left after shrinking, does not exceed 1% by the U.S. test method, CCC-T-191a. 2. Tests to determine residual shrinkage have been checked and approved by the trademark owner.

**SANFORIZER:** A finishing machine on which controlled mechanical shrinking is accomplished.

**SANGLIER:** From the French, meaning "wild boar." This dress goods is a plain cloth of wiry worsted or mohair stock, closely woven and given a rough surface finish. Material is supposed to represent the coat of the boar.

**SAPONIFICATION:** Chemically, this process, used primarily for soapmaking, is the hydrolysis of a fat by alkali with the formation of a soap, or salt of a fatty acid, and glycerol. It implies, also, the hydrolysis of a fat by any method. The process is also used in the changing of acetate rayon into a regenerated type.

**SAPONIFIED ACETATE RAYON:** A high-tenacity acetate rayon which is insoluble in acetone and is dyed like viscose rayon.

**SARAN:** A manufactured fiber in which the fiber-forming substance is any long chain synthetic polymer composed of at least 80% by weight of vinylidene chloride units ($-CH_2-CCl_2-$).

The purposes and commercial uses of these products are: Saran is known in popular language as a thermoplastic resin; that is, a plastic which is softened by heat and hardened into shape by cooling. It can be quickly and economically molded, and little waste is occasioned because it can be softened and reshaped again and again.

Saran was first made by Firestone Plastics Company in 1941. Its properties include resistance to chemicals, stains, abrasion, corrosion and moisture. It is nonflammable, tough and flexible. Its chief end-uses are for screen cloth, draperies, luggage, shoes and upholstery. Saran monofilaments are comparatively stiff and soften at low temperature. Saran's weight is too great for wide use as a textile material.

**SARSANET:** A net or veiling fabric used in the millinery and veiling trades. Originally a silk fabric of Arabic origin.

**SATEEN:** From the construction standpoint it is the same as satin. The term is used to specify that the cloth is made of cotton and not silk or rayon. Cotton-back sateen is an important fabric in the sateen group.

(*Top*) Satin weave interlacing. (*Bottom*) Satin warp effect.

**SATIN:** A term which signifies that silk or rayon have been used to make the fabric. Satin weaves are used to make satin and sateen. They will give a warp-effect or a filling-effect as desired. When compared with the other two basic weaves, plain and twill, this weave does not have the tightness of interlacing of the warp and the filling yarns or threads.

Satin effects are ideal in many silks and rayons, particularly for evening wear, since they represent an almost solid color-effect on the face of the goods.

Satin fabric may be recognized by its luster, smooth, soft feel; and face-effect. There are many types of satin on the market under specific names. Satin is the best known of all rayon or silk cloths; originated in China.

Some of the characteristics of satin are excellent draping qualities, some durability, launderability, and slipperiness. The cloth may be difficult to manipulate because of its slipperiness. Comes in white and colors and can be made into rather brilliant form-revealing garments of good texture, for evening wear.

**SATIN-BACK:** A two-faced fabric much used in the drapery trade. One face is dull finished; the other, or back, is a lustrous satin weave.

**SATIN CREPE:** See CREPE-BACK SATIN.

**SATIN WEAVE:** A manner of weaving in which the warp interlaces with the filling at points scattered over the fabric surface. Produces smooth, lustrous fabrics, with relatively long floats of the warp or filling on the face of the fabric.

**SATURATION or INTENSITY, COLOR:** A measure of the strength or purity of a color. Purity increases with increasing concentration of dye on the fiber.

**SAXONY:** Cloth made of very high-grade wool raised in Saxony, Germany. The name is also applied to soft-finished woolen fabrics of similarly fine stock, in fancy-yarn effects on the order of tweeds.

**SCALES:** Protective covering of the wool fiber.

**SCHAPPE SILK:** Considered the same as spun silk in the United States. Technically, however, there is a difference because of the manner of removal of the gum from the waste silk which is often done by a rotting process of fermentation in manure.

Schappe silk is cut into short lengths and spun into yarn on the spun-silk method of spinning; it can also be mixed or blended with other major fibers. This silk has good strength but poor, irregular luster.

Formerly, all European systems differed from the English and the American methods. Now, all European silk of this type is classed as schappe silk.

**SCHIFFLI EMBROIDERY:** A machine type of embroidery made on a loom-like mechanism. The process originated in Switzerland.

**SCHREINER FINISH:** A fabric-finishing process which gives the cloth luster by pounding it with steel rollers on which fine lines are engraved. The fine lines are thus impressed onto the fabric and reflect light to produce a luster finish. Similar to a mercerized finish.

**SCOTCH BLACKFACE:** A well-known breed of sheep which produces much long carpet wool. The fibers are very strong, rugged, and ideal for use as "filling fiber" in the manufacture of rugs and carpets. The sheep are wild, hardy, and withstand the rigors of weather very well.

**SCOTCH FINISH:** Name applied to overcoatings of the tweed, homespun, and cheviot group that possess a loosely shorn nap.

**SCOTCH TWEED:** Made on a 2-up and 2-down twill with white warp and stock-dyed filling or vice-versa. The stock colors are usually rather vivid in order to give contrast in the fabric. Fiber staple in the yarn is usually variable and is irregular in appearance; often this shagginess seems to add to the looks of the material. Always popular, the cloth is used in suiting, topcoating, sport coating, some overcoating.

**SCOURING:** The freeing of wool from yolk, suint, dirt, and all other foreign matter. It may be done by washing with soaps and alkalies, by treating with solvents or chemicals, or by naphthalating the stock at below-freezing temperatures. Loss in weight in scouring the fleece ranges from about 35% in low-grade wools to about 65% in the best types. Yolk serves as the basis for cosmetics, salves, etc., while the dried perspiration or suint is used in making potash.

**SCREEN PRINTING:** Somewhat like stencil printing, except that a screen of fine-silk mesh is employed. Certain areas of the screen are treated to resist the coloring matter. The paste color is forced through the untreated parts of the screen onto the fabric. A separate screen is used for each color in the pattern. See PRINT.

**SCRIM:** A durable, plain-weave cotton cloth. Usually made of ply-yarn and low in pick count. Somewhat similar to voile but a much lower texture. Cheesecloth with a special finish is often referred to as scrim. Comes in many variations. Usually carded but a few combed varieties are on the market.

**SCROOP:** The peculiar crunching or rustling sound noted in some silk fabrics. It is secured by treating the fabric with certain acids. Used in iridescents, petticoating, taffetas.

**SCULPTURED RUG:** A floor covering with jacquard designs in different heights of pile.

**SCUTCHER:** Another name for the opener picker machine, which is a device for cleaning fine-quality cotton.

**SEA ISLAND COTTON:** The finest cotton in the world, originally grown upon the archipelagoes along the Southern states in the United States. Some is now grown in the West Indies. It is generally fine in staple and has a high degree of spirality or "hook." Some staple is 2½ inches long. Compared with other cottons, the yield is very small.

**SEAM SLIPPAGE:** The amount a fabric pulls away at the seams. There are laboratory tests to determine this.

**SEBASTOPOL:** Twilled-face shaggy woolen material of characteristic finish. Named after the famous fortified town of the Russians.

**SECONDARY COLORS:** Secondary or compound colors—violet, green and orange—are made from a mixture of two of the primary colors (red, blue and yellow). See Primary colors.

**SECONDS:** A classification for usable imperfect goods.

**SELVAGE or SELVEDGE:** The woven edge portion of a fabric parallel to the warp.

PLAIN SELVAGE: Plain selvages are woven with extra warp ends for additional strength and in the same weave as the body of the cloth. This selvage is also defined as a wire selvage.

TAPE SELVAGE: The tape selvage consists of two or more additional threads woven in basket weave, different from body of the cloth. The additional threads and weave give added strength and resist curling.

LOOP SELVAGE: A loop selvage retains the count at the edge of the cloth the same as the body of the cloth, and is principally used by the coating trades.

CENTER SELVAGE: Double width cloth woven on single width looms have a split selvage in the center of the cloth. The split is obtained by leaving out two or more threads in the center of the selvage and cutting the cloth where the threads are missing.

**SEERSUCKER:** Cotton, rayon, or nylon crepe-stripe effect fabric, made on plain-weave variation, crepe weave. Light in weight. Colored stripes are often used. Uses are in summer clothing, boys' suits, slacks, bedspreads, and slip covers.

Launders very well, not necessary to iron; durable and gives good service and wear. Crepe effect is permanent; a popular knockabout cotton cloth.

**SEMI-STAPLE:** Fabrics considered partly as staple cloths. Some fabrics in the grouping might be coverts, grey serges, whipcords, gabardines, duvetynes, florentines, henriettas, zibelines

**SERGE:** Popular staple, diagonal worsted cloth, dyed in piece and may be made in mixture or fancy effect. It is possible to stock-dye and yarn-dye the material, but piece-dyeing is preferred. The name is derived from the Latin *serica*. This would imply that the cloth was originally made of silk. The weight of serge runs from 10 ounces upwards and it is one of the most staple of cloths. Made of wool, worsted, cotton-worsted and in other combinations. Clear finish is given the material although unfinished and semi-finished serge is on the market. Mohair serge is used as a garment lining. A 2-up and 2-down right-hand twill is used in constructing the cloth, 45-degree angle. The quality and price range is from the lowest to the highest because of the call for all types of serges. It is a formal, dressy type of cloth and is conventional at all times. Serge holds the crease very well but will shine with wear. This shine cannot be removed permanently. It is a good cloth in tailoring as it drapes and clings well.

**SERICIN:** The natural gum in raw silk that forms a most essential protective agent through the various manufacturing processes. The total amount present in raw silk ranges from about 15 to 25 per cent by weight.

**SERIGRAPH:** Instrument for testing the tenacity, stretch and elastic point of yarns. Standards set up by the ASTM.

**SET MARK:** A defect; a horizontal mark across the cloth in which there are an abnormal number of picks per inch.

**SHADE CLOTH:** Heavy cotton cloth that has been treated with starch, oil and chemicals so that it is opaque. One variety of this is holland shade cloth.

**SHADOW LACE:** A thin, filmy lace made in any design so long as shadowy.

**SHADOW PRINT:** See PRINT.

**SHADOW STRIPE:** A blended stripe effect of darker or lighter shade than the body of the goods.

**SHADOW WEAVE:** An effect on cloths in stripes or plaids produced by the immediate duplicating of the weave formation after a definite repeat in darker tones or shades of yarn which gives the appearance of reflected shadows being cast upon the lighter parts of the fabric. Upon staple goods, as black or blue, it is produced by the yarns used in part of the pattern being twisted in spinning in an opposite or reverse direction to those elsewhere required, which, in the woven cloth, will give a "shadow" effect. In worsted suitings such as herringbones, bisected block and diamond patterns, etc., it is particularly effective.

**SHAFT:** Another name for the harness on a loom. In speaking of satin weaves this term is interchangeable with harness or end. Thus, an 8-end, 8-shaft, 8-harness satin weave. See HARNESS.

**SHAKER FLANNEL:** Wool, cotton, or mixed material that is napped on both sides. Usually softer and thicker than regular flannel and is used for underwear.

**SHAKER KNIT:** The term is derived from the Shaker sect who first developed this type of heavy yarn ribbed stitch.

**SHANTUNG:** Low in luster, heavier and rougher than pongee. A plain weave silk in which large, irregular filling yarns are used. Sometimes used to describe a heavy grade of pongee made in China. Sometimes referred to as nankeen, rajah, tussah. Also made from several major fibers.

**SHANTUNG (COTTON):** Plain-woven cotton with a nubby, irregular rib effect formed by an uneven slub yarn. Slubs are thick, soft sections of the yarn which contain less twist than the thinner portions.

**SHARKSKIN:** A fine worsted quality fabric made from small color-effect weaves or fancy designs in which the effect noted in the finished cloth resembles the skin of the shark. The cloth is given a substantial finish and it wears very well. High texture is used and the fabric comes chiefly in shades of grey or brown. Ideal for office wear, since it is a dressy, conservative material.

The material is also made in acetate, rayon, spun rayon, and in various blends. This popular fabric which has a rather heavy, semi-crisp texture, is used in men's and women's summer sportswear garments.

**SHEARED WOOL:** See FLEECE.

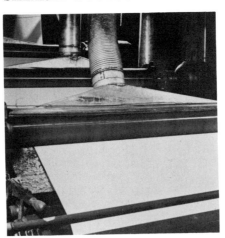

Shearing machine.

**SHEARING:** The operation of leveling the nap on cloth is much used in the woolen and worsted trades, as well as in the case of certain cotton fabrics. Shearing regulates the height of the nap or protruding fibers found on the surface of goods. The machine used may have one or two shear blades or more. A blade is exceedingly sharp in order to shave, shear, or cut off the undesirable portions. It can be arranged or set to leave a certain height of even, uniform nap on goods, since the blade can be raised or lowered, as desired. The blade is regulated to the thirty-second part of an inch. Thus, a nap could be 4/32 or 6/32 of an inch in height.

The blades are on the principle of those on a lawn mower. The material to be sheared passes under the blade and all fibers longer than the setting of the blade are taken off neatly and cleanly. There remains an evened-off surface on the fabric that leaves a sort of pile effect.

Goods may be run through the shear any number of times to produce a good surface. The operator has to be on guard constantly to watch for knots, loops, or other parts of the cloth that may be cut, and thereby rip a goodly portion of the material. When these raised places come around to the blade the shearer raises the blade to admit the passage of the cloth underneath. These blemishes are later cared for by the menders and sewers before the cut is finally passed.

**SHEARLING:** English term for yearling or a one-year-old sheep. Also means short wool pulled from the skins of sheep prior to slaughtering.

**SHED:** Passageway or opening of the warp threads in the loom made by raising and lowering warp threads by the heddles, allowing for the insertion of the filling thread by means of the shuttle.

**SHEEP:** An animal of the ruminant or chewing-the-cud genus *Ovis*. Closely allied with the goat, sheep are raised for mutton and carcass.

**SHEER:** Any very thin fabric such as organdy. Used for summer and evening clothes.

**SHEETING:** Plain-weave, carded-yarn (or combed) cloths in medium and heavy weights. Sheeting for converting purposes is about 40 inches wide. Textures are lower than those used in print-cloths and the cloth is usually made from heavier yarns—from 10s to 30s. Warp yarns in sheeting are often heavier than the filling yarn used in construction; they can also be the same count.

Sheeting comes in the following classifications: coarse, ordinary, lightweight, narrow, soft-filled, and wide. Width of sheeting will vary to suit the consumer needs. Textures may range from 40 square to 68 x 72. Sheeting is usually cotton, but also of nylon, silk, etc.

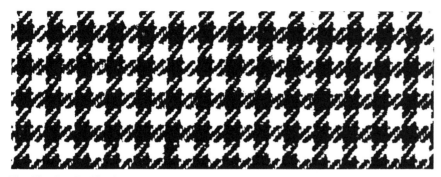

The Shepherd's Check of the Scottish Borders is the foundation on which the entire series of District Checks rests. The Shepherd's Check consisted of about a quarter inch of white and a quarter inch of black, so that the number of threads in the pattern was controlled by the size of yarn used in the fabric. This "plaidie" or shawl measured around four yards long and about a yard and a half wide.

**SHEPHERD'S CHECK OR PLAID:** Used for suitings, cap cloth, coatings, dress goods, sportswear. Made of cotton, woolen, worsted, or silk. The cloth shows black and white checks or plaids. Other color combinations are used as well. The design resembles the Scotch shepherd plaid or check. Some of the cloth, because of the color combinations used, has the tendency to cause the eyes to "jump" and some people soon tire of the cloth. Conservative designs, however, are much in demand by the trade. There is a wide range of quality and price. In producing the check, the warp and filling arrangement is four black and four white, ends and picks. The weave should begin with the "raisers" up in the lower left-hand corner of the weave. If this is not adhered to, a straight check will result which is not, strictly speaking, what is known as shepherd's plaid.

The pattern is found in particular fabrics made from any of the major fibers.

**SHETLAND:** 1. A suiting fabric made wholly or part of shetland wool. The cloth has a raised finish and a rather soft handle. Very popular for suiting and sportswear.

2. A soft knitted fabric made of shetland wool.

3. Loosely applied to various soft-handle woven or knitted fabrics that do not contain shetland wool.

**SHETLAND WOOL:** This sheep produces fine, lustrous fiber and the real wool is the undergrowth found under the long fibers. It is not shorn, but is pulled out by hand in the spring of the year. Comes in white, brown, and grey casts and is classed as a costly fiber.

**SHIFTING:** Term applied to the distortion of a fabric due to shifting of yarns out of place.

**SHODDY:** A cloth made of ground-up rags in their composition, wholly or partly wool. It is an odious term signifying refuse of "shod" or cast-off material and such fabric is in general disrepute. Many of the cheaper woolen goods are adulterated with shoddy stock.

**SHODDY WOOL:** Remanufactured wool fibers are obtained from the garnetting machine treatment, which tears apart and shreds the discarded garments fed to the machine. Shoddy comes from woolen, worsted, or knitted garments. The shoddy or mungo fibers are mixed with better quality and longer-staple fibers to make up new material to be made ultimately into fabric.

**SHOE CLOTH:** Worsted cloth made with the corkscrew weave and used in spats and shoe cloth. Cloth ranges from 12 to 18 ounces per yard and the texture of the warp and filling is very high, 80 to 140 each way. Two-ply worsted yarn is used as the warp, the filling is worsted, wool, or cotton and is usually single ply.

**SHOT SILK:** Term signifying the use of two differently colored sets of yarn, warp and filling, in order to give a changeable effect in cloth. Silk taffeta is often made in this manner.

**SHRINKAGE CONTROL:** Various processes, either mechanical or chemical, are used to minimize shrinkage of fabrics and garments; compressive shrinkage of a cotton fabric holds residual shrinkage to less than 1% in either width or length.

**SHRINK RESISTANT:** Term used to describe fabrics that have been chemically treated against shrinkage. See PRE-SHRUNK and SANFORIZED.

**SHROPSHIRE:** This county in England is the home of this popular British Down breed. Noted for both wool and mutton production. Staple is about 3 inches, the fleece weight averages 9 pounds and the quality ranges from 50s to 56s.

**SHUTTLE:** The device which carries the filling yarn in its course through the shed of the loom in weaving fabric. Power-loom shuttles are made of dogwood or persimmon, properly aged. There is a metal tip at each end of a shuttle. The filling bobbin is set into the open space provided for it in the shuttle and there is an eyelet at one end so that the filling may unwind rapidly as it is shot through the shed from the shuttle box on the one side of the loom to the box on the other side of the machine. Worsted looms average about 125 picks per minute, that is, the shuttle flies back and forth that number of times per minute from box to box. This number may vary somewhat, dependent on fabric being made and other local conditions.

**SHUTTLELESS LOOM:** Shuttleless looms are either air-jet or water-jet. With the air-jet loom, the filling yarn is propelled by a jet of air. With the water-jet loom, the yarn is propelled by a jet of water. The shuttleless looms are considerably faster than conventional looms, and thus generally more economical. However, water-jet looms are confined to filament yarns and fibers which are non-absorbent and do not deteriorate in water. Rayon, for example, would not qualify for water-jet looms.

**SICILIAN:** Was first made on the island of Sicily. Cotton warp and mohair filling were used for this lining fabric which is still popular at present when made from these or other yarn combinations. Another fabric of the same name, used for dress goods and also made in Sicily, used silk warp and woolen filling in which the rather bulky crosswise threads formed a rib effect in the material.

**SILENCE CLOTH:** See MOLLETON.

**SILESIA:** Generally a lightweight cotton-twill lining with a calendered glaze finish; a rather sturdy fabric used for lining in garments.

**SILICONES:** A class of organic chemical compounds, based on the partial substitution of silicon for carbon, which are finding important applications in making textiles water-repellent.

**SILICONE-TREATED FELT:** See FELT.

**SILK:** The end product of silk moths which are raised for commercial purposes to obtain the filament, which will range from about 300 yards to about 1,600 yards. The middle third of the filament is even in diameter, the beginning and end are rather uneven, often split and coarse. The genus *Bombyx* and other genera of the *Bombycidea* family serve as the basis for commercial yarn.

The cultivated member of this family is the *Bombyx mori,* or common silkworm. It feeds on mulberry leaves and their juices. The undomesticated silkworms belong to the Yama-Mai or other species, and develop what is known as tussah or wild silk. They feed on practically any type of leaf with which they come in contact.

(*A*) Bombyx mori, or silkworm. (*B*) Silk moth laying eggs. (*C*) Silk cocoon from which silk is taken.

**SILK FLOSS:** 1. Very short fibers of tangled waste silk.

2. Erroneously used to describe the soft fibers from the kapok tree which are blended together and used as stuffing for pillows, mattresses, and life preservers.

**SILK-MIXTURE CLOTH:** Worsted and cassimere material used for suitings and dress goods produced by interspersed weaving of all-silk threads or by the use of woolen material twisted with silk.

**SILK NOIL:** The waste from the last dressing operation in spun silk; it is often too short to be used again in silk manufacture. Noil is sold to cotton and woolen merchants who mix the stock with longer staple fibers for spinning. Fancy, nub and novelty yarns are often made with this noil in them. It adds brilliance to the yarn and often shows up in little balls or nubs in the fabric.

**SILK WEIGHTING:** A process often used in connection with silk dyeing to compensate for the loss in weight because of the removal of the silk gum or sericin, or to increase the weight and consequently decrease the cost. Generally done with tin salts (stannic chloride) but iron salts may be used for blacks.

**SILVERTONE AND GOLDTONE:** A coating cloth made from woolen or worsted warp with woolen filling. Fabric is stock-dyed and weight goes from 16 to 24 ounces per yard. Material is heavily napped. Construction may be single or double. The cloth gets its name from the fact that strands of gold- and silver-colored threads are worked into the face of the material.

**SIMULTANEOUS CONTRAST:** When two colors are juxtaposed, each undergoes surprising changes. When red is juxtaposed with yellow for example, it takes on the cast of the color which is the complementary of yellow—violet— which is composed of the other two primaries absent from yellow, namely red and blue. In sum, when two colors are juxtaposed, each takes on the cast of its neighbor's complementary color.

**SINGEING:** A process which smoothes out the surface of a fabric by passing it over gas jets to singe off the protruding fibers.

**SINGLES or SINGLE YARN:** One strand of yarn not plied. A mass of fibers or number of filaments bound together in a coherent yarn.

**SINGLE WARP:** In regard to yarns, per se, the warp threads in the cloth are single, as distinguished from two or more ply. In reference to fabric construction it is a single system of warp threads where there is, perhaps, a double system of filling threads.

**SINGLE-WOVEN FABRIC:** Cloth made with two sets of threads; one set, the threads of which run vertically in the goods, is known as the warp; the other set, the threads of which run horizontally in the material, is known as the filling. The terms *ends* and *warp* are considered synonymous; picks and filling are likewise synonymous.

**SISAL:** A bast fiber used in the manufacture of ropes. It is grown largely in British East Africa and the Dutch Indies.

**SIZING:** The addition of starch or other similar substances to stiffen warp and/or filling yarns, and certain fabrics which benefit from its application.

**SKEIN:** A length of yarn wound onto a reel, usually about 120 yards long. A skein is from 44 to 54 inches in circumference.

**SKEIN DYEING:** DYEING METHODS.

**SKI CLOTH:** See MACKINAC.

**SKINNER'S SATIN:** Trademarked satin made by William Skinner and Sons.

**SKIP-DENT:** A type of open weave much used in men's summer shirtings. The term is derived from the dent, or opening between the two wires which make up part of the reed through which the warp ends are drawn. When one of these dents is "skipped" an open skip-dent weave results.

**SLAG WOOL:** This is prepared by blowing steam through molten lead. It can hardly be called a textile fiber, but since it is used the same as some fibers in packing, it may be classified as such. Slag wool is not spun into yarn like asbestos, the greatest of mineral fibers. It is used as a felt because it is made up of fine interlocking mineral fibers that enclose a mass of minute air cells, which give it the property of a good nonconductor of heat.

**SLASHER:** The device which coats warp threads with a protective sizing to strengthen them for the weaving.

**SLATER, SAMUEL:** Often called the father of the United States cotton textile industry. He came to America from England in 1789 and reconstructed from memory at least five important textile machines which became the foundation for some of the early New England mills.

**SLEAZY:** Thin, lacking firmness, open meshed. Usually said of poor grade fabrics.

**SLEY:** The number of warp yarns per inch.

**SLICKER-FABRIC:** Plain-weave rayon, silk, nylon, or cotton cloth treated with linseed oil or pyroxylin to make it waterproof. For raincoats and fishermen's outfits.

**SLIPPER SATIN:** A strong, compactly woven cloth used chiefly for evening footwear. Textures are high and the material comes in black, white, colors, or brocaded effects of silk or man-made fibers.

**SLIVER:** A strand or rope of fibers which are soft, loose, and untwisted. Obtained from the delivery end of the carding machine in yarn manufacture. Other machines which may produce sliver are drawing frames, combers, slubber frames, and roving machines. It is the first form in which the stock being processed is delivered in a ropelike form. Sliver is greater in diameter than slubbing and roving; slubbing is larger in diameter when compared with roving, the last operation before spinning yarn. See SLUBBING, ROVING.

**SLIVER KNITTING:** A technique for making high pile fabrics. See Dictionary of Knitting Terms.

**SLIVER SPINNING:** The name for the system of spinning yarn directly from sliver instead of from roving; appropriate for machines where the sliver stock is wound into a ball form instead of being fed into the machine from a sliver can. Can spinning is so called because the creel of the spinning frame is a group of sliver cans of stock. Sliver spinning and can spinning should not be confused with pot spinning since this term refers to the receiving element in which the yarn is set in a pot-shaped receptacle by centrifugal force. See POT SPINNING.

**SLUBBING:** A term applied to the condition of a group of fibers in rope form, heavier and larger in diameter when compared with roving. An enlarged roving but not the roving that is sent through the spinning frame for manufacture into spun yarn. Generally speaking, slubbing is the name given to the strand of fibers as they appear between sliver and roving. See ROVING, SLIVER.

**SLUBS:** Imperfections made by nubs, tufts, or little balls of yarn in cloth. They are noticeable and have to be fixed in dry finishing.

**SLUB DYEING:** See DYEING METHODS.

**SLUB YARN:** Yarn of any type which is irregular in diameter; may be caused by error, or purposely made with slubs to bring out some desired effect to enhance a material. Slub yarns are popular as novelty threads in summer dress goods and find much use in hand woven fabrics.

**SLUG:** A yarn defect consisting of an abruptly thickened spot.

**SMASH:** A relatively large hole in the cloth characterized by many broken warp ends and floating picks.

**SOAPING:** Treating cloth with a soap solution. Dyed and printed fabrics are soaped thoroughly in hot solution to remove excess color.

**SODA ASH:** The technical grade of sodium carbonate. Its aqueous solution is strongly alkaline and is used in washing and scouring operations.

**SOFTENER:** Any material used in warp sizing and cloth finishing to impart a soft mellow hand to the fabric. Examples of softeners include sulfonated oils, glycerine, waxes, silicones, etc. There are durable types of cationic softeners that remain in the fabric after dry cleaning and washing.

**SOFT-FILLED SHEETING:** Usually a cotton sheeting fabric with a filling which is soft-spun and much lower in yarn count than the warp of the fabric. It is often used as a base for napped fabrics like cotton flannel.

**SOIL-RELEASE:** The property of a finish to allow a fabric to hold stains less tenaciously and thus to release the soil more readily in cleaning.

**SOIL REPELLENCY:** The capacity of a fabric to resist absorption of soils or stains. Water repellents resist waterborne stains and oil repellents resist greasy or oily stains.

**SOLEIL:** Is the French for sun, and many allied types of silk fabrics are given this name because they show bright satin-face effects which simulate sunrays.

**SOLUTION-DYED:** Refers to fabrics of rayon or synthetic fibers which are dyed by adding color to the chemical liquid before the fiber is formed through the spinneret.

**SOUFFLE:** Means puffed, and the large designs seen in crepon and other cloths which are made with a raised or puffed motif are thus named.

**SOURCE:** The first major bi-constituent fiber, from Allied Chemical, of nylon and polyester. See Bi-Constituent.

**SOYBEAN FIBER:** The fiber produced from the soybean is of protein base. It resembles wool in resiliency and feel; it is insulative, and has a tensile strength about 80% that of wool. It excels wool in resistance to alkalies.

**SPANDEX:** A manufactured fiber in which the fiber-forming substance is a long chain synthetic polymer comprised of at least 85% of a segmented polyurethane.

**SPACE DYED YARN:** Yarn dyed in single color or multi-color spaces along a given lineal length of yarn in either repeat type or random type patterns.

**SPANISH LACE:** See LACE.

**SPECTROPHOTOMETRY:** A method of measuring reflection factors of a color, by comparing various wavelengths and the intensity to a standard. The measurements can be plotted on a chart. The chart is ruled one direction for wave-lengths (the spectrum), and the other direction for reflection (the intensity).

**SPINDLE:** A long, thin rod that is used on certain textile machines for twisting and holding textile fibers in manipulation from sliver form to spun yarn. This upright device is found on slubbers, roving frames, jack frames, spinning, winding, and twisting machines. Revolving at a very high rate of speed to perform its work, drawing, twisting and winding, the spindle has a bobbin, tube, or cop set around it so that the finished stock may be wound evenly and easily.

The spindle is one of the oldest textile devices known to man. It is driven on machines of today by means of spindle banding which can drive a spindle over 12,000 r.p.m., if needs be.

585

**SPINNERET:** An essential device in the production of man-made fibers like rayon. It looks much like a thimble punctured at its end with holes of from 2 to 5 thousandths of an inch. A solution is forced through these holes at speed to produce a fine filament which is solidified in an acid bath. Spinnerets are usually made of platinum and iridium.

**SPINNING:** 1. The drafting of roving fed into the spinning frame to produce yarn of the required counts, to insert the proper number of turns of twist per inch, and to wind the newly-made yarn onto a bobbin, cone, cheese, or some other suitable holder. The three essentials in spinning are drawing of the fibers, twisting of the yarn, and the winding of the yarn onto some device. Cotton yarn is spun on the mule frame or the ring spinning frame; the same method applies to woolen yarn, while worsted yarn may be spun on the ring, cap, flyer, or mule frames.

2. The extrusion of a spinning solution through the orifices of a spinneret to form filaments. Used in manufacture of man-made filaments.

3. Collectively, spinning covers all the operations used to produce yarn from man-made filaments. There are three methods for spinning man-made filaments: dry spinning, wet spinning and melt spinning. In the dry-spinning method, a polymer solution in a solvent is forced through tiny holes into warm air. The solvent evaporates in the warm air and the liquid stream solidifies into a continuous filament. In the wet-spinning method, a polymer solution is forced through tiny holes into another solution where it is coagulated into a continuous filament. In the melt-spinning method, a solid polymer is melted and forced through tiny holes into cool air, which solidifies it into a continuous filament.

**SPINNING BATH, COAGULATION BATH:** A bath used in the manufacture of filament yarns made from man-made or synthetic bases. The solution is extruded through spinnerets for solidifying or precipitating the filaments. The minute openings in spinnerets are known as orifices, while the spinneret resembles a capped thimble and is made of platinum and iridium compound.

**SPINNING JENNY:** This was the first machine to spin more than one yarn at a time. James Hargreaves worked on this machine from 1754 to 1768 and tradition has it that the machine was named in honor of his wife or "some female." The date of his birth is unknown and he died in 1778. He was a carpenter and weaver of Standhill, near Blackburn, England. He "received the original idea when he saw a one-thread wheel overturned on the floor while both the wheel and the spindle continued to revolve." The spindle had thus been thrown from a horizontal position to an upright position and, if a number of spindles were placed upright and side by side, several threads could be spun at one time. For his contribution to the Industrial Revolution his home was sacked in 1768 and he fled to Nottingham for refuge.

Hargreaves improved his machine to spin eight yarns and later on increased it to 100 yarns at a time. He perfected the first practical frame for spinning cotton yarn.

**SPINNING, POT:** See Pot Spinning.

**SPINNING SOLUTION:** Chemical solution prepared for extrusion through a spinneret. Refers to man-made fibers.

**SPITALFIELDS:** A fabric, originally silk, with a small all-over design. Usually associated with neckwear fabrics, its name comes from the London district of Spitalfields where French Huguenot weavers settled in the 16th Century.

**SPONGING:** A shrinking process usually applied to woolens and worsteds before they are cut up. It simply calls for dampening the fabric with a wet sponge or steaming.

**SPOOL:** A wood or metal cylinder which holds the spindle on which yarn is wound.

**SPOT AND STAIN-RESISTANT:** Fabric which has been treated to resist stains. The fabric must be laboratory tested before any such claim can be made. See Water Spotting.

**SPUN DYED:** See Solution Dyed, under Dyeing.

**SPUN LINEN:** See Linen.

**SPUN RAYON:** The long, continuous rayon filaments produce rayon fabrics having smooth surfaces or crepe surfaces. The filament can be adapted for other effects by cutting it into short uniform lengths of from $\frac{1}{2}$ to 9 inches. These lengths are spun into yarns similarly to the spinning of cotton or wool.

Spun rayon yarn (*A*) compared with filament rayon yarn (*B*).

Such spun-rayon yarns have an entirely different character from the filament rayon yarns.

According to the amount of twist inserted in the spinning process, spun-rayon yarn can be made stronger, less lustrous, and adaptable to napping and other finishes, thus producing fabrics that resemble wool, linen, or cotton. Such short-staple rayon can also be combined with any of the natural fibers to make effective and useful fabrics; this blending would not be possible with the long rayon filament. Thus, spun rayon provides new finishes and a variety of low-priced fabrics that formerly were made only from natural fibers, with a consequently higher production cost.

Some spun-rayon fabrics are known by such trade names as Avisco, Fibro, etc.; there are many others that do not have specific trade names.

**SPUN-BONDING:** A process of making nonwoven fabrics from continuous filament fibers, which are bonded at cross-over points immediately after the fibers have been extruded from the spinneret.

**SPUN SILK SYSTEM:** A system of yarn manufacturing developed to process silk waste, and presently used also to a limited extent for the processing of rayon staple. The waste is usually a tangled mass of material and the first step is to break it up into short fiber lengths; then it is dressed, drawn and finally spun into yarn. The process is rather lengthy and slow and is falling into disuse.

**SPUN YARNS:** 1. Yarns made of fibers of controlled lengths (synthetic fibers).

2. Spun silk yarn made from short fibers of silk that cannot be reeled.

**SQUARE CLOTH:** A fabric in which the number of yarns per inch in the warp is the same as the number of yarns per inch in the filling.

**STABILIZED:** A resin finish on cotton or spun rayon fabrics which helps a material to keep its original finish, whether it is soft or crisp. Trade name of U.S. Finishing Co.

**STAPLE:** From Anglo-Saxon, meaning "fixed, not variable." This term is applied to cloths and apparel of conservative nature as to weave, color, construction, and quality. Dress worsteds, diagonals in blues and blacks, meltons, kerseys, beavers, broadcloths, serges, cassimeres, etc., are classed as staples. They are always in demand as contrasted with fancy and novelty cloths that come to the fore in economic cycles. The cycle of style, fashion, design, and vogue shows that some cloths come into their own about every seven or eleven years; chinchilla, for example.

**STAPLE FIBER:** Filaments of the cellulosic or man-made groups of fibers which have been cut to the length of the various natural fibers. This staple fiber may be spun alone or with cotton, wool, worsted, linen, or spun silk based on the system of spinning which involves the particular natural fiber with which it has been blended or mixed. Staple stock is obtained from acetate, rayon, Dynel, nylon, Dacron, Orlon, etc.

**STARCHING:** The addition of starches to cellulosic fabrics to add weight, and firm hand and body, to the cloth.

**STARCHLESS FINISH:** A durable finish which lasts through several washings, obviates the use of starch for body and crispness. See FINISH.

**STEAMING:** 1. Subjecting a printed or dyed fabric to steam to assure penetration and fix the color on the cloth.

2. Treating woolens with steam for controlled shrinkage.

**STENCIL PRINT:** See PRINT.

**STITCH-THROUGH:** A system of fabric construction which locks together yarns, or a web of fibers, by the use of needles and thread. Examples are Malimo and Arachne methods.

**STOCK DYEING:** See RAW STOCK DYEING under DYEING.

**STOCKINETTE:** A knitted, worsted, part worsted or cotton elastic fabric on the so-called jersey order. A product of the "stocking frame" and usually made with a "fleeced wool" back. Used as a material for working, house, and smoking jackets.

**STRAW:** Fabric made by braiding, plaiting, or weaving natural plant fibers such as stems, stalks, leaves, bark and grass. Used for making hats, bags and shoe uppers.

BAKU—Fine, lightweight, expensive straw with a dull finish. Made from fibers of buri palm along the Ceylon and Malabar coast.

BALIBUNTAL—Fine, lightweight, glossy straw obtained from unopened palm leaf stems.

LEGHORN—Finely plaited straw made from a kind of wheat grown in Tuscany, cut green and bleached, woven by hand in Italy.

MILAN—Fine, closely woven straw used in fine quality women's hats, made in Milan, Italy. Imitations must be clearly described as such.

PANAMA—Fine hand-plaited, creamy colored Toquilla straw used for men's and women's hats, made, curiously enough, primarily in Equador.

TOQUILLA—Strong, flexible fiber obtained from Jippi-Jappa leaves. Used in weaving Panama hats. No other hat should be labeled "Panama" or "Genuine Panama."

TUSCAN—Fine, yellow straw woven from the tops of bleached wheat stalks grown in Tuscany. Often woven in lace-like designs.

**STRETCH SPINNING:** A term used in the manufacture of rayon. Man-made filaments are stretched while moist and before final coagulation. This gives the filament increased strength.

**STRETCH YARNS:** Made from thermoplastic fiber, usually in continuous filament form, they possess a considerable degree of stretch and quick recovery. Deforming, heat-setting, and developing treatments are features of these yarns. There are two main types—1. Crimped or non-torque in which the deformation is in wave-like formation. Crimp may be obtained by passing the yarn over an edge, passing it through a stuffer box, or in the case of a "crinkled yarn," knitting a yarn into a fabric, then heat-setting the material followed by "back-winding" the yarn from fabric.

2. Twist or torque yarn in which the deformation is obtained by a desirable combination of heat-setting and twisting. This may be accomplished by twisting, heat-setting, and then detwisting; by false-setting and heat-setting simultaneously, or by heat-setting and twisting in the case of a monofilament. Such yarns are usually plied to control the elasticity of the finished product.

**STRIP TEST:** A method of measuring the breaking strength of cloth. The test sample is six inches long with exactly one inch width.

**STRIPPING:** Removing the dye or print color from a fabric by bleaching action.

**STRUCTURAL DESIGN:** A woven-in design, as opposed to one printed on a fabric.

**STUFFER:** An extra yarn woven in warp or filling direction to give weight or bulk to a fabric.

**S-TWIST:** A direction of twist in yarn or cord similar to the spiral part of the letter S. Formerly called "left" or "reverse" twist.

**STYLON:** Sometimes referred to as fiber-dust, the product may be applied to an adhesive-treated fabric under air-pressure, following a definite and previously arranged motif or design. Stylon is suitable for dress fabrics.

**SUBSTANTIVE DYES:** Dyes applicable to cotton and other vegetable fibers without the use of a mordant. They are used extensively where fastness properties are not important. Also known as *Commercial Dyes*.

**SUCCESSIVE CONTRAST:** The after-image which appears before a person's eyes after looking concentratedly at an isolated color. Each after-image is the complementary of the original color, e.g., red has an after-image of its complementary green.

**SUEDE CLOTH:** Sheeting napped on one side to resemble leather suede. Duvetyne, when made in cotton, is similar to suede but has a longer nap. Used considerably in jackets and sportswear.

**SUFFOLK:** British Down breed of sheep derived from crossing Southdown rams with Norfolk ewes. The medium wool obtained sorts to ¼-blood or low ⅜-blood; fibers are of moderate length and the fleece weighs about 9 pounds. Shrinkage is about 40 per cent.

**SUITING:** General term for fabrics used for coats and suits for both men and women. Includes many novelties of weave and texture, and can be made of all fibers and/or blends. See F.T.C. Rules.

**SULPHUR DYE:** See DYES.

**SULTANE:** Named for the first wife of a Sultan, is a very old textile. It was made of silk warp and wool filling on a twill weave and given a rough finish without any shearing or singeing. It is used for dress goods, shawls, mantle cloths, and cloakings.

**SUNFAST:** A colored fabric which will resist fading by sunlight.

**SUNN:** One of the bast fibers, used in India in making twine.

**SUPIMA:** Trademark for a superior type of extra-long-staple fiber, 1⅜ inches and longer. This is an exceptionally high-quality American-Egyptian cotton grown in the Southwest.

**SURAH:** A soft, twill woven silk often made in plaid effects. If made of some fiber other than silk, the fiber content must be declared. Uses include neckwear, mufflers, blouses, and dress goods. Named for Surat, India.

**SWANSDOWN:** A heavily-napped cotton fabric like flannel.

**SWATCH:** A small sample of cloth.

**SWISS:** Fine sheer cotton fabric which may be plain, dotted or figured. Usually is crisp and stiff. Often known as DOTTED SWISS. Used for dresses and, in a heavier form, for window curtains. So called because first made in Switzerland. Domestic fabrics are known as domestic dotted Swiss.

**SWIVEL:** Extra filling or swivel yarns make small clipped woven-in designs in a cloth, i.e., in marquisette or dotted Swiss.

**SYNTHETIC FIBERS:** Term used

loosely for all man-made fibers. Actually the term includes only textile fibers made by chemical synthesis.

**SYNTHETIC RESINS:** Chemical compounds used widely in recent years in the finishing of textiles. There are many kinds of synthetic resins. Cloths are generally impregnated with them to give one or more desired properties to the finished cloth, or they may be used in the coated fabric field.

**SYNTHETIC TEXTILE FILAMENTS:** They were officially recognized in 1925, when the Federal Trade Commission permitted the use of the name, rayon, for man-made yarns obtained from cellulose or its derivatives. As there are several methods of making synthetic textile yarns and materials, and as the production and types of yarns had increased and had been given various trade names, the Federal Trade Commission ruled again in 1937 that any fiber or yarn produced chemically from cellulose must be designated as rayon. Since that time, however, there have been a number of new synthetic filaments and yarns produced that do not necessarily have a cellulose base; generally speaking these are classed as synthetic or man-made.

# T

**TABBY:** Synonym for plain weave.

**TABLE DAMASK:** A cloth of cotton, linen, rayon, or mixed fibers used as a

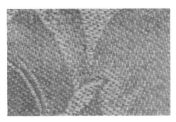

Linen damask weave.

table cover. The pattern is woven with warp satin-weave floats over a background of filling satin-weave floats and vice-versa on the back. The pattern is reversible. These contrasting floats, at right angles to each other, reflect light differently and produce dark effects on

damasks. The designs are reversed on the other side. Double damask is finer and more tightly woven than single damask.

**TABLE PADDING:** Soft cotton fabric napped on both sides or quilted. Used to protect tables from heat or pressure; also used on ironing boards. Sometimes called SILENCE CLOTH or MOLLETON.

**TACKING:** Sewing the selvages together of cloth that has been folded lengthwise, with the face side in. This is done during various finishing operations to protect the face of the fabric and also to prevent wrinkles.

**TACKLE TWILL:** A very sturdy fabric much used for athletic clothing. It is a twill weave with lustrous, smooth rayon or nylon face and cotton back. Made with steep-twill weaves. The name is a trademark of Wm. Skinner & Sons.

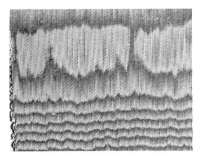

Taffeta moiré.

**TAFFETA:** A fine plain-weave fabric smooth on both sides, usually with a sheen to its surface. Named for Persian fabric *taftan*. May be solid colored or printed, or woven in such a way that the colors seem "changeable." Used for dresses, blouses, suits. Originally of silk, now often made of synthetic fibers. There are several taffeta classifications, such as:

ANTIQUE TAFFETA—A stiff, plain weave fabric woven of Douppioni to resemble fabrics of the 18th Century.

FAILLE TAFFETA—Taffeta woven with a pronounced crosswise rib.

MOIRÉ TAFFETA—Rayon or silk taffeta fabric with moiré pattern. In acetate, moiré can be fused so it is permanent.

PAPER TAFFETA—Lightweight taffeta treated to have a crisp paper-like finish.

PIGMENT TAFFETA—Taffeta woven with pigmented yarns which give the fabric a dull finished surface. See PIGMENTED.

TISSUE TAFFETA—Very lightweight transparent taffeta.

**TAKE-UP or CONTRACTION:** The difference between two points on a yarn and the same two points after the yarn has been woven into a fabric. Take-up is a mill term used in relation to looms and indicates the percentage the yarn will be shortened by weaving.

**TAMBOUR CURTAINS:** Panels of imported Swiss, heavily embroidered batiste or lawn, used for draping a window.

**TAMISE:** A close-mesh fabric first made of silk and wool and now made of man-made yarns. The name comes from *tamis*, the French word for sieve, since the fabric is of the diaphanous type, such as marquisette.

**TAPA:** A fabric native to the Pacific Islands. It is most often made from tree bark.

**TAPESTRY:** An ornamental woven fabric in which the design is usually a picture which illustrates a story. The design is an integral part of the weaving and is not embroidered. Originally made by hand, tapestries can now be woven by machine.

**TARLATAN, TARLETAN:** Originated in Italy where it was made of linen and cotton, the cloth was coarse and low in texture. Today, tarlatan is made of either carded or combed cotton yarn, and is a thick or thin scrim, heavily starched and net-like in appearance. It is used for fruit packing, dresses, coat linings, and in the sewing and millinery trades because of the heavily-sized finish, which makes it ideal for waist banding and hat lining. Tarlatan comes in white and in colors. When flame-proofed, it is used for theatrical gauze and stage draping.

**TARNISH PREVENTION:** Chemically treated, napped cloth used to wrap silver and to line silver chests to protect them from tarnishing.

**TARPAULIN:** 1. Canvas or nylon fabric usually coated to make it waterproof so that it may serve as a protection against inclement weather. Finds great use in covering athletic diamonds and fields.

2. A sailor's storm hat can be called a tarpaulin.

**TARTAN PLAID:** A conventionalized, multi-colored fabric, the outstanding material of which is kilt cloth. Plaids are used for blankets, robes, many types of dress goods, neckwear, ribbon, silks, etc. This cloth was given to the world by the well-known Scotch clans of Campbell, Cameron, MacPhee, Stewart, Douglas, MacDonald, MacPherson, MacTavish, etc. In woolens and worsteds, in subdued effects, it has use in suiting cloth. The word, formerly spelled "tartanem," was borrowed from the English who took it from the Spanish term *tiritana*. The Spaniards gave this name to colored cloths as far back as the 13th Century. There is also a tradition that tartan originated in France where similar designs in cotton are still in popular use. The Scotch have capitalized on tartans more than any other nation and the general belief is that these plaids were Scotch in origin. The Gaelic term is *brecan*. It takes about 17 yards of material to make a complete kilt outfit for an adult. Plain weave or 2-up and 2-down twill weaves are used in construction.

Tartan effects often appear in goods made from any of the major fibers.

It should be borne in mind that the word *plaid* initially described the cape portion of the Scottish Highland costume, rather than the design. But over a period of time, and most likely because the pattern in the plaid was always a distinctive cross-stripe, the terms became interchangeable, and finally *plaid* came into common use as the name for this type of design.

**TATTERSALL:** Heavy woolen fancy vesting cloth of "loud" appearance. The name is taken from the famous mart for thoroughbreds and racing stock in London. Cloth is in demand only spasmodically.

**TATTING:** A narrow lace used mostly for edging. It is made with a small hand shuttle.

**TEAR DROP:** A fabric defect characterized by crescent-like distortions in the fabric due to deviations of one or more picks.

**TEAR STRENGTH:** The force required to start or continue a tear in a fabric under specified conditions.

**TEASELS:** They are grown in Belgium, France, and other European countries and in Oregon and Washington in this country. Auburn, N.Y., is known as a teasel-raising center in the East. Teasels grow from 1 to 2 inches in length and about 1 inch in diameter. They are tough and have the appearance of a porcupine. The teasels, as used in textile finishing of fabrics, are set snugly in grooves in the napping machine cylinder which comes in contact with the cloth and raises the loose fibers to form a nap. Because teasels wear down in about a week's time, every sixth row is usually replaced each morning. Since the teasels cover the entire surface of the napping roller, the cloth receives a rigid brushing which creates the nap effect.

**TEFLON:** A trademark of DuPont for its tetrafluoroethylene fiber. Noted for its resistance to extremes of temperature and chemical action.

**TENACITY:** The breaking strength of a fiber, filament, yarn, cord, etc., expressed in force per unit yarn number.

**TENDER, TENDER GOODS, TENDERING:** Raw stock, top, yarn or fabric which has become weakened at some time during manipulation. The causes for tendering are many and may include scouring liquors which may have been too hot, over-scouring, over-carding, poor selection of raw materials, too much draft, poor tensions, faulty dyeing, excessive napping, gigging or singeing, construction defects, etc.

**TENSILE STRENGTH:** The breaking strength of a material stated in the force per unit of the cross-sectional area of the original sample.

**TENTER FRAME:** A machine that dries and stretches cloth to its finished width, and straightens its weave by the action of two diverging endless chains. Each chain is equipped with a series of clips that hold an edge of the cloth and convey it over gas flames or through a hot-air drying compartment.

**TERMINAL USE:** See END USE.

**TERON:** The counterpart of Terylene manufactured by Imperial Chemical Industries, Ltd., and sold throughout the world under this name with the exception of the United States. Terylene was discovered in 1941 by J. R. Whinfield and J. T. Dickson in the laboratories of the Calico Printers Association in Lancashire, England.

Imperial Chemical Industries, Ltd., and Celanese Corporation of America formed the Fibers Corporation, Inc., as a jointly-owned company to sell this polyester textile fiber, similar to Dacron polyester fiber of E. I. duPont de Nemours & Co., Inc. The product comes in filament and in staple forms and is used in blends with cotton, wool, and worsted.

**TERRITORY WOOL:** A term well-known for its various meanings. Originally it meant wool raised west of the Mississippi-Missouri rivers—then known as Indian Territory. At present the term means wool raised west of the 100th meridian but exclusive of wool grown in California, Oregon, and Texas; these three wools have special designations. Incidentally, other wools in this Territory Region are quoted individually.

Territory wool is chiefly of the fine type and it shows heavy shrinkage and low yield. Much of the wool is dull, dark, and dirty in-the-grease but it scours to a good white. Other names for this wool include Western, Range, Modoc.

**TERRY CLOTH:** A cotton fabric having uncut loops on one or both sides of the cloth. Woven on a dobby loom with terry arrangement. Various sizes and numbers of yarns are used in the fabric construction, forming different versions of terry cloth. Can also be woven on a jacquard loom to form designs. Can be yarn-dyed in different colors to form patterns. Bleached, piece-dyed, and even printed for beach wear and robes.

**TERYLENE:** The term is coined from the words terephthelate and polythylene, synthetic substances. Somewhat resembling Dacron. Terylene can be stretched five times its original length without losing firmness. Made in various thicknesses and widths, it can withstand bright light, and will iron, launder, and press without any special precautions. Terylene is not affected by moisture, chemical mixtures, or micro-organisms. Product of Imperial Chemical Industries, Ltd., England.

**TEXTILE:** Comes from the Latin word *textilis* (from *texere*, meaning to weave).

**TEXTURAL DESIGN:** The design in many fabrics is made by the weave rather than the color. Modern pile rugs and drapery fabrics in self-color show patterns by novel weave effects.

**TEXTURE:** The first meaning is the actual number of warp threads and filling picks, per inch, in any cloth that has been woven. It is written, say, 88 x 72. This means that there are 88 ends and 72 picks per inch in the fabric.

When texture is the same, such as 64 x 64, the cloth is classed as a "square" material.

Sheeting, with regard to texture is often referred to, for example, as a Number 128, Number 140, etc. Consideration of the number 128, means that the total number of ends and picks per inch is 128. Thus, there might be in the texture 72 ends and 56 picks, or 68 ends and 60 picks, or 64 ends and 64 picks which is a square-fabric texture. A 140 sheeting would be better than a 128 sheeting since there would be more ends and picks to the inch in the former.

Texture is also much used by the public and in advertising circles to mean the finish and appearance of cloth for sale over the counter or in the finished garment state.

**TEXTURED YARN:** Any yarn modified in such a way that its physical and surface properties have been changed. The term principally implies that a different texture has been imposed on the yarn that will in turn manifest itself in fabrics made of such yarns.

Textured yarns can be produced by mechanical or chemical means. The various ways of texturing by mechanical means are: three-stage, false twist, duo-twist, stuffer box, knit-de-knit, edge crimp, air jet, Stevetex, and gear crimp. The chemical process for texturing yarns is usually referred to as producer-textured, since such yarns are textured at the source.

**THEATRICAL GAUZE:** Thin, open-curtain fabric in plain or leno weave stiffened with sizing. Inexpensive and available in many colors. Originally used as background for stage scenery,

it is now often used for window curtains because of its transparency and interesting texture.

**THERMOPLASTIC:** Term applied to substances having the property of softening at higher temperatures. Specifically applied to certain synthetic resins and to the true synthetic fibers. All the true synthetic fibers are thermoplastic.

**THERMOSETTING:** Applied to substances which harden and set with heat. Many plastics and synthetic resins are thermosetting.

**THIBET:** Used in heavy suitings, it is piece-dyed and given clear finish; runs from 12 to 30 ounces per yard in weight. Wool, worsted, shoddy, and waste fibers are used in making the several qualities on the market. Broken weaves are employed in the construction and the filling is usually double—a face filling and a back filling. A soft and smooth plain-finished face, woolen or part woolen, features much fabric of this name. Genuine Thibets are made from the fleece of the mountain sheep of Thibet, Asia. Now usually spelled Tibet.

**THICK-AND-THIN:** A fabric woven with uneven yarns to create the effect of a homespun cloth.

**THICK-SET:** Low-quality cloth of the fustian variety used for rough wear and work and resembling a cheap velveteen or corduroy.

**THIRD-GENERATION FIBERS:** Fibers which are customed tailored for specialized markets. The most representative of the third-generation fibers are the bi-components, the bi-constituents and the blended filament yarns. See these respective definitions.

**THREAD:** 1. Slender strand or strands of a specialized type of yarn used for some particular purpose such as basting, sewing, darning, embroidery work. etc. Thread is the result of careful drawing and winding of the fibers that make up the product which has to be wound onto some form for handling, such as cop, cone, bobbin, cheese, spool, etc. Thread is made from yarn, but yarn is not made from thread.

2. Any fine cord made from one of the major textile fibers.

3. A cord made of two or more yarns twisted or plied, and then finished for a definite purpose.

**THREAD COUNT:** See COUNT OF CLOTH.

**THREE-EIGHTHS BLOOD WOOL:** A classification used in the blood system; numerical value is about 56s; below ½-blood wool and above ¼-blood wool in the Blood System of Grading used in some parts of the United States.

**THREE-QUARTER BLOOD WOOL:** A classification used in the Blood System of Grading Wool; comparable with ¾-merino stock and rated just below XX wool and above ½-blood wool.

**THROWING:** While not exactly the same as treatments given to wool, worsted, and cotton stock, throwing means the actual twisting, without drawing, of the continuous fibers or filaments of silk and man-made fibers.

**THROWSTER:** The operator who takes on the job described under THROWING.

**TIBET:** See THIBET.

**TICKING:** Made in small-twill constructions, ticking belongs in the loom-finished group of cloths: chambray, duck, canvas, denim, webbing, etc. Boiling-off or wet-finishing treatment are not applied to the material. Ticking may be recognized by its alternate stripes of white and colored yarns. A typical ticking construction would be 64 ends of 12s warp and 50 picks of 14s filling. Uses include furniture covering, lining harness, mattress coverings, and base for rubberized materials.

**TIE-DYEING:** An early method of dyeing which gave the fabric a design at the same time. Areas of the cloth are gathered up and tied tightly into a knot or bunch. When the cloth is dipped into the dye, parts of the tied areas do not take the dye but remain white and so create a design on the fabric.

**TIE SILKS:** This broad term is given to silks which are used for neckwear and cravats. Tie silk is plain or fancy and there is a great range in the cycle of cloths used.

**TINSEL:** Metallic thread used from

Toile de Jouy

earliest times in ornamental fabrics. Traditionally it was made of fine copper wire twisted with silk or cotton.

**TINTING:** 1. Application of a very light color to material.

2. Application of a fugitive color to yarn for identification purposes. A color is selected that will wash out during subsequent finishing.

**TIRE BUILDING FABRIC:** A fabric consisting of hawser cord yarn in the warp with single yarn filling at intervals to keep the warp threads in order. See HAWSER CORD YARN.

**TISSUE:** Means light-weight as applied to fabrics such as gingham, faille, taffeta, and chambray.

**TISSUE GINGHAM:** A sheer-weight gingham cloth, usually cotton.

**TISSUE TAFFETA:** See TAFFETA.

**TJAP PRINTING:** A method of block printing native to Java and other areas of the East Indies. The word *tjap* means block. Designs are made by imbedding strips of copper in the wooden blocks. The finished block is dipped into heated wax and pressed down onto the cloth. When the cloth is dyed, the wax areas resist the dye, thus creating a design. The wax is then removed.

**TOBACCO CLOTH:** Of the three basic cotton grey goods, printcloth is the best, followed by cheesecloth and tobacco cloth, respectively. Cheesecloth and tobacco cloth are the lowest in texture of any cotton materials made on a loom.

Narrow cheesecloth is under 36 inches wide; beyond this width the material is called wide cheesecloth. When the goods

are 36 inches wide, they are called tobacco cloth. Constructions as to texture are square, 8 x 8 up to 48 x 48. Warp yarns are 28s; filling yarns, 30s to 40s.

General uses for tobacco and cheesecloths in the finished state are: back-filled gauze, bandages, bedspreads, buckram, crinoline, curtaining, dust cloths, flag bunting, flour bagging, fly linings and nets, gauze, hat lining, interlining, label and sign cloth, netting, play suiting, shading cloth for tobacco and other vegetable plants, tea bags, theatrical gauze, wrapping cloth for cheeses.

**TOILE:** 1. A French term used to describe canvas and plain or twill linen fabrics. The word is now most often associated with the famous Toiles de Jouy designs printed in Jouy, France, by Oberkampf, beginning in 1759.

2. In lace, toile refers to the solid design section.

**TOP:** Found in worsted stock in all-worsted or worsted-mixes. Top is made up of fibers taken in the combing operation. It comes in slubbing or sliver form that is wound into a ball effect a foot or more in thickness and two or three feet in diameter. It resembles a cheese in appearance. The fibers in a top are parallel and of the same length. They are smooth, uniform, even, and have no foreign matter to speak of. The short fibers taken from the combing operation are called noil. These are used as a substitute fiber and may be high or low in quality. Tops are sold on the Worsted Top Exchange in New York City. Quotations are in cents and tenths of a cent per pound, and a top contract is 5,000 pounds.

**TOP-DYED:** Refers to wool which is dyed when in the form of the loose rope

591

of parallel fibers made by a combing machine, prior to spinning the fibers into worsted yarn to make worsted cloth. See DYEING METHODS.

**TOQUILA:** The fibrous veins obtained from the leaves of the Carludovica palmata and other palms, including the Toquila palm of Ecuador. The trees are native to Central and South America. The fibers are commonly known as Paga toquila or jipijapa, and the variety found in Ecuador are about a yard long. They are used to make Panama hats and mats.

**TORCHON LACE:** Simple bobbin lace, formerly made by the peasants in Europe. See LACE.

**TORQUE:** When used in describing the performance or characteristic of a yarn, the term torque refers to that property which tends to make it to turn on itself as a result of twisting.

**TOW:** A continuous, loose rope of man-made filaments drawn together without twist.

**TOWELING:** General name given to birdseye, crash, damask, glass, honeycomb, huck, huckaback, twill, turkish or terry, fancy, novelty, and guest towelings. Many of these cloths have colored or fancy borders; some of them may be union in fiber content. All toweling has property of good absorption.

**TRACING CLOTH:** Fine, close woven plain cloth; coated to give smooth surface. For making tracings and reproductions of tracings (sensitized cloth).

**TRAM:** Name for a two-ply silk filling yarn used in woven goods; spun loosely, and the opposite of organzine, the warp yarns, which is spun tightly. In the knitting trade, tram signifies the loosely-woven twisted thread of pure silk yarn that is used for men's and women's hosiery.

**TRANSPARENT VELVET:** See VELVET.

**TRANSPORTATION FABRIC:** Upholstery fabric used for seats in railroad cars, buses, and other vehicles. May also include the curtains on Pullman cars but does not include head linings. It is a rugged fabric that must withstand much friction, abrasion, strain, and be soil- and fade-resistant.

**TRAPUNTO:** A type of quilting in which the design is outlined with single stitches, and padding is drawn from the back, filling each part of the design separately, giving a high-relief effect.

**TREVIRA:** The polyester fiber developed by Hystron Fibers.

**TRIACETATE FIBER:** Fiber made from cellulose acetate as a base is known as diacetate. Triacetate fiber differs from diacetate because of different degrees in acetylation afforded and the ultimate degree of solubility in acetone. Arnel (a product of Celanese Corp.) is an example of the fiber in the United States, while Courpleta is made by Courtaulds Ltd., in England.

**TRICOLETTE:** See MIGNONETTE.

**TRICOT:** 1. The most important of the warp knit fabrics. Characterized by fine vertical wales on the face and more or less pronounced crosswise ribs on the back. May be made in stripes, mesh and elaborate designs. Used for underwear, dresses, gloves, etc. Rayon and nylon tricot are the most important tricots commercially.

2. An all-wool woven fabric made only in France, with a twill weave, having a woolen warp and single filling, warp faced and with fine lines running in the warp direction. It may also have cotton warp and woolen filling, with fine lines running in the filling direction. Both are generally piece dyed. The word tricot in French simply means knit, and the tricot stitch is the simplest of crochet stitches. It is worked with a long hook of uniform size and produces a plain, straight pattern. Tricot long refers to fabrics with rib running lengthwise; tricot cross to fabrics with a rib running across.

**TRICOT KNIT:** See KNITTING.

**TRICOTINE:** Of the family of whipcords, coverts, and gabardines. Made from a 63-degree twill that gives the characteristic double twill line on the face of the cloth. A good weave to use in making the material is

$$\frac{3 \quad 3 \quad 1 \quad 1}{1 \quad 1 \quad 2 \quad 1}$$

Other weaves of similar nature may be used as well. This 13-harness fabric is dyed in all staple colors. The cloth drapes well, is easy to tailor, and is a smart conventional fabric. A staple cloth.

Skein-dyed tricotine is on the market. Cloth is usually of medium and best quality wool or worsted, and is used in men's wear and women's wear.

Tricotine weave.

**TRIPLE SHEER:** Made of novelty-twill weaves from Bemberg yarn. A popular rayon material that wears, drapes, and washes well. Comes in many types of prints. This fine, flat-surface cloth is almost opaque. Recently there has been the tendency to get away from the twill effects which first characterized the material.

Tropical weave.

**TROPICAL:** Fancy suiting material of plain and rather open weaves. It is a lightweight worsted of the semi-staple group. Fabric is ideal for summer and tropical wear, and somewhat resembles palm beach cloth. Weight goes from 6 to 12 ounces per yard. Warp and filling are of high counts, usually 2/60s or better. Material is skein- or piece-dyed, and clear finish is given. Tropical mixtures and heathers are popular cloths in the tropical range and these cloths are stock-dyed to give the desired pattern effect.

**TROUSERING:** Use is obvious. The material is woven firmer and tighter than suiting cloth. It is also heavier in weight. Stripings are the main feature of the fabric. Used for dress occasions and in ordinary everyday wear. Made from combinations of basic weaves. The garment has a dark or black background to better enhance the striping effect. The cloth is often of double construction in warp and filling or may be made of two warps and one filling. Of worsted or cotton.

**TUBULAR FABRICS:** Any fabric woven or knitted in a tube form with no seams, such as seamless pillowcases, most knit underwear fabrics and seamless hosiery. See CIRCULAR KNIT.

**TUCK STITCH:** A variation of a basic stitch in weft knitting designed to make a bumpy, knobby, texture.

**TUFTED:** Surface yarns stitched into a woven cotton backing, usually by multiple-needle sewing machines.

**TUFTED CARPETS AND RUGS:** Manufactured like any other tufted material, either in a regular design or chenille pattern. The tufts are pulled through from bottom to top by a needle and then sliced off above the surface.

**TULLE:** 1. Sheer silk, nylon, or rayon cloth with hexagonal mesh, stiff, used much in ballet materials. White and in colors. Cool, dressy, delicate, and difficult to launder. In dress goods it is a stately type of material. Used with other cloths, overdraping. Also known as rayon net, silk net, nylon net.

2. Very fine net made at one time in Tulle and adopted by the French courts in place of patterned lace.

**TUSCAN STRAW:** See STRAW.

**TUSSAH SILK:** Sometimes called wild silk, it is the product of the uncultivated silkworm, which feeds on leaves of the oak tree, castor oil plant, cherry tree, and uncultivated mulberry tree. Little care is given to the raising of these worms, whose product is a sturdy and rather tough silk fiber. Tussah is easily reeled but it is not as soft as true silk. Shantung and similar fabrics are made of tussah.

**TWEED:** A rough-surfaced woolen material with a homespun surface effect. Tweed was originally made by hand in the homes of the country people near the Tweed River which separates England from Scotland. Yarn is usually dyed before weaving, and often woven in two or more colors to obtain some sort of pattern, check or plaid. All wool, unless otherwise stated.

CHEVIOT TWEED—Differs from other tweeds in that warp and filling are stock-dyed the same color. Wide range of colors are noted and quality varies much. Popular cloth.

DONEGAL TWEED—A plain weave woolen fabric characterized by colored slubs woven into the cloth.

HARRIS TWEED—Trade name for an imported tweed made of virgin wool from the Highlands of Scotland, spun, dyed and handwoven by islanders in Harris and other of the outer Hebrides Islands. Must be properly labeled.

IRISH TWEED—Made of white warp with filling of dark shades of grey, blue, brown and black. Weave is 2-up and 2-down twill.

MONOTONE TWEED—Tweed of mixed effect produced by weaving together yarns of different shades of the same color.

SCOTCH TWEED—Cloth with a white warp and stock-dyed filling, or vice

Tweed weave.

versa. The colors used are often vivid and much contrast is noted in the garment. This tweed often has shoddy, mungo, extract wool, etc. used in its construction. Yarn is very irregular and the fibers are of all lengths. Also refers to any Scotch homespun tweed.

**TWEED (COTTON):** A woven-design suiting, containing nubs and flakes of contrasting color, made of dyed yarns in stripes and checks and finished in a rough, tweedy texture.

**TWILLS:** In this sense, the name given to cloths that show a twill-weave construction on the face of the material. In short, twill cloth shows a diagonal or bias effect on any material in regular repeat formation. From the Scotch, *tweel*, to make a diagonal effect. There are many varieties of twill—right hand, left hand, broken, herringbone, twilled baskets, twilled ribs, steep, reclining,

even and uneven, single and double, braided, entwining, etc.

Small twill weaves find much use in giving small novelty effects to rayon and other synthetic fiber materials. These fabrics are strong, durable, dressy, and wash well. Used for dress goods.

**TWIST DIRECTION:** This is given as "S", if the direction of the spirals formed by the twist in the yarn conforms with the direction of the central part of the letter "S". In a "Z" twist, the spirals lie in the same direction as the central part of the letter "Z".

**TWIST ON TWIST:** A ply yarn in which the twist in the ply is in the same direction as the twist in the component single yarns. Frequently abbreviated T.O.T.

**TWISTS:** Woolens or worsteds of which the yarns entering same are of two colors, doubled or twisted together. This gives an effect that is rather mottled in the pattern appearance. In the trade, many cloths are spoken of as "twists."

**TWISTS PER INCH:** The number of turns in one inch of a yarn. Also called turns per inch.

**TYPP:** System of numbering yarns based on the number of thousands of yards per pound. If 5,000 yards of a certain yarn weigh one pound, its typp number is 5.

**TYPEWRITER RIBBON FABRIC:** The highest constructed cotton fabric made today. Combed Egyptian, Pima, or Sea Island cotton is used and the thread count ranges from 260 square to 350 square. Some imported British fabric has a texture of 400 square. Yarns range from 70s to 120s. Also made of nylon.

# U

**ULSTER:** Heavy overcoating cloth, loosely woven with warp of right-hand-twist yarn, and filling of left-hand-twist yarn. All types and kinds of fibers are used in the material, depending on the quality of the cloth wanted. May be piece-dyed, or stock-dyed for mixed effects. The long nap given the cloth in finishing is pressed down. Fabric weight is from 24 to 30 ounces.

**UMBRELLA CLOTH:** A cloth used for making umbrellas. Usually made with a cotton warp and silk, rayon or nylon filling which is then treated for water-repellency. It can also be made of other synthetic fabrics. It is sometimes called Gloria goods.

**UNBLEACHED MUSLIN:** A cotton sheeting cloth before bleaching which shows the characteristic slubs, specks, and impurities. Since it is unfinished it has some of the qualities of native hand-woven cottons.

**UNCUT PILE:** A pile structure in which the pile threads are not cut but form a surface consisting of small loops. The loops may be formed by means of smooth wires as in frise, or by means of a terry motion as in the terry towels.

**UNFINISHED WORSTED:** Worsted with a light nap which somewhat obscures the weave. The term is a misrepresentation because this nap is a finish on worsteds, which are ordinarily left with a smooth surface after they are woven.

**UNIFORM CLOTH:** A family of serviceable woolen cloth on the general order of kerseys and flannels as the most important. Colors are blue, grey, khaki, brown, and mixed effects. The cloth is used as uniform material for military, naval, police, fire, postal, railway, bus, public service, chauffeurs, regal livery, and other public and private groups. As most of these cloths are furnished under certain approved and decreed specifications, according to contract, a very exact demand is made on the goods to meet requirements.

**UNION CLOTH:** Woolens and worsteds which have textile fibers from other fiber kingdoms in them, e.g., a cloth that has a cotton warp and worsted filling is classed as a union.

**UNION-DYED:** Refers to a fabric consisting of two fibers which are dyed in one bath to produce simultaneously in each type of fiber a different color or a single uniform shade.

**UPHOLSTERY:** A material used on furniture and to cover walls, as curtains and hangings; also fabric coverings and treatments in automobiles, airplanes, and railroad passenger cars. The outstanding fabrics classed as upholstery include brocade, brocatelle, damask, cretonne, chintz, tapestry, jacquard fabrics of special make, denim, linen, and fabrics of the man-made fibers.

**UPLAND COTTON:** The largest part of the world's cotton crop is of the Upland type. It is also used as the standard with which other cotton types are compared. See AMERICAN, under COTTON.

**UREA-FORMALDEHYDE:** A resin used in producing an anti-crease finish on cellulose fibers. Obtained by the condensation of urea with formaldehyde, the resin is polymerized on and chemically cross-linked with the fibers by application of heat and catalysts.

**URENA:** A fiber derived from plant grown in Philippines. Similar to hemp.

**URETHANE:** Chemical family of cross-linked polymers subject to reactions which cause foaming. The foams are used for bonding and laminating fabrics. The term has gradually replaced the term polyurethane.

# V

**VALENCIENNES LACE:** One of the most easily distinguished of the net laces. The designs are all flat. See LACE.

**VAN DYKE:** Refers to a pointed edge in collars of lace.

**VAT-DYED:** Refers to materials that have been dyed by a process which employs oxidation. Vat dyes are considered the most resistant dyes to both washing and sunlight. See DYES.

**VEGETABLE FIBERS:** Refers to all textile fibers of vegetable origin: cotton, flax, ramie, jute, hemp, abaca, henequin, istle, sisal, pineapple, etc.

**VEILING:** This lightweight plain or doup material, made in many designs and constructions, is given careful treatment in finishing since this has much to do with the final appearance and sale. Veiling comes in plain or solid colors and is used for bridal veils.

**VELOUR:** From the Latin, *villosus*, meaning hairy. Cloth is used as coating material, and in velour-check form, is used for dress goods and coating cloth. The material is a thick-bodied close-napped, soft type of cloth. The name is used rather indiscriminately and is applied to suiting fabric as well. Generally speaking, a velour is a cloth that runs from 10 to 20 ounces per yard, and given a face finish. Various types of yarn are used in making the several types of velour on the market. Twills or broken constructions are used in laying out the pattern. There are several fabrics of the same construction, but of slightly different finish, to be found in the trade —suedyne, suedette, lustora, duvedelaine, valora, etc. The cloth is made in the finishing and much of the best-grade velour is really beautiful cloth. Some velour is now made with spun rayon and wool blends. Used for drapery fabric, women's coats, upholstery.

**VELVET:** Fabric with a short, soft, thick, warp pile surface. Usually made of a silk or synthetic pile with a cotton back. Also of all silk or cotton. The fabric is often woven double, face to face, and then, while still on the loom, it is cut apart by a small shuttle knife. Velvets can be finished to make them crush-resistant and water-repellent. The velvet pile is less than 1/8 inch; if 1/8 inch or more, the fabric is plush.

BAGHEERA—Fine, uncut pile piece-dyed velvet with a roughish surface that makes it crush-resistant. Used for gowns and evening wraps.

CHIFFON VELVET—Lightweight soft velvet with cut pile. Closer woven than transparent velvet. Used for dresses, suits, evening clothes.

CISELE VELVET—A velvet with a pattern formed by cut and uncut loops.

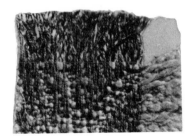

FACONNÉ VELVET—Patterned velvet made by the burn-out print method. See BURN-OUT PRINT under PRINT.

LYONS VELVET—A stiff, erect, thick piled velvet; made of silk pile and cotton or rayon back. When made of 100% synthetic fibers, the fabric is called Lyons-type velvet.

NACRE VELVET—Velvet with the back of one color and the pile of another, so that it gives a changeable pearly appearance.

TRANSPARENT VELVET — Lightweight, soft, draping velvet made of silk or rayon back with a rayon pile.

**VELVET (COTTON):** A double-woven, short-pile fabric in which two cloths are woven together, face to face, with interlacing warp yarns that are cut to form the pile. Heavier velvets are often called velours.

**VELVETEEN:** A filling pile fabric constructed in the same manner as corduroy but having a surface which is uniformly covered by a short, full, cut pile. Commonly made wholly of cotton, but sometimes also made of rayon. The construction ranges from around 175 picks per inch to over 600, with about 80 ends per inch. The filling yarn is soft spun, and in the better quality velveteens is of combed long staple cotton, which, when cut, gives a soft, smooth and velvety pile. The pile may be waxed in the finishing to improve the luster. Velveteen is usually piece dyed but it is also sometimes printed. Velveteen plush is a cotton velveteen woven with longer floats than the ordinary velveteen. These floats are firmly bound in and, when cut, give a longer pile.

**VENETIAN:** Used in men's wear and in linings. A fine, worsted-twill cloth light and medium in weight, piece-dyed, and given a high-luster finish. The name is taken from the resemblance noted to silk venetian, a cloth of real artistic value that was made in Venice. The cloth can be used as a dress worsted, the same as crepe.

**VENETIAN LACE:** The needle-point lace of Venice is called Venetian Point, the beginnings of which were the application of the needle-point to cut-work. Modern Venetian laces are made with a bobbin and are known as Flat Venetian Point. See LACE.

**VEREL:** A modified acrylic fiber made by Eastman Chemical Products, Inc. In cross-section, Verel is peanut-shaped, and it turns a deep reddish-brown without dissolving when heated with pyridene, a behavior which positively identifies the fiber. An ideal fiber for blending with other major fibers, it is used in woven and knitted fabrics such as dress and sportswear fabrics, sweaters, men's hosiery, and flannel-type men's suitings; pile fabrics in which Verel may be used for either face fabric or back fabric.

Verel can be mixed with cotton to produce lightweight fabric such as batiste, and with wool for dense industrial materials. In the non-apparel field, it can be used in blankets, paint rollers, wash mitts, toys, and polishing fabrics because of its high resistance to chemicals and flammability.

**VESTING:** Covers a large range of cloths used as vests and for dress purposes. The range of material called vesting is very wide. Vesting does not have the same meaning it formerly had. The term used to include many cloths that have now become individualized and are found under their accepted names in the trade such as bedford cord, piqué, dress goods, riding habit cloth, novelties, etc. Little genuine vesting is now to be seen because of the changes from the style, fashion, vogue, and demand of some years ago.

**VESTMENT CLOTH:** See ACCA.

**VICUNA:** The animal is found at elevations approximating 12,000 feet in the almost inaccessible regions of the high plateau area in Peru, northern Bolivia, and southern Ecuador. Vicuna, which live above the clouds, are about 3 feet high and weigh from 75 pounds to 100 pounds. The animal has a life span of about 12 years.

The fiber varies from golden-chestnut to deep rich fawn shades to a pallid white beneath the body and on the surface of the extremities, with light markings on the face and jaws.

Vicuna fibers, which are strong and resilient, have a marked degree of elasticity and surface cohesion. These fibers are the finest of all known animal fibers, being less than one two-thousandth of an inch in diameter, being little more than one-half the diameter of the finest

sheep's wool. The respective diameters of the two fibers are vicuna, .00043; fine sheep wool, .00080 inches.

The outer beard hair of the animal serves as a coat and is not used in making good-quality fabrics. The inner hair, which grows close to the skin on the neck, under shoulders, and on the sides and under-portions of the body, is very soft and silken-like.

Vicuna, the aristocrat of fibers, may be used to best advantage in the natural state; however, proper dyeing does not destroy the original beauty of the fiber itself. However, if dyed, it is necessary, because of the tendency of the fibers to resist absorption of dyes, to remove at least 50% of the natural grease and oil.

Forty fleeces are required to make enough fabric for a single coat.

**VIGOREUX PRINTING:** The printing of worsted-top fibers by passing the sliver through a printing machine which has a roll with raised bars to carry the dyestuff. The sliver is impregnated with the dyestuff when it comes in contact with the revolving bars or rollers. Black is used chiefly in Vigoreux work, but shades of blue, brown, and green may be printed by this method for coloring what will be finished spun yarn when manipulation is completed.

**VINAL:** A manufactured fiber in which the fiber-forming substance is any long chain synthetic polymer composed of at least 50% by weight of vinyl alcohol units ($-CH_2-CHOH-$), and in which the total of the vinyl alcohol units and any one or more of the various acetal units is at least 85% by weight of the fiber.

**VINYL FIBERS:** This category includes several dissimilar but related fibers:

1. Those which are co-polymers of vinyl chloride and vinyl acetate, such as vinyon. See Vinyon.

2. Polyvinyl chloride fibers.

3. Co-polymers of vinyl choride and acrylonitrile, such as Dynel modacrylic. See Dynel.

**VINYON:** A manufactured fiber in which the fiber-forming substance is any long chain synthetic polymer composed of at least 85% by weight of vinyl chloride units ($-CH_2-CHCl-$).

**VIRGIN WOOL:** The Federal Trade Commission considers this term synonymous with New Wool. It states that "the term virgin or new wool as descriptive of a wool product or any fiber or part thereof shall not be used when the product or part so described is not composed wholly of new or virgin wool which has never been used, or reclaimed, reworked, reprocessed or reused from any spun, woven, knitted, felted, or manufactured or used product. Products composed of or made from fiber reworked or reclaimed from yarn or clips shall not be described as virgin or new wool, or by terms of similar import, regardless of whether such yarns or clips are new or used or were made of new or reprocessed or reused material."

Another meaning of the term is that it is the first clipping from a sheep that has never heretofore been sheared, a shearling or yearling sheep. The first clip from the animal will be the best to be obtained, as each successive clip becomes inferior in quality; the older the sheep, the poorer will be the grade of the fiber.

Another concise and brief meaning of the term is that it is wool, irrespective of the clip, that has not been manipulated into yarn and cloth. See WOOL.

**VISCA:** When a viscose solution is forced through a narrow slit instead of a small single hole in a spinneret, a lightweight but strong ribbon-like synthetic material is produced that resembles straw. It is called visca. These narrow strips are useful in making costume accessories and in the manufacture of upholstery and millinery. They can be combined with other fibers to produce lustrous effects.

**VISCOSE:** The spinning solution used in the preparation of viscose rayon, as distinct from the solution used in the cuprammonium process of rayon manufacture. This solution is highly viscous and of a golden brown or orange red color. It is a solution of cellulose xanthate which is made from wood pulp or cotton linters, impregnated with sodium hydroxide and dissolved in carbon bisulphate, then evaporated. The cellulose xanthate crumb is then mixed with dilute sodium hydroxide solution to give the spinning solution, termed "viscose" which is then forced through the orifices

of a spinneret into the spinning bath, where it is coagulated. This process forms filament rayon.

Historically this is the third method for the making of rayon, and stems from the patents taken out by two Englishmen, Cross and Bevan; it now accounts for by far the greater part of all rayon manufactured throughout the world.

**VISCOSE RAYON:** See RAYON.

**VIYELLA:** A trademark for a lightweight British twill fabric, 55 percent wool and 45 percent cotton. The fibers in the yarn are blended before spinning; the weave is usually a two-up, two-down twill. The fabric is made in qualities and weights suitable for many purposes, including shirts, pajamas, underwear, dresses, etc.

**VOILE:** Light, sheer, thin, transparent cloth with a two-ply warp. Classed with organdy, lawn, and other sheer materials. Comes in white, dyed, or printed. Used in dress goods, blouses, draperies, scarves, lamp shades, children's clothes, difficult, however, to handle in manipulation, since it has a clinging effect. Voile has always been one of the most popular fabrics on the market since it drapes very well and is quite versatile. Good organdy and voile fabrics have the best of cotton or rayon yarns in them, with more man-made fibers penetrating the market.

**VULCANIZED FIBER:** A laminated plastic made of cotton cellulose material, layers of which are bonded by chemical treatment and converted into an entirely new homogeneous structure. It weighs about half as much as aluminum, and can absorb sudden repeated shocks and impacts without failure. Depending on its use, the material can be as hard as bone or as soft as wet rawhide. As a plastic it can be bent, formed, drawn, swagged into intricate shapes without sacrificing strength in an area, and it has stubborn resistance to wear and abrasion.

Vulcanized fiber is used industrially for electrical power-line lighting arresters, in tiny protective washers for hypodermic needles, as insulation for railroad tracks, in shuttles for textile looms, bobbins of many types, etc. It is ideal for use where durability, smoothness, and lightness of weight are required.

**VYCRON:** The polyester fiber made

by Beaunit Corporation as filament, staple, tow and fiberfill.

# W

**WADDING:** 1. A fabric made of wool fibers felted into a compact mass through the application of heat, moisture, and pressure without weaving. It is used in laundry presses, padding machines, tailoring, and upholstery.

2. An extra set of filling threads which lie dormant, without interlacing, between the face and the back fabrics in double- or treble-cloth constructions. The yarn is usually heavy and bulky, with little twist, to add weight and bulk to material.

**WAGON COVER DUCK:** A flat duck, usually double filled, made in wide widths of 48 to 90 inches. It is made in weights of 8, 10 and 12 ounces based on a width of 29 inches, and known as regular, heavy and extra heavy.

**WAIST:** 1. A garment, or that part of a garment, which covers the body from the neck or shoulders down to the waistline, more or less. Specifically the bodice or upper part of a woman's dress.

2. An undergarment for children, similarly worn, to which other clothes may be buttoned.

**WAISTBAND:** A band or sash or similar fabric which encircles the waist and generally serves to support clothing or to keep clothing in place. It is also specifically used to denote the band in the upper part of trousers or skirts which serves as an inner belt in the construction of the garment.

**WAISTLINE:** A line surrounding, or thought of as surrounding, the narrowest part of the waist; in dressmaking, the line at which the waist and skirt meet.

**WAISTCLOTH:** A loincloth.

**WAISTING:** A fabric suitable for manufacturing shirtwaists.

**WAFFLE CLOTH:** A textured cotton, similar to piqué but woven on a dobby loom in a fine honeycomb weave.

**WALE:** In a knit fabric the wale is the series of loops, formed by one needle, which run lengthwise in the material. In a woven fabric, like corduroy or bedford cord, the wale is the rib or raised cord which runs lengthwise with the warp. The word wale comes from the Anglo-Saxon *walu* which meant to mark as with stripes.

**WARP:** 1. The yarns that run lengthwise in a woven fabric. Also called chain or twist. An individual thread of warp is termed an end.

2. The yarns that run generally lengthwise in a warp-knit fabric.

3. The sheet of yarns laid together in parallel order on a beam to form a warp.

**WARP BEAM, WARP ROLLER:** A large wooden beam onto which the warp ends are snugly wound. This is followed by drawing-in and reeding before setting the beam into the sockets located at the back of the loom.

By means of friction bands and weights the warp yarn is fed evenly into the loom while the cloth is being woven. These weights are removed from time to time in order to keep proper tension on the warp ends as the warp decreases in diameter and the winding-off requires less tension in the control of the warp. Too much weight would cause some ends to break and thus impede production.

**WARP-KNIT FABRICS:** A fabric with a flatter, closer, less elastic knit than the weft or jersey knit. Very often knit so that the fabric is run resistant. Tricot and milanese are typical warp-knit fabrics.

**WARP PRINT:** See PRINT.

**WARP PRINTING:** Achieved by printing the warp threads before the fabric is woven. The pattern has blurred or mottled effects because of the subsequent weaving.

**WARP ROLLER:** See WARP BEAM.

**WASHABLE:** Fabrics which will not fade or shrink when they are washed. This term should always be qualified by careful directions in methods of handling, preferably based on lab tests.

**WASHABLE WOOL:** A resin finishing process which allows wool to be washed and dried at normal machine temperatures without shrinking or felting.

**WASH AND WEAR:** A term applied to any garment which can be washed, dried and then worn again with little or no ironing. The characteristics of pleat-retention or crease resistance may be incorporated in the fabric either through the use of hydrophobic (water-resistant) fibers or by the proper application of a good resin finish on a hydrophilic (water-attracting) fiber cloth such as cotton. More and more consumers expect that a garment sold to them as Wash and Wear should deliver satisfactory performance with either mechanical or hand washing and machine or air drying, although they do look for the less-ironing feature as a strong factor.

**WASHING TESTS:** A series of laundry tests developed by the A.A.T.C.C. to determine quickly (in an hour or less) the amounts of color fading and of abrasion encountered in five average commercial or home launderings.

**WASTE:** Fiber and yarn by-products created in the manufacturing or processing of fibers or yarns.

**WASTE SILK:** The short, unreeled filaments that are left before and after the long cocoon filaments have been removed. These short noils are carded, sometimes combed, and spun.

**WATERPROOFING:** Its purpose is to make fabrics highly resistant to water. It may be done in several ways by using insoluble substances with various methods such as: vulcanizing crude rubber and applying it to the goods, or by the application of acids, fats, oxides, gutta-percha, paint, paraffin, wax, or silicones.

The test is carried out by spraying the fabric for 24 hours at the rate of 1000 c.c. (more than one quart) per minute at a height of four feet. The chemical or physical properties of the tested material should not be affected; there should be no change in pliancy of the cloth, nor should the entrance of air be prevented.

**WATER-REPELLENT:** Treating cloth with chemical mixtures to make it moisture- or spot-proof. Laundering or dry cleaning will partially or totally remove the treatment. However, the material may be treated again with the repellent. These finishes may be resistant to perspiration, spots, stains, and water.

**WATER-RESISTANT:** Cloth that is water-resistant repels water for a limited time. Paraffin or wax methods are used to make material water-resistant. The aluminum stearate method is also used to give cloth this property; Impregnole is an example.

**WATER SPOTTING:** A physical change produced in a fabric by a drop of water. Very difficult to remove.

**WATT, JAMES:** This noted Scotsman applied steam to drive textile machinery. He took out his patent in the same year (1769) as Arkwright for the spinning frame. In 1785, Watt applied his power by steam in Robinson's cotton mill in Nottinghamshire, England. In 1790, Arkwright was using steam in his mill. By 1800, steam was generally used.

**WEAR RESISTANCE:** The resistance of a fabric to deterioration caused by normal or excessive use. It takes place on account of breaking, cutting, abrasion and wearing out or removal of fibers.

**WEAR TEST:** A method for testing the durability and end-usage performance of fabrics by evaluating suitable garments that have been worn.

**WEATHER-OMETER:** An apparatus that duplicates the combined effects of sunlight, rain, heavy dew and thermal shock and accelerates the deteriorating effects of these conditions so that the equivalent of years of actual outdoor exposure is reproduced in a few days of testing in the laboratory.

**WEAVING:** The interlacing at right angles of two systems of threads known as warp and filling. The former runs lengthwise and may go over or under the latter, which runs crosswise in the cloth. The fundamental weaves are: Plain, Twill, Satin, and it may said that all other weaves, no matter how complex, are based on one or other of these three fundamental types.

**WEAVE ANALYSIS:** The process of determining the actual construction of a fabric by physical examination of the fabric, usually with the aid of pickout glass and pickout needles. Constructions generally recognized are: plain, tabby or taffeta; twill; satin, both warp-effect and filling-effect; basket; rib, both warp-rib and filling-rib; piqué; double cloth or ply cloth; backed cloth; pile; jacquard; leno or doup; lappet, swivel or clipspot. They are as follows:

PLAIN, TABBY OR TAFFETA: One warp over and one warp under the filling throughout the cloth construction.

TWILL: Diagonal lines on face of cloth— to the right, to the left, or to right and left in broken twill.

SATIN: Smooth, shiny surface caused by floats of warp over the filling or vice versa. Diagonal lines on face of the cloth are not distinct to the naked eye but can be distinguished through a pick glass.

BASKET: Two or more warp ends over and two or more warp ends under, in parallel arrangement, interlacing with the filling yarn.

RIB: Made by cords that run in either the warp or the filling direction. The corded yarn is covered up by the tight interlacing of the system that shows on the face and back of the cloth.

PIQUÉ: The cloth has a corded effect, usually in the warp, but may also have cord in the filling, or in both directions. The cords are usually held in place by a few ends of plain weave construction.

DOUBLE OR PLY CLOTH: Two cloths woven together and held in place by binder warp or filling: not pasted. The back is usually different from the face of the cloth.

BACKED CLOTH: Cloth of one warp and two fillings or two warps and one filling. The face is much more presentable than the back of the cloth. The back is usually dull in appearance.

PILE: Extra yarns form the pile on the face of the cloth. The pile effect may be cut or uncut on the surface. Basic constructions hold the cloth in place.

JACQUARD CONSTRUCTIONS: The pattern or design is woven into the cloth. A wide range of persons, places, objects and designs may be rendered by this construction, which is used in silks, cottons and man-mades.

LENO OR DOUP: The warp yarns are often paired and half- or fully-twisted about one another. In some cloths of this type the porosity is high. Two sets of harnesses are used—standard and skeleton.

LAPPET, SWIVEL AND CLIPSPOT: Dots or small figures are woven or embroidered into the cloth by the use of an extra fill-ing in the case of swivel weave, and by an extra warp in lappet weave. The effects are based on plain weave background.

**WEAVER'S KNOT:** Much resorted to in tying knitting yarns. The knot is small and evenly distributed around the yarn. It will not slip nor untie. This knot may be omitted when threading a machine for the setting-up of new work.

**WEBBING:** Strong, rugged, closely-woven cotton material used for belts and straps of many types. It is usually heavier than the so-called woven tapes, since stronger and stouter yarns are used to make webbing. Elastic webbing is woven with rubber threads as part of the warp. Most webbing is made of cotton, but it can be made from any of the major fibers and in combinations of fibers.

**WEDGWOOD PRINT:** See PRINT.

**WEFT:** Allied with the British term, woof. Both terms are derived from the verb to weave and refer to the yarn woven by the shuttle; they are used interchangeably. In Britain the word weft is used in the sense of filling. The terms are often resorted to in the advertising of textiles since they seem to give an English "quirk" which may attract the reader's attention. Other names for weft are pick and "pick-and-shot." In the carpet trade in this country the term weft is used instead of filling in most instances and is accepted in lieu of the American term.

**WEFT-KNIT FABRIC:** Knitting process in which the thread runs back and forth crosswise in a fabric. The opposite of warp knit.

**WEIGHT DIFFERENCES IN WOOLENS:** British imported fabrics are based on a 58-inch finished width to a 37-inch yard with one quarter of a yard "thrown in" in every ten yards for "good measure."

The 58-inch by 38-inch yard gives 2204 square inches to the piece yard against the domestic yard of 56 inches by 36 inches or 2016 square inches in the yard. Thus, an 18-ounce British weight would be the equivalent of a 16½-ounce domestic:

$$\frac{18 \times 2016}{2204} \text{ equals } 16.5,$$

the approximate weight of the domestic fabric in ounces per yard.

Briefly, it may be stated that the Ameri-can cloth is approximately 11/12ths the weight of a comparable British woolen.

**WEIGHTED SILK:** Silk whose weight has been artificially increased by the addition of metallic salts to compensate for loss of sericin in the course of processing. If the cloth is overweighted it will tend to degenerate.

**WEIGHTING:** The addition of substances to add weight to a yarn or fabric, or to act as a filling agent to the fabric. A finishing process.

**WEIGHT OF FABRICS:** Three types of weights are used in cloth (1) Ounces per yard. (2) Yards per pound. (3) Ounces per square yard. See FABRIC, WEIGHT OF.

**WEST OF ENGLAND:** Woolen cloth of high reputation made in Stroud, Gloucestershire, and other western districts of England. Cloths which come from the West Riding of Yorkshire are not to be confused with West of England cloths.

**WET DECATING:** A finishing process designed to produce a bright, sheen face and soft hand to woolens. Also known as *Potting*.

**WET FINISHING:** Signifies the wet operations, chemical in nature, that may be given to cloth so as to make it, in time, presentable to the consumer. Some of the operations are washing, dyeing, soaping, fulling, milling, scouring, mercerizing, souring.

**WET SPINNING:** A manner of producing man-made or synthetic filaments into a form obtained from the spinneret of the spinning-box, in which the filaments take on form by the extrusion of a solution of the filament-forming material through a spinneret into a coagulating bath. See POT SPINNING.

**WET STRENGTH:** The wet strength of a fabric may be evaluated by thoroughly wetting before testing.

**WHIPCORD:** Dress woolen or worsted of fine and high texture. The twilled yarn is sharply defined with some fancy suggestions to whiplashes or cords. There are several cloths, some major and some minor in this group—coverts, tricotines, poirets, twill-cords, chicotines, piquetines. The yarn in a whipcord is bulkier than the yarn of the tricotine or gabardine. The cloth is lower in texture and heavier in weight than these two materials. Weight ranges from 12 to 20 ounces per yard. Whipcord finds use in livery cloth, topcoats, uniform cloth, suitings, and in public-utility materials. The cloth may be made of cotton warp and worsted filling. Whipcord is made from a 63-degree twill weave and is always a compact, rugged, good-wearing material.

Nylon and rayon whipcord is much used in riding habit, sportswear, uniform cloth. Cotton whipcord is used for automobile seat covers, boys' play suits, caps, riding breeches, uniforms.

**WHITE ON WHITE:** Fabric with a white woven-in dobby or jacquard design on a white ground. For example, white on white broadcloth, madras, or nylon shirtings.

**WHITNEY:** A soft-bodied, tufted-face overcoating cloth not unlike chinchilla. The effect, however, in finishing is that of a transverse wave-like series of lines rather than the well-known nubs or knots of the chinchilla. The lengthwise treatment of the cloth produces the "Whitney-long finish." Name is derived from the man who invented the finish to perfection in the finishing process. One of the best of wool overcoating cloths that is extremely popular.

**WHITNEY, ELI:** The American who invented the cotton gin in 1793.

Eli Whitney.

**WIDE-WALE CLOTH:** Comes from the Anglo-Saxon term *walu* meaning to mark or flail with stripes, as with a rod. The weave is indicated by wide-twilled or straight edges or ridges on face of the fabric. It is the opposite of narrow wale. Cloth under this caption

is coarse, boardy material of the serge, cheviot, and clay worsted variety. Some mackinac cloth is made with wide wales, which give a serpentine effect.

**WIGAN:** A cotton cloth that is firm, starched, plain calender finished, and devoid of luster. Usually dyed black, grey, or brown and converted from light-weight sheeting or print cloth. Used chiefly as interlining for men's and boys' clothing to give body and substance.

**WILTON CARPET:** Originated in Wilton, England, and is a variety of Brussels carpet, which now ranks second to chenille in quality and price. Woven in the same manner as Brussels, it is possible to cause some of the yarn to become "buried" in the back in order to add resiliency and quality. Wilton differs from Brussels in the fact that when the cut pile of the former is made, flat wires are used; Brussels is cut by using round wires; the knife edge cuts the loops to make the pile in both instances. Wilton is made on a jacquard loom.

**WINCH:** Any machine that treats fabric in endless belt or rope form. Used in washing, scouring, fulling, milling, dyeing, etc.; the machine consisting of an open vat for the liquor and rollers that move the cloth along in the bath.

**WINCH-DYEING:** Piece-dyeing done in a slack condition without tension, in a winch, vat or kier.

**WINDBREAKER CLOTH:** Name given to men's and women's sports jackets or reefers made of poplin, tackle twill, and similar materials which have been given repellent finishes.

**WOAD:** An ancient blue dyestuff made from the leaves of the woad plant, which was sometimes known as dyer's weed.

Whitney's Cotton Gin.

Woad is an herb of the mustard family, *Isatis tinctoria.*

**WOOF:** See WEFT.

**WOOL:** Strictly speaking, the fibers that grow on the sheep fleece. The Textile Fiber Products Identification Act of 1960 states that wool means the fiber from the fleece of the sheep or lamb, or the hair of the Angora or Cashmere goat (and may include the so-called specialty fibers from the hair of the camel, alpaca, llama, and vicuna) which has never been reclaimed from any woven or felted wool product."

This Commission also defined the following:

*Reprocessed Wool:* The resulting fiber when wool has been woven or felted into a wool product which, without ever having been utilized in any way by the ultimate consumer, subsequently has been made into a fibrous state.

*Reused Wool:* The resulting fiber when wool or reprocessed wool has been spun, woven, knitted, or felted into a wool product which after having been used in any way by the ultimate consumer, subsequently has been made into a fibrous state.

Wool from the sheep is unique in that it is the only natural fiber that will felt in a natural manner. The fiber is made of overlapping scales or serrations which vary with the several grades of wool; there are from 600 to 3,000 to the inch. The structure of the fiber is comparable with the scales on a fish or an asparagus tip. Wool is warm, springy, elastic, may be harsh. It is the weakest of all major fibers, is a generator of heat, thereby giving warmth to the body in cold, crisp weather.

There are five general types of wool: fine wools, medium wools, long or luster wools, carpet wools, cross-breed wools. On the four-point method of classifying wool the table includes combing, carding, clothing, carpet wools.

Wools are graded according to fineness, color, length of staple.

ALPACA: Fine, long woolly hair of the alpaca, a South American goat-like animal. It is superior to ordinary qualities of sheep's wool.

ANGORA: Long, soft hair-like wool of the angora goat. Used in combination with wool, and in making mohair.

BOTANY: Fine, merino-type wool shipped from Botany Bay, Australia. Also trade name of Botany Mills, Inc.

CASHMERE: Soft, very fine wool found beneath the outer hair of goats raised in the Himalayan region.

COMBING WOOL: Wool of longer fibers which are combed to straighten them out. Suitable for worsted yarns.

KEMP: Short, harsh wool used mainly in carpets.

LAMB'S WOOL: Soft, elastic wool of lambs, from seven to eight months old. Used for the best woolen textiles.

MERINO: Very fine wool, obtained from Spanish Merino sheep.

SHETLAND: Very fine wool from sheep raised in the Shetland Isles off the coast of Scotland.

SHODDY WOOL: Remanufactured wool obtained by shredding discarded woolen, worsted and knitted garments, mill waste, clippings. Shoddy material must be so labeled. Can be a mixture of fibers with wool.

TOP WOOL: Continuous strand of long wool fibers from which short fibers have been eliminated by combing.

VIRGIN WOOL: Fabrics or products that have not used any wastes from preliminary processing of new wool.

**WOOL-BACKED CLOTH:** Cloth that has an extra warp or filling used on the back of the cloth in its construction. Weight, warmth, and texture is increased by this manner of weaving cloth.

**WOOL CREPE:** See CREPE.

**WOOL-DYED:** Fabric in which the fibers are dyed before spinning into yarn. Also called "stock dyed."

**WOOL PRODUCTS LABELING ACT:** A law requiring that all wool products moving in "commerce" shall be properly labeled. Carpets, rugs, mats, and upholstery fabrics containing wool are exempt.

**WOOLENS:** Cloth made from woolen yarn but not always 100% wool in content. The average woolen has a rather fuzzy surface, does not shine with wear, does not hold the crease, has nap, and, in the majority of cases, is dyed. Woolen finish is easily recognized on cloths to determine the difference between this cloth and a worsted material.

**WOOLEN SYSTEM:** Used with regard to the manufacture of woolen yarn from short-staple stock, noil, soft or hard wastes, reused wool, remanufactured wool, reclaims, etc. The operations include sorting, scouring, blending, oiling, mixing, carding, and mule spinning. Within recent years ring-spinning has made some progress. Woolen system may be used for spinning man-made staples.

**WOOL TOP:** The continuous sliver form of long, choice woolen fibers which are to be manufactured ultimately into worsted yarn. The combing operation takes out short, immature, undesirable wool fibers, known as noil, from the choice stock.

**WORSTED, COTTON:** See COTTON WORSTED.

**WORSTEDS:** Popular class of cloths made of choice woolen stock using fibers of approximately the same length in staple. The process of making worsted cloth originated in the little village of that name in Norfolk County, England. Today, the procedure of making worsted cloth has changed somewhat because of the improvement in up-to-the-minute modern machinery.

**WORSTED SYSTEM:** The method of manufacture resorted to for medium and higher types of wool of good staple properties. Fiber length used may range from 1½-inch stock for the French or Franco-Belgian system and from around 2-inch staple for the Bradford or English system of making worsted yarn. Six- or seven-inch staple is about the limit that may be employed for worsted yarn manufacture. The main operations include carding, combing, gilling, drawing, and spinning on the mule, ring, cap or flyer frames. In some mills gilling may precede combing.

**WORSTED, UNFINISHED:** See UNFINISHED WORSTED.

**WORSTED YARNS WITH REGARD TO COLOR:** In the following information, black and white are considered as colors:

1. DOUBLE MARL: Yarn made of one end of mixture shade or solid color twisted with one end of two colors which have been roved together; that is, the colored strands entered the roving frame singly and were delivered as a single yarn effect, from the roving frame. Roving is fiber stock one step removed from being finished spun yarn.

2. HALF MARL: Yarn made of one end of mixture color or shade, twisted with one end of two colors which have been roved together.

3. MARL: Yarn made of two identical ends twisted together, the single ends used having been made up of two colors that have been roved together.

4. MELANGE: Yarn made from worsted top that has been Vigoreux or melange printed.

5. MIXTURE: Yarn made from the fibers of two or more colors blended together.

6. SINGLE MARL: A single yarn made up of two colors that have been roved together.

7. SINGLE MOTTLE: A single yarn made as a single marl yarn with regard to the combination of colors. The marl effect, however, is obtained by spinning from two halfweight rovings of different colors into the single end. The effect is a clearer contrast of color than that noted in single marl yarn.

8. SOLID COLOR: Yarn made from fibers of single color.

9. TWIST: Yarn made of two single ends of different colors, twisted together, with the single ends being solid colors or mixture shades.

**WOVEN SEERSUCKER:** See SEERSUCKER.

**WRINKLE RECOVERY:** The ability of a fabric to eliminate wrinkles by its own resilience. Wool fabrics have the greatest natural resilience but thermoplastic synthetic fibers and chemical-treated cotton and rayon also exhibit considerable wrinkle recovery. Laboratory tests can be made to determine the degree which a fabric recovers from wrinkling.

**WYATT, JOHN AND PAUL, LEWIS:** In 1738 these two interesting English inventors introduced the principle of drawing rollers that made possible the spinning of yarn without the use of the fingers. Their invention gave to the world the use of excess speed of rollers and the principle of drawing and drafting textile fibers.

In 1748 they invented the revolving cylinder carding machine.

**YACHT CLOTH:** Stoutly made, unfinished worsted and blends in blue, white, and delicate stripes. Used in yachting circles.

**YARD:** Is a 36-inch measure in America, while the English yard is a standard established by the government, indicated by two marks on a metal rod embedded in the masonry of the House of Parliament in London. The American yard, which is 1/100,000 of an inch longer than the English yard, is not fixed by government standards. The foot of today, which measures 12 inches, is supposed to have been the length of the foot of James I, 1603-1625.

**YARN:** Spun yarn is the product of the spinning frame characterized by being a continuous, evenly distributed, coherent arrangement of any type of fibers of varying or similar staple length, the relative positions of which are maintained by the introduction of a definite lateral twist to produce strength or coherence imparted in the final operation.

**YARN-DYED:** Yarns dyed in the skein or package before weaving.

**YARN NUMBERING SYSTEMS:** The fineness of single yarns is defined below in the units currently used for the common fibers. The definitions also apply to the equivalent single number of ply yarns.

ASBESTOS (cut): The number of 100-yd. lengths per pounds avoirdupois.

COTTON (hank): The number of 840-yd.

hanks per pound avoirdupois.
(typp.): The number of thousands of yards per pound avoirdupois.

GLASS (cut): The number of 100-yd. lengths per pound avoirdupois.

JUTE (spyndle): The weight in pounds avoirdupois of a spyndle of 14, 400-yd. of yarn expressed as "pounds per spyndle."

LINEN (hank or lea): The number of 300-yd. hanks or leas, contained in one pound avoirdupois.

RAYON, CONTINUOUS FILAMENT (denier): The number of grams per 9,000 m. length.

RAYON, STAPLE (denier): The number of grams per 9,000 m. length.

RAYON, SPUN (typp): The number of thousands of yards per pound avoirdupois.

SILK, RAW or BOILED OFF (denier): The number of grams per 9,000 meter length.

SILK, SPUN (hank): The number of 840-yd. hanks per pound avoirdupois.

WOOLEN (cut): The number of 300-yd. "cuts" or hanks per pound avoirdupois.
(run.) The number of 1600-yd. hanks per pound avoirdupois.

WOOLEN or WORSTED (typp): The number of thousands of yards per pound avoirdupois.

WORSTED (hank): The number of 560-yd. hanks per pound avoirdupois.

**YARN PER INCH:** The number of warp yarns per inch and the number of filling yarns per inch in a fabric. Same as *Construction*.

**YARN SIZES:** Yarns (same as threads) are numbered according to weight: the higher the number, the finer is the actual yarn. A *1's* cotton yarn has 840 yards in one pound; a *10's* yarn runs 8400 yards, or ten 840-yard lengths to the pound; a pound of *160's* yarn would stretch nearly 80 miles. A medium yarn is a *30's*. A 30/1 is a one-ply *30's* yarn; a 30/2 is a two-ply yarn, containing two strands of *30's*.

**YARNS, STRETCH:** See STRETCH YARNS.

**YOLK:** The natural grease in sheep wool. When purified it is known as lanolin.

**ZEFRAN:** The acrylic fiber produced by Dow Badische Company as staple and tow.

**ZEIN:** A protein fiber made from corn meal. The fibers are obtained by extruding the zein solution through spinnerets into a coagulating bath while simultaneously contacting the zein with a reactive aldehyde, such as formaldehyde, and subsequently subjecting the resultant fibers to elevated temperatures.

**ZEPEL:** Zepel is a fluorochemical produced by Du Pont which is applied to fabric as a stain repellent. Zepel is applied to a fabric by padding from an aqueous bath or by spraying from a solvent dispersion. Curing links the molecules of Zepel firmly into place, forming an invisible chemical shield around the fibers.

**ZEPHYR:** Originally was a lightweight worsted yarn of good quality. Fabric made of the yarn was also known as zephyr. Today, many lightweight cottons and man-made fabrics are advertised as zephyr to attract attention to the sheerness or lightness of the material. The name is from *Zephyrus*, classical god of the west wind.

**ZEPHYR FLANNEL:** Name given to flannel of ordinary nature that has silk mixed with the stock in making the yarn.

**ZIBELINE:** Used for cloakings, coats, and capes in women's wear. The cloth is made from cross-bred yarns and the fabric is strongly colored. Stripings, sometimes noted in the cloth, work in very well with the construction and appearance of the finished garment. The finish is a highly raised type, lustrous, and the nap is long and lies in the one direction. The cloth may or may not be given a soft finish and feel.

**ZIPPER:** Same as *Mispick*. A cloth defect due to a missing filling yarn.

**Z-TWIST:** Direction of twist in yarn or cord called Z twist as the spirals conformed in slope to the middle part of the letter Z. Also called "right" or "regular" twist.

# INDEX